Roaring Camp

Roaring Camp

The Social World
of the
California Gold Rush

SUSAN LEE JOHNSON

W. W. Norton & Company
New York   London

First published as a Norton paperback 2001

For information about permission to reproduce selections from
this book, write to Permissions, W. W. Norton & Company, Inc.,
500 Fifth Avenue, New York, NY 10110

The text of this book is composed in Stone Serif
with the display set in Caslon Open.
Composition by Tom Ernst.
Manufacturing by Quebecor Printing, Fairfield, Inc.
Book design by Lane Trubey.

Library of Congress Cataloging-in-Publication Data

Johnson, Susan Lee.
    Roaring Camp : the social world of the California Gold Rush /
Susan Lee Johnson.
        p.   cm.
    Includes bibliiographical references and index.
    ISBN 0-393-04812-8
    1. California—Gold discoveries—Social aspects.   2. California—
Social life and customs—19th century.   3. Sierra Nevada (Calif. and
Nev.)—Gold discoveries—Social aspects.   4. Mining camps—Sierra
Nevada (Calif. and Nev.)—History—19th century.   5. California—
Ethnic relations.   I. Title.
F865.J675 2000
979.4'04—dc21   99-33684
                                                                          CIP

ISBN 0-393-32099-5 pbk.

W. W. Norton & Company, Inc., 500 Fifth Avenue, New York, N.Y. 10110
www.wwnorton.com

W. W. Norton & Company Ltd., 10 Coptic Street, London WC1A 1PU

7 8 9 0

For my father, Bud,
   in memory of rivers;
For my mother, Jan,
   in honor of seasons;
To my lover, Camille,
   for the wisdom of arroyos.

It takes a long time to remember, it takes generations, sometimes nations, to make a story.

—Betty Louise Bell, *Faces in the Moon*

Contents

Contents

List of Illustrations

Preface

Until about the twentieth of September, the Indians had worked constantly
around us. All the companies let them go freely where it seemed good to
them, even in our ditches, to gather the paydirt in their pans, carry it on
their heads and go wash it at the river. The women especially did this
work; however, I have never seen an Indian woman cede to her husband
the gold she gathered, which made me suppose that each one worked for
herself.

—Jean-Nicolas Perlot, *Gold Seeker: Adventures of*
a Belgian Argonaut during the Gold Rush Years

FOR MANY OF US, thoughts of the California Gold Rush do not evoke
scenes like the one described in this epigraph, in which French
and Belgian men mine for gold side by side with Miwok Indian
women. Since we do not envision such scenes, we also cannot ask
why European miners might think of themselves as "letting" native
peoples pan for gold in California, and why a Belgian man might
conclude that Miwok women worked only for themselves. Our failure
to consider such scenes and ask such questions is part of a larger
problem of collective memory. After the decline of California's surface diggings in the 1850s, the Gold Rush increasingly came to be
remembered as the historical property of Anglo Americans, especially
Anglo American men, and came to be associated in everyday language with facile notions of fast fortune. It is the task of this book
both to interrogate and to dismantle the stories white Americans
have told themselves about the California Gold Rush, and to offer
instead a pastiche of tales that will help us think as complexly and
critically about the conquest of history as we have begun to think
about the history of conquest.

To accomplish this task, I focus on the region that Gold Rush participants called the Southern Mines, or that area in the Sierra Nevada
foothills drained by the San Joaquin River. The Southern Mines are
particularly illuminating for my purposes because the region's popu-

lation was more diverse than that of the Northern Mines (the foothill area drained by the lower Sacramento River). Mexicans, Chileans, French, and Chinese were prominent in the southern region, and Miwok Indians maintained a strong presence there. African Americans, both enslaved and free, also worked alongside Anglo Americans in the Southern Mines. Indeed, the Gold Rush was not only among the most demographically male events in human history, it also—particularly as it transpired in the Southern Mines—was among the most multiracial, multiethnic, multinational events that had yet occurred within the boundaries of the United States. In addition, unlike the Northern Mines, the Southern Mines failed to follow what historians have described as the typical trajectory of industrialization for western mining, in which placer (surface, individualized) techniques gave way in an orderly fashion to hardrock (underground, industrialized) mining. Not surprisingly, then, the Southern Mines have constituted the area least studied by historians, though diggings in the far northwestern corner of California share with the southern region a history of neglect.

The stories I tell about the Gold Rush have in common a concern with relations of difference and domination, relations frequently defined along lines of gender and race or ethnicity or nationality, and often made manifest in economic terms. In this, I have placed Anglo American men as squarely within social constructs of gender and race or ethnicity or nationality as, for example, women (of all races, ethnicities, and nationalities) and emigrants, white ethnics, and peoples of color (both women and men). And I have identified the pursuit of dominance on the part of some white American men in the diggings as a first step in the long discursive process by which whole pieces of California's Gold Rush past fell by the wayside of history. Those pieces could not be reconfigured in memory until the wholesale transformation of the "subject" of history began over three decades ago, with the painstaking work of scholars of class, race, sexuality, and gender. In the end, it is the social movements that inspired such scholarship that have most deeply influenced my thinking in this book.

The avid reader of mining histories may hear echoed in the title of this work the name of a fine book about mining in British Columbia, Jeremy Mouat's *Roaring Days: Rossland's Mines and the History of British Columbia* (1995). I don't mean to be a claim jumper. My title actually comes from the famous Bret Harte story "The Luck of Roaring Camp," which I analyze in the epilogue.

Earlier, abbreviated versions of two chapters of this book have appeared in print elsewhere: "'Domestic' Life in the Diggings: The Southern Mines in the California Gold Rush," in *Over the Edge: Remapping the American West*, ed. Valerie J. Matsumoto and Blake Allmendinger (Berkeley: Univ. of California Press, 1999), and "Bulls, Bears, and Dancing Boys: Race, Gender, and Leisure in the California Gold Rush," *Radical History Review* 60 (Fall 1994).

Beyond my overriding debt to activists for race, gender, sexual, and economic justice—who first won my admiration when I was growing up during the 1960s in Madison, Wisconsin—I am obliged to a good number of individuals and institutions. This book began as a dissertation, for which I received support from the Mrs. Giles Whiting Foundation (Whiting Fellowship in the Humanities); the Woodrow Wilson National Fellowship Foundation (Charlotte W. Newcombe Dissertation Fellowship); the Huntington Library (Research Fellowship); and Yale University (John F. Enders Fellowship). At Yale, Florence Thomas cheerfully charted my progress through the graduate program. At the University of Michigan, both the Women's Studies Program and the Department of History granted me funds for last-minute research assistance as I was finishing the dissertation. Staff in both units, particularly Judy Mackey and Janet Fisk, helped me manage these funds and navigate a new academic environment. They and their coworkers deserve raises, roses, and utmost respect.

The journey from dissertation to book was long and full of detours, as matters of love and death kept me packing, unpacking, and repacking my things in an effort to live in accordance with what mattered most to me. In the meantime, I was fortunate to receive extraordinary support from the University of Michigan in the form of a Faculty Grant and Fellowship as well as a Michigan Faculty Fellowship at the Institute for the Humanities. I am most grateful not only for this material assistance but for the encouragement both fellowships offered me at a time when family matters weighed on my heart. I also have continued to benefit from the generosity of the Huntington Library, which gave me a National Endowment for the Humanities Fellowship that allowed me an entire academic year at that institution. It was during that year that I produced most of this book's final two chapters as well as the epilogue. When I was in the final hours of finishing the book, I received a Dean's Summer Research Fellowship at the University of Colorado at Boulder, which allowed me to return to California to gather illustrations. Thanks to Dianne Johnson for helping me manage those funds.

Archivists, librarians, local historians, and other kind folks made sure I had access to the necessary materials for this study. George Miles at the Beinecke Library walked me through the closed stacks and explained the intricacies of cataloging there well before this project took shape as a dissertation, and then continued to be of tremendous assistance in the years that followed. Waverly Lowell gave me tips on California archival resources generally. Nicole Bouché helped me at the Bancroft Library, and, when I went back there to search for illustrations, Jack von Euw made sure I found what I needed in record time. During an early research trip to the Bancroft, I was fortunate to find a seat next to the Berkeley graduate student Michael González, now of the University of San Diego. Michael not only pointed me toward source materials but also helped me survive the 1989 earthquake. Another Berkeley graduate student, Judy Yung, now of the University of California, Santa Cruz, assisted me in all matters related to Chinese Gold Rush experiences, for which I will always be indebted. I am also grateful to Sally McCoy, who took me into her El Cerrito home while I was working at the Bancroft. The staff at the California State Library in Sacramento and the Holt-Atherton Center for Western Studies at the University of the Pacific at Stockton, especially Daryl Morrison, also gave me much aid.

At the Huntington Library, Martin Ridge, Roy Ritchie, and Peter Blodgett all took interest in my work and helped me make good use of my time at that institution. For a model of curatorial expertise, collegiality, and basic human decency, one need look no farther than Peter Blodgett; I am proud to call him a friend. In 1998, as Peter's energies increasingly were occupied by the Huntington's Gold Rush exhibit, I was fortunate to be able to turn to Jennifer Martínez for able assistance. For additional help in acquiring illustrations from the Huntington, my thanks to Kristin Cooper, Lita García, Lisa Ann Libby, and Jennifer Watts. Indeed, there is probably no staff member at the Huntington who has not helped me at one time or another; to all, my deepest gratitude. I also benefited from conversations about my work with other readers at the Huntington, particularly Bill Deverell, Amelia Montes, Terri Snyder, and the late Wilbur Jacobs. And I am very thankful to Carol and Luther Luedtke of South Pasadena for opening their home to me both times I was in residence at the Huntington.

For assistance in locating and gaining access to illustrations for this book, I am also grateful to Craig Bates, curator of ethnography for the National Park Service Museum at Yosemite National Park; the photographer Leroy Radanovich in Mariposa, California; and Aisha Ayers, Marcia Eymann, and Claudia Kishler at the Oakland Museum of California. Three private collectors, too, allowed me to use images reproduced herein; my gratitude to Stanley B. Burns, M.D., Matthew R. Isenburg, and Charles Schwartz.

Up in the gold country, in the four counties that constitute the geographic focus of this study, I relied on a whole host of friendly people to direct me to everything from county court records to the nearest cup of coffee: Larry Cenotto, historian of Amador County, at the Amador County Museum and Archives; Sheldon Johnson, Amador County clerk and recorder; Lorrayne Kennedy at the Calaveras County Museum and Archives; Willard Fuller at the Calaveras County Historical Society; Judith Cunningham of Foothill Research Associates; Sharon Marovich at the Tuolumne County Historical Society; Carlo De Ferrari, historian of Tuolumne County, who literally unlocked the vaults for me at the Tuolumne County Courthouse; Muriel Powers at the Mariposa Museum and History Center; Scott Pinkerton, historian of Mariposa County; and Darden Gilbert in the County Clerk's Office at the Mariposa County Courthouse. Though not in the business of history, one other person made my travels in the gold country memorable; Barbara Saunders, then manager of El Campo Casa Resort Motel in Jackson, went far beyond the call of duty in making my first shoe-string-budget research trip more comfortable.

My training as a historian began two decades ago, at Carthage College in Kenosha, Wisconsin. There, Angela Howard and Jonathan Zophy introduced me to the field of women's history and John (Ben) Bailey to the American West. I am grateful to them for sending me down those trails, and for being such fine teachers. I also owe more than I can say to Jane Gronholm, Laurie Poklop, and Kären Schultz for growing up with me there, and especially for that train trip we took to Montana in 1976. Look where *that* led! And to Kim House, poet and fisherman, my belated gratitude.

At Arizona State University in Tempe, where I pursued my master's degree, I worked with a number of wonderful scholars. Over the years, my adviser there, Mary Rothschild, has continued to take interest in my work and well-being, for which I thank her. Likewise, Christine Marín, a fellow graduate student and head of the Chicano Studies Collection at Hayden Library, early on had a great influence on my work. I am also grateful for the continued support of Susie Sato, then of the Arizona Historical Foundation. And although Julia Velson (granddaughter of Clara Lemlich Shavelson, who called for the general strike vote in the Uprising of the Twenty Thousand) is a Californian, I first met her in Arizona. Since then, I've learned more from her about the way the world works than from most of the books I've read.

In the early 1980s, I worked for the journal *Signs* at Stanford University and had the good fortune to know and learn from an extraordinary group of graduate students there, including David Gutiérrez, Valerie Matsumoto, and Peggy Pascoe. Dave, you are my model for intelligence, integrity, and irreverence, perfectly proportioned. Estelle Freedman and Barbara Gelpi also took time out of busy schedules to nurture my work and academic career. And it was at Stanford that I hooked up with Kath Weston, from whom I learned a good deal of what I know that's worth knowing. There I also met Clare Novak, my coworker at *Signs* and now a friend for life. Stanford introduced me to Yukiko Hanawa as well, who early on prompted and influenced my thinking about issues of difference and domination. I continue to marvel at Yukiko's breathtaking intellectual range, her keen sense of justice, and the integrity with which she conducts her life, and I offer her my deepest appreciation. It was in these years, too, that I had the great good fortune to meet a trio of scholars whose work on gender in the mining West has been an inspiration for my own; my gratitude to Elizabeth Jameson, Mary Murphy, and Marion Goldman.

At Yale University, I was surrounded by friends, colleagues, and advisers who believed in the worth of this project and in my ability to carry it out. My dissertation committee consisted of Nancy Cott, William Cronon, Ann Fabian, Howard Lamar, and David Montgomery, but other faculty members also took interest in me and my work. Of these, Emily Honig and Jonathan Spence offered assistance and support at key moments. It was Howard Lamar who first counseled me to study the Southern Mines. Thank heavens I took his sage advice. Generations of his students have filled their acknowledgments with paeans to his kindness and generosity, and I can but join the chorus. I only hope that this book, begun at his suggestion, will start to repay him for the many gifts he has given me. From the earliest stages of this project, Ann Fabian saw clearly in my work things that I could only dimly envision, and in several key places, the material that follows took shape as much in her hands as in mine. Her wisdom and quick wit not only saved me from numerous errors of interpretation; they made this a more graceful and nuanced work. Thank you, Ann. This book began as a seminar paper in a course David Montgomery taught in 1985–86 on industrialization, and the questions I learned to pose in that class are the most important questions I address herein—indeed, they may be the most important questions one can ask about social relations of difference and domination. I deeply appreciate his advice, his vision, and his integrity. Nancy Cott's own early work in antebellum U.S. women's history laid the foundations for much of what I have said about antebellum U.S. men, and her constant engagement with the ever-changing world of feminist scholarship has frequently saved me from reinventing the interpretive wheel. Throughout this project, she displayed that rare talent for offering nothing but constructive criticism when I strayed down dead-end roads, and lavish praise when I struck out in more promising directions. Many, many thanks. Last, but certainly not least, I thank Bill Cronon for caring about me and my work, and for providing a model of what it means to be a scholar engaged by the ethics of everyday life. We have different intellectual and political passions, but these differences have only helped me see more clearly how to live within such passions and remain true to what matters. I am also profoundly grateful to Bill for first telling our now mutual editor, Steve Forman, about my work. That act has made this a more daring and less dutiful book—which made it much more fun to write. There is no end to my gratitude.

At Yale as well, I was surrounded by graduate students who nurtured and challenged me, including George Chauncey, Phil Deloria, Debbie Elkin, Faulkner Fox, Amy Green, María Montoya, Katherine Morrissey, Gunther Peck, Dorothy Rony, Beryl Satter, Barbara Savage, Tom Smith, Brian Wescott, and David Yoo. Although she was a fellow graduate student, it was in her professional capacity that Ann Garland helped me through some difficult times at Yale. My dissertation reading group offered me the most thorough and thoughtful critiques I received of early versions of my work. To Michael Goldberg, Yvette Huginnie, Reeve Huston, and Karen Sawislak, a thousand thanks. A special thanks to Yvette for keeping the faith. I couldn't have survived my years at Yale without the love of other close comrades who helped me live my daily life with dignity. In addition to many of those named above, my deepest gratitude to Adrienne Donald, Leslie Frane, Regina Kunzel, Susan Larsen, Mary Renda, and Lynn Yanis.

I accumulated many intellectual and personal debts at the University of Michigan. A junior faculty women's reading group gave me excellent comments on my work. The members included Elsa Barkley Brown, Miriam Bodian, Sueanne Caulfield, Laura Downs, Kali Israel, Sue Juster, Valerie Kivelson, and Kathryn Oberdeck. Thanks as well to Elizabeth Anderson, Andrea Hunter, Carol Karlsen, Terri

Koreck, George Sánchez, David Scobey, John Shy, Pat Simons, and
Domna Stanton. My years in Michigan were not easy ones for me
personally, and no one helped me more through those times more
than Abby Stewart and Elsa Barkley Brown. I miss you both. My gratitude, too, to the matchless Betty Bell for her many gifts. Several
Michigan graduate students worked as research assistants at various
stages in this project, including Lorena Chambers, Mary Coomes,
Cathleen Craighead, Richard Kim, David Salmanson, and Peter
Shulman; many, many thanks. Elizabeth Kodner (now Shook), then
an undergraduate, distinguished herself as an effective research assis-
tant for me as well—so effective, that I recruited her several years
later to come to graduate school at the University of Colorado at
Boulder, and also engaged her research assistance once again.

A brief interlude at the University of California, Los Angeles,
allowed me to get to know Michael Salman and Muriel McClendon,
from whom I have learned much about living and working with
dignity. That interlude gave me time with Deena González and
Alicia Gaspar de Alba as well, from whom I also have learned a great
deal. I am especially grateful to Deena for her continued support of
my work.

I completed this book after I joined the faculty of the University of
Colorado at Boulder, and have called on several colleagues to read or
otherwise consult with me about my work as it neared publication.
Martha Hanna, Patty Limerick, Ralph Mann, and Tim Weston all felt
the weight of the manuscript on their laps when it reached the last
draft and saved me from important errors. I am especially grateful to
Ralph Mann for his intellectual generosity toward me and this book.
And for her support of and enthusiasm for my work, I am grateful,
too, to Nan Alamilla Boyd. María Montoya of the University of
Michigan also read key portions of the final draft and offered helpful
suggestions. Katherine Morrissey of the University of Arizona read
that draft as well, and provided essential assistance at the final hour,
for which I offer my thanks. And over the last few years, I also have
benefited from the insight of Krista Comer of Rice University.

I consider it a singular privilege to be publishing this book with
W. W. Norton & Company. I am more grateful than I can say to my
editor, Steve Forman, for his astounding patience and his warm
encouragement. I work best in silence and isolation, and Steve has
honored these penchants by leaving me alone until I was ready to venture out of my cocoon. And then he shepherded the book through the
production process with acuity and forbearance. I also am thankful to
Don and Jean Lamm for their wonderful hospitality in Santa Fe just

after I completed the book manuscript. My profound gratitude, as well, to Jacques Chazaud for the handsome maps, and to Otto Sonntag for the superb copyediting. Since I love maps and have worked as a copyeditor, I especially appreciate this labor on my behalf.

With so much help, this should be a flawless work of scholarship. But alas, I couldn't respond to every piece of advice these students, friends, colleagues, editors, and teachers offered me, and so difficulties, no doubt, still abound herein. Whatever remains that is graceless, contradictory, or just plain wrong is my responsibility alone. Credit for whatever is artful, coherent, and right-minded must be shared among many.

This book openly yearns for social relations in which difference and domination are not so closely, so predictably, and so devastatingly linked to one another. While I was writing it, I happened briefly upon a human community that gave me hope for the future as well as sustenance in the here and now. This was the congregation of Christ the Shepherd Evangelical Lutheran Church in Altadena, California, a multiracial congregation that welcomes lesbian, gay, and transgender people. It is not an affluent community, but a community rich in respect, warmth, and humor—a community that does justice and loves kindness, to paraphrase a biblical admonition, as a matter of course. I am grateful to members of that church for all that I learned from them.

I owe it to my parents, Jan Johnson and the late Bud Johnson, that I could recognize what was happening in that community of faith and yearn for the same in the world around me. After this project was completed as a dissertation but before it became a book, my father's terminal illness began to take its slow, inexorable, and painful march toward death. Nothing I have ever witnessed has taught me as much as my father's death—and no lessons have I so not wanted to learn. But learn them I have—not from death alone but from the grace with which my father faced it. This book is in part dedicated to his memory. It is also dedicated to my mother, who has given me an extraordinary model for living with loss and growing in grace. This is for you, too, Mom. I am grateful as well to my sister and brother, Lynne and Scott Johnson, for early on teaching me to assume nothing, to question everything—even if that questioning sometimes grew tedious for our parents. And also I thank the rest of my family: Kerrie, Ron, Mike and Caryn, Marlisa, and Michelle and Rodrigo. Special thanks to the five lights of my life, our dear grandchildren: Casey, Mason, Courtney, Michael, and Kelcey.

No one deserves more thanks, however, than my lover and life partner, Camille Guerin-Gonzales. Also a historian, Camille has read every word of this book and talked with me not only about how to make it better but about how to make it *matter*. From very different life histories, from very different positions in the contemporary world, we share visions for social justice, and those visions motivate our daily work. We also love each other with abandon. This book, then, is also for her.

Roaring
Camp

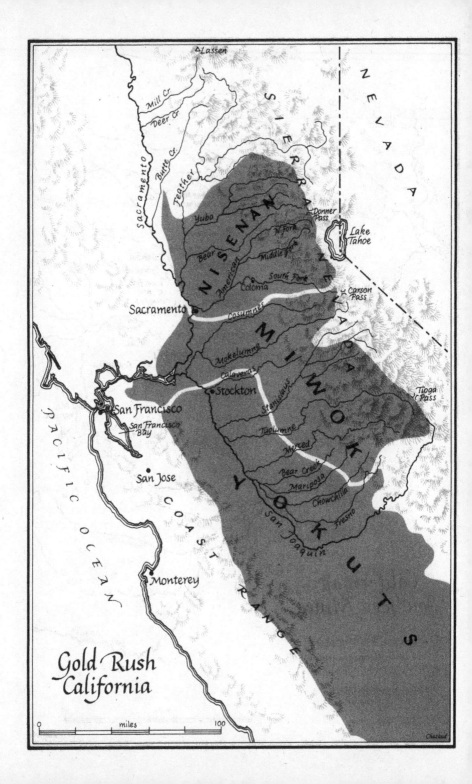

Gold Rush
California

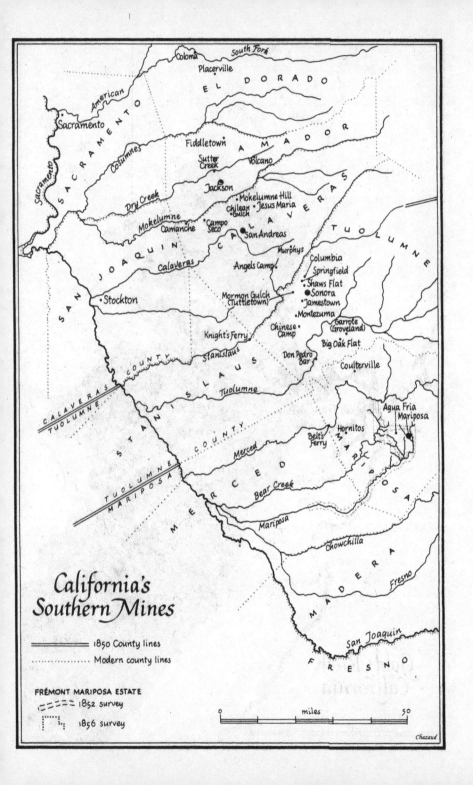

California's Southern Mines

Coloma
Placerville
South Fork
EL DORADO
American
Sacramento
Costumnes
Fiddletown
AMADOR
Sutter Creek
Volcano
Sacramento
Dry Creek
Jackson
Mokelumne
• Mokelumne Hill
Chilean • Jesus Maria
Gulch
SAN • Campo Seco
JOAQUIN
Camanche
CALAVERAS
• San Andreas
Calaveras
Murphys
TUOLUMNE
Angels Camp •
Columbia
Springfield
• Stockton
• Shaws Flat
Mormon Gulch
(Tuttletown)
● Sonora
• Jamestown
• Montezuma
Garrote
(Groveland)
Knight's Ferry
Chinese Camp
Big Oak Flat
Stanislaus
Don Pedro Bar
Coulterville
CALAVERAS COUNTY
TUOLUMNE
Tuolumne
STANISLAUS
Agua Fria
Mariposa
COUNTY
Merced
Hornitos
Belt's Ferry
MARIPOSA
TUOLUMNE
MARIPOSA
Bear Creek
MERCED
Mariposa
Chowchilla
MADERA
San Joaquin
Fresno
FRESNO

California's Southern Mines

────── 1850 County lines

· · · · · · Modern county lines

FRÉMONT MARIPOSA ESTATE

⌐¬⌐¬⌐¬ 1852 survey

⌐ ⌐ ⌐ 1856 survey

0   miles   50

Chazaud

Prologue

Joaquín Murrieta and the Bandits

Chances are whatever memory you have of the California Gold
Rush depends in part on where you grew up—San Francisco,
Santiago, Paris, a New England port town, or somewhere off the
winding path of California Highway 49, in what tourist culture calls
the gold country. It depends on the people you grew up with and the
stories they told you about the past. If you are Chicano, you may
have a different sense of what the Gold Rush was about than if you
descend from the native peoples of interior California, or if, like me,
your northern European forebears took root in the American Midwest
after the Civil War. If you grew up in the United States, or received
much of your formal education here, chances are your early book
learning about the Gold Rush placed the event as an episode in a
larger story about westward expansion, Manifest Destiny, and the
inevitable march of civilization. If you are a historian, you may have
accumulated more specialized knowledge about the discovery of gold
in 1848 and its consequences, but chances are collective memory of
the event still informs your impressions. It does mine—schoolbook
pictures of abandoned ships in San Francisco's harbor, a portrait of a
bewhiskered white fellow gripping a pan in which flecks of gold
catch the midday sun.

The Gold Rush is that kind of event. Like "Civil War" or
"Depression," the term we use to describe what happened in the
Sierra Nevada foothills during the midnineteenth century rolls easily
off the tongue, slips naturally into discussions of present-day concerns, particularly economic concerns. You know what a gold rush

is—at least that it has something to do with sudden pecuniary gain. You probably can remember when the Gold Rush happened, if only by recalling the name of a professional football team. But even if you must consult contemporary popular culture to "date" the event, the term is still largely sufficient to itself, relatively self-referential. You can know it outside of a clear historical context in a way that you cannot, for example, know the War of 1812, the Uprising of the Twenty Thousand, or Angel (as opposed to Ellis) Island, though the tale of westward expansion is no doubt close at hand when one speaks of the Gold Rush. The event exists in that tension between memory and history described by the French historian Pierre Nora when he writes of *les lieux de mémoire*, roughly "sites of memory." According to Nora, *les lieux de mémoire* "capture a maximum of meaning in the fewest signs"; they have a remarkable "capacity for metamorphosis, an endless recycling of their meaning."[1]

For that reason, your recollections are important. They hint at the varied uses to which the Gold Rush has been put in the last century and a half, and as such they are as much my concern as the century of scholarship that began with Charles Howard Shinn's and Josiah Royce's tomes of the 1880s, that continued with Rodman Paul's and John Caughey's volumes in the 1940s, and that finds its most recent expression in the work of Ralph Mann, J. S. Holliday, David Goodman, and Malcolm Rohrbough.[2] I do not attempt to resolve the tension between memory and history that gives the Gold Rush its salience. I write within that tension, now indulging in what two scholars call the "rules of recording and interpretation that . . . belong to historical discourse," now in the more "unreflective, erratic operations of memory."[3] I am concerned both with what happened in California after 1848 and with what the Gold Rush has come to mean.

Since the California Gold Rush occurred in a time and place wherein diverse peoples competed over resources, notions of social order, and definitions and distributions of wealth and power, I am particularly concerned with how the event has been construed more and more narrowly over time until it has come to connote merely fast fortune. In this process, some collective memories, such as mine of the independent Anglo American prospector, have come to carry more truck than others. Likewise—in a multiethnic, multiracial social world of entrenched gender hierarchies and vast political and economic inequities—some Gold Rush recollections predictably have died quiet deaths or have been nurtured only among particular peoples, now kept on the margins, now endangered by the voracious appetite of the "main plot." My task here, then, is not so much to

construct an accurate narrative of what happened in the Sierra
foothills after 1848, to create a *new* main plot, but to take issue with
received wisdom about the Gold Rush by encouraging the proliferation of alternative plot lines, stories not customarily nourished by the
dominant culture, broadly defined, or even by most historical scholarship. I start, then, with a tale born of strife in what was, in the gold
era, known as the Southern Mines.

The Southern and Northern mines, along with the Shasta-Trinity diggings in the far northwest, were California's premier gold-producing
regions after 1848.[4] The northern and southern sections were both
located in the foothills of the Sierra Nevada. The Northern Mines constituted the drainage of the lower Sacramento River, while the
Southern Mines fanned out over the drainage of the San Joaquin
River—the Cosumnes, Mokelumne, Calaveras, Stanislaus, Tuolumne,
and Merced rivers and their tributaries. Today, the Southern Mines

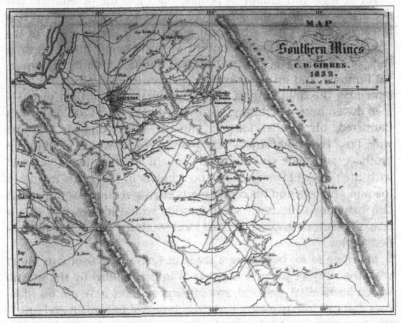

An 1852 map of California's Southern Mines with the supply town of
Stockton. Note Spanish- and English-language place-names, as well as those
derived from Miwok dialects, such as Tuolumne and Moquelumne (now usually spelled Mokelumne).

Reproduced by permission of the Huntington Library, San Marino, California.

would roughly comprise Amador, Calaveras, Tuolumne, and Mariposa counties. Prior to 1848 the area was home to Sierra Miwok Indians and other native peoples; within a decade, Miwok *rancherías* still remained, but were overshadowed by Anglo American–dominated towns like Jackson and Mokelumne Hill to the north, Sonora and Columbia in the midsection, and Coulterville and Mariposa to the south. Stockton, down in the San Joaquin Valley, was the regional supply center.

It was from this southern area in 1853 that a Mexican family fled from a well-armed, state-sponsored band of Anglo rangers. Some of the Mexican men got caught, and some were killed. At least one had his head cut off; another, a three-fingered hand. Both body parts were preserved in alcohol and put on exhibit until they apparently were lost in the San Francisco earthquake and fire of 1906. If this story sounds familiar, you are probably a California native, a student of western or Chicano history, or an aficionada of western movies, or you have read one of the many fantastic accounts of Joaquín Murrieta. It was his head, so they say.[5]

For at least two groups of people, the short life of Murrieta has become a Gold Rush parable of resistance. According to the researcher Frank Latta, who spent much of his life in search of the "historical Joaquín," branches of the Murrieta family in the Mexican state of Sonora have sustained an oral tradition regarding Joaquín, "El Famoso," and his lesser-known relatives for over a century. They remember the Gold Rush as a series of outrages upon their people— men driven from rich mining claims by Anglos, Jesús Carillo Murrieta murdered, his brother Joaquín Murrieta horsewhipped, Joaquín's wife, Rosa Felíz de Murrieta, raped—outrages for which Joaquín, his brothers, and male cousins finally sought revenge, and then paid with their lives.[6] Likewise, Chicano scholars in the 1970s reclaimed Joaquín Murrieta and his counterparts elsewhere in the Southwest as "los bandidos Chicanos," social bandits whose insurrection in the face of American invasion thrilled local Mexicans as much as it horrified Anglos.[7]

My impulse for beginning a study of California's Southern Mines with the story of Joaquín Murrieta is in part guided by the uses to which his familial, political, and intellectual heirs have put his life— uses that call into question traditions invented to explain and justify the imposition of Anglo American dominance in the diggings. It is also guided by the many key historical and historiographical issues raised by the Gold Rush incidence of Mexican insurgency and by the separate but related construction of the problem of Mexican ban-ditry. And because Murrieta met his fate in 1853, roughly midway through the period under study here, his activities serve as a bench-mark for the changes that characterized the Southern Mines from the discovery of gold in 1848 to the departure of gold seekers for new western bonanzas starting in 1858. That the alleged banditry of Murrieta and his relatives came at a moment of constricted economic opportunity for most Gold Rush participants is easily established. That it also marked the culmination and ultimate demise of armed resistance to Anglo rule by disenfranchised peoples in the mines is only a little more difficult to document—as is the contention that Anglos' hysterical response to perceived brigands in their midst indi-cated the fragility of that rule before 1853. That the showdown between Murrieta's men and the California Rangers was as well a des-perate struggle over the content of gender (what was it to be a woman or a man?) and entitlement to work (who had a right to get a living from the earth?) is less evident in what has been written to date about Mexican banditry. But these issues, along with the more often asked and still crucial questions of opportunity and insurrec-tion, guide my reading of the events of 1853.

As near as anyone can tell, people who went by the name of Murrieta had been migrating north toward what became the Mexican state of Sonora for over three centuries by the time of the Gold Rush, with long periods of residence in the present-day states of Michoacán and Sinaloa. Family tradition identifies the forebears of Joaquín Murrieta as *pobladores*, pioneers, who stayed in the northern and western reaches of what was, until 1821, part of the Spanish empire. By the time they settled in southern Sonora, family members recall, the Murrietas engaged regularly in three activities—digging gold, raising stock, and fighting Indians.[8]

That one collective memory suggests the ways in which people named Murrieta have conceived of their past and the ways in which historians might further understand it. First, it is a past lived by women and men related to one another by marriage and by what is called blood; that is, it is a familial past of cousins, siblings, spouses, grandparents. Second, it is a past remembered primarily through the activities of men—mining, ranching, warring—and only incidentally through the deeds of women.[9] Third, a historian might note, the Murrieta past is one of people living on the periphery, making com-modities of natural resources and sending them off to more popu-lated areas. Finally, it is a past of frontier people, of those in the New World who vied with native peoples for control of the land. This is the background against which occurred the troubles in California.

No written records document the Murrietas' response to news of the Gold Rush. But oral tradition places at least one Murrieta, a half brother to Joaquín, in the diggings just months after the discovery of gold at Sutter's mill in January 1848. He would have been among compatriots: Mexicans from Sonora were among the first to arrive, following close on the heels of Californios and South Americans, as well as assorted North Americans and Europeans already in the territory.[10] Within a year, a dozen family members followed, among them Rosa Felíz de Murrieta and her young husband, Joaquín. Rosa may have been the only woman in the party, but on the trail and in the mines she would not have been all that exceptional. Mexican women accompanied their menfolk to the diggings more frequently than women of any other immigrant group. After all, California was not only close to Mexico; until recently it had been *part* of Mexico.[11] Once in the gold region, the Murrieta clan, like a majority of Mexican gold seekers, went to work in the Southern Mines.[12]

No record survives, either, of how Rosa Felíz de Murrieta spent her time in the diggings. If she was like other Sonoran women, though, she may well have done her share of panning for gold. When Monterey's alcalde Walter Colton went up into the foothills to survey the placers in the fall of 1848, he saw at least two Mexican women at work alongside men. One announced, Colton reported, that she was taking out an ounce of gold a day (about sixteen dollars worth), and the other he observed indignantly tossing the contents of her *batea*, or pan, back into the water when it yielded a mere half dollar.[13] Chances are, these women were not full-time gold washers; an ounce a day was not a particularly high take for 1848, and frustration at a half-dollar pan indicates that the second woman was hoping for a quick bonanza.[14] Both probably mined in the time they could spare from their other tasks.

Their other tasks must have been formidable, too. Although Mexican women were not so rare as Anglo American or European women in the mines, even among Mexicans, men made up the majority of immigrants. As a result, women's perceived capabilities were in demand. Antonio Franco Coronel, a Californio who arrived at the Stanislaus placers in the fall of 1848, recalled that a female servant not only cooked for her own party but sold frijoles and tortillas to other miners for one peso a plate. Coronel claimed that she left the diggings after three months with more than thirteen pounds of gold.[15] Both Mexican and non-Mexican men ate food prepared according to Mexican practices; William Perkins remembered how Mexican women sold "the national dish of meat and chile pepper, wrapped within two tortillas" from carts in the Gold Rush town of Sonora, and R. A. Appling, an Anglo southerner, wrote to a relative at home about how much he paid for frijoles, which he knowingly explained was pronounced "free holders."[16] Likewise, Mexican women not only washed the clothing of those with whom they had come to the mines but also sold their laundry services to men who traveled without women.[17] Someone like Rosa Felíz de Murrieta, then, probably looked after the cluster of tents that sheltered her male relatives, and perhaps brought income into the camp by selling her domestic skills and by working the placers—that is, the surface diggings—in her spare time.

Rosa's husband, Joaquín, and his brothers and cousins, relieved from daily domestic concerns, turned their attention to familiar pursuits—gold mines and livestock—pursuits that they hoped would prove more lucrative in California than they had in Mexico. In the state of Sonora, Indian resistance often frustrated settlers' efforts to eke out a livelihood from the land—Apaches, Yaquis, Seris, and Mayos all challenged the Murrietas and related families in the hinterlands.[18] California Indians too resisted invasion, but Sonorans headed for the Sierra foothills found that native peoples there were inundated by immigrants to an extent unheard of by northern Mexican Indians.[19] Then, too, the United States had just acquired California in the late Mexican War; Sonorans accustomed to Spanish and Mexican styles of conquest that stressed incorporation and exploitation of native peoples over elimination may have known they were headed to a country where an aggressive Indian policy touted removal of Indians from areas settled by whites as an ultimate goal.[20] In such a place, perhaps, the Murrieta men could finally make their fortune.

Maybe it would be a fortune in gold, or maybe a fortune that galloped out of California on its own hooves. It seems likely, in fact, that Joaquín Murrieta and his kin were compelled to turn their attention from gold to horses over the four or five years they spent in California. If Mexican miners in Sonora had been hounded by Indians, in California they faced equally indomitable foes—hostile Anglo Americans backed by an arrogantly anti-Mexican state legislature. The story of nativist agitation in the diggings is a complicated one, but Anglo American opposition to Mexicans in the mines took three basic forms: individual incidents of harassment; mining district "laws" that excluded Mexicans and other non–U.S. citizens from particular areas; and a statewide foreign miners' tax, approved in 1850, that charged foreign nationals twenty dollars a month to work the placers.[21] What evidence exists for Murrieta's treatment in the mines concerns harassment—in this case violent attacks by Anglo men in Calaveras County—but such incidents took place in a larger context of systematic exclusionary and discriminatory measures against Mexican nationals.

Anglo intimidation assured that the Gold Rush would be more boondoggle than boom for the Sonorans who accompanied Murrieta to the Southern Mines in 1849. Joaquín, Rosa, and their relatives probably were driven from the Stanislaus placers at least once, maybe more than once, during their California sojourn. No contemporary written accounts describe their expulsion, but everyone from former Murrieta associates to one of the California Rangers later agreed that Anglos evicted Joaquín from rich mining claims. Likewise, not only Murrieta descendants but the grandson of a Calaveras County sheriff told Frank Latta of at least three brutal assaults on the Sonorans: Anglo ruffians raped Rosa, and then, after a dispute with Joaquín's half brother, Jesús Carillo Murrieta, over either a horse or a mule, English-speaking toughs lynched Jesús and horsewhipped Joaquín.[22]

By this time Joaquín may have given up mining altogether—Rosa too would have abandoned whatever use she had made of the *batea*—and the couple seems to have turned to keeping a gaming table near Angels Camp. There Joaquín is said to have dealt monte, a popular Mexican pastime that drew in miners of all nationalities during the Gold Rush. Rosa, depending on how wary she had become of the Anglo men who were then swarming into the foothills like so many hornets, may have frequented the monte table herself; Mexican women in the town of Sonora were doing so at the time, and prior to the American conquest that began in 1846, women's gambling was not uncommon on Mexico's northern frontier.[23]

Ultimately, though, according to Murrieta descendants and associates, Anglo outrages in the Southern Mines proved intolerable. Economic siege was one thing. Just as Sonoran forty-niners knew more about mining than Anglos did, so too they knew more about surviving in what was until so recently the Mexican hinterlands; they knew other ways to create commodities out of California's abundance. Refusing to be driven out of the area altogether, most of the Murrieta men seem within a year or two to have turned to rounding up wild horses in the San Joaquin Valley and driving them south into Mexico for sale to wealthy rancheros.[24] The animals themselves were evidence of earlier decades when Miwok and other interior Indians raided Spanish and then Mexican coastal settlements, capturing horses for their own use and, after the entry of Anglo American fur trappers over the Sierra Nevada in 1826, for trade as well. The vast mustang herds that the Murrietas found in the valley were progeny of those stolen steeds, and the Sonoran immigrants, so familiar with running live-stock on the open range, could put the animals to immediate use.[25]

But economic siege accompanied by flogging, rape, and murder was something else altogether. These were personal, physical assaults that called for different strategies of resistance. Driven from mining claims, Sonoran men could profitably herd wild horses—and steal some Anglo mounts for good measure. In the memories of Murrieta descendants, however, an unholy trinity of events at long last unleashed the vengeance of their forebears. When asked in the 1960s what had happened to Joaquín in California, one aging Murrieta woman replied, apparently through an interpreter, "What happened? Just that the Americano miners assaulted Joaquín's wife, hung his brother and whipped him." The woman's cousin recalled what he had heard from Sonorans who returned with news from the diggings: "They said that Joaquín Murrieta was an honest, hard-working man in . . . Alta California . . . and that the miners in las placeras assaulted Joaquín's wife, whipped him and hung his brother."[26]

Why might these details be so firmly anchored in family memory? Perhaps the events recall a time when Spanish and Mexican notions of communal and familial honor were in decline, disrupted by the incursion of market forces and eclipsed by concomitant values of individual achievement.[27] The very migration undertaken by the Murrietas is evidence of the economic transformations at work in the Mexican north, though Sonora's ties to urban markets were by no means stable in the 1840s and 1850s.[28] The persistent stories of Gold Rush violence and vengeance hark back to an earlier ethic, not yet archaic in the 1850s, under which rape, lynching, and whipping took on meaning as affronts to male honor. Of course rape, in particular, had its own meanings for women, as did the notion of honor.[29] For men, however, sexual violation of a woman called not for her retribution but for the retaliation of her menfolk. And, indeed, however Rosa Felíz de Murrieta reacted to her assailants, it is not her response but that of her husband which is remembered.

The nature of that response is remembered too. Here Murrieta family tradition and contemporary Anglo accounts of conditions in the Southern Mines for a moment converge. All agree that by early 1853 one or more men named Joaquín and his or their comrades were dodging in and out of the Sierra foothills on fast horses, stealing gold dust and livestock and occasionally killing people. Then the stories bifurcate. Murrieta associates and descendants recall that Joaquín

Murrieta carried out a personal vendetta against only those Anglo thugs who heaped shame upon his family, and that his banditry consisted of hunting down the offenders and, one by one, roping and dragging them to death. If Murrieta stole, he stole only what he needed to survive, and only from men like his persecutors; he deplored raids on stages and expresses, freighters and provisioners. In fact, family tradition holds that Murrieta's men broke ranks with a related gang led by Manuel Duarte, who was known as Tres Dedos (Three Fingers), precisely because of Duarte's penchant for highway robbery and indiscriminate bloodshed.[30]

Contemporary Anglo accounts told a different tale, with different characters. There was a Joaquin, but not until May of 1853 was that given name linked to a surname resembling Murrieta.[31] By that time, California newspapers had been running stories about "the notorious outlaw, Joaquin" and his band of desperadoes for months. Generally no family name was attached, though beginning in February accounts occasionally identified a "Joaquin Carillo" as ringleader. Under his direction, or under the direction of *some* Joaquin, Mexican bandits robbed gold miners of gold, stockmen of stock, and almost anyone of life itself. Attacks were random and unprovoked. If any group of people suffered most at the hands of the thieves and murderers, it was the newest immigrants to the Southern Mines: Chinese men.[32]

Anglos were hard-pressed to make sense of all this. Early on, some writers placed Joaquin in a recognizable cultural and historical category by referring to his men as "banditti," a term of Italian origin that conferred upon the men a daunting European lineage. Others linked Joaquin to guerrilla bands active during the U.S.-Mexican War.[33] At least one newspaperman, though, saw danger in ascribing to Joaquin the status of bandit: "It has been the fashion of the historian and the novelist to trace in the characters of their bandit heroes some redeeming traits," the writer warned, "but in the conscience of this blood-thirsty villain there appear to be no qualms, no mercy or reproach."[34] No one had yet claimed publicly that the Sonorans had any motivation other than greed and innate depravity, but this writer wanted to make sure that Joaquin and his band would not be cast in that familiar drama of decent men forced by unfavorable circumstances into brigandage.

The tension that arose out of using the language of banditry to describe the thefts and murders of 1853 continued in Anglo accounts, but newspapermen did their best to guard against the implication that Joaquin was a victim turned avenger. No decent

man, however tormented, would wreak havoc on the innocent and
defenseless, and this is what Joaquin did. White women and children—customary candidates for the cultural category of "innocent
and defenseless"—were few and far between in the diggings, and so
Anglos took to assigning Chinese men such roles: "[Joaquin] rides
through the settlements slaughtering the weak and unprotected. . . .
So daring and reckless is he, that he marches in the day time through
thickly peopled settlements and actually correls [*sic*] the Chinese by
the score."[35] According to newspapers, Joaquin would bully his way
into Chinese tents and force the residents to cook for him. If a
Chinese man resisted, one of the bandits might draw a knife and
"run the unfortunate celestial through the body."[36] The process by
which Anglo Americans came to terms with Asian immigration in
part by assimilating Chinese men to dominant notions of female
gender is a complicated one, but one aspect of that invidious process
began here, where white men momentarily proclaimed themselves
defenders of Chinese miners.[37]

If Joaquin proved himself unmanly by attacking the "weak," he
did so in other ways as well. To Anglos, particularly those from the
northeastern United States, Joaquin had all the fortitude and bravery
of a man, but none of the conscience, all of the lively impulses of a
man, but none of the self-control. He was both "daring and reckless,"
his deeds both "bold and heartless."[38] His thieving ways further challenged the emerging discourse of manliness by lampooning the belief
that success, increasingly defined as economic gain, resulted from
hard work and prudent plans. After one incident in which Joaquin's
band apparently stole several thousand dollars, a Calaveras County
correspondent lamented, "once more has the hand of industry been
forced to yield its hard earnings to depraved and reckless outlaws."[39]
For Anglo Americans, Joaquin must have been a sort of gender nightmare, embodying the potency of manhood without its customary
restraints. Indeed, when white men tried to chase him down in
locally organized posses, Joaquin easily eluded them: "so fertile is he
in expedients," one account read, "that he baffles his pursuers and
defeats the plans of the many thousands who are lying in wait for
him."[40] For Anglo men, Joaquin was like their own worst selves set
loose in the diggings—dark, sensual, impulsive, out of control.[41]

Something had to be done. At first, Anglo men in Calaveras County
took it upon themselves to clear out what they deemed to be the robbers' den, known to the English-speaking as "Yackee Camp" (located
first by Yaqui Indians, who, like other Sonorans, had journeyed north
to the California placers). According to newspaper reports, a posse

from nearby San Andreas rode into the camp and found a Mexican "who boasted of having killed Americans . . . and who was supposed to have been concerned in the present murders." On that evidence, they strung him up. Then the Anglos moved on to Cherokee Flat (another camp first settled by Indians) "and came up with two other Mexicans," who tried to flee. The Americans shot one and hanged the other.[42] In the meantime, other Anglos did their part in San Andreas and along the forks of the Calaveras River, forcing Mexicans one by one out of the area: "If an American meets a Mexican," one account explained, "he takes his horse, his arms, and bids him leave." A mass meeting at Double Springs called for more sweeping measures, passing a resolution to make it "the duty of every American citizen . . . to exterminate the Mexican race from the county."[43] As another item declared, "Violent diseases require violent remedies . . . and we should remember that in Calaveras county no man can retire to his pillow without the fear of the intrusion of some villain, no man's life is safe, there is no settlement that is not liable to an attack."[44]

The hysteria reflected in newspaper reports was not the whole Anglo story, however. Anglo American men in the Southern Mines who kept journals were more temperate in their response to the events of 1853. Many diarists did not mention the commotion at all. Others devoted one or two entries to the events during the winter months, noting down whatever they could learn from conversation and from the local papers.[45] Alfred Doten, a twenty-three-year-old New Englander who was keeping a store in Calaveras County, was in an unusually good position to gather information, and indeed, he wrote more about the excitement than did others. As early as September 1852, Doten mentioned a "Mexican rascal" who frequented the tent to buy provisions and on whom Doten had pulled a revolver in a dispute over liquor; Doten claimed the "scamp" was one of a band of six thieves headed by a man named Cladne.[46] In January 1853, Doten noted that "the Mexicans on the upper part of the Calaveras have taken to robbing, murdering, stealing horses, & c," and he described the exodus of Mexican women, men, and children from the area after the cleanup at "Yankeeville" (Yaqui Camp).[47] Even at the height of the excitement, though, on February 17—when hundreds of Anglo men were combing the hills of Calaveras County in pursuit of "Joaquín, Cladne, and his band"—Doten reported no widespread terror in the area, save that among Mexicans who were being driven from the diggings. On a night when no man was supposed to be able to go to bed without fear for his life, the habitual reveler Doten noted, "Evening, the boys were in and we had a *soirée*."[48]

The newspapermen and the diarists, of course, were telling different stories for different reasons. Stockton's *San Joaquin Republican*, in particular, had joined in a larger campaign among Anglo men in the Southern Mines to persuade the California state government to accomplish what they had proved themselves incapable of accomplishing—ending Mexican insurgency once and for all. What good was the Treaty of Guadalupe Hidalgo, which had ended the war with Mexico in 1848, if Mexican men in California were free to resist Anglo dominance with arms and at will? The short-lived foreign miners' tax of 1850, which similarly had sought to contain and control the Mexican presence in the diggings, had been a fiasco; so many Sonorans simply headed for home that commerce in the Southern Mines collapsed.[49] Some Mexicans defiantly stayed on, and now it seemed Anglo Americans were reaping what they had sown. Individual Anglo men could and did sign petitions begging California Governor John Bigler, first, to offer a reward for the capture of Joaquin (he did—a thousand dollars), and then, when local posses failed, to deputize a company of rangers to bring the bandit in.[50] But the newspapers could dramatize the plight of law-abiding citizens in a more disinterested fashion.

At long last the campaign bore fruit; on May 17, 1853, Governor Bigler approved "An Act to authorize the Raising of a Company of Rangers," designating Harry Love as commander.[51] Mariposa County petitioners had first suggested Love because of his "experience in border warfare and a long residence on the frontiers of Texas."[52] The legislature must have thought those were good qualifications for chasing Mexicans. In fact, once the troops were mustered in, a Mariposa correspondent assured newspaper readers that *all* of the men had "smelt powder either in Mexico or Texas."[53] More and more, the rangers seemed soldiers engaged in a rearguard action designed to shore up the gains of the late expansionist war.

The drive for state intervention had not gone uncontested. Though little publicized at the time, California Assemblyman José María Covarrubias had protested the "violent remedies" debated by the legislature. Covarrubias, a native of France who had become a naturalized citizen of Mexico and married into the prominent Carillo family of Santa Barbara, drafted a minority report on the matter in his capacity as chair of the Committee on Military Affairs.[54] Addressing a proposal for a bounty to be placed on Joaquin, the legislator cited a basic Anglo American legal tenet: "To set a price upon the head of any individual who has not been examined and convicted by due process of law," he wrote, "is to proceed upon an assumption of guilt." Neither was Covarrubias impressed by the source of such assumptions: "floating rumor and mere statements of newspapers should not be taken as conclusive evidence." These accounts, he observed, were "somewhat erroneous." Then his understatement gave way to incredulity: "Unless the said Joaquin be endowed with supernatural qualities he could not have been seen at the same time in several places widely separated from each other." Besides, the assemblyman argued, a reward might encourage the acquisitive "to magnify fancied resemblance," resulting in "dozens of heads" being turned in for identification.

Finally, Covarrubias took up the matter of the name Joaquin Carillo (at this point Carillo was the only surname accounts had attached to the bandit): "there are citizens of this State, descendants of ancient and honorable families, who bear the name of Joaquin Carillo."[55] One of them happened to be the legislator's brother-in-law, a district judge in Santa Barbara.[56] Covarrubias may have been more concerned about the "ancient and honorable families" of old California than the countless Sonoran *pobladores* who had answered the call of gold since 1848. Increasingly, though, the fates of affluent Californios were tied to those of poorer Spanish-speaking immigrants. The Anglo pursuit of a vaguely identified Mexican could produce dozens of heads with "black hair" and "black eyes"; the search for a "Joaquin Carillo" could bring dishonor to once preeminent men who were fast losing ground, both literally and figuratively, in their native land.[57]

In the end, Covarrubias's appeal to Anglo American notions of equity and his plea for respect for Californio notions of honor fell on deaf ears. By late May, Harry Love and his rangers were in the field, hot on the trail of men who suddenly had become known as the "five Joaquins"—Joaquin Muriati, Joaquin Ocomorenia, Joaquin Valenzuela, Joaquin Botellier, and Joaquin Carillo.[58] It is hard to know whether the proliferation of Joaquins represented Anglo attempts to explain the geographic spread of reported depredations or instead reflected information gathered from months of chasing the supposed perpetrators.[59] Most likely, both phenomena were at work and were mutually reinforcing. New intelligence about the bandits, who were reported to number in the hundreds, came in from each self-appointed posse, but somehow only men with the name Joaquin stuck in Anglo memories.[60]

And so it was, according to the accounts of Love and his men, that on July 25, when the rangers finally rode into a camp at Arroyo

Cantúa near the Diablo Range on the Tulare Plains (south and west across the San Joaquin Valley from the Southern Mines), one of them was able immediately to point out which of the Mexican men gathered there was Joaquin. After all, there were so many from which to choose. When that man tried to escape, first by horse and then on foot, the rangers took aim and shot him. At least two of Love's men claimed that as he fell the man called out to them to stop shooting, as he had had enough, *"No tere mas, yo soy muerto."*[61]

Meanwhile, Anglo reports say, Love killed three more suspects and detained two others, as the rest of the Mexicans encamped at Arroyo Cantúa fled into the hills. The rangers then cut the heads off of two of the four slain men, and Love sent two of his charges to the U.S. outpost at Fort Miller to have the heads preserved in alcohol there. One of the beheaded men, all agreed, was the man identified as Joaquin when rangers first rode into the arroyo.[62] But when Love wrote to the governor announcing news of the battle a week later, he insisted, "There is not the least doubt that the head now in my possession is that of the noted Joaquin Muriatta the Chief and leader of the murderers and Robbers of the Calaveras and Mariposa."[63]

The "noted Joaquin Muriatta," of course, had only recently been named in Anglo newspapers as one of the "five Joaquins," and he had never been identified as the ringleader. And so perhaps it is not surprising that some Anglos wondered just whose head Love's men had taken to Fort Miller. The *Los Angeles Star* and San Francisco's *Alta California* poked fun at the whole business, and the *Alta* editor went so far as to suggest, "Although I will not say that interested parties have gotten up this Joaquin expedition, yet such expeditions can generally be traced to have an origin with a few speculators."[64] Writers for Stockton's *San Joaquin Republican*, the newspaper that had pushed so hard for state intervention, continued to champion their man Love and his detachment, and chastised the skeptics: "Why do they . . . cast a slur on the reputation of as brave a body of young men as ever entered the field?" But even such staunch advocates could only add to the confusion; the same article that took rival papers to task went on to declare, "In our mind, there is no doubt that Joaquin Valancuela (not Carillo) has been killed." To further persuade readers, the editor quoted a Mariposa correspondent on this Joaquin Valancuela: "'He is the Simon Pure Joaquin, and you will see his head in the course of a week in Stockton.'"[65]

And the other *cabeza*? Love claimed only that the second head had belonged to one of Joaquin's "principal men," or again to Joaquin's "Lieutenant."[66] But even before Love filed his report the newspapers had a name for the decapitated Mexican man—"Three Fingered Jack." This "Jack" was also described as "notorious," though no Anglo accounts before the conflict at Cantúa had ever used that sobriquet or mentioned a bandit whose hand had but three digits.[67] Be that as it may, this second head suffered an even more ignominious fate than the one said to belong to one or another of the Joaquins. Love reported to the governor that the head of the "Lieutenant" had been so disfigured by a shot through the skull that the rangers had to bury it at Fort Miller.[68] Apparently, though, some prescient, or just blood-thirsty, Anglo soldier had wittingly or unwittingly prepared for this turn of events by slicing off the dead man's three-fingered hand as well, because ten days or so after the raid at the arroyo, the *San Joaquin Republican* reported the arrival of one of Love's men in Stockton with "the head of Joaquin and the hand of 'Three Fingered Jack.'"[69] Six days later, broadsides appeared in the streets of Stockton announcing a one-day exhibition of:

THE HEAD
of the renowned Bandit!
JOAQUIN!
AND THE
HAND OF THREE FINGERED JACK!
THE NOTORIOUS ROBBER AND MURDERER.[70]

It all happened so quickly that no one seemed to wonder how it was that rangers commissioned "for the purpose of capturing the party or gang of robbers commanded by the five Joaquins" returned from the field not with prisoners to be turned over to county authorities (only one arrested man survived and landed in the Mariposa county jail), but with a head and a hand to be preserved in glass jars.[71] José María Covarrubias probably was not surprised; although there was no official order to murder men and mutilate corpses, Covarrubias assumed that the bandits' pursuers would return with heads for identification.[72] Why? Surely live prisoners—or even full corpses—although more difficult to transport, could have been identified more easily than the distended visages on heads soaked in alcohol, and hence would have guaranteed a quick reward. Perhaps Covarrubias understood that the Mexican men and their Anglo enemies were caught up in a pernicious affair of honor that would likely end in dishonorable death. The legislator took as a matter of course that decapitation of someone named Joaquin Carillo could shame not just that man and his family but other, more affluent Joaquin Carillos as well. Besmirching the family name, beheading—these were dishonoring acts, and Covarrubias both anticipated and sought to prevent them.[73]

What the legislator probably did not know was that some of the Anglo Americans were operating under not entirely dissimilar assumptions about male honor. All sorts of U.S. men—northern men, southern men, urban clerks and farmhands, African American slaves, free blacks, and displaced American Indians—had gone to California in search of gold, and most likely many sorts of American men joined the war on Joaquin. The particular discourse of manliness that pervaded newspaper accounts of 1853 indicates that northern, white, aspiring middle-class men were prominent actors in the struggle not only to catch the bandits but to mold perceptions of the problem of banditry as well.

But a faint trail of evidence suggests that southern frontiersmen were also among Joaquin's most determined opponents—men whose understandings of personal honor may have resembled Mexican beliefs as much as white northerners' notions of manhood. Virtually all Anglo accounts agree that among the rangers was a lieutenant, William Byrnes, who had known Joaquin personally in the early years of the Gold Rush; many further agree that Byrnes and Joaquin played monte together. This man Byrnes is variously credited with having identified Joaquin either when the rangers rode into Arroyo Cantúa or after the shooting had stopped, when corpses littered the ground. Many say it was Byrnes who cut the heads off two of the dead men (and perhaps the hand as well?), and all agree that Byrnes was one of the rangers who took the body parts to Fort Miller for preservation.[74] Who was this man Byrnes, who seems to have known a Joaquin and who played a key role in seeing to it that the head and the name of a Joaquin would live in infamy?

Leonard Withington Noyes, a New Englander who wrote his reminiscences in later years, recalled knowing a "Bill Burnes" and his brother Mike at Murphys Camp in Calaveras County, not far from where Joaquin Murrieta was supposed to have dealt monte. Although the spelling differs, it seems likely that "Bill Burnes" and "William Byrnes" were the same person. According to Noyes, Mike Byrnes was one of four men who worked together on the Texas Claim and called themselves the "Texas Rangers." Noyes claimed that these Texans made "enormous sums of money which was all plaid off at *Monte* and expended for bad Whiskey." He added that they "delighted in swagaring around Town with a Big Six Shooter and Boey Knife . . . usually half drunk and acheing for a quarel." William Byrnes seems not to have mined with his brother's company, but he lived in the area and Noyes knew him, at least by reputation: "Bill Burnes . . . Gambled was a Shooter from Texas and inclined to quarel." Noyes recalled that Byrnes "was said to have shot the Notorious Joaquin Muriatta whose Head Harry Love had on exhibition afterwards." William Byrnes would also have known his brother's mining partner Sam Green, another of the "Texas Rangers," whom Noyes depicted as constantly "Making an exhibit of his Revolver & Knife and threatening Vengance to all who happened to disagree with him."[75] When Noyes described Sam Green and the Byrnes brothers, he was evoking a characteristi-cally Yankee portrait of white southern frontiersmen: it was a portrait that captured all the quick-tempered violence of that male world without comprehending its roots in notions of honor that could turn taunts, insults, and even practical jokes into deadly challenges.[76]

Joaquín Murrieta may have set up camp next door to that male world in 1850 or 1851. The relations between Green, the Byrnes brothers, and Murrieta's family are likely to remain largely lost to his-torians, but what little evidence there is points to complicated alliances and enmities. William Byrnes may well have known Joaquín Murrieta, or else one of his close male relatives, and the setting for their acquaintance might well have been the monte table. Given Byrnes's later cut-throat activity at Arroyo Cantúa, one might assume that he and Murrieta were not friends. Sam Green was also apt to have known Murrieta, but chances are Green was on better terms with the Murrieta clan. A Calaveras County sheriff remembered,

> There was bad blood between Sam Green and Bill Lang over the lynching of Jesus Murrieta, Joaquin's brother, in Murphys New Diggins when Lang accused Jesus Murrieta of stealing a mule that he, Lang, had sold to Jesus. . . . Green sometime after this meets Bill Lang and as Green was in his cups, denounced him. "You cowardly cur you had nothing on them Murrieta boys, Jesus paid you for that mule. You are a born scoundrel. . . . I ought to kill you and I guess I will."

He did. And he was hanged for murder in 1852 at Mokelumne Hill.[77]

The point here is not so much to determine who shot whom, who lynched whom, who tangled with whom over a game of cards, but rather to suggest what kind of social world gave rise to a larger con-flict that finally ended with state-sponsored Anglo rangers galloping off to a U.S. military base with two Mexican men's heads and one hand. Sam Green's doubly fatal fight with a man who was probably among the Murrietas' harassers indicates that when southern back-country notions of male honor shared ground with those of Sonoran *pobladores*, unlikely alliances could develop. They were not long tolerated, though, among Anglos, who quickly put an end to Green's pugnacious ways. After the hanging of Sam Green, there is scant evidence of any cross-ethnic ties, as Mexican men intensified their resistance to Anglo depredations and Anglo men nervously imagined the worst—every robbery, every murder became the act of an elusive, omnipresent, omnipotent Joaquin.

William Byrnes, the "shooter from Texas," may have had his own reasons for chasing down a Mexican man with whom he had once played monte, but Byrnes was content to subsume his individual tale of enmity within a larger Anglo story about amoral Mexican men who preyed on "defenseless" Chinese and imperiled American habits of industry. His personal narrative may have been resolved by the deeply dishonoring act of decapitation; the shared Anglo tale found its denouement in a heroic battle that reenacted, one more time, the American conquest of Mexico's upper extremities.

The story was not over, however, as long as people kept on retelling and, indeed, reinventing it, as I have here. I began my retelling with the voices of twentieth-century Sonoran descendants and elderly associates of the Murrieta clan, filtered through the research agenda of the author Frank Latta and my own strategy for introducing the Gold Rush with one of its most intriguing conflicts. Some of those same voices, just as they contest contemporary Anglo accounts of the cause, extent, and meaning of the events of 1853, similarly contest the story's outcome. In effect, Murrieta descendants and associates contend that Anglo readings of banditry and its suppression in the Southern Mines are lies.

This is especially true of the account of the Cantúa raid offered by Avelino Martínez, who told Latta that he had been hostler for Joaquín Valenzuela, cousin of Joaquín Murrieta, in California. Martínez—who Latta says was of Spanish Mexican, Indian, and Chinese descent—was convinced throughout his life that Harry Love and his rangers were a detachment of the U.S. Army.[78] He claimed they wore soldiers' uniforms and carried soldiers' guns, and that Murrieta, Valenzuela, and the others, having left the mines and taken up mustang running, knew that they were being pursued by the military. When Love caught up with the Sonorans at Arroyo Cantúa, Martínez explained, they were rounding up horses for one last drive down into Mexico.

The night before the raid, Joaquín Murrieta and a few others were encamped on higher ground at Las Tres Piedras, above and to the west of the arroyo, and hence were not at Cantúa when Love arrived the following morning. Valenzuela had dispatched Martínez to Murrieta's camp to pick up some things they needed for the trip south, and so the hostler was not at the arroyo either. Murrieta's hostler, on the other hand—a California Indian called Chappo, who was raised at Mission San Carlos Borromeo—*was* at Cantúa (caring for Murrieta's lame horse), along with Valenzuela and the man known to Martínez as Tres Dedos.[79] Martínez recalled that Tres Dedos and Murrieta had argued bitterly over what course of action they should take now that the U.S. Army was after them—Tres Dedos advocated another round of robberies so that all could return to Sonora with plenty of gold, and Murrieta refused. That was the last Martínez knew of those camped at Arroyo Cantúa until late on the morning of July 25, when another of Valenzuela's men rode up with news of the army attack at the lower camp.[80]

Although anxious to see what had happened at the arroyo, the men at Las Tres Piedras did not dare ride down that afternoon, for fear soldiers would discover them. So they spent a sleepless night up in the hills, and then followed circling buzzards into the camp the next day. They found eight corpses there, according to Martínez, two of them mutilated—those of Chappo, the Indian hostler, who had lost his head, and Tres Dedos, who had lost both head and three-fingered hand. Joaquín Valenzuela was also among those killed. All of the dead men had been robbed, their clothes and boots cut open, and the entire camp had been swept clean of horses, saddles, blankets, guns, knives, and gold—save a few ounces someone had hidden in a coffee pot on the morning of the raid. Martínez was emphatic about the identity of the decapitated men—one was Tres Dedos, who became known to Anglos as Three-Fingered Jack, and the other was his fellow hostler Chappo. Murrieta was not among the dead; he helped bury them. The "head of the renowned bandit Joaquin" exhibited first at Stockton in August 1853, then, belonged to a mission Indian named Chappo.[81]

In the telling and retelling of stories like this one and the ones about harassment of the Murrietas in the mines, family members and associates have over the years found ways to get the last word, at least among themselves, in their exchange with Anglos. Faced with a Yankee discourse of manhood and morality that cast their forebear as a godless fiend, they could point to the lust, greed, and cruelty of Anglo men in the diggings and on the horse trails. Faced with a southern discourse of male honor that sought to shame their fore-bear, they could turn the tables and offer the ultimate insult to hon-orable men—call them liars. Encountering a drama that ended with a Mexican man deeply dishonored, they could rewrite the final scene by substituting for their kinsman a California Indian—since native peoples, by definition, already were dishonored in Spanish Mexican cultures.[82] Encountering yet another story about U.S. victory, they could tell their own tale about Americans hell-bent for glory—grim, grasping, and gullible. None of this could bring back the dead or give the women and men of the Murrieta clan another chance to hunt for their fortune unmolested, but it could preserve a sense of dignity that Anglo Americans had tried to destroy.

In this project, the Sonorans whom Latta interviewed and other champions of Murrieta's legacy have had some help, because from the start California's newspapers whispered Anglo culpability. Simply calling Joaquin a bandit invoked a larger narrative about downtrod-den men, compelled by repeated injury or injustice to turn to a life of crime. One editor had confronted this problem head-on, and tried valiantly to assure readers that *this* bandit had no such sad story to explain his malevolence. As long as Joaquin was on the loose, his opponents were able to check this discursive flow. But once the dan-gers of life in the diggings seemed to wane, and the bandit's wicked brain appeared to be separated from his murderous and thieving hands, the floodgates opened.

The first freshet came in the form of a small book entitled *The Life and Adventures of Joaquín Murieta, the Celebrated California Bandit,* pub-lished in 1854. The author's name as it appeared on the title page was Yellow Bird; to others he was known as John Rollin Ridge, son of a Connecticut Yankee, Sarah Northrup, and John Ridge, now deceased, but formerly a leader among those Cherokees who urged compliance with the federal policy of removing native peoples from the south-eastern states to Indian Territory in the 1830s. The elder Ridge had been killed in 1839 at his new western home by those outraged at his support of the Treaty of New Echota, by which Cherokees ceded their land claims in the East.[83] John Rollin Ridge—who witnessed his father's murder and participated in the deadly feuds that marked the redefinition of the Cherokee Nation in the midnineteenth century—emigrated, like many Cherokees, to California at the time of the Gold Rush.[84] Ridge failed there at both mining and trading; indeed, recall-ing his background among Cherokee planters, he complained in a letter, "I have worked harder than any slave I ever owned or my father either. All to no purpose."[85] *The Life and Adventures of Joaquín Murieta* was his first literary venture.

Starting where Anglo newspapers left off in 1853, Ridge took up the language of banditry with a vengeance. For Ridge, Murrieta was "a man as remarkable . . . as any of the renowned robbers of the Old and New World"; he was the veritable "Rinaldo Rinaldini of California" (Rinaldo Rinaldini was the hero in a late eighteenth-century German novel of brigandage). In endearing Murrieta to readers, Ridge pulled no punches. Murrieta as a boy had been "mild and peaceable." As a young man he was devastatingly handsome. What is more, by the end of the U.S.-Mexican War, he had become "disgusted with the conduct of his own degenerate countrymen and fired with enthusiastic admiration of the American character." All to no purpose. In California, men who "bore the name of Americans but failed to support the honor and dignity of that title" ran Murrieta off mining claims, whipped him, raped his "mistress" Rosita, and hanged his half brother.[86] The rest, so to speak, was history.

And memory. Once Ridge published his tale of atrocity and its retribution in 1854, Anglo recollections of unprovoked Mexican attacks on mining camps would never again seem so credible. The Ridge version of Murrieta's life, which teased out the narrative of banditry embedded in even the most rabidly anti-Mexican newspaper accounts of 1853, became the basis for countless plays, operas, poems, crime stories, dime novels, and histories about Murrieta in a number of languages. The Spanish-language versions, popular in Mexico, Chile, and Spain, featured either Mexican or Chilean bandidos, reflecting the origins of most Spanish-speaking Gold Rush immigrants. In English, the story probably reached its widest audience with the Depression-era biography by Walter Noble Burns, *The Robin Hood of El Dorado,* and the Hollywood film version with the same title, released in 1936 and starring Warner Baxter.[87]

Ordinary people who had lived in Anglo communities in the Southern Mines·told similar stories as they grew older. Mrs. Lee Whipple-Haslam's reminiscences, for example, echoed aspects of Ridge's version. Even though Whipple-Haslam insisted that "mob violence" was justified during the Gold Rush "to put the fear of the Lord . . . into the hearts of Mexicans," she claimed that Murrieta "was painted blacker than he deserved." Three white "brutes of the lowest order" had robbed Murrieta, "heaped every indignity on his wife," and burned down his cabin. While other accounts attributed Murrieta's subsequent vendetta to his sense of honor, Whipple-Haslam traced the violence to his "untutored, savage heart." Still, she

"I am Joaquin! If any of you want to shoot me, now is your time; I dare you to shoot!"

A representation of Joaquín Murrieta from *The Life of Joaquin Murieta the Brigand Chief of California; Being a Complete History of His Life, from the Age of Sixteen to the Time of His Capture and Death at the Hands of Capt. Harry Love, in the Year 1853* (San Francisco: Office of the "California Police Gazette," 1859).

Courtesy of the Bancroft Library.

could not really blame him. At least, she reasoned, he was "never known to molest women and children."[88]

Both English- and Spanish-language accounts of Joaquín Murrieta, then, have depended on bandit narratives to make intelligible the events of 1853. Indeed, the Sonorans who raided Anglo gold and horses in the diggings may have seen themselves as bandits, thereby helping to create a historical hall of mirrors in which substance and reflection have been indistinguishable. Nevertheless, the stories of banditry inscribed in conversations, newspaper articles, plays, and the like over the past century and a half have had different narrative purposes. Consider, for example, the varied strategies of Ridge, of Anglo chroniclers, of Murrieta family members, and of recent Chicano writers.

For Ridge, the moral of Murrieta's story rang clear as a bell: "there is nothing so dangerous in its consequences as *injustice to individuals*— whether it arise from prejudice of color or from any other source; that a wrong done to one man is a wrong to society and to the world."[89] Cherokee accommodationist, southern slaveholder, northern academy-educated forty-niner, Ridge drew from an unusual repertoire of experiences to write a story that he hoped would bring in "a great deal of money," with which he planned to start up a newspaper that would give voice to the "leading minds in the different Indian nations."[90] But his pamphlet novel owed a debt to the genre of cheap fiction that has been analyzed as a site of cultural conflict in which "signs with wide appeal and resonance"—the bandit hero, for example—take on different masks, in which "conflicting groups of people become giant characters."[91]

For Anglo chroniclers, Murrieta's banditry had another significance. First and foremost, it established Murrieta's band—and by extension other Mexican adversaries—as worthy opponents for Anglo American men. (That Anglo men themselves were the root cause of Murrieta's marauding was a problem for which Ridge had already provided a neat solution; the Sonorans' Anglo tormentors were Americans in name only, men from whom real Americans could readily dissociate themselves.) Ridge's editor had made this aim more explicit when he described Murrieta in the book's preface as "a manifest contradiction" to the belief that Mexicans were "'A Nation of Cowards.'"[92]

The history of U.S. westward expansion is replete with examples of male antagonists who, in the heat of combat, seem spineless knaves; later, in the soft light of victory, they become noble foes. The foremost instance of this gendered process, of course, is the construction of the American Indian "brave"—a construction close at hand when Whipple-Haslam indulgently attributed Murrieta's vengeance to his

"untutored, savage heart." Implicit in this reinvention of adversaries
is a variant of what has been called "imperialist nostalgia," by which
agents of colonialism yearn for "what they themselves have transformed."[93] Romantic memories of a dashing, but defeated, Mexican
bandit, then, reflected back upon his presumably equally dashing,
and victorious, Anglo opponents. At the same time, such memories
mourned the passing of a stalwart enemy whom Anglos had left
headless on the battlefield.

Or so it was among some of those who had lived through the Gold
Rush. In the case of Joaquín Murrieta, it took only a generation or
two for some Anglos to abandon nostalgic constructions. Thus, in the
same month that *The Robin Hood of El Dorado* appeared in movie theaters across the United States, an Anglo humorist who wrote for the
San Francisco Chronicle took aim at the Gold Rush bandit in a story
provocatively titled "My Grandfather Debunks Murietta, Who Was a
Sissy." The writer Earle Ennis reported that Murrieta's mother "liked
the Lord Fauntleroy style of dress and made [Joaquín] retain his curls
into manhood." Thus coiffured, Murrieta would "flip his long, raven
locks out of his eyes when he was angry." Furthermore, the bandit
"walked like Clark Gable"—not the walk of a (white) man's man. As
for Murrieta's exploits, the humorist dismissed them as the overreac-
tions of a hysteric: "Once he shot a whole company of infantry
because they marched through an old lady's cornfield. On another
occasion he chased a general in full uniform from Tuolumne
Meadows to Oregon because the general was mean to his horse."
Indeed, while successive generations of white people indulged ever
more freely in imperialist nostalgia with regard to the Native
American "brave," the legacy of the Mexican American "bandit" has
been more erratic and ambiguous. But questions of gender, as well as
race, have remained at the center of changing Anglo constructions.[94]

Murrieta family members and contemporary Chicano writers have
used the language of banditry differently than have Ridge or Anglo
chroniclers, though family and ethnic strategies owe a debt to Ridge's
storytelling, which contributed to a cross-national ennobling of
Murrieta's memory. Murrieta descendants and associates recall a fore-
bear who did all within his power to defend, not degrade, the family
name. Most likely, oral "tradition" about Murrieta has undergone
considerable reinvention over the years, as tale tellers have reconciled
conflicting reminiscences and tailored a narrative of the California
years consistent with present family circumstances.[95] But over the
many years that Frank Latta spoke with women and men named
Murrieta, Valenzuela, and Felíz in Sonora and California, certain

memories held relatively constant: the journey north; the harassment in the mines, including rape, whipping, and lynching; the turn to mustang running; the rift between Murrieta and Tres Dedos; and the fight at Arroyo Cantúa—which Murrieta was said to have survived. As significant as these details is the consistent pride family members voiced as they talked to Latta about a man who, far from dying a dishonorable death, disappeared after the final battle, so to live on in memory.

Chicano writers, activist and academic alike, similarly have made use of the bandit narrative, but for larger purposes. Identifying Murrieta as a social bandit—a man engaged in individual insurrection who is heralded among the oppressed as a hero—Chicano historians have given him an important place in an ethnic past plagued by domination that can serve as a source of remembered power in creating a more just and equitable ethnic future.[96] This hopeful creation of ethnicity through the arts of memory occurs as well in the epic poem by the Chicano activist Rodolfo "Corky" Gonzales, *I Am Joaquín—Yo soy Joaquín*, first published in 1967.[97] A searching study of the ambiguities of Chicano history—a past both Indian and Spanish, Mexican and American, a past of both "tyrant and slave"—the poem begins with uncertainty, "I am Joaquín / lost in a world of confusion," and ends in anticipated triumph, "I am Joaquín / . . . I WILL ENDURE!" Between uncertainty and triumph, the reader meets the presumed Joaquín of the poem's title:

> all men feared the guns of
> Joaquín Murrieta.
> I killed those men who dared
> to steal mine,
> who raped and killed
> my love
> my wife.[98]

The familial drama of female shame and male honor is finally played out on a larger stage, and in that drama Anglo American men, cowering in the hills of California, pay a high price for their unmanly ways. Remembered victory, then, becomes a wellspring of renewed resistance.[99]

What of my own purposes in retelling—indeed, reinventing—the story of Joaquín Murrieta? I have done so in part because the story illustrates in microcosm some of the tensions between memory and history that characterize knowing the Gold Rush itself, and hence underscores the difficulties inherent in studying something so utterly common. But while the Murrieta tale engages the dialectic of history and memory, it does so from a perilous position. If the Gold Rush benefits from a habit of ritual remembering in mainstream Anglo American culture, Joaquín Murrieta—despite all of the books, poems, paintings, and films—suffers from an Anglo habit of ritual amnesia. I ought to know; I was well into my research on the Southern Mines before I "remembered" that Mexican "banditry" was central—both chronologically and conceptually—to my study of social relations during the California Gold Rush decade, 1848 to 1858.[100]

And so it is. In telling the tale, I have tried to create a vivid but also mercurial picture of the decade at its midpoint in order to persuade you that the Gold Rush, particularly as it occurred in California's Southern Mines, marked a time and place of tremendous contest about maleness and femaleness, about color and culture, and about wealth and power. I have hinted that there was something special about the Southern Mines that kept these contests close to the surface of daily life, so that they easily erupted into violence of all sorts—economic, physical, political, sexual. All over the gold regions, the relative absence of women, the overwhelming presence of men of many nations and colors and creeds, and the wild fluctuation of local economies ensured that white, American-born, Protestant men who aspired to middle-class status would be anxious about issues of gender, of race and culture, and of class. After all, many such men assumed that they, collectively, should subdue and rule the newest territorial acquisition of the United States.

But what was true everywhere in the diggings was especially true in the Southern Mines, where the foreign-born predominated in numbers, where Miwok Indians stubbornly persisted, where the small female population included a large proportion of non-Anglo women, and where the capitalist trajectory of gold exploitation and the accompanying elaboration of class hierarchies were thwarted by inadequate underground deposits suitable for industrialized mining. On this meandering, even dead-end, path to industrialization, the dominance of Anglo American men and institutions was often—as we have seen—difficult to enforce, and groups of people united by shared interests could create for themselves spheres of autonomy and strategies for interdependence.

Still, historical study of the Gold Rush has concentrated on the Northern Mines, where the trajectory from surface, individualized (placer) mining to underground, industrialized (quartz or hardrock) mining was most clear.[101] Why do we know more about rich diggings, like the Northern Mines, than about relatively poorer diggings, like .

the Southern Mines? (The same is true for their analogues outside California; consider, for example, Virginia City, Nevada, and Virginia City, Montana.) How is it that poorer diggings came to be populated disproportionately by people born outside the United States? To what extent has the protracted boom economy—searched for but not found in the Southern Mines—become a metaphor for American expansionism, optimism, and "staying power"? To what extent do these constructs in turn reflect dominant nineteenth- and twentieth-century discourses of gender, of race and ethnicity, and of class? How did the California Gold Rush become part of an American language of success? In that process, what has been remembered and what forgotten?

These are some of the questions I address in the chapters that follow. Key in my reading of the Gold Rush is a commonplace of women's and ethnic studies—that, in the United States, women of all races and ethnicities and both women and men of color constitute "marked" and white men "unmarked" categories of human experience, the unmarked category serving as the normative, the more inclusive, the less "interested" and particular.[102] It is among my purposes in this study to foreground the lives of women of color, men of color, and white women, and to "mark" the categories of Anglo and male experience—to show them to be as historically and culturally contingent, as deeply linked to understandings of gender and race, and as limited in their ability to "explain" the Gold Rush as that of any other group of participants. Sometimes I will do so by emphasizing the peculiar specificity of the lives of the dominant; at other times I will pointedly "change the subject."[103] I will continue to talk about the ways in which all-male events have been about gender, and about how white women's and men's doings have been about race. I will also have occasion to read nondominant peoples into Gold Rush stories that have seemed not to be about them at all.[104]

This latter strategy I have already employed in my not-too-subtle efforts to read Rosa Felíz de Murrieta back into the tale of Joaquín Murrieta—efforts that faltered once the tempo of the narrative picked up and took a forced march into paramilitary conflict. Her disappearance in my story reflects her virtual absence in all accounts of the events of 1853 after the remembered rape in the mines. Anglo accounts generated prior to the battle at Arroyo Cantúa had always ignored her existence, and Murrieta descendants and associates, when they mention her, place her out of harm's way at a rancho in Alameda County, in the San Francisco Bay area, during the face-off between the bandits and the rangers.[105] Then she—like her husband, for that matter—vanishes altogether.

Of all the scores of Murrieta family members and acquaintances
Frank Latta interviewed between 1920 and 1980, only one person
(and then her offspring) remembered what had become of Rosa and
Joaquín. In 1936, in Hermosillo, Sonora, a woman who described
herself as the widow of Joaquín Murrieta's nephew explained to Latta
that once Joaquín had finished the burials at the arroyo, he rode with
a male companion north and west to meet Rosa in Alameda County,
where she was living with Joaquín's sister and nephew. En route, the
two men ran into some Anglo officers and, assuming the officers
were looking for them, tried to escape. But the Anglos began shooting and injured Joaquín before he and his companion got away.
Joaquín made it to the rancho, but died of the gunshot wound two
days later. Before he died, he insisted that Anglos never learn of his
fate, and so Rosa, Joaquín's sister, and the male companion buried
him beneath the hard-packed dirt floor of the rancho's saddle room.
Then, Latta's informant said, "Rosita [as she was known to family
members] sold everything and went to San Francisco. She married
the compañero who had brought Joaquín home and helped bury
him. The newly married couple went to Mexico on a boat."[106] No one
ever heard from them again.

Built within the structure of this memory is an obvious explanation for why Rosa and Joaquín disappear without a trace in other recollections; Joaquín demanded that his death and burial be kept
secret, and Rosa, having remarried quickly and departed with the
profits from Joaquín's mining and horse herding and her work keeping up the rancho, would have been disinclined to maintain family
ties. Whatever one makes of the story—it does not contradict what
most scholars would take to be the historical record—it is telling that
Latta found the only keepers of the tale to be the woman who first
related it in 1936, her daughter, and a granddaughter, who in 1972
was business manager for an appliance company in Hermosillo. No
simple story of a helpless woman raped and then widowed as her
husband seeks vengeance, this reinvented female tradition brings
Joaquín home to a household and ranch managed by his womenfolk,
and buries him in the safety of its foundations. Then, as if to frustrate
any lingering sentimentality or nostalgia, the tale ends as Rosa sells
the land, the livestock, and the adobe house; she leaves California for
good and sails off to Mexico with the proceeds and a new husband.[107]
An ambiguous legacy, perhaps, but one that three women thought
important to remember.

Part I

Rush

Chapter 1

On the Eve of Emigration

When Rosa Felíz de Murrieta and her husband, Joaquín, chose to leave Sonora in 1849 and start out on the overland journey north to California, they were trying to improve their lot in life. Theirs was a constrained choice. The very concrete constraints the Murrieta family faced involved three abstract categories of relationships. First, there were local, regional, and international economic ties. Second, there were formal political and diplomatic relations. Third, there were bonds forged over cultural ideas and practices of work, gender, and migration. In other words, going to California depended on the extent to which and the ways in which the commercial and industrial revolutions of the nineteenth century had permeated emigrant homelands and tied those homelands to other places and peoples around the globe. Emigration also depended on the extent to which and the ways in which those links were reflected in the political and diplomatic ties between such homelands and the United States, which had so recently acquired California. Finally, the decision to emigrate—and sometimes, the coercion that dictated emigration—depended on how people in various places understood and acted on interrelated cultural constructions of work (what constituted work and who did it?), gender (what was required for someone to be regarded as a woman or as a man?), and migration (who could leave the homeland, for what purpose, and for how long?).[1]

The Murrieta family was caught up in just such a dense web of interrelationships, the nature of which will become clearer in the following pages. Similar constraints faced women and men in other parts of the world. For some, the constraints were such that going to California was out of the question: Gold Rush migration was global but selective. Chileans went; Argentineans and Brazilians, for the most part, did not. Cantonese speakers from South China went; people from Shanghai and Nanjing did not. African Americans, both enslaved and free, went; Africans did not. France sent many fortyniners; Spain, hardly any. Men immigrated in droves; women, in comparatively small numbers.

It was not so much, then, that "the world rushed in," but that more men and fewer women from very particular places at very particular times left their homes and made their way by water and by land, as quickly as they could, to the California diggings.[2] What tied these disparate movements together was the imminent, and selective, triumph of capitalist market economies, whose representatives sent tentacles out around the globe, linking many peoples, products, and places to each other in their pursuit of wealth. In this world of commerce and, increasingly, of industry, gold was money, or wealth, that could be turned with human labor and tools of manufacture into capital. That is not, emphatically, to say that all who dug for gold were capitalists—far from it. But all had been touched by capitalism's expansive tendencies. Some sought gold to create capital; others, to ward off capital's dynamism and its definitional habit of turning human energy into labor power. The discovery of gold in California in 1848, then, must have seemed wildly fortunate to a wide variety of people coming to terms with such monumental economic changes.[3]

But emigrants' movements were governed, too, by shifting geopolitical relations, and these relations helped shape the conditions under which people left their homelands as well as their reception in California. Western liberal political notions were on the ascendance in certain parts of the world, sometimes in lockstep with leaps of commercial faith, sometimes not. Political liberalism and commercial ambition often colluded—in Britain's relations with China, for example, or the United States' with Mexico. In these cases, the arrogance of colonial power could be stunning. But people came from these places so recently defeated in war, often hoping against hope for a better life in California.[4]

The nature and the degree of freedom people exercised in participating in the Gold Rush varied greatly, from the craftsman who aspired to a better life he could not find in New England to the Parisian prostitute frustrated by dull times after the French debacle of 1848 to the northern Mexican *peón* or southern U.S. slave who left home at someone else's behest but who might use the tumult of the diggings for his or her own ends. One group of Gold Rush participants, of course, was not an immigrant group at all. Native peoples of the Sierra foothills—and in the Southern Mines these were primarily Miwoks—played unwilling hosts to the hordes of sojourners who descended on their gathering and hunting grounds. Some Indians actually migrated *out* of the area after 1848, pushing farther up into the Sierra Nevada, though most stayed and adapted to the radical changes underway in the foothills.

My purpose here is to suggest some of the momentous local and global forces that worked together to bring sixty or seventy thousand immigrants in less than a decade to an area that had once supported perhaps six or seven thousand native people.[5] These forces had everything to do with what would happen in the Southern Mines between 1848 and 1858. Gold Rush social relations, then, arose out of the backgrounds and aspirations of polyglot peoples differently affected by worldwide economic and cultural change. Among these, Miwoks, Mexicans, Chileans, French, Chinese, African Americans, and Anglo Americans would come to play important roles in what I identify as central dramas in the gold era of the Southern Mines.[6] It is clear that there were as many stories that led to the banks of the Mokelumne, Stanislaus, and Merced rivers as there were women and men in the mines. From these stories, however, particular patterns emerge. Consider first those who hailed from the former Spanish empire in the New World.

Mexico and Chile sent more emigrants north to California than any other Latin American nation did. Both were in the throes of political, economic, and social change that followed their declarations of independence from Spain earlier in the century (Chile in 1817, Mexico in 1821) and their increasing incorporation into world markets. Those changes, however, took distinctive courses in the two countries. Furthermore, the differences between Mexico and Chile that shaped their emigration patterns were reinforced by the regional origins of Mexican and Chilean emigrants; Mexicans came from the isolated northwestern state of Sonora and Chileans from the thriving central area of their country.[7]

The migration of the Murrieta clan, for example, suggests some of the conditions that prompted Sonorans to consider leaving home. Recall that Murrieta family members remember a Mexican past of digging gold, raising stock, and fighting Indians. The Murrietas lived in what one historian calls the "periphery of nineteenth-century Mexico."[8] The area that became the state of Sonora in 1831 lay on the western slope of the formidable Sierra Madre Occidental, a rugged mountain range that cordoned the state off from the rest of Mexico. Like the Sierra Nevada foothills in California, the region west of the Sierra Madre was distinguished by mineral-rich streams that flowed out of the mountains, carving valleys that broadened as the rivers drained into the Gulf of California. Home to such native peoples as the Yaquis, Mayos, Seris, Pimas, and Opatas, the area drew Jesuit missionaries in the late sixteenth century. In the seventeenth and eighteenth centuries, a larger white and *casta* (mixed-race) mining, farming, and ranching population followed, settlers who alternately vied with Sonoran Indians over land and sought to engage them as laborers. In the late eighteenth century, the Spanish crown expelled Jesuits from the northern frontier and sent in the military to break Indian resistance where missions had failed. Indians responded variously, but violent retaliation against cultural, economic, and military dominance was a regular feature of relations between native peoples and Spanish Mexican interlopers in northern Mexico.[9]

In the decades before Rosa Felíz and Joaquín Murrieta were born, their Sonoran homeland was relatively removed from settlements to the north in California and from the seat of colonial power in Mexico City. But its isolation was hardly complete. Oceangoing commerce with Pacific neighbors and land links to New Mexico continued, and Sonora was also touched by the momentous economic and political changes of the era. These transformations would set the stage for mass emigration by the late 1840s. Since the precarious Spanish Mexican communities of Sonora had depended on the royal military presence and on royal promotion of the mining industry for peace and prosperity, the nationalist movement that swept New Spain after 1810 found little support in Sonora. But nationalism prevailed elsewhere, and independence came in 1821, leaving Sonora on the margins of national development. During the war for independence, Sonoran mining suffered from severed lines of trade and loss of royal protection. The industry, and hence the people whose livelihood depended on it, never fully recovered in the following decades. Agriculture also suffered during the war. But from the 1820s on, owners of large haciendas and small farms alike benefited from renewed access to interregional markets and especially from the new participation of foreign merchants who brought increased access to Pacific trade. Workers on farms and haciendas and in mines were often Indians. With the decline of mining, more and more mine laborers became tied to the growing agricultural sector as *peónes*.[10]

In southern Sonora, where Rosa and Joaquín grew up, Yaquis and Mayos prevented rapid agricultural expansion. They did so by holding on to fertile commons in the Yaqui and Mayo valleys, maintaining pueblos to which Indians dispersed throughout Sonora returned with regularity. Squeezed by white and *casta* encroachment and denied the special legal status they had enjoyed under Spanish rule, Yaquis mounted armed revolts in 1825 and 1832. Meanwhile, farther north, Apaches took advantage of the decline in frontier defense to renew their raids on Spanish Mexican settlements and trails, and found eager buyers for their booty among Anglo American traders who poured into New Mexico after 1821. Mexico City could do little for the beleaguered northern Sonorans, and in 1835 the Sonoran state legislature declared war and created local militias, which proved no match for determined Apache opponents. Through the 1830s, then, life in sparsely populated rural areas of Sonora, particularly in the far south and far north, became increasingly untenable for Spanish Mexican settlers. Because of this, and because of increased foreign trade since independence, cities in the middle of the state—Hermosillo, Ures, and the port of Guaymas—grew apace.[11]

In the 1840s, when Rosa and Joaquín came of age, courted, and married, the situation went from bad to worse. The national political conflict between federalists and centralists became a kind of race war in Sonora, as Indians allied themselves with local centralists who vowed to protect native land claims. (Federalists were liberals who railed against hereditary privilege and established authority, while centralists were proclerical conservatives who favored a strong central government.) Then, in 1846, as if such regional strife were not ruinous enough, war broke out with the United States, disrupting all overseas commerce through Guaymas. Despite the American naval blockade, central Sonora was spared some of the worst ravages of the civil and foreign wars, because of the comparative shelter offered in the cities and because the centralist political majority there was able to maintain peaceful relations with native peoples. Rural Sonora, however, was not so fortunate. By the time gold was discovered in California in the winter of 1848, much of northern and southern Sonora had been laid waste by years of unremitting turmoil.[12]

It comes as no surprise, then, that some ten thousand people, maybe more, left Sonora for California between 1848 and 1850.[13] The precise racial/ethnic makeup of the migration is unclear, though one historian notes that a sizable number of Yaquis were among those who departed.[14] Perhaps these were Yaquis, primarily men, who had left their central Sonoran homeland to work as miners for Spanish Mexicans elsewhere in the state. The precipitous decline in regional mining since independence would have made tales of rich placers in

California all the more enticing. Such men, accustomed to migrating for labor within Sonora, may have seen mining in California as a better alternative than debt servitude on haciendas and farms closer to home. Not all Sonorans, however, whether Indian or Spanish Mexican, avoided *peón/patrón* labor relations by emigrating to California. While many, like the Murrieta clan, traveled north as *gambusinos,* or independent prospectors, others went to the mines under the control and protection of a wealthy *patrón*—recall the servant of the Californio Antonio Franco Coronel, who cooked for her own party and sold beans and tortillas to other hungry miners as well.[15]

Coronel's female servant notwithstanding, the vast majority of Mexican Gold Rush emigrants were men. In April of 1850, for example, a Sonoran newspaper reported official emigration figures for five towns, including Ures and Hermosillo. Out of almost six thousand emigrants, only a hundred were adult women; another hundred were children.[16] Adult men, then, made up over 96 percent of the travelers. Unlike the Murrietas, these emigrants left Sonora's more urban areas; the extremely small proportion of women might reflect how much easier it was for female-headed households to survive in towns and cities. Indeed, according to newspaper reports, some municipalities lost so many men that political offices, long a male province, went vacant.[17] Given the state of the Sonoran countryside, particularly in the north and south, one might assume that rural families, more than urban families, left for California together, rather than leaving women and children behind to fend for themselves. Rosa Felíz de Murrieta's migration is a case in point.

Still, Murrieta family tradition suggests that Rosa was the only woman of the clan to accompany her male relatives to the diggings. What of those rural Spanish Mexican women who stayed behind? Their ability to maintain family farms and ranchos must have depended in large part on their relationships with local Indians and their proximity to Apache raiding trails that entered the Sonoran heartland from the north. It seems likely, though, that a good number of rural women embarked upon their own migration—not to distant California, but to the towns and cities of Sonora. Evidence of heavy female migration to Mexico City and to other Latin American municipalities in this period suggests that women may have been overrepresented among Sonoran rural–urban migrants as well—just as men were overrepresented in the exodus to California.[18] Urban areas offered rural women work as domestic servants for affluent families and as food vendors on city streets.[19] Not surprisingly, female-headed households abounded in urban centers, as also they must have in Yaqui pueblos.[20] The seemingly male world of the California mines, then, may well have been linked to virtual cities of women in northern Mexico.[21]

The many men and few women who journeyed by sea from central Chile north to California left behind a very different homeland. Unlike the Murrietas, they did not come from an area that had been remote in colonial times and that remained peripheral after inde-

A Gold Rush–era Chilean sailor who jumped ship in San Francisco Bay. His name is unknown. From a daguerreotype by William Shew.

Courtesy of Stanley B. Burns, M.D., and the Burns Archive.

pendence. Chilean emigrants came from a core agricultural and commercial region that witnessed a population boom and saw a more decisive incursion of foreign economic interests in the nineteenth century than did Sonora. From the sixteenth-century Spanish conquest until the independence period of the early nineteenth century, the fertile central valley and its environs defined Chile. Desert country farther north did not come under Chilean control until the 1880s, and the southern region remained in the hands of Araucanian Indians. The central valley, with its port at Valparaíso and the national capital inland at Santiago, resembled California's Sacramento and San Joaquin valleys in climate and in suitability for orchard, vineyard, cereal, and livestock production. The towering Andes Mountains formed a barrier to the east, and coastal hills lay to the west. Because of this geographic unity and natural abundance, and because of Araucanian resistance to the south, Spanish settlement took root in the central valley. Araucanians' warlike opposition bequeathed to those settlers a legacy of militarism and a habit of colonizing those Indians whom they were able to subdue. In central Chile, a relatively homogeneous *casta* population was thus among the main fruits of conquest.[22]

Early on, the Spanish encomienda system—whereby the crown granted men rights over native peoples as a reward for military service—consolidated land and labor in the central valley and helped create a colonial elite that would pass on its wealth and power to later generations. As Indian workers in these agricultural areas succumbed to disease and the severity of forced labor, or as they simply fled, *casta* workers began to take their place. Although encomiendas were abolished in 1791, large estates still dominated central Chile into the nineteenth century. To a greater degree than in northern Mexico, then, relations and conditions of labor in Chile maintained continuity from the late colonial era on into the post-independence years.[23] That continuity would affect the nature of Chilean emigration to California.

The *castas* who worked the land of large proprietors included both inquilinos, or service tenants, and *peónes* or *gañanes*, who engaged in seasonal day labor. An inquilino man assisted in rodeos and harvests, and worked as well at various tasks on the estate perhaps two or three days a week. In exchange, he received a small plot of land that he and his family could farm. He might also be required to supply one full-time worker to the landowner from his own household or from smallholders or landless men in the area. An inquilino woman might provide domestic labor for the landholder, but she also engaged in extensive household industry, especially in dying, spinning, and weaving woolen cloth for rugs, blankets, ponchos, and other apparel. After independence, increased foreign trade brought cheap British cotton into Chile, and women's wool production decreased, though woolen ponchos continued in use and cotton cloth itself still had to be made into garments.[24]

Unlike inquilinos, who called a piece of land their own, *peónes* or *gañanes* lived in the interstices of the large estates and were not themselves small proprietors. In part because of rapid population growth in the eighteenth and early nineteenth centuries, an increasing number of Chileans formed a class of unattached, landless, and mobile people who engaged in seasonal labor and lived precariously off the natural abundance of the central valley. Some of the men looked for work in the area just north of the valley called the *norte chico*. There a mining economy rivaled agricultural pursuits, and a smaller number of women found employment in *pulperías*—store-saloons where men drank, gambled, danced, and sought sexual services from prostitutes. Others must have found their way to Valparaíso, which nearly quadrupled in population with the opening to foreign trade after independence and started to become, as one historian notes, a "rough-and-tumble, bawdy Pacific port." But many formed the backbone of the central valley's transient rural labor force. Proprietors hired them at harvest or roundup time for remuneration that might amount to bountiful food and drink and a setting for exuberant song and dance.[25] These rural workers, along with more affluent men increasingly involved in commerce, would contribute disproportionate numbers of those who answered California's call of gold after 1848.[26]

Just as the lives of the Murrietas help demonstrate the particularities of Mexican Gold Rush emigration, so does the life of the *patrón* Vicente Pérez Rosales, who traveled to California with *péones* and inquilinos, help illuminate Chilean emigration. Pérez Rosales was born in 1807 to a landowning family in the central valley. He grew up in the years of Chile's independence movement. During the period of adjustment to independence that characterized Chile in the 1820s, Pérez Rosales was in France completing his education. He returned to his homeland, but by 1830 found that financial difficulties caused the loss of his parents' estate. The young Pérez Rosales spent the following years trying to recoup family fortunes—searching for Chilean gold, operating small factories, engaging in commerce, smuggling cattle over the Andes from Argentina.[27]

News of California's gold discoveries, which arrived at Valparaíso in the autumn of 1848, seemed to offer Pérez Rosales a new opportunity to regain the affluence of his youth. Without extensive landholdings and control over large numbers of laborers—both of which assured a life of relative comfort and a means of participating in Chile's fledgling export sector—Pérez Rosales's last best chance lay in finding a way to prosper in an evolving cash economy. Trade, manufacturing, running livestock—all moneymakers—proved insufficient, and Chilean gold seemed in short supply. What could be more auspicious, therefore, than word of astounding quantities of placer gold in California? Cash in rivers, cash in ravines, cash in hand! Already oceangoing commerce—dominated by British, North American, and European merchant marines—linked Valparaíso with the port of San Francisco. It would not be hard to get there. As for mining, Pérez Rosales had spent a good deal of his young adulthood looking for, if not finding, precious metals, and he would not have trouble finding other inveterate prospectors to accompany him. Indeed, one foreign observer claimed that Chileans panned for gold after every good rainfall.[28]

And so Pérez Rosales assembled his band of argonauts, including three half brothers surnamed Solar Rosales—Ruperto, César, and Federico—and a cousin or brother-in-law (or both) named Felipe Ramírez. These patricians of small means were able to bring with them two tenant laborers—inquilinos—from Las Tables estate, and three *peónes*, hired on contract. The conditions of that contract are unclear, as is the labor arrangement made with the tenants. Although Pérez Rosales kept a diary of his California adventures, he did not mention the terms under which he engaged these five men.[29] The inquilinos as well as the *peónes* were subservient to Pérez Rosales. But the inquilinos seem to have maintained a relationship with their Gold Rush *patrón* that included a modicum of personal regard, while bounded by habits of paternalism and deference. Pérez Rosales recorded the inquilinos' names in his diary—Cipriano Avello and Juan Urbina—and routinely noted tasks they completed, mishaps they suffered, and remarks they made.[30]

The *peónes*, however, remain shadowy figures; the *patrón* mentions only a "mulatto" who was with the brothers and a *peón* called Chinguillo.[31] The social distance and relative power that defined relationships among *patrónes*, inquilinos, and *peónes* is inscribed in the writings of Pérez Rosales as degrees of silence. Still, the distinctions he makes between categories of workers—tenants and contract laborers—are not always clear and fixed. He calls Avello, one of the Tables men, a *"peón"* on occasion and routinely refers to *"los peónes"* as an undifferentiated group. And it is as a group that the *peónes* made Pérez Rosales most nervous. At sea less than a month, he noted in his diary that although all business matters had long since been settled, disputes had arisen nonetheless between *peónes* and *patrónes*. Pérez Rosales was alarmed by the *peónes'* behavior: "They refuse to obey now; how will they act later?" The prospect of vast gold deposits in California, much as it thrilled men like Pérez Rosales, made them worry as well that their customary relations with men like Avello, Urbina, "the mulatto," and "Chinguillo" might be in jeopardy.[32]

Pérez Rosales and his companions boarded the French ship *Staouelí* bound for San Francisco in December of 1848. His narrative of shipboard adventures reveals that other social and labor relations sailed north from Chile to California as well. Among the passengers who caught the attention of Pérez Rosales was a woman traveling under the name Rosario Améstica. Pérez Rosales wrote his diary as a sort of extended letter to his mother, and the coyness with which he discussed this particular shipmate may have been his way of trying to entertain his mother without entirely offending her sensibilities. Améstica, Pérez Rosales implied, had made the rounds of Chilean towns and cities before boarding the *Staouelí*—he reported that she had been known as Juana in Concepción, Pancha in Talca, and Rosa Montalva in Valparaíso. A port officer challenged her right to passage on the *Staouelí*, though she had paid her fare of six *onzas* (about $125). According to Pérez Rosales, she pleaded her good character to the officer, and finally was allowed to board, all the while intending to recoup her fare among the all-male passengers and crew and then make her fortune selling sexual services in California.

Pérez Rosales did all he could in his diary to titillate his mother, and whoever else he thought might read it, with suggestive remarks about "Rosita's" shipboard activities. Meanwhile, he insisted that he had opposed her passage and that he and his brothers alone had been "virtuous, chaste; or finicky and choosey" during the voyage. He did admit to hosting "Rosita" and her guitar in the cabin one evening to hear her perform French and Chilean tunes, both lewd and patriotic. What his diary does not reveal is whether his mother was at all amused, and whether "Rosita" was able to earn back her fare, in spite or because of men like Pérez Rosales.[33] The intricacies of Chilean class and gender relations suggested by the diary of Pérez Rosales would soon be played out on a new stage crowded by an international cast of characters, and *peónes*, *patrónes*, and prostitutes would reevaluate their roles accordingly.

Meanwhile, in the southern U.S. state of Arkansas, an African American man by the name of Stephen Spencer Hill was at work as a slave for a white master named Wood Tucker. In 1849, the two would go west in search of gold. Regarding the backgrounds of Hill and Tucker, the California record reveals little—how long they had been in Arkansas, what kind of enterprise Tucker ran there, how many other people lived under Tucker's control.[34] Chances are they had not been in Arkansas long. They probably had migrated there from a southern state farther east, contributing to the phenomenal population growth in states like Mississippi and Arkansas that accompanied the expansion of southern agriculture before the U.S. Civil War. That expansion occurred largely in response to the emergence of an industrial economy in the North Atlantic region, spearheaded by the extraordinary growth of English textiles in the late eighteenth century. By the early nineteenth century, the northeastern United States had established its own textile industry. Thus demand for cotton increased dramatically, and southern agriculturalists hurried to plant more and more acres of the crop, always moving westward in search of new lands.

Black slavery long predated the cotton boom, but whites found it particularly suitable for cotton production. So slavery moved west with agricultural expansion. Although the grand plantation with its vast slave quarters epitomizes the antebellum South in popular memory, a modest farm in a state like Arkansas where a white man like Wood Tucker oversaw a handful of African Americans like Stephen Spencer Hill was probably more common. Tucker may have moved west to Arkansas in the company of family members—siblings, parents, cousins, perhaps a wife. But Hill is less likely to have done so. The cotton boom meant that masters sometimes sold slaves into the western territories without regard for black kin ties. Whether or not Tucker or Hill had been living with relatives in Arkansas, the two men seem to have set out for California alone. Tucker left no record of his reasons for emigrating; perhaps his farm had failed, or perhaps he sought quick capital to expand his holdings.[35]

While some slaveowners traveled west alone with only a single slave in 1849, a handful of white southern men went to California accompanied by their own families and those of their African American slaves. Like Tucker and Hill, they came primarily from western slave states—Mississippi, Arkansas, Texas, Missouri. These large parties of black and white gold seekers were not common in the California migration. But once in the diggings they were highly visible—because whites and blacks lived side-by-side, because the parties so obviously depended on coerced labor, and because they included black and white women and children. Thomas Thorne, for example, a New Jersey–born white man who had married a white woman, Mary, from North Carolina, seems to have followed the cotton boom west to Arkansas and Mississippi, where two of the couple's children were born, in 1840 and 1845. A third child must have been conceived en route to the diggings, because the Mariposa County census taker found the Thornes with a four-month-old baby in 1850. Close in age to Mary and Thomas, Diana and Lewis Caruthers, the Thornes' African American slaves, hailed from North Carolina and Virginia, respectively. Diana had given birth to all three of their children in Arkansas in the mid to late 1830s.

Similarly, the white McGee family of Tennessee—two brothers and their wives—had stopped for a time in both Missouri and Texas, where each of the women had six children. The two white families brought with them a forty-five-year-old black slave named Silas, himself a native of Tennessee, and seven young African Americans who ranged in age from three to twenty-one years. The 1850 census does not reveal how the twenty-one-year-old black woman who accompanied the party was related to Silas—she might have been his wife or his daughter—though she too was born in Tennessee. The six black children with them all were natives of Texas. The McGee masters and their slaves, like the Thorne and Caruthers families, had been on the move for decades, following King Cotton west, before they answered California's call of gold.[36]

When slaves and their masters left Texas or Arkansas in 1849, they could not be certain how their distinctive style of labor relations would be received in the California diggings. In just three years, between 1845 and 1848, the United States had added over one million square miles to its domain, an increase of two-thirds over its earlier lands resulting from the annexation of Texas (1845), the treaty with Great Britain over the disputed Oregon boundary (1846), and the conquest of California and most of the Southwest from Mexico (1848). Territorial aggrandizement threatened earlier sectional compromises that kept slavery a southern labor system, while the North moved toward a predominance of "free" wage work. Texas entered the union as a slave state in 1845, and Oregon would do so as a free state in 1859. But slavery's fate in California was not assured, even though the Treaty of Guadalupe Hidalgo had called for the United States to honor the Mexican abolition of slavery in former Mexican territories. The sudden influx of tens of thousands of Americans into California after the discovery of gold in 1848 dictated that the slavery question would be called there sooner rather than later.

In the fall of 1849, delegates met at Monterey to draft a constitution for California, preparatory to applying for admission as the thirty-first state of the Union. The document they produced prohibited slavery, not so much out of abolitionist sentiment as out of fears that slave labor could limit opportunities for free white miners and that some slaves might eventually be emancipated in the diggings, thereby augmenting California's free black population. Indeed, some at the convention sought unsuccessfully to prohibit free black immigration as well. The U.S. Congress finally did admit California as a free state, but not until statehood had been balanced with a number of other measures designed to placate the white South; the entire package became known as the Compromise of 1850.[37]

All of this occurred as black and white southerners traveled to and arrived in the diggings, and even with free labor established as the letter of the law in California, none could be sure how it would be enforced. Masters took their chances bringing slaves to the Gold Rush. But many must have been willing to face the prospect of losing their human property given the promise of placer bonanzas in the Sierra Nevada foothills. Indeed, some slaveholders planned in advance to grant slaves their freedom in California once the slaves had worked for a set period of time or had dug a certain amount of gold—in this way masters benefited from coerced labor while minimizing the potential conflicts they might face in bringing slaves to a free state. Enslaved African Americans, for their part, could exercise little choice in emigrating. But they must have learned on the way to California or in the diggings that placer mining in a nonslave state could offer new roads to freedom. Slaves might live less at the whim of masters in a place where the legal status of their relationship was in question. Blacks might also find new possibilities when surrounded by a diverse population that encompassed a variety of labor systems and that included some antislavery northerners—both whites and free blacks. For many, the potential would never be realized; for others, digging for gold meant an opportunity to buy themselves, and perhaps even their loved ones, out of bondage.[38]

Nonslaveholding white southerners who went to California had entirely different hopes and fears. Their hopes and fears, however, arose out of a shared past with black slaves and white masters. John Paul Dart, for example, a Mississippi surveyor and civil engineer who had fought in the Mexican War, had little sympathy for the most powerful men of the southern social order. Even from far-off Tuolumne County, where he arrived in 1850, Dart filled letters home with criticisms of white planters, deriding their devotion to cotton and their ironic dependence on the "Free Soil States to which they appear to have such an antipathy." Decidedly Whig in his political leanings, Dart thought the South should pull itself up by its own bootstraps by raising more corn and less cotton. But his dim view of planters did not include a critique of the labor relations that underlay their regime. Indeed, that regime permeated his own understanding of himself. In the diggings, despite the boom-and-bust nature of local economies, Dart determined that he would always live "like a white man." This, he wrote to his brother, "I have always done, if it took the last shot in the locker."[39] In California "whiteness" was defined in opposition to a variety of "nonwhite" peoples, but for a southern white man like Dart, black slaves were the first point of reference. So too for Jefferson Martenet, a young man from Baltimore who went to California to establish his economic independence. While still in the East, he incurred substantial debt, which he considered a "cause of great mortification." "I have been made to feel my dependence," he lamented to his mother, "to blush at being compelled to submit to degradation, to negro treatment, all because misfortune placed me under obligations which I cannot as yet cancel."[40] Anguished that he had to blush as he imagined a white woman would, to submit as he imagined a black slave would, Martenet believed he deserved better. In California, southern white men such as Martenet, Dart, and Wood Tucker would search for the good life to which they felt entitled.

On January 24, 1849, two northern white men—Jason Chamberlain, a carpenter by trade, and John Chaffee, a wheelwright—set sail from Boston together on the ship *Capitol*, bound for San Francisco. Chamberlain was twenty-seven years old and Chaffee twenty-five. Neither had married. They arrived in California 176 days later, after a voyage around South America's Cape Horn. Immediately, they found employment in San Francisco at the astounding *daily* wage of twelve dollars—an amount that exceeded the *weekly* wages of most antebellum workers in the Northeast.[41] Within two weeks, however, they could no longer withstand the temptation of gold in the foothills. As Chamberlain told a female correspondent half a century later, "We . . . then were stricken badly with the mining fever and at times I think it as the worsed moove we ever made in leaving the City so full of bustle & business for the uncertainty of the mines."[42] It was a move Chamberlain never reversed, as he and Chaffee joined the minority of Gold Rush participants who spent the rest of their lives in the diggings. After fifty years, though, in June of 1903, Chaffee made one more trip down to the Bay Area. Afflicted with a painful skin disease and other ailments, Chaffee accompanied a professor friend "below" to see a doctor. The fellow forty-niners never saw each other again. On August 2, 1903, Chamberlain wrote in his diary, "went for mail heard the sad news of my Dear Partner Chaffee he died 2 oclock The morn of 31."[43]

The story of Chamberlain and Chaffee—a Gold Rush narrative that stretched out over half a century—has become a part of local color in Tuolumne County, where the two men grew old together. Some say it became part of American popular culture with the publication in 1869 of the short story "Tennessee's Partner" by Bret Harte, who more than any other writer helped codify collective memory of the California Gold Rush in the United States. According to some accounts, Harte heard about the partnership of Chamberlain and Chaffee in the 1860s from a mutual friend and used it, loosely, as the basis for his famous tale.[44] But whatever the uses to which Chamberlain and Chaffee's California sojourn has been put, it began in an utterly common New England manner.

The two young men were artisans in a changing northern economic and social order that had begun to disrupt preindustrial labor relations, especially for white men. In earlier times, a man might learn a trade first as an apprentice and then proceed to the intermediate status of journeyman working under the direction of a master craftsman. The first half of the nineteenth century, particularly in the Northeast, brought a revolution in markets, in transportation, and in manufacturing that threatened customary paths to self-sufficiency for men like Chamberlain and Chaffee. More and more, journeymen in various trades found that an entrepreneurial spirit began to infuse craft production. This shift opened opportunities for some to achieve unprecedented economic rewards as master craftsmen in a newly commercial milieu, while others remained locked in a dependent, subordinate status that had once represented only one stage in a working man's life. Labor historians have shown how some such men actively resisted these changes, developing new forms of solidarity and a language of class to articulate their wants and needs. This was a male language, but it encompassed the concerns of men as providers for their families as well. Other men sought more individualist solutions to the precarious position into which economic transformation put them and their families. These men, along with their womenfolk, forged a new middle class of prosperous artisans and shopkeepers and, in time, clerks, managers, and professionals as well.[45]

It is important not to draw these distinctions too sharply, however, for the period under study here. The process of industrialization was a gradual one that affected different localities at different times. Even the same New England town could, for example, support both an industrially organized textile mill and more traditionally organized artisan workshops.[46] The Gold Rush occurred at a pivotal point in these economic transformations, when the languages of class and the languages of individualism were only beginning to diverge. Nonetheless, fear of subordination for male artisans like Chamberlain and Chaffee was in the air, and the discovery of gold in California provided an answer to such fear that leaned toward individualism rather than solidarity.

Another forty-niner, Nathan Chase, explained such motivations in a letter to his wife and the mother of their sons: "Jane i left you and them boys for no other reason than this to come here to procure a littl property by the swet of my brow so that we could have a place of our own that i mite not be a dog for other people any longer."[47] Chamberlain and Chaffee had no such obligations, but the young men were at an age where they might be expected to marry and assume familial responsibilities. It seems reasonable to surmise that the two did not depart for California intending to live out their days together in the shadow of the Sierra Nevada. Instead, like Nathan Chase, they probably sought to navigate northeastern economic change by finding a quick western way to achieve what was known as a "competency"—a couple of years of diligent gold digging and then economic independence. Whatever their intentions, they could hardly have predicted a lifetime of labor in the Southern Mines.[48]

Mary Harrison Newell, a white woman from Wilmington, Delaware, could hardly have predicted the twists and turns the Gold Rush brought her life either. Although she grew up in a border state between North and South, Mary Newell spent the early days of her marriage to William Newell in his hometown of Utica, New York, where she probably gave birth to their son, Jesse. There William experienced a business failure. So when news of the Gold Rush arrived in late 1848, he formed an association with nine other men to go to California and share the costs of shelter and provisions there.[49] After William left, Mary headed south with Jesse to her father's home. In Wilmington, her family—father, a sister close in age, and other siblings—ran a bakery, and Mary soon settled into the rhythms of a baker's life. Her father, Benjamin Harrison, was proprietor, and it fell to him to work late at night preparing cakes, pies, and breads for the following day's customers while his daughters watched over the household. But during the day everyone took turns at the shop. All hoped that William's sojourn in California would be brief, and that he and Mary would be reunited to continue their young lives on firmer financial footing.[50]

But the Newell and Harrison families were restless in this uncertain economic era, and letters sailed back and forth between California and Delaware debating the merits of various schemes to augment family fortunes. Mary pleaded with William to come home, gold or no gold, that they might search for prosperity together. Benjamin Harrison asked his son-in-law about a tract of land the younger man owned in Pennsylvania. Would William sell the land to Benjamin? Could William return and join his wife's family on the land, turning it into a productive homestead? What were the prospects for bakers in mining towns like Columbia, where William lived? Should Benjamin, Mary, and other family members relocate and open a shop there? Mary insisted that if William would not come home, she must join him in the mines. William insisted that she must wait until he had himself established in his own business, so they could avoid the financial straits they had faced in Utica. Meanwhile, William's Utica relatives joined in the fray, at first imploring him to return east, and then sending his less than industrious younger brother out to California so that William could "make a man" out of him.[51]

Mary's requests grew more urgent six months after William departed, when their son, Jesse, died suddenly in June of 1849. William did not learn of his child's death for months, and that news came in a letter from Mary announcing that she too was in poor health. Although she recovered quite quickly, slow mails and lost letters meant that William spent most of the winter wondering whether his wife had succumbed to illness as well.[52] Still, the bereaved father was determined to stay the course in California. In this, he sounded a little like Nathan Chase (who went west so as not to be "a dog for other people any longer"): "How can I now leave all and go home to be dependent on others to be a clerk a servant of servants." But William's goals were not nearly so modest as those of Nathan Chase. By rejecting the occupation of clerk, William scoffed at what some took to be a sure entryway to middle-class manhood. In 1852, he scolded his wife for asking him to come home: "I can not go home this fall when I go Home I must carry with me enough to support us through life." Finding a "place of our own"—Nathan Chase's aspiration—was not enough for William: "if I should return home I could only bring enough to start in some kind of business and then if I should again be unfortunate it would be worse than before."[53] One white man's competency, it seemed, was another's empty purse.

Although Mary urged William to return, or to send for her to join him, it was not William's financial ambitions that troubled her. What Mary seemed to reject was her husband's assumption that their common prosperity should depend on his efforts alone. The increasing separation of home and workplace that accompanied northern industrialization gave some newly middle-class women a standpoint from which to question emerging commercial values— even as the home itself, however paradoxically, became a "launching pad" for middle-class men.[54] Mary Newell was not one of these crit- ics. She was a valued partner in a family enterprise controlled by her father but dependent on her labor. Indeed, once she left Wilmington, her father complained that the shop's profits declined, that the undependable boys in the family were no substitute for her. So Mary rightly chafed at the idea that her husband was responsible for their welfare. In the end, her persistence bore fruit. On December 12, 1853, William penned these words to his wife, "Now you and I shall live separate no longer than I can help and I will leave it alto- gether for you to say whether you will come out here and stay two years or whether I shall come home next spring"—though his description of business prospects in California indicated he had no desire to return east.[55]

Six months later, Mary Newell set sail from New York City and by July of 1854 was safely situated in the new house William had built in Columbia. Mary immediately began to lobby her sister and father about relocating to California, assuring them that this was the place to make money, particularly if they would leave the boys behind and bring with them only the hardworking (and marriageable) girls. But before the Harrisons could arrange their affairs and prepare to move, Mary wrote to tell them that William, whose health had been failing since before she arrived, was dead. After five long years apart and after the loss of their son, one might assume that Mary would return to Wilmington as soon as she could dispose of her husband's assets in Columbia. Instead, the young widow continued to press her relatives to come west, now suggesting that she and her sister Lucy take up the family's entrepreneurial banner:

> I think Lucy and I had better make arrangments to go into some
> kind of business. . . . I want to be doing something. you know I
> cannot keep still eny more than you can Lucy I think you had
> better get some childrens Patterns for clothes and some trim-
> mings such as buttons Pins Tape dress trimming . . . coton
> thread neadles sewing silk . . . and you had better get a cloak . . .

plain black velvet I would get if I were you. . . . I think you had better get some nice dresses as they dress as much here as at home and get Father some nice things.[56]

Materials for a clothing business, respectable apparel for the family— middle-class husbands might be mortal, but middle-class dreams died hard. Among her many resources, Mary Newell could fall back in a sorrowful time on the knowledge of her own economic competence in a increasingly commercial world. With that knowledge, with family members who saw her welfare as tied to their own, and with the privilege that arose out of being a "respectable" white widow in a town like Columbia, Mary was well situated to realize her hopes in California.

Mary and William Newell, Jason Chamberlain and John Chaffee— each pair illustrates some of the local, regional, national, and even global forces that drew northerners to California after 1848. All four people were trying to make their way in a changing economic milieu, but the aspirations of Chamberlain and Chaffee, on the one hand, and the Newells, on the other, were not the same. Chamberlain and Chaffee sought to avoid the threat to artisan independence that industrialization seemed to portend. The Newells had different dreams. They were already on the path to middle-class life at the time of the Gold Rush, and California became a new venue in which to follow that star. And indeed, Chamberlain and Chaffee maintained what they understood as their independence over the years as small-time miners and cultivators in rural Tuolumne County. Mary Newell, for her part, remained in the town of Columbia and remarried quickly. Her new husband was an officer of the Tuolumne County Water Company, one of the grandest entrepreneurial schemes the Southern Mines ever saw, and one of the economic anchors of Columbia's homegrown white middle class after the boom years of the Gold Rush.[57]

Years earlier, in the adjacent town of Sonora—a more heterogeneous town than Columbia—another group of women sought access to the gold dust that seemed to pass so freely from hand to hand in the diggings. They served liquor in saloons; they tended gaming tables; they had sex with men, sometimes for profit in brothels, sometimes in intimate relationships—men whose pockets seemed lined with gold. The women were from France, and, if we can credit the recollections of the Canadian-born forty-niner William Perkins, they wore stunning clothes and could turn men inside out with their winning ways. Unlike many immigrants who took up unfamiliar tasks such as gold-mining in California, these French women knew their work and practiced it with aplomb. Perkins himself must have been a bit unnerved by their poise, because he went to great lengths to assail their collective character in his reminiscences, which were probably written a decade after the Gold Rush: "Artificial in the extreme, [the French woman] adapts her manners, as she does her dress, to circumstances. . . . she is a lady, a gambler, a coquette, a fury, a bachante and a prude by turns. . . . for money to the Frenchwoman is the real object of her adoration, and to acquire it there is nothing she will not do."[58] That adaptability and unalloyed ambition were useful to any Gold Rush participant was lost on Perkins, who felt sure that anyone who embodied such traits was, by definition, not a woman. Who were these people who so troubled Perkins, and why had they come to work in Sonora?

No letters or diaries written by French women who worked in the saloons, dance halls, and brothels of the Southern Mines have survived in the historical record. Their names, however, abound in Gold Rush legal proceedings: Anne Lyons worked at a dance house and barroom kept by Rose Cartier in Sonora, for example, and Emilie Henry ran a saloon in Mariposa.[59] One can only assume that many of these women hailed from the extensive French demimonde of the midnineteenth century. Prostitution flourished in Paris and other French municipalities under a distinctive system of rules, called regulationism, that had roots in the ancien régime but came into full flower only after 1802. In that year, Parisian administrators established facilities in which to examine prostitutes for sexually transmitted diseases. From there, officials made the medical examination mandatory and then began to require all prostitutes to register with the police. As an older begrudging tolerance of sexual commerce joined with newer anxieties about contagion and public hygiene, women who sold sex for cash found themselves caught in a legal limbo that matched their customary economic marginality. If they followed regulationist procedures, they could ply their trade. But if they then broke a rule, or missed a medical exam, or created any other sort of trouble, they were arrested and imprisoned without trial. Thus by complying with registration, prostitutes could easily put themselves outside the law. Of course, not all women who sold sexual favors registered with the police, and officials began early on to register suspected prostitutes against their will. Over the course of the nineteenth century, concern about "clandestine" prostitution increased, until nearly any working-class woman who raised suspicion might be subjected to arrest and examination. The real hysteria over unregistered prostitutes came decades after the Gold Rush, but the arbitrary harassment of working women, both those who were registered as prostitutes and those who were not, was common practice by the time Paris received word of California's gold discovery in late 1848.[60]

The freewheeling world of the Gold Rush must have looked good to women accustomed to the strictures of regulationism, which represented an attempt to stabilize unstable sexual and economic categories among urban women. In the mines, such Parisians might or might not engage in sexual commerce, since the demand for women in a variety of service occupations seemed to equal the demand for prostitutes. Women could serve men drinks, or deal them cards, or set up housekeeping with them. Informal union with Gold Rush men had its advantages over prostitution: companionship, reduced risk of sexually transmitted disease, greater protection from the fluctuation of local economies, maybe even better sex (or, if not, then less of it). Then, too, simple sex for cash was always an option, since gold dust and men willing to pay were rarely in short supply. And in California, a woman did not have to register with authorities or submit to a medical examination, nor was she as likely to be arrested as she had been in Paris. In short, the diggings offered the tolerance of home without the constant surveillance.

Even the structure of prostitution was looser in California, particularly in the early years and particularly outside of San Francisco. In Paris a registered prostitute was likely to work in a *maison de tolérance* under the watchful eye of a madam, who usually split a prostitute's earnings with her after deducting the costs of room, board, clothing, and other incidentals. A madam might induce a prostitute to run up a substantial debt, so that the latter could ill afford to leave the bordello. And brothel life itself could be tedious and confining. While it offered possibilities for intimacy among women who worked as prostitutes—if we can believe the fevered commentators who wrote about French prostitution in the nineteenth century—it fostered same-sex eroticism in the context of enforced proximity, economic coercion, and the constant scrutiny of public authorities.[61] By comparison, while California promised no bed of roses, it seemed to offer a kind of autonomy to women schooled in social constructions of male need and desire.

More than repression made French prostitutes in the late 1840s think about traveling thousands of miles in search of a living. Regulationism might be grim, but in good economic times it did allow women to support themselves through sexual commerce. These were not good times. At midcentury, prostitutes faced the same conditions that other French working people faced—the severe economic depression that preceded and precipitated the abortive revolution of 1848. Depression, in turn, begat emigration.

Indeed, 1848 is one of those years that fascinate historians—a year during which a number of seemingly unconnected but nonetheless transformative events happened at once. In North America, the events included the signing of the Treaty of Guadalupe Hidalgo, which so drastically altered the boundaries of the United States and Mexico; the first women's rights convention, held in Seneca Falls, New York; and the discovery of California gold. In Europe, the events included the series of revolutions that rumbled through Paris, Vienna, Berlin, and Milan, along with the appearance of two works that would come to exert tremendous influence over ideas about economy and society—John Stuart Mill's *Principles of Political Economy* and Karl Marx and Friedrich Engels's *Communist Manifesto*. Taken together, the events of 1848 signaled the emergence of an expansive liberal capitalist order based on notions of civil equality, popular sovereignty, and the free play of market forces. At the same time, the events gave voice to critics of that system—from those who demanded extension of ideas about civic equality to those who rejected the capitalist trajectory of change.[62]

In France, proponents and opponents of the new order joined forces to defy the reign of King Louis Philippe, who sought in vain to contain the revolutionary alliance of workers and bourgeois republicans. The revolution of 1848 was set in motion by the poor harvests of 1846, which led to social unrest among rural people and urban workers alike and which brought about a larger financial crisis as well. Louis Philippe ultimately abdicated and fled the country. Into the power vacuum created by abdication stepped a provisional government that included the socialist Louis Blanc. As that government tried to address the problems of the laboring poor by proclaiming the "right to work" and establishing national workshops, and as mass mobilization ensued, the infrastructure for profound social change emerged.[63] Had that change occurred, perhaps emigration to California would not have looked so enticing. But the radical coalition quickly came apart. Beginning with the abolition of the national workshops and the bloody suppression of Parisian workers' protests, the Second Republic devolved into a repressive regime that repudiated many of the revolutionary goals upon which it had been founded. By the end of 1848, Louis Napoléon Bonaparte, nephew to the former French emperor Napoléon Bonaparte, had been elected president, and over the next three years his government dismantled the opposition. In late 1851, when Louis Napoléon faced the refusal of the National Assembly to pass a constitutional revision that would allow him to serve a second term, he engineered a coup d'état. One year later, on the anniversary of the coup, France was once again proclaimed an empire.[64]

Meanwhile, the economic crisis of 1846–47 that had set the stage for revolution continued to plague the French. Some signs of recovery appeared in 1850 and 1851, no doubt aiding Louis Napoleon in his imperial designs. But until then unemployment and underemployment left workers scrambling to eke out a living. To make matters worse, the bad harvests had brought about food shortages and exorbitant prices.[65] Imagine the excitement, then, when official news of the California gold discovery reached France in December 1848. Struggling urban workers and rural peasants were not the first to respond, but rather men with capital who could finance their own voyage or join with others in entrepreneurial plans to transport people or goods to the mines and markets of California. Speculators and promoters, in fact, went wild with the news, announcing their schemes to would-be shareholders and emigrants in half- and full-page newspaper advertisements and broadsides posted all over Paris. Between 1849 and 1850, French men established eighty-three companies and societies devoted to exploiting California's newfound wealth, some of them offering inducements to "associated workers" such as inexpensive shares and three-year labor contracts (during which, as shareholders, they could expect to earn astounding dividends). The largest of the companies, La Californienne, sent six teams of workers to the diggings, pledging food, shelter, and tools, but delivered on none of the promises. Like those who joined other French societies (and like members of most Anglo American companies organized to go to California), the Californienne emigrants were on their own once they reached their destination. Neither did shareholders who stayed behind in France see dividends. Still, between company-sponsored and individual emigration, well over twenty thousand French-speaking people traveled to California during the Gold Rush.[66]

At least one of the French emigration schemes caught the attention of Karl Marx, who saw in it a symbol of failed revolution. Authorized by the Paris prefect of police, the Société des Lingots d'Or in 1850 organized a lottery, the proceeds of which would be used to transport five thousand poor emigrants to California. The grand prize was a 400,000-franc gold ingot. Although lotteries were illegal in

France, government officials hoped by this plan to rid themselves of a good number of the Parisian radicals of 1848 as well as other undesirables. Writing in 1852, Marx lambasted the scheme: "golden dreams were to supplant the socialist dreams of the Paris proletariat." The laborers, he lamented, "did not recognize in the glitter of the California gold bars the inconspicuous francs that were enticed out of their pockets."[67] However Parisian workers understood their purchase of lottery tickets from the Société des Lingots d'Or, Marx indeed captured the irony of a gold rush that followed on the heels of a failed revolution. Not so long before—on the streets of Paris in February of 1848—some French people had bolder dreams.

Halfway across the world, a sixteen-year-old named Fou Sin was leaving his job in a Hong Kong store to board an American ship called the *Captain Tiger,* on which he would serve as cabin boy. Little did he know that ten years later, in 1858, he would stand in a California court and be sentenced to death by hanging—having been accused, along with four other Chinese, of robbing a water company safe and murdering a white clerk who worked for the company manager. In part because Fou Sin was charged with such a crime, his life at first glance seems unlike those of most Chinese immigrants to California. Nonetheless, Fou Sin's biography reveals much about the Gold Rush emigration of people from Guangdong Province, in South China.

At an early age, Fou Sin traveled the global trade routes that linked most of the continents, and learned as well what role a young man from the Pearl River Delta could expect to play in the expanding capitalist markets of the world. Speaking to a white newspaperman in 1858, Fou Sin explained that he had been born in the 1830s on a tiny farm "about three day's travel from the city of Hong Kong," where his father also worked as a stonecutter. His mother died young, leaving her husband with two sons. When Fou Sin was about twelve, he boarded a British brig as a cabin boy. A year and a half later, he went back and took up work at the Hong Kong store, where he learned to speak English. Then, in 1848, he returned to seafaring labor, now on the ship *Captain Tiger.* When that vessel docked in Singapore, Fou Sin stayed behind and worked as an "English officer's boy" for three years.[68]

The next few years of Fou Sin's life read like a lesson in the geography of market connections. He spent three seasons as steward on a French whaling ship that traveled between the Sandwich Islands (now Hawaii) and New Bedford, Massachusetts, by way of Cape Horn.

A Gold Rush–era Chinese emigrant. His name is unknown. The daguerreo-typist Isaac Wallace Baker may have asked this man to display his queue, thereby creating a more exotic image for Anglo American viewers.

Courtesy of the Oakland Museum of California.

Settling for a time in Honolulu, Fou Sin worked as a cook for an American merchant's family. Then, after a brief stint as a steward on an interisland schooner, he headed for the Amur River, stopping briefly in Japan. (The Amur River drainage, though nominally Chinese territory, was an area of Russian expansion in the 1850s.) Boarding a Russian man-of-war at the mouth of the river, Fou Sin stopped for a few days in Petropavlovsk-Kamchatski, where he saw the effects of British and French attacks on the city during the Crimean War. Finally, the Russian ship sailed east for California. On New Year's Day in 1857, Fou Sin arrived at San Francisco.[69]

In San Francisco, Fou Sin set himself up at a sailors' boardinghouse kept by an African American man named Overton. Finding intermittent work as a cook in a white-owned boardinghouse and a black-owned hotel, Fou Sin kept himself employed for a few months, before he had to settle for sleeping and eating at a Chinese barbershop. In the meantime, he got into a fight at a "Spanish dance house" with a black man, who Fou Sin claimed called him a "d——d Chinaman." That incident landed Fou Sin in jail. But no witnesses appeared against him, and so he was released. Fou Sin then took two jobs in quick succession as cook for a Panama steamer and a San Francisco hotel. Once again unemployed, he got into another scrape, this time at a Chinese brothel, but he managed to escape arrest. Down on his luck, Fou Sin was fortunate to run into an old friend from his Sandwich Islands days—Chou Yee, a man who had grown up in the same district near Canton as Fou Sin. Chou Yee was in San Francisco just briefly and was preparing to return to the Southern Mines. He assured Fou Sin that there was plenty of work for Chinese cooks in the diggings and offered to lend his friend the thirty dollars it would cost to travel to the town of Jackson and find a position. Fou Sin accepted, and the two men left the city for the mines in September of 1857.[70]

Unlike Fou Sin, most Chinese immigrants to California had not spent years sailing the world's oceans, dropping anchor at far-flung Pacific and Atlantic ports. Most did not speak English, and few had spent as much time as Fou Sin working for European and U.S. employers. But Fou Sin was not an anomaly. His experience instead was an extreme example of the changes at work in the lives of people in South China, especially since the Opium War of 1839–42. Some of those changes were the immediate result of European and American attempts to draw China more firmly into the ever-expanding economic sphere of North Atlantic nations, and of attempts among southern Chinese to nurture a market-based economy of their own. Other changes had longer histories.

Fou Sin, for example, told newspapermen that his father's farm in South China was really "a very small piece of land." Having some sense of what Americans meant by the term "farm," Fou Sin was trying to convey the situation rural people faced in his homeland. Ever since Europeans in China had introduced new crops such as peanuts and sweet potatoes that could be cultivated on marginal lands, the Chinese population had increased rapidly. By the early nineteenth century in South China, that growth had outstripped the region's ability to support its inhabitants, and people lived on small plots that amounted to a quarter acre per person. This turn of events, however, did not necessarily bespeak widespread rural poverty: the Pearl River Delta supported a well-developed market economy, and some foodstuffs were imported from other areas.[71] Then, too, emigration from South China was not a new phenomenon, and Fou Sin's father's decision to send one of his sons abroad followed older regional practices as much as it responded to recent upheavals. From the time that the Han Chinese had moved south into the area that became Guangdong Province, a process that took many centuries, they had been relatively isolated from the interior of China by mountains and thus oriented toward the South China Sea. Foreign trade was conducted largely through South China ports, and emigration was common. Indeed, by the time of the Opium War, large settlements of overseas Chinese thrived in the Philippines, Indonesia, Thailand, and elsewhere in Southeast Asia.[72]

Other changes in South China had more immediate antecedents. It was this complicated set of transformations that created the global lines of trade and migration Fou Sin followed before he arrived in California. The British, voracious tea drinkers and lovers of Chinese silk and porcelain, had found in the eighteenth century a commodity that could stop the one-way flow of English silver into Chinese coffers. That commodity was Indian opium. The conquest of India allowed Britain to develop a profitable triangular trade engineered by the East India Company. The trade's success depended on an eager market of Chinese opium smokers, and indeed, between 1730 and 1830, British sales of opium to China increased a hundredfold. The ending of the East India Company's monopoly on Asian trade in 1834 only increased sales of opium, as North American and other European merchants rushed into the breach. Chinese officials, of course, deplored the spectacular expansion of the opium trade and the drain of Chinese silver to the West. To an already rigorously regulated system of foreign commerce, the emperor in 1838 added an all-out war on opium. A war on opium was a war on Britain, and as English merchants withdrew from Canton to Hong Kong, the Chinese fortified coastal waterways. Battles ensued, and as the war moved north out of Guangdong and Fujian provinces toward Nanjing in 1842, the Chinese sued for peace. The Treaty of Nanjing forced concessions that would haunt Chinese diplomatic and trade relations for the rest of the century. Not to be outdone, the United States and France quickly demanded treaties that gave them the same rights as Britain.[73]

Yet after the Opium War, Cantonese people in South China made it difficult for foreigners to go about their business as the Treaty of Nanjing stipulated, mounting urban riots and attacks by local militias emboldened by participation in the recent conflict. Meanwhile, secret societies known as the Triads stepped up their activities in the Pearl River Delta, drawing on social discontent, economic dislocation, and antigovernment sentiment to move from older practices of banditry and smuggling to open rebellion. In an 1854 conflict known as the Red Turban Revolt, for example, bands joined together to capture the city of Fatshan and threaten Canton itself. Government forces eventually crushed the uprising, but nothing seemed to arrest the wave of violence that washed over South China in the 1850s—clan feuds, antiforeign riots, secret-society warfare, battles between Hakkas (migrants from the north and their descendants, who came to constitute an ethnic minority in South China) and Puntis (Cantonese speakers whose forebears had lived in the region longer). Hakka-Punti conflicts took on new meaning in the 1840s when Hong Xiuquan, a Hakka man from Guangdong influenced by Protestant missionaries, gathered converts to his Society of God Worshipers in neighboring Guangxi province. The movement he started evolved into the bloody Taiping Rebellion of 1851–64, which nearly toppled China's Qing dynasty. Although the heart of the uprising was located from Guangxi north to Nanjing, it was rooted in the ubiquitous foreign presence and social upheaval of South China, and its impact reached back to Guangdong as well.[74]

These transformations, along with the firmly market-oriented economy of South China and the established trade ties between the region and North America, contributed to widespread emigration from Guangdong in the midnineteenth century.[75] Although South China had long sent many of its sons and a few of its daughters abroad to augment household economies, the Gold Rush migration in some ways represented a new departure. Earlier emigrants tended to come from southern Fujian Province and northeastern Guangdong, while California-bound Chinese came from the Pearl River Delta area in south-central Guangdong.[76] When white authorities charged Fou Sin with murder in Amador County in 1857, they alleged that he had acted in concert with four other Chinese, including his friend Chou Yee. One of the men was never apprehended, and another took his own life in jail. But the three other men implicated in the murder grew up within a hundred miles of each other in the Pearl River Delta area, where market economies were most developed and where dislocations accompanying foreign incursion were most acute. Fou Sin and

Chou Yee had grown up in the shadow of Canton itself and were drawn into the web of global commerce early—Fou Sin left South China in the mid-1840s, and by the mid-1850s he had crossed paths with Chou Yee in the Sandwich Islands. The third man, named Coon You, seems to have grown up in the Heungshan district, closer to Macao. He told newspapermen through a translator that he was only twenty years old and had come to California just a year or so before he was arrested for murder. Unlike Fou Sin, who at twenty-six had not married, Coon You left a wife behind in China.[77]

Coon You—young, recently married, non-English-speaking, probably a direct migrant from Guangdong to California—had more in common with most Gold Rush Chinese than did the much-traveled Fou Sin. When Fou Sin first left home in 1845, he did so with his father's approval and no doubt contributed to his family's well-being either through his earnings or simply by his absence. But by the time he boarded his second vessel in 1848, he did so without his father's consent, a point he emphasized when he was interviewed in jail. So it seems likely that his movements from that time on were not part of a household economic strategy. By contrast, Coon You, who was eager to speak of his marriage, probably still thought of himself as his family's emissary to Gam Saan ("Gold Mountain," the Cantonese term for California). Like other Chinese in the mines, Coon You likely did what he could to send home remittances to relatives. Before his arrest, in fact, he had been working his own placer claim along a creek in Amador County. By late 1857, however, when he was arrested, it was clear that some of the prime gold deposits left in the Southern Mines were not in the creeks but in the coffers of water company managers. It is not clear if Coon You, along with Fou Sin and Chou Yee, would have been willing to mine a safe and bludgeon a clerk to get a bigger share of those riches.[78]

The vast majority of Chinese emigrants to California were—like Fou Sin, Chou Yee, and Coon You—young men sent at least initially by families to augment household incomes in the Pearl River Delta. But a small minority were women. A handful of these were merchants' wives or else servants, but many more were young women who contributed to family economies by working as prostitutes abroad. Their financial contributions generally took two forms: First, procurers paid parents a price for each daughter sold, and, second, remaining family members gained when there was one fewer mouth to feed. Most of these women ended up in San Francisco—recall that Fou Sin got into one of his fights at a Chinese brothel—or the supply centers of Sacramento and Stockton. But by 1860, census takers found over four hundred Chinese women in the Southern Mines.[79] As in the case of French prostitutes who went to California, Chinese women who sold sex for cash left behind no first-person accounts that document their emigration experiences. But the work they did, the lives they lived, and the deaths they died would prove crucial to the evolution of social relations in the Southern Mines.

Finally, then, we return to the Sierra Nevada foothills, where Rosa Felíz de Murrieta, Vicente Pérez Rosales, Stephen Spencer Hill, Jason Chamberlain, Anne Lyons, and Fou Sin all were headed—and where native peoples braced themselves for change. It was a French-speaking man who left behind one of the richest accounts of Indian strategies for coping with rush of immigrants into Miwok gathering and hunting grounds. This Belgian-born gold seeker, Jean-Nicolas Perlot, had lived through the events of 1848 in Paris and had joined one of the California-bound companies there, arriving in the Southern Mines in 1851. Three years later, in the fall, when the salmon were running in the Merced River, Perlot met up with a young Miwok leader. Perlot thought that this man's name was Scipiano and that he was a chief of the Yosemite band. Most likely this was the leader whom other immigrants called Cypriano, a leader of the Awal Miwoks. This Scipiano complained to Perlot about the changes the Gold Rush had wrought in the lives of his people. Scipiano had spent some time in a Spanish Mexican mission, and so he spoke to Perlot in both his native dialect and the Spanish language. As for Perlot, he had been learning Scipiano's Miwok dialect and could understand some Spanish as well (he carried a Spanish dictionary with him in the mines), though he was a native speaker of French. By the time Perlot sat down to write his reminiscences years later, he recorded Scipiano's complaints in French, with a few Miwok and Spanish words retained along with their French translations and a few potentially puzzling phrases explained parenthetically.[80]

One can only hope that something of what Scipiano was trying to say to Perlot in 1854 has survived these linguistic, cultural, and temporal leaps. According to Perlot, Scipiano explained that his people had to be allowed to come down from the mountains "to gather the acorns on their flats, where *Nangoua* (God) calls them, since he plants their food there." The Miwok man, Scipiano said, "is not a *hin-hin-mèti* (bear) of the mountains, he is born in the plains and flats which you now take from him." Before the Gold Rush, men like Scipiano never went to the mountains "except during the days of sun (summer) to refresh himself." Now he was forced to take refuge there.

Jean-Nicolas Perlot, a Belgian-born emigrant from France. Perlot mined alongside Miwok Indians and learned something of their beliefs and cultural practices.

Courtesy of the Bancroft Library.

Whether Scipiano indicated that he was speaking exclusively of native men or whether some of the gendered references entered in translation is unclear. But as Scipiano went on, he spoke specifically of native women: "Our women that *Nangoua* gave us so that we could remain without end (so that our race could perpetuate itself) have more trouble remaking us (giving us children)." This was because of the move into the mountains: "they have to give birth in the cold (the snow), and the *piquini* (the child) perishes." Scipiano's demand, then, was this: "Look for *l'olo* (gold) where you want, let the *Ochà* (Indian woman) seek her seeds where they are and *Oualai Nang-à Blanco* (and the Indian will be the friend of the White)."[81]

If Scipiano truly envisioned a way for his band to coexist with non-Indians in the Sierra Nevada foothills, perhaps it was because it had been only six years since Miwoks had held sway over much of the drainage of the San Joaquin River. To be sure, newcomers had already impinged upon the autonomy of these native peoples by 1848, and Miwoks had engineered uneasy strategies of interdependence with the interlopers, just as they had interacted with neighboring Indians in the past—Yokuts to the south, Nisenans to the north, and Monos and Paiutes on the "other side of the sky" (that is, east across the Sierra Nevada).[82] But the Sierra Miwoks, unlike the linguistically related Bay and Plains Miwoks, had not been forced to forfeit control over their communities before the Gold Rush. By contrast, Bay Miwoks, who lived inland from the edge of the San Francisco Bay area east to the Sacramento–San Joaquin Delta, were among the native peoples of California's interior whom Franciscan missionaries sought as converts when disease and hard labor began to take its toll on coastal Indians; Bay Miwoks first appear in Mission San Francisco records in 1794. Likewise, Plains Miwoks, whose territory covered the valley lands of the lower Sacramento and the area where the Cosumnes and Mokelumne rivers empty into the San Joaquin, soon faced pressure from the Franciscan fathers; Mission San José began to record Plains Miwok baptisms in 1811. Following on the heels of missionization, malaria inadvertently introduced in the Central Valley by British Hudson's Bay Company trappers in 1833 killed perhaps twenty thousand people, wiping out human habitation in parts of the valley, once the most densely populated area of native California.[83]

Both microbes and missionaries had a difficult time following the tributaries of the San Joaquin River above the valley into the Sierra Nevada foothills where Scipiano grew up. Indeed, some lowland Miwoks took refuge up-country when life in the valley—or in the missions—became untenable. Conversely, some Sierra Miwoks must have found their way down to the coastal settlements, because Scipiano's brother Juan told Perlot that their family had spent at least a few months at a mission when the boys were very young. Scipiano himself had stayed longer, Juan explained, and so of the two brothers, Scipiano spoke the better Spanish. Scipiano's father, José, was a chief, and, as his eldest son, Scipiano stood to inherit his father's position; indeed, Juan told Perlot that *Nangoua* (Perlot's rendition of a Miwok word for god), was so eager to produce an heir to the chief that Scipiano "had come into the world after seven moons." Perhaps Scipiano's parents, too, had high hopes for their son and thought a short stay at a mission where he could learn Spanish would serve the future leader well in a world where newcomers controlled the lands to the west. At any rate, the brief contact Scipiano's family had with the Franciscans—so unlike the earlier missionization of Bay and Plains Miwoks—suggests that relations between Sierra Miwoks and Spanish Mexicans were not relations of dependence and domination before the Gold Rush.[84]

Actually, by the 1830s the distinctions scholars have drawn between Plains and Sierra Miwoks began to break down, as lowcountry bands were disrupted by solicitous missions and infectious disease. Those who survived both incursions headed up into the foothills and reconstituted their communities or joined up-country bands. By the time of the Gold Rush, then, the native peoples of the foothills were a mixed lot of valley Indians, mission Indians, and Sierra Miwoks.[85] As newcomers joined up-country peoples, they brought with them a new subsistence strategy developed in the years since Spanish Mexican settlement began on the California coast in the late eighteenth century: horse raiding. Miwoks in the Central Valley had been stealing horses from *padres* and *pobladores* for decades, but the raids increased once the missionaries began to come into the interior in search of new converts. In 1833, the year of the malaria outbreak and the year Mexico secularized California missions, raiding briefly declined as valley residents succumbed to illness or fled to the hills. But within a year or two Miwoks started stealing horses again, now from the Californio rancheros, who were quickly gaining control of mission lands and labor. Indians used the horses to hunt elk and antelope, and they also grew fond of horsemeat as a supplement to their customary diet. Around the same time, however, a new use for Mexican horses emerged, as American fur trappers ranged into California and found there not only the beaver they sought but also Indians adept at rounding up livestock and willing to trade with these new intruders from the east. The mountain men, in turn, took the horses to the annual fur trade rendezvous, that riotous, multilingual gathering of trappers, company men, and Indians which disturbed the peace of some Rocky Mountain valley every summer from 1825 to 1840. In trading horses with American trappers coming west over the Sierra Nevada, Miwok men—for horse raiding had been assimilated to notions of male responsibility in native divisions of labor—were drawn into a global arena of market relations.[86]

Closer to the Miwoks' home, immigrants were moving into California's Central Valley, creating other tentative links between native and non-native economies and further blurring the boundaries between the two. These immigrants were taking advantage of the exodus of native peoples and the largesse of California officials, who, since the Mexican declaration of independence in 1821, had been trying to guard the fragile string of Spanish Mexican settlements along the Pacific from Indians to the east and from Russian, American, and British interests on the coast. The first non-Mexican to try ranching in the interior was the Massachusetts-born "Dr." John Marsh, who had a habit of passing off his Harvard bachelor's diploma as a medical degree. With the money he earned treating patients, he was able in 1838 to purchase a rancho in the San Joaquin Valley, where he lived and prospered until disgruntled Mexican workers killed him in 1856. A year after Marsh went into business on the San Joaquin, John Sutter, a German-Swiss immigrant who liked to tell people he was a French captain, approached California Governor Juan Bautista Alvarado for permission to start a colony on the Sacramento River. Alvarado agreed, eventually granting Sutter nearly fifty thousand acres and full civil authority in the valley. The governor hoped that Sutter's settlement would end Indian horse raiding, frustrate the designs of American and other fur trappers, and check the ambitions of Alvarado's uncle, Mariano Guadalupe Vallejo, who was gaining power as a military commander to the north at Sonoma.[87]

Sutter's New Helvetia colony indeed became a focal point of the interior in the 1840s, though it hardly had the effect Alvarado intended. Sutter welcomed Anglo Americans who had started to trickle into California via the Overland Trail, and his fort, at present-day Sacramento, began to serve as a magnet for emigrants. Marsh, too, encouraged Americans to make the journey by posting letters to eastern friends and newspapers extolling the virtues of his new homeland: the rich soils; the herds of wild horses, elk, and antelope; the local Indians who became "willing serfs" for white farmers. But it was Sutter, not Marsh, who knew the most about native labor, for in the decade during which he ruled the lower Sacramento Valley, Sutter became California's premier employer of Indians. In this he adopted Spanish Mexican practices of using native workers, but forsook the incorporative style of conquest that had characterized Mexico's northern frontier; Sutter had no interest in what Franciscans thought of as Indian souls.[88]

Native peoples, for their part, responded to Sutter's presence in a variety of ways. When he first headed up the Sacramento to set up camp, Gualacomne Miwok men met Sutter at the delta and thoughtfully guided him north, out of Miwok country and into the gathering and hunting grounds of Nisenans. Indeed, Nisenans may have constituted a large proportion of Sutter's Indian workforce. They had been hard hit by malaria and had not adopted the extensive horse raiding practices that kept Miwoks strong to the south. Many Nisenans and perhaps a smaller number of northern Miwoks saw employment at New Helvetia as a way to supplement their subsistence and to gain protection in what must have seemed an increasingly dangerous local world. Such Indians constituted Sutter's entire labor force, save a handful of Hawaiians and a few overseers. They harvested wheat, washed and sewed clothes, distilled liquor, made hats and blankets, tanned leather, trapped beaver, killed deer, caught salmon, sailed goods up and down the Sacramento, constructed the buildings of New Helvetia, and served in Sutter's militia. They helped build, but never quite finished, a sawmill in Nisenan country that looms large in collective memory of the Gold Rush; it was in the tailrace of Sutter's mill that the overseer James Marshall discovered gold in January of 1848.[89]

Indians did not adjust smoothly to the work discipline Sutter tried to impose. Wheat was the colony's main crop, and consequently the wheat harvest, which occurred in the summer and fall, required by far the largest number of native laborers. But it coincided with key moments in the seasonal subsistence patterns of Nisenans and Miwoks alike—when seeds ripened, when acorns dropped from the oak trees, when salmon swam up the tributaries of the Sacramento and San Joaquin. This native harvesttime provided much of the food Indians stored for winter months, when neither the Sierra foothills nor John Sutter could give much nourishment. So Indians employed at New Helvetia felt obliged to come and go at will during the very months when the colony needed them most. Sutter did what he could to get and keep workers, offering trade goods and extending credit whenever possible but also resorting to capturing Nisenan men and holding them under armed guard.[90]

Still other Indians, among them many Miwok bands that lived farther south, kept out of Sutter's reach altogether and continued with their customary round of activities, which had long since included stealing horses. In fact, Sutter's presence on the Sacramento gave some Miwoks a new target for their raids, which in turn inaugurated new patterns of warfare in the foothills, as Sutter sent his Indian militiamen out after the resourceful thieves. But even with all of these changes at work among the Miwoks, the rhythms of everyday life in the up-country drainage of the San Joaquin were largely familiar ones. Perhaps six or seven thousand Indians lived along the rivers of what came to be the Southern Mines—from north to south, the Cosumnes, Mokelumne, Calaveras, Stanislaus, Tuolumne, and Merced. They organized themselves into groups of perhaps one to

three hundred people (such as the Awal Miwoks), who used a certain
territory for gathering and hunting and honored a common leader
(such as Scipiano's father, José). If a chief did not have a son, the
office might pass to his daughter, and so female leaders, while rare,
were not unknown. Before the Gold Rush, the Awals probably
counted as their own a few semipermanent settlements, which
through Spanish contact came to be known as *rancherías*, and a number of seasonal campsites. *Rancherías* were often home to people of a
particular lineage, which consisted of men related by blood, women
who married into the kin group, and the children women bore.[91]

Just as native labor practices proved important in Sutter's venture,
so too would they influence Indian-immigrant relations during the
Gold Rush. Miwok practices depended on the natural abundance of
the foothills, an abundance immigrant miners often were hard-
pressed to recognize. Starting in the spring, for example, Miwok
women headed out from the *ranchería* to begin their annual round of
gathering wild foods. First came the new greens from plants like
columbine, milkweed, larkspur, and "miner's lettuce." Then, in May
and throughout the hot, dry months of summer, women gathered a
variety of seeds from balsam root, evening primrose, summer's dar-
ling, farewell-to-spring, and countless other plants. In August,
Miwoks set fire to the land to encourage the growth of seed-bearing
annuals and to ensure forage for deer as well. Then women turned
their attention to collecting digger pine nuts, until the foothill oaks
began to yield their crop later in the fall. Acorns were far and away
the most important staple in Miwok diets. Thus the quintessential
image of autumn in California—dark green foliage of oak trees
against parched golden hills—held for Miwok women and their menfolk a promise of winter comfort.[92]

Miwok men busied themselves with hunting, fishing, horse raiding, and, occasionally, warring—though most non-Indian observers
insisted that the men were never as busy as the women.[93] Still, hunting and particularly stealing horses could take Indian men farther
away from *rancherías* and sometimes for longer stretches of time.
Men of the foothills hunted deer most of all, using communal methods to surround the animals or more solitary tactics whereby individuals wearing deer's head disguises stalked their prey. Men also fished
for trout and salmon, using nets and spears of their own design (they
made their own bows and arrows, too, just as women constructed
baskets for gathering). And it was men who engaged the newcomers
from the other side of the sky—no longer just Monos and Paiutes but
now American trappers who brought trade goods to exchange for

stolen horses. In all of this, Miwok men knew themselves to hold more power than their womenfolk, even as they acknowledged that men would soon perish if women stopped "remaking" them and gathering acorns below where *Nangoua* planted oak trees.[94]

Still, if the reminiscences of the Belgian miner Jean-Nicolas Perlot are even a remotely reliable guide to Indian ways, it seems likely that Miwoks saw their style of gender relations not so much as natural but as contingent. Just as important, Perlot's recollections hint at Miwoks' ability to imagine the most fundamental kinds of changes— an ability that would serve them well during the Gold Rush. One exchange between Perlot and Juan, brother of Scipiano and son of José, helps illustrate this. Juan had been trying to explain to Perlot why Miwoks tried to conceive their children so that they would be born between March and June: "It is . . . because the Spirit wishes it, and proof that he wishes it is that *Ouatou* [the sun] is climbing then." Perlot was confused. Was the sun not climbing in January and February as well, after the winter solstice? Juan was patient: "at that time it is *Commè* [the moon] who rules, she is superior to *Ouatou,* but she makes nothing grow." Perlot could not understand the relation-ship among *Ouatou,* the sun; *Commè,* the moon; and *Nangoua,* whom he took to be the Miwok god. So Juan went back to the beginning, as he might with a child. *Nanguoa,* whom Juan further characterized in both his own dialect and Spanish as "god thought of motion," had created two suns and entrusted them with the task of "making and directing everything that moved." One sun made a woman, while the other made a man, and the two suns argued with each another about the relative value of their creations. The sun who had made the man struck the sun who had made the woman, and the latter sun lost thousands and thousands of pieces of light that spread throughout the sky. That diminished sun is now the moon, and the stars are her missing pieces that she tries to gather to herself for fifteen days out of every month. But each time she collects her strength, *Ouatou* once again defeats her, shattering her reconstituted self sometimes with such force that one can actually see stars hurtling across the sky.[95]

Perlot, an eager pupil, was transfixed. Did Juan think that *Commè* would eventually prevail over *Ouatou,* the moon thereby regaining her status as a sun? "Oh yes," Juan replied, "already in spite of [*Ouatou*], the snows are appearing on the mountains, and *Commè,* who gathers her *î-attissa* [pieces of light] and who does not throw them, is keeping them to make use of them when she has enough." He went on ominously, "Look carefully when she has grown big and you will see a large bundle of *î-attissa* she is hiding so that *Ouatou* doesn't see them, but she lets them be seen enough so that *Oscha* (woman) always hopes that *Ouatou* will be conquered at last." On that day, Juan concluded, "it will be so much the worse for the *Nang-à* (man), that *Ouatou* made, and so much the better for *Oscha* (woman), who is the work of *Commè;* then the latter will rule the world, which will begin again, and the *Oscha* will rule the *Nang-à,* and she will avenge herself on him, if he has mistreated her."[96]

Perhaps Juan had perceived a change in climate of late, or perhaps the growing cold had something to do with his people's move up into the mountains, or perhaps he was simply entertaining himself with his naïve guest. Whatever was the case, Juan's words indicated an intellectual penchant for imagining transformations of the most elemental sort. It was this sense of the grand potential for change— along with this notion of the contingency of power and the responsibilities of those who held it—that would carry Miwoks and their allies through the Gold Rush years.

Much of what made life after 1848 so difficult for the six or seven thousand native people who lived in the foothills of the Sierra Nevada was the influx of immigrants that increased the human population there tenfold in a few short years. A dense web of economic, political, and cultural transformations, both global and local, brought Mexicans, Chileans, Anglo and African Americans, French, and Chinese to Miwok gathering and hunting grounds in response to the discovery of gold in California. Miwoks, too, had participated in some of these transformations before the Gold Rush, but not to anywhere near the extent they would after 1848. Once assembled in the Southern Mines, this diverse array of people would contend with one another to determine whose interests would be best served by the rush for riches. Like the relationship Juan described between *Commè,* the moon, and *Ouatou,* the sun, Gold Rush relations of domination were achieved through struggle, maintained by constant vigilance, and always threatened by subordinates' will to come out from the shadows. *Commè* continued to wax and wane over the Sierra Nevada foothills. In the meantime, she witnessed many a contest like her own.

Part II

Boom

Chapter 2

Domestic Life in the Diggings

66 I have heard of Miners at some diggins subsisting for days on Acorns of which we have a very fine kind in this Country," Helen Nye wrote to her mother in 1853. Nye, a Massachusetts-born white woman whose husband was a merchant at Don Pedro's Bar in Tuolumne County, went on to explain how immigrant men learned to make use of the oak tree's bounty: "The Indians make great account of gathering [acorns] for their winter store." Newcomers to the Sierra Nevada foothills watched the autumn harvest with interest. And though they preferred to purchase rather than hunt for or gather their own provisions, in hard times, and especially on prospecting tours, they might follow Miwok practices. While looking for new diggings in Tuolumne County during November of 1849, for example, William Miller and his Anglo companions baked acorns for supper, and a few days later, farther south in Mariposa County, the clergyman Daniel Woods and his prospecting party boiled a kettle of acorns with a bit of venison for their evening meal. In general, though, Gold Rush immigrants saw the food that Miwoks most valued as something to be eaten only in dire circumstances. As Charles Davis explained to his daughter in 1852, while acorns, grass, and wild oats abounded in the Sierra foothills, "these serve for Wild Indians and Wild Animals."[1]

As Davis's disdain for Miwok sustenance suggests, cooking and eating could be sites of contestation, as well as of communion, in the Southern Mines. That was because culinary practices fit into a larger constellation of activities in the diggings that signaled for many a world of confusion—men mending trousers and caring for the sick, Anglos dining on acorns and frijoles. Edmund Booth captured one aspect of that confusion when he complained to his wife in 1850, "Cal. is a world upside down—nothing like home comforts and home joys." Booth was a New Englander by birth and an Iowan by migration, and he wrote to his wife, Mary Ann, from the Tuolumne County town of Sonora. He lived at a boardinghouse there kept by a young Mexican man and two African American men from Florida. Edmund told Mary Ann that his daily routine began when he awoke from a night's sleep on the bare ground, rolled up his blankets, and sat down to a breakfast of coffee, meat, butter cakes, and applesauce. Then he walked half a mile below the town to the diggings. "The evening passes," he wrote, "in reading, talking, thinking of home, or as I am now—writing." Booth stayed in towns and at boardinghouses more frequently than did many placer miners, perhaps in part because he was deaf and thus lived most safely in densely populated communities of hearing people.[2] But if Booth's privations were less severe than those of most gold seekers, what did he mean when he complained to his wife about the absence of "home comforts and home joys"? Why did California in the 1850s seem like a world standing on its head?

To answer these questions, one must ponder the multiple meanings of such common activities as eating acorns, digging gold, thinking of home, and inhabiting a race or a gender.[3] Even in so short a time as the Gold Rush years and even in so small a place as the Southern Mines, meanings proliferated, evolved, collided. By attending to daily life in the diggings—to the work people did to maintain and enrich themselves and to the ways they filled the rest of their Gold Rush hours—one can begin to comprehend why so short a time was so transformative and why so small a place was so volatile. While native people in the Southern Mines lived in communities with roughly equal numbers of women and men, among immigrant peoples, skewed sex ratios meant drastically altered divisions of labor in which men took on tasks that their womenfolk would have performed back home. Analyzing how immigrant men parceled out such work and how they thought about what they were doing shows us much about the content of gender in the Gold Rush. Examining the meanings of the domestic and personal service work that the small number of non-native women did in California opens a window on the same subject. And studying the perceptions Indian and immigrant peoples held of one another's ways of manufacturing material life provides yet another view.[4]

Skewed sex ratios in the diggings were accompanied by an extraordinary demographic diversity: people came to California from many parts of the world, producing and reproducing ideas about color, culture, and nation that, on U.S. soil, often coalesced into conversations about race.[5] Race, like gender, is a changing set of ideas about human difference and hierarchy, and a relation in which those ideas are put into practice. In Gold Rush California, its meanings pulsed through everyday life like an erratic heartbeat. For instance, the way that certain tasks, such as cooking or laundry, came to be associated with particular groups of non–Anglo American men demonstrates how constructions of race could be mapped onto constructions of gender in the diggings.[6]

Not everyone in the Southern Mines dug gold, but everyone did perform, or relied on others who performed, life-sustaining and life-enhancing tasks such as procuring provisions, preparing meals, and providing companionship. Since few could reproduce in California the divisions of labor that made the performance of these tasks seem more or less predictable and culturally coherent back home, Gold Rush participants devised new ways to provide for their needs and wants. But all the while they wondered and worried about what it meant, for example, that Anglo men were down on their knees scrubbing their shirts in a stream, that Mexican women were making money hand over fist selling tortillas on the streets of Sonora, or that French men seemed so good at creating homey cabins in the diggings.

Distinguishing between two kinds of work—domestic and personal service work, on the one hand, and work in the mines, on the other—may seem to reify categories of labor. Surely placer mining sustained and enhanced human life as much as baking bread or caring for the sick did. In making such distinctions, one invokes the discursive division between home and the workplace that accompanied the growth of industrial capitalism in the nineteenth century, especially in the northeastern and urban United States. One also echoes more recent Marxist-feminist delineations of productive and reproductive labor, which have placed "reproductive" chores (often women's work) on a par with those "productive" chores (often men's work) assumed to constitute true economic activity. But impulses similar to those that split home life off from labor in the nineteenth century—impulses scrutinized by twentieth-century feminists—also led most Gold Rush participants to view mining as qualitatively different from and more important than their other daily tasks. This makes intuitive sense, especially since immigrants traveled hundreds or thousands of miles to dig gold or to profit from those who did. Yet performing this privileged activity required that miners pay attention

English-speaking miners used lettersheets such as this for correspondence with friends and relatives back home. This lettersheet expressed nostalgia for domestic comfort.

Reproduced by permission of the Huntington Library, San Marino, California.

to the exigencies of everyday life. And, in fact, evidence shows that gold seekers paid great heed to their more immediate desires—for shelter, for food, for company, for pleasure, for some way to make sense of what was for most a novel situation. Then, too, for one group of people in the Southern Mines—Miwok Indians—gold digging rarely became the most important, community-defining kind of labor performed. So the distinction drawn here between mining labor and domestic and personal service work is at once heuristic *and* grounded in some, but not all, relevant historical circumstances.[7]

In the end, though, the distinction serves yet another purpose. During the 1980s, historians learned to use poststructuralist analyses of language that show how binary oppositions work—oppositions such as the one between productive and reproductive labor. In the productive/reproductive labor distinction, for example, the leading term (productive or "breadwinning" work) takes primacy, while its partner (reproductive or "domestic" work) is weaker or derivative. This hierarchical relation mirrors some social relations of dominance and subordination based on gender and race. So foregrounding reproductive or domestic labor in a history of a mining area, where mining labor might be assumed to take precedence, is itself a gesture toward unsettling that hierarchical relation.[8] I begin, then, not in the mines themselves but in the brush and bark houses and canvas-topped cabins Gold Rush participants built in the Sierra foothills.

Indeed, one of the first needs immigrants had to meet was that for shelter. Only occasionally did immigrants imitate Miwok practices that made use exclusively of local materials to shield people from the elements and to bind them together in small groups that shared a common living space. Sierra Miwoks built two kinds of dwellings, one primarily for the warmer months, when people were on the move in search of food, and another for the colder months, when bands tended to stay in one place, living off the summer and autumn harvest and waiting out the winter rains. Both were conical structures—to a Canadian and a Belgian gold seeker alike, they looked like beehives—but summer houses were thatched with brush and grass, while winter shelters were made of long slabs of bark.[9] Immigrants sometimes constructed brush camps too, especially in the heat of the summer and when they were on prospecting tours. At least one observer acknowledged the miners' debt to native peoples in this, using a term for Indian dwellings of eastern origins: "Some comfortable wigwams are made of pine boughs thrown up in a conical form, and are quite dry."[10] French, Mexicans, and Americans all seem to have built such houses. An Anglo chronicler claimed that Chileans and Mexicans also made structures of hides laid over wooden frames.[11]

Still, by far the most common material Gold Rush immigrants used for shelter was canvas, and this may have been even more true in the Southern Mines than in the Northern Mines. When J. D. Borthwick, a Scottish artist and writer, toured the diggings in 1852 and 1853, he noted that in the north, "log cabins and frame houses were the rule, and canvas the exception; while in the southern mines the reverse was the case."[12] Winters farther south were milder, which accounts for some of the difference, and the persistence of placer mining—which characterized the southern region throughout the 1850s and which necessarily encouraged transience—may explain it as well. Placer miners were always on the move, taking up new claims when old ones gave out or situating themselves near riverbeds during the dry months and on smaller creeks in the rainy season; they relocated so often that "vamos the ranch" was often the first "Spanish" English-speaking miners learned.[13]

Though most did live in canvas homes, the word "tent" actually described a wide variety of structures. Some people lived in cramped quarters, such as the Chinese men Borthwick saw in 1852, the first year of mass Chinese immigration to California, and who were organized "in a perfect village of small tents." Likewise, the Pennsylvanian Enos Christman shared with two others a nine-foot-square dwelling that ran up to a ridge pole in the center. "Within this house," Christman noted in his journal, "we eat, sleep, rest and tell each other good yarns."[14] Tents like these were not only small; they also offered little protection. John Doble's canvas home in Calaveras County got damp with every rainfall, and, since it had no fastenings, camp dogs ran in and out with impunity, sometimes carrying off mouthfuls of provisions.[15]

So when miners stayed still for any length of time, they built more elaborate shelters. For instance, although the Belgian Jean-Nicolas Perlot and his five French companions lived at first in a small tent and a brush hut, within a year the four men who remained in partnership built a typical structure, "a sort of cabin of tree trunks, topped with canvas to form [a roof] composed of two tightly stretched pieces of canvas, one six inches above the other."[16] Such canvas-topped cabins were ubiquitous in the Southern Mines. In them, immigrants could set up rough bedsteads and construct fireplaces, though at least two Anglo men remembered how improvised chimneys forced smoke into their living quarters instead of drawing it out.[17] Heavy rain could impair the draft of even a well-built fireplace, and Welsh-born Angus McIsaac, situated near Mariposa, noted in his diary that men living with such irritants often compared their smoky cabins to scolding wives or leaky ships.

McIsaac's observation suggests how readily Gold Rush participants saw in their material world metaphoric possibilities, how easily the frustrations of camp life took on gendered meanings. McIsaac himself thought a smoky home was "ill compared" to a scolding spouse or a leaky vessel. An unmarried man with a sweetheart back home and a seafaring past, he noted, "were I compelled to take charge of either, I would on all acations choose the former."[18] Wives, ships, cabins—men grumbled about the responsibilities entailed in their dominion over each of these when the objects of their authority proved unmanageable. McIsaac may have thought a woman the most pleasing ward, but he took for granted the gender hierarchy his words implied. Meanwhile, he and his neighbors took charge of their more immediate surroundings by christening their cabins with names that suggested, even celebrated, the absence of sharp-tongued spouses: Loafers' Retreat, Main Top (a cabin of sailors), Temperance Hole, and Jackass Tent. Like the Anglo miners a bit to the north who called their camp Whooping-boys Hollow, McIsaac and friends took a certain pleasure in the canvas-covered world without women they created.[19]

Not all shelters in the Southern Mines bespoke the ambivalent bachelorhood of men like Angus McIsaac. Among immigrant peoples, more Mexican men than others came to California with their womenfolk. Although descriptions of the dwellings they built are few and written primarily by non-Mexicans, it seems likely that some Mexican Gold Rush communities celebrated social possibilities different from the ones celebrated by Whooping-boys Hollow. By far the most perspicacious observer of Mexican camp life was Canadian-born William Perkins, a merchant in the town of Sonora who claimed he was known among Spanish-speaking people there as *el amigo de los extranjeros*, friend of foreigners.[20] Perkins found among Spanish-speaking people an otherness that attracted him as much as it repelled many of his English-speaking neighbors. Hence his rhapsodies on Mexican life in Sonora:

I had never seen a more beautiful, a wilder or more romantic spot. The Camp . . . was literally embowered in the trees. The habitations were constructed of canvas, cotton cloth, or of upright unhewn sticks with green branches and leaves and vines interwoven, and decorated with gaudy hangings of silks, fancy cottons, flags, brilliant goods of every description; the many-tinted Mexican *Zarape*, the rich *manga*, with its gold embroidery, Chinese scarfs and shawls of the most costly quality. . . .

For Perkins, the scene was at once novel and familiar; he could not help recalling "the descriptions we have read of the brilliant bazaars of oriental countries." Whatever the scene evoked for the orientalizing eyes of Perkins and men like him, there is no reason to doubt that Mexicans did indeed decorate their dwellings with brightly colored flags and fabrics and serapes. Perkins noted that it was Mexican men who built the brush houses for their families and who, "leaving their wives and children in charge," went off during the week to dig gold. However few and far between, then, even in Gold Rush California there were eye-catching, well-tended worlds without men.[21]

For the most part, though, miners fended for themselves. Once they constructed cabins or pitched tents, inhabitants had to organize domestic labor such that all stayed reasonably well fed and healthy. By far the preponderance of evidence about camp life describes the subsistence strategies of Anglo American men—particularly diary-writing northerners. Still, a handful of sources generated by French- and Spanish-speaking immigrants, as well as descriptions of non-Anglo camps by Anglo writers, help round out the picture of daily sustenance in the diggings. Then too, multiethnic, multiracial tents and cabins were by no means rare in the Southern Mines, and white men who worked in partnership with men of color, for example, sometimes left a record of shared domestic duties.

Probably the most common type of household in the Southern Mines during the boom years of the Gold Rush was that of two to five men who constituted an economic unit: they worked together in placer claims held by household members, alternating tasks and placing the gold in a common fund from which they purchased food and other necessities. Profits, when there were any, were divided among the partners.[22] But such households were not universal. Often the men of several cabins would band together, for example, to dam a river and work its bed. In this case, domestic concerns were the province of the cabinmates, while the larger group distributed the proceeds of labor in the diggings. Likewise, a household might include members who worked separately and did not pool resources, but did share household tasks and provisions. The variations on these themes were endless, and the unpredictability of placer claims meant that a miner might find himself in a variety of domestic situations over the course of a year or two in California. At times he might even end up, as Anglos put it, "on his own hook," mining and tenting alone. But most men spent a good deal of time living and working in cooperation with other gold seekers.[23]

These generalizations probably hold for most white men, both North American and European, and most free African Americans during the Gold Rush. It is likely that they hold for a large number of Mexican and Chilean and perhaps some Chinese men as well. But for those North Americans, Latin Americans, and early-arriving Chinese who went to California under conditions of slavery, debt peonage, or contract labor, other domestic arrangements may have obtained. And whenever women of any background were present in the camps or whenever men lived in or near towns with boardinghouses and restaurants, daily subsistence was a different matter.

All types of households in the Southern Mines, save those of Miwoks, relied on tenuous market relations to supply most of their basic needs. (In time, even Miwoks would turn to the market for many provisions.) Out in the camps, men traded in gold dust for provisions at the nearest store, generally a tent or cabin located a fair hike from home and stocked with freight hauled overland to the mines from Stockton.[24] In the first year of the Gold Rush, some goods came straight from Mexico, as merchants in northern Sonora emptied their shelves and hurried their wares on pack animals to the mines. Rancheros from southern California also bypassed the new trade routes, driving their cattle directly to the diggings and reaping healthy profits.[25] But Stockton was a conduit for most trade goods. Beef, pork, beans, flour, potatoes, and coffee ranked high on miners' lists of provisions purchased. In flush times, they might also be able to buy onions, dried apples, or a head of cabbage, though fresh fruits and vegetables were the hardest items to find.[26]

Limited foodstuffs spelled monotonous meals for most, but also encouraged people to exchange cooking techniques. Men from Europe and the United States, for example, sometimes adopted Mexican practices. Perlot and his French companions, en route to the mines in 1851 and low on provisions, met a party of Mexicans who were eating what looked to Perlot like turnips dipped in salt and pepper, fresh tortillas, and hearty beefsteaks cooked on sticks over an open flame. The Mexican men gave Perlot some raw meat, and he returned with it to his own party's fire, proclaiming, "Messieurs . . . in this country, this is how beefsteak is cooked."[27] Howard Gardiner, a Long Islander, was less enthusiastic about the Mexican-style foods he learned to prepare during lean times, recalling that he and his part-

ners lived "more like pigs than human beings." But those meals
based around pinole, a fine flour of parched corn that had been
pounded in a mortar, sustained him until he was able to buy what
seemed to him more appropriate Anglo fare.[28] While not all English-
speaking miners were as disdainful as Gardiner was, the contrast
between Perlot's and Gardiner's responses to Mexican dishes would
be echoed in later conflicts between Anglo Americans, on the one
hand, and Spanish- and French-speaking immigrants, on the other.
Just as Gold Rush shelters took on gendered meanings, so too could
Gold Rush food become racialized in its procurement, preparation, or
consumption—recall Charles Davis's comment about fare that was fit
only for "Wild Indians and Wild Animals."

Among Latin Americans in the diggings, men might try to appeal
to one another's tastes, especially when commercial interests were at
stake. When Vicente Pérez Rosales, the Chilean *patrón* who went to
California with his brothers and five laborers, learned in mid-1849
that non-Anglos were being driven from the mines, he turned his
attention to trade. He and his companions set up a store filled with
goods purchased in San Francisco—Chilean cheese and beef jerky,
toasted flour, dried peaches, candied preserves, and two barrels of
brandy. All items sold well except the jerky, which was full of what
looked like moth holes. In desperation, the Chilean merchants laid
the jerky out in the sun and coated it with hot lard to fill up the aper-
tures. Then they piled it up in a pyramid shape and doused it with a
"devilishly" hot sauce made from Chilean peppers. The pungent
smell of the jerky caught the attention of some Mexican customers,
and so the traders thought fast: "We told them it was the most select
jerky," Pérez Rosales recalled, "the kind served to the aristocracy in
Santiago." He went on, "We lied like experienced merchants who
assure a trusting female customer that they are losing money on an
item, and would not sell it at such a low price to anyone but her."
Here Pérez Rosales turned Mexican unfamiliarity with Chilean foodstuffs to his advantage, playing on envy of aristocratic privilege and,
in his own mind, making women out of Mexican men, thereby
underscoring Chilean manliness. While this incident took place in
Sacramento, entrepôt for the Northern Mines, similar interethnic gas-
tronomic and commercial episodes, which were charged with taken-
for-granted notions of gender and tinged with class meanings, must
have occurred in Stockton and the Southern Mines as well.[29]

Most immigrants, like these Mexican customers, preferred to purchase their provisions in the diggings. But during the first few winters
of the Gold Rush, floods in the San Joaquin Valley and treacherously

muddy roads between Stockton and the foothills brought severe shortages of even the most basic supplies. In mid-October 1852, for example, Moses Little wrote from Sandy Gulch in Calaveras County, "We have been living rather short for the past few days. On Baked beans & bread—no potatoes." A month later: "No provision up yet and the last flour in the loaf." In another month, his tone was more ominous: "Frank and friend C went over to the store. . . . but they were all out of Flour Meal & Pork. We have now not more than enough to last for 2 or 3 days longer."[30] During the same winter, Perlot and his Belgian partner, Thill, living in Bear Valley near the Merced River, could find no provisions at all until they learned of a lone merchant at Big Oak Flat who was distributing beans and flour in equal portions to hungry miners regardless of their ability to pay. A number of men did receive their rations gratis, but at times such as these food was often scarcer than gold.[31]

Thus many miners tried to supplement store-bought provisions by hunting and fishing, and a few gathered greens in the hills or planted small gardens. Not all who hunted met with success. Moses Little managed to bring down some quail just in time for Christmas dinner during the lean winter of 1852, but he spent most of his shot at target practice. Timothy Osborn, another white New Englander, and his cabinmates were similarly ineffective in late 1851 despite the abundance of deer, antelope, and bear near their Tuolumne County camp. They depended instead on neighboring Texans, "genuine backwoods-men," to supply them with venison.[32] William Miller had better luck. He and his fellow white partners were camped near a group of free black men in the fall of 1849, and in addition to coming together to dam the river and work its bed, the two parties went out deer hunting with one another and otherwise shared provisions. Heavy rains foiled the plans of the damming company, but the African and Anglo American residents of the camp continued to exchange gifts of fresh venison. By Christmas, one of the black men, Henry Garrison, had moved into Miller's tent, and all parties spent the holiday together indulging in a "Splendid Dinner" and dancing to the music of Garrison's fine fiddle playing.[33]

Fewer men planted gardens or gathered greens. So visitors were astonished by Perlot's singular store of herbs and vegetables. After serving salad to an incredulous miner in the mid-1850s, Perlot took him on a stroll: "I led him a hundred paces from the house . . . where I gathered chervil; a few steps farther to a place where cress was growing well . . . ; a little farther, I found lamb's lettuce," and so on. One of Perlot's partners, the French Louvel, had planted the garden the year before. On seeing it, the newcomer exclaimed, "My God, . . . how stupid can you be! to suffer four years as I have, without having had an idea as simple as that."[34] A few others had that same idea. William Miller planted cabbage and onions in 1849; the preacher Woods put in potatoes, turnips, and cabbage the next spring; and the following year A. W. Genung cultivated two acres from which he boasted he could raise a thousand dollars worth of vegetables—a claim that had as much to do with their scarcity and high price in the diggings as with his confidence as a gardener.[35]

Still, most immigrant men suffered from the dietary deficiencies created by their ignorance of the wild plants that Miwok women gathered and by their unwillingness to grow more familiar crops. Perhaps they hesitated to plant vegetables because their campsites were temporary or because kitchen gardens were generally women's responsibility back home. Whatever the reason, their reluctance made them sick. George Evans, for example, could not fathom why he was too ill to work in the mines during the winter of 1850, until doctors told him he had scurvy: "They advised me to get all the vegetables afforded by these hills." So he had friends gather what looked to him like wild cabbage and onions, and he bought some Irish potatoes and a bottle of lime juice. Within two days, his health took a clear turn for the better.[36]

Evans, given his condition, was wise to eat his vegetables raw, but miners cooked most of their food and had to determine among themselves how to share culinary duties. What evidence exists about such divisions of labor reveals more about Anglo American men than other Gold Rush participants, but Europeans and free African Americans, at least, seem to have followed similar practices. The Belgian Perlot claimed, in fact, that most men in the diggings organized cooking in like fashion: "The rule generally observed between miners in partnership . . . was to do the cooking by turns of a week." Similarly, John Doble explained to a correspondent, "sometimes one does the cooking and sometimes another and one only cooks at a time and cooks for all who are in the Cabin." Moses Little approved of this common arrangement: "As we take turns to do the cooking we shall know how things are done."[37]

Indeed, there were many things to do. A man's "cook week" began on Sunday, when he prepared for the days ahead, as Little recorded: "It being my week to cook I have been somewhat busy—more so than on other Sabbath—Coffee to burn A box full of nuts to fry Bread to bake & Beef to cut up & take care of." George Allen's Sunday journal entries note a similar round of tasks—boiling meat, making bread, stewing grapes, cooking rice and beans, frying doughnuts, bak-

ing apple pie and bread pudding. During the week, the cook continued to make large quantities of staple foods like bread and beans, in
addition to getting up three meals a day. Little, for example,
described his evenings as punctuated by the rhythm of domestic
duties: "I sit & mended a shirt while my bread is baking & my Beef
boiling"; and two nights later, "I am writing My Beans are stewing &
Bread baking."[38] The days around New Year's 1850 must have been
the cook week of Henry Garrison, the African American fiddle player
who lived with William Miller and his dancing partners, because
Miller's journal for that period is filled with references to Garrison
cooking breakfast, making apple pudding ("the Best Pudding I had
Eaten Since Leaving home," Miller wrote), and stirring up a
"Beautiful Stew" of squirrel meat. Miller must have looked forward to
Garrison's cook weeks, because at least one of his other partners had
trouble even lighting a fire, to say nothing of preparing meals for the
men.[39] Domestic competence was hardly universal in the diggings,
but men valued it when they found it among their comrades.

It is much more difficult to determine from English-language and
translated sources whether or not Mexican and Chilean men working
in partnership with their compatriots adopted similar divisions of
labor. While Anglo Americans, particularly northerners, occasionally
remarked about household arrangements that differed from their
own—those in which women or male subordinates such as slaves
took on cooking duties—they wrote little about camp life among, for
example, Mexican men who lived in groups of four or five. It is hard
to say whether this silence represents indifference or whether the
divisions of labor were similar enough among small parties of Anglos
and Mexicans that Anglos found in their neighbors' habits little upon
which to remark. Perhaps Perlot's contention about "the rule generally observed between miners in partnership" was widely applicable
in the Southern Mines.

Anglos did occasionally write about Chinese men, who arrived in
the Southern Mines in large numbers toward the end of the boom
years of the Gold Rush. But white observers were more apt to note
how odd they found Chinese foods, cookware, and eating imple-
ments than to describe how Chinese men divided up domestic work.
Borthwick, the Scottish traveler, visited Chinese camps in both the
Northern and the Southern mines, and claimed that Chinese men
"treated in the same hospitable manner" all those who approached
them. On each visit, Chinese miners invited Borthwick to eat with
them, but the traveler declined, finding their dishes "clean" but
"dubious" in appearance. He added that he much preferred "to be a

The Scottish artist and travel writer J. D. Borthwick's rendering of a domestic scene at a Chinese camp.

Courtesy of the Bancroft Library.

spectator," a role chosen by many a white man in his dealings with Chinese miners. The spectacle Borthwick described was that of a Chinese camp at dinnertime, with men "squatted on the rocks in groups of eight or ten round a number of curious little black pots and dishes, from which they helped themselves with their chopsticks."[40] Borthwick's word picture evoked white men's visions of the Chinese; there was something both delicate and animal-like in the circle of squatting Chinese and their curious cookware. While his words said as much about white visions as about Chinese practices, they did suggest that Chinese miners working in large parties broke into smaller groups of men who shared meals and that they used cooking and eating utensils from their homeland.

Some white men were more gracious than Borthwick when invited to join Chinese circles. John Marshall Newton was camped with a partner near five hundred Chinese miners in Tuolumne County in 1852. After helping the Chinese secure their title to a claim that had been challenged by English miners, Newton fancied himself a "hero" in his neighbors' eyes. The Chinese men did bring him plates of "rice flavored with sweetmeats" and other small gifts. They also invited him for meals, a practice Newton described with nostalgic flavor and a dash of exoticism: "many a pleasant dinner have I had eating their outlandish dishes." No doubt the Chinese miners appreciated Newton's assistance in what often proved for them an inhospitable local world. But however much they credited his actions, they also relished making him the butt of dinnertime jokes. Invariably when Newton sat down to eat, someone would hand him chopsticks. "Of course I could do nothing with them," Newton remembered, and so "the whole 500 seeing my awkwardness would burst out into loud laughter."[41]

To the Chinese miners, their neighbor must have looked a bit like an overgrown child fumbling with his food. Still, despite this momentary, ritual reversal of a dynamic in which Anglo American men disproportionately held the power and resources necessary to ensure survival in the diggings, more often Chinese men found it expedient to curry favor with whites. In a situation where white men missed more than anything "home comforts and home joys," Chinese men could turn Anglo American longings to their advantage. Indeed, although Newton sometimes offered his Chinese neighbors cups of coffee, neither he nor other white men whose personal accounts are readily accessible left behind evidence of having shared their own meals with Chinese miners; the dinner invitations flew in one direction, from the Chinese to their Anglo neighbors. Howard Gardiner, for example, the one who loathed Mexican foods, lived for a time by himself near the tent of a Chinese man. Sometimes Gardiner would stay late working on his claim, and when he went home, he recalled, "I found that the Celestial had preceded me and prepared supper."[42] Gardiner's neighbor must have found some benefit in looking after the white man. Meanwhile, for Gardiner the arrangement seemed so unremarkable—so familiar, perhaps—that he granted it only passing mention. In everyday events like these, where men of color performed tasks white men associated with white women, Gold Rush race relations became gender relations as well.

Among some groups of men in the diggings, such domestic practices were institutionalized. In 1850, Timothy Osborn, a white man from Martha's Vineyard, lived near a Mississippi party headed by a planter named Gaster, whose sons had persuaded him to try his luck in California. Gaster brought four of his thirty black slaves with him from home, men who Osborn observed were "prompt in executing the commands of their master." Osborn, who did his own domestic work, remarked that the African Americans "were very useful fellows about a camp . . . some of them being occupied . . . in cooking and keeping everything 'decently and in order.'" Northerners sometimes remonstrated against slave labor in the mines, but, if Osborn's sentiments were at all common, the idea of having someone else prepare meals for white men and clean up around their camps had its appeal.

After all, this was a culturally intelligible division of labor, even if back home it usually followed what were understood as lines of gender rather than race. As another Anglo man complained to his mother, "If, as at home, we had others to attend to the household arrangements, it . . . would be different, but here everything must be done by ourselves."[43]

Osborn did not stop to think why Gaster's slaves were so "prompt" in obeying their master—after all, California was admitted to the union as a "free" state as part of the Compromise of 1850. The New Englander later learned that at least one of the enslaved men had left behind a wife and two children in Mississippi; this could have provided good motivation for helping Gaster achieve his goals as quickly as possible. Then too, although four black men accompanied Gaster to California, by the time the group left for home, only three joined the return party. Perhaps one of the black men had been able to buy his way out of bondage after a few months of diligent work in the diggings. This was a common occurrence in California, where the price of freedom was generally around a thousand dollars. Whatever motivated the African American men's behavior, Osborn himself could not help looking longingly at the services they provided.[44]

In still other camps, men who were not in hierarchical relationships with one another nevertheless chose divisions of labor that resembled the habits of home. Sometimes the practices were temporary. When Pérez Rosales, his brothers and workers, and three other Chileans first went to the mines, all of the men hauled their belongings over rugged terrain and all went to work in the diggings—all save a man named Hurtado, who, because he was sick and unable to do heavy work, was assigned cooking duty. When the others returned from a day of mining, Pérez Rosales recalled, "Hurtado was awaiting us with beans and rice he had been keeping good and hot." It was not unusual for convalescing men to do extra domestic work, which for some must have reinforced the notion that such tasks were best suited to the weak.[45]

On occasion, however, a healthy man in partnership with another took over food preparation entirely. When Perlot teamed up with Louvel, the French man who gardened behind the cabin, the two came up with such an agreement. According to Perlot, Louvel had a "refined palate" and was a superb cook, while Perlot's skills were "mediocre." So the men decided to forgo cooking in weekly rotations: "Louvel . . . consented to do it alone, on condition that I would go hunting every Sunday. He concocted the stew, I furnished the hare; each one found his satisfaction in this arrangement." In the

long run, the plan had its costs. During their first summer together,
both Louvel and Perlot spent most of the time digging a ditch for
water to make it easier to wash gold-bearing dirt once the winter
rains began. When they finished and found the skies still clear,
Louvel grew restless. As Perlot recalled, Louvel "had nothing for dis-
traction but his culinary occupations," while Perlot kept busy hunting. After several weeks of inactivity, Louvel left Perlot to join a
fellow countryman working farther north. Perlot was on his own for
several months until he finally found a new partner, for whom he
immediately prepared a welcoming feast. This partner was the fellow
who was so taken by Perlot's succulent salads—so taken that the newcomer, like Louvel before him, agreed to take on cooking duties
indefinitely. Perlot had a way with men.[46]

No doubt similar domestic arrangements existed elsewhere in the
diggings. But most who could rely on someone to make all their meals
by definition either lived in or near a boardinghouse, owned a slave,
or had a wife. Thomas Thorne must have been in Gold Rush heaven.
An Anglo Texan, Thorne came to the Southern Mines with enslaved
black women and men *and* a white wife. The party ran a boardinghouse renowned in Mariposa County for delicacies such as buttermilk
and fresh eggs. In 1850, three Anglo American men lived with the
Thorne family in the shingle-roofed cabin that the merchant Samuel
Ward, brother of the soon to be famous Julia Ward Howe, called
Thorn Villa. Many others spent a night there when traveling through
the area, and some who lived nearby took their meals at the cabin for
a weekly fee. Neighbors like Charles Davis ate there only on occasion,
when their taste for finer fare got the best of them, as Davis explained
to his daughter: "here in California we can get . . . a great plenty of
common food of every kind. . . . But no eggs, no Turkey, no Chickens
no pies no doughnuts no pastry . . . unless we take a meal at Mrs.
Thornes." Mary Thorne, mother of three children, managed the
boardinghouse with the assistance of Diana Caruthers and her two
daughters, Caroline and Georgeanne, three of the ten African
American slaves who lived with the Thornes in the diggings.[47]

Even when black labor helped create such plenitude, white men
associated domestic comfort largely with white women. Thus both
Ward and Davis attributed the bounty they encountered at the boardinghouse to "Mrs. Thorne." When Mary Thorne was ill, Davis acknowledged that there was "nobody except the Old darkey Woman & her
two daughters to serve up for the boarders"; but his preface of "nobody
except" defined the presence of the Caruthers women as a sort of
absence. Indeed, while white men might credit the usefulness of slave

labor for household chores, it was white women's domestic abilities that most enthralled them. After eighteen months of cooking for himself, Lucius Fairchild, a future governor of Wisconsin, moved into a sturdy frame dwelling where one of the residents lived with his wife and infant daughter. The Vermont woman kept house for the men, and Fairchild was ecstatic: "You can't imagine," he wrote to his family, "how much more comfortable it is to have a good woman around." Enos Christman, who gave up mining to work for the first newspaper in the Southern Mines, the *Sonora Herald*, echoed Fairchild's sentiments. Christman lived in the two-story adobe building that housed the newspaper offices, and when his partner's wife and children finally arrived in 1851, he beamed, "Everything now goes on quite comfortably. A woman about a house produces a new order of things."[48]

It was not only family homes that triggered gendered and racialized imaginings. Roadside houses where white women cooked for travelers also proved perfect sites for conflating things culinary and things female. When P. V. Fox described his stop at Richardson's Ranch en route to the diggings, he was especially vivid: "Had beef steak, Pickled Salmon, Hash, Potatoes, Bread, biscuit, Griddle cakes & Sirrup, Tea & coffee. Pies & cakes, Peach sauce, and a chat with the land lady (The rarest dish)." It was indeed the case that meals at white women's establishments were more elaborate than white miners' usual fare. In particular, where an Anglo woman served food, milk and eggs were sure to be found—not surprising, since cows and chickens had long been a special province of women in rural American divisions of labor. In California, the prospect of indulging in such items could take on the urgency of romance. Sam Ward, traveling to Stockton from the mines, hesitated to stop at a new wayside inn rather than the one kept by a male acquaintance on the Tuolumne River. But, he recalled, "a smiling hostess in the doorway and a tethered cow hard by tempted me." Then he completed the metaphor: "This infidelity to my friend, the landlord of the Tuolumne, was recompensed by the unusual luxury of eggs and milk, for which I felt an eager longing."[49]

As Ward's turn of phrase suggests, men's longings and men's loyalties could be confusing in California. Domestic concerns were somehow female (were they not?), and so it was only natural (was it not?) that men would prove inept at caring for themselves and one another in the diggings. Often enough, this was so. But for every case of scurvy, for every burned loaf of bread, for every man who could not cook a decent meal for his partners, there were daily domestic triumphs in the diggings.[50] When he first arrived in the mines, for example, Enos Christman complained that his flapjacks "always came out heavy doughy things" that no one could eat. "Want of a teacher," he thought, made learning to cook difficult. But trial and error brought good results, as Christman proudly noted: "We can now get up some *fine dishes!*" Likewise, William Newell, writing to his wife Mary, was emphatic about the improvement in his own culinary skills: "I have got to be a great Cook." Others, like Perlot, found that a new man about the house could produce a different order of things. Likewise, Daniel Woods was especially thrilled when a young sailor came into his life, "a man with a brave heart in danger, but with a kind heart to those he loves—rough or gentle like the ocean he has navigated." The fellow was a "first-rate cook," and he also built camp stools and a bedstead, Woods noted, "so that our mining home presents an unusual air of comfort." What were men to make of the domestic contentment they found in the diggings? What did it mean when a New Englander sat down to his journal after a sumptuous trout dinner and wrote, perhaps with some exaggeration, "French cooks we consider are totally eclipsed and for the reestablishment of their reputation we can do no less than recommend a visit to our camp"?[51]

French miners relax at lunch, not looking particularly domestic.

Courtesy of Matthew R. Isenburg.

For English-speaking men to liken themselves to French cooks was no empty gesture. Anglo American and British immigrants considered exaggerated domesticity a national trait among French men. The Englishman Frank Marryat was delighted to find a large French population in the town of Sonora, "for where Frenchmen are," he wrote, "a man can dine." Likewise, A. Hersey Dexter, who suffered through the hard winter of 1852–53, was saved by "the little French baker" next door who allowed neighboring miners a loaf of bread each day. Yet it was the traveler Borthwick who best elaborated upon this vision. Borthwick described a French dwelling along Coyote Creek in Calaveras County that resembled Perlot and Louvel's—a "neat log cabin," behind which was a "small kitchen-garden in a high state of cultivation." Alongside stood a "diminutive fac-simile of the cabin itself," inhabited by a "knowing-looking little terrier-dog." Along with Dexter, Borthwick insisted on fashioning French men and things French as somehow dainty (small, little, diminutive)—echoing Borthwick's descriptions of Chinese men huddled around their "curious little black pots."[52]

But in the domestic lives of the French Borthwick found nothing exotic—the cabin was neat; the garden was cultivated; even the dog had an intelligent face. Instead, Borthwick found among the French a magic ability to create a homelike atmosphere: "without really expending more time or labor, or even taking more trouble than other men about their domestic arrangements, they did 'fix things up' with such a degree of taste, and with so much method about everything, as to give the idea that their life of toil was mitigated by more than a usual share of ease and comfort."[53] The experience of Perlot and Louvel, of course, indicates that among French-speaking men some more than others were inclined to "fix things up." But the Anglo propensity for casting all French men as a sort of collective better half in the diggings is telling. More explicitly than back home, where gender could be mapped predictably onto bodies understood as male and female, gender in California chased shamelessly after racial and cultural markers of difference, heedless of bodily configurations.

California *was*, for many, a "world upside down." Even in hotels and restaurants, all the help might be male. When Hinton Rowan Helper— who would soon be known as a southern critic of slavery but who first took aim at California—passed through Sonora and breakfasted there, he noted that the male proprietor and two male workers cleared the table. "Women have no hand in these domestic affairs," he exclaimed. "There is not a female about the establishment." In case the reader missed the point, he added, "All the guests, owners and employees are men." (The breakfast was dull, too—pork, beans, and flapjacks.)[54] The future governor Lucius Fairchild himself became such an employee for a time and felt compelled to explain the situation to his family: "Now in the states you would think that a person . . . was broke if you saw him acting the part of *hired Girl*. . . . but here it is nothing, for all kinds of men do all kinds of work." Besides, he went on, "I can *bob around the table,* saying 'tea or Coffee Sir.' about as fast as most *hombres.*" Although Fairchild insisted it all meant nothing in California, his explanation suggested that it meant a great deal—white men bobbing around tables waiting on other white men. If he could act the part with such enthusiasm, did gender and race have less to do with bodies and essences than with performing tasks and gestures? No doubt Fairchild thought he could tell a "natural" hired girl from one just "acting the part." But the anxiety such situations produced could be striking. Fairchild, for example, compared his own performance not to that of "real" women but to that of other *hombres*—as if the English word might not adequately insist upon his own essential manhood.[55]

It was true that people who thought of themselves as "*hombres*" rather than "men" had less call to wait on or be waited on by other male gold seekers. Recall that Mexican men came to California with their womenfolk more often than did men of any other immigrant group. Mexican women, while few in number, provided domestic labor not just for husbands and brothers but often—at a price—for larger communities. Remember, for example, the party assembled by Antonio Franco Coronel, the southern California ranchero. Coronel traveled with two Indian *peónes* and two Sonorans who were indebted to the *patrón* for the cost of the journey north—Benito Pérez and his wife, whose name was not recorded. The wife of Pérez received half an ounce of gold (about eight dollars) each day to buy provisions for the group. Of her own accord, she started preparing more food than she and the four men could eat; the extra she sold. She charged a peso a plate for tortillas and frijoles, and eventually earned three or four ounces of gold (fifty dollars or more) per day. It must have been women such as Coronel's cook whom the French journalist Étienne Derbec encountered, prompting him to conclude that tortilla making was "the sole occupation of Mexican women when they do not have an Indian to take care of that job." (And if Coronel's party was at all typical, more male Indian *peónes* were employed in the mines than over campfires.) Derbec thought it a hard life for a woman. It may have been tedious, but no miner would have scoffed at a steady income of three or four ounces a day, even in 1848; by 1849, an ounce per day was considered a respectable yield.[56]

In the town of Sonora, Mexican women made a magnificent display of their culinary talents, cooking in open-air kitchens huge quantities of wheat and corn tortillas to serve along with a *sopa* of meat cooked in a chile sauce. William Perkins recalled that Indian and Spanish Mexican women alike sold their wares in this manner, while native men who had once lived in Spanish missions passed through the weekend crowds carrying buckets of iced drinks on their heads and singing out, *"agua fresca, agua fresca, quatro reales."* Meanwhile, stalls and stands tempted passersby with "sweetmeats of every description, cooling beverages, with snow from the *Sierra Nevada* floating in them, cakes and dried fruits, hot meats, pies, every thing in the greatest abundance."[57] Some white women also sold food in quantity—at Curtis Creek, Benjamin Butler Harris met an Oregon woman "who cooked and sold from early morn to dewy eve dried-apple pies for $5.00 each." But nowhere did Anglos create the extensive commercial domestic world that Mexican women, along with mission Indian men, set up on the streets of Sonora. It was a world that was reminiscent of Mexican cities where women supported themselves and sometimes their families by hawking tortillas, tamales, and fresh produce from homes, market stalls, and street corner stands.[58] Even Hermosillo and Ures could not have produced as many willing customers for women's wares as the Gold Rush town of Sonora, however. There is no way to quantify how much gold dust passed from men's hands to women's hands in this domestic marketplace, but it must have been considerable.

Still, as Lucius Fairchild's waitressing suggests, this commercial sphere included men who provided goods and services as well. Fairchild was not alone in serving his fellow (white) man, but more often men who did such work were not Anglo Americans. When Vicente Pérez Rosales gave up on mining and storekeeping, for example, he opened a café in San Francisco called Citizen's Restaurant. Perhaps the name was defiant; noncitizens like Pérez Rosales were already subject to harassment in California. Indeed, his decision to leave the diggings had everything to do with such treatment. The Chileans built their café and immediately hired a French cook, who Pérez Rosales claimed was famous and whom he paid more than twenty dollars a day plus room and board. There is no evidence to explain why this particular French man took this particular job, but French-speaking as well as Spanish-speaking immigrants faced Anglo opposition in the mines, and so the domestic marketplace may have been an attractive alternative. Nonetheless, restaurant work, even proprietorship, seemed to hold stigma for men thus employed. As

Pérez Rosales complained, "We were, at one and the same time, the masters and the servants of the restaurant," a statement that may also have reflected the *patrón*'s affluent youth.[59]

In the diggings, too, non-Anglo men provided many of the services the largely male population wanted. Helen Nye, the white woman whose husband was a merchant at Don Pedro's Bar, was in a good position to keep track of the demand, in particular, for non-Anglo cooks. Her home on the Tuolumne River was also a boardinghouse, but she did not prepare the meals. In letters to her mother and sisters, Nye explained her absence from the kitchen in a variety of ways. Once she intimated that her husband and a boarder had decided to hire a French cook, seemingly over her objections. On another occasion, she wrote that although she wanted to help out, "about all who hire as Cooks prefer to do the whole and have the regular price." In yet another letter, she complained that the cook Florentino had "left in a kind of sulky fit" and that his job landed in her hands: "I found it was too much as it kept me on my feet all the day." "If we were a private family I should prefer to do it," she reasoned, but keeping a boarding-house was a different matter. The shifting ground of Nye's explanation suggests that she worried about what her female relatives might think of her circumstances. Whether or not Nye herself wanted to stay out of the kitchen, the male cooks kept on coming. Florentino got over his fit and returned to Don Pedro's Bar, and he was preceded and fol-lowed by others—a fellow named Scippio, for example, and an African American man whom Nye, in spite of her stated wish to help with the cooking, disliked because he worked slowly, forcing her to assist. And although she implied that her husband made hiring decisions, she once revealed her own hand in the process by writing to her sister, "I think I shall try a Chinese cook next they are generally liked."[60] Nye's compulsion to explain her relationship to domestic duties—like Fairchild's to explain his—and her inconsistent descriptions indicate that novel divisions of labor could unsettle notions of womanliness as well as manliness. What *did* it mean for a white woman to turn over cooking to a black man, a French man, a Chinese man? For a Chilean *patrón* to wait tables alongside his *peónes*?

It was confusing—the way that gender relations, race relations, and labor relations coursed into and out of customary channels in California, here carving gullies out of hard ground, there flowing in familiar waterways, whereby women waited on men, darker-skinned people served lighter-skinned people, and a few held control over the labor of many. Beyond food preparation, other kinds of domestic and

personal service work became sites of such confusion. This was especially true of laundry and sewing as well as the care of convalescing
men, activities that were often gendered female in immigrants'
homelands.

Washing and mending clothes was an endless preoccupation for
miners, who spent much of their time shoveling dirt, sand, and
gravel. Out in remote camps, men did their own laundry in rivers
and streams. Although most left no record of using anything but
water to clean their clothes, some used a plant of the lily family, the
bulb of which has the properties of soap. John Doble may have
learned this trick from a native man who stopped to wash his pants,
shirt, and vest at the river where Doble was working. Likewise, Mrs.
Lee Whipple-Haslam recalled that Indians taught her mother to use
the soap plant, while the French journalist Derbec claimed that
Mexican men often made use of such bulbs.[61] Like ways of cooking,
washing techniques could be shared across the various populations in
the diggings. In this, native peoples and those from nearby held a
premium on knowledge of how best to use the local environment.

Miners, particularly Anglos, did their laundry on Saturday afternoon, after half a day of work in the mines, or else on Sunday. Some
found that digging gold was such dirty work that they had to wash
themselves and their clothes more often, as Leonard Noyes recalled:
"every morning we would take a swim, put on our blue drilling pants
and shirt work all day in the mud go home at noon. jump into the
water wash mud off, put on our flannels and let our cloathes dry
while we got dinner—at night go through the same motions." It
must have been a common scene in the diggings—men bathing
naked together in the river and walking about camp in flannel drawers, trousers draped over bushes and drying in the sun. Some men
hated the work—both Enos Christman and Howard Gardiner called
laundry "detestable"—but others seemed to revel in the washing-and-
bathing ritual. Timothy Osborn, in particular, looked forward to his
Saturday afternoon plunge into the slow, deep waters of the Merced
River, allowing himself to be drawn out into a swift current that
whirled him downstream until rapids forced him to scamper up the
bank and return to his friends.[62]

If washing and bathing proved a site of homosocial bonds among
some Anglo American men, so too did sewing. Although John Doble
moaned to a female correspondent about the task—"One thing troubles us old Bachelors sorely and that is mending our clothes"—others
recorded the repair of shirts, pants, and socks without complaint.
Most knew that sewing was work that could be done while beans

were boiling or friends were "spinning long yarns," and it also passed
the time when sickness or bad weather confined miners to their
tents.[63] Some even elevated the care of clothing to a moral impera-
tive, as did William Miller when he wrote in his diary, "I am sorry to
say there is one in my Camp who . . . chooses to Lay Down and Sleep
rather then mend his Cloths, or eaven wash them . . . he does not
Improve his time as he Should." But it was the Reverend Woods who
articulated the gendered meanings that some men could not help
attaching to their rainy-day sewing circles. In January of 1850 Woods
wrote, "In our visits to each other these days, like the ladies at home,
we often take our sewing with us. Today I took a pair of stockings to
darn, one of my shoes to mend, and the 'Democratic Review' to read.
While we plied our needles, our tongues were equally busy speaking
of mutual friends and hopes."[64] Busy tongues and needles, mutual
friends and hopes—these were intimate terms for an everyday task
shared among miners.

Still, while some seemed to enjoy such scenes, many jumped at the
chance to turn over the care of personal belongings to someone else.
More often than not, that someone else was a woman, frequently a
Mexican woman, or perhaps an African American or Chinese man. In
the town of Sonora, the all-male milieu of laundry work in the diggings was replaced by settings in which Mexican women washed
clothing while Mexican men—and often Anglos as well—looked on.
William Perkins, ever the voyeur, described one such tableau:

> O, for a camara lucida to enable me to delineate some faithful
> pictures of mining life and scenery! I thought thus, as I sat
> watching a party of Mexican women, who, in a little stream
> behind the house were busy . . . washing clothes. There they
> were, all squatted on their haunches, and naked to the waist, for
> they are obliged to disembarrass their arms and shoulders from
> the folds of the *rebosa*. . . .

He went on to explain how Mexican men—Perkins called them "lazy
Greasers" in "dirty zarapes"—lounged on the stream bank, "keeping
up a continual clatter of not the most chaste conversation" with the
women. Whether or not Perkins's own participation in the scene was
"chaste" was not an issue he addressed, but rather one he projected
back onto the Mexican men. Although Perkins thought of himself as
el amigo de los extranjeros, in fact his "friendship" with "foreign"
women seems to have been based on visions of them as erotic, even
animal-like others ("squatted on their haunches, and naked to the

waist"). And his relationships with non-Anglo men were of a discrim-
inating sort—French and South American men always excited his
sympathies, while Mexican men often seemed to him lewd, filthy,
and indolent.[65]

Given that Perkins is the only known chronicler of the scene in
Sonora, can one read the scene from a different vantage point? From
the perspective of women who toiled in the cool water while banter-
ing with countrymen and wondering about the Anglo who watched
from his window? From the perspective of the voluble men on the
stream bank who relaxed while their countrywomen worked under
the gaze of a "friend of foreigners"? It was a volatile combination—
Mexican women, Mexican men, and Anglo men in close proximity,
Anglos seemingly taking for granted that Mexican women labored,
that Mexican men lounged, and that Anglo men did whatever they
pleased. In a town like Sonora, where Mexicans and other Spanish-
and French-speaking immigrants lived in large numbers, men like
Perkins had to watch their step; leering from a window might be the
extent of their intrusion into social worlds not their own.

Out in the diggings, however, in more sparsely populated areas
with scattered concentrations of various immigrant men and few
women at all, those who took in washing could find themselves in far
more danger. Howard Gardiner, for example, recalled a story one of
his partners had told him about an incident at a Mexican woman's
washhouse in Tuolumne County. The partner, Stephen, had taken his
dirty clothes to this establishment, but then lost in a card game the
dollar he needed to pick them up. So he borrowed a dollar back from
the victor and proceeded with his three companions to "the Spanish
woman's." The laundry doubled as a saloon, and Stephen's friends,
having had more luck at cards, bought several drinks there. According
to Gardiner, the drunken Anglos "became hilarious and disorderly to
an extent that offended the woman's husband." The Anglos, in turn,
took offense at the suggestion that they were behaving badly, and one
called out to another, "what had we better do with this Greaser?" The
rest happened quickly; one grabbed the Mexican man, another bound
his hands, and a third threw the man's own reata over his neck and
strung him up from a tree outside his own door. "This summary execution," Gardiner claimed, "staggered Stephen," who, fearing punishment, fled from his friends. Fear—for her own safety—also kept the
Mexican woman silent; she answered all inquiries about the identity
of her husband's murderers with "*quien sabe?*" (who knows?).[66]

All this for what started as a hike to pick up a dollar's worth of clean
clothes. One cannot help wondering if the Anglos' hilarity and disor-

derliness involved what William Perkins might have called "not the most chaste conversation" with the Mexican woman, provoking yet one more interethnic Gold Rush drama revolving around notions of male honor and ending—like the story of Joaquín Murrieta—with the murder of one more Mexican man. Indeed, by invoking the term "greaser," an epithet usually reserved for Mexican men, the Anglos could have been justifying their unlimited access to the personal services—domestic or otherwise—of the Mexican woman. Whatever the Anglo misbehavior that prompted the Mexican man's anger and led eventually to the Anglo murder, it was clear that even the act of picking up freshly laundered clothes could prove deadly in the diggings.

Usually, laundry establishments were sites of more benign interactions, but ones nonetheless that bespoke some of the social hierarchies of the Gold Rush. Non-Anglo men joined Mexican women in the laundry business. In particular, those men who were subject to systematic harassment as miners, such as the Chinese, worked in washhouses, but so did other men of color. An older African American in Calaveras County, for example, ran a laundry as early as 1850. Although free blacks in the diggings did not face the strictures of the foreign miners' tax, they did face countless daily insults and informal prohibitions, which might have encouraged entry into the commercial domestic sphere.[67] Friedrich Gerstäcker recalled that the Calaveras County man charged half the going rate for shirts—twenty-five cents each rather than half a dollar each—and yet "lived exceedingly well by it." The demand for laundry services must have been great, because when Gerstäcker went to pick up his wash at this man's establishment, he found a huge pile of clean but unironed and unmarked shirts, which the proprietor told him to sort through on his own. In frustration, Gerstäcker randomly picked out six wrinkled shirts that he liked. The laundryman, not one to coddle his white customers, just shrugged, "Ebery gen'leman did the same."[68]

As the number of Chinese immigrants to California increased after 1852, and as the state government reinstated a foreign miners' tax (the first tax, imposed in 1850 and directed primarily at Spanish- and French-speaking miners, had been repealed), Chinese men moved into the laundry business.[69] Documentation for how and why Chinese started opening washhouses is frustratingly slim. Most scholars acknowledge that the process began during the Gold Rush and assume that it is explained by the absence of women in California and the harassment that encouraged some Chinese to provide goods and services to miners rather than engaging in mining themselves. Historians argue that both ethnic antagonism and the low capital and equipment requirements of washing accounts for the prevalence of Chinese laundries in California. And they remind readers that washing was women's, not men's, work in South China—that the "'Chinese laundryman' was an American phenomenon."[70]

Gold Rush sources do not reveal much more about the process. Hinton Helper, in his 1855 book *The Land of Gold: Reality versus Fiction,* claimed that washing clothes provided "the most steady and lucrative employment" for Chinese men. He noted a sign outside one establishment that read, "Wong Cho. Washing and Ironing—$3 per Doz.," indicating that like the black laundryman in Calaveras County, Wong Cho charged twenty-five cents for each piece of clothing. The Chinese man, however—probably a proprietor in a larger town where he would have had competitors—also did ironing. Helper's observations appear in a full chapter on Chinese in California, the main point of which is to suggest why "the copper of the Pacific" will likely become "as great a subject of discord and dissension as the ebony of the Atlantic." That such race trouble, actual or potential, was also by definition gender trouble is suggested by the fact that Helper's reflections on Chinese laundries immediately follow his discussion of the preponderance of men among Chinese immigrants, the lack of virtue among the few Chinese women in California, and the difficulty whites have in "reading" Chinese gender: "You would be puzzled to distinguish the women from the men, so inconsiderable are the differences in dress and figure." Helper is no guide to the meanings Chinese men may have attached to their work as launderers, but his observations suggest that Chinese immigrants—like much else in the Gold Rush—generated gender and race anxiety among Anglo Americans.[71] When it came to California, Helper had an ax to grind. Just as he would soon condemn southern slavery for its deleterious effects on poor whites, so too did Helper worry over the impact of the Gold Rush on the honest (white) laborer. A larger purpose of his book was to discourage emigration to the golden state, and one of his key strategies was to stress the different sorts of moral peril white women and men would face there. The heightened ambiguity of gender relations in a multiracial, predominantly male social world seemed to him heavy artillery to deploy in this battle for perceptions of the Gold Rush, and his discussion of Chinese laundry workers arises in this context.[72]

J. D. Borthwick, on the other hand, saw the "whole Golden Legend as one of the most wondrous episodes in the history of mankind," and so his descriptions of Chinese washhouses had a different aim. For him, the laundrymen were picturesque—part of the exotic human landscape of Gold Rush California—even while whites might sometimes find them repugnant. Borthwick explained that "the great scarcity of washerwomen" gave "Chinese energy" room to show itself in laundry work. Like Helper, Borthwick noted the large number of washhouses with their English-language signs, but the latter also stepped within such establishments to give the reader a sense not only of the work process but also of the social relations fostered by the preponderance of Chinese in the business: "Inside these places one found two or three Chinamen ironing shirts with large flat-bottomed copper pots full of burning charcoal, and, buried in heaps of dirty clothes, half-a-dozen more, smoking, and drinking tea."[73] Like Borthwick's description of Chinese cooking, this passage reflects as much his own ideas about Chinese men—that they were hardworking and gregarious and yet accustomed to squalor ("buried in heaps of dirty clothes")—as it does Chinese habits. But it also suggests that washhouses were not only work sites but centers of sociability for Chinese men.[74]

Care of the sick proved another kind of work that encouraged men to stretch, twist, invert, or even temporarily abandon customary ideas and practices. If one ignored the near absence of all women save Miwoks in the diggings, one could see much that was familiar. Timothy Osborn thought so: "A mining camp very closely resembles a country village, in its domestic concerns . . . sickness . . . excites the enquiry of neighbors, and the little exchanges by way of mutual relief is one of the beauties of camp life." William McCollum, a doctor from western New York State, went even further, claiming that the sick and destitute got along better in California than anywhere else in the world: "There is fellow-feeling there, a spirit of active, practical benevolence." According to McCollum, men made charity offerings for the ill on a scale that matched the extravagance of the Gold Rush itself: "$1000 could be raised easier there . . . than $5 in any of our large villages."[75]

Enthusiastic as some men could be about such "fellow-feeling" in 1849 or 1850, those who wrote reminiscences decades later could be positively enraptured. Benjamin Butler Harris, recalling the manly democracy of the diggings (and misquoting Shakespeare) was breathless: "Was this Utopia? Was it the Isle of the Blest? What largeheartedness, what floods, what gushes, what warm glows of friendship and kindness one for the other. One touch of their grand natures made them all akin." In Harris's memory, such male homosocial desire could transcend even racial and ethnic hatred. During the winter of 1849, scurvy was common in the mines. Harris thought the disease was particularly widespread among Mexicans, and he remembered that at one point seven hundred in his camp were "sheltered, doctored, nursed, and maintained by miners' subscriptions alone." Recalling this scene prompted Harris to condemn the "bigot," the "loud-mouthed Pharisee" of the "civilized" world in favor of those "whole-souled pioneers" who constituted "a superior society." Elsewhere Harris's reminiscences are filled with accounts of Mexican and French resistance to the foreign miners' tax, of Indian-immigrant conflicts, of the Australian "flood of scoundrels" that "polluted the mines" (floods could bring danger as well as pleasure), belying his romantic constructions of ubiquitous male harmony in the diggings.[76] But something about the way men cared for one another prompted Osborn and McCollum and then Harris after them to celebrate the manly benevolence they saw manifest in the mines.

As the inconsistencies in Harris's reminiscences suggest, that benevolence was hardly universal. Whether or not miners' subscriptions actually maintained seven hundred Mexican men in the winter of 1849, other kinds of cross-racial, cross-ethnic incidents revolving around care of the sick did occur in the diggings. For example, George Allen, who belonged to a damming company of twenty-odd men, noted in his diary during the summer of 1850 that two members were ill, one of whom he called simply "the Mexican." The men voted that one of the Anglos would "take charge of the sick Mexican . . . and see that he is taken cair of and provided with things to make him comfortable." Although this man was part of the company, he was the only one whom Allen failed to mention by name. This suggests the Mexican man's marginal status in the largely Anglo operation; he was a coworker whose health was important, but he would never be a member on the same footing as Allen and the other Anglos. For the unnamed Mexican, this was neither utopia nor the isle of the blest, but rather a local world in which loyalties among men reflected limits as well as largeheartedness.[77]

An incident with similar implications occurred at William Miller's camp in December of 1850. Henry Garrison, the black man who cooked beautiful stews and played a fine fiddle, had moved into Miller's tent (Garrison's own having been too thin to withstand heavy rains). Shortly thereafter, neighbors tried to persuade Miller to take in a sick white man. The invalid was one of a party from the Sandwich Islands whose tent had also been threatened by winter storms. One of the sick man's partners came to Miller drunk and railed: "he begun with Blowing up Garrison the Colard Man for not Comeing to lend him A hand & . . . then Commenced throwing out his hints to me that I had a fine tent And that the Sick Man was A Laying on wet Blankets And on the wet Ground." Garrison, though born in New York, had come to California from the Sandwich Islands; he knew the white men camped nearby and apparently thought little of them. As for Miller, he found the intoxicated intruder obnoxious, perhaps in part because the man was Irish; although Miller always described cordial relations with African Americans, his every reference to Irish immigrants was racialized and derogatory. Miller refused to care for the ailing white man, commenting, "It is D-D [damned] hard . . . If People . . . that are in Partys together And have Sick men Amongst them that they Should be Unwilling to take Care of them." A few minutes later, another white neighbor came by, someone who was friendly with both Miller and the islanders, to try to talk Miller and Garrison into taking the invalid in. Miller refused, and then Garrison "knowing the whole Party And their Proceedings Explained things more clearly." The neighbor turned to leave, muttering that the sick man "was a White And Should be takeing care off." Miller and Garrison stood their ground, as Miller recorded in his diary: "I . . . Said to him that the Partey the Sick man belonged to Should be made to take Care of him or they Should be Drove from the Mines." Apparently they convinced the skeptic, because he returned to the islanders and told them they must nurse their own. "Fellow-feeling" knew clear boundaries in the diggings, and often those boundaries followed racial and ethnic lines. When they did not—as when Miller welcomed Garrison into his tent—miners could expect challenge, particularly from white men who felt entitled to certain kindnesses in California.[78]

As fractured as "fellow-feeling" could be by race trouble, it was also full of potential for gender trouble. In the eastern United States, at least, and probably in other emigrant areas as well, caring for sick people was more often women's work than men's. Male physicians, to be sure, intervened from time to time, especially in cases of serious illness, but wives, sisters, mothers, female slaves and domestics, and sometimes hired home nurses (who were women) provided much of the daily maintenance for convalescents—the kind of maintenance that men needed most often in California.[79] So when Gold Rush men took care of each other, it was not surprising that some read that care as gendered female. George Evans is a case in point. Before Evans discovered he had scurvy, he had been sick on and off for weeks. He worried about the scarcity of doctors in the diggings, but more than anything he missed "the tender care and unceasing attentions received from loved hands at home"—hands, no doubt, of his womenfolk. Nevertheless, in California other hands were busy attending to his needs, as he recorded in his diary: "Mr. Parker, an excellent and attentive nurse in sickness . . . baked us some apple pies . . . the only food relished by me in the past four days. These pies could not have been better if baked at home." Much as Evans longed for the care of the women he left behind, men like Mr. Parker proved that the diggings were full of tender, competent nurses.[80]

Offering such tenderness could put men in compromising situations, however. When a man in A. Hersey Dexter's camp became so ill as to require constant attention, Dexter took on the role of caretaker. He remembered long days and nights spent alone with the invalid, broken up only by visits from his mining partners on their way to and from work. Occasionally, the sick man became delirious and tried to embrace Dexter forcefully, a situation Dexter felt might have proved dangerous had not the two men been of equal strength. Dexter recalled: "He seemed to have taken a fancy to me, and in his calmer moments would beg me not to leave him." Although the nurse did not articulate the kind of danger he thought he faced from his ward, his description of an incident that occurred the night before the man died can be read as saturated with erotic imagery. That evening, Dexter remembered bending over with his back to the patient to pick up wood chips off the floor. Suddenly the sick man leaped up from the bed and grabbed Dexter from behind: "we both fell on the floor, he on top and holding me with a grip of iron." Were the man's actions involuntary? Dexter described them that way: "This contraction of the muscles did not last for long . . . and in a short time he released his hold and lay as if he were dead." Whatever else the caretaker may have felt for the invalid, there was something in the nursing role that left Dexter feeling alternately protective of and vulnerable to his charge—feelings probably shared by many women who attended sick men in isolated domestic settings in the nineteenth century.[81]

Beyond these daily struggles over cooking, laundry, and caretaking, one of the clearest indications that life in the diggings raised questions for immigrant men about the content of gender and race is the extent to which Gold Rush personal accounts are filled with painstaking descriptions of sexual divisions of labor among native peoples. Such personal accounts, of course, were written disproportionately by literate, white Americans and Europeans, and hence tell little about the responses of black, Chilean, Mexican, or Chinese men to California Indian practices. But it is no exaggeration to say that Gold

Native gender divisions of labor interested Anglo American and European men. Here, John Hovey, who illustrated his own diary with watercolors, depicts an Indian man hunting. Given that Hovey lived and worked in the Southern Mines, the man represented was probably Miwok. From the John Hovey Journal.

Reproduced by permission of the Huntington Library, San Marino, California.

Rush letter, diary, and reminiscence writers were obsessed with the ways in which Miwoks organized men's and women's work. No other group's daily habits so interested white people, and no aspect of those habits proved so fascinating as the seemingly endless round of native women's work. This was not a new fascination. For nearly three centuries, Europeans and then white Americans had observed, described, and commented on native divisions of labor all over North America, far more often than not concluding that Indian women did most of the work while Indian men frittered away their time hunting and fishing. Historians have paid close attention to this Euro-American practice, pointing out the actual differences between native and white divisions of labor that gave rise to such perceptions as well as the ways in which such perceptions bolstered Euro-American ideologies of conquest.[82] These elements infuse descriptions of California Indian practices as well.

But Gold Rush accounts were written in a particular historical context—one where men far outnumbered women, where a stunningly diverse population inhabited a relatively small area, and where most turned their attention to an economic activity that offered potential (however seldom realized) for quick accumulation of capital. In this context, where differences based on maleness and femaleness, color and culture, and access to wealth and power were so pronounced and yet so unpredictable, curiosity about the habits of native peoples took on a special urgency. In particular, immigrant men who had assumed, often for the first time, responsibility for much of their own domestic and personal service work now seemed preoccupied with how differently Indian women maintained themselves and their communities.

White men were especially interested in how native women procured and prepared acorns, perhaps the single most important food Miwoks ate. If a Gold Rush writer wrote nothing else about Indians in his letters or diary, he generally included at least a brief mention of acorn gathering or processing. In November of 1852, for example, Moses Little noted that his "neighbors the Indians" had come "to their old winter quarters" nearby and that the "Squaws [were] out pounding Acorns to make their bread."[83] But many included more elaborate descriptions of women's work—gathering up acorns, hulling and then pounding them on limestone outcrops to make a fine meal, leaching the meal to remove the bitter-tasting tannic acid, and then preparing acorn-based soups and breads. During February of 1852, for example, John Doble watched as a nearby Miwok encampment grew from three bark huts to four hundred in preparation for what he called "a big Fandango." Doble's curiosity got the best of him, and he decided to take a look. As he approached, he found half a dozen Miwok women at work. Suddenly he realized why he had seen in the foothills so many "large stones with flat surfaces . . . & all the flat surface filled with small round holes in the shape of a physicians Morter." It was on such surfaces that women sat pounding acorns with large, oblong rocks; the holes were created by the repeated impact of stone against stone. It was hard work. Women built brush shades to protect themselves from the burning sun, but even so, some perspired enough to dampen the stone around them for several inches. Once the acorns were hulled and ground, women leached the meal and then, unless they immediately made it into bread, boiled it, a process that involved dropping red-hot rocks into tightly woven baskets filled with water.[84]

Other white men's descriptions of this process shared Doble's obsessive attention to detail, an obsession matched rarely in Gold Rush personal accounts, save in explanations of placer (and, later, quartz) mining techniques. Even miners' own culinary efforts did not receive as much attention as those of native women. It was almost as if, in their diligent representations of the seemingly reproductive work of Miwok women and the seemingly productive work of mining men, diary and letter writers tried to reinscribe ideas about gender difference that life in the diggings had so easily unsettled. But ideas about gender difference were always already ideas about race difference, and those processing acorns were not the women whose absence white miners bemoaned. Indeed, in California difference piled upon difference until it was hard for Gold Rush participants to insist upon any one true order of things. After all, no one could deny that white miners also performed "reproductive" tasks. Nor could anyone deny that native women's customary chores were "productive"—or that Miwok women panned for gold as well. Besides, there were few simple parallels between California Indian women's labor and the Euro-American category of "domestic" work. So immigrant men tried to make sense of what they saw by drawing on an older discourse that opposed native women's drudgery and native men's indolence.

It was a familiar refrain. The French journalist Étienne Derbec knew the tune: "It is generally believed that the Indians live from the hunt; but, mon Dieu! they are too lazy." Hinton Helper, employing the generic term whites often used for native peoples of California and the Great Basin, echoed Derbec: "The male Digger never hunts—he is too lazy for this." Both Helper and Derbec claimed Indian women fed their communities; Derbec thought they spent "their entire lives in the hardest toil." What is more, women always struggled under heavy burdens—either baskets of seeds and nuts when out gathering or family provisions when traveling from place to place—while men carried only their bows and arrows. Enos Christman, watching a party of Miwoks pass through the town of Sonora, noted this too: "The women appeared to do all the drudgery, having their baskets . . . well filled with meat." A more thoughtful diarist might have wondered whose work produced the animal flesh the women carried.[85]

Friedrich Gerstäcker, the German traveler, assessed Indian divisions of labor differently. He acknowledged that a woman had to collect seeds, catch insects, cook meals, rear children, bear heavy loads, "and, in fact, do nearly every thing," while a man merely walked about "at his leisure with his light bow and arrow." But Gerstäcker thought he understood why: "though this seems unjust," he wrote, "it is necessary." He went on, "in a state of society where the lives of the family depend on the success of the hunter, he must have his arms free . . . for action at every minute."[86] Still, the seemingly contradictory

HUTCHING'S
CALIFORNIA SCENES.

THE
CALIFORNIA INDIANS.

AN INDIAN FANDANGO.

GATHERING ACORNS.

CATCHING GRASSHOPPERS

GATHERING SEEDS.

GRINDING ACORNS, &c.

MODE OF TRAVELING.

BURNING THEIR DEAD.

COOKING FOOD

Another popular lettersheet represented the California Indians whom English-speaking miners observed in the diggings. In accordance with white men's interest in native gender divisions of labor, this lettersheet concentrated on Indian women's labor. Although at least one of the images depicted native men working, the text read, "The women do the work, the men the eating, grumbling and sleeping."

Reproduced by permission of the Huntington Library, San Marino, California.

impulse either to castigate native men for their sloth or to elevate their economic role to a position of dominance arose from a common, culturally specific concern about the meanings of manhood.

This concern had its origins in the changing social and economic order that sent such letter, diary, and reminiscence writers off to California in the first place—one in which the transformation from a commercial to an industrial capitalism was accompanied by an increasing separation of home and workplace and by shifting distinctions between male and female spheres. White men who aspired to middle-class status were quickly caught up in this whirlwind of change, and the uncertainty of their own positions in the emerging economic system made the potential for quick riches in California all the more enticing.[87] What most found in the diggings was no shortcut to middle-class manliness but rather a bewildering array of humanity that confounded whatever sense of a natural order of things they could find in midnineteenth-century western Europe or eastern North America. They might try to remember gender difference through ritual descriptions of Miwok women's "domestic" chores and their own "breadwinning" labor. But in the selfsame gesture, that reinscription produced and reproduced race difference as well. Besides, the content of both immigrant and Indian lives in the diggings defied such easy oppositions.

Then too, Miwok people talked back. Recall, for example, how the Awal man Juan explained his people's style of gender relations to the Belgian miner Perlot. Juan located the greater power of Miwok men in an ancient battle between two suns of equal brilliance, one of whom had created woman and the other man. The fight ended in victory for the sun who created man; the sun who created woman shattered and became the moon and the stars. But Juan claimed that the moon gathered to herself her lost brilliance every month, and, in spite of her waxing and waning, she was slowly and secretly retaining more and more of her splendor until the day when she could again do battle with the sun and at long last conquer him. The present order of things, then, was just that—a contingent set of relations constantly undermined by the life-sustaining tenacity of women who gathered strength from their surroundings.[88]

Still, while such relations might be contingent, Miwok women and men alike took pride in them and looked with incredulity at the ways in which immigrant peoples organized their lives. Helen Nye found that her curiosity about a Miwok encampment near her home at Don Pedro's Bar, especially about "the women with their little ones their mode of cooking & [such]," was returned in kind. Nye told her sister that Indian women watched her as closely as Nye watched them: "they come round to my door and gaze at me and my movements as if I was a seventh wonder." The Miwoks not only looked; they talked. Nye could not understand what they were saying—to her it was all "jabber"—and hence we cannot know what these particular women made of what they saw. But in other situations, Miwok women spoke plainly—probably in Spanish—to immigrants about white gender relations. Leonard Noyes recalled that an older Indian woman one day gave him "quite a Lecture on White Women working [too] little and Men [too] much." "She became very much excited and eloquant over it," Noyes remembered, "saying it was all wrong." In exchanges like these, Gold Rush contests over the meanings of gender and race—contests never far from the surface of everyday life—were articulated emphatically.[89]

And Miwok sexual divisions of labor were not unchanging; they were dynamic constructions that shifted according to the exigencies of local economies increasingly impinged upon by market forces. At times, Indians resisted the changes, continuing older subsistence practices to an extent that bewildered immigrant observers. As Timothy Osborn put it, "so long as a fish or a squirrel can be found . . . they will not make any exertions towards supplying themselves with any of the luxuries so indispensable to . . . the white man!" He watched in October as Miwok women gathered acorns, and wondered why they continued to do so, "while with the same labor expended in mining they could realize gold enough to keep them supplied with flour and provisions for the entire winter!"[90] Osborn might have noted a few other things—that immigrant miners often had trouble supplying *themselves* with flour and provisions during the winter; that non-Indians, too, relished an occasional meal of squirrel stew, or acorn soup, or fresh-cooked salmon; and that Miwok women did, in fact, dig gold and use it to buy flour and other goods. Still, Osborn's descriptions of Indians persisting in old habits may not have been all that selective. Miwok subsistence patterns varied a great deal from place to place in the Southern Mines and from year to year during the Gold Rush, and Osborn's neighbors may well have been able to sustain themselves through gathering and hunting alone in the fall of 1849.

Elsewhere and at other times, immigrant observers saw different strategies. As Gerstäcker put it in 1853, "the gold discovery has altered [Indians'] mode of life materially." On the one hand, he thought, "they have learned to want more necessaries," while on the other "the means of subsistence diminishes." More and more, Miwoks supplemented customary ways of getting food with gold mining in order to buy nourishment. Perlot recalled that in 1853 he regularly saw Indians traveling to Coulterville, in Mariposa County, and Garrote, in Tuolumne County, to purchase flour with gold they had dug.[91] At Belt's Ferry on the Merced River, where Sam Ward lived, the situation was different; there native people probably spent more time mining than they did gathering and hunting. Following an Indian-immigrant conflict in early 1851 known as the Mariposa War, the merchant George Belt received a federal license to trade with local Miwoks (and one Yokuts band) as well as a contract to furnish them with flour and beef in order to keep the peace. Ward watched over Belt's Ferry between 1851 and 1853 and got to know native people who felt their best chance for survival lay in setting up camp near an Indian trader. Mining along the Merced kept the Indians supplied with gold, which they used to trade at the store. Still, problems multiplied in the government contract for provisions, and even goods for purchase failed to appear on the trader's shelves. So Miwok women frequently fanned out in search of seeds and nuts, and Miwok men watched for salmon runs or headed down to the San Joaquin Valley to hunt for wild horses.[92]

The more things stayed the same, the more they changed. Miwok men watched for salmon, but found the fish had been waylaid by dams built downstream. Miwok women gathered, but just as their menfolk had added horse raiding to hunting duties decades before, so might women now pan for gold as often as they collected acorns. White men looked for women to wash their clothes, but instead of seemingly willing wives or mothers, they found a mart for laundry dominated by Chinese men and Mexican women. White women, few in number, set up housekeeping in California, and learned—to their delight or their dismay—that there were plenty of men for hire to help lighten the burdens of everyday life. African Americans who came to the mines enslaved worked as hard as ever making their masters and mistresses comfortable, but found, too, that the Gold Rush opened up new possibilities for freedom. Mexican women sold tortillas and frijoles on the street, just as they had in Sonoran towns and cities, but discovered that in California the market for their products seemed as if it could not be glutted. And thousands of Chilean, French, and Mexican men engaged in one more strategy to help themselves and their families out of precarious situations back home. Some of these men were not lucky enough to escape the diggings with their lives—for this was no utopia for those who were not white and English speaking. If they did, though, they learned that mining the white miners—with their incomparable nostalgia for "home comforts and home joys" and their sense of entitlement to the same—was both safer and more lucrative than washing gold-bearing dirt.

Still, as often as Anglo American men patronized a commercial domestic sphere peopled largely by non-Anglos, they also turned inward to create for themselves something of the comforts and joys of home. Some men reveled in the fellow-feeling—the floods, the gushes, the warm glows of friendship—that grew out of shared domestic tasks and intimate caretaking one for the other. Many more bemoaned the absence of women—for whom household chores increasingly were considered not only a responsibility but a natural vocation—and belittled their own, often manifest abilities to sustain and enhance life.[93] Indeed, in the diggings, the process of idealizing the home and woman's place in it was uncomplicated by the day-to-day tensions of actual family households. Thus, gold or no gold, newly married Moses Little could write confidently from his Calaveras County cabin that there were "riches far richer" awaiting him back east with his "companion in Domestic Happiness." Benjamin Kendrick was similarly emphatic in his recommendation to would-be gold seekers: "I would not advise a single person that has a comfortable home in New England to leave its comforts and pleasures for any place such as California with all its gold mines." But A. W. Genung went farthest in giving the gold country's missing quality—domestic comfort—an explicit gender and, implicitly, a race. Acknowledging its advantageous physiography, fine climate, and economic potential, Genung nonetheless was adamant about California's chief deficiency: "The country cannot be a great country nor the people a happy people unblessed by woman's society and woman's love."[94] The society of Miwok and Mexican women did not figure in Genung's equation; the woman whose love California lacked was white. For men such as these, the more things changed, the more things stayed the same.

Was this utopia? Was it the isle of the blest? For many, the gold boom created what seemed an unnatural state of affairs—even so, a state of affairs to which they were ineluctably drawn. Benjamin Kendrick might not advise a single person (read "man") to leave a comfortable eastern home for California, but he and thousands upon thousands of others did just that. And in spite of the tremendous diversity such men found among their neighbors in the diggings, it was striking how the dominant metaphor of domesticity—a metaphor specific to a particular people from a particular place—came to insinuate itself into the lives of all sorts of Gold Rush participants. Consider an episode Enos Christman recorded in his diary in 1852. One January night, two Mexican women happened by a group of Anglo miners who were settling into their blankets at Cherokee Camp, near Sonora. The traveling musicians produced guitars and a tambourine, and the men set aside their bedding, listened to the serenade, and then got up to dance with each other. As the night wore on, the music's tempo slowed, until finally the women started strumming the chords of "Home, Sweet Home." They did not intone the lyrics; these women had watched Anglo miners long enough to know that the familiar tune alone would evoke the desired reaction. The men responded apace: "Suddenly a sob was heard, followed by another, and yet another, and tears flowed freely down the cheeks of the gold diggers."[95] The musicians walked away, their tambourine filled with pieces of gold.

Chapter 3

Bulls, Bears, and Dancing Boys

For a good many men who went to California after 1848, the notion of a "social" history of the Gold Rush would have been a contradiction in terms. For them, "society," like domestic comfort, was one of the very things the diggings lacked. Angus McIsaac said it well on Christmas Day in 1852 when he lamented, "This day I . . . thought of my situation here in this wild mountain 'hamlet and the very few pleasures it is adapted to afford deprived of social society & of mingling with . . . tender hearted friends." Other men modified "society" differently—"good society," "congenial society," the "sweets of society," the "pleasures of home and its society," "quiet home comfort and the society of friends."[1] But however they modified it, they found it missing in the Sierra foothills and themselves the poorer for its absence. What was this "society" that did not exist in California? Why did "the social" as a category of human experience seem empty to some Gold Rush participants as they went about their everyday lives together in the diggings?

In describing California as devoid of society, Anglo American and European men invoked a peculiarly nineteenth-century, middle-class notion of "the social," one in which the influence of white women and their perceived attributes was axiomatic. "The social" was thought to revolve around familial, relational, and community concerns, around human interaction and connectedness. At the same time, women were thought to constitute a kind of glue that held families, relationships, communities—indeed, society—together. "The social," in this womanly construction, was an antidote to the manly anomie that increasingly seemed to characterize a changing economic milieu, wherein individual men were encouraged to "make themselves." It was no wonder, then, that life in the mines provoked male nostalgia not only for the "comforts of home" but for the "sweets of society" as well. Men missed women they recognized as sisters, wives, mothers, sweethearts, to be sure. They also missed an intricate mosaic of meaning seemingly embodied in female friends and relatives, a mosaic they felt themselves incapable of piecing together on their own.[2]

But Anglo American men's vexation over the lack of society took on a special meaning in the Southern Mines, where the absence of Anglo women was matched by the presence of large numbers of Miwoks, Mexicans, Chileans, French, and, later, Chinese. Of these, only the Miwok population included roughly as many women as men. Among immigrants in the Southern Mines, two years after the gold discovery, men still constituted 97 percent of the population. Of these, only Mexican women accompanied their menfolk to the diggings in noticeable numbers, though handfuls of Chilean and French women and, later, Chinese and Anglo American women lived in the larger camps and towns.[3]

J. D. Borthwick, the Scottish artist and writer, described the difference between the Northern Mines and the Southern Mines this way:

> In the north, one occasionally saw some straggling Frenchmen . . . , here and there a party of Chinamen, and a few Mexicans. . . . The southern mines, however, were full of all sorts of people. There were villages peopled nearly altogether by Mexicans, others by Frenchmen; in some places there were parties of two or three hundred Chilians forming a community of their own. The Chinese camps were very numerous; and besides all such distinct colonies . . . every town of the southern mines contained a very large foreign population.[4]

Nevertheless, for many Anglo immigrants, this presence equaled an absence of "good" and "congenial" society. And it was not only white men whose astigmatic vision of the social was as racialized as it was gendered. In 1908, over fifty years after she had lived as one of the few Anglo children in the Southern Mines, Mrs. Lee Whipple-Haslam had herself photographed with two Indian women who had been her playmates in the 1850s. She included the picture in her published reminiscences and captioned it "Photograph of the author and two friends. This picture will exemplify a lonely childhood." Likewise, though without direct reference to his non-Anglo neighbors in Tuolumne County, Jesse Smith complained to his sister in 1852, "The society I think is not as good here as farther north, there is fewer families. Where men have their wives and children and settle down everything looks and *is* better than where the population is of the transient unsettled kind."[5]

These transient, unsettled people, however, turned the diggings into a grand field for human interaction and connectedness, not only in the ways they organized mining labor and domestic and personal service work but also, and perhaps particularly, in the ways they occupied themselves during their leisure hours. Just as differentiating reproductive from productive labor highlights a problematic opposition, so too does distinguishing between labor and leisure. Notions of labor and leisure were in flux in the nineteenth century, especially in industrializing areas such as the northeastern United States. In such places, as wage work and accompanying notions of time discipline began to replace older labor systems, the distinction between work and leisure was growing more pronounced.[6] Yet even Gold Rush immigrants who came from industrializing areas found themselves plunged into largely preindustrial work patterns in the diggings—patterns determined by daily cycles of light and dark, and seasonal cycles of heat and cold, downpour and drought. Whether they came from industrializing areas or not, all immigrants in the mines were part of the global movement of people, goods, and wealth that accompanied the proliferation of market economies and the colonial ambitions of North Atlantic nations in the nineteenth century. Given this context, all participated in marking mining as the "work" of the Gold Rush.

But people in every Gold Rush community, immigrant and Indian, sought diversion from the business of producing material life—they sang and prayed, they told stories and wrote letters, they gambled and got drunk, they danced to one another's drumming or fiddle playing and cheered at bull-and-bear fights. Leisure, defined loosely to include both diversion and sacred practices, was often a contested terrain upon which gold seekers drew boundaries that separated them into opposing camps—camps divided by language or religion or nationality but also by different notions of what constituted appropriate behavior in a disproportionately male "social" world. Still, the twain did meet: polyglot peoples bartered for companionship at fandango houses; Chilean and French men met at Mass; Anglos and Mexicans sat cheek by jowl over games of chance. Meanwhile, in towns like Sonora, some Spanish- and French-speaking women created a market for heterosocial pleasures that became key in redistributing Gold Rush wealth and in challenging Anglo notions of what would *count* as society. Indeed, whenever a miner cut loose and stopped working, someone else started—a Mexican matador, a Protestant preacher, a French woman at her gaming table. The worlds of labor and leisure, then, were bound together.

Opposing "labor" to "leisure," of course, obscures the extent to which—in profoundly material ways—the two terms and the social practices they represent depend on one another for meaning. The leading term, labor, and the social practices it represents generally take precedence in studies of mining rushes because of the predominance of men among the migrants and the prevalence of cultural constructions of labor as male.[7] No historian could deny the central importance of mining labor to life in the Sierra foothills after 1848. But in mining—a new occupation for many but one most identified as suitable for men—immigrants found a daily practice in which to ground a sense of themselves as appropriately gendered. Leisure, by contrast (along with reproductive labor such as cooking and sewing), proved a site in which oppositions such as male versus female and white versus nonwhite were thrown into disarray. So here my focus is on leisure because, like domestic and personal service work, leisure was one of the key locations in which gendered and racialized meanings got made, unmade, and remade during the Gold Rush. When immigrant men laid down their picks and shovels, they found that the oppositions which created both social order and social relations— that is, society—back home were all out of kilter in California.[8]

This was especially true of Anglo American men, who assumed postures of domination in an expanding nation-state that had just acquired continental breadth, and who were best positioned to reap the benefits of the emerging class system that accompanied industrialization (though many would fail miserably in their efforts to achieve middle-class status, and others would contest the emerging class system itself). For such men, the Gold Rush created a kind of crisis of representation, because so much of what they imagined as society was unavailable or unrecognizable in California, and what was within reach did not look suitably social. How, then, would they make sense—for themselves, for each other, and for folks back home—of what they *did* find and see and touch in the diggings? Posing the question in this manner is not meant to suggest that Gold Rush participants who were not Anglo and male were somehow accustomed to life in the mines. However familiar the rise and fall of the foothills may have been to Miwoks, for most participants, a gold rush was something new under the sun. Nor does the question mean

This lettersheet depicts the ways in which the Gold Rush disrupted customary boundaries of gender and race for Anglo American men.

Reproduced by permission of the Huntington Library, San Marino, California.

that the representational practices of such peoples were unaffected by the upheaval of the Gold Rush. But few Miwoks, Mexicans, Chileans, French, and Chinese in California conflated their daily lives with a project of national expansion and economic growth infused with notions of progress and "manifest destiny." All, however, would be touched—some violently—by the will to dominance of those for whom such conflations came easily.

For Miwok people, for example, the Gold Rush was about invasion on an unprecedented scale, despite earlier contact with Spanish Mexicans on the California coast and white fur trappers coming west over the Sierra Nevada. Miwok responses to conquest were many, from armed resistance to petitions on their own behalf, to assimilation of gold digging into women's gathering activities, to retreat from the foothills up into the mountains.[9] When they laid down the woven baskets they used to pan for gold and the weapons they used to fight off the invaders, though, Miwoks worked to represent their new situation by incorporating symbols of conquest into customary ceremonies. Key among these was one called the *pota* ceremony, a commemorative gathering that reminded participants of unnatural or unusual deaths, generally by violence or witchcraft, within a lineage group. Much of the ceremony involved relatives of the deceased dancing around vertical poles to which were attached effigies of murderers or others held responsible for the death; dancers attacked the effigies with arrows, clubs, and knives.[10]

In August of 1855, the white immigrant Alfred Doten walked five miles to attend a *pota* ceremony on the south fork of the Cosumnes River. When he arrived at what he called the "Indian 'fandango,'" he found Miwoks dancing around a flagstaff that supported not only the customary effigy of a man but a U.S. flag as well. An English-speaking Indian, whom Doten took to be a chief, explained to the Anglo that this ceremony recalled an earlier time when a neighboring group of Indians had come to a festival, but brought with them "a kind of poison" that made the local people ill. Medicine men learned the nature of the poison, however, and could now prevent the sickness; the ceremony was held "in commemoration of the time of the poisoning." The effigy on the flagpole, then, probably represented the bearers of the sickness that had afflicted local Miwoks years ago. The dance was a way of remembering.[11]

If Doten asked about the meaning of the U.S. flag that waved above the effigy, perhaps he got no answer. If he did, he chose not to record it either in his diary or in an account he sent to his hometown newspaper in Massachusetts, the *Plymouth Rock*. But something about the proximity of the flag and the effigy must have troubled him. He noted the presence of both in his diary ("Old 'Santiago's' tribe was . . . dancing about a flag staff, with the stars and stripes flying at the top, and a small effigy of a man hung by the neck"). But his *Plymouth Rock* article ignored the effigy altogether, portraying the dance as an innocent romp around the Star-Spangled Banner ("the Cosumnes tribe were dancing around a pole about twenty feet high, with a small American flag flying at the top"). Doten's discomfort may have been well placed. Items that were displayed on poles in *pota* ceremonies (generally effigies and bear hides that also represented killers) always became objects of derision and violence.[12]

Given this, the act of dancing around a U.S. flag during a *pota* ceremony was, at best, no compliment. The incorporation of the flag into the customary practice of attacking effigies suggests an understanding of the U.S. conquest as something altogether different from other tragedies that had beset Cosumnes Miwoks, tragedies that could be represented adequately by effigies of those who brought death by foul means. And, indeed, while this *pota* ceremony commemorated an earlier time of loss, sickness and death were everywhere in the summer of 1855 as well. Just two days before Doten attended the ceremony, for example, a native boy whom area white men called Jack—who had been adopted, abducted, or otherwise taken in by two of Doten's friends—had died after "slowly wasting away with consumption." Miwok women in the area, including the boy's aunt, loudly mourned the child's passing. Likewise, the day after the *pota* dance, elders brought several sick children to healers who gathered for the ceremony, in hopes of saving them from Jack's fate.

With death all around—no doubt occasioned by disease and hunger as much as by overt violence—the 1855 *pota* ceremony looks like evidence of a new means of representation, whereby a flag stood for a people who took what they wanted in the name of a nation. The *crisis* of representation, then, was Doten's: he could not find a way to communicate what he had seen along the Cosumnes River to *Plymouth Rock* readers without challenging their understanding of the national project of westward expansion. Nor could he explain it to himself, even if he noted privately the proximity of effigy and flag. Miwoks found the flag's presence compatible with collective memory of an earlier period of suffering, and with the losses of the present time. For Doten, the link between death and the flag was unrecognizable, or perhaps unspeakable.[13]

Pota gatherings were just one of the many Miwok ceremonies and celebrations immigrant miners witnessed during the Gold Rush. Indeed, all extant accounts of such events were written by white American or European observers, who rarely knew enough about their Miwok neighbors to understand or contextualize what they saw. Half a century after the Gold Rush, at a time when Indian populations had dwindled from several thousand to several hundred and settled village life had superseded an earlier seasonal mobility, anthropologists ventured up into the Sierra foothills to make social scientific observations of Miwok ceremonies. In this, scholars relied both on native informants and on ethnographic assumptions about "primitive" cultures. Whatever their deficiencies as observers, however, white miners and, later, early anthropologists did witness Miwok ceremonies and speak with Miwok people about their meanings.[14] These were ceremonies situated in time that might otherwise be lost to the historical record, given the precipitous decline and restructuring of native populations that was underway even before 1848 but that the Gold Rush itself accelerated. For historians, then, such sources are indispensable.

John Doble, who took such pains to describe Miwok acorn processing, was also an especially careful observer of Indian ceremonies.[15] When he happened upon the Miwok women grinding acorns on a limestone outcrop near the Mokelumne River in February of 1852, for example, he was watching preparations for what he described as a "big fandango." The women themselves might have used the Miwok word *kote* to describe the upcoming events, though Spanish terms like "fandango" and "fiesta" would have been as familiar to them as they were to Doble. Hundreds of Indians had filed into the camp the day before, men carrying bows and arrows and women toting children as well as large, conical shaped baskets suspended from straps around their heads. No doubt the travelers were responding to an invitation from local Miwoks sent out by runners days before; the invitation took the form of a knotted string, the number of knots indicating the number of days before the *kote* would start. After watching the women grinding, Doble came upon Miwok men readying themselves for a dance. His description of the men's costumes and of their procession toward the ceremonial assembly house, a round, partly underground earth lodge, suggest that they were preparing for a particularly sacred dance—this because the men were covered with a profusion of owl and hawk feathers, arranged in elaborate headdresses and glued to faces, torsos, and limbs with a mixture of pitch and grease. For Miwok people, feather regalia were enormously powerful; if they were not made or handled correctly, or if someone accidentally touched them, illness was sure to follow. So it seems likely that the dancing men Doble followed to the ceremonial lodge were involved in a ritual not meant purely for entertainment.[16]

Nonetheless, plenty of entertainment went along with such a dance. Doble noted that only a hundred of those who had come for the *kote* could actually fit themselves into the dance lodge, and so "those outside kept time by hooping yelling singing & dancing . . . keeping up a perfect and most *beautiful* confusion." No doubt Doble was more confused by what he saw than the hooping, yelling, and singing Miwok women and men who gathered outside the lodge and danced to the rhythms emanating from the foot drum inside. Still, Doble appreciated what he heard—"they keep good time . . . & some of their tunes are good"—that is, until he went back to his own camp and was kept awake by the hollow log drum into the wee hours of the morning.[17]

The *kote* Doble observed was not a timeless expression of Miwok culture but an event situated historically. When Indians arrived for the ceremony, those coming from the lowlands, closer to the San Joaquin Valley, came in cast-off Euro-American clothes, having learned from repeated contact with immigrants that few things irked white people more than minimally clad Indians. Miwoks arriving from more mountainous areas had learned this particular method of appeasing whites imperfectly. Some men came just in loincloths and some women in simple skirts, while others sported Euro-American items in a haphazard manner that bedeviled white people—"from a shirt above to a full and fine cloth dress with calf boots & a high top beaver with a belt and revolver." Likewise, as Indians passed a white-owned store on their way to the *kote*, they traded gold dust for beef and cognac. Doble noted that many gathered outside the ceremonial lodge were intoxicated (Doble himself was an expert on this subject, having just spent his twenty-fourth birthday in drunken revelry) and that some of the young men were in ill humor, picking fights with one another. One wonders if these youths were subjected to the same kinds of speeches that an anthropologist heard elders make when he attended a Miwok ceremony fifty years later: "The young men were admonished to let drink alone, to keep away from quarrelsome people, to be slow to anger; to avoid hasty replies, particularly when talking to white men who might say exasperating things."[18] Euro-American clothing, store-bought beef and cognac, white men watching sacred dances (some, like Doble, clambering to the top of the ceremonial lodge and peering down through the smoke hole)—these were signs of the times.

While dances such as the one John Doble observed were central to Miwok spirituality, few other Gold Rush participants incorporated dance into spiritual observances. For most, this reflected distinctions some Christians made between body and soul, in which the bodily intensity of dance seemed a threat to religious rectitude. This is not to say that practicing Christians did not dance, but rather that dance and worship for them separated easily into profane and sacred domains, respectively. In the sacred domain resided church services and other religious rites performed by clergy, as well as private and informal spiritual observances such as prayer, Bible reading, and hymn singing. Catholic and Protestant immigrants alike re-created these familiar rituals in the diggings.[19]

Mexicans, Chileans, and French constituted the bulk of the Catholic population in the Southern Mines; Irish, Peruvian, German, Italian, and American-born Catholics rounded out the numbers. As one Gold Rush–era Benedictine missionary put it, "It is very difficult to obtain useful priests for this country because a priest should be able to speak at least three languages—English, Spanish, and French. Everywhere the population is a mixture." Not all gold seekers raised Catholic were practicing Catholics in the diggings, but as the same priest explained, "Even the bad ones still want to be counted as Catholics and die as such."[20] Good or bad, by clerical standards, a majority of Catholic Gold Rush participants were concentrated in the Southern Mines. Indeed, two of the three established Catholic churches in the diggings were located in the southern towns of San Andreas and Sonora.[21] Few descriptions of these early churches survive, but services held in them must have resembled one that a French-born Chilean, Pedro Isidoro Combet, attended when he took refuge from the rigors of mining down in San Jose: "Nothing could have been more impressive and picturesque than this gathering of the faithful of all Catholic nations: the types and manners all mixed together. . . . This assembly of men of many races, wearing the same kind of clothes . . . and worshipping the same God, all of this did affect me deeply."[22]

The San Jose church, located in a low-country town still dominated by Californios, featured a Spanish-speaking priest who was fluent in French. Up in the foothills, however, at the tent that served as the San Andreas church, a French priest who was fluent in Spanish officiated. When J. D. Borthwick passed through San Andreas, he noticed the structure, which was distinguished only by the wooden cross over its door. He found the interior spare, with the exception of an altar that was draped with colored cloth and covered with candlesticks, "some of brass, some of wood, but most of them regular California candlesticks—old claret and champagne bottles." Closest to the altar stood a number of Mexican women, and behind them the church was filled with Mexican men, except for Borthwick and a few curious Anglo Americans standing near the door. Suddenly, though, two of the Anglos—"great hulking fellows," Borthwick called them—swaggered in, making it clear "that their only object was to show supreme contempt" for the service. Borthwick himself, a native of Scotland, had little sympathy for Anglo American impudence. Thus when the Mexican congregation and their French priest dramatized that impudence, Borthwick was gleeful: "the entire congregation went down on their knees, leaving these two awkward louts standing in the middle of the church as sheepish-looking a pair of asses as one could wish to see."[23]

Here the crisis of representation belonged less to Borthwick or the Mexican churchgoers than to the "great hulking fellows" who tried to disrupt the Mass.[24] That disruption was, in effect, an attempt to define the meaning of the service—that is, as a foolish exercise of piety on the part of a benighted, dark-skinned people and their foreign spiritual father. When the congregants fell to their knees, the sacredness of the space was restored, and the Anglos momentarily lost their power to establish meanings. While Mexican (and French) resistance to Anglo dominance in the diggings took more purposeful forms outside of Mass, this intervention into the control of definitions was probably unconscious—yet no less effective for being deployed in the course of everyday habits.[25] Still, while Borthwick enjoyed the contest of meanings, his own sense of order was disrupted by other aspects of the scene he observed. He claimed, for example, that the Mexican churchgoers spent the rest of the Sabbath gambling. For Borthwick, this accentuated the proximity of the sacred and the profane in California—altar candles in champagne bottles, obnoxious American louts standing in a roomful of prayerful Mexicans, prayerful Mexicans leaving Mass for the gaming tables.

Indeed, these kinds of juxtapositions were especially troubling to certain Protestant argonauts, for whom the Gold Rush itself was a site of moral peril. Such gold seekers—would-be middle-class white men from the northeastern United States—generated and preserved by far the greatest volume of primary sources that address the sort of daily concerns of interest to social historians (this from men convinced "society" was lacking in California). In fact, the act of generating those texts—letters, diaries, and reminiscences—was part of the way in which many such men tried to come to terms with the moral ambiguity of their participation in the Gold Rush. That ambiguity arose in part out of a discursive shift in the meanings of white manhood in the industrializing United States, such that self-control became one of the hallmarks of manliness. Restraint may have seemed wise to a variety of men whose lives were rendered precarious by the nation's fitful economic transformation. But it was particularly well suited to men who aspired to the emerging middle class—master craftsmen, shopkeepers, clerks, and their sons—whose interpretation of success in the new order emphasized individualism and competition over cooperative enterprise.[26]

Two aspects of Gold Rush life ensured that questions about male self-control would assume increased relevance in California. First, there was the means by which most men earned a living. Elsewhere men might find greater congruence between their own experience as economic actors and the notion that success, increasingly defined as the accumulation of capital, resulted from hard work and prudent plans. Placer mining gave men cause to dispute that belief. For one, the average daily yields of white miners declined precipitously over the boom years of the Gold Rush. In addition, though few made a fortune in California, those who did relied as much on luck as hard work. Placer mining exaggerated the economy's capriciousness to such an extent that men could seriously question the value of self-control.[27] Second, the absence of white women—and their discursive presence—contributed to debate over male restraint. At the time of the Gold Rush, northeastern Anglo American women and men were enacting the transformation of domestic life that accompanied industrialization. That shift included a new emphasis on the sentimental heterosociality of the privatized home, which entailed gendered responsibilities for its realization—for men, the diligent exercise of self-control, and for women, the application of superior moral sensibilities.[28] In the diggings, then, battles raged over whether white men had either reason or ability to practice restraint when apart from their collective better half. Was the discursive presence of women alone enough to encourage self-control?

In the absence of women, many aspiring middle-class white men from the Northeast turned to organized Protestant worship for support in their efforts to stay on the moral high road in California. Finding that support, however, was often no simple task. Sometimes trouble arose from the physical distance to the nearest services. When P. V. Fox was situated in the remote area of Chilean Gulch on a Sunday in April 1852, he complained, "There was no meeting nearer than Mokelumne Hill but I did not feel like walking five miles and back so I staid at the cabin." The next month, when he relocated to Mokelumne Hill, he began to attend the Methodist church there regularly.[29] For other men, it was not only miles that separated them from worship. Timothy Osborn wrote twice in his diary that he would gladly walk five miles on the Sabbath, if he could find but one minister in the mines who had "enough of the true Christian spirit." His complaint may have been disingenuous, however, because when he moved down to Stockton, a bustling supply town with a number of established churches, Osborn still proved a restless soul. He attended Methodist Episcopal services there a couple of times, but spent as much time in his diary describing the "*low* necked dress" of a young woman in the congregation, Miss Isbell, as he did the sermon and music. By the end of the month, not even Miss Isbell could lure Osborn back to Sunday worship, as he noted in his diary, "there is but little inducement for one to sit an hour upon anything but an easy seat and be bored with a dull stereotyped sermon." For New England boys like Osborn, the thrill of the profane triumphed daily over the tedium of the sacred. Indeed, the eve of the following Sabbath found Osborn and a male companion window peeping at a young French woman of "fair proportions" as she undressed for bed.[30]

Protestant ministers in the diggings longed for men to find relief in true religion. Some did. After several months mining at Rich Gulch in Calaveras County, George Allen went down to San Francisco to buy provisions for the winter. There he went to church and found himself "verry happy to have the privalege of meeting with Gods People and to worship him in his sanctuary once more."[31] The diary of Lemuel Herbert, however, suggests that some found more than mere happiness in Protestant worship. Herbert was a Methodist minister from Ohio who dug gold and preached salvation in the far northern reaches of the Southern Mines. At Drytown, Upper Rancheria, Fort John, and Volcano, Herbert presided over Sunday services as well as temperance meetings, the latter sometimes held in the street, where large crowds, "a mixture of every grade and colour," would gather. Church services themselves may have drawn primarily Anglo Americans, but even on a Sunday Herbert could look out on his flock and see the faces of men whose homelands had been touched by the Protestant missionary impulse and the proliferation of market economies. On one occasion Herbert turned his gaze upon a dark-skinned man who exclaimed, "Bless God," during the sermon, only to learn after church that the man was a Hawaiian whose father, "the king of the Island," had sent him to New York as a youth to learn English "so as to fit him for to do business between the different countries." As this man's enthusiastic participation in the Sunday service suggests, Herbert tended toward ecstatic worship of the camp-meeting variety, where men shouted and cried and declared themselves "seekers of salvation." The bonds among men who worshiped this way were strong, and yet the transience of placer mining populations meant such ties were severed regularly. On a Sunday when one of Herbert's temperance societies was about to dissolve, the men gathered "lost all ballance and found relief in giving way to sighs sobs 'and gushing tears." They sang and embraced one another and then, after they had recovered from their "passion and grief," turned their conversation to the prospect of meeting again in heaven. "This hope cheered us," Herbert wrote in his diary. In California, the love of God and the love of man for his fellow man, through which Christians "lost all ballance" and sought relief in each other's arms, seemed especially compatible.[32]

Still, the incongruities of a pious life in the Southern Mines could be striking. Like the Catholic priest who used champagne bottles for candleholders, a Protestant minister might find himself preaching at a store with a brandy cask for a pulpit or in a gambling tent where men sat at monte tables for worship. He might have to refuse donations from a man who staged a footrace on the church's behalf, raising funds by encouraging spectators to bet on the outcome. Even those who attended services were sometimes surprised at what they heard there. When Jason Chamberlain and John Chaffee, the partners who spent half a century together in Tuolumne County, first attended church in 1851, they listened to a Dr. Moore, who exhorted them "to lead sober temperate lives to get gold as fast as possible" and then head back east. But Moore went on to tell the congregants a number of stories, "some of them very humerous," Chamberlain recalled, "perhaps . . . [too] much so for preachers . . . at home." Chamberlain had an explanation for this comic sermon, however: "California is an exception to all rules of propriety every one seems to have a kind of way of his own preachers as well as others."[33]

And, indeed, gold seekers of many descriptions had ways of their own when it came to spiritual matters. In part because of the scarcity of established churches, some men gave themselves over to private devotions and informal hymn singing to a greater extent than they might have back home. The French journalist Étienne Derbec wrote that Mexican miners sometimes knelt at the foot of a tree on which they had carved a cross; there they would "celebrate the divine services in their own way." And passing by an early quartz mine at Carson's Creek just after a Catholic holy day in 1852, J. D. Borthwick spotted a ten-foot-high cross erected by Mexican miners and "completely clothed [with] beautiful flowers." Such men might also sing hymns in two- or four-part harmony late into the night, punctuating the refrains, according to Derbec, with shouts and gun shots. Unlike Borthwick, who was convinced Mexican churchgoers gambled after Mass, Derbec was sure that Mexicans refrained from gaming on the Sabbath, though the latter felt such abstinence was "a great privation for them."[34] No doubt some Mexicans gambled and others did not. Of those who did not, some probably felt deprived while others were just as happy to avoid the monte tents and spend their Sundays in prayer and song.

Likewise among Anglo Americans. As Charles Davis complained to his wife, in the diggings even godly men would "join the ranks of Satan and spend their Sabbaths with little or no restraint." Davis exempted himself from this indictment, as would have other men who regularly set aside time for private worship. Perhaps it was not surprising that a clergyman like Daniel Woods did so. After conducting what he called "family worship" with a friend on New Year's Day in 1850, for example, Woods exclaimed at "the refreshing fountain of comfort which springs up in the soul while kneeling before the throne of 'our Father in heaven.'" But laymen also found fountains of comfort in private devotions, and even in quiet correspondence with pious relatives in the East. Singing hymns together could bring "silent but eloquent tears" to men's eyes, as familiar tunes prompted thoughts of home. Scripture reading, alone or with tentmates, could do the same, particularly because Bibles were often gifts gold seekers had received, on departing for California, from female friends and relatives. As such, Bibles were tangible reminders of the female moral influence posited in nineteenth-century middle-class notions of gender. Reading correspondence from home had a similar effect. As Lucius Fairchild explained to his sister, "your good kind letters have done much towards keeping me *within sight* of the straight & narrow path."[35]

Keeping that path even within a white man's peripheral vision was a constant struggle. In August of 1850, George Allen was shocked to learn that some of his fellow miners had turned against him: "I know not for what cause other than I will not Join with them in their *Profanity* and *Vulgarity*." Allen was outraged, but also worried that he too might fall prey to evil influences. He had watched as professing Christians in the diggings had learned to "roll sin as a sweet morsel under the[i]r tong[ue]s." For himself, Allen prayed that he would outride such temptations, and thus land his "weather beaten bark on the fair banks of deliverance."[36] This imagery calls to mind the ways in which white men of Allen's class believed in concentrating their ener-

gies—economically, for success in the market place; genitally, for pro-
creation; and morally, for the life hereafter. For some, then, the Gold
Rush itself was incitement to profligacy. Consider the long diary entry
P. V. Fox wrote on his thirty-first birthday chronicling his life to that
point. Fox intertwined the economic, the sexual, and the moral, gloss-
ing over childhood and identifying the start of his life odyssey as his
first acquaintance with female friends. Such contact gave him "exqui-
site pleasure," he wrote, demonstrating that his "domestic organs were
large or active or perhaps both." His vital energies thus confirmed, Fox
took his place in the "busy world" of men and money, and soon thereafter married and became a father. Suddenly, however, "there was a
great stringency in the money market," and Fox could not collect on
debts, sell property, or satisfy his creditors. Desperate, he left for
California in February of 1852. But after seven months in the mines, he
had accumulated a mere $150. Meanwhile, his wife bemoaned his
absence, and Fox could only conclude, "Surely I must be wicked to
remain away so long . . . for the little gold I am getting."[37]

Such worrying white men, however, were surrounded by others who
had indeed learned to roll sin as a sweet morsel under their tongues.
For those who had, notions of sin themselves gave way to the sweetness of Gold Rush pleasures—card playing, strong drink, easy sex,
and even the license to cuss with impunity. These were the "vices"
the clergyman Daniel Woods felt substituted for "common amusement" in California.[38] Just as men could worship outside established
churches in the diggings, so too could they seek pleasure in private
moments or together in twos and threes, far from the din of the
monte tent or dance hall. But documenting these often relatively private practices is not easy. Those men driven to generate and preserve
the kinds of primary sources most apt to shed light on the dailiness
of pleasure seeking in the mines were also the men most likely to
have internalized Protestant moral codes—since diary writing itself
was seen as a way to keep a record of one's soul.[39] Such moral codes,
if they did not prevent untoward behavior, at least discouraged men
from keeping a written record of their indulgence in sex, cards,
liquor, and strong language. It is easy enough to find white men's
accounts of such activity among their neighbors—particularly but by
no means exclusively if their neighbors were non-Anglo—but much
harder to find white men who wrote about their own private patterns
of excess. Those few who did used a variety of narrative strategies to
explain the relationship of their behavior to their larger sense of
themselves as white, Protestant-raised, American men.

Three examples illustrate some of the different ways in which men confronted the crisis of representation the Gold Rush wrought: the diaries of Alfred Doten, from Plymouth, Massachusetts; of John Doble, from Sugar Creek Township in southeastern Indiana; and of Timothy Osborn, raised in Edgartown, Massachusetts (on Martha's Vineyard), but emigrated from New York City. All three men were in their early twenties; Doble and Doten, at least, were younger sons in large families. Doten's and Osborn's fathers seem to have been sea captains, while Doble grew up on a farm. At least two of the three had been apprenticed to a manual trade, and at least two of the three had done some clerking or bookkeeping as well. In short, all three had followed typical trajectories for midnineteenth-century northern white men who struggled to be part of the emerging middle class.[40]

Of the three men, it was Alfred Doten who most reveled in what many Protestants experienced as the moral ambiguity of the Gold Rush. Although he joined with fellow passengers in singing temperance songs during his sea voyage to California, once in the diggings Doten rarely advocated self-control. The sheer number of terms Doten used to describe his drinking patterns, for example, indicates how central liquor quickly became in his life. One day he might write that he had been on a "bender" or a "tall spree," on another that he had been "tight," or "wild," or "obscure," or, more to the point, "infernally drunk." Doten does not seem to have been an inveterate gambler, but he did know how to curse. Once, when convinced Mexican men had stolen some of his gold-bearing dirt, he exhibited his talent in writing: "God damn their thieving Mexican souls eternally to the hottest corner of hell." Needless to say, there was no love lost between Doten and many of his non-Anglo neighbors. As he recorded in his diary one day while keeping a store in Calaveras County, "I had plenty of Chinese, Mexicans, indians, and other scrubs to deal with and several drunken ones to bother me, but the day passed off without too many rows." Still, Doten saw fit to carouse with other such men. During just one week in September 1852, for example, he got "tight" with some French men, had a "big fandango spree" with four Mexicans, and, with a friend named Alfaro and other Chileans, did both: "we had a hell of a spree and . . . got a little tight."[41]

Not all of Doten's non-Anglo "friends" were men, however. His diary includes reference to sexual encounters with both Miwok and Mexican women, and to a contemplated encounter with a black woman.[42] For instance, Doten detailed the visit of two Indian women to his store, a young mother with a baby in tow and an older woman who, given that Doten describes her as having "short stiff grizzly hair," was probably in mourning—Miwoks cut off their hair when a close relative died. Doten claimed to have wooed the younger woman with presents and taken her into his tent, where he was "about to lay her altogether," until the older woman burst in and "gave the young gal a devil of a blowing up." Doten was convinced the younger woman appreciated his attentions: "She didn't get cross at all but gave me a slap in the face and ran away laughing." Meanwhile, the older woman shook her fist at Doten and gave him a piece of her mind in her native language, as Doten returned her fire, "cussing her in good round English." Neither could understand the other, but their mutual displeasure was clear enough. As the women left, Doten pleaded with his would-be sexual partner in Spanish to come back to the store alone when she could. She replied that she would try, though there is no evidence that she ever returned.[43]

Doten's diary, then, offers one reading of his encounter with the young Miwok mother, a reading in keeping with the meaning-making strategies of white men who gave themselves with some enthusiasm to the moral peril of the Gold Rush. But other readings are possible, if elusive in evidential terms, and must be ventured for historical situations such as this, where so much was at stake for all involved—even the future of customary ways of living and thinking and being in the world. Without information about sexual practices and their meanings among nineteenth-century Miwoks, one can but guess at what this encounter meant to the women involved.[44] Perhaps Doten was right in assuming that the younger woman was a willing partner who was thwarted only by the older woman's intervention. Then again, maybe the two women were actually of like mind, and their visit was an elaborately planned ruse to trick a white man out of some trade goods but deny him the payment—in sexual favors—he expected. Or perhaps Doten's advances were unwanted, the young woman's laughter when she broke free of his embrace a way of mocking the failed assault, and her parting promise a ploy to discourage him from tracking her down later.

Whatever the encounter meant to the women, the meaning for Doten is clear enough. Doten thought himself "quite a hunk of a boy," and he hated for anything to dampen his ardor. On his twenty-first birthday, for example, he saluted himself, "Hurrah old man how's your *crotch rope*," and then complained because a cold kept him "not in a condition to enjoy it." Enjoying it, it seems, was somehow easier with women he presumed would not bring their moral authority to bear upon him. While Doten maintained a chaste correspondence with a white sweetheart back home and politely pursued a young

white woman in Calaveras County, his relationships with women of
color were shorn of the trappings of courtship or, as he satirically put
it, "happy hearts, fluttering gizzards, honey sugar." The only potential
dalliance with a non-Anglo woman that gave him pause was one proposed by a light-skinned black woman, as Doten wistfully recorded in
his diary: "'Maria' has fell in love with me and wants me for her *lover*
as she is a yellow gal and it would hardly do for me to *marry* her
legally. . . . She is a real good looking girl of fine shape and no doubt a
fine bedfellow." An antislavery northerner who within a week read
Uncle Tom's Cabin for the first time, Doten seems not to have been
able to reconcile this particular temptation with his belief in the moral
superiority of Yankee race and class relations. No such misgivings
entered into his relationships with Miwok or Mexican women, however. In fact, nothing slowed Doten down until September 7, 1855, six
years after he arrived in California. While prospecting that day near
Volcano, Doten was crushed from the waist down by a cave-in. He was
partially paralyzed for a time, and even a month later, though he had
begun to take a few steps, he noted, "no feeling in my crotch yet." By
December, still lame, he left the diggings for good.[45]

John Doble was more ambivalent than Alfred Doten about mining
camp life, and thus provides a second example of the ways white
men negotiated the phantom "society" of Gold Rush California.
There is no evidence that Doble was sexually active with women;
indeed, he frowned on the kind of behavior Doten took in stride.
When friends once approached an Indian camp in search of sexual
partners, for example, Doble declined to accompany them. And
when a cabinmate announced that he planned to have an overland
emigrant woman move in without benefit of clergy, Doble would not
allow it.[46] Indeed, Doble seems to have been quite comfortable with
the homosociality of the diggings. His relationship with James
Troutman is a case in point. Nothing affected Doble more deeply
than Troutman's untimely death in September of 1853, nine months
after the two moved in together in Volcano. For ten days, Doble
attended his sick friend—sitting up with him each night, giving him
medication, and watching as his body and then his mind succumbed
to a high fever. The day Troutman died, Doble wrote in his diary,
"Now am I again alone the only heart that I have found that beat in
unison with mine suddenly torn from me." Doble's description of the
heart that "beat in unison" with his own is especially instructive: "I
have never met a Man in life as generally respected as was Jim. . . . he
was entirely clear of all the Vices for which *Cal* is so noted he used
strong drink in no form. . . . he made use of no profane Language at

all." The bond between the two men at first seems curious, because Doble himself was hardly "clear of all the vices" for which California was notorious. But Doble's misgivings about these habits ran deep, and his friendship with Troutman marked a period of intense efforts at self-reformation. Troutman possessed the attribute that was so elusive in Doble's life; he was self-control incarnate.[47]

John Doble's early months in the Southern Mines bore some resemblance to Alfred Doten's. Doble, for example, recorded in his diary a precise definition for the miner's "spree": "to go the Grocery & drink as much liquor" as one could. But Doble's particular weakness was gambling. From the start, he disapproved of the practice. After a night of poker in which he lost forty dollars, Doble confessed that he had "a love for that game" even though he knew that "Money thus gained is of no Value"—that is, it was money gained without labor. He thought he ought to quit. He did not. After a long losing streak a few months later, Doble finally won a dollar and a half. Again he thought he should quit: "If I can resist the temptation I surely will now henceforth & forever." He could not. For six months he played only for liquor, but then joined another cash game and lost a dollar and a half. This time, he wrote in his diary, he was "determined to quit the evil practice of Gambling." He may or may not have kept his resolve, but he recorded no more gambling in his diary. By that time, he had lived with Jim Troutman for three months, and his commitment to learning habits of restraint was at an all-time high. For Doble, then—in contrast to Doten—seasons of indulgence brought seasons of regret. Troutman's death six months later shook Doble, but never again did he give in to temptations as he had during his first months in California.[48]

Timothy Osborn, a third miner who dared keep record of his flirtation with vice in California, followed neither Doble's trajectory of earnest self-reformation nor Doten's antipathy toward the strictures of middle-class manhood. Osborn's self-representation did not read as a triumph of the forces of good over those of evil or as a devil-may-care embrace of dissipation. Instead, his was a delicate oscillation between propriety and the pull of illicit pleasures. This back-and-forth motion takes literal shape in the way Osborn chose straightforward prose to describe most daily concerns in his diary, and more coy and allusive language to refer to situations fraught with moral ambiguity. Sometimes not even allusion was obscure enough, though, and then Osborn abandoned conventional writing altogether, substituting shorthand in its place, as he did when describing his window peeping at the naked French woman in Stockton. Osborn also used shorthand to record private, though less morally questionable, musings about white women back home on Martha's Vineyard—marriage prospects, kisses dreamed of, memories of parting from his special favorite, Cousin Annie Coffin.[49] But the remainder of the coded entries refer quite explicitly to Osborn's curiosity about sex and the opportunities the Gold Rush offered him to indulge it.

Indeed, while Osborn took a drink from time to time and was also quick to acknowledge the "peculiar fascination in card playing" (which, nevertheless, had to be "kept within proper bounds"), his sexual inquisitiveness knew fewer limits.[50] Miss Isbell's "*low* necked dress" aside, it was Miwok women who most often captured Osborn's imagination. Mining along the Merced River during the late summer and fall of 1850, Osborn lived and worked in close proximity to native peoples, both Indians of the foothills and lowland Indians who had left coastal missions to join up-country bands. He frequently remarked at the scant clothing of Sierra Miwoks, taking particular interest in the women's bare breasts. He acknowledged that his curiosity "was exercised rather more freely than strict propriety would allow under other circumstances," but insisted that the women's "*modesty did not seem to suffer much*," underlining that phrase for good measure. All of this Osborn recorded in his diary with just a hint of moral inhibition. But in shorthand Osborn indicated that his exercises went beyond observation. He had heard, he wrote, that Indian women, like animals, had "certain times for seeking the man." And his own experience inclined him to believe this pernicious bit of white wisdom: "I have seen Indian girls, who, when they were 'in heat,' would fondle around you and in every possible way would ask you to relieve them, while at other times it would be an impossible thing to get your own wishes gratified." Like Doten's description of his attempt to "lay" a young Miwok woman, Osborn's reflections were steeped in dominant discourses regarding native women's "animal" proclivities. Such discourses precluded other readings of Miwok sexual practices in the context of conquest: for example, Miwok women might have their own reasons for wanting sex at one time and not at another; some Miwok women might have welcomed intimacy with white men, for whatever reason, while others abhorred the thought; one white man might have appealed to a Miwok woman, while another repelled her.[51]

Despite this indication that Osborn may have had sex with Miwok women, most often he seems to have gratified his own wishes simply by watching—or else by spending lazy Sunday afternoons alone in his hammock. In addition to his voyeuristic observation of Miwok and French women, Osborn found other opportunities for looking. In the mines, he and a partner once shared a meal with a mission Indian couple who were traveling through and who seemed particularly enamored of each other. When the couple bid the white men *adiós*, Osborn and his partner followed them surreptitiously until the Indians left the trail and stole into a cluster of willows. The miners got as close as they could and then, Osborn wrote in his diary, "we stood almost breathless lest we should be discovered and spoil our fun!" That was as much as Osborn would commit to paper, fearing "the displeasure a description of after scenes might bring" upon him. Once settled down in Stockton, Osborn found more visual enticements. On a Saturday night, for example, he met up with a French man crying out, *"Ici, il y a vue de Paris,"* and offering a look into a "camera of very powerful size." Osborn gave him two bits, and saw something he could only record in shorthand: "Naked men and women in the *very act.*" Shifting back to conventional writing, Osborn concluded "it *was a very good view of Paris.*"[52]

Still, most of the scenes Osborn contemplated were ones he conjured up in his own mind. While mining along the Merced, Osborn's favorite spot to dream was in a hammock of Peruvian netting that he rigged up beneath an oak tree overhanging a ravine. Here, on a Sunday or early on a weekday afternoon when he and his partners enjoyed a siesta, Osborn would nap or read a borrowed novel or let his thoughts drift to women back home.[53] He may also have masturbated. In one diary entry, his description of cigar smoking in the hammock seems full of double entendres. The entry begins with Osborn "smoking away . . . at a third rate 'short six,'" and imagining women he knew walking to church. In no time, the diarist found himself taking a pleasure "in the curling smoke of an ordinary 'long nine' which the unpracticed do not know." Osborn himself must have been practiced, because he knew that a smoker was a contented man who, "impotent of thought, Puffs away care."[54]

At other times, Osborn counted on slumber to bring him contentment. Early on, he was frustrated that dreams of hometown girls had left him unfulfilled: "I never have had a 'golden dream' yet!" But within a few months sleep brought results. Once, after dreaming about hours spent alone with a woman in an Edgartown hotel, he awoke uncovered, undressed, and exposed to the December chill—but happy. On another occasion, an afternoon nap delivered up "a romantic dream" about a woman in Mexico City who was wealthy, worldly, and "over-anxious to see '*Los Estados Unidos.*'" Osborn was equally anxious to show her *estadounidense* valor, though domestic life in the diggings intervened. With sweet regret, he noted in his diary, "Had I not awoke by the cry of 'supper!' I should have gratified her."[55]

Even in their dreams, then, the sights and sounds of the Gold Rush haunted Anglo American men, disrupting the ways in which they had imagined the world was ordered, showing them that such conventional terms of ordering required, at the very least, refinement in California. Different men negotiated the crisis of representation differently. Some tried to ignore it, projecting "social" disorder onto cultural "others"—Mexican gamblers or French prostitutes, for example—collapsing race and culture into questionable leisure practices. Men such as Doten, Doble, and Osborn, however, located themselves in the very belly of the beast and struggled to represent themselves—wholeheartedly or ambivalently, with or without a trajectory of self-reformation or dissipation—as aspiring middle-class white men in a world where constructions of gender, class, and race were unfamiliar and in flux.

It was not only in the private pursuit of pleasure described by men like Doten, Doble, and Osborn that Gold Rush participants faced this crisis of representation, because such men were also relentless in their search for companionship. Both heterosocial and homosocial ties flourished in California, but the paucity of women along with cultural constructions of male needs and desires meant that, for many men, contact with women was at a premium. Women knew this. In fact, the small number of non-native women in the Southern Mines—in 1850, maybe 800 in an enumerated immigrant population of 29,000—occupied an extraordinary position in what quickly became a multiracial, multiethnic market for male-female interactions.[56]

This is not the same thing as saying prostitutes abounded in the diggings. The sexualized geography of gender and race in the Sierra foothills was far more complicated than such a statement suggests. A smug Anglo man like Enos Christman living in a predominantly non-Anglo town like Sonora might claim that the women there were "nearly all lewd harlots," but even he knew the situation in Sonora was more elaborately alluring. On any given Sunday he might attend an auction, a bullfight, a circus, or an exhibition of "Model Artists" (with naked women posing), and then he might go to a dance house, a gambling hall, or a fandango. No matter where he went, part of what he paid for was often, quite simply, proximity to women. Not that sex itself was not for sale—it was. But men would lay down gold dust for far less. Christman himself, after a long Sunday working in the office of the *Sonora Herald,* for example, drank wine with a friend and then rushed uptown to spend his earnings at a fandango, "looking at the Americans dancing with the Mexican señoritas." No doubt the dancing Yankees were willing to pay a little bit more.[57]

Dance houses, sometimes called fandangos, dotted the Southern Mines and the supply town of Stockton. They were so common that men rarely bothered to describe them. As one miner offhandedly noted, "Went to some of *the houses,* saw *some of the senoritas."* Spanish-speaking women may have predominated among those who worked in such houses, but it was not only Anglo men who paid for their company. John Wallis, a God-fearing, Cornish-born emigrant from Wisconsin, once wandered into a dance hall in Stockton and saw "a set of teamsters" (teaming was an overwhelmingly Mexican occupation in the mines) and some Mexican women *"Dansing* and drinking and Cutting Up and a thousand other fooleries." The Mexican women and men must have continued their lively fandangos, though Wallis was sure *he* never wanted to "See a Nother." Up in the foothills, such establishments, like businesses of all sorts, came and went with astonishing rapidity. In late June of 1852, for example, John Doble mentioned Volcano's "Spanish Dance house" in his diary. Within two weeks, the dance hall had closed down, its proprietors arrested for grand larceny. While they lasted, though, fandangos were like magnets to men who mined in the surrounding gulches and ravines. And although Mexican and Chilean men frequented them to dance with their own or each other's countrywomen, the halls were not havens from Anglo American hubris. Alfred Doten and his drunken companions, for example, took the occasion of the Fourth of July in 1855 to march into Fiddletown playing "Yankee Doodle" on fife and drum. They stopped at the "Spanish dance hall" to dance, then marched downtown and "up again into the dance hall, three times round inside" and then paraded out of town. Like the impudent display of the two Anglos in the San Andreas tent that served as a Catholic church, the march through the Fiddletown fandango was another instance in which white Americans tried to regain control over meaning making in the Southern Mines. Ethnic social spaces might be permitted in the diggings—and patronized by Anglos—but men such as Doten and his friends made sure that the recent Anglo American conquest of Mexican California, and the dominance it implied, would remain fresh in the minds of all Gold Rush participants.[58]

One spot in the Southern Mines held out more successfully against such Anglo indignities, at least until the passage of the foreign miners' tax in 1850.[59] The town of Sonora, between the Stanislaus and

Sonora, California, in 1852, home to an unparalleled world of commercialized leisure. Note the diverse group of gold seekers in the foreground, who
appear to be Anglo American, Latin American, and French.

Reproduced by permission of the Huntington Library, San Marino, California.

Tuolumne rivers, had been established by Mexican miners well before
the flood of immigrants from the United States and Europe arrived in
the latter half of 1849. For a time, it was known as "Sonoranian
Camp" to the English speaking, "Camp Sonoranien" to French speakers, and "El campo de los Sonoraenses" to those who founded it.
Eventually the shorter name Sonora took hold, reflecting the birth-
place of the town's founders. When the California state legislature
tried to change that name to "Stewart," local businessmen prevailed
in their arguments that "no foreign or Atlantic communication
directed to 'Sonora' would ever reach 'Stewart,'" whether that communication came from Mexico, Chile, Peru, or the United States. In
this, the merchants acknowledged the diversity of Sonora's population as well as its international ties.[60]

One of those businessmen, William Perkins, who arrived in the
summer of 1849, left behind a detailed account of life in this
Tuolumne County town during its heyday, from 1849 to 1852. Recall
that Perkins, who was Canadian-born, thought of himself as "a great
favorite with the foreign population," though he extended the hand
of friendship more often to well-situated South American and French
men than he did, for example, to Mexican *gambusinos* or Chilean

peónes. As an English-speaking merchant (he could also converse in French) in a largely non-Anglo town, Perkins did what he could to maintain ties with his neighbors. One of the ways he did so was by participating fully in the social life of Sonora—going to the fandangos; frequenting the dance halls and gambling saloons; and attending the "celebrations, balls and dinners," often patriotic in tone, given by French- and Spanish-speaking people.[61]

The Sonora that Perkins described encompassed an unparalleled Gold Rush world of heterosocial leisure. Or so it seemed to the men who participated in it; for the women of Sonora, it was also a world of work. Moreover, it was a world of work stratified by race and national origin. According to Perkins, "A lady's social position with white gentlemen was graduated by shades of color, although we would sometimes give the preferance to a slightly brown complexion, if the race was unmixed with the negro." The "social position" to which Perkins referred was that of mistress: Chilean and Mexican women who appeared to be of Indian and European descent, as well as French women, all could make their way in Sonora by attaching themselves to men of some means in the diggings. Perkins claimed that the typical Mexican or French woman preferred informal union to marriage—the former, he presumed, because she would not "*marry a heretic*," and the latter because she would rather not "bind herself by ties" that in time would seem "irksome."[62]

Perkins's characterization of the differences between Spanish- and French-speaking women who cohabited with men says a great deal about how white men came to terms with the presence of female people who did not fit comfortably in the category of "women" upon which such men's understanding of "the social" rested. If Perkins is a reliable guide to this process, Anglo men felt compelled by Gold Rush social relations to create new typologies of women—new hierarchies of gender, race, and ethnicity. For example, Mexican and Chilean women met Perkins's approval because they, "even in the equivocal position of mistress," maintained a certain dignity, while French women did not. French women's chief sin, it seems, was their love of money. By contrast, Perkins claimed, "the spaniard" would not allow men "a glimpse of interested motives." The latter, then, "remain[ed] a *woman*," while the former was "made up of artificiality; profligate, shameless, avaricious and vain." Now, disinterestedness was hardly a useful trait in a gold rush, and so it seems likely that Spanish-speaking women simply made sure that Perkins could not read their motivations. And undoubtedly, more than one Mexican or Chilean woman benefited from his romantic naïveté.[63]

Part of what distinguished French women from Mexican and Chilean women in Perkins's eyes was that the former tended bars and gambling tables, while the latter, at least in these early years, did not. By May of 1850, Perkins contended, French women had monopolized the "Lansquenet tables and the liquor Bars," so that "no decent place" where liquor was sold failed to employ "a pretty and handsomely dressed Frenchwoman behind the counter." Despite his contempt for such women, even Perkins sometimes deigned to drop a "few quarters for the enjoyment of a genial smile" from a Parisian bartender. In the end, Perkins judged women by what they sold. While Spanish Mexican women in New Mexican towns like Santa Fe ran saloons, in the town of Sonora during the boom years, French- and Spanish-speaking women seem to have filled different niches in the Gold Rush market for heterosociality: French women took gold dust from men for a drink or a bet on cards, while Mexican women, in particular, specialized in selling prepared foods and working in dance halls. Mexican women did gamble in the saloons of Sonora; Perkins once watched two young Mexican women at a table by themselves "betting, flirting, and smoking cigaritos" until they lost all their money on a single card, bid Perkins *buenas noches*, and "glided away" together. French women, by contrast, not only gambled but tended gaming tables, overseeing men's winnings and losings, for which Perkins dubbed them "the forms of angels in the employ of Hell."[64]

Like many men, Perkins felt compelled to impose some kind of moral hierarchy on a market in which he was a willing consumer, and from first to last, he held the French, Mexican, and Chilean women of Sonora responsible for emptying men's pockets and tempting their weak natures.[65] That French women earned Perkins's special disapprobation (and his patronage, too) no doubt reflected the means by which they emptied those pockets. As mistresses of gaming tables, French women put Anglo men's control of their own resources at risk. This potential loss of control mocked dominant definitions of manhood, in which manly restraint was supposed to coexist in symbiotic relationship with womanly moral sensibilities. Here, in California, were whole new species of women, living and working not alongside emerging bourgeois neighborhoods—as, for example, prostitutes did in cities like New York—but at the very center of Gold Rush society, with few middle-class Anglo women physically present to contest newly sexualized, racialized, and commercialized notions of womanhood.[66]

Given how hard men like Perkins worked to develop ways of ordering this new world, ways to make sense of this novel situation, it is no wonder that the eventual arrival of middle-class Anglo women in the Southern Mines proved disconcerting. As Perkins put it, "It is too much to expect from weak male human nature in California, that a man ever so correctly inclined, would prefer the lean arm of a bonnetted, ugly, board-shapen specimen of a descendant of the puritans, to the rosy cheeked, full formed, sprightly and elegant spaniard or Frenchwoman."[67] Having struggled to find new ways of representing gender relations that could accommodate the presence of Miwok, Mexican, Chilean, and French women, now Anglo men had to relocate Anglo women in an altogether new discursive field. So in spite of white men's frequent complaints that the mines lacked the "sweets of society," not a few such men paradoxically bemoaned the arrival of increasing numbers of Anglo women in California.[68]

The arrival of a "board-shapen specimen of a descendant of the puritans" was a harbinger of things to come. There were other harbingers as well. J. D. Borthwick saw a hint of the changes when he visited Sonora in 1852. He delighted in the Sunday scene, when men came into town from miles around, some dressed in rough miners' togs, but others "got up in a most gorgeous manner." Many wore silk scarves of orange or scarlet hanging over one shoulder and tied loosely across the chest. Some attached feathers, flowers, or squirrel tails to their hats, while others braided their beards in a whimsical style. Mexican men sported brightly striped blankets, while French men, with neatly trimmed whiskers, flaunted caps of red or blue. The men caught Borthwick's eye first, but he admitted that the "Mexican women with their white dresses and sparkling black eyes were by no means an unpleasing addition to the crowd." But Borthwick ended his description on a dark note. He was alarmed at the occasional man in a black coat and stovepipe hat—"a bird of evil omen among a flock of such gay plumage." Writing in the same year, Perkins was more blunt: "Sonora is very dull compared to what it used to be." Indeed, the more the town took on the look of an eastern seaboard city in the United States, the less Perkins liked it: "What with peaceable citizens, picayunish yankees, Jew clothing shops and down-East strong-minded women, Sonora will soon be unbearable." While other gentile argonauts echoed such antisemitic comments, it was notable that Perkins saw the presence of Jewish merchants as a marker of a larger shift in Gold Rush relations of gender, class, and ethnicity.[69]

Some gold seekers did not wait for the arrival of Jewish merchants and "down-East strong-minded women" to begin bemoaning the

changes that were in the air. For such men, the presence of any
women at all foretold an end to male camaraderie in the diggings.
John Doble, for example, touring the town of Jackson in May of
1852, noted that the "Gamblers & women were busily engaged at
their different avocations which lead to misery and wretchedness,"
possibly referring to women employed at two Chilean dance houses
in town. Jean-Nicolas Perlot, the Belgian miner, who spent more time
in the mountains with Miwok Indians than in the immigrant towns
of the Southern Mines, had managed to avoid contact with non-
native women for the better part of four years. When he finally
noticed the influx of women into the diggings in 1855—an influx
that had begun much earlier—he was stunned: "From that moment,
everything changed! Farewell to the peaceful life of the placers! . . . .
People worked less and spent more; illnesses were more frequent,
more numerous, more deadly."[70]

As Perlot's lament suggests, the equation of "women" with all that
constituted "the social" as a category of human experience was not
ubiquitous in the Gold Rush. Granted, Perlot and Doble both were
making thinly veiled allusions not to married, middle-class women
but to those who sold companionship to a variety of male customers
(and who presumably caused "misery" and "illnesses"). Yet Doble
and Perlot were also among the men most content with the homosociality of mining camp life. Indeed, beneath the complaints about the
absence of "society" in California ran an undercurrent of pleasure
taken in the constant company of men. It was not so much that gold
seekers fit into neat categories of those who preferred either the
homosocial or the heterosocial—though some, no doubt, did—but
rather that the meaning of "social" life in the diggings was hotly contested. In the end, a particular vision of "society" would assume an
uneasy dominance in the Southern Mines, but in the meantime,
struggles continued both within argonauts and between them over
what the Gold Rush had wrought.

The tension exhibited itself even in a single text produced by an
individual Gold Rush participant. On the one hand, the German gold
seeker Friedrich Gerstäcker could remark at the "perfectly social body"
that he and his fellow miners constituted at Rich Gulch in Calaveras
County—"a little world of ourselves, in closest neighborhood and
amity, eating, working, and sleeping together, and not caring more for
the world around us, than if it did not exist." On the other hand,
when he reflected on the long-range potential of California, he
insisted that "social life" would come about there gradually, "princi-
pally by and through the presence of the gentler sex."[71] Likewise J. D.

Borthwick acknowledged that "society—so to call it" lacked a certain polish in the diggings. But, he reasoned, that was all to the good, because it meant that each man was "a genuine solid article . . . the same sterling metal all the way through which he was on the surface." Benjamin Butler Harris went so far as to applaud the "superior society" of the mines, made up as it had been of "people culled from every race and nation . . . [a] varicolored, and Babel-tongued group . . . free in every sense, standing on an equal plain, a nobility whose title was *manhood*." In a world where dominant constructions of gender were disrupted by the physical absence of white women, what was it about the socialities of the mines that could prompt for some such romantic memories? After all, as a New York friend reminded Timothy Osborn one Sunday when the men in camp dressed up in order to look "fascinating" for one another, "Ah! Tim, this isn't going up Broadway with a pair of bright eyes by your side."[72]

That, it was not—not Broadway, not the Bowery, not the streets of Valparaíso or Paris or Hermosillo. Nonetheless, men in California sometimes had bright eyes for each other. As Borthwick's description of Sonora's "gay plumage" and Osborn's of his friends' "fascinating" Sunday styles suggest, miners could take great pride in their appearance and great interest in the appearance of others. One of Osborn's Sunday visitors, "a little fellow," Osborn called him, came dressed in white pants like a sailor, "looking decidedly 'cunning' as the girls would say." But even more than his Anglo friends, Osborn noticed his Mexican neighbors. "Their peculiar dress always excites my attention," he wrote in his diary, "the loose bottomed under pants of snow white, and the gay woolen outside, open at the sides with long rows of brass buttons, and their black velvet tunic so short . . . as unable to reach the top of their pants." Neither was John Marshall Newton afraid to be caught looking. He recalled that one of his partners in Tuolumne County in 1851, a tall Dane named Hans, was "one of the most magnificent looking young men I ever saw." He had "massive shoulders and swelling muscles" that stood out "like the gnarled ridges of an oak tree." Newton remembered himself as a slight, soft-hearted boy who "yearned intensely for a friend" and who at first had so much trouble handling heavy mining tools that he often fainted from exertion. The magnificent Dane, then, was a perfect partner, because when Newton could not budge a boulder with a crowbar, he recalled, "Hans would . . . thrust me aside, take hold of the stone . . . and throw it out of the pit."[73]

Such differences in age, strength, and inclination could contribute to a cross-gendering of men's relationships with one another. At

Howard Gardiner's camp on the Tuolumne River in 1853, for example, one "handsome youngster" was christened Sister Stilwell because
of his "fresh complexion, lack of beard, and effeminate appearance."
The reveler Alfred Doten made an even more tantalizing reference in
one of his diary entries. In May of 1852, he described a Sunday fandango with visiting Chileans that included an expedition across the
Mokelumne River to a store kept by a man named Brooks. When
Doten returned home that night, he noted in his diary, "There is a
Chileno *hermaphrodite* camped near Brooks' store."[74] To date, the historical record offers up no other definitive clues about Brooks's neighbor.[75] S/he could have been a cross-dresser or someone with unusual
genitalia. Whatever qualified h/er for Doten's designation of "hermaphrodite," s/he seems not to have kept it to h/erself. S/he was, in
other words, a public "hermaphrodite"—someone everyone "knew"
to be anatomically female or male but who cross-behaved, or else
someone everyone "knew" to have, for example, what no one could
easily recognize as a clitoris or a penis, testicles or a vagina. Whatever
s/he had or whatever s/he did, s/he was "known" for miles around,
and no one—least of all Alfred Doten—seemed especially troubled
about h/er presence.[76]

Perhaps this is because Brooks's store on the Mokelumne and
Gardiner's camp on the Tuolumne were not isolated sites of cross-
gender gymnastics in the diggings. Not every ravine had a "Sister
Stilwell" or a Chilean "hermaphrodite," but most saw men coming
together in novel ways on a daily basis. If devising domestic divisions
of labor did not create gender trouble enough, there was always dancing. Miwok ceremonial lodges and Mexican fandango houses were
not the only venues for itchy feet in the Southern Mines. In fact, in
the diggings, all that was needed for what one argonaut called "the
tallest kind of dancing" was a handful of men and a fiddle. From the
very first night they shared a tent, William Miller, a white man from
Massachusetts, enjoyed the company of Henry Garrison, a black man
born in New York but emigrated from Hawaii: "he being a Mucision
And haveing his Fiddle the Eavening was Spent very agreeable."
While neighboring white men disapproved of Miller's relationships
with African Americans, that disapproval did not prevent the black
and white men from celebrating Christmas together in 1849. They
spent all afternoon and evening dancing to Garrison's fiddle, inter-
rupted only by a "Most splendid Dinner," a "fine Cold Lunch," and
then more of the "hot stuff" just before midnight.[77]

Alfred Doten's holiday bashes, characteristically, always sounded
a bit wilder than anyone else's, perhaps because he was, in a word, a

drunk or perhaps because he would commit to paper what other men kept to themselves. Christmas of 1853, for example, found him at Fort John in Amador County, throwing for his friends "a glorious game supper of fried deer tongue, liver, quails, and hares" and a *"Christmas spree"* replete with bottomless bottles of cognac and the music of violin, flute, banjo, clarinet, and accordion. Doten himself was a fiddler, and he made sure the tunes were right for inebriated men afflicted with barnyard wit: "The *'Highland fling'* was performed to a miracle, and the *'double-cow-tird-smasher'* was introduced with *'tird-run variations.'*" Of course, Doten did not wait for Christmas or the Fourth of July to carouse, and he did not carouse only with Anglos. In the summer of 1852, for instance, he had "quite a fandango" with some Mexican men, one of whom played the violin and another of whom tripped the light fantastic with "rattles on his feet." The dancer may have been a Yaqui Indian, because Doten noted the fellow's "Yacky deer dance with Coyote accompaniment."[78]

Diary-keeping men like Doten and Miller, however, wrote next to nothing about the way men interacted with one another when they danced in the diggings. Fortunately, J. D. Borthwick took time to describe a ball he attended at Angel's Camp, a largely Anglo American town, in 1852. Such balls were common, he thought, in the gulches

The Scottish artist and travel writer J. D. Borthwick's rendering of a Gold Rush ball, seemingly attended by white Americans and Europeans. Note the lone fiddler on the left who provides the music.

Courtesy of the Bancroft Library.

and ravines of the Southern Mines.[79] At Angel's Camp, a fiddle and a flute provided the music, and the fiddler led the dancers through their steps, singing out "Lady's chain," or "Set to your partner," or, a favorite call, "Promenade to the bar, and treat your partners." Here lancers were special favorites—sets of five square dances for several couples, each one of the sets in a different meter. "The absence of ladies," Borthwick noted, "was a difficulty which was very easily overcome." All agreed that every man "who had a patch on a certain part of his inexpressibles" would be a woman for the night, indicating just how successfully Gold Rush demographics and contests for meaning had unsettled normative notions of gender. Borthwick thought the patches themselves quite "fashionable"—large squares of canvas on dark pairs of pants. Elsewhere in the diggings, another miner noticed men wearing pants patched front and back with sacking that read "SELF RAISING HAXHALL," a favorite Virginia-made flour, or else bearing the name of some brand of hot chile. If the "ladies" of Angel's Camp announced their potentialities in this manner, Borthwick declined to comment. He did, however, remark at a Scottish boy who spelled the men from their lancers for a time by performing the Highland fling. The boy danced and shouted furiously, while the men cheered and clapped. After a quarter of an hour, he retired to the bar, where, Borthwick noted, "if he had drunk with all the men who then sought the honor of 'treating' him, he would never have lived to tread another measure."[80]

Did the "gentlemen" see their "ladies" home, or the "men" their "boys"?[81] The Gold Rush did occur in an era of increased possibilities for same-sex eroticism. Sex between seafaring men was common enough, for example, that it had its own name. The "boom cover trade" referred to the sex sailors had with each other under the covering that protected ship masts.[82] This was also the period in which Walt Whitman walked the streets of New York in search of working-class male lovers, and in which the Reverend Horatio Alger was dismissed from his Massachusetts church for having sex with boys.[83] It was a time when moralists generally considered sex between men a sin or vice, but not necessarily an indicator of an identity or sense of self. In this context, most Anglo American Gold Rush letter and diary writers would have been just as wary about keeping a record of sexual contact with other men as of drunkenness, gambling, or, for that matter, nonmarital sex with women. Indeed, the only unambiguous extant record of sex between men in the Southern Mines occurs not in a letter or diary but in the divorce proceedings of Hanna and Jeremiah Allkin of Calaveras County. Jeremiah had come to California in 1851, and Hanna joined him there in 1854. Two years later she divorced him, in part because "of his frequently sleeping with certain men, in the same house then occupied by her as his domicil—for the diabolical purpose of committing the crime of bugery."[84]

But ambiguous records abound. Alfred Doten, never one to tiptoe around what some thought of as vice, habitually noted the individual men with whom he spent the night, using language not unlike Whitman's. As early as February of 1850, when he first approached the mines from San Francisco, Doten noted, "I picked up a companion on the road & got behind my party and night overtaking us, we had to spread our blankets & pass the night on the ground." In March of 1852, Doten took in a friend, James Flynn, who was fighting with his own tentmate. "We slept together at my house," Doten remarked. Flynn seems to have stayed only a few days, though a week later Doten was referring to him as "Jimmy, my little partner." But Doten was a rolling stone, and so in the same diary entry he wrote that he had gone to a store where he was to begin work the next day, "and slept there all night" with a "Dr. Quimby." Doten could make life in the camps sound like a game of musical beds. One night he wrote, "Moody and John Spicer went down to the ranch—Newt came down and passed the evening with me—slept here," and the next, "Newt and Moody stopped at the Gate—Young slept with John—I slept in the house alone for the first time."[85]

Moody and John, Newt and Moody, John and Young, Doten and Newt, Doten and Jimmy, Doten and Dr. Quimby—we cannot know what transpired when beds in the diggings were thus occupied. Certainly bed sharing was a common practice in the nineteenth-century United States, perhaps particularly in frontier areas, and it would be foolhardy to suggest that bed partners commonly shared sexual pleasures.[86] But Doten and his friends bedded down together in a particular setting—one characterized by the presence of curious young men and lonely husbands, by close dancing and hard drinking, by distance from customary social constraints and proximity to competing cultural practices. In this context, it would *also* be foolhardy to suggest that Jeremiah Allkin was the only man in the Southern Mines who ever reached for a friend in the heat of the night.

This, then, was the Gold Rush world that some white men complained deprived them of "good," "congenial," or simply "social" society. Although it was abundantly clear that connections of all sorts flourished in the diggings, Anglo men did not always know how to represent those connections, which often failed to follow customary rules for negotiating oppositions that constituted the realm of the

During the Gold Rush, this popular image circulated as that of a "girl miner." More recently, it has been reproduced as that of a "woman miner." Actually, according to Jennifer Watts, curator of photographs at the Huntington Library, it is an image of John B. Colton, a lad whose countenance has transfixed many a male viewer for a century and a half. See Jennifer A. Watts, "From the Photo Archives: 'That's no woman . . .,'" *The Huntington Library, Art Collections, and Botanical Gardens Calendar*, July–Aug. 1998.

social. For such men, the absence of white women and the overwhelming presence of Miwoks, Mexicans, Chileans, French, and, later,
Chinese, upset the gendered and racialized oppositions upon which
notions of social relations and social order rested—male/female,
white/nonwhite, sacred/profane, even labor/leisure. Indeed, the profusion of California letters, diaries, and reminiscences is itself evidence
of the crisis of representation the Gold Rush wrought.

Of course, all Gold Rush participants had to renegotiate their usual
modes of representation in California, where everything from the natural environment to demographics to local economies was strange and
unstable. Just as Anglos could march into a Mexican dance hall playing
"Yankee Doodle," as if to give their personal stamp of approval to the
Treaty of Guadalupe Hidalgo, so too, for example, could Miwok
dancers represent their understanding of the politics of conquest in
customary *pota* ceremonies. But the *crisis* of representation—the profound dis-ordering of conventional oppositions and conventional hierarchies—may have been peculiar to Anglo American men, who in
situation after situation found their power to establish meanings in
jeopardy. These were, after all, the people in whose favor industrialization and westward expansion were supposed to work. But for all their
faith in these processes, white men found unanticipated discursive
contests in the Southern Mines, contests with material consequences.

These material and discursive contests were nowhere brought into
sharper relief than in such popular leisure practices as gambling and
blood sports.[87] In the Southern Mines, games of chance like monte
and bloody spectacles like bull-and-bear fights reflected Gold Rush
enmities that were rooted in the will to dominance of some Anglo
American men in the diggings—enmities that were played out simul-
taneously on a broader stage where expulsion from mining areas,
excessive taxation, and paramilitary campaigns plagued Miwok,
Mexican, Chilean, and French Gold Rush participants.[88]

Gambling was far and away the chief entertainment in the diggings, and perhaps the most popular pastime in the Southern Mines
was the Mexican game of monte. As early as October of 1848, just ten
months after the discovery of gold at Sutter's mill and well before
most emigrants from Europe and the United States arrived, the
Californio Antonio Franco Coronel and his servants, mining with
great success near the Stanislaus River, watched as a Sonoran *gam-
busino* dug enough gold in seven hours to set up a monte bank.
Dealing out the cards on a woolen blanket and drinking from a bottle
of brandy, the Sonoran lost all that he had in less time than it took

him to make it, leaving him with nothing but the blanket, his pants and shirt, and an empty bottle. Such losses might have ruined a man in the Southern Mines a year or two later, but with rich diggings still plentiful, the Sonoran probably recovered. Coronel did not stay long at the Stanislaus. He wintered in the town of Sonoma and then worked the placers in the Northern Mines. But when he returned ten months later to purchase a mule team, he found the area overrun with gambling tents. A large landowner who controlled the labor of many servants, Coronel was surprised by what he saw there: "men who . . . nobody would give a cent for in normal times, plac[ing] on a bet bags of gold each one of which . . . would insure to a family as much happiness as money can buy."[89]

Gambling took on a special significance in a setting like California, where it shared with the primary economic activity, placer mining, elements of unpredictability and irrationality.[90] Then too, in an intensely multiethnic, multiracial place such as the Southern Mines, gambling could also expose deadly fault lines in communities bent on digging what was thought of as cash from the earth. In popular games such as monte as well as an Anglo favorite, faro, gamblers ostensibly competed not with one another but with the "bank" of gold and silver coin managed by the man or woman who dealt the cards. Even though the games' design did not entail direct competition between players (as mining did not between miners), jealousies over big winnings at the monte table (as over high yields in the diggings) could foster ill will. Fear of cheating (as of unfair advantage in the mines) also ran rampant; no man wanted the deck stacked against him.[91] Indeed, no other activity in the diggings, aside from mining itself, provoked as much rancor as gambling.

Leonard Noyes, who in 1851 worked near Murphys Camp in Calaveras County, may have exaggerated when he remembered, "Every Sunday someone was shot in a Gambling den and often times during the week." As if it was part of the same thought, though, he went on to describe the "loss of life" occasioned by "quarels about [mining] claimes." In this, he suggested the symbiosis between mining and gambling as well as their common progeny—"every one was compelled to be on the Fight enough to take his own part." Noyes actually thought Murphys "was not so bad as many other places," because there were fewer Mexicans and so "Miners got along better." In the next breath, however, he acknowledged that these same Anglo miners "frequently made rades on Mexican communities" in which the Anglos would "commit all sorts of Degradations." It was, in fact, the area around Murphys and neighboring Angels Camp that is said to have witnessed the rape of Rosa Felíz de Murrieta, the lynching of Jesús Carillo Murrieta, and the horsewhipping of Rosa's husband and Jesús's half brother, Joaquín.[92]

Another incident that took place near Murphys in 1851 helps illustrate how monte could make bad blood boil. Noyes recalled that Mexicans had "quite a camp" at Indian Gulch that year, just north of Murphys. The camp boasted three tent stores, one of them kept by a Chilean man named José María and his wife. Two Anglo gamblers, Hugh O'Neil and Dick Williams, opened a monte table at María's tent, where in the space of a couple days, eight or ten Mexican and Chilean men "lost all their dust." O'Neil claimed that he overheard the men plotting in Spanish to murder the Anglos and reclaim the $10,000 monte bank. So when a scuffle broke out and the Anglos thought the Mexican and Chilean men were robbing the bank, O'Neil tore through the back of the tent with his knife and escaped with what money he could grab. Williams, also trying to run off with part of the bank, met a different fate; as Noyes heard it, a Mexican man put a knife through the gambler's chest. That was all it took for neighboring Anglos to tell a familiar tale: "by daylight everybody was out having been told the Mexicans had raised and were murdering all the Americans in Indian Gulch."

A story started this way and told by Anglos tended to move inexorably toward a predictable denouement, and so it was that fifty or sixty Anglos rushed into Indian Gulch that morning, a dozen of them intent on holding a makeshift inquest and the others hungry for quick revenge. The supposed murderers were long gone, and so the mob turned to a dark-skinned Chilean man (perhaps of African descent) who, along with his light-skinned wife, had kept a boardinghouse where the Mexican monte players took their meals. Noyes recalled that he and the handful of Anglos committed to a more orderly form of vigilantism pleaded with the others to let the Chilean man go. In the end, the more vengeful Anglos prevailed, forcing the Chilean to run up a hill while they opened fire on him, killing him instantly. When his wife "burst forth in a tirade of curses," the Anglos set fire to her tent. Next the mob went after José María and his wife, at whose store Williams and O'Neil had set up their monte table. Both husband and wife were nearly hanged. Again the calmer minority of Anglos interceded, arguing that María was "a very nice Gentlemanly Chilano" who had begged for his life in English. Noyes and his comrades won this debate, perhaps by emphasizing perceived class and race differences that distinguished the English-speaking María from the dark-skinned man who kept the boardinghouse: José

María and his wife escaped lynching, though they lost everything but their lives. Then, according to Noyes, the Anglos continued their depredations at Indian Gulch, burning, robbing, and killing until they were satiated. Among the mob was a Texan named Sam Green, later hanged for murdering a fellow Texan, William Byrnes, the supposed headsman of Joaquín Murrieta.[93]

It was striking how rapidly the death of an Anglo at the hands of a Mexican became for some Anglos the opening line of a larger story about a Mexican uprising replete with murder and mayhem. Such hysterical narrative responses to ethnic tensions in the mines indicated how fearful Anglos could be over the lack of control they were able to exert in the Southern Mines—whether control over meanings, control over the proceeds of mining, or control over the complex interactions between the two. Indeed, when the new widow of the dark-skinned Chilean man "burst forth" with her "tirade of curses," no doubt turning the charge of murder back onto the Anglos, they burned down her tent. Contests over meanings mattered. They drew blood; they destroyed homes; they brought death.

Perhaps tensions at monte tables frequented by Mexican miners and Texas Anglos were predictable, but racial/ethnic violence spilled over into gambling tents patronized by non-Texans as well. One Sunday evening in December of 1851, Alfred Doten was sitting down to write to his hometown sweetheart, when he heard cries of "to arms!" and "get your rifles!" He soon learned why his Anglo neighbors—a collection of northerners and southerners—were so excited. According to the Anglo rumor, some Anglos had stepped up to a bar at a Mexican tent to order a drink. One of them, a man named Alexander McDonald, had asked some Mexican men standing there if they were going to drink. One of the Mexicans retorted, *"no sabe,"* or at least that is how the Anglos remembered it, and so McDonald replied, "Well if you are not going to drink, we are, so just stand back." When he got no response, McDonald took the man by the shoulder and pushed him aside ("not roughly," Doten insisted). Then, according to the Anglos, the Mexican man and his partner left the tent, only to return later swinging swords at McDonald and another Anglo. One thing led to another, until both McDonald and one of the Mexicans had gunshot wounds.

By the next morning, Doten had managed, by means of a dare, to gather half a dozen Anglo men to pursue the Mexicans believed to have wielded the weapons at the bar. Other Mexicans in the neighborhood gave the Anglos no assistance, until a boy tipped them off about an older man who knew where the men were hiding. The

Anglos tied the older Mexican up and threatened his life until he told what he knew. Eventually the Anglos rounded up two Mexican men presumed to have been the sword swingers. Meanwhile, Alexander McDonald died, and shortly thereafter his mining partner, Dave Keller, rode in on horseback and begged Doten and his vigilante gang, which had grown considerably from the original half dozen, "Oh, let me kill them with my own hands." When the mob refused, intent on their own version of justice, Keller broke down and sobbed in another man's arms, calling out, "Alex! Alex! Alex!" Doten himself was touched by the scene, and confessed, "I cried too and many a rough hardy miner turned away . . . to wipe away their tears which came rolling down their bronzed and manly cheeks." At once, the tearful men assembled a jury of twelve. Only half of the witnesses summoned had to swear to the prisoners' identities before the jury cried out impatiently, "enough, this is evidence enough." After deliberating fifteen minutes, the "jury" found the Mexicans guilty of murder and sentenced them to death. In no time at all, both men were hanging by the neck from a pine tree.

Doten insisted that other Mexicans in the neighborhood "hated and feared" the lynched men, and that one of the two was a "noted highway robber" in Mexico. Nonetheless, a large party came the next day and asked to bury the corpses, and a week later two compatriots threatened the life of the older Mexican who had been coerced into revealing the whereabouts of the wanted men, indicating a good deal more community support for the deceased than Doten recognized. For his part, Doten was deeply affected by the hangings, and suggested that even the weather reflected the situation's solemnity: "The night was dark and fearful and . . . the howling and roaring of the wind through the tall pines and the warring of the elements rendered the scene awful and terrific." It was not a night to spend alone, as Doten recorded in his diary: "I slept at my camp with James Flynn and John (a Mexican boy) for company." As awful as Doten found the night, the terror must have run much deeper for those neighboring Mexicans who, unlike the boy sleeping with Doten and Flynn, were not in good graces with their Anglo neighbors.[94]

If antagonism at monte tables and liquor bars could escalate quickly to bloodshed, another popular pastime in the Southern Mines itself dramatized Gold Rush tensions rather than playing them out on human flesh. Animal flesh did not fare as well. Like monte, bull-and-bear fighting was a Mexican cultural practice, one particularly well suited to the Sierra Nevada foothills, home to both grizzly and black bears and within trading distance of low-country ranchos. Bull-and-bear fights were only one of the blood sports common in the mines. Mexicans staged bullfights and cockfights too, as well as engaging in splendid displays of horsemanship. In one amusement, for example, men buried a rooster in the sand and then dashed past the bird at full tilt, trying to grab it by the neck without toppling from their horses. But bull-and-bear fights were clear favorites among gold seekers of many descriptions—Mexicans, Anglos, and French to be sure, and perhaps others as well. Leonard Noyes contended that almost every good-sized camp in the Southern Mines had a circular arena constructed of wood and surrounded by tiers of seats and a high fence to keep out nonpaying spectators. Mexicans held not only bull-and-bear fights but bullfights in these arenas. For variety, a mountain lion might be put into the ring. P. V. Fox, for instance, once witnessed a "fight" where the bull and bear were reluctant to tangle; eventually the pacific duo was removed from the ring and replaced by another bull and a matador. All in all, it proved a quiet afternoon, because this second bull was not in a "fighting mood" either.[95]

More often, pitched battles ensued. Practices varied from camp to camp, but bears were generally roped or chained to a post in the middle of the arena and given ten or twenty feet of slack in which to maneuver. Sometimes bulls were similarly restrained, and some proprietors also sawed off the tips of the bulls' horns. Spectators gasped and whooped and shouted as the fight began, often with a charge by the bull that was met by a snout-crushing chomp of the bear's teeth. Bulls were the real crowd pleasers, enjoying as they did a special relationship to notions of manhood among Spanish-speaking peoples. Women and men alike marveled at the daring and determination of the bulls. Indeed—in California, at least—bullfights in particular seemed quite conducive to gender play, constituting a kind of liminal space in which attributes of manhood could be extracted from larger constellations and claimed by anyone willing to look a bull in the eye.

At Sonora, for example, Enos Christman watched as a stunningly dressed Mexican woman entered the arena after picadores had taunted the bull. In an intricate dance, she parried with her foe until, at an opportune moment, "she plunged the sword to the hilt into the breast of the animal." A shower of silver dollars fell at her feet, and the cheer of the crowd was deafening. Likewise, J. D. Borthwick attended a bullfight at Columbia where it had been announced that Señorita Ramona Pérez would be matador. In this case, however, the woman turned out to be an exquisitely cross-dressed man, who made short order of the bull and then ran out of the arena, "curtsying, and kissing her hand" to the audience. As for the bull-and-bear fights, Mexican women thronged to them, hollering and laughing and waving handkerchiefs along with the other spectators, whom Hinton Rowan Helper described as men of "all sizes, colors, and classes such as California, and California alone, can bring together."[96]

Helper was always disturbed by California's multiracial, all-too homosocial population, and so his reflections on the audience had an anxious, disapproving tone. But J. D. Borthwick, himself an artist as well as a writer, romanticized human diversity in the arenas, representing it (as he did in his description of Sonora's streets) as a riot of color, turning spectators into spectacle. Borthwick's description of an 1852 Mokelumne Hill bull-and-bear fight began with the two fiddlers—"a white man and a gentleman of color"—who played while the crowd gathered. The arena itself, he thought, was "gay and brilliant," and the "shelving bank of human beings which encircled the place was like a mass of bright flowers." There were the blue, white, and red miners' shirts; the men's bronze faces; the variegated Mexican blankets; the guns and knives glancing in the sun; the red and blue French caps; and always, the "Mexican women in snowy-white dresses." The bear seemed a dull brute, but Borthwick's bull was a gorgeous beast, "of dark purple color marked with white. . . . his coat . . . as smooth and glossy as a racer's." Once the fight began, however, the purple and white, the bronze and blue, and the glint of steel all dissolved into crimson. The bull's nose turned "a mass of bloody shreds," and a red flag taunted a bear brought low. While it began as a celebration of human diversity, Borthwick's depiction of the bull-and-bear fight now took an ominous twist—the circle of bright human flowers blanched by the animal carnage within the ring.[97]

Some representations dispensed with romantic images altogether. At Mokelumne Hill, for example, proprietors advertised an upcoming event throughout the area on placards that read,

WAR! WAR!! WAR!!!

The celebrated Bull-killing Bear,

GENERAL SCOTT

will fight a Bull on Sunday the 15th inst., at 2 p.m.

at Moquelumne Hill.

General Winfield Scott, then a Whig presidential candidate, had led the invasion of Mexico in 1847, taking fourteen thousand U.S. troops from Veracruz into Mexico City in what proved the decisive campaign of the war. Like the bull-and-bear fight Frank Marryat described a year earlier in Sonora—where the bear was christened America—the Mokelumne Hill event, while rooted in Mexican cultural practices, took on particular Gold Rush meanings. In this case, General Scott did indeed vanquish his foe, and the proprietor took up a collection from the spectators to pit the bear against yet another bull (one "equally handsome," Borthwick noted). This bull, too, met defeat, but a few weeks later the grizzly himself perished when a bull's horns tore through his ribs and ruptured vital organs.[98] Still, in the 1850s, a bear probably did not need to be called America or General Scott for Anglo/Mexican tensions to be invoked. Bull-and-bear fights called to mind not only the association of bulls with Spanish Mexican culture but also the recent Bear Flag Rebellion of pre–Gold Rush Anglos against Mexican rule in California. In that conflict, a grizzly bear and a lone red star graced the flag of the short-lived Anglo "California Republic."[99]

In bull-and-bear fights, then, enemies could meet in the ring again and again, spectators could place bets on the action, and the outcome of the contest, now freighted with ethnic as well as gendered meanings, could change from one Sunday to the next. All over the Southern Mines, events like this drew gold seekers from their diggings, dealers from their gaming tables, even some preachers from their makeshift pulpits. Perhaps the unpredictable endings of bull-and-bear fights and the mutual high spirits of the spectators provided some relief from the relentless tensions of life in the mines.

But in the end, those tensions were reproduced in the spectacles, which themselves became representational just as surely as the practices of writing letters and diaries, attacking effigies (and flags), assigning gender by means of a patch on a pair of pants, or marching into a dance hall playing patriotic tunes. Such contests over meanings in California revolved around a central question: Who would *own* the rush for riches in the Sierra foothills? Coming as it did at a pivotal moment in the course of industrialization, westward expansion, and class formation, the Gold Rush seemed to Anglo American men an opportunity whereby they might secure for themselves dominant positions in the emerging social order. Once in the Southern Mines, however, such men found that the absence of white women and the presence of native peoples, Latin Americans, Europeans, and later, East Asians, confounded their notions of what constituted "good" and "congenial" society. The crisis of representation that followed erupted with particular force across the terrain of leisure. There the boundaries of the social—the boundaries that make meaning—blurred, transmogrified, and reconstituted themselves again and again in the diggings, with different consequences for different Gold Rush participants.

Chapter 4

Mining Gold and Making War

Out of the day-to-day world of fiddles and fandangos, fresh greens and frijoles, tensions arose that turned the entire Southern Mines into an arena of conflict that came to favor certain contenders over others. Such struggles were bound up not only in the daily act of digging gold—the presumed "work" of the Gold Rush—but in daily acts of nursing and laundering, whoring and hymn singing as well. Most stories of the mining boom in California tie turmoil tightly to contests over gold—who would have access to it and who would profit by its acquisition.[1] This makes good historical sense for a period in which a key state legislative act taxed "foreign" miners, in which litigation over mining claims clogged county court dockets as quickly as courts could be established, and in which some miners exchanged picks and shovels for knives and rifles at the drop of a hat. What is lacking in many stories, however, is sustained attention to the social contexts and cultural meanings of battles over mining labor and its product, gold.

For in the end, if one is to understand something of what happened in the Sierra Nevada foothills after 1848, there can be no separation between productive and reproductive work, or between labor and leisure. Enmities might arise as easily out of disdain for how people got gold, shared food, or played cards. Alliances might be forged over a deer hunt organized cooperatively, over a dance performed admirably, or over a water ditch dug in common so that miners could wash gold-bearing dirt. Central to all of these enmities and alliances were gendered and racialized notions of what it meant to live appropriately in a gold rush. And central to the ways in which observers have seen (and not seen) such enmities and alliances are gendered and racialized notions of what a gold rush is.

So while I reintroduce herein what many take to be at the center of Gold Rush history—that is, the work of mining and the conflicts it provoked among miners—it is not happenstance that this set of stories follows rather than precedes those already told. In ordering my narrative in this manner, I have not meant to suggest that digging gold was less important, in relative terms, than were other daily activities in constituting what came to be called the Gold Rush. But I *have* meant to dis-order customary accounts of the period so that the salience of gender and race, both in what happened and in how those events have come to be remembered, would be more evident.

Here, then, the shovel hits the dirt, the woven basket swirls the water, and women and men look over their shoulders to see who might be gathering more gold than they, and where, and how. And they think about how much gold might be enough gold for whatever reason they started getting it in the first place, and, in some cases, about who might help them get that amount, and what that help might cost. All of these stories placed end to end would not together constitute an adequate Gold Rush narrative; but no adequate Gold Rush narrative can be constructed without them. These are tales that arise out of the complex set of mining labor relations that evolved in the Southern Mines—relations based on the work habits and social practices of diverse immigrant and native populations but patterned as well by the exigencies of an extractive economy emerging in the newest territorial acquisition of the United States and by the overwhelming predominance of men among the immigrants. Work in the diggings proceeded according to a dizzying array of systems that included independent prospecting and mining partnerships as well as altered Miwok gathering practices, Latin American peonage, North American slavery, and, later, Chinese indentured labor. Wage work among miners was much more prevalent after the initial boom, but when it occurred in the early years of the Gold Rush, it fell disproportionately to non–Anglo American men.

More than narratives of mining labor itself, however, these are stories about the conflicts work in the diggings provoked. In fact, nowhere is the contested nature of Gold Rush social relations clearer than in the series of mining-related ethnic and racial "wars" that plagued the Southern Mines: the Chilean War, the "French Revolution," the Mariposa War, and a whole host of skirmishes less extravagantly labeled by either participants or historians. Another key set of struggles revolved around white opposition to black labor in the mines. Many of these conflicts reflect the vigorous, often violent resistance that attempted imposition of Anglo dominance could provoke in an area like the Southern Mines, where non-Anglos frequently predominated in numbers. In spite of numerical superiority, though, Miwoks, Chileans, Mexicans, French, African Americans, and, later, Chinese found that U.S. whites were backed by an anti-Indian, antiforeign, and antiblack state government that did not hesitate to levy onerous taxes on "foreigners," send out militias after troublesome Indians or Mexicans, or return fugitive black slaves to their white masters. Once these struggles were resolved, organized and armed resistance to Anglo control in the Southern Mines—which now began to take shape as class rule too—would become increasingly difficult. Hence the story of individual retribution that began this study of the Gold Rush in California's Southern Mines—the tale of the "bandit" Joaquín Murrieta and his plucky, til-death-do-us-part partner, Rosa Felíz de Murrieta.

In order to comprehend the battles that raged in the Southern Mines over access to gold, one must understand something of the methods by which miners extracted the precious metal. Gold in California was found in three types of deposits, which miners called placers, gravels, and quartz. In the boom years of the Gold Rush, most gold seekers set their sights on the placers, surface deposits that were relatively easy to exploit with simple tools such as picks and shovels and buckets. Sometimes placer gold was located in the bed of a stream or river, and so argonauts had to divert these bodies of water in order to work their beds. What miners recovered, however, was not pure gold but gold mixed with dirt and rocks. In order to separate the metal from the debris, miners relied on one of gold's key attributes—its weight. Gold is heavy, and so miners could wash gold-bearing dirt with water and expect the gold to sink to the bottom while the water washed the debris away. In a pan, a gold seeker simply swirled water and auriferous dirt around and around until the water and dirt sloshed over the sides and gold was left gleaming in the bottom. But most turned to devices such as rockers, long toms, or sluices to get at the gold. Rockers were the smallest and simplest and sluices the largest tools, but all relied on the same principle. Miners washed gold-bearing dirt through these boxlike wooden devices, which were lined at the bottom with cleats, or "riffles," that caught the gold. To exploit the placers, gold seekers most often worked in small, cooperatively organized groups, not in big, hierarchically organized companies with large numbers of wage laborers.

As time passed, miners realized that the placers were like the tip of an iceberg—that far more gold lay deeper beneath the earth's surface. Some of those deposits were "deep gravels," or ancient placers that had long since been covered by debris. Other underground deposits were composed of gold that was embedded in solid rock—vein or quartz gold, it was called. Extracting gold from these kinds of deposits required more technical know-how, greater outlays of capital, and often larger numbers of workers than did placer mining. Their exploitation eventually turned mining into a full-fledged industry in California and led to an elaboration of class relations similar to those that characterized other industrializing areas in the United States and around the world. Although miners had no way of knowing this in the earliest months and years of the Gold Rush, there were actually fewer deposits of these sorts—deep gravels and quartz gold—in the Southern Mines than in the Northern Mines. Accordingly, economic development and class formation followed different patterns in much of the Southern Mines. But in the boom years of the Gold Rush, these distinctions between the Northern Mines and the Southern Mines were only beginning to emerge, and placer mining remained the chief concern of most gold seekers throughout the gold regions.[2]

Some disputes over labor in the diggings echoed those raging in the eastern United States. Important in a few conflicts was the language of "free labor," which, by the time of the Gold Rush, was fast becoming the rallying cry of certain northern white men on the make, and which soon proved decisive in reshaping the political party system in the United States and in the sectional antagonisms that threatened to destroy the Union by the end of the 1850s. Not surprisingly, free-labor ideology lurked around the edges of struggles involving African American miners, but it also cropped up in other disputes as well. In the end, however, given the prevalence of a variety of "unfree" labor systems in the mines, it is striking how modest the drive for free labor could be in the boom years of the Gold Rush.

The language of free labor fused an older Protestant belief in the worthiness of work with new attention to upward mobility and economic growth more appropriate to the evolving industrial capitalism of the Northeast. In this, hard labor for wages held a certain dignity, but only as a stage in a man's life before he began to work for himself. As one historian explains, "The aspirations of the free labor ideology were . . . thoroughly middle-class, for the successful laborer was one who achieved self-employment, and owned his own capital—a business, farm, or shop." Implicit, and often quite explicit, in this was a relentless critique of African American slavery in the South, which to many northerners thwarted economic development and negated possibilities for social mobility. For some, this critique was consistent with a desire to end the enslavement of black people and offer them the perceived benefits of a dynamic, expansive, capitalist social order. For others, it reflected a desire to end the degradation of nonslaveholding, poor whites, who had no opportunity to rise in an economic system that lacked a substantial middle class.[3]

Free labor, antislavery, and, sometimes, antiblack rhetoric permeated California's early state legislative debates, though such ideologies played themselves out differently in the mines.[4] In the senate and assembly, California's initial admission to the Union as a nonslave state gave way to continued disagreements over whether or not even free African Americans should be allowed to immigrate. At the same time, California law before 1852 was silent on the question of what would happen to slaveholders who entered the state with enslaved blacks, and attention to the question was minimal, especially in the diggings.[5] As one young master wrote to his father with regard to a slave named Patrick, "I don't consider there is any risk in bringing Patrick . . . as no one will put themselves to the trouble of investigating the matter."[6] And the Martha's Vineyard–born Timothy Osborn noted that enslaved blacks near his Tuolumne County camp worked hard for their Mississippi master, "notwithstanding the laws of the land that make them free."[7] Despite their antislavery reputations, white people from states like Massachusetts often did nothing to interfere with men such as this Mississippi planter. Charles Davis, himself an advocate of colonization schemes for African Americans, was sure that he had chosen a path of moderation in his dealings with neighboring slaveholders in Mariposa County: "Everybody here knows that I am a friend to the slave, but for all this, his master is a friend to me. I can say and do just as I wish with the slaves around me, and their masters have no suspicions of my injuring them, and every black man that knows me, manifests the greatest respect toward me."[8] Out in the diggings, the "laws of the land" were largely irrelevant, and it was northern white men like Osborn and Davis who helped ensure that black slave labor would thrive in the Southern Mines.

Indeed, the Southern Mines were the first destination of many white slaveholders, traveling overland as they did along southern trails to California.[9] Mariposa, the southernmost county in the region, seems to have been a special haven for slave-owning whites. The county's rugged terrain and small immigrant population may have made ignoring the "laws of the land" all the more simple. The evidence is circumstantial, of course, since as a "free" state California gathered no statistics regarding slaves and slaveholders. But the immigrant population of Mariposa County in 1850 (4,379 people in all) included 4.5 percent African Americans, while the larger populations of Calaveras and Tuolumne counties (16,884 and 8,351 people, respectively) included only .5 and .75 percent black people, respectively. And the 1850 manuscript census for Mariposa County reveals a number of large groups from southern states that included both black and white families—parties, no doubt, of slaves and their masters.[10]

Despite this relatively hospitable climate for slave owners in a nominally "free" state, enslaved African Americans recognized that the ambiguities of both law and custom in California offered unusual opportunities for escape from bondage. The frequency of fugitive slave cases during the first few years of the Gold Rush makes this clear. And, indeed, the judge in one such case in 1851 found that the federal fugitive slave law, passed as a part of the Compromise of 1850, had no bearing on cases in which slaves fled their masters in California and did not cross state lines in their flight. In 1852, however, the friends of slavery in California succeeded in shepherding through the legislature a state fugitive slave law that allowed white slave owners to reclaim black slaves who had escaped within the state. This law was renewed in 1853 and 1854, and then finally allowed to lapse in 1855.[11]

Flight from slavery was not the only means by which African Americans seized their freedom. Perhaps in part because of the tenuous legal status of slaveholding in California, enslaved blacks not infrequently were able to buy their way out of slavery in the diggings. Thomas Gilman, for example, an African American man in his twenties, purchased his freedom for $1,000 in 1852 at Shaw's Flat, a placer mining area in Tuolumne County. Born in Tennessee, Gilman seems to have worked in the diggings until he accumulated the capital to free himself. He lived in Tuolumne County for the rest of his life, mining and paying taxes on personal property and real estate assessed for as much as $725 during flush years, as little as $25 in hard times. Likewise, Peter Green purchased his freedom from Thomas Thorne, one of the largest slaveholders in Mariposa County, for $1,000 in 1855. Perhaps Green and Gilman, like the black men Leonard Noyes observed at San Antonio Bar in Calaveras County during 1851, had had mining claims of their own that they were allowed to tend on Sundays; these "Sunday claims" may have been the resource many African American men tapped to obtain their "freedom papers" in California.[12]

Unlike Thomas Gilman, many black miners who bought or otherwise appropriated their freedom were unable to live in peace in the
diggings. Stephen Spencer Hill, who accompanied his Arkansas master to California in 1849, claimed to have bought his way out of
bondage in April of 1853.[13] The former master, Wood Tucker, went
back home, and in October 1853 Hill filed claim to 160 acres of land
near Gold Spring in Tuolumne County. He cleared 40 of those acres,
planted wheat and barley, and, in his spare time, built a cabin and
kept mining for gold. Six months later, however, a friend of Hill's former master named Owen Rozier arrived at Hill's ranch, asserting that
Hill had never been freed and that the land Hill owned was thus
actually the property of Tucker, who was now back in Arkansas. On
the advice of a proslavery attorney, Rozier wrote to Tucker asking to
be appointed Tucker's agent in California, so as to reclaim Hill as well
as the cabin, the fields, and the diggings. When Hill received word
that his former master had authorized Rozier to seize him under
California's fugitive slave law, Hill fled. He was quickly arrested.
Meanwhile, a handful of white neighbors rallied on Hill's behalf. As
the British-born John Jolly recorded in his diary four days after the
arrest, "Hames, Chips & myself collecting subscriptions for conducting Steves case. Engaged Mr. Wolcot & Barber as his lawyers."[14] Other
neighbors harvested Hill's crops and cleared the ranch of everything
from which Rozier and Tucker could profit, and hounded Rozier so
mercilessly that Rozier finally pistol-whipped one of them, which
landed the would-be slave-catcher temporarily in jail alongside Hill.
But in the end, the lawyers engaged for Hill could not prove his freedom, and so Rozier made plans to transport the former slave back to
Arkansas. Rozier made it as far as Stockton. There Stephen Spencer
Hill made good his final escape, along with, according to the local
newspaper, "the gold watch of Mr. R, some thirteen dollars in cash
and a draft on Miles Greenwood & Co., of New Orleans, for $500."[15]
Rozier's loose change may not have made up for the land Hill had
lost and the work that had gone into the improvements, but there
must have been, nonetheless, a sweetness to the taking.

   It was not only recently freed slaves such as Hill who faced harassment in the diggings. James Williams, an African American man who
had escaped from his Maryland master as a boy of thirteen, made his
way to California when he was twenty-six to dig gold and live in a
place of relative safety from those who would enforce the federal
fugitive slave law. In the Southern Mines, however, he found his troubles did not cease. As he recorded in a narrative of his life that began
with his flight from bondage, Williams worked for a white man in

the diggings for six months until the employer turned on him: "he either raised a false report, or caused one to be raised in order to get a certain class of men to pursue me, to make me leave the place, to elude paying me my money, and he accomplished his design."[16]

Williams did not reveal the nature of this "false report," but other white miners' responses to black men in their midst provide some clues. In the fall of 1849, William Miller, the Anglo American man from Massachusetts who lived and worked with free African Americans on the Tuolumne River, got into a fight with southern white men over who would be allowed to work adjacent gold claims. Miller and his white partners had joined forces with a party of black miners ("Coulard Gentlemen," Miller respectfully called them in his diary) to dam the river and work its bed. As the company of black and white men walked downstream together to locate the best spot for damming, they came upon a group of white southern miners and asked whether the damming project would interfere with their digging. The southerners said it would not. But soon enough, as Miller put it, "a Swaggering Looking Fellow Came Along," and announced that "a White Man might come in [work in the vicinity] but a Black Man Could Not no how." From there things went from bad to worse, as the southern men came after Miller's party first "Armed to the Teeth with Rifles. Revolvers. Bowie Knives. and one Pick Ax," and then with a vow to go to the law. The latter threat proved decisive, as Miller recorded in his diary, "Our Committee thought It was a going to accumulate Considerable expense in the Co[mpany] Concluded to give up to them and went to work below them."[17]

In all of this, racialized understandings of "free labor" haunted the everyday work lives of African American men in the mines. Ironically enough, this was particularly true for those who were indeed free laborers; such miners could face opposition from both northern and southern whites. A few of these men, like Thomas Gilman, were able to carve out niches of relative safety in the foothills, living out their lives beneath the Sierra Nevada. More often—even when they had white allies like the Gold Spring men who helped Stephen Spencer Hill or the associates of William Miller who stood by their "Coulard Gentlemen" friends—free African Americans faced harassment in the diggings. Meanwhile, enslaved blacks benefited little from the attentions of white northerners like Charles Davis, who thought slavery "a great evil" but fancied himself equally the friend of both master and slave.[18] Indeed, free-labor ideology rested on an important ambiguity in its critique of slavery; it was never entirely clear whether it was the institution of slavery itself or the presence of black workers that ideologues thought degraded (white) labor.[19] In this, the "friends" of African Americans in the mines could bear an eerie resemblance to their enemies.

If the Southern Mines were no haven for African Americans, neither was the area a refuge for Latin Americans. Chileans and Mexicans who worked in parties led by a *patrón* faced their own set of Anglo hostilities in the diggings, but those hostilities at times resembled black-white conflicts. Several historians point to Latin American peonage as a central concern for Anglo Americans who wished Chileans and Mexicans out of the mines. Such scholars argue that Anglo treatment of Spanish-speaking miners "hinged . . . on the slavery question" as it was evolving in the United States, a debate that encouraged immigrants from northeastern states to see "parallels between Negroes and masters, on the one hand, and peons and patróns, on the other."[20] Some evidence for this interpretation exists. For example, when Theodore Johnson entered a gorge near Weber's Creek, just to the north of the Southern Mines proper, he noted, "we met a large party of Peruvians and Chilians, with their Indian *peones* or slaves, besides a considerable number of Mexicans from Sonora." In this, Johnson indicated how closely connected North American slavery and Latin American peonage could be in Anglo men's minds.[21] And in the summer of 1849, San Francisco's *Alta California* reported that a mass meeting of Anglos along the Tuolumne River had issued a proclamation complaining about "the sudden and unexpected appearance among us of influential men from distant provinces of Mexico, Peru, Chile, the Sandwich Islands & c., with large bands of hired men, who are nominally slaves." This proclamation called for the "immediate expulsion from the diggings . . . of all classes of slaves or hired serfs coming from distant countries."[22] Instances such as these demonstrate that, as another historian puts it, "in the gold camps, individual Anglo-Americans feared that Sonoran peons or Southern capitalists with gangs of slaves would exploit the gold fields in such an efficient way that free labor would be driven out."[23]

Yet in situations where one might most expect to hear the voice of free labor rising in protest, one listens in vain.[24] In the spring of 1849— before the bulk of Anglo Americans and Europeans immigrated—the Californio Antonio Franco Coronel returned to the diggings after wintering at a Sonoma rancho.[25] Coronel seems to have had four servants with him—Benito Pérez and his wife, and two "mute Indians," as Coronel called them, one of whom was named Augustin. Augustin was probably a *genízaro*, a detribalized New Mexican Indian captured and eventually traded to Californios for horses.[26] When Coronel returned to the mines with Augustin and the others, he settled in for a time at

An artist's rendering of an early Gold Rush scene, with a Californio *patrón* and Indian miners working alongside Anglo Americans. Both women depicted appear to be Spanish Mexican. From *The Shirley Letters from the California Mines in 1851–52* (San Francisco: Thomas C. Russell, 1922).

Reproduced by permission of the Huntington Library, San Marino, California.

the "dry diggings" along Weber's Creek, where Theodore Johnson had encountered Chileans, Peruvians, and Mexicans. Coronel found a similar mix of argonauts, along with Californios like himself and some Anglo Americans and Germans. As Coronel recalled, "All—some more, some less—were profiting from the fruits of their labor." Yet one Sunday, Coronel arose to find armed Anglos on patrol and notices posted on trees ordering all who were not U.S. citizens to leave the area within twenty-four hours. In response, according to Coronel, a number of people "of various nationalities" gathered in a defensive position atop a hill. But twenty-four hours passed, and then three or four more days, and not much more transpired than verbal taunts, warning shots, and some drunken revelry. "Finally," Coronel remembered, "we returned to . . . our work, although daily some of the weak were despoiled of their claims by the stronger." A few days later, however, a French-speaking man and a Spanish-speaking man were summarily hanged by inebriated Anglos for allegedly stealing four pounds of gold. For Coronel, this was the last straw: "This act dismayed me. . . . Two days later I picked up camp and went to the northern mines."[27]

Dictating his reminiscences of the Gold Rush nearly thirty years later for the Bancroft collection of Californiana, Coronel tried to make sense of what had happened to him and his workers in the diggings. Nowhere did it occur to him that the disputes in which he became embroiled were disputes about his use of *peón* labor, though Coronel went on to become a high-ranking official in Los Angeles city and California state governments and was thus well versed in Anglo American political culture. Instead, Coronel thought that the main reason for Anglo antipathy to Spanish-speaking miners was that "the majority of them were Sonorans who were men used to gold mining and consequently more quickly attained better results— as did the Californians by having come first and acquired the same art."[28] Indeed, historians have noted the frequency with which Anglo miners first learned placer mining techniques by watching Mexican or Chilean miners in action, and Southern Mines sources underline this conclusion.[29] When he arrived in the diggings, for example, Timothy Osborn saw Spanish-speaking mission Indians washing out gold in wooden *bateas:* "It was the first mining we had ever seen and we watched them carefully." Osborn questioned them in Spanish about how much gold they were finding, and the miners replied, as Osborn wrote in his diary, "*'Poquito medio once esta dia'* (little—half an ounce today)." That sounded good enough to Osborn and his two cousins; they staked a claim nearby.[30]

With Mexicans, Chileans, Californios, and mission-educated Indians as frequent gold-mining teachers and guides to gold deposits, Anglo Americans rarely took quick offense at the labor practices that produced the first glint of yellow metal they saw in California, whether those were the practices of independent *gambusinos* or teams of *patrónes* and *peónes*. In June of 1850, for example, Timothy Osborn noted, "The Spaniards (more especially Sonorians) are hospitable to the Americans in their own country, and it is due to them that every opportunity to reciprocate their kindness should be seized upon." In fact, it took Osborn a full six months in the diggings to learn to use the racial epithet "greasers" when writing about Mexican miners in his diary. These later references were a far cry from journal entries written when he first arrived in the Southern Mines.[31] As Osborn's early observations suggest, little more than curiosity often characterized initial meetings between English- and Spanish-speaking peoples. The Reverend Daniel Woods, for instance, came upon a large Chilean camp in January 1850 south of Sonora. Woods noted that the Chileans had "come from their own gold mines to try their fortune here." He took particular interest in a family at work in the diggings—the father and older children panned for gold, while the mother washed clothes and kept an eye on an infant swinging in a basket from branches overhead. Meanwhile, a five-year-old girl "with a tiny pick and spade" worked at a hole already two feet deep, washing the dirt down at the stream and placing a "scale or two of gold into a dipper a little larger than a thimble."[32] This was not the stuff of ethnic war in the mines.

But war there was. What happened in the diggings near the Calaveras River during the winter of 1849–50 was the first of three key ethnic conflicts that occurred during the boom years in the Southern Mines. These are conflicts that demonstrate the delicate interplay between global economic change and individual actions in creating the event that is remembered as the Gold Rush. They also demonstrate the decisive role of the state on behalf of white Americans in the diggings, though that role itself could be contested among competing groups of Anglos. In all of this, the language of free labor was often muted by the overwhelming desire of many Gold Rush participants to gather gold as quickly as possible and then return to their homelands. But that language, along with the rhetoric of the European revolutions of 1848, sometimes surfaced—for example, in Anglo American men's expectation that the state would surely support them (as true independent producers) and in the French deployment of symbols of revolutionary ferment.[33]

The first of these three conflicts has often been called the Chilean War. Documentation for what happened in the Calaveras diggings includes articles from San Francisco's *Alta California;* an unpublished account by an Anglo participant, John Hovey; another by an Argentinean-born Chilean observer, Ramon Jil Navarro, published as a series of articles in Concepción's *El Correo del Sur;* and a reminiscence by another Anglo participant, James J. Ayres, written in the 1890s but published in the 1920s. The accounts diverge in both particulars and in narrative intent.[34] Taken together, however, the various accounts suggest the following. In late 1849, parties of both Chileans and Anglos decided to winter south of the Calaveras River in a ravine that had come to be known as Chile, or Chilean, Gulch. At some point, Anglo miners called a mass meeting, elected a judge or alcalde for the mining district, a man named Collier, and ordered the Chileans out of the diggings. Few Chileans left. Around the same time, some Chileans drove some Anglos off a mining claim in the vicinity. After the Chileans were ordered out of the district, they sent a delegation to Stockton to plead their case to a regional judge there, a man named Reynolds. Reynolds sympathized with them and issued a warrant for the arrest of Judge Collier and the Anglos who had tried to expel the Chileans. Fortified by the writ of arrest, but lacking Anglo officials willing to enforce it, the Chileans returned to the gulch and planned a surprise attack on the Anglos in order to make the arrest. Sometime between eight and ten o'clock on the night of December 27, 1849, somewhere between twenty (a Chilean estimate) and two hundred (an Anglo estimate) Chileans fell upon the Anglos, who numbered between a handful (according to the Anglos) and a horde (according to the Chileans). At least two Anglos and perhaps one Chilean died in the ensuing struggle. The Chileans finally subdued the Anglos, tying some to trees while capturing others, and then began marching them in the middle of the night to the regularly commissioned local alcalde, a man named Scollan, who apparently offered the Chileans no assistance. Then the whole party started toward Stockton, several of the Chileans dropping out of the procession along the way. En route, however, an Anglo rescue party overtook the captors and their captives, and now the rescuers marched the Chileans back toward the Calaveras, while the former Anglo captives continued on toward Stockton to deal with the authorities there. Back in the Calaveras diggings, Anglo miners organized a makeshift trial for the Chileans. The jury sentenced three men to death, perhaps two to have their ears cut off, and several to fifty lashes or more.

The *Alta California* seems to have lost track of events in the diggings by this time and failed to report on the final outcome. At first, the *Alta* noted that two hundred Chileans had attacked about twenty Americans, killing several and then marching the prisoners toward Stockton, "not even allowing the wounds of the unfortunate men to be dressed." The paper reported that "the Chilenos said they were acting under orders from the authorities," and warned that "this outrage will be the signal for a general outbreak between the Americans and foreigners in the mines."[35] Two days later, however, a letter from a Stockton correspondent provided more details, some of which contradicted the earlier story. The correspondent explained that it was Anglos who had decided to winter near the Calaveras first, though they had chosen a spot where "Chileans or other foreigners" had worked the summer before. Soon after the Anglos settled down for the rainy season, Chileans moved in nearby. This led to the mass meeting of Anglos, which produced the order for Chileans to leave the area. The correspondent acknowledged that the Chileans had secured a writ of arrest for the Anglos from the Stockton judge, but added that "none of the Chilians spoke English, nor did they show any authority for the arrest of the Americans." In the process of the arrest, two Anglos and one Chilean were killed. The Chileans marched Anglo prisoners to the tent of the local alcalde, Judge Scollan, who "refused to have anything to do with them," and then started off toward Stockton. Stopping at a store along the road the next morning, the Chileans had breakfast but offered the Anglos only "a little cold coffee." Meanwhile, "some of the Chilians . . . had either given out or vamosed." By now, according to the correspondent, the Chileans began to fear an Anglo rescue attempt, and so they came to "an understanding with the Americans, and agreed to loosen their arms . . . provided they would intercede for them in case of an attempt at rescue by other Americans." Deliverance came soon enough. The Anglo rescuers bound the Chilean captors and marched them back toward the Calaveras, while the freed Anglo captives went on to Stockton "and gave themselves up to the authorities." The correspondent had heard that the eleven Chilean prisoners "unable from exhaustion to proceed to the Calaveras, were hung upon the road," though he emphasized, "I give this as a rumor."[36]

Five days after this report, a final letter from the Stockton correspondent appeared in the *Alta*, detailing the efforts of an Anglo delegation from the Calaveras that had come to Stockton, as the correspondent put it, "for the purpose of laying before our citizens a correct account" of the conflict in the diggings. The delegation included four white men, all "most respectable and intelligent gentlemen," who appeared before a meeting "of the citizens of Stockton." These "gentlemen" succeeded in convincing the "citizens" that the Chileans, "by false swearing," had obtained a writ of arrest from the Stockton judge for the Anglos, including Judge Collier, who had ordered Chileans out of the mines. "If this writ had been placed in the hands of a proper officer," the correspondent explained, it would have been obeyed. Instead, "it was given to a parcel of the lowest order of Chileans—none of whom could speak a word of English—who . . . stole upon their unsuspecting victims in the dark . . . murdering all who offered the least resistance." Those at the meeting passed resolutions applauding the conduct of the Anglos and offering to "unite with the miners to render any assistance they may desire in bringing the guilty to a just punishment." The correspondent closed his letter by reporting that "there is no truth to the rumor that the [Chileans] were executed on the road," and warned that those Chileans left near the Calaveras were reinforcing their position and might also be "endeavoring to induce the Indians in the neighborhood to join them."[37]

For readers of the *Alta California*, then, the Chilean War was a conflict that arose when "the lowest order of Chileans," legitimately banned from Anglo diggings, sought the aid of corrupt Anglo officials, to whom the correspondent referred as "certain persons who would now wish to shirk from all responsibility." In the end, for English-speaking readers, the event became a kind of warning against the possibility of "a general outbreak between the Americans and foreigners in the mines" or, alternatively, of a deadly alliance between Chileans and Indians in the diggings. Conspicuously absent in all of the *Alta California* articles was any mention of competing sets of labor relations or of conflict between the ideological underpinnings, for example, of Chilean *patrón/peón* practices versus small-scale Anglo mining partnerships.

For John Hovey, one of the Anglo miners who participated in these events, recognition of distinctive Chilean labor relations in the diggings was something of an afterthought. Hovey recorded what he observed in his diary, and also inserted a separately titled narrative, "Historical Account of the troubles between the Chilian & American Miners in the Calaveras Mining District." According to Hovey, "the troubles" began when Anglo prospectors strayed into a mining area claimed by Chileans and were ordered to "*vamos.*" The Anglos, "for they were staunch men," responded by organizing a mining district in which only "*bona-fide* citizens of the United States working for themselves" could take up claims. Significantly, the district laws included provisions for a "Military Captain" as well as a president, secretary, and judge. The president himself was no pacifist, and Hovey remembered that the white miners' leader made a speech at the founding meeting in which he railed that "the foreigners, and especially the d[amne]d copper hides, every s[o]n of a b[itc]h of 'em, should be driven from our diggings." When the Anglos of the newly created mining district approached the Chilean camp to enforce the new laws, they learned that many of the men there were "*peons* or slaves." But nowhere did Hovey suggest that Anglos wanted to exclude Chileans *because* of unfree-labor practices. The point was to drive out foreigners, dark-skinned men, illegitimate sons of immoral women. The remainder of Hovey's version of the events at the Calaveras roughly follows the chronology of other accounts, ending with the trial of Chileans, the execution of three *patrónes*, and the whipping of the *peónes*. The only Anglo act that seemed to give Hovey pause was the execution of one of the three Chilean leaders. This man had come to California with his son, who had taken ill. "Think of that little boys feelings," Hovey exclaimed, "left alone in a foreign land sick without a friend and only eleven or twelve years of age."[38]

An absence of concern about questions of free labor characterized the account of Ramon Jil Navarro as well. Navarro's is by far the most elaborate and dramatic of the narratives, sparing nothing in its portrait of the aggrieved Chilean miners as men of high principle, uncommon bravery, and peerless hospitality. For example, Navarro pointedly distinguished Chileans in California from Mexicans, who,

The Anglo miner John Hovey's rendering of the makeshift jail and court-house where Chilean participants in the "Chilean War" met their fate. From the John Hovey Journal.

Reproduced by permission of the Huntington Library, San Marino, California.

though perhaps the most skilled miners in the diggings, nonetheless "allowed themselves to be treated like cowards by the Americans." As for his countrymen, Navarro boasted, "There is not a single example of a Chilean letting himself be forced off his claim without a struggle."[39] Navarro's story begins as several groups of Chileans settle in for the winter of 1849–50, each building a cabin and hauling in supplies for the rainy months ahead. On December 10, however, Anglos in the area—having decided to "act as an authority independent of Calaveras County, the state of California, or even the United States

201 *Mining Gold and Making War*

itself"—issued an order to the Chileans to abandon their camp. As Navarro understood it, Anglos justified this act by arguing that it was wrong that "Chileans, as foreigners, not paying any fees, should exploit the mines at the expense of themselves who were citizens of the United States and who had come by land with so much toil and privation and who were rightful owners of mines bought from Mexico with Yankee blood." The Chilean men who headed the companies, however, refused to leave, citing the severity of the winter, the law of the land, and "the right of possession, which was even more sacred in California." Yet two days later, several Anglos walked into the Chilean camp, saying, "You, Chileno, *largo de aquí*" (get out of here). The leader of the group working in the placers, José del Carmen Téran, simply replied, "You, Yankees, *largo de aquí*."[40]

A few days after this incident, according to Navarro, hostilities moved beyond such mutual posturing, as Anglos infiltrated the Chilean camp, separating the men working in the diggings from their *patrónes* in the cabin area. Some Anglos hid among the trees nearby as the district's alcalde, Judge Collier, and some unarmed Anglos approached the cabins in a seemingly friendly manner. The Chileans welcomed the Anglos, serving them "coffee and a light lunch." Finally, on cue, the armed Anglos rushed in from the woods and surrounded the Chileans at gunpoint and then moved out to seize the men at work in the diggings. This accomplished, the Anglos robbed the Chileans, marched them to the Anglo camp, and forced the stronger captives to help stow the stolen goods in Anglo cabins. Navarro considered this the work of "bandits" and compared the Anglos unfavorably with highwaymen from Guadalajara or Apache raiders in northern Mexico, who, though they were thieves, never mistreated their victims with bodily insult or injury.[41]

In Navarro's account, then, these are the provocations that forced the Chileans to seek help from officials in Stockton. There they received the sympathies of the judge, the sheriff, and the town's leading merchants. So they returned to Judge Scollan, the appointed alcalde in Calaveras County, with the following order, which Navarro, himself the official translator for the Stockton court, interpreted for the Chileans:

By these presents, Messrs. Concha and Maturano are authorized to arrest and bring to Stockton either freely or by force all of the individuals residing in Calaveras who have defied the legal authority of this subprefecturate and who have recognized Mr. Coller as judge. They are authorized likewise to arrest and bring to Stockton all individuals who took part in the robbery, violence, and expulsion carried out against the aliens living in Chile Gulch. . . . The lawful judge of Calaveras, Mr. Scollen, will authorize the execution of this order by his presence.

Judge Scollan dutifully accompanied two of the *patrónes* to the Anglo camp and served the warrant, but when the Anglos refused to comply, Scollan claimed he could do no more.[42]

It was at this point that the Chileans took matters into their own hands, feeling the need, as Navarro put it, "to avenge their outraged honor." Three of the Chilean *patrónes*—Terán and two others, named Ruiz and Maturano—led their parties into battle. There were only twenty men in all, the *patrón* named Concha having departed with his workers for Stockton. The tiny band of Chileans approached the Anglo camp, bursting through cabin doors and shouting, "*Subprefecto orden, vamos* for Stockton." The Anglos went for their weapons and immediately felled one of the Chileans. In retaliation, Maturano and Ruiz killed an Anglo each. The struggle continued until the Anglos were finally subdued, and then, finding that the captured Anglos outnumbered the Chileans two to one, Terán reluctantly ordered that the "the most vicious of the Americans" be tied up. The Chileans further revealed "their generosity of character and their good hearts" by refraining from taking anything from the Anglo camp, not even the goods that had been stolen from Chileans days before.[43]

The Chileans then proceeded to Judge Scollan's residence, to demonstrate their respect for legitimate government. There, they treated the wounds of those Anglos who had been injured, exhibiting tenderness, Navarro contended, to the point of tears. Then the captors and their captives continued toward Stockton, stopping for breakfast at a roadside store where "all sat down together at the same table without any ceremony and in perfect harmony." According to Navarro, "a kind of intimacy had grown up" among the men by daybreak. Still, at each stop along the way, a few Chileans dropped out of the march, too "sick or too worn out to continue walking." Finally, their numbers reduced, the Chileans encountered a band of a hundred armed Anglos at a roadside inn, and, unable to resist, the captors surrendered. The Anglos bound the remaining Chileans so tightly that the ropes drew blood. But what "distressed the Chileans most," Navarro wrote, "was the vile ingratitude with which their good treatment of their prisoners was requited." Some of the Anglos then started the Chileans back toward the Calaveras, while others "went on to Stockton to seize the subprefect" (who had already left for San Francisco).[44]

Navarro's account continues in this vein, stressing the countless deeds of inhumanity the Anglos inflicted upon the Chileans, especially the refusal to feed the captives; once back in the diggings, the Chileans were herded into a cold room and "treated exactly the way captains of slaving ships treated the unfortunate Negroes who fell into their hands." Soon enough, however, on December 31, the makeshift trial began. It did not last long. By ten o'clock that night, the sentences came down: Terán and two others were to be thrown off of Mokelumne Hill; three men were to be whipped, have their heads shaved, and their ears cut off; and several others were to be whipped and have their heads shaved. The last two groups of convicts asked to be shot rather than suffer such dishonoring punishments, but the Anglos refused their request.[45] Before New Year's morning arrived, however, Anglos from the Mokelumne mines intervened and demanded leniency for the Chileans. They succeeded only in protecting one man, Maturano, and in insisting that the death sentence for Terán and the two others be carried out in a more humane fashion. So it was that on January 1, 1850, three Chilean men died by firing squad; three others were whipped and shaved, and lost their ears to an Anglo's knife; and the rest were tied to branches and "whipped so that blood spurted from their lungs." Not even the "sobbing pleas" of the son of one of the dying men could "inspire pity" among the Anglos, "such men as they were."[46]

Throughout, Navarro took pains to underline the manly stoicism of his Chilean protagonists, and particularly of the *patrónes* among them, who chose violence only when provoked but then were quick to defend their own honor to the death. At the same time, theirs was a style of manhood that mixed courage with compassion, as evidenced by the tender care and comradeliness (and especially the breakfast) they offered their Anglo captives, despite the Anglos' rapacious acts. The Anglos, by contrast, were cheap hoodlums who knew nothing of either honor or manhood, not to mention hospitality. As if to underscore the bankruptcy of Anglo gender in the diggings, Navarro placed at the scene of the final trial a woman, wife of one of the jurors. This Anglo woman, Navarro wrote, failed to act "in keeping with the mission of her sex" by consoling the prisoners and pleading on their behalf. Instead, she "was an endless torment to the Chileans." She stood in the doorway at the trial, alternately drinking and swinging a noose at the prisoners, demonstrating "the horrible facial expressions they would have in their last agonies." And then, when death called, she "watched the spectacle in as cold blooded a manner as the worst of the Yankees."[47] How better to represent the disorder of the diggings, where racial and ethnic violence cost men their honor, their ears, and their lives, than as a disorder of gender?

The final account of the Chilean War appears in the reminiscences of James J. Ayres, *Gold and Sunshine*, which he wrote fifty years after the events. The book, which was not published for another twenty-five years, opens as Ayres and his partners settle in for the winter of 1849–50 near the Calaveras River. Two miles away was a Chilean settlement, watched over by a Dr. Concha and several "lieutenants." The military allusion was no accident. The rest of the camp was made up of *peónes* Concha and others had brought from Chile, who, according to Ayres, "stood in relation to the headmen as dependents, in fact as slaves." Neither was the reference to slavery incidental.[48] Conflict arose when "small parties of Americans" would discover new diggings, but then be "driven off by a superior body of these Chileans." So the Anglos called a mass meeting and drew up mining laws. As Ayres put it, "In other mining districts where Americans from the South had brought their slaves with them, a law was adopted which prohibited masters from taking up claims for their slaves." In the Calaveras diggings, this principle was applied to situations where Chilean *patrónes* took up claims for their *peónes*. Soon after the meeting, some Anglos were driven "under peculiarly aggravating circumstances" from a gulch they were working (one hears echoes of Terán's mocking, "You, Yankees, *largo de aquí*"). The district's alcalde, Judge Collier, called another meeting, which "came together in a temper of great exasperation," adopted a resolution to order the Chileans out of the mines, and then "marched in a body to Chilean Camp, and served the notice upon the headman present."[49]

According to Ayres, the Anglos had almost forgotten the "Chilean imbroglio," when one evening their tent flaps flew back and they found a dozen guns aimed at them. Ayres was among those bound to a tree by the attacking Chileans. But because Ayres spoke some Spanish, the Chileans took him to another camp in case they needed an interpreter. This put Ayres in a cabin where two Anglos had been shot, and introduced him to the person he assumed had led the raid, a man Ayres thought the Chileans called Tirante. "He was not misnamed," Ayres added. (Terán was at the center of Navarro's narrative too, but as hero rather than tyrant.)[50] Ayres numbered the Chilean captors at five dozen and the Anglo captives at thirteen. The party proceeded to the tent of Judge Scollan, who Ayres acknowledged was the "regularly appointed alcalde." Ayres learned later that the Chileans had tried to persuade the alcalde "to give a tone of legality to their murderous proceedings by certifying to our arrest by the authority of a warrant that had been issued by Judge Reynolds, of Stockton." The alcalde declined to intervene, so the Chileans pushed on with their prisoners toward Stockton. In the morning, when they stopped at a trading tent, Ayres noted that the Anglos were "allowed to get some coffee and food." There Ayres learned that some Anglos were planning a rescue, and he also noticed that the Chileans had "diminished in numbers" along the way: "Some of the peons had dropped out from sheer exhaustion; others had furtively deserted."[51]

As the remaining Chileans recognized their increasingly perilous situation, they began to argue among themselves about what to do. According to Ayres, "Tirante proposed that the prisoners be dispatched," and that the Chileans disperse. But "a large, fine-looking Chilean called Maturano . . . opposed the proposition not only as cruel and inhuman, but as one that would surely bring upon them the vengeance of the whole American people." Maturano won this debate, and Ayres vowed to repay him for "the manly and humane stand he took in this terrible crisis of our fate."[52] By evening, all were so weary that they stopped for the night and lay down around a campfire. Eventually the Chileans fell asleep, and the Anglos were able to loosen their ropes and quietly gather their captors' weapons. On signal, then, the Anglos turned on the Chileans and tied them up. "The peons," Ayres noted, "gave us no trouble when they saw that their patrones were in our power." At daybreak, the Anglos marched their former captors toward Stockton, until they ran into a party of rescuers at a roadside inn along the way. After a grand reception and a good meal, the rescue team headed back toward the Calaveras with the prisoners, while Ayres was appointed "to go to Stockton and lay the facts before the people and the authorities"—but not before he paid his debt to Maturano. Ayres took Maturano aside and told him to escape by running for his life through the wild oats that grew near the inn. As Maturano prepared to leave, Ayres recalled, "he kissed my hand and thanked me."[53] Then Ayres went on to Stockton, finding "the community intensely excited" and particularly outraged at Judge Reynolds, who had issued the warrant for the Anglos' arrest and who now had escaped to San Francisco. That evening, Ayres attended a mass meeting, where a nephew of Judge Collier "delivered a powerful, eloquent and impassioned address" that exonerated the Anglos of all wrongdoing. His good name cleared, Ayres headed back to the Calaveras, where he learned that miners from Mokelumne Hill had conducted a trial and pronounced the following sentences: "Tirante and two others . . . were sentenced to death; some four or five . . . were sentenced each to receive fifty to one hundred lashes on the bare back; and two . . . were condemned to have their ears cut off."[54]

Such was the story of James Ayres—a story that, not surprisingly, frequently contradicts that of Ramon Jil Navarro. Yet even with a narrative structured to shed the best possible light on his own and other Anglos' actions, half a century later Ayres felt compelled to write an apologia for the story, a brief chapter entitled "Obvious Observations upon the Bloody Episode." What was obvious to Ayres by 1896 was that "mutilation can at no time nor under any circumstances be justified." The death sentences, even the whippings, did not trouble Ayres so much as the act of cutting off Chilean ears, which he confessed had not troubled him at all in 1850. In what must have seemed a fitting argument to make in the 1890s, Ayres wrote, "This only goes to prove that our civilization is, after all, but a veneering, and our inherent nature is that of the savage, only requiring the proper circumstances, conditions, and surroundings to draw it out" (surroundings many called the frontier).[55] Besides, Ayres had placed himself in Stockton at the time of the trial and had made other miners responsible for the brutal sentences.[56] His conscience assuaged, Ayres went on to lay responsibility for the affair at the feet of the Stockton judge, who ignored local mining district laws. And, Ayres added, "If I am told that we had no right to forbid the Chileans to locate claims for their peons, the answer is obvious, that we had the same right . . . as the other districts had to forbid the slave owners among our own people to stake out claims for their black bondsmen." He concluded by explaining that his purpose was to set the story straight not only in the United States but in Chile as well. A few years earlier, he noted, a mob in Valparaíso had "maltreated and killed sailors belonging to a United States cruiser" (this was the cruiser *Baltimore*). Chilean newspapers had identified this uprising as retribution for the 1849 "Chilean Massacre" in California. "This venomous spirit," Ayres claimed, made its way even to the "higher orders of Chile, and at one time it looked as if we would . . . have to bring the peppery little republic to its senses by our national strong arm." No doubt, such comments failed to endear Ayres to any Chilean reader who happened upon *Gold and Sunshine* after it finally was published in 1922.[57]

A great deal is kaleidoscoped in Ayres's brief justification of the Chilean War. First, there is the retrospective insertion of concern over Chilean peonage, which Ayres likened to slavery. Accounts generated during the Gold Rush—the *Alta California* coverage, John Hovey's diary, and Ramon Navarro's articles in *El Correo del Sur*—downplayed conflicts over labor relations and the ideas that informed them. Ayres and men like him may indeed have been concerned about questions of free labor in 1849. But such concerns were unlikely to produce a clear consensus among Anglos in the Southern Mines, where southern whites, some with black slaves in tow, were overrepresented. It seems likely, then, that aversion to unfree-labor practices was peripheral rather than central to the Chilean War of 1849–50. By 1896, however, when middle-class white northerners and southerners were mending all sorts of ideological fences, it would not have been unseemly for Ayres to map the "slavery question" onto other kinds of disputes that arose in the diggings.[58]

Second, there is the self-assured Anglo Americanism reflected in Ayres's didactic use of the Gold Rush past to placate "peppery" Chileans who dared challenge U.S. imperial power—Chileans who had a historical memory all their own. Indeed, decades before the 1890 attack on U.S. sailors from the cruiser *Baltimore,* a Chilean author had claimed John Rollin Ridge's Joaquín Murrieta as Chile's own Gold Rush hero, christening him El Bandido Chileño. To an audience schooled in such Gold Rush tales of resistance, *Gold and Sunshine* shed little light on the subject. As the easy Chilean appropriation of Murrieta suggests, outside of the United States, battles over the meanings of the Gold Rush have been resolved less frequently in white Americans' favor. As recently as 1966, for example, the Nobel Prize–winning Chilean poet Pablo Neruda transformed the Murrieta story into an anti-U.S. opera titled *Fulgor y muerte de Joaquín Murieta* (The Splendor and Death of Joaquín Murieta). The opera was translated into a number of languages and performed widely in Latin America, Eastern and Western Europe, and the USSR (and on some U.S. college campuses in 1968).[59] In a song that introduced the opera, Neruda, like Ramon Navarro before him, reclaimed the Gold Rush for Chilean audiences:

> Today they kill blacks like this
> before it was Mexicans,
> thus they also killed Chileans,
> Nicaraguans, Peruvians,
> those unrestrained gringos
> with their inhuman instincts
> . . . .
> Who disputed their ground
> and who challenged them face to face?
> It was a Chilean bandit!
> It was our Joaquín Murrieta![60]

Such tales of resistance—stories retold and retooled by each generation, each collectivity—were rooted in the everyday struggles of Gold

Rush participants. Those historical struggles, while they have been recounted in wildly disparate ways according to the varied interests of tellers, had in common the pursuit of dominance in the diggings by some Anglo American men and the tacit approval of many others. The will to rule reflected in such conflicts as the Chilean War had as much to do with processes unfolding in cities and villages like Boston, Philadelphia, and Boscawen, New Hampshire, as with anything happening in camps and towns like Mariposa, San Andreas, and Mokelumne Hill. It reflected the transformation underway in the eastern states that entailed industrialization and the commercialization of agriculture, shifts that had a monumental impact on the lives of young men uncertain about how to negotiate the changing economic landscape. Going to California was a deeply individualistic, if also familial, response to the industrial and commercial revolution of the midnineteenth century. As such it was a kind of middle-class project, although, to be sure, many of the men who engaged in the project were at most aspirants to that class status. And many would fail miserably in their desperate attempt to avoid what free-labor advocates saw as the degradation of lifelong wage work. One Ohio man put it this way: "Being a shoemaker, and ambitious to rise somewhat over the bench, it is no wonder that the discovery of gold in California excited my fancy and hopes." Such men would go to great lengths to protect the object of their dreams. They would be challenged, of course, by other Gold Rush participants caught up in what was ultimately a global economic transformation. What would prove decisive in the diggings, however, was the power of the state to back up the Anglo will to rule.[61]

The most common means white American men devised to protect California's gold from the aspirations of other Gold Rush participants was the creation of mining districts with laws barring non–U.S. citizens from the diggings. This is the route John Hovey and James Ayres took at Chilean Gulch in late 1849. A couple of months earlier, "the People of Lower Mocalime Bar" (along the lower Mokelumne River) passed a similar set of resolutions, arguing that when U.S. citizens arrived in California, they found "a large proportion of its mineral resources in the hands of a people who have no right whatever to the soil on which they are trespassing—No interest in the perpetuity or prosperity of our government, and strangers alike to its laws, its language, and its institutions." The Anglo men thus appointed an alcalde to notify the "foreign population" that they must immediately stop mining and "prepare to leave the country with all convenient dispatch."[62]

Sometimes exclusionary practices were more ad hoc. For example, while mining at Mormon Gulch in Tuolumne County during the winter of 1850, the Reverend Daniel Woods noted that his neighbors quite unceremoniously had "driven off a large number of French miners from what is called 'French Bar.'"[63] Another such expulsion involved a more diverse set of miners. William Shaw, who had emigrated from England to Australia in 1848 and then moved on to California in 1849, traveled to the diggings with two other white men and two men of color. The latter included a Chinese man, who had been a crew member on the ship Shaw took from Australia, and a young Malaysian, who Shaw said had been adopted by one of the white men as a child and over whom the white man exercised "paternal controul." Shaw referred to these two as "followers" whom he and his associates had brought along "thinking they might be useful"; the men of color, in other words, were employed by the white men. Once up in the foothills, Shaw's party found themselves accused as trespassers by Anglo Americans, who offered a variety of reasons for trying to eject Shaw's party from the diggings. As Shaw put it, "The presence of our black confederates they made a source of complaint: evidently imagining them to be in a state of slavery or vassalage to us." Shaw assured them that he "exercised no compulsion over the blacks." But the white Americans also argued that "coloured men were not privileged to work in a country intended only for American citizens." And then some among them "were inconsistent enough to ask the Celestial and the Malay to work for them for pay."[64]

Shaw went on to explain that over time "this feeling against the coloured races rose to a pitch of exasperation." Some of the antipathy arose, he thought, because "capitalists" were hiring Chinese, Hawaiian, or native laborers in what he called a "system of monopoly." "The obligations and agreements entered into" between such employers and workers, Shaw reported, were frequently "cancelled and annulled by the fiat of the vox populi." At the same time, independent bands of Mexican, Chilean, and, increasingly, Chinese miners were at work in the diggings, and Anglo Americans, "relying on their numerical strength, commenced acts of hostility and aggression on any 'placer' inhabited by coloured people, if it were worth appropriating or excited their cupidity." The results of such appropriations were not hard to predict. As Shaw put it, "retaliations were made, and where might was right, retributions upon unoffending individuals often took place, which were nigh producing a war of race against race."[65]

This near "war of race against race" created some unexpected alliances, particularly after April 1850, when the California state legislature imposed a licensing tax of twenty dollars per month on all non–U.S. citizens at work in the diggings.[66] Officially, the law was called "An Act for the better regulation of the Mines and the government of foreign miners," but it was known to most as the foreign miners' tax (or as one disgruntled French immigrant called it, "the miserable law of 20 piastres").[67] In and around the town of Sonora, response to the tax was especially swift and ultimately decisive. Friedrich Gerstäcker, the German travel writer who published his observations of the Gold Rush soon after his sojourn in California, called what happened in Tuolumne County the "French Revolution," though the uprising against the foreign miners' tax included not only French but Mexican and Chilean miners and some Germans as well.[68] Anglo American merchants in Sonora (indeed, throughout the Southern Mines and the supply town of Stockton) rallied in opposition too. Other merchants, such as the Canadian-born William Perkins, joined them, since all faced tremendous business losses as a direct result of the tax.

Although the foreign miners' tax was approved April 13, 1850, and its text printed in California newspapers within the following two weeks, it was not until May that organized resistance began. When the tax collector, Lorenzo A. Besançon, arrived in Tuolumne County to begin his appointed duties, Mexican, Chilean, and French miners gathered outside of Sonora, responding to notices posted throughout the town and the nearby American Camp (soon to become the town of Columbia).[69] To date, no Mexican, Chilean, or French accounts of these cross-ethnic meetings have been uncovered, though Anglo newspaper stories abound and Gerstäcker's fanciful tale of "Die französische Revolution" provides a non-Anglo counternarrative. (Gerstäcker's account seems particularly fanciful because it recounts verbatim conversations to which he was unlikely to have been party.) The *Stockton Times* reported that some had seen Chilean, Mexican, and French flags hoisted in defiance where miners gathered at the ironically named American Camp. Gerstäcker recounted a different meeting at Murphys New Diggings, where German miners were also in attendance, Alsatians prominent among them, and Basques among the French.[70]

All were dismayed by the new tax. As one Sonora correspondent to the *Stockton Times* (who signed himself "Leo" but was actually the merchant William Perkins) explained, the miners insisted "that it was impossible that such an amount could be paid; . . . a great many diggers hardly getting more gold than sufficed for a mere livelihood."[71] Out of these assemblies came delegations sent to authorities in

Sonora "to ascertain if any action of the Governor could arrest the consummation of the contemplated taxation." The delegates memorialized the governor, complaining that the tax would lay waste to all of their hopes, not to mention all commerce in the Southern Mines. Leo translated a bit of the memorial for the *Stockton Times* to demonstrate how reasonable the petitioners were:

> Without doubting for a moment the power of the present government to make a difference between American citizens and those of other countries, we humbly draw your excellency's attention to the fact that it is altogether contrary to the institutions of the free Republic of the United States, to make such a difference as amounts in reality to a prohibition of labor. Without assuming any tone other than that of the deepest respect for the government under which we live and are protected, we beg humbly to suggest to your excellency that a larger state income could be raised, and that too, without causing the slightest dissatisfaction, by the imposition of four or five dollars per month, instead of the large sum of twenty.[72]

For some, however, reasonable petitions did not suffice to express their indignation. Nor did all Anglo Americans and their allies respond to Spanish- and French-speaking people's protests with as much sympathy as Leo, or William Perkins, who wasted not a day in pronouncing the tax "illegal, unjust, abortive and extremely prejudicial to the best interests of the state."[73]

Accounts of what occurred on Sunday, May 19, 1850, are vague and sometimes contradictory, but they suggest that the delegates sent into Sonora to reason with authorities were backed up by three to five thousand French, Chileans, and Mexicans. Perkins placed these men outside the town of Sonora, while another correspondent indicated that at least some of that number "proceeded tumultuously into town, sweeping through the streets, boasting of their strength, and threatening in many instances to burn the town that night." Writing his reminiscences years later, Benjamin Butler Harris suggested that the "turbulent convention" of "foreigners" itself took place in Sonora and was dominated by a French man, Casimir Labetoure—who, as it happens, was Perkins's next-door neighbor, a fellow merchant, and a member of the Sonora town council. Harris recalled that Labetoure "made a 'liberty or death' speech in both French and Spanish in which he encouraged the Mexicans with the averment that the foreigners on the Coast largely outnumbered the

Americans, that the Americans here could not fight like those of the
Mexican War, being servile peons sent here by their masters to delve
in the mines."[74] Nevertheless, none of the accounts reported any violence, save an incident, seemingly unrelated to the revolt, in which a
Mexican man resisted arrest. Perkins claimed that another Mexican
drew a knife to protest the arrest and that yet another bystander, presumably Anglo, interceded, wounding the armed Mexican man
severely with a bowie knife (the Mexican later died). Harris, on the
other hand, recalled that it was the deputy sheriff himself who had
"cut off with a bowie knife the head of a Mexican who, with drawn
pistol, had resisted arrest under a warrant."[75] Whatever happened, a
Mexican seems to have died at the hands of an Anglo, which must
have added to the tension seething in Sonora.

Meanwhile, Anglos and their allies sent messengers out to the surrounding camps, drawing in hundreds of armed miners, who, according to Perkins, "marched through the streets with guns and rifles on
their shoulders." The Mexicans, French, and Chileans seem to have
left Sonora, regrouping at American Camp, where they raised their
flags and considered their options. Incensed, armed Anglos swept
into the camp the following morning "to avenge the insult." One
correspondent insisted that when the Americans arrived, "they found
all things in order." But Harris recalled that the Anglos marched in
just as "the foreigners, with streamers, banners, and flags, were parad-
ing the streets . . . preceded by a naked Indian daubed in war paint,
all singing the *Marseillaise* and other Revolutionary Songs." Along
with the report that Labetoure denounced Anglo miners as peons,
Harris's description of this demonstration suggests that the language
of free labor and the rhetoric of revolution could easily be tapped
once tensions surfaced in the mines. Another observer, however,
described no such dramatic encounter and maintained instead that
the Anglo warriors "liquored up" once they reached the quiet camp
and sat down en masse to a banquet served up at the principal hotel.
All agreed that no battle ensued, though Harris was sure that the
Anglos had intimidated the French- and Spanish-speaking miners
into retreat, and the protesters' flags, now full of bullet holes, were
replaced by the Stars and Stripes.[76]

Gerstäcker reported that, in the meantime, the French, Germans,
and "Spaniards" at nearby Murphys New Diggings got word that two
French men and a German had been arrested at Sonora while protesting the tax, and that the sheriff there had "been killed with a knife by
a Spaniard." In response, a crowd of French-, German-, and Spanish-
speaking miners gathered, "each talking in his own language" (occa-

sionally resorting to English to make themselves understood), and decided to march into Sonora in defense of their compatriots. Among them was a particularly eager soldier, a woman who worked the gaming tables and habitually dressed in pants and a short jacket, "sporting a felt cap clapped jauntily on the side of her head." On this day, she tied a red ribbon around the hat, mounted her horse, and urged a few of the more reluctant (and inebriated) men to join her. Some of the men hung back, but a Madame Louis—herself already clad in "dark colored pantaloons, a red woolen shirt, a large felt sombrero over one ear"—leaped into her saddle, her less enthusiastic husband, Monsieur Louis, falling in behind. "Here were our two Amazons," Gerstäcker exclaimed, "galloping, laughing, and singing as they went."[77] It took a German observer to recognize, or perhaps to produce, the revolutionary panache of these French women's attire.

As it turned out, when the soldiers arrived in Sonora, they learned that the report about the imprisoned men and the murdered sheriff was false: "The whole affair was merely an extravagant story that had had as its consequences the embroiling of the Americans with the foreigners."[78] An extravagant story indeed, but a story that had a particular resonance for certain Gold Rush participants. It was not hard for French-, Spanish-, and German-speaking miners to believe that Anglo Americans had thrown their compatriots in jail without just cause, or that one of their own might have become so enraged at discriminatory treatment that he would have stabbed a sheriff. Even lies tell truths. Likewise, it was not hard for readers of Gerstäcker's tale to imagine that French women in the mines had donned pants, shirts, jackets, caps, and even Mexican sombreros, given the perceived blurring of gender and ethnic boundaries that the Gold Rush entailed. Of course, part of this blurring recalled the European revolutions of 1848, but it took on new meanings during the Gold Rush. Hardly a contest in the diggings narrated by participants or observers lacked its cross-gender, cross-racial component, whether it was a fiery French orator denouncing Anglos as peons to a Mexican audience or an "unhappy husband" searching for his "gentle better-half" among a bunch of red-shirted miners. In the latter case, when camped for the night en route to Sonora, Monsieur Louis had to survey closely each face among his party "until at last he discovered Madame, stretched under a tree at the side of her friend." In true Gold Rush fashion, that is, "without regard for the rights of the first occupants," Monsieur Louis "chose as his place of repose the space between the two fair ladies."[79]

William Perkins, as Leo, seems to have heard about Madame Louis and her comrades, as he noted that "a large body of Frenchmen under arms" had arrived in Sonora, having received word that "the French inhabitants were in danger of their lives." When they realized the report was false, "they peaceably dispersed." In fact, a good number of French- and Spanish-speaking miners not only dispersed during the "French Revolution"; they left the Southern Mines altogether. One Anglo who had swept into American Camp with his compatriots, for example, noted the "scene of confusion and terror" that marked the men's march: "Mexicans, Chilenos, *et id genus omne*—men, women and children—were packing up and removing." In retrospect, this participant wondered, "What could have been the object of our assembly, except as a demonstration of power and determination, I know not; but if intended as an engine of terror, it certainly had the desired effect." At the time of these events, however, most Anglos and their allies who worried about the effect of the tax had more practical concerns. Leo had warned in his very first letter to the *Stockton Times* about the antitax uprising in Sonora: "This state of affairs, if allowed to last, will ruin the prosperity of the whole southern mines, and your own town of S¦ockton will be the first to suffer thereby." It took only a week for the *Stockton Times* editors to offer their wholehearted agreement. On June 1, the newspapermen noted, "As we expected, the collection of the new tax is producing a ruinous effect upon the traders in the southern mines. Business, in many places, is at a complete stand still; confidence is shaken; there exists a universal feeling of distrust among the miners; man is set against man."[80]

Accompanying this report was a memorial addressed to the governor of California and signed "by nearly every merchant in Stockton," which complained that the foreign miners' tax had succeeded only in stopping "the labor of thousands of miners," destroying business, and creating "a feeling of disorder and discontent in the mines, where the most perfect order and harmony" had previously prevailed. The merchants argued—like the French, Chilean, and Mexican petitioners before them—that the tax ought to be set at a rate of five dollars a month instead of twenty. And the *Stockton Times* heartily endorsed the memorial, urging the governor to consider "the claims of the vast interests embarked in the district of San Joaquin, where the burden of the tax is most severely felt."[81] Indeed, merchants in the Southern Mines had taken the middle-class project of Gold Rush emigration one step farther, by plowing their profits into commerce in California rather than taking gold east to advance business prospects back home. Anglo American miners might want the Southern Mines all to themselves, but Anglo American merchants wanted customers. And in the Southern Mines, customers were just as likely to be Mexican or French or Chilean as they were to be white people from the eastern states. By the summer of 1850, then, just two years after the discovery of gold in the Sierra Nevada foothills, the meanings of Anglo dominance in the diggings had begun to bifurcate. What began here as diverging interests between white miners, on the one hand, and white merchants, on the other, would evolve into full-fledged class conflict in the years to come.[82]

The protests of Mexican, French, and Chilean miners and—probably more important—the petitions of merchants in the Southern Mines eventually had their intended effect. On August 10, 1850, the *Stockton Times* announced that the foreign miners' tax had been reduced from twenty dollars per month to twenty dollars for a four-month period. By March of the following year, the tax had been repealed altogether.[83] Residents of the Southern Mines, however, knew it was far too late for the repeal to bring back old times in the diggings. Two years later, Anglo men still remembered "the long train of fugitives" leaving the mines: "Some were going North; some South; the great body was probably bound for home; some by way of the sea; others by Los Angelos and the Great Desert." As early as July 20, 1850, the *Stockton Times* had reported a mass exodus from the area tributary to the San Joaquin River: "the evil is done—the foreign population, we mean the Mexicans, Sonorians and Chilians are on the march home. . . . The San Joaquin district will loose from twenty to thirty thousand of her working population in the space of a few months."[84] The newspapermen, allies more to Anglo merchants than to Anglo miners, mourned especially the departure of Mexicans, protesting that "the land of their adoption is no longer a land for them." To those who doubted Mexican immigrants' desire to settle in California, the newspaper challenged, "look at their wives and families; see them . . . becoming proprietors of lots for the erection of stores. Speak with them and learn their ultimate intentions." For the *Stockton Times*, a tax on "foreign miners" was a "direct tax on labor," and as such it impeded efforts to create "a permanent laboring population" in California. Members of what would become a middle class in the Southern Mines argued that it was customers and wage workers—not competitors for U.S. gold—who were driven off by the foreign miners' tax.[85]

Yet not all left, and those who stayed did not adjust easily to the tax and the relations of dominance it evoked. The Reverend Daniel Woods heard in July of 1850 that a dozen men had been murdered in and around Sonora in the space of a week. Woods imagined, "This state of things is no doubt owing in part, to the heavy tax imposed

on foreigners, which deprives many of them employment. In consequence, they [are] destitute of the means with which to purchase
their daily supplies. They are accordingly driven to steal and murder."
Woods probably exaggerated the extent to which the responsibility
for mayhem in Sonora could be laid solely at the feet of disgruntled
"foreign" miners, but his assessment of the situation was in fact more
generous than that of many Anglos. Woods, unlike others, also recognized that the tax drove increasing numbers of the Mexicans who
remained into wage labor.[86] Violence and theft in the Southern Mines
did seem to surge in the summer of 1850 and continue unabated at
least into the following year, no doubt in part as a consequence of
both the economic destitution and the ethnic tensions created by the
foreign miners' tax.[87] In response to the turmoil, Anglos in Sonora
gathered late in July at what one unsympathetic Anglo wag called
"The great Greaser Extermination meeting." Those in attendance
voted for resolutions claiming that "the lives and property of the
American citizens are now in danger, from the hands of lawless
marauders of every clime, class and creed under the canopy of
heaven." Because the men gathered felt sure that they had in their
midst "the Peons of Mexico, the renegades of South America, and the
convicts of the British Empire," they resolved that "all foreigners in
Tualumne county, except persons engaging in permanent business
and of respectable character, be required to leave the limits of said
county, within fifteen days." Five hundred copies of these resolutions
were distributed throughout the county.[88]

So it was that, by the summer of 1850, some Anglos in the
Southern Mines had tried to drive French miners from French Bar,
Chileans from Chilean Gulch, and Sonorans from Sonora, the town
founded by northern Mexicans in 1848. From here on, struggles
between Spanish- and French-speaking Gold Rush participants, on
the one hand, and Anglo Americans, on the other, would not erupt
into events observers could hyperbolize into "wars" or "revolutions."
For one, too many Chilean, French, and Mexican miners left the diggings for such skirmishes to continue unabated. In addition, two
years of discriminatory and exclusionary practices—from the most
local disputes over a single placer claim to the systematic, state-sanc-
tioned persecution of "foreign" miners—had a profound effect on the
strategies of resistance and accommodation remaining Spanish and
French speakers pursued. Chileans had learned that civil authorities,
however sympathetic to Chilean complaints about expulsion from
the diggings, would not defy angry crowds of white Americans to
offer Chileans protection. And French- and Spanish-speaking men

alike had found that, without the backing of Anglo merchants, their challenges to extortionist legislation met with outraged reprisals from Anglo miners. In retrospect, even some white Americans recognized the horror that they, collectively, had visited upon Mexican, Chilean, and French Gold Rush participants. Benjamin Butler Harris, for example, invoking the name of the nativist Know-Nothing Party of the later 1850s, claimed that the foreign miners' tax was "so outrageously extortionist in its terms as to make an angel weep or a Know-Nothing laugh." And the man who called the exclusionist gathering in Sonora "The great Greaser Extermination meeting" penned a poem by that title which satirized a rabidly anti-Mexican speech delivered there by a man named John Cave:

> . . . that speech, it is sure to immortalize Cave,
> And I hope coming folks will take warning,
> And choose (if they would their property save)
> *Some American place to be born in.*[89]

The warning Mexican, Chilean, and French Gold Rush participants took from the events of 1849 and 1850 led to new tactics of survival, evasion, and revenge. Many simply left. Others moved to or created camps and towns with non-Anglo majorities. Mokelumne Hill and nearby Jesus María, in Calaveras County, for example, retained an international appearance. An American dentist named John Baker lived there in the mid-1850s and described the population of Jesus María in particular as consisting of "Chilians, Mexicans, Americans, Peruvians, Dutchmen, Italians and Indians." He added, with some trepidation, "they present to me a mixed mass, I can assure you. The principal language is Spanish." Indeed, Baker had to learn Spanish in order to work in the area. Several years later, a German traveler to Mokelumne Hill found the French influence still strong there, though he noted an increasing number of German residents as well. The principal inn, the Hotel Leger, he described as "an establishment half way between a German beer hall and a French restaurant," perhaps not surprising, since the innkeeper was Alsatian. Farther south, in Mariposa County, the town of Hornitos became a place of refuge for a variety of non-Anglos, but particularly for Mexicans. A smug young Anglo woman visited there in 1857 and noted that she "wasn't much taken with it. Most of the inhabitants are spaniards & Indians." Four years later, another traveler noted of Hornitos that "to this day there seems to be an omnipresent struggle between the Mexican and American element . . . . Even the very signs seem to fight it out, or compromise. The stage house is the 'Progresso Restaurant'; the bakery is a 'panderia'; the hotels invite both in Spanish and English; the stores in Italian as well as American and Spanish; while Sam Sing or Too Chang outrival the 'lavado y plan[c]hado.'"[90] For some non-Anglos who stayed in the Southern Mines, living in camps and towns with non-Anglo majorities was a ticket to economic and cultural survival.

Others fought Anglo dominance tooth and nail. When they did, often as not, they in turn faced dire legal or extralegal consequences. If the *Stockton Times* coverage of killing and stealing in the Southern Mines after the imposition of the foreign miners' tax is any indication, it would seem that individual and anonymous retaliation against Anglo usurpers became more common over time than the earlier organized forms of resistance practiced in the Chilean War and the "French Revolution."[91] Response to such retaliation was swift and furious, and no doubt fell upon many a Mexican or Chilean who had *not* participated in and perhaps did not even countenance acts of violent retribution. The sheriff of Tuolumne County, for example, kept a record of his expenditures for 1851—the year *after* the exodus of Mexicans and Chileans—which indicates that of 115 suspects he arrested, over half had Spanish surnames.[92] Just as often, however, "suspects" faced not a sheriff and a court hearing but a vigilante mob, sometimes organized enough to call itself a vigilance committee. Misbehaving white Americans were by no means exempt from the workings of lynch law in the Southern Mines, but for every well-publicized whipping or hanging of a suspected Anglo thief or murderer, probably several Mexicans met a similar fate. In the summer of 1851, for instance, when Sonora's vigilance committee was most active, the hanging of a white man named Hill received the most publicity. But Enos Christman detailed in his diary just one week of the committee's deeds: "the Sonora Vigilance Committee hung another horse thief. The following Sunday three Mexicans were tied to the whipping post, and each received twenty-five lashes well laid on. Another Mexican was found with a stolen horse . . . and sentenced to receive 150 lashes, to have one-half of his head shaved, and to leave the country in 48 hours under penalty of being hanged if he ever returned."[93] With such odds, it is little wonder that in some cases, strategies of individual and anonymous retribution evolved into instances of social banditry in the diggings, as they did with Joaquín Murrieta and his compatriots.[94]

In the meantime, however, there was yet another population in the Southern Mines that interfered daily with the project of asserting Anglo American dominance in the diggings. Native people in the foothills—including both Sierra Miwoks and mixed bands of Miwoks, Yokuts, former mission Indians, and other peoples from the San Joaquin Valley—had adopted a variety of strategies in response to the unprecedented invasion of Miwok gathering and hunting grounds after 1848. The most important among these were placer mining and livestock raiding. Miwoks and their allies started mining long before the bulk of Anglo and European immigrants arrived in the Sierra foothills. In fact, on the day that Antonio Franco Coronel, Benito Pérez and his wife, Augustin, and the other "mute Indian" got to the Stanislaus diggings in the fall of 1848, they had barely settled in when "seven Indians, each one with little sacks of gold," approached the campsite. One of these Indians, who were most likely Miwoks, took hold of Coronel's saddle blanket—a worn cover that had cost only two pesos—and then pointed to a certain spot on his elongated sack of gold, indicating how much he was willing to offer for the purchase. Coronel hesitated, blankets being scarce in the mines, but relented when one of his *peónes* volunteered to make him a cover of woven grass. Coronel sold the blanket for more than seven ounces of gold (about $112), and then a second for more than nine ounces (about $144). Meanwhile, Benito Pérez sold another Miwok a New Mexican serape for two pounds, three ounces of gold (about $560).[95]

Pérez, himself an experienced miner, marveled at how much gold the Miwoks carried in their sacks. He urged his *patrón* to send him and Augustin after the Indians to learn the whereabouts of their placers, and Coronel agreed. Pérez and Augustin followed the seven miners back to their *ranchería*, and camped a ways off so as not to be seen. The next morning, the two *peónes* trailed the Miwoks to their diggings and surprised them while they worked. According to Coronel, although the Indians "seemed hostile," Pérez "insisted in digging in a place next to theirs." In no time at all, Pérez had gathered three ounces of gold (about $48).[96] When Pérez and Augustin returned and told their *patrón* the news, Coronel sent them back, along with the other "mute Indian," to "take possession" of the most productive ground. Coronel came close behind, "followed by some of the Spanish people who had been there in camp." Shortly, Californio *patrónes*, Indian *peónes*, and Sonoran *gambusinos* filled the ravine Coronel called Cañada del Barro (no doubt because of the *barro*, or clay, that made washing the gold so difficult). Coronel did not mention what became of the seven Miwoks who had led them to these extraordinarily rich claims; he himself mined there only for a couple of months before leaving the diggings for the winter.[97] Mexicans, Californios, and mission Indians may often have introduced Anglo prospectors to profitable diggings, but long before, Spanish-speaking men and women themselves had followed Miwoks into the mines.

Some historians have stressed the extent to which California Indians were incorporated into the placer mining economy as wage or contract laborers, following the pattern of Spanish Mexican use of native workers in the service of settlement. This practice, such historians argue, declined with the ascendancy of Anglo Americans in the diggings, who, as a group, pursued a policy toward Indians of extermination rather than incorporation and exploitation. And indeed, there were early examples in the Southern Mines of widespread white employment of native workers. John Murphy, for whom Murphys Camp in Calaveras County was named, struck it rich in 1848 and 1849 by contracting for Indian labor in the diggings in exchange for supplying the workers with clothing, blankets, and food. Murphy seems also to have cemented trade and labor relations by marrying a native woman. These laborers may well have been Miwoks, who were native to the area. But Murphy himself had come to the Southern Mines from Charles Weber's camp farther north, where Yokuts Indians seem to have worked for Weber's Stockton Mining Company. So it is possible that some of Murphy's laborers were Yokuts as well.[98] After establishing one work site, John Murphy and his brother Daniel moved on to nearby Angels Creek, where they took up a second set of claims, which became known as Murphys New Diggings (the spot from which Gerstäcker's French "Amazons" would depart for Sonora a year or so later). The New Englander Leonard Noyes arrived at this camp in the fall of 1851, after the Murphy brothers had left, and heard "Fabulous Stories . . . of the amounts of Gold" taken there by Daniel Murphy, "who had all the Indians working for him." Noyes recalled that Murphy had "had a trading post there [where] he sold Indians coarse white blouses or over shirts for their weight in Gold."[99]

But by far the most well-known early white employer of native labor in the Southern Mines was James D. Savage (the name prompted a French Gold Rush participant to insist that Savage had been kidnapped as a child and raised by Indians).[100] Savage was actually an overland emigrant from Illinois who worked for a time at Sutter's Fort before the Gold Rush began. But by the time the massive influx of immigrants started, in 1849, Savage was already established as an Indian trader to the south of Sutter's Fort in the area that was becoming the Southern Mines. Eventually, he set up trading posts on the Fresno, Mariposa, and Merced rivers; learned a number of Indian dialects; and married several native (probably Miwok and Yokuts) women. Everywhere Savage set Indians to work in the diggings, not only around his Mariposa County trading posts but also to the north at what would become Jamestown and Big Oak Flat in Tuolumne County. White observers consistently described Savage as the acknowledged "chief" of the native communities with whom he was associated, but given the difficulties whites had in understanding Indian habits of social organization, it seems likely that the relationship between Savage and the Miwok and Yokuts workers was more complicated. It is clear that Indians routinely exchanged with Savage the gold they gathered for clothes, blankets, and provisions, just as the native peoples to the north did with John and Daniel Murphy.[101]

The reasons some Miwok and Yokuts people worked for Savage and the Murphy brothers are not hard to imagine. Increasingly, native peoples found themselves hungry and cold as a consequence of invasion and the subsequent decline of animal populations in the foothills. Likewise, they found themselves the target of harassment and violence from immigrant miners. The Reverend Daniel Woods visited one of Savage's camps in the late fall of 1849 and warned that although the Indians there were "*openly* friendly," they in fact harbored a "growing distrust of the emigrant miners," who subjected Indians to "the most cruel and barbarous impositions." Woods predicted that "the time will come when they will seek revenge." He was right. In the meantime, although immigrants responded with outrage at the first signs of Indian resistance, most, like Woods, were well aware of the situation they had created for native peoples in the diggings. Lafayette Houghton Bunnell, who participated in the hostilities that eventually erupted, remembered, "We had sufficient general intelligence . . . to know that we were looked upon as trespassers on [Indians'] territory, but were unwilling to abandon our search for gold." And the *Stockton Times* could not have been clearer about the causes of Indian-immigrant tensions in the Southern Mines: "The complaint on the part of the Indians is that the white men have driven the game from their accustomed haunts; that the rivers which aforetime so abundantly supplied them with fish, cease to afford them food; and that the Americans kill their young men." In circumstances like these, working under the protection of a white man such as Savage and gaining access to immigrant trade goods made sense.[102]

Still, most Sierra Miwoks did not choose this strategy for coping with invasion. Indeed, both Savage and the Murphys probably employed not only Miwoks but Yokuts, whose hunting and gathering grounds lay to the south and west of Miwok territory. The Yokuts were native people who, like the Plains Miwoks, had been forced into Spanish Mexican missions earlier in the century and who generally had more experience with non-Indian labor practices than did those Sierra Miwoks who, up to the time of the Gold Rush, had remained largely beyond the reach of Spanish Mexicans and later European and Anglo settlers such as John Sutter and John Marsh.[103] Hence, it seems likely that proportionately fewer Miwoks worked initially for white men than did Yokuts in the south and Nisenans in the Northern Mines.

Sierra Miwoks did dig for gold, however. Throughout August, September, and October of 1850, for example, Timothy Osborn worked and lived alongside Indian miners near the Merced River, noting in his diary mostly friendly exchanges with his neighbors. The Miwok women and men came and went as they pleased, carrying not only bows, arrows, and animal carcasses, but *bateas* and crowbars as well, indicating that they had begun to supplement customary means of subsistence with mining. Likewise, Friedrich Gerstäcker, passing through Murphys New Diggings in late 1850, encountered a band of Miwoks and watched them dig gold there, noting that Indians in the Southern Mines were far less likely to work for whites than those farther north. These Calaveras County Miwoks labored in family groups, the men breaking up the hard ground with pickaxes and the women and children carrying the gold-bearing dirt off and washing it at the river.[104] Few such early descriptions of Miwok mining practices exist, but it seems likely, given Gerstäcker's account and a scattering of later reports, that women were central in the Miwoks' turn to gold digging. Sam Ward, brother of Julia Ward Howe, lived among Miwok and Yokuts miners at George Belt's ferry and store on the Merced River in 1851 and 1852.[105] There he, like Gerstäcker, saw Indians mining in families, "the father scooping into his *batea* the invisible mud and sand of the riverbed, and the mother bearing it to shore to perform those skillful gyratory manipulations by which the water is made to carry away . . . the earthy matter until . . . there remain at the bottom of the pan the yellow spangles surrendered by the incongruous mass."[106]

Among other Miwok bands, women seem to have assumed responsibility for virtually all aspects of mining. This was the case in early 1851 when Ephraim Delano dug gold at Dusty Bar on the Stanislaus River. There, he wrote to his wife back in Maine, he saw "plenty of the Indian woman at the mines." In fact, he said, "The Woman does the principale part of the Labor I have seen some of the squaws digging gold all day with a Child on there Back slung in a Basket." As late as the summer of 1854, Jean-Nicolas Perlot saw similar sights when he followed Miwok miners deep into the Sierras to what he hoped would be rich diggings along the south fork of the Merced River. Once Perlot and his companions located the Indian placers, they began working nearby—according to Perlot, in perfect amity. Indeed, Perlot seems to have forgotten who first discovered these diggings, noting in his reminiscences, "The Indians worked constantly around us. All the companies let them go freely where it seemed good to them, even in our ditches, to gather paydirt in their pans, carry it on their heads, and go wash it at the river."[107] Perlot was quick to point out who the miners were in this Miwok community: "The women especially did this work; the occupation of the men consisted almost entirely in watching the women's work." In this situation, then, gold digging seems to have been assimilated into women's gathering activities, leaving Miwok men their customary, more episodic work of hunting, fishing, and horse raiding. Perlot probably mistook this symbiotic sexual division of labor for Miwok women's economic independence when he wrote, "I have never seen an Indian woman cede to her husband the gold she gathered, which made me suppose that each one worked for herself." In fact, around the same time, Miwok women also were selling Perlot and his companions fresh salmon—the products of Miwok men's work—indicating the mutual dependence encouraged in native divisions of labor.[108]

Whether Miwok women mined on their own or worked alongside their menfolk, their labor was key to the survival of native peoples in the Southern Mines. When J. D. Borthwick arrived in the vicinity of Mokelumne Hill in 1852 after a stint in the Northern Mines, he was immediately struck by the relative prosperity of the Miwoks, compared with the Nisenans he had seen farther north. Borthwick was sarcastic about the causes of Miwoks' well-being, suggesting that they must have been "a slightly superior race" because they "had more money, and consequently must have had more energy to dig for it." What Borthwick probably did not understand was how different the recent histories of Nisenans and Miwoks had been. Nisenans had lost a great deal of their autonomy well before the onset of the Gold Rush: They were hard hit by malaria in the 1830s; they formed the backbone of John Sutter's Indian labor force in the 1840s; and they, unlike Miwoks, had not engaged in extensive livestock raiding and trading to offset pre–Gold Rush incursions. What Borthwick saw when he compared Nisenans and Miwoks, then, were native peoples differently affected by conquest.[109]

The Miwok practice of livestock raiding—developed decades before to cope first with horse-rich Spanish Mexicans coming from the west and, later, horse-poor Anglo American fur trappers coming from the east—proved particularly adaptable to Gold Rush circumstances.

Immigrant miners falsely attributed all manner of depredations to Indians in the diggings, and they probably exaggerated Miwok livestock raiding as well. But when it came to horse and mule stealing, there was no denying both Miwok propensity and Miwok prowess. Miwok men increasingly came to supplement hunting with livestock raiding, particularly as deer populations declined, so it was not farfetched for immigrants to look about for signs of Indians when they woke up in the morning to a missing mule. The Reverend Daniel Woods put it most simply when he described thefts by Miwoks at Sherlock's Diggings in Mariposa County during November of 1849: "Mules are stolen, and driven away to be eaten." A few days earlier at nearby Agua Fria, George Evans recorded in his diary that local Indians had proved "very troublesome to the miners, having stolen

The Anglo miner John Hovey's rendering of his camp at Red Bluff Bar, with Jenny and Jerico in the foreground. Such mules were favorite targets for native livestock raiders. From the John Hovey Journal.

almost all the mules brought here." But Evans also wrote that these same Indians were meeting with miners a few miles away to "enter a treaty" with them: "[The Indians] seek to camp in some of these ravines during the winter months and wish to first secure a peace with the palefaces now holding possession of their old winter quarters." Peace seems not to have been secured, however, because two days later Evans noted that eighteen mules and several horses were missing when the immigrant men arose for breakfast. The miners gathered to plan revenge, vowing "to follow, kill, and plunder this thieving horde of savages."[110]

Immigrant men were sorely troubled by the loss of their pack animals, but they were also irritated and sometimes frightened by the brazen defiance Miwoks displayed in their interactions with the miners. Alfred Doten wrote about a February 1850 incident in Tuolumne County in which forty miners chased a party of Miwoks assumed to have stolen some mules, only to find the Indians safely ensconced on a hill "in too great numbers to drive them from their position." The Miwoks stood on the hilltop mocking their pursuers, using "the most insulting gestures and language, slapping their arses and daring the Yankees to come up there." Enraged, one of the miners picked off one of the Miwoks with a rifle bullet. Later, the miners retrieved the Indian's bow and arrow as well as his scalp, but they never recovered the mules.[111] Similarly, William Miller and his companion, Mr. Savory, were unnerved one night in March 1850, while en route south from the Tuolumne to the Merced River. They had pitched their tent near an Indian encampment. Later in the evening, an older Miwok man was carried in with a bullet hole in his neck. The women at the camp began to yell and moan and "Kept It up all night," according to Miller. Concerned, Savory helped dress the old man's wound. But neither of the white men could sleep that night, as Indians kept passing near their tent, "Damning the Americans in Spanish." The Miwoks may have known little English, and the Anglos little of whichever Miwok dialect these Indians spoke, but both groups understood enough Spanish for the Miwoks to make clear their general disdain for Anglo invaders, Savory's wound dressing notwithstanding.[112]

Sometimes fear of the consequences of such disdain, along with a fervid belief in widespread Indian "depredations," could unite not only Anglo Americans but French and Mexican miners as well. Such was the case during the winter of 1850–51 around the headwaters of the Calaveras and Mokelumne rivers, an area the *Stockton Times* noted was "in a state of great excitement in consequence of the irruptions of large bodies of the hostile Indians." The newspaper acknowledged that the Miwoks were "irritated by their former sufferings," but complained that "they now murder and rob all that comes within their reach." No longer content to take one or two horses or mules at a time, early in January, "immense swarms of Indians poured down and drove off every animal they could find," or so a white miner told the *Stockton Times*. In response, some number of French, Anglos, and others—two different newspaper articles estimated 100 and 500, respectively—set out after the presumed livestock thieves.[113]

The French men, all accounts agree, were members of the famed Garde Mobile, volunteer troops who had helped suppress street rioting in Paris during the revolution of 1848 but who since, as one historian puts it, "had become somewhat obnoxious." To rid themselves of potential troublemakers, French government officials shipped 140 of the Gardes Mobiles off to California in November 1850. These soldiers ended up in Calaveras County, sporting arms, flags, and other accoutrements of war, much to the dismay of Anglo American miners, who no doubt remembered the past summer's "French Revolution" in Tuolumne County. Tensions ran high, and more than one high-spirited, if not particularly lethal, skirmish erupted. In one threatened conflict, a group of Miwok warriors actually weighed in on behalf of the Anglos, though no war ensued. Another struggle prompted the *Stockton Times* to run a tongue-in-cheek article titled "The Garde Mobile versus the Anglo-Saxon," which closed with assurance that "the Anglo-Saxon was victorious."[114]

But Anglo-French tensions fell by the wayside when neighboring miners banded together to chase supposed Indian livestock thieves. According to two newspaper reports, the miners chased the raiders to the north fork of the Stanislaus River, but found them ensconced "in a bold and strong position," on a table-shaped mountain far above the river bed. It must have been a capacious table, because the *Stockton Times* contended that 500 Indians and "upwards of 700 mules, horses, and cattle" were camped there. Nonetheless, these Miwoks, like those that Doten's neighbors found "slapping their arses and daring the Yankees" from a hilltop, continually "defied the white man" to retrieve the animals. A second article concluded with the kind of suggestion that always put fear in the hearts of Anglo miners—that is, the possibility that a single struggle was actually evidence of a broader, interracial coalition against the majority of white men in the mines. In this case, a participant in the hostilities told the *Times* that he thought the belligerents were actually "a mixture of Northern and Pale Indians, a few 'Niggers' and white men."[115]

After following these events for a couple of weeks, the *Stockton Times* suddenly fell silent, failing to report on how the conflict ended. There could have been a number of reasons for this silence, but one particular explanation suggests itself in an account of the struggle Leonard Noyes recorded in his reminiscences. Noyes was camped near the south fork of the Calaveras River, in the heart of the livestock-stealing area, during the winter of 1850–51. He recalled that cattle and horses regularly were found missing that winter, and the "Indians were charged with being the thieves." Noyes joined the makeshift troops that organized to go after the Indians, a group he remembered as including "50 Americans 25 Mexicans and 75 of the Guard Mobile, French refugees." The soldiers advanced to the Miwok camp near the Stanislaus River. There they planned for the Anglos and Mexicans to circle around behind the camp, which was up in the hills, and then run the Indians toward the waiting French men.[116] But when Noyes's contingent got to the Miwok camp, the Indians were gone. Furthermore, there were "no signs of their ever having Cattle there or Horses as no tracks appeared," though there were "plenty of bins made of bushes very neetly constructed, all filled with Acorns." Some of the Anglos and Mexicans proposed burning the acorn granaries, but others prevented this action because, as Noyes put it, "most of us concluded that we had been lied to in regard to the Indians having stolen the Cattle." Noyes closed his account of this nonengagement by describing how his party fired a few volleys to make their French allies believe that the Anglos and Mexicans had done battle with the Miwoks, and how one man instructed the rest to tell the French men they had encountered fifteen hundred Indians rather than about fifteen (and those "[too] far off to shoot"). "Always after," Noyes recalled, when he would run into one of the Gardes Mobiles, he "got a hearty shake of the hand" for his bravery. If Noyes was correct that the combined Anglo, Mexican, and French troops never saw more than fifteen Indians and never found any sign of stolen livestock, perhaps the *Stockton Times* editors concluded that under these circumstances, no news was the best possible news to print.[117]

There must have been dozens of such not-so-close encounters in the Southern Mines during the early years of the Gold Rush, and thus it is not surprising that one set of incidents finally led to genuinely warlike conditions in the diggings. The Mariposa War began in December of 1850 when native people in the employ of James Savage, while he was away, attacked his trading post on the Fresno River, killing three white men, wounding another, and ransacking the store. According to one account, the Indians took this action most immediately because the men left in charge refused to slaughter a cow for their use. Upon his return, Savage located the attackers and tried to negotiate with them. The Indians tried to negotiate too, asking Savage to join them in war against immigrant miners, or a least to return to his trading post and remain neutral in the hostilities. Savage refused, and in fact signed on as commander of the volunteer force organized to chastise the Indians. This force, known as the Mariposa Battalion, consisted of just over two hundred soldiers, with white frontiersmen from Missouri and Texas overrepresented among them but including as well a strong contingent of white men from New York State, a handful of Europeans, and at least one African American from Philadelphia and one Hispano from New Mexico.[118]

One of the New Yorkers, Robert Eccleston, is the only soldier in the Mariposa Battalion known to have kept a journal during the military campaign, which lasted officially from February to July of 1851.[119] The outbreak of hostilities between Indians and immigrants included not just the contingent that attacked Savage's trading post in December but a broad, if loose, coalition of Miwok, Yokuts, and mixed bands in Mariposa County. Tensions spilled over into Tuolumne and Calaveras counties as well—though the *Stockton Times* may have exaggerated when it reported in late January, "It now appears that with few exceptions the whole of the Indian tribes from the Cosumnes to King's river are in a state of insurrection." A majority of the struggles occurred in Mariposa County, not coincidentally the site of the most widespread white use of native labor in the Southern Mines. Though actual battles took place, Eccleston's diary reveals the Mariposa campaign, for the soldiers, as a tedious pursuit of individual Indian bands through the relentlessly rugged terrain of the Southern Mines' southernmost reaches. The warriors of one band might give themselves up to the troops, calling their womenfolk, children, and elders out of the mountains and taking them down to the plains where the government wanted native people to settle. Meanwhile, another band would keep themselves well in advance of the soldiers, traversing the ravines and canyons of Mariposa County with ease while Eccleston and his comrades lumbered along behind.[120]

Even Savage himself, no stranger to the local geography, had trouble keeping up with Indians. Before the Mariposa Battalion had been mustered in, he chased after three hundred former employees who had attacked and then bolted the Fresno River post. Eccleston noted that Savage "was but an hour behind the Indians in his start & not with standing they were heavily packed could not overtake them . . .

& Savage is no slow traveller." The whole of the Mariposa War was like this. Once, in March, when some of the troops thought they were closing in on the Yosemite band (a mixed group of Miwoks, Paiutes, and Yokuts), they arrived at the *ranchería* only to find it deserted, save a few dogs and a hundred-year-old woman. When the soldiers asked where her people had gone, she retorted, "Go look." Frustrated, the troops burned over five thousand bushels of acorns and "any quality of old Baskets"—all the products of native women's work. Indeed, burning acorn granaries, and sometimes whole *rancherías*, was one of the most common acts of the soldiers, who had such difficulty catching up to the Indians themselves.[121]

Native women (like native men) played contradictory roles in the conflict, from the aged Yosemite woman who baldly defied a detachment of the Mariposa Battalion to a young woman who served as guide to the troops in their campaign against the Chowchilla Yokuts band. This particular woman delighted Eccleston, with her "black & straight hair hung down gracefully upon her shoulders," a scarf "thrown negligently over the left shoulder," her bodice of white muslin and skirt of blue calico, and "her small feet & ankles showed to advantage." Of course, native men also served as guides to the soldiers, though none of them caught Eccleston's eye. Sometimes, women could be used as pawns in the struggle, as when the Nuchu Miwok band, once members had surrendered and agreed to move down to the plains, offered to help the Mariposa Battalion. As Eccleston recorded in his diary, "The chief here offers to send with us 50 warriors to fight against the Yoosemita's providing we give them the women as prisoners." Perhaps Yosemite women were renowned for their work habits. Indeed, when the Mariposa Battalion finally did make contact with the Yosemite band, through the leader named Tenaya, Tenaya balked at the idea of settling in the San Joaquin Valley and receiving government annuities: "We do not want anything from white men. Our women are able to do our work," he boasted.[122]

Whatever role native women and men played in the Mariposa War, some maintained remarkable dignity even in defeat. Benjamin Butler Harris, for example, recalled that when several bands gave themselves up to the troops, a very old woman among them was asked her age. She replied, knowing that her people were being sent to live on the plains, "I am the mother of all these mountains." Surrenders such as these came slowly, however. Six bands signed treaties in March, and another fifteen in April, while others still eluded their pursuers. On hand to sign these treaties were federal Indian commissioners, who would return these and future agreements to the U.S. Senate for ratification.[123] While the treaties showed little or no understanding of or respect for native cultures or modes of subsistence, neither were they stingy in what whites perceived as material benefits. As Eccleston recorded in his diary, the treaties proposed that the Indians settle in the San Joaquin Valley, "allowing them 10 years provision & clothing for 20 yrs, a pair of pants, shirt & blanket every four mo[nth]s to each Indian. They also give them 1 Farmer, a Carpenter, a Schoolmaster & Preacher, and a Blacksmith." Eccleston noted as well James Savage's assessment of such treaties. Savage predicted that not all of the native people would come down out of the mountains, but only "young men & fast travelling women." These would accept government "presents" and build temporary shelters, but then "as soon as they get a good chance, steal a large band of horses & kill a few white men & run back to the mountains."[124]

It did not happen just this way, but Savage was correct to predict that, for the most part, Miwoks would not become reservation dwellers. For one, the treaties negotiated by the federal commissioners were never ratified by the U.S. Senate (in part because of resistance to the treaties from the California state government), though the vote against ratification would not come about until the following year. In the meantime, federal Indian agents and commissioners considered the treaties already in effect, and so spent freely on food and equipment, and granted licenses to traders to operate within the ill-fated reservations. James Savage was one of these licensed traders, and for a little more than a year he settled back into an uneasy peace with those Indians who had gathered, for the time being, down in the valley on the Fresno Reservation—most of them probably Yokuts.[125] But in the summer of 1852, Savage became embroiled in a dispute with a competing trader, Walter Harvey, over native treaty rights; in this case, Savage seems to have taken the Yokuts side in the controversy. Harvey was furious with Savage not so much over their opposing views but over remarks Savage had made questioning his status as a gentleman. In a fight, Harvey shot Savage and killed him. Thus ended the career of the largest employer of native labor in the Southern Mines. As for Harvey, within a year he would join Harry Love's state-sponsored rangers in pursuing the latest lion in the path of Anglo dominance in the diggings—Joaquín Murrieta.[126]

The Mariposa War had a less profound impact on Sierra Miwoks and their allies than one might expect. In Calaveras County, for example, Miwoks continued to combine mining with customary subsistence strategies, using gold to buy what hunting and gathering could no longer supply and what contact with immigrant society made indispensable—especially clothing. When Indians did turn to reservation resources, one historian suggests, they often did so "as part of their seasonal round," though this mixed economy became more difficult to sustain as the decade went by.[127]

Events at Belt's ferry and store on the Merced River illustrate another path Miwoks followed after the war. George Belt had received one of the coveted licenses to trade with native people, and later a contract to supply two groups of Indians with cattle and flour as stipulated by the soon to be unratified treaties of 1851. The native settlements located in and near the Merced Reservation included several bands of Miwoks and one of Yokuts. Sam Ward arrived there late in the summer of that year, anxious to cast his lot with the newest entrepreneurs in the diggings—those investing in quartz mining. Although Ward came from an old and affluent banking family in New York City, he had not been able to maintain family fortunes. On the advice of "an old Chilean miner who had once [overseen] similar works in his native country," Ward and other Anglos eagerly bought shares in a quartz company. One of Ward's fellow shareholders, Henry Drought, also became a partner of Belt's ferry and store. Since Drought preferred to manage his business affairs from San Francisco, he enlisted Ward to watch over operations at the Merced River or, as Ward put it, to "see the hands played out which had been dealt to my friend in the double game of Indian trading at the river and of quartz crushing" at Quartzburg, a few miles east of the ferry and store.[128]

Thus Ward settled in at Belt's, where the Miwok and Yokuts bands had already established their *ranchería* and were hard at work placer mining. Indeed, when Ward first arrived, they had been so successful in the diggings that they had cleaned out the store's shelves of all trade goods. So the proprietors were obliged to sell the Indians a small herd of cattle at reduced rates in order to prevent them from taking their business to a rival trading post. Once Ward assumed his duties, he assessed the situation and concluded, "Unlike most producers . . . our market lay under our eyes; the demand depended . . . upon the success of our consumers in their gold washings." Hence, Ward decided to turn his attentions to "the habits and customs of the Indian tribe," of which he now considered himself "the vicarious *paterfamilias*." A chance visit by James Savage, who was en route to San Francisco and who spoke at length to the Indians at Belt's in their native dialect, convinced Ward that he, too, must learn the Miwoks' language: "My plans were soon formed to approach, if not to rival, the white Savage in this particular influence over the red."[129]

The Miwok miners tried to help Ward with his language lessons, just as they patiently watched him try to learn how to pan for gold sometime later, but there is little evidence that he was a particularly apt pupil. What Ward did learn, however, was how adaptable these native women and men were to changing economic circumstances. Ward taught some of the youngsters to grow melons, while their parents balanced gold digging with gathering, hunting, and fishing. In fact, when a dam built farther down the river prevented salmon from swimming up as far as the *rancheria* at Belt's, Ward intervened on the Indians' behalf and persuaded the immigrant men downstream to remove the obstruction. All over the Southern Mines, Indians like these negotiated their needs with interlopers like Ward. Native people turned immigrant commercial ventures to their immediate advantage when they could, and adjusted to the loss of autonomy gold-centered social and economic relations spelled when they could not. All in all, many Indians in California saw to it that the Gold Rush did not destroy native communities or ways of life, though the dislocations of the former and the transformations of the latter were often monumental in scale.[130]

Miwoks were especially successful in this regard. The Belgian miner Jean-Nicolas Perlot learned this in the years following the Mariposa War, as he pushed up farther into the Sierra Nevada in search of gold. Indeed, while men such as Ward stayed in the foothills investing in quartz mines and trying to profit from licensed Indian trading and federal Indian contracts, Perlot worked to prolong the Gold Rush—a phenomenon centered on the quick exploitation of surface deposits—by ranging far and wide in pursuit of undisturbed placers. In his perpetual prospecting in Mariposa and Tuolumne counties between 1852 and 1854, Perlot found Indians there engaged in a wide variety of activities. During the hard winter of 1852–53, for example, Miwoks from the Tuolumne River area seized Perlot's only pack animal ("alas! our donkey, our poor donkey," Perlot recalled), and killed it for food, leaving only the head and hooves behind. And that spring, Perlot ran into three Miwok men who were hunting— safer work, when Indians could find it. After exchanging friendly greetings, Perlot realized that he had met one of the men many months before along the Fresno River, when the man had helped Perlot balance a heavy load of supplies on a mule.[131] And in the fall, when camped along the Merced River, Perlot watched Miwok women gathering a cornucopia of seeds and berries in the neighborhood. One morning in October, however, Perlot awoke to the sound of native women and men "singing, and running with all the speed which with they were capable in the direction of the Merced." This coming and going went on for two days, and Perlot began to worry that the Indians might be preparing for battle. But then two Mexican men passed by who understood something of the local Miwok dialect. They informed Perlot that the words of the song he kept hearing meant simply, "The acorn has fallen." What Perlot was witnessing was the start of the annual celebration that marked the beginning of the acorn harvest. He was a bit chagrined: "Those whom we saw passing by . . . , so noisy and joyful, were therefore not animated by . . . bellicose intentions," Perlot recalled, "they were going to celebrate the acorn festival."[132]

It was in the following year, however, 1854, that Perlot saw Miwok women regularly passing by his camp en route to Coulterville, in Mariposa County, or Garrote (later Groveland), in Tuolumne County. On their way to town, the women traveled unencumbered, but on their return they walked with heavy baskets of flour carried on their heads. Perlot concluded that these women must be coming from rich Indian placers located up in the mountains. So he decided to inquire about these diggings with Indians he knew—a man Perlot called "Flesno" (because this was the fellow who helped Perlot with his mule on the Fresno, which Perlot thought Miwoks pronounced "Flesno") and one named Juan, with whom Perlot could communicate in Spanish. Juan and "Flesno" eventually led Perlot to these placers, where Perlot entered a world seldom encountered by white Gold Rush participants. It was here that he saw Miwok women at work in the mines, those who he thought ceded none of the gold they gathered to their husbands. It was here that he talked with the leader of a Miwok band—José, father of Juan and Scipiano—who had memorized his people's treaty rights by heart. And it was here that he met with José's son, Scipiano, who spoke his desires to Perlot with the hope that this relatively sympathetic white man might have some influence with those who lived below: "Look for *l'olo* (gold) where you want, let the *Ochà* (Indian woman) seek her seeds where they are and *Oulai Nang-à Blanco* (and the Indian will be the friend of the White)."[133]

Of course, immigrants did not invade Miwok gathering and hunting grounds to find friends, but to get gold, and the mutual respect that came to characterize Perlot's interactions with Miwoks—often a grudging respect on Perlot's part—was the exception rather than the rule in the Southern Mines. Perhaps it was Perlot's ascribed status as a "foreigner" in California that helped shape his own historical memory of Indian-immigrant relations there.[134] For men like Perlot knew what it was either to steer clear of white Americans bent on economic dominance or to negotiate an interdependent existence on the margins of Anglo settlement—margins that were centers for those Miwok, Mexican, Chilean, and French people who survived the "wars" of 1850 and 1851. Still, European men—Belgians like Perlot along with the majority of French-speaking immigrants who came from France—stood a far better chance of insinuating themselves into the dominant culture and class of the Southern Mines, where law and custom barred Latin Americans, native peoples, and also African Americans from even the prospect of free participation in civic and economic life there. This would also be true for Chinese immigrants, who began to pour into the Southern Mines only in 1852, once these initial ethnic and economic tensions had been resolved largely in white Americans' favor.

After the Chilean War, the Mariposa War, and the "French Revolution," middle-class Anglo men—for more and more there *was* a recognizable middle class in the mines—asserted control in a variety of ways. They bought up water rights and sold use of the water to men who persisted in the declining placers; they invested in quartz mining; and, perhaps most significantly, they sent for their wives and other female relatives from the East. Together, these white women and men would seek to realize their vision of "good and congenial society" in the Southern Mines. And they, particularly the men among them, would also remember the boom years of the Gold Rush in a manner that would obscure much of what these pages recall—that is, a Gold Rush in which some of the riches of the Southern Mines may have sailed off to Mexico in the hands of Rosa Felíz de Murrieta, widow of the late Joaquín.

Part III

Bust

Chapter 5

Dreams That Died

It was autumn 1852, and Miwok people were facing their fifth acorn harvest since Gold Rush immigrants had arrived in the foothills. The Mariposa War was over. The foreign miners' tax had come and gone. In the town of Sonora, a local correspondent to the *San Joaquin Republican*, a Stockton newspaper, sat down to pen a column entitled "Enterprise at Sonora." His was a booster's prose, designed to lure even more settlers to the town "at the centre of the placer diggings." He was writing about Sonora, but to speak of Sonora was to speak of the Southern Mines. And to speak of the Southern Mines in late 1852 was to speak of change—change that had occurred already, change that was now underway. From the correspondent's point of view, change was all to the good. "Since the first settlement of this country by the Americans," he wrote, "the southern mines have been filled with foreigners." No more. Now, he bragged, "We see around us in every direction the results of the indomitable energy and perseverance of an American population."

What did American energy and perseverance look like? First and foremost, they looked like huge canals that took water from rivers such as the Stanislaus and Tuolumne and diverted it to the mines, so that paydirt could be washed not just during the rainy season, but in the dry summer months as well. American energy and perseverance had an urban look as well: towns like Sonora boasting broad streets and fireproof buildings. And there were churches, printing offices, newspapers, and express companies, which the correspondent thought spoke well "for the morality, intelligence and enterprise of our citizens." In Sonora, there was a schoolhouse and a post office, as well as a hotel with "neat and well supplied tables," "attentive and obliging servants," and "clean and well appointed rooms." Not only in Sonora but in the nearby communities of Jamestown, Columbia, Shaw's Flat, and Springfield as well, there were "neat cottages, surrounded with gardens," evidence of that which white miners had found lacking in the boom years of the Gold Rush: "domestic comfort." Finally, American energy and perseverance looked like a world in motion. With pride, the correspondent described the four daily stages that arrived in Sonora from Stockton, and the innumerable conveyances that traveled on the hour between Sonora and surrounding towns, all of which gave "our mountain city an air of bustle and activity."[1] Elaborate waterworks in the diggings; permanent buildings, community institutions, and conventional family homes in the towns; transportation to the outside world; a population becoming more "American" than "foreign"—to more than one white man's eye, these were welcome signs of change in the Southern Mines.

All observers agreed that the mining regions were changing, but different observers measured the causes, extent, and consequences of change differently. Although the identity of the Sonora correspondent is lost to the historical record, that of a writer from Amador County who published in San Francisco's *The Golden Era* is clear. Signing herself "Lenita," Lorena Hays was an unmarried white woman who had accompanied her widowed mother from Illinois to California in 1853. She was twenty-seven years old when her columns first appeared in the paper. Writing in September 1854 about change in California, Lenita was less sanguine, and a good deal more prescriptive, than the Sonora correspondent.[2] Of course, she was living in a mining camp called Cook's Bar, not a thriving town like Sonora. And hers was not a booster's voice, but rather a voice for reform in California. Still, some of the differences between her column and that of the Sonora writer are differences in perspective attributable to ideas about and experiences of gender that were becoming more common in the Southern Mines during the 1850s. These ideas and experiences originated among Anglo Americans who were struggling to constitute a middle class in the mines. And struggle they did. White people who identified with the project of American nationhood generally took for granted that they *should* achieve and sustain economic and cultural dominance in the diggings, but they did not necessarily agree about the process. Sometimes their disagreements followed lines of gender.

Recall that the Sonora correspondent, probably an Anglo American man, found the locus of change in the Southern Mines in such accoutrements as flumes, fireproof buildings, and family homes. Lenita took another tack. Advances in mining and construction were important, and Lenita remarked that Cook's Bar boasted "a number of very good buildings." Nonetheless, the water ditch in her neighborhood was under repair, and so miners were idle. The kind of "American energy and perseverance" that the Sonora correspondent heralded, in her view, was not enough to bring about change in California. For just as quickly as a flume could be built or a ditch dug, it could fail. Then men, whom Lenita did not hesitate to call "children of a larger growth," had a surfeit of energy and a lack of employment, and got themselves into a world of trouble. The answer, for Lenita, was reform. Rhetorically, she asked, "Shall California be a 'lesser light' in the moral firmament?" Certainly not. Her adopted state would yet "become a light among nations": "But where are we to look for this influence—the lever that is to set the ball in motion? Towards what point are we to look for the light that is to break forth as sunlight to purify, cleanse, and irradiate our moral atmosphere? Where is the star that is to illumine our social horizon?" The lever, the point of light, she boasted, was "WOMAN." It was foolish to think that "man, all-powerful as he is," could do the work of reform alone, while woman's hands were "folded in luxury, thus tacitly giving consent to the vice and immorality in which our land abounds." Privately, in her diary, Lorena Hays wondered what caused vice and immorality in California: "Is it because of our peculiar situation—the mixed and incongruous mass of our population or the predominance of the male element in society, or is the evil attributable to inefficient Legislation[?]" But publicly and privately, she was sure that "WOMAN"—by which she meant white, middle-class, Protestant women—would be instrumental in bringing about a cure.[3]

Between them, Lenita and the Sonora correspondent provide a good, if interested, introduction to the transformations that characterized the Southern Mines beginning in 1852 and intensifying throughout the rest of the decade. The changes hinged on two processes already in motion. The first was the consolidation of Anglo American dominance, which had been established through such conflicts as the Chilean War, the Mariposa War, and the "French Revolution."[4] The second was the decline of rich placer diggings, which encouraged some to develop new ways of seeking wealth. As important were the increasingly close ties between local political and economic contests, on the one hand, and national and international developments, on the other. It was by these developments that a gold rush which had been global in scope came to be seen as *the* Gold

Rush, an episode in American nation building. As a part of this process, the Southern Mines began to slip from view.

The consolidation of Anglo dominance, the decline of the placers, and the tightening bond between the Southern Mines and eastern centers of power had different but complementary effects in the smaller world of the diggings and the larger foothill world within which gold-based economic practices were embedded. Because all of these causes and effects were so deeply interrelated, it is impossible to sort into neat categories things pertaining to mining and things pertaining to the complex human communities that emerged in and around the diggings. But by 1852, class relations indigenous to the Southern Mines had begun to take shape. These were relations rooted firmly in the productive process of gold mining. They were also relations rooted in the continuing—though slowly diminishing—demographic predominance of men in immigrant communities and in the tacit agreement among those men that mining was the "work" of the Gold Rush. Here, then, I return to the diggings, which white men scrambled to preoccupy, battling Chinese miners with one hand and Anglo "monopolists" with the other.

Consider first the consolidation of Anglo American dominance, an always unfinished process that required constant vigilance and considerable solidarity on the part of white Americans. Events such as the 1849 Chilean War and the imposition of the foreign miners' tax in 1850 drove many Spanish- and French-speaking gold seekers from California altogether. But others stayed, especially in the Southern Mines. Among those who remained, some moved far out of the reach of Anglos, as when Jean-Nicolas Perlot headed up into the Sierra Nevada in search of Miwok placers or when Mexicans and Chileans— including, it is said, Joaquín Murrieta—congregated in Spanish-speaking communities such as Hornitos, in Mariposa County. As for native peoples, after the 1851 Mariposa War, most continued to combine mining and customary subsistence strategies, here walking to immigrant settlements to trade gold dust for flour, there fanning out among the oaks to gather acorns. But now a new population of Gold Rush participants appeared on the scene: immigrants from South China. Some Chinese had arrived in California as early as 1848, but the majority came beginning in 1852. Unlike Mexican and Chilean gold seekers, Chinese immigrants did not settle disproportionately in the Southern Mines, but instead spread out over all of California's mining districts, including the Northern Mines and the Shasta-Trinity diggings in the far northwest. Nonetheless, they came in great numbers to the south. Indeed, by the end of the decade, Chinese immigrants made up one-fifth of the population of the four counties that constituted the Southern Mines.[5]

When they arrived in towns such as Mariposa and Mokelumne Hill or moved to remote camps in Amador and Tuolumne counties, they entered areas with a recent history of intense racial and ethnic conflict, conflict that had been resolved largely in Anglo Americans' favor. So, like the Mexicans who built Hornitos or those Miwoks who pushed up into the mountains, many Chinese steered clear of white Americans (and sometimes of Mexicans and Miwoks as well), buying up placer claims that Anglos thought were played out or working in jobs that white people shunned. Chinese gold seekers could not, of course, avoid all conflict. They, too, would face a foreign miners' tax, in addition to daily indignities at the hands of other Gold Rush participants. Their patterns of resistance and accommodation were predicated on the prior establishment of Anglo American dominance in the diggings; no "Chinese War" or "Chinese Revolution" ever disturbed the uneasy peace of the Southern Mines.

Consider as well the decline of the placers. Scholars who talk about change over time in western mining generally describe a steady progression from individualized, surface (placer) mining to industrialized, underground (vein or lode or quartz) mining. As an intermediate stage between placer and quartz techniques, they sometimes include the exploitation of deposits called deep gravels. Miners worked such deposits through tunnels, and they also turned to "hydraulicking"—a kind of glorified placer mining in which men shot extraordinarily powerful streams of water against hills thought to be rich in gravels. In California, the Northern Mines roughly followed this trajectory of industrialization. The Southern Mines, on the other hand, industrialized only by fits and starts. There were notable exceptions, especially in Mariposa and Amador counties. But relatively sparse deposits suitable for hydraulic or quartz mining meant that industrialization was the exception rather than the rule. That is, quartz mines financed by moneyed men and worked by hired hands did not come to characterize mining in the south nearly so much as in the north. Instead, persistent placers were the rule.

The world of surface mining, however, did change substantially after the boom years. One key transformation involved the increasing number of Chinese at work in the placers. There was another shift, too. Anglo American entrepreneurs, frustrated by declining yields and weary of backbreaking work, hit on a moneymaking scheme tailor-made for the Southern Mines, which early on had been known as the "dry diggings." Such businessmen banded together to form water companies, building systems of ditches and flumes and then selling use of the water they tapped to placer miners, who needed it to wash gold-bearing dirt. These water company officials became part of the first real Gold Rush elite. Company directors, along with mining town merchants and professionals, were among the first Anglo men to send for their female relatives from the East, and so gender and race relations took on new class meanings as well.[6] All of this inaugurated a set of social relations that pit groups of white men against one another. Independent white miners, a dying breed, took to struggling against "water monopolies" and "striking" for lower water rates. But the culture of placer mining and the decline of rich diggings put limits on collective resistance. As a result, truncated class formations emerged, and miners set their sights on new bonanzas elsewhere in the North American West.

Finally, consider the ways in which the transformations of the 1850s tied the Southern Mines ever more tightly to the political and economic capitals of Anglo America in the East. The diggings continued to draw emigrants not just from the eastern United States but from around the world. Increasingly, however, newcomers, relative old-timers, and native peoples alike were incorporated into, and sometimes excluded from, communities on the basis of political and economic cultures that took their cues from the East. Local representatives to state and national legislatures, large water companies, county court systems, quartz mining investors, even a local landowner who ran for president: these entities and these people demonstrated that the Southern Mines—no matter who lived there—was becoming not just a more Anglo American place but a place obliged to eastern centers of power. That is to say that Gold Rush participants and observers began to map local relations of domination onto national relations of gender, race, economics, and politics—as explosive as these were in the decade before the U.S. Civil War. But social relations in the Southern Mines were crucially different from those in eastern places. This in part is why they have proven so difficult to remember in the century and a half that has passed since.

The social relations of gold seeking, always in flux, convulsed in the early 1850s. First, Chinese men burst into a world of work already fraught with contention and inequity. Second, white entrepreneurs began to channel river water through flumes and sell use of the water to struggling miners. Many expected a third shift, too: a transition from placer mining to the exploitation of quartz gold and deep gravels. This shift never took hold in the Southern Mines the way it did in the Northern Mines, because there were fewer such deposits in the south. Unaware of this geologic disparity, however, miners to the south lived in anticipation of a boom in quartz or gravels. In a few isolated spots, their hopes (and fears) were realized. The most noted of these was the Mariposa Estate, owned by the famed explorer John C. Frémont. There the dream of unlocking subterranean wealth turned for many to a local nightmare, in which bogeymen from eastern and European capitals haunted the Southern Mines.

All of these changes, both actual and anticipated, were caught up in the steady decline of rich surface deposits, which began just as soon as gold seekers swarmed into Miwok hunting and gathering grounds in 1848. By 1852, the average daily yield for placer miners was less than a third of what it had been in 1848—just $6, down from a high of $20 in the year following the gold discovery. Frustrated miners were sure the decline was even steeper. In 1851, for example, A. W. Genung wrote home from Tuolumne County that he had given up on making his "pile" quickly, complaining, "It can be done only by a slow and laborious process." Genung believed that "the first digging of the river banks and beds of the creeks . . . gave from four to six ounces a day," or $64 to $96. Provisions ran $5 a day, and a glass of whiskey cost $2. "The second digging and washing," he wrote, "which I arrived in time to get a parting glance at, gave from one to 2½ ounces per day," or $16 to $40. Daily provisions went for $3, and a glass of whiskey sold for 50 cents. Now, he thought, an individual miner made only $4 or $5 each day. Daily provisions cost him a dollar, and a glass of whiskey set him back 12 or 13 cents. Genung nonetheless predicted that the area would "all be worked over again at one or two dollars per day," adding, "I don't wish to be here then." An 1853 correspondent to the *San Joaquin Republican* put such disillusionment in similarly blunt terms: "California, is herself, no more. The mines are much too crowded for all to do well."[7]

Most Chinese gold seekers arrived in California during this season of dashed hopes, taking up placer claims others abandoned. Perhaps because they had missed the earliest days of the Gold Rush, or perhaps because most could not communicate easily with their disappointed neighbors, or perhaps because circumstances in their homeland were dire, Chinese miners did not seem to share white men's pessimism. By all reports, this lack of pessimism served them well. As late as 1858, an Amador County newspaper reported that Chinese men were digging gold not at some remote foothill stream but at the creek that ran right through the center of Jackson, the county seat. Although this was ground that had been "worked over at least a dozen times," the paper said, the men were making "from $2.50 to $8 per day to the hand" and showing off specimens that weighed from an ounce to six ounces each. Similar reports appeared in newspapers from other counties in the Southern Mines. In 1854, for example, a Mariposa County paper noted that the Guadalupe mining district had "gone over to China," and that the men there were making from $3 to $5 per day. And in Calaveras County in 1856, a newspaper remarked that in just three months, Chinese miners had bought up over $21,000 worth of claims along the Mokelumne River. Employing the name Anglo Americans used for all Chinese men in California, "John Chinaman," the paper noted that such purchases proved the value of area mines, since "John is a good judge of diggings, a close prospector, and a successful miner." These, of course, were reports of especially fortunate Chinese miners, but they indicate that a "slow and laborious process" could still yield plenty of gold a good half dozen years after A. W. Genung penned his complaints.[8]

Chinese men took much of that gold out of claims such as those staked out along the Mokelumne River in 1856. Over the course of the 1850s, in fact, river mining increasingly became the province of Chinese gold seekers. In the last days of 1850, for example, Timothy Osborn, mining along Little Humbug Creek in Tuolumne County, noted in his diary that a group of Chinese men had set up camp nearby. This early-arriving Chinese party mined in the same area and probably used the same methods Osborn did, shoveling bucket after bucket of gold-bearing dirt and washing it out in a rocker. As for himself, though he had been in the diggings only six months, Osborn was tired of it all: "I am sick . . . of the dog life of a miner . . . and would give all I have to be at home . . . and *forget* the word California and *never* hear it spoken again!!" He left the diggings for good just days later, settling in the supply center of Stockton. Meanwhile, Chinese men poured into the areas white men like Osborn left behind. Some continued to work at out-of-the-way spots such as the Little Humbug, but more and more, Chinese miners turned their attention to claims along the major rivers of the Southern Mines— the Cosumnes, the Mokelumne, the Calaveras, the Stanislaus, the Tuolumne, and the Merced. Indeed, by late 1853, Osborn wrote from Stockton that the Chinese had a "'life lien' upon the rivers" of his old stomping grounds. And just as Chinese miners had bought up the claims along the Mokelumne River in 1856, a Mariposa newspaper noted in 1857 that Chinese men were busy working the bed of the Merced: "The whole flat along the river has been staked off by them."

Rumor had it, in fact, that these miners recently had unearthed a seven-pound piece of gold. Such a lump would have been worth almost $1,800.[9]

True or not, reports like these must have galled white men who had given up on gold as well as those who hung fire in the mines. For those, like Timothy Osborn, who left the diggings, Chinese miners' accomplishments belied the Anglo axiom that the placers were all but played out. For those who stayed but complained about decline, Chinese success made white men seem like whiners. Anglos knew that the river claims Chinese men mined already had been worked by teams of Americans and Europeans, who diverted water by means of dams and flumes and then washed out the gold-bearing dirt in exposed riverbeds using rockers, long toms, or sluices. It must have been hard to see Chinese men come in and repeat this labor to good account, sometimes using pumps to help remove water that lingered in the riverbed.[10] After all, many Anglos had struggled during the first years of the Gold Rush to circumscribe both the presence and the activities of non-Anglos so as to gain, as far as it was practicable, pre-emptive access to California's riches.[11] Once reasonably secure in that access, however, Anglo miners found that digging gold simply was not as easy as it had been in 1849. In response, many left altogether, while others adapted not only labor practices but their own expectations in order to cope with changed conditions. But just as they made this transition, a new group of gold seekers arrived on the scene. The "wars" and "revolutions" of 1850 to 1851 were fresh in Anglo men's minds—conflicts in which Miwoks, Mexicans, Chileans, French, and other Europeans in the Southern Mines tried to stand their ground against white Americans. So Anglo response to the influx of Chinese and to their enterprise in the diggings was swift indeed.

Some white men were content to deny that enterprise altogether, ridiculing Chinese mining practices as crude and inefficient. One effective way to do this was to feminize Chinese men, as the Scottish writer and artist J. D. Borthwick did when he published his account of an 1852–53 tour of the diggings. Borthwick claimed that the "individual labor" of Chinese men "was nothing compared with that of other miners." He maintained that the Chinese lacked the "force" and "vigor" of the Americans and Europeans, that they handled their mining tools "like so many women, as if they were afraid of hurting themselves." Indeed, Borthwick noted, American men called Chinese mining methods "scratching."[12] Some of this was sheer silliness, as Chinese involvement in large-scale river mining showed. But there was some truth to the contention that many Chinese men mined in ways that differed from those of than other gold seekers. Many did, for example, limit their gold-washing tools to the smaller rocker rather than the larger long tom or sluice.[13] They did so in large part because of discrimination. Chinese soon learned that whites would not hesitate to expel groups of Chinese men from mining claims. Smaller tools simply were easier to gather up and cart to new diggings when the need arose—hence the reputation for the "backwardness" of Chinese placer mining.[14] Calling the use of such techniques womanish, of course, was deeply ironic, since these were techniques most white men had used—sometimes only months earlier. Where Chinese men only "scratched" the surface, they learned to do so chiefly from white men, who also guaranteed by their discriminatory actions that the portable rocker would become the Chinese miner's stock-in-trade.

For many white gold seekers, the situation called for more than dismissing their new neighbors as men with small tools, which they handled "like so many women." For such white men, expulsion seemed the better solution. One of the first widely reported attempts to drive Chinese miners from the Sierra Nevada foothills occurred in the Southern Mines.[15] It came less than halfway into the first year of increased Chinese immigration—1852—and just two weeks after an alarmed Governor John Bigler addressed the California state legislature on the dangers such immigrants represented. Tellingly, it happened at the site of the most vociferous French, Mexican, and Chilean resistance to the foreign miners' tax of 1850, the town of Columbia, in Tuolumne County.[16] In May of 1852, San Francisco's *Alta California* declared that the people of Columbia had proven themselves "entirely without a precedent or a parallel in their hatred and hostility for the Chinese." Men of that town, styling themselves simply "the miners," had passed in a mass meeting resolutions designed to assure that "no Asiatic or South Sea Islander" would work in local diggings. The resolutions included a charge to create a vigilance committee that would both enforce exclusion in Columbia and encourage white men throughout the Southern Mines to follow suit.[17]

"The miners," however, singled out for verbal abuse not only Chinese men but those "shipowners, capitalists, and merchants" who supported "the importation of these burlesques on humanity." The resolutions argued that such moneyed men loved California's "rocks and rills" as well as "her woods and templed hills" only for the "gold they can filch from the one, and the lumber they can obtain from the other." A man named John A. Palmer (of whom, more anon) chaired the meeting, while the secretary was Thaddeus Hildreth, widely cred-

ited among white people as the man who "discovered" gold at
Columbia in 1850—though by most accounts, Mexicans mined there
first.[18] In choosing Hildreth as secretary, "the miners" chose one who
could represent them in both senses of the word: he could stand for
them literally in dealings with those outside their group—Hildreth,
no doubt, reproduced and circulated the miners' resolutions—and he
could stand for them symbolically as well. In his role as "discoverer"
of gold at Columbia, Hildreth embodied white miners' own best
hopes for themselves as independent producers, untrammeled from
above by "shipowners, capitalists, and merchants," unabased from
below by Chinese "burlesques on humanity." Here, then, is a
moment of conception (again, in both senses of the word) for a
homegrown working class in California's Southern Mines, in which
white miners figured themselves as humanity itself, over and against
Chinese "burlesques," and as husband-like lovers of California, over
and against rapacious "shipowners, capitalists, and merchants."[19]

As this bold characterization suggests, by 1852 the fissure that
started to separate miners from merchants during the fight over the
1850 foreign miners' tax was widening. The divide yawned wider
when California's legislature settled on a new foreign miners' tax as a
way of dealing with Chinese men in the diggings. In 1852, legislators
debated a variety of measures designed to regulate Chinese immigrants, from laws that would have made labor contracts drawn up
abroad enforceable in California (a favorite of the men miners called
"capitalists") to those that would have expelled Chinese from the
mines altogether (a popular idea among white miners). In a sense,
reviving the foreign miners' tax was a compromise between these two
extremes, though one that ultimately leaned toward merchants'
interests over those of white miners.[20]

At first, however, merchants and their allies—notably newspaper
editors—worried that a new tax would simply bring back old troubles. The *San Joaquin Republican*—which, under its first banner, the
Stockton Times, had denounced the earlier tax—could not forget that
the 1850 bill had "convulsed society in the southern mineral region."
What the Southern Mines lost in 1850, and stood to lose again in
1852, were prospectors, laborers, and customers, though now these
were Chinese:

Have not this race of men . . . discovered new placers, and been . . .
the hewers of wood and drawers of water for *our* citizens? In the
cities are they not our attendants in our houses, and in our public rooms? Do they not wash our shirts? The Chinese, in this

city alone, must expend, and thus throw into circulation, money to the amount of $500 a day, at the very smallest calculation. This money goes into the hands of our merchants.

The Stockton editor denounced the 1852 act as "The Dog in the Manger Bill," but in fact legislators did seem to recall the 1850 fiasco.[21] This time around, they levied a foreign miners' tax at a substantially lower rate—three dollars per month as opposed to the earlier twenty dollars a month, a rate that had driven so many Spanish- and French-speaking gold seekers out of the mines.

The 1852 tax did not scare Chinese miners away.[22] To be sure, some resisted paying the fee. In 1855, for example, groups of Chinese men attacked collectors of the foreign miners' tax at least twice, once in Tuolumne County and once in Mariposa County. In each case, the tax collectors survived, but one or more Chinese lay dead by the end of the incident.[23] More common was the kind of evasion described by a white man who had been a young boy in Mariposa County in the 1850s and 1860s. He recalled that the "tax collectors had a hard time collecting," because when Chinese men saw one coming "they would run & hide in holes & some would climb trees."[24] But many Chinese must have decided to pay the moderate fee and go on about their business. Indeed, by 1856, the once-worried *San Joaquin Republican* could blithely report that Tuolumne County received more revenue from the foreign miners' tax than from any other single source, including property taxes.[25] What had once been a bugbear was now a bullish sign of growth.

White miners generally did not see it that way. Shortly after the tax became law, the *Alta California* drew a sharp contrast between what increasingly were class-motivated points of view—one a vision of those who were coming to constitute an Anglo middle class (a vision shared by a majority of state officials), and the other belonging to Anglo miners. "The difficulty now," the editors wrote, "is to reconcile" the two perspectives—the first, which condoned "licensing foreigners to work the mines for a consideration," and the second, which refused "to let them work upon any consideration."[26] The *Alta California* cast its lot with those who stood to benefit from a foreign miners' tax—the emerging white middle class and the state. Anglo miners, meanwhile, continued to oppose the tax. Six months after the act's passage, for example, a constituent wrote from Tuolumne County to the state legislator James Mandeville, reminding him, "As regards the Foreign Tax Bill you are well aware of the opinions of a large portion of the American Miners That is we want no tax levied on them except such as will amount to a prohibition."[27] The foreign miners' tax of 1852 never amounted to a prohibition on Chinese labor, and thus the "American Miners" lost their bid for exclusion. Instead, the tax survived through the 1860s and became a key source of revenue for the new American state of California.[28]

Although Anglo miners railed against the "shipowners, capitalists, and merchants" who flooded the state with "degraded Asiatics" and forced a "system of peonage" on the mines, there is no evidence that a group of Americans orchestrated Chinese immigration and imposed upon Chinese miners a system of coerced labor. As historians of Asian America have shown, most Chinese men came to California having paid for their own passage or having borrowed the fare, intending to repay it out of their earnings as miners.[29] Contrary to white miners' beliefs, the vast majority of Chinese men were not unfree workers. A Stockton restaurateur insisted on this to newspapermen in the spring of 1852: "Chinese John . . . requests us, flatly, to contradict the statement which is going the round of the papers . . . that his countrymen come to California either as slaves or under contract."[30] Entrepreneurial Americans who introduced unfree Chinese labor in the mines were few and far between.

The arrival of Chinese in the diggings, however, coincided with the growth of local capitalist enterprise that threatened the autonomy of white placer miners. In the minds of white miners, then, the two phenomena must have seemed related, since anti-Chinese and anticapitalist agitation shaded into one another and drew in common from emerging languages of class.[31] In the Northern Mines, large mining companies represented the greatest threat to individual miners. But in the south, where a relative lack of deposits suitable for hydraulic or quartz mining was matched by an abundance of persistent placers, large water companies took center stage. As a result, in the Southern Mines, antipathy toward Chinese miners and white water company managers went hand in glove.

In fact, on the very day that the *Alta California* reported Columbia's mass meeting to expel Chinese miners, the paper also ran a notice that the Tuolumne County Water Company had succeeded in bringing water to Columbia through a ditch that connected the diggings to Five Mile Creek, a tributary of the Stanislaus River: "Their race is complete at last!—and the water is actually running through it! Hundreds, we say thousands of miners are rejoicing." These men may not have rejoiced for long, since the race was small and the company's flumes were built with green timber that warped and shrank. The grand potential of the company would not be realized until a larger race, then still under construction, reached the Stanislaus itself and tapped the waters of that formidable river for the Columbia placers.[32] But when miners saw that first fledgling ditch fill with water from a distant creek, their relief must have been alloyed with unease. Water had always been scarce in the Southern Mines, but its use had been free. Now it might be more plentiful, but miners would have to pay to use it. And those they would have to pay looked a good deal like "capitalists" in the making: in the case of the Tuolumne County Water Company (TCWC), a group of men who formed a joint stock corporation capitalized at more than $200,000.[33]

White miners' unease did not erupt immediately into opposition to this or any other of the many water companies that were organized in the Southern Mines.[34] Indeed, the anger that erupted at this historical moment was aimed at Chinese miners and only incidentally at Anglo "capitalists." But the timing of the anti-Chinese meeting at Columbia along with its anticapitalist tenor suggests that white miners' twin anxieties about the flow of water and the influx of Chinese compounded each other. When Anglo miners finally did cry out against the TCWC, another connection between anti-Chinese and anticapitalist impulses emerged. For its first years of operation, the TCWC was the only venture of its kind in the vicinity of Columbia, though smaller ditches brought water to placer claims elsewhere in the county. Hence the company was able to command high prices. In January of 1853, just eight months after the anti-Chinese meeting, white miners gathered again in Columbia, this time to protest the exorbitant rates they paid for the use of water supplied by the TCWC. These miners likely resembled the group that voted for Chinese expulsion, since they chose as their chairman John A. Palmer—the same man who had chaired the anti-Chinese meeting. As the conflict between white miners and the TCWC unfolded over the next two years, Palmer continued to serve as a leader.[35] It would not be until 1855 that the miners succeeded in forcing the company's hand, but the 1853 meeting did serve to unite them against the TCWC and to broadcast their complaints far and wide.[36]

Anti-Chinese activity in the diggings continued throughout the 1850s, but not with the same intensity as in 1852. White miners came to tolerate the foreign miners' tax as a means of policing and exacting tribute from Chinese miners. And Chinese men themselves carefully orchestrated their gold seeking in order to minimize contact and conflict with Anglo Americans, concentrating their efforts in river claims abandoned by white men and using mining tools that were easy to carry off to new diggings when Anglo hostility erupted.

Beyond the mining districts, white men committed a range of anti-Chinese acts; they attacked Chinese brothels, for example, and also turned armed struggles between rival groups of Chinese men into a spectator sport for Anglos.[37] In the diggings, however, an aggrieved and anxious peace emerged.

Even as anti-Chinese agitation quieted in the Southern Mines, proliferating water companies continued to worry white miners into the mid-1850s. If debates over the proper response to Chinese in the diggings revealed the outlines of emerging class divisions among Anglo American men, then arguments about water companies laid those divisions bare. No longer did white miners inveigh against nameless "shipowners, capitalists, and merchants"; now gold seekers targeted local white businessmen who had pooled resources to create large enterprises such as the TCWC and its counterpart in Calaveras County, the Mokelumne Hill Canal and Mining Company. In the end, environmental limits and cultural constraints militated against sustained consolidation of white miners' interests. Though stillborn, the white working class in counties such as Calaveras and Tuolumne had a momentous gestation.

Documentation for Tuolumne County, home of the TCWC, is by far the richest.[38] Company records reveal the process by which managers, beginning in 1852, bought up land in the Stanislaus River drainage on which the TCWC constructed flumes, cut tunnels, and shoveled out reservoirs. The company also purchased working ditches dug previously by individual miners or smaller water or mining companies. Prices for these land transactions ranged from a low of $25 for a tunnel near Gold Springs to a high of $8,000 for the extensive Yankee Hill Ditch. In addition, company men took up individual 160-acre claims that were then used as TCWC reservoir sites.[39] These managers set their own salaries at $7 or $8 per day (in addition to stock dividends as they became available) and then paid laborers, such as ditch diggers and ditch tenders, at a rate of $5 a day.[40] Wages fluctuated—and generally dropped—over the course of the 1850s, though those who managed the TCWC lost proportionately less over time than those who tended the company's growing system of flumes, tunnels, and reservoirs.[41]

Meanwhile, no company besides the TCWC had succeeded in bringing water to the rich placer claims of the Columbia mining district. So gold seekers there were compelled to pay the $6 per day demanded for the use of water. By March of 1855, miners had had enough. They held a mass meeting in Columbia and drafted resolutions in which they pledged themselves collectively to refuse to patronize the TCWC until the price of water was reduced to $4 a day. Calling their action a "strike," the miners charged that they had long been "oppressed by the exorbitant exactions" of the TCWC, the managers of which had grown fat "by the sweat of the brow of the careworn working man." Now white miners declared themselves "at *war*" with the "controling cormorants of this *monster monopoly.*"[42]

The war was not between miners and monopolists alone. In addition to refusing the TCWC's water, miners called on one another to withdraw any money they had in banks in Tuolumne County or elsewhere in the state. Surplus cash, the resolutions directed, was to be deposited in the safe of a "friendly merchant," where it would be beyond the reach of well-connected TCWC managers. But the bulk of miners' money was to be invested in what the resolutions called the "new water company."[43] Though newspaper reports of the mass meeting did not name this enterprise, local miners knew whereof the resolutions spoke. The newcomer was the Columbia and Stanislaus River Water Company (CSRWC), organized less than a year earlier to compete with the TCWC. Trustees of the CSRWC had held public meetings in various camps during the preceding months to drum up support. Very little actual ditchdigging had been done, however, before the mass meeting in March. According to one CSRWC trustee, John Jolly, the miners' action against the TCWC was just what the new company needed. On the eve of the Columbia miners' meeting, Jolly noted in his diary, "A mass meeting called for tomorrow which I trust will start our new ditch." Jolly was not disappointed. Within days, he could write triumphantly that the "old [company] surrendered to the will of the miners," adding that "the new [company] has distanced [the TCWC] by getting the start we so long wished for."[44]

The white miners, then, were not alone. Both local merchants and a rival water company supported their cause, and TCWC managers were forced to reduce water prices just days after the miners' mass meeting. Merchants, as they had with the initial imposition of taxes on "foreign" miners in 1850 and 1852, worried about their customers, far more of whom were miners than water company managers. In fact, the "Traders, Mechanicks and business men" in and around Columbia drafted a polite petition to the TCWC to express their collective "anxiety and alarm" over the breach between miners and company men. Unlike the miners, these merchants and their allies disclaimed "all right or disposition to intermeddle or dictate" to the TCWC how it should conduct its "own concerns," acknowledging that "much of the prosperity that our town enjoys is justly attributa-

ble to [the company's] enterprise." From their ambivalent position
within emerging Anglo American class relations, however, the petitioners argued that "the rates the Miners have been paying for water
are higher than the diggings will justify." The merchants closed with a
deferential plea: "We most earnestly express the hope that your circumstances will permit you to reduce the price of your water."[45] The
circumstances that permitted such a reduction included both the
backing of the merchants and the competition offered by the CSRWC.

In addition, the TCWC's decision to reduce rates for the use of
water probably depended on the ambivalence of men within the
company itself. Many company men had come to California initially
with dreams of making their fortune in the diggings, and only
recently had abandoned those dreams in favor of entrepreneurial
enterprise. Even as they built the Southern Mines' grandest business
venture, they remembered the backbreaking labor of mining as well
as the exacting work. of exclusion, whereby Anglo Americans
attempted to arrogate the placers to themselves. One such man was
Joseph Pownall, who collected water rents for the TCWC in the
Montezuma mining district. Pownall had trained as a physician in
New York and practiced medicine in the South. He went to California
in 1849 at the age of thirty-one. Pownall tried his hand at mining for
several years before he joined the ranks of the TCWC. Just days after
the miners' mass meeting in March of 1855, he wrote to the company secretary, concerned about the "piping times" in Columbia.
Pownall reported that his own policy with Montezuma miners had
been to be "as conciliatory as possible." In fact, he had unilaterally
lowered the price of water for his customers: "I took the responsibility to reduce and let the Board [of Trustees] raise the price again and
censure me if they saw fit." Calling "the great majority" of miners
"honourable and high minded men," Pownall argued that the TCWC
should go so far as to reduce managers' salaries before allowing the
company's reputation to be tarnished by a dispute with miners.[46]

Joseph Pownall's letter to the company secretary also sheds light
on how the quarrel between white miners and the TCWC was connected to an emerging Anglo American political culture in the
Southern Mines. Pownall told the secretary that he thought the price
of water "must necessarily come down," "however galling" it might
be for the company to "succumb to such rascals as Palmer [and]
Coffroth." In naming John A. Palmer and James W. Coffroth as
adversaries, Pownall looked backward as well as forward. Palmer, as
we have seen, was a leader among white miners early on, both when
they agitated for Chinese exclusion in 1852 and when they protested

TCWC water rates starting in 1853. Coffroth, on the other hand, for many embodied the Tuolumne County of the future. Though he was only twenty-six, he was already a veteran of California's legislature, having won his first election to the state assembly in 1851; he later became a state senator. Locally, Coffroth was known as "Columbia's favorite son." He was a frequent orator at community events, and his poetry appeared in area newspapers (given his famous verbal felicity, one might attribute to Coffroth that well-turned epithet—"the controling cormorants of this *monster monopoly*"). He was also—and this is what most galled TCWC managers—president of the rival Columbia and Stanislaus River Water Company. Not all in Columbia and the vicinity, then, were so taken with James Coffroth. In his letter to the TCWC secretary, for example, Pownall reported that a "deputation" had "waited on the miners" in Montezuma, asking for their cooperation. These deputies, no doubt, came either from the CSRWC or from the protesting Columbia miners. Pownall told the secretary that he thought the Montezuma miners would refuse to cooperate with the deputation, adding sarcastically, "they are perfectly aware that the interests of the dear people here are not much cared for by Columbias favorite son, poet [and] 'song-clad [seraph]'"—referring, perhaps, to Coffroth the legislator as much as to Coffroth the water company president.[47]

What Coffroth represented was a particular kind of political actor in the Southern Mines—a Democrat who claimed the mantle of Jacksonian Democracy by championing the cause of independent white miners. In the process, he secured his own political, and perhaps economic, fortunes. Meanwhile, the Democratic Party in the diggings, as elsewhere in the United States, was in turmoil, wracked by disputes over slavery and by the growth of the American, or Know-Nothing, Party. The full extent to which the battle between the TCWC and the white miners reflected the machinations of party politics is a topic for a different—and necessary—kind of history of the Southern Mines. But there are clear indications that a local political crisis was implicated in the battle.[48] According to Joseph Pownall, the disfavor into which the TCWC had fallen by 1855 resulted from "the wire pullings of harpies who for years have been hovering about Columbia ready to pounce upon and fleece the unfortunate who may have been caught in their toils."[49] The "unfortunate," of course, were the aggrieved white miners. The "harpies," no doubt, were their grassroots leaders, such as Palmer, as well as their powerful political ally, Coffroth. What Pownall was saying was that Columbia's miners had been hoodwinked into fighting the TCWC by such men. What

A stock certificate from the Tuolumne County Water Company, 1854. Most stockholders were white men, but the owner of this share was an Elisabeth Klemm. Note the signature of the Democratic politician James W. Mandeville.

Courtesy of the Bancroft Library.

Pownall was not saying was that the TCWC had its own friends in high places. Chief among them was another Tuolumne County Democratic legislator, James W. Mandeville. Mandeville was a quieter brand of Democrat than Coffroth, but one who also kept his thumb in the local pie, searching about for a golden plum. From the start, Mandeville was a stockholder in the TCWC. Indeed, his incoming correspondence from 1852 on is filled with answers to what must have been repeated queries about the company's prospects. In 1854, Mandeville was elected a trustee of the TCWC.[50] Two Democratic politicians in Tuolumne County, then, lined up squarely behind two rival water companies: James Coffroth as the highly visible president of the CSRWC, and James Mandeville as the more circumspect stockholder in and trustee of the TCWC.

The full texture of this rivalry may be lost to the historical record, but surviving pieces of the fabric hint at what it all felt like in the hands of varied participants. Just as the politics of water spilled over into the politics of state, so too did it seep into the everyday politics of sex, of race, and of gender. For example, a month after the Columbia miners called the TCWC's bluff and won lower water rates, newspapers reported that CSRWC President Coffroth had challenged TCWC President Alexander M. Dobie to a duel. Now the issue was not water but character. "A certain lady," according to Dobie, had informed him that Coffroth had made remarks "derogatory to [Dobie's] character." Not to be outdone, Dobie told the woman that Coffroth himself was a "frequenter of houses of ill-fame in Columbia." Coffroth, in turn, demanded "gentlemanly satisfaction" of Dobie. Dobie refused, smugly reminding Coffroth the lawmaker that dueling was not only "barbarous and inhuman" but illegal.[51] For some, such crossing of swords made life in Tuolumne County read like a Shakespearean drama. After the miners' strike in March of 1855, Coffroth broke loose from his Democratic moorings and drifted briefly into the Know-Nothing Party, which was making significant inroads into California politics. On the one hand, mainstream Democrats excoriated Coffroth. One partisan newspaper, for instance, racially taunted the nativist Know-Nothings by denouncing "the late political somerset of Mr. Coffroth into the embrace of the Hindoos."[52] On the other hand, not all Know-Nothings welcomed Coffroth into the fold, particularly not those who had ties to the TCWC. One of the original stockholders in the TCWC, who had recently left the diggings, wrote to Joseph Pownall several months after the miners' uprising, anxiously inquiring about the state of his business affairs in Columbia. He also expressed glee that California had "gone K[now] N[othing]" in the late elections. "Hip Hip Huzza," he penned, adding, "I hope however that our mutual *friend* the Hon J W Coffroth has been consigned to the 'tomb of the Capulets.'"[53] It was no accident that this TCWC stockholder identified Coffroth with Juliet's family line rather than that of Romeo. When it came to white men hurling insults in the Southern Mines, manhood as well as whiteness were always on the side of the detractor.

All of these circles of intrigue, interest, and meaning, then, came to swirl around an economic contest between white miners, who had fought hard for exclusive access to the placers, and white water company managers, who had created a commodity out of the one thing placer miners most needed if that access was to translate into hard cash. In their opposition to the TCWC, the Columbia miners questioned not a company's right to put a price on water but rather its right to set that price without regard for what white men reasonably could be expected to spare out of their daily earnings. Whatever the original intentions of the CSRWC managers, then, when the miners fell in behind them in 1855, the rival water company did indeed evolve into a different kind of animal. The TCWC, for example, had been incorporated with a capital stock of $220,000, divided into 275 shares of $800 each.[54] The CSRWC, however, was organized with a capital stock of $300,000, divided into 1,500 shares of $200 each, allowing many more to become shareholders for much less.[55] What is more, when striking miners threw their support to the CSRWC, a good number left their long toms and sluices and went to work digging ditches for the new company, accepting CSRWC stock in lieu of wages.[56] This action not only forced the TCWC to accede to the miners' demands (lest the old company continue to lose ground to the new); it also gave white miners a very real stake in the fortunes of the CSRWC. Newspapermen sympathetic to the miners—and to the miners' allies—wrote in glowing terms of what became known as the "Miners' Ditch":

> This ditch is one of the most magnificent achievements of enterprise which the records of California industry can produce. Conceived under . . . a pressing demand, . . . the work . . . was commenced by private enterprise and individual labor, and without the aid of a single dollar from the treasury of the organized company. In giving . . . encouragement to labor, Hon. J. W. Coffroth . . . deserves distinguished praise, as through his eloquent representations, he induced scores of laborers to shoulder their picks and shovels and march to the line of labor, with no other promise of remuneration than that which would arise from the profits of the ditch, after its completion. And yet, perhaps, the greater credit is due to the hardy sons of toil. . . .

Seldom, this editor concluded, did "individual enterprise, without the aid of capital" succeed in completing "a work as grand and extensive" as the CSRWC ditch.[57]

In fact, the work was not completed for three more years. When it finally was finished, Columbia turned itself out as never before.[58] On November 29, 1858, the CSRWC faithful and their friends assembled in a grand procession that wended its way through the town, replete with brass bands, military and fire companies, carriages carrying company officials and town dignitaries, as well as hundreds and hundreds of men on foot—among them, those who had helped dig the "Miners' Ditch." Many carried banners, including one that pictured two miners sitting at a roughly hewn table, a barrel of pork and a sack of beans at their side; one man pointed to the provisions, declaring, "In these we trusted." Some men marched together under the banner of a "Miners' Union"—though sources are frustratingly opaque as to the origins and activities of this group.[59] Finally, all assembled in the center of town, where James Coffroth held forth to the teeming crowd on the history of the CSRWC. A free public dinner followed and then, to end the day, a spectacular display of fireworks and an elaborate ball.

What must have appeared at the time as the triumph of independent white miners, however, looks in retrospect like a swan song for a dying breed. Plentiful, cheap water, the miners learned, was not enough to ensure their independence. There had to be gold in the ground. As they had since the beginning of the Gold Rush, placer yields continued to decline over the course of the 1850s. Indeed, in 1858, when the Columbia miners celebrated the completion of their ditch, California's gold production was only 57 percent of what it had been in 1852, when the TCWC stockholders signed their incorporation papers.[60] The CSRWC, then, having come of age in this climate, slipped into arrears. Columbia area miners again came to the aid of the company, staging demonstrations, threatening violence, and demanding that the "Miners' Ditch" remain "a lasting monument of the energy and perseverance of the laboring class of Tuolumne County." But in 1860, creditors forced the sale of CSRWC properties at a public auction. The purchaser of the "Miners' Ditch" was that *monster monopoly*," the TCWC.[61]

By then, California was no longer the only field where aspiring white men could establish themselves as "independent miners." In British Columbia, word of gold at the Fraser River drew thousands of California miners northward in 1858. More promising still was the discovery of both gold and silver in Nevada's Carson River basin in 1859. Thousands more rushed east across the Sierra Nevada to that destination. News of gold in almost every western territory followed in subsequent years, creating a patchwork of western places where Anglo American men might escape the economic dependence that both eastern places and played-out western placers seemed to portend. Never mind the demise of the "Miners' Ditch," then; there would always be another gold rush.

Over the course of the 1850s, dramas similar to these played themselves out elsewhere in the Southern Mines, though perhaps nowhere with as much swagger and flair as in Columbia, an exceptionally rich gold district that was known as the Gem of the Southern Mines. Far less common in the south was a trajectory that came to characterize much of the Northern Mines in the 1850s, as men with capital turned their attention away from the placers and toward gold that was buried deeper beneath the earth's surface. These deposits included quartz or vein gold as well as deep gravels. Yet such deposits were relatively scarce in the Southern Mines, at least when compared with the diggings to the north. Of course, there were crucial exceptions to the rule. Much of the gold mined in the vicinity of Columbia, in fact, came out of a rare patch of ancient gravels that had never been buried by debris. Likewise, substantial quartz gold turned up at the northern reaches of the Southern Mines, in Amador County, and far to the south as well, in Mariposa County. But these deposits paled in comparison with the spectacular veins and gravels of the Northern Mines.[62]

Many residents of the Southern Mines and the supply town of Stockton refused to believe, or at least to admit, that the diggings to the north held this advantage. As early as 1850, the *Stockton Times* denounced as "anti-south" an *Alta California* article which implied that "the probable amount of metaliferous quartz in the southern mines" was limited. Boosters for the southern diggings shot back that the area boasted "mountains of auriferous quartz," which were "already, with eminent success, being worked by companies."[63] By the mid-1850s, some Mariposa County residents, in particular, insisted that "the richest quartz veins in California" were found within their county lines.[64] Later, in 1857, one writer claimed that the quartz resources of Tuolumne County alone, "if the proper appliances existed for their development," could "supply the whole world with gold . . . for a century—perhaps a dozen centuries to come." Despite the hyperbole, this last statement actually reflects a decline in confidence that characterized the Southern Mines in the later 1850s. The writer nowhere said that Tuolumne County quartz deposits were greater than those elsewhere in the state, and he was careful to add that their development would require "proper appliances." In fact, the writer's purpose was to caution residents against a "quartz mania," whereby "men rush heedlessly [into quartz mining], expecting sudden and fabulous profits without preliminary investment of capital or labor, or both."[65] By the end of the 1850s, then, if none conceded the advantage of the Northern Mines in quartz mining, at least fewer insisted that the diggings to the south had the edge.

One man who especially hoped that the Southern Mines were concealing a buried treasure in quartz was John C. Frémont, the nationally acclaimed explorer. As luck would have it, Frémont had become a major landowner in the area just before gold was discovered in 1848. His career in the Southern Mines—along with that of Jessie Benton Frémont, his wife—illustrates something of the fortunes of quartz mining there, while also illuminating a much wider set of concerns. Stories about the Frémonts invariably encompass a panoply of themes in U.S. history, generally, and the history of westward expansion, in particular. Those set in 1850s California are no exception. In just a dozen years, the Frémonts' lives became touchstones of not only far-flung capitalization in western mining but the disposition of Mexican land claims; the administration of the U.S. public domain; the pursuit of wealth through contracts to provision dispossessed Indians; the spread of black slavery into the territories; the making of national reputations through western ventures; the transformation of U.S. political parties; the rise in white women's political participation; and the local emergence of racialized and gendered class relations that reflected both national and international economic upheavals.

It all began before the Gold Rush. John C. Frémont's third western expedition took him to California on the eve of the U.S.-Mexican War, where he participated first in the Bear Flag Rebellion against Mexico. Ultimately, U.S. Brigadier General Stephen Watts Kearny marched Frémont back east in the summer of 1847, after Frémont placed himself on the wrong side of a struggle between Kearny and Commodore Robert F. Stockton over whether Stockton legitimately could appoint Frémont as governor of occupied California. Frémont was court-martialed for mutiny and disobedience. Before he left California, however, he had purchased—with the assistance of Thomas O. Larkin, U.S. consul in Mexican California—a vast tract of land known as Las Mariposas from the prominent Californio Juan Bautista Alvarado and his wife, Martina Castro de Alvarado.[66] Located in what would become Mariposa County, the tract was a "floating grant" that Alvarado had received in 1844 from California's governor (because of Mexican community property law, Castro de Alvarado also gained an interest in the property). The boundaries of the grant were not specified—only that it was to cover ten leagues between the Sierra Nevada to the east and the San Joaquin River to the west, and between the Merced River to the north and the Chowchilla River to the south. Alvarado had hoped to survey this stretch of land and take possession of the ten leagues that best suited his needs, but the resistance of native peoples foiled his plans.[67]

But for the gold discovery, Frémont's claim to the land might have met the same fate. Like all of what became the Southern Mines, Las Mariposas was within the hunting and gathering grounds of Sierra Miwoks, among whom had settled other Indians who were escaping the twin scourges of malaria in the Central Valley and missions on the coast. Frémont met up with these mixed bands late in 1845, after crossing the Sierra Nevada into California. The outcome was not a happy one for the explorer. The native peoples who had joined up-country Miwoks in the decade before the Gold Rush, as Frémont

knew, included many who were adept horse raiders. So when
Frémont entered the land that he would later purchase and saw signs
of horses, he sent out four scouts (two white men and two Delaware
Indians) to track down the responsible "Horse-thief Indians," as he
called them. The plan backfired. Not only did the local band surround the scouts, separating them from their horses and shouting at
them in Spanish, even when Frémont's men retrieved the scouts and
their mounts, the Indians circled the explorer's camp and, as Frémont
remembered,

> harangued us, bestowing on us liberally all the epithets they
> could use, telling us what they would do with us. Many of them
> had been Mission Indians and spoke Spanish well. "Wait," they
> said, "*Esparate Carrajos* [sic]—wait until morning. There are two
> big villages up in the mountains close by; we have sent for the
> Chief; he'll be down before morning with all the people and
> you will all die. None of you shall go back; we will have all your
> horses."

Frémont and his men slipped away, out of the foothills, before the
local people could make good on their threat. He did not return to
the neighborhood for over three years. In the meantime, Frémont
had gained title to the land, though Indians repelled four early
attempts by his representatives to take possession.[68] It took the Gold
Rush for him to be able to return to the scene of this particular
humiliation.

And return he did, though in the long run Frémont's greeting by
gold seekers who invaded Miwok lands proved only marginally
warmer than his reception by Indians. It did not help that he was the
largest landowner in the Southern Mines, and that his title to the
land and its gold was contested. It did not help that Jessie Benton
Frémont was a daughter of the powerful Thomas Hart Benton, expansionist Democrat from Missouri, and that Benton alternately championed and then shunned his peripatetic son-in-law (who had eloped
with Jessie when she was but seventeen).[69] It did not help that John
Frémont's loyalty to the Democrats—the majority party in the
Southern Mines—proved a good deal more brittle even than that of
James Coffroth, the local Democrat who only briefly abandoned his
party for the Know-Nothings. Frémont, by contrast, became the first
presidential candidate of the new Republican Party in 1856. All
things considered, newspapers exaggerated only slightly in saying
that Frémont had "no friends in the mines."[70]

The enmity started early. By the end of 1849, California had ratified its constitution and elected its first officials. The new state legislature, in turn, elected Frémont as one of two U.S. senators, though he drew a short two-year term in Washington. While in office, Frémont introduced a number of bills, but none were more important to Californians than those involving mines and land claims. Frémont's land bill proposed a board of commissioners to examine land titles established under Mexican law. Frémont did not stay in the Senate long enough to shepherd the measure through Congress, but his foes suspected that the bill would have favored his own interests, as the holder of a Mexican land grant, as well as those of Californios over the interests of Anglo Americans.[71]

"Frémont's Gold Bill," as it was called in the press, generated even greater resistance. A Stockton newspaper took Frémont to task for trying to restrict mining privileges to U.S. citizens, reminding readers of how the late foreign miners' tax had depopulated the Southern Mines. The editor accused Frémont of "basely pander[ing] to what he supposes to be the prejudices of the miners in the San Joaquin region."[72] A newspaper correspondent from Tuolumne County denounced the provisions of Frémont's bill that would have sent federal agents to the diggings to grant miners permits for thirty-foot-square "placer lots" (or two-hundred-plus-foot-square lots for quartz mines). The agents also would have managed local juries appointed to settle mining disputes. The Tuolumne correspondent protested, "[F]or nearly three years we have peaceably and quietly settled our own difficulties . . . and my opinion is that a jury of six practical miners will adjust any disputes . . . as efficiently as a man with a fat salary, sent out from the old states, who does not know a quartz vein from a slate lead."[73] Finally, Frémont's neighbors in Mariposa County drafted a memorial to the U.S. Senate, complaining that the bill's provisions would drive them "to a fugitive life, having so small a quantity of soil apportioned to each, in the placer diggings." Likewise, they argued, the lot size for quartz mines, which were worked by large companies, was insufficient: "no company can be formed limited to so small a portion of any vein yet found in California."[74] Indeed, criticisms of the bill were so varied that taken together they seem to represent resistance to any interference whatsoever in the affairs of California miners by the federal government. Frémont himself asked Californians to believe that his sole intent had been "to exclude all idea of making national revenue out of the mines—to prevent the possibility of their monopoly by moneyed capitalists—and to give to natural capital, to LABOR and INDUSTRY, a fair chance in fields of its own choosing."[75] It was perhaps too much for Frémont to ask, since he was so deeply identified with national interests—through his government expeditions, his Senate seat, and his family connections—and, through his promotion of Las Mariposas, with moneyed capital.

Las Mariposas, in fact, was only one of Frémont's schemes for making his fortune in California. He owned or claimed interest in a number of other properties, including Alcatraz Island, three San Francisco city lots, the orchards of Mission Dolores, land along the San Joaquin River, and ranchos in present-day Kern and San Joaquin counties.[76] In addition to these properties, Frémont made money from beef contracts with the federal Indian commissioners who were sent to California in 1851. Although the U.S. Senate never ratified the treaties these agents negotiated with native peoples, the agents went ahead and made contracts to provide Indians with the beef the treaties promised, and then paid contractors with drafts drawn on the Secretary of the Interior. The contracts themselves were plagued by fraud and speculation, and California Indians were hardly the chief beneficiaries of all the meat and money that changed hands. Frémont himself took in over $180,000 worth of the commissioners' drafts, all of which the federal government at first refused to honor. Through a special authorization by Congress, however, Frémont was able to collect on his drafts, plus interest, which amounted to $58,000.[77] Unlike his other economic and political ventures, Frémont's beef contracts drew but little criticism. Years later, a former member of the Mariposa Battalion, the mostly white volunteer force that had fought in the Mariposa War, charged a "California Indian Ring" with profiteering off such contracts. He claimed to have warned no less an Indian trader than James Savage, who received much contracted beef, that Savage was surrounded by "sharp men" who were using him "as a tool to work their gold mine."[78] Few others seemed to care that "sharp men" such as Frémont may have fleeced Indians to finance quartz mines.

In the end, it took more than beef contracts to keep Las Mariposas up and running. The difficulties Frémont faced were deep, many, mutable, and always compounded by his inexperience in business. In 1864, he lost control of the property altogether. In the meantime, Frémont was sitting, quite literally, on a gold mine. He discovered as early as 1849 that the Mariposa Estate, as it was called by English speakers, included a gold-studded quartz vein over five miles in length—this in addition to the hundred pounds of placer gold Sonoran miners were washing out each month and dividing equally with Frémont, who had engaged the Mexicans to work on his behalf.[79] Quickly, Frémont turned to a system whereby he leased often unlocated portions of the vein to whoever agreed to mine it and to return to him one-sixth of all gold found. He also took on partners to attract Europeans to the property, with the hope that British capitalists, in particular, would jump at the chance to finance the concentration of men and machinery required to extract gold from solid rock. His representative in England, David Hoffman, was often exasperated with Frémont. Hoffman complained that Frémont failed to keep him informed of developments in California and that he allowed other interested parties to complicate what Hoffman saw as an exclusive business arrangement. In 1851, Thomas Hart Benton himself stepped in and tried to force the sale of Las Mariposas, arguing that his son-in-law was "not adapted to such business." The sale was stopped, but not before John and Jessie Benton Frémont traveled to London to put matters aright. This 1852 trip started out pleasantly enough, with Jessie presented to Queen Victoria. But as John boarded a carriage one evening, he was arrested for drafts he had drawn on the federal government during the war with Mexico; the drafts had been sold to a British concern and had gone unpaid. Hoffman posted bail for Frémont—after the famous American spent the night in lockup. Affairs such as these made attracting and retaining European capital for Mariposa's mines no small task.[80]

To make matters worse, Frémont's title to the estate was in constant jeopardy. When gold was discovered in the Sierra Nevada foothills, miners quickly fanned out over the entire area. This included Las Mariposas, virtually the only tract of land that was not, according to provisions of the Treaty of Guadalupe Hidalgo, part of U.S. public domain. But gold seekers treated it as if it was, setting up tents, staking claims, and digging paydirt on land that Frémont claimed, or would later claim, as private property. Some eventually took up leases with Frémont, but many did not. Locally, then, the stage was set for battles between an often absentee landowner and those who worked on the land in question. These local contests were overlaid with legal contests that went all the way to the U.S. Supreme Court. Following the multiple paths of these struggles is not easy. The historian who has followed them most carefully explains that the overlapping systems of mining law in California are perplexing enough: "Compound the situation with a superimposition of . . . claims and claim jumpers, leases and subleases, original companies and reorganized companies, sales of both mineral claims and surface lands, authorized agents and unauthorized," she writes, and recon-

struction becomes a herculean task.[81] That the original grant to Juan
B. Alvarado was a "floating grant" only complicated matters further.
Without definite boundaries, for example, Frémont was able to claim
one tract of land in 1852 and then a substantially different tract in
1856. The 1852 Mariposa Estate was shaped like a pan with a long
handle; it included a circle of gold mines up in the foothills and then
followed the Mariposa River downstream to the San Joaquin Valley.
The 1856 Mariposa Estate dropped the handle, and then increased
the size of the pan to include the rich quartz mines of upper Bear
Creek Valley.[82]

Frémont's claim to Las Mariposas was the first case considered
under the provisions of the Land Act of 1851—though this bill is perhaps best known for the role it played in the dispossession of the
Spanish Mexican elite in California. The land commissioners confirmed Frémont's title in 1852. The District Court for the Northern
District of California, however, reversed the commission's decision in
1854. So Frémont took the case to the U.S. Supreme Court, where,
the following year, he won on appeal. In its decision, the Supreme
Court ordered a new survey of Las Mariposas, which inaugurated
another round of legal maneuvers. In the meantime, Frémont completed the required survey, by which he claimed important new mineral lands in Bear Valley. But with the legality of the survey in
question, Frémont was still without final certification and a patent
from the federal government. The case returned to the Supreme
Court once more. Finally, on February 19, 1856, President Franklin
Pierce signed the patent for Las Mariposas and, in a White House
meeting, personally handed it to Frémont. By then, it was widely
known that Frémont himself was a potential candidate for the presidency of the United States.[83]

Observers in the Southern Mines and the supply town of Stockton
kept close tabs on these proceedings. Some actually wished Frémont
well, arguing that "when quartz mining companies can get title to
their claims, a large amount of capital will be brought into the country."[84] More common, though, were the sentiments expressed in
Stockton's Democratic newspaper, the *San Joaquin Republican*, which
took Frémont to task at every turn. There was the issue of foreign capital. As early as 1852, the Stockton paper exclaimed that Frémont had
"actually leased a portion [of Las Mariposas] to a French company"
and that it was his intent "to move Heaven and Earth to possess himself of that immense tract of land." Six months later, the editors were
more direct about what it was they thought Frémont was doing to
foreign, and especially British, investors, choosing a metaphor that

had fond associations in the homosocial world of Gold Rush California: "Col. Fremont has 'diddled' John Bull . . . sliding into his 'tender affections' in the slickest manner imaginable."[85] And then there was Frémont's title to the land itself, which the *San Joaquin Republican* took as a symbol of capitalist greed. If confirmed, Frémont's claim would sound the death knell of the independent Anglo American miner:

> The once independent miner is cut off . . . by the title of the capitalist; he cannot work "on his own hook" . . . ; he must either rent a tract of land, or he must go to work . . . at the wages offered; and if there should be a large increase in the labor market, his wages must necessarily [fall] until they reach the level of labor in other countries. Doubtless, all this time, the capitalist is growing richer and is making gigantic improvements: but, what boots it? Labor is his footstool; labor is the sacrifice.[86]

Anglo American labor as his footstool, foreign capital as his bedfellow: Frémont's appendages were everywhere they ought not to have been.

In 1856, when the title to Las Mariposas was confirmed and Frémont became the Republican presidential candidate, critics shifted gears, now tying his financial and political ambitions together into a single oppressive bundle—one that was destined to land squarely on white miners' shoulders. "It must be admitted," taunted the Stockton paper, "that John Charles Mariposa Claim Fremont . . . possesses great *claims* to the suffrages of the people of California, particularly the miners." The article went on to explain why it would be "perfect madness" for miners to support Frémont, reminding them of the legislation he proposed while senator and of the leasing he promoted on Las Mariposas. In a stunning prediction, the newspaper argued that Frémont as president would abolish "free mining" altogether and enforce the sale or leasing of mineral lands, which would "either create a civil war or cause to be instituted the worst system of white slavery ever known."[87]

Critics also linked Frémont's ambitions to the aspirations of those who stood outside the customary circle of Jacksonian Democracy—particularly women and African Americans. The new Republican Party actually embraced a range of antislavery views, from abolitionism, at one end, to opposition to the westward expansion of slavery, at the other. Frémont himself was chosen as candidate in part because his views on slavery were less well known than those of other potential nominees. Nonetheless, Democrats in the Southern Mines painted Frémont as the consummate race traitor. Taking issue with a Sacramento newspaper that supported Frémont because of his western explorations, the *San Joaquin Republican* answered in the language of antiblack race hatred. That Frémont had once "regaled himself on horse flesh," the Stockton editors retorted, did not entitle him to "his present woolly horse ride for the Presidential stakes." Other explorers were more deserving of the honor—"even," the editors mocked, "Jim Beckwith," the famous black fur trapper.[88] Democrats in California, as elsewhere, also identified Frémont with the woman movement, in part because of the active role Jessie Benton Frémont played in his campaign (a role that seemed all the more remarkable because her father, Thomas Hart Benton, campaigned against John). Indeed, back east, Republicans sported ribbons emblazoned with slogans such as "Jessie's Choice," and woman suffragists, both prominent and obscure, championed John. In all of this, Anglo American women entered into the fray of national party politics as never before, much to the horror of many.[89] Even in the Southern Mines, reform-minded women took courage from the "Frémont and Jessie" campaign. An Amador County white woman, for example, sat down to her diary and penned confidently, "I go in for Fremont and freedom." Meanwhile, local Democrats found themselves forced to reckon with Jessie, who, they complained, "declare[d] herself to be a black republican!" What was worse, according to many, was that her declaration mattered.[90]

In the end, since the Republican campaign failed (though it surely succeeded in launching the new party into a national orbit), no one learned what a Frémont presidency might have meant for women, abolitionists, blacks, California miners, or other Americans. But Frémont, along with his creditors, still owned the Mariposa Estate, and so the Southern Mines had not seen the last of him. In fact, with the election over and his title to the land secured, Frémont returned to California to manage his property. In 1858, he traveled east, and then west once again, now accompanied by Jessie Benton Frémont and their children. By that time, the stage had been set in Mariposa County for a showdown between John Charles Frémont and his local detractors. His claim to the land might be secure, but claiming the minerals that land contained was another matter. This was not, after all, a land rush. It was a gold rush. And "gold" was a fighting word.

Almost as soon as Frémont received the patent to Las Mariposas, critics began to argue that his title to the land, because it was based on a grant made under Mexican law, did not include title to the mines.[91] And, in fact, in Spanish and then Mexican law, minerals did occupy a peculiar place. That is, if one person discovered and then exploited a mine on land that had been granted to another, or even if one person took up a mine that had been abandoned by another, then in either case, the person working the mine could rightfully lay claim to it. In Frémont's case, the size of the original grant to Alvarado, the abundance of gold therein, and Frémont's infrequent presence on his property before 1857 all worked together to ensure that claimants to the mines of the Mariposa Estate would be many and restive. In addition, when Mariposa County residents learned that the 1856 federal patent to the estate included rich diggings in Bear Valley that Frémont had never before claimed, the simmering pot began to boil. When Frémont began to press his claim to these mines, all hell broke loose.

Much of the controversy surrounded the quartz mines and mills of the Merced Mining Company (MMC). On the last day of 1856, for example, one of Frémont's agents sent a notice to MMC officials demanding possession of their reduction works at Mount Ophir. As many Mariposa County residents recognized, this was simply an opening salvo in Frémont's campaign to expropriate the gold of Bear Valley. They responded accordingly, forming a miners' and settlers' association in the first weeks of 1857. Those gathered resolved that

> in the event of John C. Fremont [or his associates] attempting to interfere with, molest, or eject any number of, *or even one* Miner, Settler, or resident upon [land claimed as part of the Mariposa Estate], we do hereby solemnly pledge ourselves to make common cause against him, or them—for the *plundering* of one is that of all, and a blow at one is an aim at each and all, Miners and Settlers, upon said tract.[92]

Making common cause against Frémont, however, was easier said than done. This because he rarely used force to interfere with, molest, or eject miners and settlers from Bear Valley, but rather a series of legal maneuvers. The MMC responded in kind, until, by March of 1857, as many as twenty suits between the two parties were wending their way through Mariposa County's district court—not to mention those that had gone or were going all the way to the California supreme court. Especially important were MMC injunctions to stop Frémont from seizing ore and other property, and injunctions by Frémont and his agents to prevent the MMC from pursuing their work on land that Frémont claimed.[93]

From the complicated matrix of suit and countersuit, a ground zero emerged for the fight between Frémont and his detractors: Bear Valley's Josephine and Pine Tree mines. The MMC had worked these sites longer, but Frémont now claimed them. Despite pending lawsuits, both parties continued extracting gold from the mines, though through separate tunnels. In October of 1857, for example, the *Mariposa Gazette* reported that "men in the employ of both the Fremont and Merced Mining Companies are working in close proximity to each other at the Pine Tree vein." MMC employees had just received a writ of injunction ordering them to stop mining there, but they persisted nonetheless. "No serious disturbance has yet occurred," the *Gazette* noted, but then added that "the prospect looks squally at the 'seat of war.'"[94] Squalls came and went throughout the fall and winter. In February of 1858, the *Gazette* found both companies "still busily engaged in quarrying, hauling and crushing quartz from the celebrated vein near Bear Valley," and reported with relief that the "excitement which . . . has threatened to end in violence between the rival companies, has cooled down to a healthy temperature."[95]

When summer came, tensions and temperatures rose. By now Jessie Benton Frémont had arrived in Bear Valley, bringing to the summer's events their best chronicler. She brought with her the three Frémont children—Lily, Charley, and Frank—as well as two maids, women identified in Jessie's letters only as Mémé and Rose.[96] Although many residents of the Southern Mines hated the Frémonts and all they represented, there were enough supporters in the valley to offer the family a rousing welcome. As Jessie wrote to her friend and distant cousin Elizabeth Blair Lee, "They had a great bonfire on Mount Bullion the night we got in & they fired off quicksilver flasks which sounded just like cannon echoing through the hills grandly."[97] Indeed, the mountain itself had been named for her father, who was called "Old Bullion" for his hard-currency views. (Sadly, Jessie's father, with whom she had reconciled after John's presidential bid, died in Missouri just as the Frémonts arrived in San Francisco on their way to the mines, though Jessie did not learn of his death until she was settled on the Mariposa Estate.).

At Bear Valley, the family took up residence in a modest whitewashed cottage, but one that was filled nonetheless, according to Jessie, with "velvet carpets & a fine piano, bronze clocks, [and] marble-topped furniture."[98] Mémé, who probably had come to the United States after a Frémont sojourn in France, and Rose attended to the children and to the well-appointed cottage. In addition, a Spanish-speaking black woman from the West Indies came by the day

The home of John C. Frémont and Jessie Benton Frémont at Bear Valley on the disputed Mariposa Estate, or Las Mariposas.

Courtesy of the Bancroft Library.

to do the Frémonts' laundry.[99] Meanwhile, two menservants long associated with John, both experienced frontiersmen, labored on the grounds and took a special interest in young Charley and Frank. One was Albert Lea, a free black man whose mother had worked for Jessie's father and who himself had served on one of John's western expeditions. The other was a man named Isaac, whom Jessie called "a spare, wiry Tennessee Indian with enough colored blood to have been a slave," but who she imagined had seized his own freedom "sharply."[100] Although Jessie claimed that this retinue offered her "slender working power," it actually was rare for white Americans in the mines, even those of the emerging middle class, to have so many servants; this much help was a mark of unusual affluence.[101] Perhaps in part because she anticipated less household service than she enjoyed back east, Jessie had long resisted settling at Las Mariposas. Only seven years earlier, she had declared, "The Mariposas is no place for me—Indians, bears & miners have made it lose its good qualities as a country place."[102]

Once resident on the Mariposa Estate, Jessie accustomed herself to

Indian neighbors, who lived in a large village nearby. And she encountered bears only when she set out on horseback to explore the Sierra Nevada.[103] But miners were still quite capable of destroying the "good qualities" of the Frémonts' "country place." In July of 1858, just as Jessie was coming to terms with her father's death and learning to live in her foothill home, she penned an agitated letter to the family friend and political adviser Francis Preston Blair (Elizabeth Blair Lee's father), announcing "news of our broken peace in this valley which was to have been our place of refuge against bad passions and bad climate." (She was referring to the "bad passions" of the 1856 presidential campaign and the "bad climate" of the eastern seaboard, which exacerbated the Frémonts' frequent respiratory ailments.) A week earlier, having just returned from San Francisco, Jessie found herself "waked from my first sleep after the journey by the alarm of regular border ruffian warfare." From that moment, she told Blair, all was "merged into one thought—how to save life & keep off

A Miwok *ranchería* near the Frémont house on Las Mariposas. Describing her home, Jessie Benton Frémont wrote, "Near by was a large Indian village, some hundreds settled there. The young women from it came constantly to our house and sat about on the grass chatting together of us and laughing as they watched our doings with frank curiosity. We were their matinée." See *Far-West Sketches* (Boston: D. Lothrop, 1890), 103.

Courtesy of the Bancroft Library.

the impending fight."[104] This was the fight that had been brewing for so long between John and his agents, on the one hand, and the Merced Mining Company, on the other. The MMC, in turn, had the support of many Mariposa County men, some of whom had organized themselves into a group called the Hornitos League.

The Hornitos League, like the earlier miners' and settlers' association, included individual placer miners and others who faced dispossession when the title to Las Mariposas was confirmed.[105] This organization of Anglo men shared a name—Hornitos (literally, "little ovens")—with the largest Mexican town in Mariposa County. In the years since the first foreign miners' tax, Hornitos had become a refuge for those Mexicans who refused to leave the southernmost reaches of the Southern Mines.[106] The members of the Hornitos League may have been from this town.[107] But it also seems possible that in calling themselves the Hornitos League, white miners ironically were likening themselves to those besieged Mexicans who had carved out a place for themselves in defiance of exclusionary practices. The naming, then, may have been double-edged. It may have invoked not only common anti-Mexican sentiments but a kind of grudging respect: these white men were not about to be pushed around as Mexican miners had been, and yet, if push did come to shove, the Anglos would stand their ground just as the residents of Hornitos had. The irony deepens when one remembers that these white men's mining claims were threatened by decisions made in American courts that had confirmed an Anglo man's title to a Mexican land grant. It deepens even further when one considers that Jessie Benton Frémont called her husband's opponents "border ruffians"—a capacious term with a rich historical resonance for Anglo Americans, and one that took on new meanings as U.S. borders expanded to include what so recently had been Mexico's northern frontier.[108]

"Border warfare" erupted in this manner. According to newspapers, as MMC employees and Frémont's miners bore down on each other through separate tunnels that exploited the same quartz vein, the MMC men insisted that "the Fremont Company were taking out the golden quartz from the other end of what they considered their property, at a rate which they did not feel justified in allowing."[109] One day early in July, the MMC miners, who had been laboring in the Josephine tunnel, approached the entrance to the Pine Grove tunnel, where Frémont's men were at work. The MMC men demanded possession of the mine, but Frémont's men refused to leave. The next morning, members of the Hornitos League joined the MMC miners, until some seventy men held the entrance to the Pine Tree Mine, with a handful of Frémont employees still holed up inside.[110] Jessie Benton Frémont wrote that the usurpers at first refused to allow her husband's workers food. One of John's men, however, was married to the woman who boarded the Pine Grove miners. According to Jessie, this "little woman," Elizabeth Ketton, "took a revolver & a basket of provisions & presented herself at the mouth of the mine." The boardinghouse keeper said that if the combined forces of the MMC and the Hornitos League "offered to touch her," she would shoot. This was no small threat, since the "men in the drift had laid a train & put their tools & old iron & blasting powder near the entrance & were ready to [make] a blast at the sound of firing." In other words, with one shot, mine and miners alike would have been blown up. After this, Ketton was allowed in twice daily, "carrying food in her hands & under her clothes pistols & powder & caps."[111]

Meanwhile, according to Jessie, the MMC men had threatened to burn down the Frémont cottage, and so Albert Lea and Isaac stood guard there. John moved back and forth between the cottage, the occupied mine, and his quartz mill, which he also kept under armed watch since it was filled, Jessie said, with "gold in amalgam & some coined & much machinery." Jessie minimized her own participation in all this to Francis Preston Blair, saying only, "whenever Mr. Frémont was in sight I was very brave."[112] According to her biographer, however, Jessie later insisted that she herself, driven by Isaac and accompanied by Mémé, had taken the note that contained the threat to her cottage and haughtily handed it back to hostile miners headquartered at a nearby saloon. Afterward, as Isaac turned the wagon toward home, Jessie recalled, "I fully expected to be shot in the back."[113] Though Jessie may have exaggerated her derring-do in hindsight, such action is quite in keeping with contemporary descriptions of her behavior. Abraham Lincoln, for example, who disliked the Frémonts, called Jessie "quite a female politician." And the Reverend Thomas Starr King, who adored Jessie, depicted her as "a she-Merrimack, thoroughly sheathed, and carrying fire in the genuine Benton furnaces"—a match, and then some, for the "little ovens" tippling in a Bear Valley saloon.[114]

John, for his part, appealed to California officials for firepower. Governor John B. Weller's third wife was a cousin of Jessie's, a connection that could only have helped when the Frémonts found themselves in such a dangerous fix. At John's request for aid, Weller telegraphed military companies in Columbia, Sonora, and Stockton "to hold themselves in readiness" in case armed conflict broke out in

Mariposa County. John also appealed to men he called "friends in San Francisco" for muskets and ammunition.[115] Shortly thereafter, the *San Joaquin Republican* reported that four cases of muskets were headed up to Bear Valley, "being forwarded by the United States Marshall."[116] State governors and federal marshals were truly good friends to have. Despite widespread animosity toward the Frémonts in Mariposa County, men of the Hornitos League simply could not claim such powerfully situated friends or useful family connections. In the end, these individual miners and settlers, along with the Merced Mining Company, had to back down. The court battles dragged on, and local controversy continued to erupt. Now and then, newspapers printed items with inflammatory titles such as "The Fremont Outrage."[117] But the Bear Valley War, as it is sometimes called, was more bluster than muster.

At the height of these hostilities, Jessie Benton Frémont had written a forty-four-page will and testament "in case," as she put it, "of loss of life."[118] But what actually died in Mariposa County in the summer of 1858 was what would expire in the town of Columbia after the celebrated completion of the "Miners' Ditch." What ended as the Hornitos League gave up its siege of the Pine Tree Mine was a local dream among white men of maintaining exclusive access to a boundless resource that would ensure their continued independence. The dream would continue for half a century in other western places where placer rushes beckoned men who felt betrayed by the promise of industrialization—Nevada, Arizona, Montana, Colorado, Idaho, Dakota, and Alaska territories in the United States, and British Columbia and the Yukon in Canada. It would continue in a diminished fashion even in western mining areas that moved much more quickly, decisively, and successfully than the Southern Mines did from individualized placer mining to industrialized hardrock mining. In such places, hardrock miners, who were often staunch union men, kept placer mining tools close at hand in their cabins or in union halls, always hoping against hope that a rich strike in their off-hours might suddenly yield them the fabled independence of white men during California's golden days.[119] Few remembered how amazingly short-lived that "independence" actually had been—and how deeply rooted in the dispossession of other Gold Rush participants, especially, in the Southern Mines, Miwoks, Mexicans, Chileans, French, and Chinese.

Chapter 6

The Last Fandango

A t the turn of the twentieth century, John Robertson was growing old in New York State. But in the 1850s, he had mined in
Calaveras County with his friend Wade Johnston, who went on to
live near San Andreas for the rest of his life. The two white men
struck up a correspondence when they were in their seventies, in
which they reminisced about the Gold Rush years. Wade also filled
John in on the changes that had taken place over the decades in and
around their old haunts. John was struck by the transformation: "In
my time," he recalled, "things were some what loose." A recent letter
from Wade had convinced him that people in Calaveras County
eventually tightened up: "Your letter goes to show," John wrote back
to Wade, "that after I left they began to live in a more civilized way—
got married, settled down, raised families, instead of keeping them
selves in hot water striveing to make a pile and leave; they settled
down and lived like white folks."[1]

Living "in a more civilized way," however, was not a simple matter
of settling down. For John Robertson, civilization involved a broad
range of social, cultural, and economic practices by which people of
European descent became "white": women and men, clearly two separate human categories, consummated (ideally) exclusive intimate
relationships that were sanctioned by the state; they conceived offspring and reared them in (ideally) cohesive social units called families; they kept one place of residence for a long period of time,
perhaps even a lifetime; and there they engaged in economic activity,
activity that allowed for the steady accumulation of capital and the

reproduction of a labor force, which in turn allowed them to continue to live in the place called home. No matter that a wide variety of peoples engaged, or tried to engage, in some or all of these practices. No matter that some people of European descent rejected or were unable to engage in some or all of them. For John Robertson and many other Gold Rush participants, the pursuit of such activities constituted whiteness, and the ascendance of such activities constituted a racial triumph.[2]

To triumph, however, one must engage in a struggle and ultimately exercise greater power than those over whom one triumphs. In an event as celebrated as the California Gold Rush, it is the struggle and the exercise of power that is forgotten, the triumph that is remembered. The most sophisticated stories told about the Gold Rush recognize that there were precious few individual triumphs in the diggings; many sought, but few made, their "pile." These stories incorporate the Gold Rush into larger narratives about nation building. But even such narratives often downplay the conflict and coercion inherent in nation building, particularly where nations are assumed to be built on a foundation of certain social, cultural, and economic practices.[3] During the Gold Rush, nowhere were conflict and coercion more evident than in the Southern Mines.

Here, then, I turn to a second set of struggles, a second broad exercise of power that helped transform the Southern Mines after 1852. Just as change emerged within the sphere of mining labor, it erupted as well across the terrain of domestic and personal service work and especially across the landscape of leisure. Outside the mines themselves, particular sites became emblematic of the transformation—saloons and fandangos, to be sure, but also the dusty streets and clapboard cottages of Jackson and Sonora and Mariposa. Particular historical actors took center stage in these dramas, especially women from every group of Gold Rush participants—Indian and immigrant; Spanish, French, English, and Cantonese speaking. But men of all descriptions were also key players—gamblers and fighters, dancers and drinkers, lovers and legislators. In the process, an earlier social world of possibility and permeable boundaries began to give way to more entrenched forms of dominance rooted in Anglo American constructions of gender, of class position, and of race, ethnicity, and nation—that is, in particular ideas about what it meant to live "like white folks."

Indeed, the older and newer social worlds of the Gold Rush started on a collision course in 1852. Recall that a Sonora newspaper correspondent saw the upheaval as a victory for "American energy and perseverance," exhibited in such structures built by white men as flumes and fireproof businesses. Meanwhile, Lorena Hays, writing under the pen name Lenita, saw the upheaval differently. For Lenita, it was the ongoing struggle of white women—working alongside, or perhaps a step ahead of, their menfolk—to illuminate California's "social horizon."[4] Still other residents of the Southern Mines saw the collision not as the imminent triumph of markets and morals but as an assault on their livelihoods and their comforts as well. These residents could include, for example, those who worked in or frequented gambling houses and dance halls, those who toiled in the dwindling placers, or those who found intimacy outside of marriage. Non–Anglo Americans were overrepresented among those for whom the decline of the Southern Mines meant a decline of possibility, but disappointment touched all manner of Gold Rush participant. Thus a Mexican woman who ran a fandango or a French woman who dealt monte might be put out of work by the efforts of reform-minded Anglo women—themselves often the wives of merchants, professionals, or water company managers. At the same time, a married white woman who had enjoyed the attentions of too many lonely men at "respectable" balls and parties might find herself in divorce court; then she, too, could lose her livelihood. And we have seen that those squeezed by the demands of water company officials or quartz mining magnates were often as not Anglo miners. Still, the transformation of the Southern Mines weighed most heavily on those who could not claim the mantle of whiteness.

Nowhere did change weigh more heavily than on the newest and oldest residents of the region—Chinese immigrants and native peoples. In addition to exclusionary and regulatory practices in the mines, Chinese faced other pressures that were predicated on the earlier resolution of racial and ethnic conflicts to the benefit of white Americans as well as on the arrival of increasing numbers of Anglo American women. Most Chinese women, who began to come to the Southern Mines a couple of years after Chinese men started to arrive, worked as prostitutes, and the brothels in which they worked quickly became targets for white men's brutality. Chinese men, on the other hand, frequently faced off in violent conflict with one another. The battles they planned and sometimes fought were rooted both in storms that raged in South China and in local disputes that pitted groups of immigrants against one another in a region of dwindling resources. These conflicts, in turn, became a gruesome spectator sport for white Americans in the mines, indicating, as one scholar puts it, "the casual value placed on Chinese life" as well Anglo attraction to the "perceived exoticism of Chinese culture."[5] Around the same time, Sierra Miwoks were learning to turn white spectatorship to their advantage. Already, because of the decline of animal populations and the constriction of grounds available for gathering plant foods, Miwok people were purchasing meat and flour in immigrant settlements. By the later 1850s, groups of Miwoks began to travel to towns such as Sonora and Agua Fria for a new purpose: dressed in ceremonial regalia, they danced in the streets, collecting cash from passersby. In so doing, Indians invented new traditions for a world invaded by gold-based social relations. Whether or not various residents of the diggings could profit from the gaze of white gold seekers, increasingly the ubiquity and power of that gaze structured social relations in the Southern Mines.

Perhaps the most emblematic site of change in the Southern Mines was the ubiquitous fandango. Before the Gold Rush, "fandango" was a term that referred not to a place for dance but to a particular kind of dance event—one popular among poorer Spanish Mexicans in California. The "fandango house," often called simply a "fandango," was a Gold Rush innovation.[6] By 1851, a newspaperman in Tuolumne County could write a tongue-in-cheek tribute to his town's most popular site of public amusement, titling it "The Fandango in Sonora." His was a romp of an article that compared Sonora's dance halls to the boulevards of Paris and the parks of New York City. Claiming that Sonora boasted five "fandango saloons," the writer described two, one French and the other Mexican. The French fandango was in "a stylish room, brilliantly lighted," where patrons danced a polka. In the tight embrace and unison gyration of couples, the writer detected "a Gallic fraternization"; only when the music stopped was it clear that "there were really two persons in the performance." The reader could not be sure whether the "two persons" were male and female respectively or, as was common in the early 1850s, both male. Next, the writer moved on to the Mexican fandango. In this saloon, it was dim and smoke filled the air. But the dancers were "going at it with a perfect looseness," urged on by a "brawny guitarist" whose music "lustily horrifie[d] the night." It was more likely here that men danced with women, since when the music ended, each "caballero" led a "fair dulcina" to the bar for refreshment. The caballeros, however, just as often as they were Mexicans, were "Sydney convicts" (that is, Australians), perfumed local officials, and youths who looked like mercantile clerks. It was the dancing women who made this fandango Mexican, women who, according to the writer, were "brown in complexion" and "blue" in moral character. At the night's end, each man left with one of the dancers, and the newspaperman drew the curtain, noting, "We only promised to daguerreotype the fandango, and would not outrage decency by introducing after scenes."[7]

Soon, Gold Rush journalists decided that describing the fandango itself—let alone the "after scenes"—was an outrage to decency. In the same issue of the Stockton newspaper that reprinted "The Fandango in Sonora" from the *Sonora Herald,* there also appeared a frightful account of a murder that had taken place at Casa de los Amigos, a Stockton fandango. Apparently, two men, Caleb Ruggles and James McCabe, had quarreled over which of them would go home with a woman named Luz Parilla. A bowie knife, a pistol, drunken men, and Luz Parilla herself, shuttling between her angry would-be lovers, all figured in the account, which ended with Jim McCabe dead from a gunshot wound and Caleb Ruggles dismissed on grounds of self-defense.[8] After the summer of 1851, the Stockton paper would print many more articles of this type about dance halls—articles that directly or indirectly condemned fandangos as sites of vice and violence—and none at all of the celebratory type from the Sonora paper.[9] Even the next piece on fandangos reprinted from the *Sonora Herald* sang a new tune: a year after Sonora's newspapermen winked at the town's most popular resorts, they ran an approving notice of a new city ordinance that prohibited fandangos, declaring, "the majority of the people are decidedly opposed to all such vile exhibitions."[10]

This was wishful thinking. There were plenty of people in Sonora, as elsewhere in the Southern Mines, who were decidedly attracted to such exhibitions, both patrons and workers. But the ordinance, along with a flood of newspaper reports about murder and mayhem in the dance halls, was evidence of a push that began in 1852 to curtail public amusements that had thrived in the early months and years of the Gold Rush, including not only fandangos but brothels and gambling saloons as well. This push was the consequence of two major transformations in the Southern Mines. The first involved the racial and ethnic conflicts, primarily among men, that had occurred between 1848 and 1851 and that had been resolved largely in Anglo Americans' favor—the Chilean War, the "French Revolution," and the Mariposa War.[11] The second involved an influx of Anglo American women, particularly women with family ties to men who were helping constitute a middle class in the more well-established towns of the Southern Mines. The resolution of the racial and ethnic clashes provided the engine for an assault on dance halls, gaming tables, and houses of prostitution. The arrival of white women from the eastern United States provided the fuel.

Census figures give an outline of the demographic change. In 1850, the non-native population of the Southern Mines was less than 3 percent female—about 800 women in an enumerated immigrant population approaching 30,000. By 1860, an influx of women brought that figure up to nearly 19 percent—over 9,000 women in an enumerated immigrant population of almost 50,000.[12] This was not a random increase. Although some women came to California on their own in the 1850s, many more came to join husbands or brothers or fathers already resident in the diggings. And those men in the best economic and social position to summon their wives or sisters or daughters to California were men who had weathered successfully the initial racial and ethnic strife of the Gold Rush—that is, Anglo Americans. Among Anglos, not all were equally able to send for their womenfolk; merchants, professionals, and water company officials, for example, were more able than most miners. Such shopkeepers, lawyers, and managers were the progenitors of a homegrown middle class in the Southern Mines. But class making in the nineteenth century was a family affair, and this was nowhere more true than in the diggings. Only when women joined these men in California did a middle class begin to take root.[13]

One such woman was Mary Harrison Newell, the baker's daughter from Delaware who in 1854 joined her upstate New York husband, William, in the town of Columbia.[14] William Newell had been in California for five years and early on had become secretary of the Tuolumne County Water Company (TCWC).[15] By the time Mary came, he had abandoned the company, sold some of his stock, and entered into partnership with a man named Marcellus Brainard. The two white men kept a store that William described to Mary in one of the last letters they exchanged before she went west: "it is the same as a Common Country Store at home Groceries Provisions Hardware Clothing Dry goods Mining Tools *Rum and Tobacco* fill a prominent place." Once Mary arrived, with all her enthusiasm for moneymaking in California, she entered easily into the world that William had described to her in letters: "Society is now growing a great deal better here a good many merchants and miners and others are sending for their Families."[16]

The wife of William's business partner, Clementine Brainard, was especially excited about Mary's arrival, noting in her diary on July 2, 1854, "Mrs. Newell arrived very unexpectedly this evening accompanied by her father: think I shall like her much." Although William

Newell and Marcellus Brainard did not remain in partnership long,
Mary and Clementine continued their round of visiting with one
another and with women married to other up-and-coming white
men in Columbia. Mary must have been a particular comfort to
Clementine, as Mary's self-assurance in household and business matters was matched by young Clementine's awkwardness at domestic
tasks and her astonishment at the pace and content of commerce in
Columbia. Mary was an experienced baker, for example, while
Clementine thought that learning to cook was "a bitter pill"—not
surprising, since in one attempt at frying doughnuts she "came near
setting the house on fire." Clementine also bemoaned her husband's
frequent business trips to San Francisco, and worried over the liquor
he sold in his store—a worry Mary did not seem to share.[17] Much as
the growing number of comfortably situated families, then, such
female friendships helped anchor the emerging white middle class of
the Southern Mines.

The Newell family, however, was not long for this world. Just over a
year after Mary arrived, William died. Now Mary turned her own sights
to business, plotting with her sister, who was on her way west from
Delaware, to open a store of their own. In the end, although Mary
briefly went into partnership with her father selling paint, wallpaper,
and glass—her father also went west after William's death—she soon
found another road to economic security. A year or so later, Mary
Harrison Newell married Joseph Pownall, the collector of water rents
for the TCWC who had challenged the trustees during the miners'
strike of 1855.[18] By the time they married, in 1857, Pownall himself
was both a trustee and the secretary of the water company. For his part,
Pownall had worried over his bachelor state for years (he was nearly
forty). He must have been pleased at long last to take his rightful place
in the changing Gold Rush world he had described to a friend in 1854:
"This country . . . is fast settling up with families of respectability wives
daughters & other permanent fixtures of this class which assist so
much in giving character & a healthy moral tone to the machinery regulating what is termed society."[19] Unlike Clementine Brainard, Mary
Pownall never seemed that concerned about Columbia's "moral tone."
But the social transformation of places like Columbia did not require
all the "respectable" wives and daughters of the white middle class to
tinker with "the machinery regulating what is termed society." To a
certain extent, it was enough that white women simply were present.
Their presence, in turn, served as a reminder of middle-class cultural
expectations whereby women acted as moral arbiters of society, thus
encouraging men to exercise self-control.

But Mary Pownall aside, some white women did bring with them a recognizable impulse for social reform. The impulse was recognizable, of course, because the social ills that white, middle-class women saw in the diggings—especially drinking, gambling, and sexual commerce—all existed in eastern places and had become targets of reform there.[20] So those who sought to do battle with public amusements in the Southern Mines came armed with an ideological arsenal—a discourse of reform, if you will. Consider, for example, Elizabeth Gunn, who joined her husband in California in 1851. Gunn's mother was an antislavery woman, Elizabeth Le Breton Stickney, who after the death of her first husband was (unhappily) married to the abolitionist Henry Clarke Wright. So young Elizabeth grew up surrounded by antislavery Quakers and other antebellum reformers in Philadelphia, and then she married an abolitionist, Lewis Gunn, as well.[21] By 1850, however, Lewis was in California, working as editor of the *Sonora Herald*—the paper that first printed the tongue-in-cheek tribute to the fandango in July of 1851. Elizabeth arrived in Sonora just weeks later. If one can judge by the articles reprinted from her husband's paper in the Stockton press, the *Sonora Herald* soon assumed a disapproving tone on the subject of fandangos. It is not clear what role Elizabeth played in this, but it is clear where she stood on such issues. In a letter to her mother and sisters, Elizabeth wrote that although there were "some good Anti-slavery and Temperance men" in Sonora, there were also many "of a different sort, lawyers and merchants who gamble and go to houses of ill fame and keep mistresses, mostly Mexican women." She went on to denounce a judge in town who had sold his house to prostitutes and who himself "kept" a native woman. It must have been evident to Elizabeth Gunn that women who worked in dance halls, gambling saloons, and brothels, as well as those who cohabited with men, had found viable livelihoods in Sonora. Up the hill from her own house, one of the finest and best situated in town, was another built by a young French woman—just seventeen years old—for herself, her mother, and her younger brother and sister. Elizabeth wrote that this woman earned her living "by going to the gaming houses and dealing out the cards to the players."[22] Reform-minded women had their work cut out for them.

Most white women who remonstrated against public amusements in the Southern Mines were not so well-connected as Elizabeth Gunn. Some, like Clementine Brainard, had had little experience in eastern reform circles, but felt that social conditions in the diggings demanded their attention.[23] Another such woman was Lorena Hays. It was Lorena Hays who wrote for *The Golden Era* under the pen name

Lenita, worrying over "vice and immorality" and looking to "WOMAN" as the star that would finally brighten California's "social horizon." She was also the woman who noted in her diary during the 1856 presidential election that she favored "Fremont and freedom."[24] Her father had died in 1848, when she was twenty-two. In 1853, her widowed mother decided to leave Illinois and follow siblings west, taking along her four unmarried daughters. When they arrived in Amador County, the Hays women supported themselves by taking in boarders and by teaching. Immigrating as they did after the initial boom, their financial situations were always precarious. So one by one, each of the women married, including Lorena's mother.[25]

As for herself, Lorena mourned her lot. She longed to attend school in Sacramento, but could not afford it. As consolation, she devoured every book and periodical she could find, from the *Water-Cure Journal* to *Hopes and Helps for the Young of Both Sexes*. Then she met an editor for *The Golden Era*, the first California publication to call itself "A Family Newspaper." He invited her to write a column, and she obliged, publishing seven letters in *The Golden Era* between 1854 and 1857. None of this altered Lorena's profound despair over her lack of schooling, which she had hoped would fit her to move in better social circles. Like her mother and sisters, she too married, though only after anguished indecision. Her suitor, John Clement Bowmer, was a man whom she "never really admired . . . as a lover," though she came to "love him for his goodness." Once married, she knew, "Friends, name, fame, all are given to husband—to one." She wondered if "in that one" she would find "an equivalent." She did not. In fact, after a brief period of bliss that probably coincided with her deepening sexual relationship with her husband, Lorena slipped back into despair over lost opportunities in her life. Her husband, it seems—though "*noble*" and "*good*" and capable of satisfying her in his "loving embrace"—shared none of her spiritual and intellectual passions. Lorena found an outlet for those passions by writing for publication.[26]

That she chose Lenita as her pen name for *The Golden Era*, borrowing Spanish speakers' practice of creating diminutive, affectionate forms of female names, suggests a curious process of identification, projection, and reversal. It was only as Lenita that Lorena could express her deepest longings. Somehow, Lorena had come to identify her otherworldly passions with what she understood as the worldly passions of her Mexican and Chilean neighbors, in whom she took a great interest. Indeed, Lorena tried to learn Spanish as soon as she arrived in California, and she tutored a young Chilean who wanted

to improve his English. Likewise, one of her longest journal entries
denounced the reign of terror local vigilance committees had visited
upon Mexicans and Chileans in Amador County after a small band of
robbers assumed to be Mexican had killed several Anglos at a remote
camp. As Lorena put it, "We fear a great deal more disturbance from
these committees and white greasers than from the Mexicans who
have been driven from their homes." "Greaser," of course, was a
racial slur Anglos routinely hurled at Mexicans; calling Anglo men
"white greasers," then, was the ultimate insult. Nonetheless,
although Lorena identified with Spanish-speaking people and projected upon them unfettered passions, the reforms she so wished for
in California necessarily spelled a narrowing of opportunities for
Mexicans and Chileans, and especially for those women whose livelihoods depended on the worldly passions of a still disproportionately
male social arena. In calling for such reforms, Lorena Hays gave voice
to sentiments common among white women who were helping constitute a middle class in the Southern Mines.[27]

Still other Anglo women were less concerned about what Lenita
called California's "moral atmosphere" than about the ways in which
social conditions in the Southern Mines intimately impinged upon
their everyday lives. In a divorce case in Amador County, for example, Chloe Cooper complained that when her husband, James, left
their home in New York State in 1849 and went to California, "he
commenced to visit fandango houses . . . and kept company with
divers women of ill fame of the Spanish race . . . and did commit
adultery, and have carnal connection with them in said houses of ill
fame." What was worse, when Chloe joined James in 1854, he continued his carousing. His behavior finally came to her attention,
Chloe said, in 1857, and she left him.[28] Another case told a similar
tale. Even though Mary Jane Anderson went west along with her husband, James, once in California this James too "spent his time among
idle and dissolute persons, and frequenters of gambling saloons and
brothels," and he slept with women Mary Jane called "spanish prostitutes" as well.[29] Likewise, Mary Ann Hayes called her husband,
Nicholas, "a frequenter of houses of ill fame" in her divorce complaint, and Tuolumne County acquaintances backed her up. A team-
ster said he had seen Nicholas go off into private rooms with a
"Spanish" prostitute in Sonora. And a neighbor claimed he had seen
Nicholas at a brothel in Columbia asking a Mexican woman "what
she charged." The neighbor recalled that the woman had said "three
Dollars," and that the two had disappeared for half an hour thereafter.[30] There is no evidence that women such as Chloe Cooper, Mary

Jane Anderson, and Mary Ann Hayes participated in campaigns to shut down public amusements in the Southern Mines, but one can imagine that they did not stand in the way.

What did these campaigns look like? Interestingly enough, it is easier to find complaints about public amusements than to find evidence of action against them. Actual reform efforts on the part of Anglo American women and their menfolk were limited. Despite their increasing cultural, economic, and political power, Anglos, according to the 1860 federal census, constituted less than half of the total population in the Southern Mines, ranging from a low of 37 percent in sparsely populated Mariposa County to a high of 49 percent in more populous Amador County. Since these figures do not include native peoples, and since non-Anglo populations in general often were underenumerated by census takers, the actual percentages of white Americans in the southern diggings may have been even lower.[31] By definition, then, Anglos in the Southern Mines pursued reform from a precarious position. And, by the mid-1850s, the white American population was fractured by growing class divisions. Furthermore, Anglo men were sharply divided over the need for reform, since many were enthusiastic participants in the leisure worlds reformers decried. Nonetheless, there were sporadic attempts to bring such worlds to an end, which took shape in temperance organizing, in campaigns for Sunday business closings and Maine-style liquor laws (which would prohibit the sale and manufacture of alcohol), and in local initiatives against dance halls, gaming tables, and houses of prostitution.[32]

White women took an active role in these efforts. Women's diaries from the mid-1850s suggest that some merchants' wives worked behind the scenes, encouraging their husbands to give up selling liquor or to close their stores on the Christian Sabbath. Clementine Brainard, for instance, prayed in her diary that her husband Marcellus would "come to the determination soon that by the help of God he will deal in no intoxicating drinks whatever." She added, "may he feel that it is not good for his soul if it is for his purse." Clementine may have made Marcellus feel that it was not good for his marriage, either.[33] Likewise, Lorena Hays Bowmer assumed a triumphant mood when her husband, John, "at last effected a settlement of his business" so that his store remained closed on Sunday, suggesting that she, too, had been an advocate for reform within her own home.[34] But there were organized efforts among white women as well. In 1855, for example, the Stockton press noted that the "ladies" of Campo Seco, in Calaveras County, were the "prime movers" in advocating a Maine law. In 1856, a Tuolumne County newspaper observed that the "Ladies of Columbia" were petitioning merchants there to close their shops on Sunday. And in the same year, the *Weekly Ledger* in the Amador County town of Volcano poked fun at women's support of Sabbatarianism, suggesting that petitions to the state legislature in that town "were put in circulation by [marriageable] but not married ladies, in order to give the young 'lords of creation' one day in the week to devote at the shrine of bright eyes and bewitching ringlets."[35] Even where white women were not distributing petitions, they were understood within their own social circles to be both inspiration for and prime beneficiaries of reform. The *Weekly Ledger* may have teased those with "bright eyes and bewitching ringlets" about their interest in a Sunday law, but the same newspaper routinely called on women readers to serve as moral beacons, whether by drawing men to church through their own regular attendance or by lending their aid in establishing schools for children and lyceums for adults. In the end, it was thought, this would all redound to the benefit of "ladies," as they would be able to walk peaceful streets that had once been "monopolized by rowdyism of every grade."[36]

The behavior of some Anglo women in the Southern Mines belied such middle-class cultural assumptions, which connected ladyhood, whiteness, and morality as interlocking links in a single chain. In addition to assaults on polyglot sites of public amusement, one of the means by which white women and their menfolk tried to redirect the leisure energies of Gold Rush participants was by creating alternatives to saloons, fandangos, and brothels. Among these alternatives were balls sponsored by community organizations and parties thrown by members of the emerging white middle class. These balls and parties often seem to have had the desired effect. But they could also become sites of contestation. In March of 1854, for example, Clementine and Marcellus Brainard received an invitation to what they thought would be such an event in Columbia. They intended to go to the party, but then Marcellus took sick. In the end, Clementine was relieved, noting in her diary, "I am very thankful something has happened to prevent our going . . . as I understand some are invited that are not fit for decent people to associate with." Her worst fears were realized when she learned that some had left the party in protest when a man named Cazneau arrived with a woman to whom he was not married. The next day, two separate duels threatened between Cazneau and the men who had departed when he arrived. (Neither fight actually materialized.) Clementine Brainard did not identify the woman who accompanied Cazneau to the party, but an 1852 court record provides a clue. In that year, an emigrant from Maine named Phoebe Quimby divorced her husband on grounds of cruelty; once, for instance, while she was pregnant, her husband had thrown her across a room. Phoebe's husband countered that Phoebe had been sleeping with Thomas Cazneau for almost a year, and that she had moved in with Cazneau after filing for divorce. Despite these accusations, Phoebe won the divorce. In 1852, it seems, a white woman could leave a cruel husband and cohabit with another white man with relative impunity. But by 1854, a couple such as Phoebe Quimby and Thomas Cazneau could no longer go to a party attended by "decent people" without trouble erupting.[37] Times were changing.

Phoebe Quimby was not the only Anglo woman who failed to advance the cause of reform. Divorce records from the 1850s are replete with accusations against unruly white women. Such charges are hardly unique to the Southern Mines or to the Gold Rush era. One historian, for example, has studied divorce in two nonmining counties of California between 1850 and 1890. He finds that although both women and men charged estranged spouses with adultery, husbands did so at twice the rate of wives. Accusations of adultery do not necessarily reflect how often women had sex outside their marriages. Instead, the charges represent a complex interaction among actual instances of extramarital sex, legal restrictions on admissible grounds for divorce, and cultural ideas about what constituted the most egregious affronts to marital vows for women.[38] None of this is unique to the diggings. But charges of marital infidelity in the diggings did reflect the particularities of changing social relations there. Some white women seem to have initiated extramarital romance, for instance, at the very balls and parties that other white women hoped would stem the tide of Gold Rush patterns of leisure.

Because there were still five times more men than women in the Southern Mines as late as 1860, even gatherings middle-class people thought of as "respectable" could become arenas of contact between single men looking for women's attention and women looking for intimacy outside their marriages. The story of Mary Ann Chick is a case in point. When Mary Ann joined her husband, Alfred, in Calaveras County in 1855, their relationship quickly deteriorated. Mary Ann filed for divorce in 1859, charging Alfred with cruelty and violence. Alfred countered, however, that Mary Ann had taken up with a boarder in their household, Frank Averill, with whom she attended balls and parties and from whom she accepted "valuable presents." That social events organized by middle-class people could become sites of moral ambiguity is also suggested by the divorce case of Emily and O. S. Davis. Emily charged her husband with extreme cruelty, and a neighbor backed her up, testifying that Mr. Davis called his wife a "damned stinking Shit ass" and a "damned wasteful bitch of Hell." Significantly, the same neighbor praised Emily by insisting that "she does not go out as other women do to balls and parties."[39] Those "other women," then—women such as Mary Ann Chick—must have used balls and parties to bask in the attentions of unmarried men.

While some white women dallied with men at "respectable" gatherings, others profited by Gold Rush gender divisions of labor, which took husbands away from family homes for much of every day and sometimes for even longer stretches of time. Sarah Philbrick of Amador County, for instance, tried to divorce her husband, William, for cruelty and violence. But William retorted that when he "was away from home at work on a Quartz lode," Sarah would visit an unmarried man named Bayerque. Furthermore, William charged, Sarah did this at night, often "dressed in men's apparel." William thought she wore men's clothing "so as to prevent being detected while on the streets." Whatever Sarah's reasons for cross-dressing when she visited her lover, according to William's friends, she showed no remorse for her actions. After Sarah gave birth to a child, for example, William complained that the baby was not his, but rather "a certain Frenchman's at Volcano." Sarah shot back that, in fact, the child did "[look] like the Frenchman." William's brother said that this kind of wrangling was common between William and Sarah. The brother recalled that when William accused Sarah of "kissing a man," she rejoined that she "would do it again." So William slapped her. In the end, the judge disallowed the divorce, arguing, "Courts of equity cannot allow a woman who boldly avows her own turpitude to her husband to complain of her husband's anger when thus provoked."[40]

Likewise, in Tuolumne County, Joseph Hall complained that his wife, Celia, had "established a system of telegraphing or signalizing to inform her paramours" whenever Joseph was away from the house working. Joseph named three men with whom he was sure Celia had been intimate. One of these men, Charles Knight, testified that he indeed had slept with Celia. He also said he had seen one of the other men in bed with her as well. Charles explained that the first time he and Celia had sex, he had gone to the Halls' house to dig a cellar while Joseph was off at work. When Charles went inside for a drink of water, he said, Celia "began to sing bawdy songs." Then she locked Charles in the house. He was able to escape, but when he went back inside later, Charles insisted, "she seized hold of me and forced me to have intercourse with her."[41] Celia, it seems, would not take "no" for an answer.

We cannot know whether the relationships between the determined Celia Hall and the reluctant Charles Knight or between cross-dressing Sarah Philbrick and the French man Bayerque bore much resemblance to the descriptions deponents provided in divorce proceedings. But the descriptions in and of themselves, because they were designed to influence the court, had to tell stories that made sense to judges and jury members (all of whom were white men). To those who heard them, stories about married white women cavorting with men at parties or forcing men to copulate when husbands were off at work made all too much sense. That such stories made sense probably said as much about white male anxieties as about white female activities. But it also suggests that while there were plenty of white, middle-class women advocating reform in the Southern Mines, there were others whose actions threatened those efforts. This would help explain why narratives of unruly, aggressive Anglo women who took advantage of Gold Rush social relations were so prevalent in the 1850s. At the very least, such stories suggest that keeping the chain linking ladyhood, whiteness, and morality in good repair required constant vigilance. The work of discursive repair must have sometimes frustrated the social practices of reform.

But there were other reasons why streets in the Southern Mines often remained stubbornly "monopolized by rowdyism." Put most simply, some Mexican, Chilean, and French women wanted it that way, for a rowdy street was a path to a living. These women had helped create not only a domestic marketplace but also a commercial sphere of public amusements in the Southern Mines. Because the early exclusions and extortions of the Gold Rush, especially the 1850 foreign miners' tax, were aimed primarily at non-Anglo miners, those non-Anglos who toiled at different pursuits were less likely to leave the diggings. Women were overrepresented among those who worked in other sectors of the boom economy, and thus were overrepresented among those who stayed on in the gold regions. They carved out for themselves economic niches that exclusionists—whose goal was to reserve the placers for white American men—at first ignored. Such women's work did not threaten the "independence" of Anglo miners. In fact, some white men came to define their access to the services French, Mexican, and Chilean women provided as part and parcel of their manly "independence." The patronage of Anglo miners, as well as that of those Latin Americans and Europeans who remained, offered a measure of economic security to women who worked in the heterosocial leisure world of the diggings.[42] Recall, for example, Elizabeth Gunn's neighbor, a French teenager, who by dealing cards in Sonora had made enough money to build a house for her entire family.

French women such as Gunn's neighbor were ubiquitous at gaming tables throughout the Southern Mines. Documents from an 1856 grand jury investigation of gambling saloons in Tuolumne County make this clear. As a result of its investigation, the grand jury filed a number of indictments against both women and men who worked at gaming tables. Just as grand jury members indicted a "John Doe" and a "Richard Roe" for gambling, so too did they indict a "French Mary," vaguely accusing such a woman of opening a "certain . . . game of chance called Monte" in a "certain house in Columbia."[43] They may have had a specific monte dealer in mind, but they made the indictment ambiguous enough that any one of a number of French women could have found herself in court. Women from France did not content themselves with just working in saloons, either. Many owned or managed such establishments. In the mid-1850s, for instance, court records show that several French women ran saloons in the town of Mariposa, including a Madame Clement, a Madame Follet, and a Madame Henry.[44] Emilie Henry seems to have been especially well situated. In 1856, the San Francisco merchants Mills and Vantine sued Henry for failing to pay them for what they claimed was almost $800 worth of supplies for her business. In the course of the suit, the court attached Henry's property, and the schedule of her belongings revealed an impressive collection of barroom furnishings in addition to large quantities of champagne, wine, brandy, port, and ale. For her part, Henry sniffed that the goods she received from Mills and Vantine were "not of the quality contracted for" and "not of the value charged."[45] When middle-class Anglo women worried about the relative affluence of women who worked in saloons, then, these worries were not sheer flights of fancy.

And it was not only French women who owned and managed sites of public amusement in the Southern Mines. Mexican and Chilean women did so as well. A woman named Isabel Ortis is a notable case in point. It is not clear when Ortis arrived in the Southern Mines, or even whether she came from Chile, from northern Mexico, or from elsewhere in Mexican California.[46] She was at least minimally literate, as she signed her own name in legal documents. Her business acumen must have been considerable. A variety of court records for a single year, 1858, show that she managed two separate fandangos in Amador and Calaveras counties. An inquest into the death of a Portuguese-born man who had emigrated to California from Chile, for example, places Ortis as the proprietor of a dance hall at Camanche Camp, in Calaveras County, and as the owner of a house there. According to the inquest, the deceased had visited the dance hall one night and had later retired with a woman at Ortis's home, where he took sick and died. Ortis was among those called to testify before the jury of inquest. She was quick to point out that the man "did not eat or drink anything in the dance house."[47] (No charges were brought against her.) In addition, Amador County records reveal that Ortis leased a building on Main Street in the town of Jackson that she used as a saloon and dance house. The building belonged to a Mexican or Chilean woman, Natividad Shermenhoof, and her German-born husband, John. When Natividad divorced John in 1856, he retained control of their common property, including the dance house on Main Street. So in 1858, Natividad sued John for her share of their property, claiming that he had earned $1,000 in rent from Isabel Ortis since the lease began. Natividad won the case, and she got her share of Isabel's rent money.[48] For both Isabel Ortis and Natividad Shermenhoof, then, the Gold Rush commercialization of leisure spelled profit, though Isabel probably reaped the most direct rewards.

So accomplished a businesswoman was Isabel Ortis that at least one Anglo American, a man named John McKay, tried to hide his failings behind her success. John may have been Isabel's lover; at least that is what one of his creditors maintained. In 1856, John McKay had joined with the attorney Armsted Brown in building a livery stable on a lot that McKay already occupied on Main Street in Jackson, down the road from Ortis's fandango. Brown supplied the capital for the stable, and McKay mortgaged his half of the property to Brown in order to secure the loan. But McKay fell behind in his payments, and, in early 1858, he applied to the court as an insolvent debtor. In the meantime, however, he quietly had transferred his interest in the livery stable to Isabel Ortis. According to the attorney Brown, McKay did this in order to shield the property from creditors. But Ortis, in turn, perhaps in order to defeat the mortgage, purchased title to the lot on which the stable stood from the prominent Californio Andrés Pico.[49] Pico was among those landowning Spanish Mexicans who had led the resistance against Anglo Americans during the conquest of 1846–48 (his brother, Pio Pico, was California's governor when the conquest began). After the signing of the Treaty of Guadalupe Hidalgo, however, Andrés Pico took his place in the new

Armsted C. Brown, attorney at law, who tangled with Isabel Ortis and her lover John McKay in court.

Courtesy of Charles Schwartz, Ltd., New York.

political order as a state legislator, while struggling to retain his land-holdings.[50] His claim to the lot in Jackson where the livery stable stood rested in his Arroyo Seco land grant, which dated from the Mexican period and was as yet unconfirmed.[51] The Arroyo Seco case was making its way through the legal system as slowly and tortuously as was John C. Frémont's claim to the Mariposa Estate. Frémont received far more attention nationally than Pico did, but locally white miners and settlers in Amador County denounced the Arroyo Seco grant just as their counterparts to the south vilified Las Mariposas.[52]

In trying to nail down her interest in Amador County real estate by linking it to a Mexican land grant, then, Isabel Ortis entered a juridical maelstrom.[53] When Armsted Brown turned to foreclose the mortgage on the stable and to challenge John McKay's claim of insolvency, the attorney went after Isabel Ortis with a vengeance, making legal mincemeat of her appeal to the Arroyo Seco grant and dragging her character through the mud as well. As he prepared for McKay's insolvency hearing, Brown drew up questions for McKay designed to expose both McKay and Ortis as morally, not materially, bankrupt: "Were you at the time [you sold Ortis a half interest in the livery stable] living and cohabiting with her . . . ? Who is this Isabel Ortiz—where does she live and what does she follow for a living?" And among his notes about issues to bring before the court, Brown wrote, "McKay has for a long time and still does keep live with and maintain a Woman of Spanish [descent] known as Isabel Ortiz the Mistress of a Dance House and house of ill fame in Jackson." The attorney's notes continued, arguing that if McKay "has incurred any losses since commencing his business of stable keeping . . . they have been lavished upon his said Mistress and not in payment of [his] debts." Brown, then, planned to use the intimate relationship between Ortis and McKay as a way of discrediting McKay's legal claims—not to mention his social claims to respectability. And Brown threw in Ortis's status as a dance hall proprietor for good measure.[54]

According to the argument Brown was going to make in court, McKay had squandered money on his "mistress" rather than losing it in legitimate business. Here Brown was disingenuous about who was keeping whom in this relationship, since it was Ortis who stayed afloat while McKay sank deeper into debt. But the attorney's argument would have been an effective one among the Anglo American men who heard it in court: a white man ought to remain master of his own resources and not spend those resources recklessly on a "mistress" of "Spanish" descent. What was the point of the military and economic conquest of California, whereby Anglo American men asserted dominance over Spanish Mexican men, if Latin American women could turn around and exact tribute from Anglo men with impunity?[55] By taking Ortis to court, then, Brown drew her into an arena of power that could re-create her as a representative of a cultural category—a "kept" woman of "Spanish" descent, the "mistress" of a notorious fandango. Thus categorized, she could be dismissed.

It is not clear from the historical record what happened to Isabel Ortis. But she may have met her match in Armsted Brown. According to a local historian, Brown was not only a prominent lawyer but also "an inveterate buyer of real estate." Indeed, when fire swept through Jackson in 1862, four years after Ortis and McKay tangled with him in court, Brown lost thirty separate properties in town. A native of Missouri but an emigrant from the lead mining districts of Wisconsin, Brown arrived in 1849 at the camp that would become the town of Jackson. Soon thereafter, he returned to Wisconsin for his wife, Philippa, a native of Cornwall, and their six offspring; they would have five more children as well. The Browns were one of the first white families in town. A Whig who turned Democrat when the Whig Party collapsed, Armsted Brown held public office in the town, county, and state off and on throughout his life. Deep pockets, family ties, legal skills, political power: this was not a happy combination to find in an Anglo neighbor if one was a Mexican or Chilean fandango manager trying to hold on to one's livelihood in the Southern Mines. Indeed, the arrival of people like the Browns presaged the end of an era. Whatever happened to Isabel Ortis in the short term, then, the long-term outcome is clear enough. Left standing after the 1862 fire in Jackson was the Browns' impressive two-story brick home built atop the town's most prominent hill. One can still visit that home today; it is now the Amador County Museum, which preserves official collective memory of Jackson and its environs. Armsted and Philippa Brown are remembered there; Isabel Ortis and the hapless John McKay are not.[56]

For every Isabel Ortis in Jackson and every Emilie Henry in Mariposa, there must have been dozens of Mexican, Chilean, and French women in the Southern Mines who worked in fandangos, saloons, and brothels without owning or operating them. Dancing with men, dealing them cards, servicing their bodies—these were not easy ways to make a living, and each grew more difficult as the 1850s progressed. Consider, for instance, the problems Laura Echeverria faced in Sonora. She had married Juan Echeverria there in 1851. It is unclear from the historical record where Laura and Juan grew up, though evidence suggests that Juan came from Monterey County in California, where he worked a rancho near Mission San Juan Bautista. Laura and Juan did not stay together long. By 1852, Laura was on her own in Sonora. In 1857, she sued for divorce, claiming that Juan, though he was worth at least $4,000, had failed to provide for her. Juan countered that since their separation he had given Laura some $6,000, which she, in turn, had "squandered in dissipation."[57]

Those who testified on Laura's and Juan's behalf, respectively, fell in behind them. Several men backed Juan up, arguing that he had given Laura money out of the proceeds of livestock he had sold and that he had allowed her to collect rent on properties he owned in Sonora as well. When asked why Laura and Juan separated, a man named Pedro, who may have worked for Juan, answered bluntly, "I believe it was the woman's fault." Pedro acknowledged, however, that Laura had lost her livelihood when the reform bug bit the Southern Mines, explaining that "she dealt [cards at the Long Tom Saloon] until the gaming law was enforced." Another man, named Bartolomé, was scandalized when he saw Laura with a child that could not have been Juan's: "I told her at the time that she was in for it," he said. According to Bartolomé, Laura retorted "that she was young and could not live without a man."[58]

Some of the men and all of the women who testified took a more charitable view of Laura. They insisted that she had worked hard in the years she had been on her own, sometimes taking in washing and sewing, sometimes keeping a restaurant, sometimes working in a dance hall, sometimes selling "cold suppers" at the Long Tom Saloon, and sometimes dealing cards there. One of her coworkers at the dance hall was a French woman named Anne Lyons. Anne explained how Laura's work life had evolved since the Echeverrias' separation, which occurred while Laura was pregnant: "In 1851," Anne testified, Laura was "in a family way, and she was cooking at her sister's house." Anne continued, with markedly French syntax, "after [Laura's] confinement she was during two months sick. I lent her then two hundred dollars. She went over to the [L]ong [T]om and used to make up cold suppers; afterwards she was washing and sewing and afterwards she has worked with me for a long time."[59] As this testimony suggests, French, Mexican, and Chilean women struggled to earn a living, moving back and forth from work in the domestic marketplace to work in commercialized leisure to work in their own households. They also relied on one another—female relatives and fellow employees, women from their homelands and women from half a world away. Indeed, when Laura Echeverria was "in a family way" and after she gave birth, not only her sister but a French coworker stepped in to help.

The women who testified on Laura's behalf during the divorce bristled at the lawyers' questions. Rose Cartier, for example, had been Laura's employer. When asked "what kind of business" she ran, the French woman replied simply, "I keep an establishment in Sonora." Only when pressed would she say that the business was a "Dance house and bar room." When asked what kind of work Laura had done at the Long Tom Saloon, Anne Lyons answered that Laura prepared meals there. When asked if Laura also gambled, Anne retorted, "I do not know as I have never been inside a gambling house." When asked what kind of business went on at the Long Tom, among the most notorious gaming saloons in Sonora, Anne claimed not to know. Most obstreperous, however, was Laura's sister, Matilda, who was angry both with her brother-in-law Juan and with the attorneys attending the divorce case. Matilda insisted that her sister was often ill and that Juan "never contributed to her support at those times." Instead, Matilda said, she herself labored to support Laura and Laura's child, until Laura's health improved and the sisters were able to work together. When Laura asked Juan for money, Matilda fumed, Juan told his wife that "she might make tortillas to maintain herself." Disgusted, Matilda explained how hard the sisters had worked to support themselves. When asked if Laura gambled, Matilda acknowledged that Laura had "had a bank" but claimed that Laura "never bet herself," adding, "that was the only mode she had of maintaining herself in Sonora." When asked if this was a monte bank, Matilda rejoined, "I don't know. I never paid any attention to it. I don't recollect." And when pressed to reveal her own occupation, she shot back, "That has nothing to do with my sister's affairs. It is nobody's business."[60]

The exasperation these women felt is palpable in their exchanges with the lawyers who handled the Echeverrias' divorce. Their anger is not hard to understand. Here were well-heeled Anglo men putting non-Anglo women's work lives under a magnifying glass, arching an eyebrow at all they saw. Perhaps the attorneys themselves were patrons of Rose Cartier's dance hall and the Long Tom Saloon. Perhaps they were not. But it would have been easy for the women to see these men as representing a cultural category, the existence of which had once assured Spanish- and French-speaking women of a livelihood. Anglo men in and around Sonora had been among the best customers of local saloons and fandangos. Now some such men—no doubt backed by their womenfolk—threatened to bring about Mexican, Chilean, and French women's dispossession. All Gold Rush participants had the power to re-create others as representatives of cultural categories. But, more and more, that power was working disproportionately to the benefit of Anglo Americans.

Indeed, it would only be a matter of time before women such as Laura Echeverria, Rose Cartier, Isabel Ortis, and Emilie Henry would drift away from the Southern Mines altogether. Gold Rush social relations persisted into the 1860s, but they began to be overshadowed by a new social order as early as 1852, when the *Sonora Herald* wrote approvingly of the city ordinance that prohibited fandangos. The arrival of women such as Mary Newell, Clementine Brainard, Elizabeth Gunn, and Lorena Hays presaged the changes. At the same time, the divorces of women such as Chloe Cooper, Mary Jane Anderson, and Mary Ann Hayes, who accused their husbands of keeping company with Mexican and Chilean women in the late 1850s, show just how protracted the struggle was between older and newer styles of heterosocial relations in this multiracial, multiethnic social world. It was protracted in part because white, middle-class women, perceived as those who both inspired and benefited from reform, were few in number; because white men were ambivalent about whether change should even occur; and because a handful of white women themselves rather liked the old order, which gave them intimate access to a wide range of lonely men. Just as important, however, was the will of Spanish- and French-speaking women to earn a living in the context of conquest.[61] The avenues that many of them followed—owning, managing, and working in dance halls, gambling saloons, and brothels—were wide open in the initial gold boom, and they narrowed only gradually over the course of the 1850s. It was not easy work and it would not last forever; but then neither would much of what constituted Gold Rush labor. Casa de los Amigos down in Stockton, Sonora's Long Tom Saloon, the fandango Isabel Ortis ran in Jackson, Madame Clement's saloon in Mariposa—for a time, these were places where California gold found its way out of the hands of men from around the world and into the hands of women from Mexico, Chile, and France. When these buildings closed their doors, just as surely as when the placers pinched out, the Gold Rush was over.[62]

Sometimes you could even see it happening. One fall day in 1858, a stage driver came to the office of a Stockton newspaper with word of a fire that had just ravaged the main street of Jamestown, near Sonora in Tuolumne County. It began, the driver said, "in an unoccupied building formerly used as a fandango house." The blaze spread quickly down both sides of the street, consuming all but the small number of fireproof structures. Many of the buildings that burned were hastily constructed wooden saloons. Next door to the boarded fandango house, however, was a dwelling that was still occupied. A woman lived there, the stage driver said, and when the fire started, she rushed out into the street with a trunk containing $3,000. In the fright and confusion that followed, the trunk was spirited away. According to the driver, many believed that whoever stole the trunk had anticipated all of this, that "the fire was started with the view of having the money thus exposed."[63] The historical record reveals nothing else about this woman. But it would not be far-fetched to imagine that she had worked in the fandango, or maybe in one of the saloons that burned nearby. Her earnings neatly stored in a trunk, perhaps she was hoping to leave the diggings with assets for a new life. The fire would have destroyed those dreams. Most women did not end their careers in the Southern Mines in so dramatic a fashion, but a fandango in flames was surely a sign of the times.

In the end, Anglo American, middle-class people did not succeed in ridding the diggings of commercialized forms of leisure in which men purchased proximity to women. Increasingly, though, the work done in that leisure sphere was performed not by self-supporting Mexican, Chilean, and French women but by indentured and enslaved Chinese women, who reaped little direct benefit from their labor. Indeed, at the same moment that French- and Spanish-speaking women were riding west in stagecoaches bound for Stockton or Sacramento en route to San Francisco, Cantonese-speaking women were riding east up into the foothills of the Sierra Nevada. By 1860, almost 450 Chinese women lived in the four counties that constituted the Southern Mines, roughly 4.5 percent of the Chinese population.[64] While a handful of these women may have been servants or merchants' wives, most worked as prostitutes. The lives of Chinese women engaged in sexual commerce, then, serve as part of a coda to stories of transformation in the Southern Mines during the 1850s. White spectatorship of two other sets of social practices complete the postscript. In the first, Chinese men faced off against each other in armed conflict. In the second, groups of Miwoks paraded into immigrant settlements, making music and dancing for townspeople, and collecting cash on the side. On the one hand, these three final topics suggest just how deeply entrenched forms of Anglo power had become in the Southern Mines by the late 1850s. On the other hand, each demonstrates how incomplete and unstable any such relations of domination remained, so long as a will to both survival and dignity existed among those with less access to power.

First, then, the world of Chinese sexual commerce: historians have demonstrated that Chinese women who sold sex for cash exercised far less control over their labor and earnings than did other women employed in Gold Rush leisure establishments, including non-Chinese prostitutes. Many died on the job, stricken by sexually transmitted disease or cut down by violence at the hands of clients or employers. Cantonese-speaking women also came to California under circumstances different from those of most of their menfolk. Chinese men often emigrated independently or under the credit-ticket system, whereby a man repaid the cost of travel out of the money he earned in the diggings. In contrast, most Chinese women arrived in San Francisco already indentured or enslaved. Secret societies, or tongs, which had roots in underground, antigovernment movements in South China, emerged in California as the major organizers of Chinese prostitution. It was a profitable business for procurers, importers, and brothel owners, if not for prostitutes. In any given year, for example, a brothel owner could make much more money off an individual woman's labor than a male Chinese worker could hope to earn. It followed, then, that Chinese prostitutes lived under strict surveillance and control.[65]

Some prostitutes may have arrived earlier, but it is clear that by 1854, tongs had established brothels throughout the Southern Mines as well as in Stockton.[66] It was during that year that newspapers began to report on a variety of largely unsuccessful attempts to close or at least regulate houses of prostitution. Fire companies in Stockton and Sonora, for example, did the job by turning fire hoses on Chinese brothels. The sexual and racial symbolism of such ejaculatory attacks could not have been lost on participants. Indeed, one such hosing in Stockton—itself an act of destruction and intimidation—provoked a wider anti-Chinese riot during which white men assaulted Chinese women. So violent was this event that newspapermen who earlier had winked at "the cold water remedy" now denounced fire hosing and upbraided those men who had perpetrated "indecent attacks upon frightened prostitutes."[67] By the late 1850s, fire itself had become a metaphor for Chinese sexual commerce, and Chinese houses of prostitution, in turn, came to stand, in Anglo minds, for the troubling persistence of Chinese settlement in the diggings. In 1857 and 1858, for example, costly conflagrations consumed parts of Columbia and Mariposa. In both cases, newspapers blamed the blazes on Chinese residents, claiming that the fires began in Chinese brothels. After Columbia's calamity, a correspondent telegraphed the *San Joaquin Republican* to report that the fire—which, it was said, created several hundred thousand dollars worth of damage—"was caused by an opium smoker" at a house of prostitution. A later report detailed the losses suffered by white people in Columbia, and the list of sufferers read like a who's who of the town's middle class: Marcellus Brainard, merchant and husband of Clementine, lost $8,000, for instance, and Joseph Pownall, TCWC official and new husband of the former Mary Harrison Newell, lost $2,500.[68] In newspaper articles such as these, Chinese communities became hotbeds of drugs and desire, threatening to engulf the self-control, industry, and sobriety of the Anglo American middle class.

Efforts to contain or curtail Chinese prostitution were ongoing in the 1850s. As early as 1854, Sonora's town council, for example, passed a "stringent ordinance for the suppression of Chinese houses of ill-fame."[69] To the north in Jackson, town fathers took yet another approach. There the marshal began collecting a licensing fee of twenty dollars a month from those who managed Chinese brothels. This practice did not last long. Within months, an Amador County grand jury indicted Jackson's trustees for pretending that they "had the legal right to levy a Tax upon Chinese houses." In case anyone missed the point, grand jury members defined such establishments as "houses of ill fame kept for purposes of public prostitution and occupied by Chinese whores." One trustee indicted was Armsted Brown, the attorney and landlord who would soon set his sights on property claimed by the dance hall manager Isabel Ortis, and whose home would one day become the county's historical museum.[70] Again, white men's ambivalence about the commercialization of sex—a process in which they might find pleasure or profit or both—limited attempts at reform.

All in all, fire hoses, town ordinances, and license fees had little lasting impact on Chinese sexual commerce in the Southern Mines. No doubt such tactics increased the daily risks of prostitution, but not to the extent of eliminating brothels as workplaces for Cantonese-speaking women. In 1856, for example, a Sonora grand jury indicted "Chinaman John" and "John Doe a Chinaman," two different men, for keeping houses where women sold sex for cash, though the local law prohibiting such establishments was already two years old. In 1858, a white woman in Amador County filed for divorce, accusing her husband of sleeping with a woman at a "Chinna Brothel" in Sacramento as well as "various women of the chinese race" elsewhere in the diggings. And later that year, under the title "Americanizing," an Amador County editor reported that two Chinese prostitutes had "astonished and amused the people of Volcano by appearing on the streets in American colors—hoops and all!"[71] Chinese sexual commerce itself was no longer astonishing to white people, only the sight of Chinese prostitutes walking the streets in American-style clothing. For some—no doubt especially for white men—that sight was a source of amusement.

It was amusing for two reasons. First, it confounded racialized gender categories in ways reminiscent of the early years of the Gold Rush in the Southern Mines, when white men did domestic work, danced with each other, and developed new hierarchies of gender and race to accommodate the presence of Mexican, Chilean, French, and Miwok women. It must have reminded such men of the "world upside down" created in the Sierra Nevada foothills after 1848. But now ten years had passed, and a new social order had taken hold in the diggings, brought about in part by an influx of Anglo American women. So the sight of Chinese prostitutes promenading in "American" garments could amuse white men for another reason: it did not threaten that social order. There is no evidence that Chinese women who labored as prostitutes in the Southern Mines were able to achieve anything like the limited financial independence Mexican, Chilean, and French women gained by owning, managing, or even just working in leisure establishments. Historians have identified a tiny handful of Chinese women elsewhere who were able to profit from sexual commerce, such as Ah Toy and Suey Hin in San Francisco.[72] But no such women emerge from the historical record of the Southern Mines in the 1850s; there are no tongue-in-cheek newspaper accounts, no revealing court records, no white women's diaries filled with fears about the relative affluence of Chinese working women. For most white men, the world by 1858 was turning right side up, and Chinese women in hoop skirts were a curiosity, not a symbol of a world gone crazy.

For the promenading prostitutes, wearing hoop skirts must have meant something else altogether. The meanings these women attached to the act, however, are lost in a historical record generated by people who knew little and cared less about the inner lives of Chinese prostitutes. There is no way to know for sure, for example, who decided what these women would wear the summer day they appeared on the streets of Volcano. Higher-status prostitutes in San Francisco, who served a Chinese clientele, often wore elaborate and expensive clothing. But mining town prostitutes were generally of a lower status, and they served a multiracial clientele. One historian contends that prostitutes in the diggings endured especially harsh treatment—that banishment to a mining town brothel was a way to punish women who defied established controls in the city.[73] Thus it seems likely that a brothel owner, rather than the women themselves, decided on the hoop skirts and then sent his charges out walking, perhaps to drum up business. There was every reason in the summer of 1858 for a businessman to dream up new ways to attract customers: it was in the spring of that year that gold was discovered at the Fraser River in British Columbia, drawing thousands away from the California diggings and depressing the local economy. Just days after the women walked the streets in "American colors," the same newspaper complained about all those who had "left Amador county and gone to Frazer river."[74]

But even if a brothel owner hit on the idea of dressing Chinese women in "American" finery, it was not he but they who promenaded two abreast in skirts that took up a good deal of ideological as well as physical space. The flavor of that emotional experience is lost to the historical record, but one can imagine that appropriating symbols of ladyhood, whiteness, and morality provided an unexpected feast for women whom most other Gold Rush participants meant to starve. It was a rich joke in a poor world. It was a mockery of gentility, that great reservoir from which white, middle-class women drew so much of their social, cultural, and economic power. As one scholar has argued, Chinese women could take courage in knowing that their sale or indenture into prostitution helped their struggling families back home in the Pearl River Delta.[75] Perhaps courage could come as well in a hoop-skirted march through the dusty streets of a town like Volcano.

Local newspaper reports on Chinese women, of course, reveal more about the discursive and social practices of Anglo American, middle-class men than about the lives of Cantonese-speaking women. But in the absence of documents generated by the women themselves, such obdurate reports must be forced to yield every shred of evidence they contain about the ways in which Chinese women were able to maneuver in a tightly circumscribed social and discursive world. Along with the account of the promenading prostitutes, a handful of newspaper references to Chinese women in 1857 and 1858 suggest that some such women pushed at the boundaries of that world to good effect. The writer of one report, for example—tellingly titled "An Honest John Chinawoman"—was astonished to discover a married Chinese woman who had helped her husband build a house and who worked alongside him mining a nearby creek bed. There is no way of knowing if this woman accompanied her husband to California or if she bought her way out of a brothel and married a suitor, though the latter is more likely. The writer's account of this house-building, gold-mining woman is drenched in his own arrogant understandings of race, gender, beauty, and morality. "The Celestial 'beauty,'" the editor gibed, "wields the pick and shovel with the air of a miniature Amazon."[76] Wring his report out, however, and there emerges an immigrant woman who with her own hands forged a different sort of life for herself in late Gold Rush California. Life with a pick and a shovel, a house and a husband improved on a servitude that might end in death.

Likewise, a second report reveals how a Chinese woman tried to use a countryman's earnings and perhaps the local court system to gain her freedom. She had been brought to California by another Chinese woman—perhaps the famous Ah Toy herself—"as a slave for *any* purpose." The enslaved prostitute, in turn, borrowed $400 from a Chinese man in Amador County to purchase her freedom, "giving him a written mortgage of *herself* to secure the payment of the money." The Chinese man, the newspaper recounted, then "endeavored to enforce his lien," perhaps by insisting on free sexual services or by forcing the woman back into prostitution. Someone—it is not clear from the report whether it was the woman herself—then charged this man with abduction and took him to court. The man who had lent the woman money failed in his attempt to enforce what he thought was his lien on her person. The judge in the case informed him that "persons could not be restrained of their liberty for evil purposes, even if they had originally agreed to it."[77] The account does not reveal what became of the woman who borrowed and bought her way out of bondage. But the act itself spoke volumes about her aspirations.

It was not only Chinese women who became workers in the world of leisure that had evolved in the foothills of the Sierra Nevada since the discovery of gold in 1848. Unwittingly, hundreds of Cantonese-speaking men became bit players in spectacles attended or at least anticipated by hundreds of white men, who seemed as hungry for the blood of Chinese men as for the bodies of Chinese women. These Cantonese-speaking men were participants in pitched battles waged among opposing groups of Chinese in the diggings during the mid-1850s. Such battles were not unique to the Southern Mines. Indeed, the most famous fight, which became known as the Weaverville War, took place in 1854 in the Shasta-Trinity diggings far to the northwest.[78] But the Southern Mines saw their share of actual and expected warfare. Major conflicts occurred in 1854 near Jackson, in Amador County, and in 1856 near Chinese Camp, in Tuolumne County. In 1856, a similar battle threatened in Mariposa County, and smaller skirmishes erupted at San Andreas, in Calaveras County, and at Knight's Ferry, near the border between Stanislaus and Tuolumne counties.[79]

The lack of Chinese-language sources describing these events in the Southern Mines and similar fights elsewhere in the diggings has left scholars unsure about the causes and meanings of militarized conflict among Chinese immigrants in the 1850s. English-language sources are concerned primarily with what white men saw as the entertainment value of the battles. Such accounts usually identify the opposing factions in fights among groups of Chinese as "Cantons" and "Hong Kongs." These divisions do not correspond to what scholars of Chinese America describe as the major bases of social organization in California's earliest immigrant communities. Chinese men who immigrated from the three counties closest to the port city of

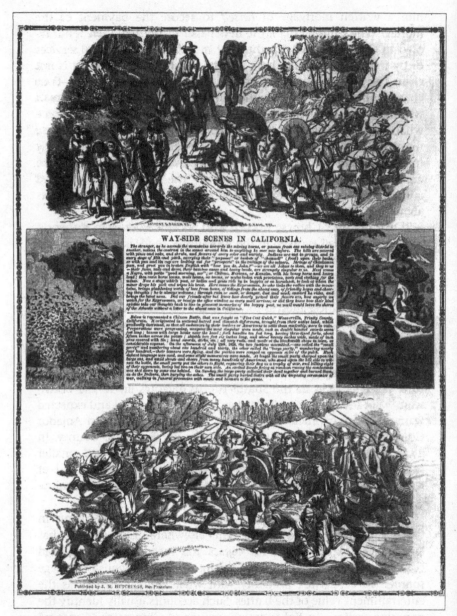

This lettersheet depicts many Anglo American preoccupations during the Gold Rush, including the place of white male prospectors in the polyglot diggings, the labor of native peoples, and the battles between groups of Chinese miners that became a spectator sport for Anglo men.

Reproduced by permission of the Huntington Library, San Marino, California.

Canton (known in Cantonese as Sam-yap, in Mandarin as Sanyi, and in English as "Three Districts") did form a district association that was known both as the Sam-yap Company and as the Canton Company. So it is possible that battle participants whom English-speakers called Cantons hailed from Sam-yap. But there is no such logical relationship between those called Hong Kongs and any identifiable group of Chinese who emigrated in the 1850s. On the other hand, Canton and Hong Kong were the most widely recognized Chinese place-names among English speakers in the midnineteenth century, since the cities those place-names represented were sites of extensive British and American incursion in China. It seems likely, then, that English speakers simply attached as monikers to opposing "armies" the two Chinese terms they knew best.[80]

In fact, various groups labeled "Cantons" and "Hong Kongs" in battles that erupted across hundreds of miles over a period of several years probably represented a broad array of opposing interests among Chinese men. These opposing interests may have originated in local, California-based enmities as much as in the social ruptures of South China in the 1850s, which included clan feuds, ethnic conflict, secret-society warfare, and small- and large-scale revolutionary movements, such as Guangdong's short-lived Red Turban Revolt (1854–55) and the calamitous Taiping Rebellion (1851–64), which almost ended the Qing dynasty.[81] Some sources suggest that Chinese battles in California were rooted in the disparate district origins of immigrants. In the case of the Weaverville War, for example, a white observer called one of the warring factions the "Young Woes."[82] Unlike other English-language appellations, this was a clear reference to the geographic origins of participants: the Yeung-wo Company was a district association created by immigrants from Xiangshan County, in the vicinity of Macao. Not only did men from Xiangshan organize a district association separate from that formed by men from the Canton area; they spoke a different Cantonese dialect as well. In addition to bringing memories of tremendous strife in South China, then, immigrants also spoke different dialects and called different places home, and these differences had profound social meanings.

That struggles among Chinese men in late Gold Rush California so often turned into armed conflicts comes as no surprise. The diggings, established as they were by a variety of immigrants committed to the pursuit of quick riches, long since had been a place of violence for opposing social groups. In addition, Chinese came into this cultural milieu from a situation in Guangdong in which foreign incursion and social upheaval had spawned widespread militarization. Ever since the

Opium War (1839–42), local militia had flourished there, and young men who emigrated to California had grown up surrounded by warfare.[83] These are among the circumstances that gave rise to the battles English speakers described between groups of Chinese.

Whatever the origins and meanings of armed conflict among Chinese immigrants to California in the 1850s, their troubles quickly became a spectator sport for white men. In late May of 1854, a local newspaper reported that Chinese men in and around Jackson were employing area blacksmiths to forge weapons for an impending fight, which the author hoped would unfold as "a Chinese version of the renowned battle between the Kilkenny cats." Another writer added that the event "was a rich 'nut' for the white citizens who were extremely anxious that the affair should come off." The conflict that did ensue, though it produced "about a dozen broken heads," disappointed white spectators, who hoped at least a few Chinese would fall in battle. One subsequent newspaper account, entitled "Great Chinese Battle at Jackson—0,000 Killed," mocked the struggle, complaining that the Chinese settled their differences "without the loss of a single life."[84] Reports of later battles in the Southern Mines took a similar tone. When a fight was brewing among Chinese men at Bear Valley early in 1856, white miners in Mariposa County eagerly headed in that direction hoping, according to a correspondent, "to see the 'Menagerie.'" The writer lamented that the miners "were obliged to come back unsatisfied."[85] Ten months later in Tuolumne County, white men got their wish, when two armies of some four hundred Chinese men each faced off, fortified with spears, clubs, and muskets. This battle, which erupted in October near Chinese Camp, was no doubt the largest such conflict in the Southern Mines. Newspapers reported that two or three Chinese men died in the struggle. According to one account, a "large number of Americans were present from all the mining camps in the vicinity, for the purpose of seeing how the moon-eyed contestants conducted warfare." The county sheriff was among the spectators; his horse was "shot out from under him by a random shot."[86]

It had come to this, then. Once, white men had worried for their own safety when non-Anglos shouldered weapons in the diggings, assuming that Anglo camps would be the target of truculence. Now white miners feared for their livelihoods, not their lives. A Chinese man-at-arms, like a hoop-skirted Chinese woman, was not a danger but rather a diversion, titillating and ridiculous all at the same time. This was so in part because Anglo American dominance was now reasonably well assured in the Southern Mines. In establishing that dominance—which was never complete or uncontested—white people had succeeded in renaturalizing the boundaries of gender and race that characterized their own lives. Chinese women and men stood outside those boundaries, and this is why hoop skirts and deadly weapons on their persons looked so comical to so many white observers. To stand outside bounds of gender and race was, in effect, to stand outside the bounds of humanity. Thus it was that Anglos who anticipated trouble among Chinese men at Bear Valley or Knight's Ferry hurried to see a "menagerie" and hoped the fight would "terminate like the Kilkenny cats."[87] For white men in the mid-1850s who made spectacles out of Chinese battles, watching human heads break and human blood flow seems to have been the moral equivalent of watching a bull-and-bear fight back in the boom years of the Gold Rush. Then, animals stood in for human hostilities, particularly hostilities between Mexicans and Anglos.[88] Now white men watched with hilarity as people stood in for animals, and human flesh gave way to spearheads and musket balls. This was the arrogance of Anglo America. One wonders, then, how random the shot was that killed the county sheriff's horse during the autumn battle in 1856. Perhaps the blast was a brutal, eloquent rebuke to the dehumanizing gaze of white miners.

Many Gold Rush participants were accustomed to the gaze of those who held greater social, cultural, economic, and political power in the Southern Mines. That gaze could, as in the case of white men who watched Chinese battles, dehumanize; it could also exoticize, fetishize, and romanticize. Sometimes, people who were the objects of such scrutiny could profit thereby, thus becoming subjects of their own survival. Spanish- and French-speaking women who worked in saloons, dance halls, and brothels were among these Gold Rush participants. So were a significant number of native people. As early as 1853, small groups of Indians dressed in ceremonial regalia began occasionally to file into immigrant towns, where they danced and made music for passersby. The native performers collected coins from the immigrant spectators, and then filed back out of town. One of the first recorded of such events took place at Mokelumne Hill in September of 1853, around the time of the acorn harvest. Miwoks were meeting about a mile away from that town for a grand celebration, and while some Indians prepared a campsite for the gathering, a local newspaper reported, "a band of nine came into town and performed a dance through the streets." Each dancer sported body paint and a feather headdress and carried a wand decorated with feathers, bones, shells, or beads. One played a whistle that sounded to white

This image of Miwok dancers on Washington Street in Sonora may date from as late as the 1880s, but the Miwok practice of dancing in immigrant towns began in the late Gold Rush era. Craig D. Bates, curator of ethnography for the National Park Service Museum in Yosemite National Park, first reproduced this image in "Miwok Dancers of 1856: Stereographic Images from Sonora, California," *Journal of California and Great Basin Anthropology* 6, no. 1 (1984), but has since learned that the image may have been made later.

Courtesy of the Yosemite National Park Research Library, National Park Service.

listeners like "the sharpening of a saw heard in the distance," and to this music the others "performed a dance, their motions being quick and well-timed." After each dance, they "passed round a hat . . . and obtained liberal contributions."[89]

Newspaper accounts of such events are rare, but immigrants who later wrote about their Gold Rush experiences frequently recalled native performances. White children seem to have been especially impressed by what they saw. Anna Lee Marston, the daughter of

Sonora's reform-minded couple, Elizabeth and Lewis Gunn, was only eight years old when her family left the diggings for San Francisco in 1861. But one of her most vivid memories from an early childhood in the mines was of Miwoks dancing in front of her house: "They wore high feather head-dresses and had grotesque stripes painted on their chests, and would grunt and dance and whistle through long reeds until we threw down some dimes."[90] George Bernhard, the son of a German storekeeper at Upper Agua Fria, in Mariposa County, grew up there in the late 1850s and early 1860s. Like Marston, Bernhard recalled later in life,

> Twice a year 25 or 30 [Indian] men & women with their face striped red & blue the squaws had black rings in their ears & nose . . . visited all of the towns, they would form a circle in front of the store 5 or 6 had tin pans or wash basins they would beat them with a stick then 3 or 4 others would get into the [center] of the ring & dance up and down & sing. . . . if there were any miners at the store they would toss them [coins]. . . . they would keep this up for an hour, then go to Princeton, Mt. Ophir, Bear Valley & Hornitos.[91]

One New Englander who was an adult during the Gold Rush, living at Murphys in Calaveras County, had similar memories. Leonard Noyes wrote that every so often, eight or ten Indians decked out in paint and feathers would "get in a line and run blowing [reed] whistles . . . arround from one Mining Camp to another occasionaly comeing to a stop and chanting some mornefull song of theirs." Then the performers would collect contributions before heading off to the next town. Noyes recalled that he "never learned why" his native neighbors did this.[92]

Indians probably did this to help supplement their dwindling means of subsistence, just as they had taken up placer mining.[93] Animal populations that Miwok people relied on for food had diminished drastically since the Gold Rush began, and immigrant mines, roads, and towns had proliferated across customary grounds for gathering wild greens, seeds, and nuts. In response, Sierra Miwok people—among whom lived former mission Indians as well as refugees from disease in the Central Valley—began to purchase food and other supplies from immigrant settlements. Placer mining provided much of the cash Indians needed to buy beef when they could not hunt deer and flour when they could not gather acorns. Dancing for immigrant audiences provided even more money.

Miwoks must have realized early on that immigrant peoples would pay to watch common native cultural practices. Leonard Noyes thought that Indians who lived around Murphys learned this when they saw their first traveling circus in 1854. They were especially taken with the elephant, which they called the "animal with a tail at each end," but they also noted that immigrants paid admission to see the spectacle. Afterward, the Miwoks held a large gathering for which they built a round assembly house, a semisubterranean structure supported by posts and beams and covered with thatch and earth in which people danced and gambled. According to Noyes, the "Young Indians taking the que from what they had seen at the circus concluded to make something out of the show so they stationed themselves at the opening demanding 2 bits each admittance, saying white man all same as Indian 2 [bits]." White men apparently paid the price, but when a native person entered, he or she handed over the cash and then, once inside, sent another Indian back out with the money so that the fee could be passed on to another native participant.[94] Thus in this instance, Miwoks in Calaveras County used market-based relations with outsiders to their own advantage without at the same time substantially altering ceremonial and social practices for themselves.[95]

Performing for audiences in immigrant towns represented a more profound accommodation to gold-based social relations than this, since it removed native dances from native communities altogether. Nonetheless, such performances seem to have been infrequent; George Bernhard remembered seeing only two a year, and Leonard Noyes recalled that Indians filed into town to dance and sing only "at times."[96] And native people controlled the location, timing, and content of the events; this was a far cry from taking up wage labor in immigrant homes or industries. Furthermore, photographic evidence suggests that the dancers may have dressed in a manner that changed key parts of Miwok ceremonial regalia. This would have neutralized the sanctity of their costumes when they performed for non-native peoples, whose gaze might otherwise have disrupted the power of Miwok ritual practices.[97] So while Miwok street dances represented deeper accommodations to changes underway in the foothills, they also represented astute perceptions of those changes. The white gaze might dehumanize, exoticize, fetishize, or romanticize, but it was clear to Indians that white people would put money where their eyes wanted to be, just as it was clear that human life in the Sierra foothills now required money. Sierra Miwoks understood, then, what immigrants such as George Bernhard thought about watching Indians dance in the street: "We kids enjoyed it," he wrote later in life, "it was as good as a Nigger Minstrel or a Circus to us."[98] That Indians acted on such racialized understandings, as older ways of maintaining communities began to fail, is hardly surprising.

By the late 1850s, social relations in the Southern Mines had metamorphosed to accommodate the presence of new Gold Rush participants, the departure of others, and the continuing needs and desires of those who stayed on in the foothills. White women and Chinese women and men were among the latest arrivals. Mexicans, Chileans, and French—and especially the women—were among those who were starting to leave. So too were a wide variety of men frustrated by the declining placers and flush with the promise of bonanzas elsewhere. Other men stayed, convinced that veins, gravels, and placers would yet yield still greater treasures, or that profits were possible in different pursuits. Miwok women and men lingered as well, perhaps hoping that the decade-long invasion of the foothills by immigrants might somehow reverse. An Indian man whom Anglos in Amador County knew as Captain Jack, for example, told a white acquaintance in 1858 that he thought the Fraser River rush could depopulate the town of Jackson. The newspaperman who recounted Jack's story did so with all the arrogance and condescension of those accustomed to uncontested narrative power.[99] Rendering Captain Jack's speech using diction that reflected white imagination as much as Indian utterance, the newspaperman nonetheless conveyed something of Miwok dreams: "Purty soon white man vamose—Ingin git him big house, heap grub, plenty blanket! White man vamose Frazer river!"[100]

White men, along with their womenfolk, had different dreams, as well as disproportionate access to the power that could make those dreams come true. That power increased manyfold when white women from the eastern United States began to join their menfolk in the mines and set about supplanting with "respectable" gatherings popular recreations that had catered to men and provided work for polyglot women. As early as 1853, the *Sonora Herald* noted the increasing numbers of "the gentler sex dispersed among the hill-sides and ravines," as evidenced by the "female habiliments in many directions hanging out to dry."[101] Like flags flying, such recognizably white women's garments announced a consolidation of Anglo American dominance in the diggings.

By 1856, the picture seemed even more promising. When white miners, white merchants, and white managers of the Columbia and Stanislaus River Water Company (CSRWC) allied themselves to ward off what they saw as the monopolistic threat posed by the Tuolumne

County Water Company (TCWC), they produced a booklet entitled the *Miners and Business Men's Directory* for Tuolumne County.[102] It was filled with advertisements, mining districts laws, names of governmental representatives and community organizations, as well as lists of all who counted as "miners and business men." The directory studiously avoided mentioning the TCWC—even though that company's system of flumes, ditches, and reservoirs represented the county's greatest business enterprise—and shamelessly promoted the interests of the CSRWC.[103] In addition, the *Miners and Business Men's Directory* included narratives detailing the history and prospects of camps and towns throughout the county. The narrative for Columbia—home of the reform-minded Clementine Brainard as well as the monte-dealing "French Mary"—was particularly revealing of Anglo American aspirations:

> This place is fast filling up with families—a surety of a permanent population and of improvement in society. The barberous amusements, introduced by Spanish customs, have long since ceased to disturb the peace of the community, while other Spanish customs that tend so much to the spread and continuance of immorality are fast dying, and in a short time will only be known as things that belonged to the past. The gambling saloon no longer, by its music, attracts the unsophisticated to squander their money on "dead things," and those who were connected with such houses have gone to other parts, or sought other occupations. . . . And as the Mexican population, and the class that are ever congregated around gambling houses are removed from our midst, the security of life and property may be soon considered equal to that afforded in most places in the older States.[104]

Things that belonged to the past; things that belonged to the future: the editors of the *Miners and Business Men's Directory* were hopeful that "Spanish customs" and Mexican people, rowdy gambling saloons and the monopolistic TCWC were all of the past, and that (white) families, secure property, and the CSRWC "Miners' Ditch" were all of the future. Things that belonged to the past were "dead things." Things that belonged to the future were alive. Already, the editors noted, forward-looking residents were planting fruit trees and vines around homes and ranches. It would not be long, the writers predicted, "before most of our citizens will sit under their own vines and fig trees, with none to molest them or make them afraid."[105]

The *Miners and Business Men's Directory* was wrong about much: neither "Spanish customs" nor Mexican people nor French monte dealers disappeared so easily, and even where they did begin to depart, "Chinese customs" and Chinese people often stood in their stead. What is more, gambling saloons and the TCWC maintained a robust health throughout the rest of the decade, while the CSRWC collapsed. And women, on whom the increase of conventional families depended, still constituted less than one-fifth of the population as late as 1860. But white women and men together did begin to turn much of the Southern Mines into a place where few dared to "molest them or make them afraid." What they could not create was a world in which, for example, no Chinese woman would fly "American colors," straining the links among ladyhood, whiteness, and morality, and rattling the social, economic, and discursive chains that bound their own lives. Neither could immigrants prevent Indians from learning the economy of conquest and turning that knowledge to sustenance. Nor could Anglo Americans deflect the stray bullets that now and then knocked them unceremoniously off their high horse.

Epilogue

Telling Tales

In the 1990s, a travel writer for the *New York Times* encouraged readers to visit the foothills of the Sierra Nevada. Her article, "Exploring the Mother Lode," begins with a spare but serviceable two-sentence history of the California Gold Rush:

> In 1848, a carpenter named James Marshall noticed flecks of gold shining in the tailrace of the sawmill he was building for John Sutter on the American River in California. Though the discovery did neither Marshall nor Sutter any good, it spurred tens of thousands of fortune hunters to struggle by land and sea, hoping to find its riverbeds strewn with the stuff of dreams.

The author goes on to assure her readers that now anyone can visit this land of dreams, "with less discomfort," by taking a three-day tour along California's Highway 49, which traverses the gold region. She recommends that tourists restrict themselves to the northern half of the highway, since it "offers a greater concentration of mining sites, museums and Victorian architecture." The southern half, she explains, "is the least densely populated part of the gold country," with the exception of the state park at the reconstructed town of Columbia and the modern county seats at Mariposa and Sonora. With the Southern Mines dispatched in two sentences (save a brief mention of towns in Amador County, which has always straddled the divide between north and south), the author goes on to detail the historical, technological, and architectural sites that dot the northern Mother Lode.[1]

Why are the Northern Mines so memorable, the Southern Mines so forgettable? It is my contention that the Southern Mines have been neglected because the area fits dominant cultural memory of the Gold Rush—as it has evolved in the United States—less well. First, the south was by far the more demographically diverse region, in that Native Americans, Latin Americans, African Americans, East Asians, and Europeans frequently outnumbered Anglo Americans there. Second, it was the area that was less successful in following what came to be the expected trajectory of industrialization in western mining. The unruly history of the Southern Mines has proven more difficult to enlist in American narratives of success, stories of progress and opportunity that are linked to financial gain and identified with people racialized as white and gendered as male. An adequate account of the century-and-a-half-long process by which dominant cultural memories have evolved and have been contested by countermemories could easily fill another book about the California Gold Rush. But an account of the origins of those discursive struggles must start here—else one key purpose of the layering of historical particularities in the preceding chapters will go unrealized.

At the same time that social relations in the Southern Mines were changing in the 1850s, dominant meanings of the California Gold Rush were beginning to take shape. Although these were contemporaneous developments, the meaning-making process that occurred on a national level in the United States almost guaranteed that social change in the Southern Mines would not capture eastern imaginations, and hence would not figure in a reimagined, now continental American nation.[2] Close readings of four texts published during and just after this period show how lived social relations in the Southern Mines, popular representations of the Gold Rush, and the project of nation building were interrelated. The first two texts—both obscure and each superficially similar to the other—illustrate the start of this interrelationship. These are pamphlets produced in the 1850s that purport to document crime and its consequences in the Southern Mines. The second two texts—well-known stories written in the 1860s by California's premier teller of tales, Bret Harte—are more tangentially related to the historical past of the Southern Mines. But the direction of those tangents indicates much about the process by which the United States claimed the Gold Rush as cultural property over and against the claims of other nations, and by which some

Americans asserted ownership over and against the proprietary rights of other Americans.

Crime pamphlets had been popular in the United States since the early nineteenth century; their appearance on the literary horizon coincided with the emergence of cheap, often sensationalist newspapers called penny papers, which appealed in both price and content to working men in eastern cities.[3] Immigrants to California from the East would have been familiar with the popular genre, while eastern readers would have welcomed new tales from the far western frontier. And indeed, the first of these stories was printed not in California but by a New Orleans publisher who had offices in Charleston, Baltimore, and Philadelphia as well; no doubt it circulated first in such eastern and southern locales. The pamphlet told the story of *Two Eras in the Life of the Felon Grovenor I. Layton. Who Was Lynched by the Vigilance Committee, at Sonora, Tuolumne County, California, June 17th, 1852.* The second of these stories, however, was published in the Southern Mines, by the printer in Jackson who produced the local newspaper. It, too, told a story of crime and retribution: *Murder of M. V. B. Griswold by Five Chinese Assassins; Fou Sin—the Principal . . . Convicted, and Sentenced to Be Hung at Jackson, April 16, 1858.* No doubt this pamphlet circulated primarily in California.[4]

Different as social relations in the Southern Mines were from those in the East, the first of these two pamphlets suggests how mightily some could struggle to incorporate those relations into stories intelligible to an eastern readership. *Two Eras in the Life of the Felon Grovenor I. Layton* tells a familiar tale of a respectable young man who travels from the Hudson River Valley home of his loving parents to New York City, the Anglo American capital of vice and immorality. Though Grovenor goes there to study medicine, he soon falls under the influence of a "dissolute and unprincipled young man" who introduces him to the city's brothels, billiard saloons, and gambling houses. Then, suddenly, Grovenor's parents succumb to small pox. What is more, he learns that his father has died insolvent, leaving Grovenor a beggar and forcing him into a career of crime. First, he forges a check. Next, he kills a man. By this time, it is the fall of 1848, and news of the gold discovery in California reaches New York. Gripped by gold fever, Grovenor forges another check in order to purchase his passage to "the El Dorado of the Pacific, the Ophir of America." In the spring of 1849, he boards a steamer bound for Panama, accompanied by his lovely but fallen paramour, Irene (Irene, too, has met her downfall in New York, having left behind a loving family in the Mohawk Valley, only to find herself seduced and abandoned in the city, where she meets Grovenor).[5]

Together, Grovenor and Irene arrive in San Francisco. There they manage a gaming house until they are run out of town by a vigilance committee for robbing and murdering a customer. So they move on to Benecia, northeast of San Francisco, and again open a gambling saloon. Here, too, they cheat and kill and must leave town. Next, Grovenor and Irene head for Sacramento, and Grovenor, under an assumed name, opens an exchange office and banking house. At first, he runs a legitimate business, but then he falls in with a gang of counterfeiters and begins to dispose of counterfeit notes to "unsuspecting miners." Eventually, however, some do suspect Grovenor, and they set up a sting to catch him in the act of exchanging hard-earned gold dust for worthless notes on eastern banks. Again, Grovenor escapes before he can be caught, and he and Irene move on to Stockton, where he works with counterfeiters under a new assumed name. Here he leaves Irene and goes on to continue his nefarious business alone.[6]

He heads for the Southern Mines, stopping at Jamestown, near Sonora. There he hears talk of some Chileans who are finding "an immensity of gold at Mormon Gulch." Grovenor starts immediately for their camp, where he finds two men and a woman sharing a cabin and "digging with might and main." They tell Grovenor that they have taken ten thousand dollars out of their claim in three short months. So he ingratiates himself with the Chileans, until they agree that he may join them in their labors and keep one-fourth of the gold dug thereafter. Grovenor works with them for a week, meanwhile plotting robbery. One day, he returns early to the cabin, complaining of sickness. Within an hour, the men send the woman back to the cabin to check on Grovenor. She catches him in the act of stealing their gold, and runs to the door to alert her mining partners. But Grovenor stops her and stabs her to the heart, and then rushes out to meet the men who are running from the claim. He slashes each of them to death. Then he drags the bodies into the cabin and, after gathering up the gold, sets the domicile ablaze.[7]

Now Grovenor goes to Sonora, "the greater part of whose inhabitants are Chilians and Sonorians," and puts himself up at "the best house of entertainment." He explains that his haggard appearance and his bloodied clothing are the result of an Indian attack. Then a party of Chileans, having passed through Mormon Gulch, comes to town. They have seen the burned cabin and found human bones amid the charred timbers. They come to Sonora laden with evidence

Illustration from the crime pamphlet *Two Eras in the Life of the Felon Grovenor I. Layton. Who Was Lynched by the Vigilance Committee, at Sonora, Tuolumne County, California, June 17th, 1852. For Robbery, Murder, and Arson, He Having Robbed Three Chilians, Two Men and One Woman, of Ten Thousand Dollars in Gold Dust, at Mormon Gulch, Murdered and Burned Them, Together with Their Cabin, May 28th, 1852.* (New Orleans, Charleston, Baltimore, and Philadelphia: A. R. Orton, 1852).

Reproduced by permission of the Huntington Library, San Marino, California.

of the murders. Many suspect Grovenor, and the local vigilance committee questions him. But he cannot be linked positively to the crime until a man from Jamestown steps forward and identifies Grovenor as the person whom he had told several weeks before about Chileans who were striking it rich at Mormon Gulch. So the vigilance committee impanels a jury and swears the Jamestown man in as a witness. Then another stranger comes forward and says that he saw the suspect digging gold alongside three Chileans at Mormon Gulch. On this evidence, Grovenor is convicted of murder and sentenced to hang. Only now does Grovenor feel remorse, and he delivers these dying words before the rope is adjusted about his neck:

> There was a time, I remember me, when I was innocent, and
> knew no guile; but a change came over the spirit of my dream,
> and I turned disdainfully from the beaten paths in which my
> fathers walked, and followed in pursuit of a phantom which

tempted me on with its luring smile and siren song. . . . If this were the only crime I have stained my soul with, I might hope to be forgiven; but I have perpetrated so many crimes that I cannot hope to be forgiven, either in this, or the world to come.

In case the reader has failed to grasp the meaning of this tale, the writer concludes that "the sad end of the felon, Grovenor I. Layton," should be "a warning to all, and deter many from taking the *first false step*."[8]

In this narrative, California in general and the Southern Mines in particular are western outposts of the moral world represented by New York City—extreme outposts where a young man's propensities toward evil go from bad to worse, where the rush for gold and the race to sin put him on a fast track to judgment. Curiously enough, Grovenor Layton may well have been a figment of that moral world's imagination. He appears nowhere in the historical record that one would expect to find him—in local newspaper reports, for example, or in the letters and diaries of people who lived in and around Sonora in the summer of 1852, when Grovenor was supposed to have been lynched. In fact, Sonora's vigilance committee was most active a full year earlier, in the summer of 1851, when reports of vigilante trials and executions in Sonora filled newspaper columns as far away as San Francisco.[9] This suggests that the story of Grovenor Layton was not simply shaped by eastern discourses of urban danger and the perils of unseemly gain, as was many a crime pamphlet tale. His absence in the historical record suggests that the story was wholly fabricated within such discourses.[10]

Yet even if eastern imaginations created Grovenor Layton's tale, the actual particularities of social relations in the Southern Mines are among the signposts that give the narrative direction. After trouble follows him from San Francisco to Stockton, Grovenor heads to the vicinity of Sonora, the heart of the Southern Mines and the virtual headquarters of gold-seeking Chileans and northern Mexicans—or "Chilians and Sonorians," as the pamphlet would have it. He learns about a party of Chilean miners, whom he finds and joins, only to rob and murder them in a week's time. He escapes the crime scene to Sonora, where he lodges at a "house of entertainment." Looking much the worse for wear, he blames his appearance on marauding Indians. But the miners Grovenor kills are part of a larger Chilean community, and so the crime is quickly discovered. A vigilance committee steps in and, with testimony that can place him at Mormon Gulch with the Chileans, Grovenor is convicted. Signposts drawn from life in the Southern Mines, then, help plot Grovenor's downfall:

Sonora's multiethnic population and its public amusements, immigrant travel and the perceived threat from native peoples, the arbitration of justice by vigilance committees.

The signposts, however, just as often as they point in historically meaningful directions, are turned upside down and backward. Put simply, vigilance committees were more concerned with punishing wrongs done to Anglo Americans than wrongs done by them, especially wrongs done by them to non–Anglo Americans. Often enough, wrongs against Anglos were perpetrated by other Anglos, so many a white man dangled from a hangman's noose. When one did, his name filled not only newspapers but letters and diaries as well. In the summer of 1851, for example, the Sonora vigilance committee went after an Anglo named Hill and eventually lynched him. Hill's name peppers the historical record for those months. During the same summer, however, a white man named Snow was murdered, allegedly by Mexicans. One must look long and hard to find any reference to the names of the Mexican men who were hanged by the vigilance committee for Snow's murder. Most typical is the kind of reference the merchant William Perkins made in his diary once the summer's hangings were over: "The summary execution of Hill and a few Mexicans has had a more wonderful effect than could have been anticipated."[11] All of this is to say that while Grovenor Layton may have been the sort of white man vigilance committees loved to hate—particularly for his bilking of innocent white miners—historically, the crime of cheating and killing Chilean gold seekers would have been an unlikely last straw to lead to a lynching.[12]

This takes us back to the eastern imaginations that produced and consumed *Two Eras in the Life of the Felon Grovenor I. Layton*. In 1852, the region known as Southern Mines did not write its own stories—at least not stories that were consumed by mass audiences outside of California. Details of life in the Southern Mines did circulate via newspapers, emigrant letters, guidebooks, and returning gold seekers—enough so that easterners could imagine Grovenor mining with Chileans at Mormon Gulch, lying about an Indian attack, boarding at a Sonora house of entertainment, hanging by the neck from a vigilante rope. But details and stories are not the same thing. In 1852, stories about the Southern Mines were rarely indigenous tales. Generated elsewhere, such narratives took crucial details of life in the diggings and familiarized them as aspects of an essentially eastern, Anglo American story: the tale of a country boy gone to ruin in the city, which, in turn, was a tale of the moral peril men faced in an increasingly market-based economy. Viewed in this way, the teller of

Grovenor's tale was not so far off in depicting the diggings as an out-post of the urban East. The growth of cities in the nineteenth century depended on the exploitation of resources in the hinterlands.[13] And just as gold moved from west to east, from country to city, in 1852, so too did information about the social relations that gold-seeking engendered. The stories easterners told about such social relations may not have made much sense to residents of the Southern Mines, but they would have helped domesticate the Gold Rush for eastern readers by assuring them that the dangers of the city and the dangers of the diggings bore a family resemblance.

By 1858, enough such stories had been told about the Gold Rush that the event had been domesticated in both senses of the word: Anglo Americans had come to understand the Gold Rush in the con-text of nineteenth-century domestic ideology, and they also had claimed the event as a domestic episode—an episode in national his-tory. That is to say that the diggings became as familiar a trope for the fevered coupling of material gain and moral hazard as the city had become—a place where a man might "make himself," but where he also might lose himself and his moral bearings to the excesses of a changing economy. Launched from a middle-class family, as Grovenor Layton was, a young man was expected to have internalized not only the domestic values necessary to work hard, make money, and provide for a family but those that would prevent him from wanting to make too much money too fast without work, since opportunities for unseemly gain abounded.[14] In the end, then, the real danger was located within individual white men. Certain settings, such as cities and mines, simply encouraged a man to abandon self-restraint or, as Grovenor put it, to turn "disdainfully from the beaten path in which my fathers walked." Just as it was incorporated into everyday eco-nomic and social thought of the dominant, so too was the Gold Rush assimilated into narratives of nation building, so that gold seeking came to represent perils and possibilities not merely for individuals but for the American nation itself. The California state legislature aided this process by imposing a foreign miners' tax in 1850 and again in 1852, which not only circumscribed the work of many gold seekers but also helped define gold seeking as a right of citizenship. And the lucky timing of the gold discovery—simultaneous with the 1848 sign-ing of the Treaty of Guadalupe Hidalgo, whereby the United States took California from Mexico—made many Americans feel that the Gold Rush was a providential gift to a favored nation. A decade later, in 1858, the event had been housebroken into just such an animal.

By then, the Southern Mines region was telling its own tales.

Whether anyone outside of California was listening is another question. The second pamphlet under consideration here was printed in the town of Jackson by the publisher of the local newspaper. And it is not only this western place of publication that distinguishes the 1858 pamphlet. Where *Two Eras in the Life of the Felon Grovenor I. Layton* reads as a single, continuous story, *Murder of M. V. B. Griswold by Five Chinese Assassins* is fragmented. Where one voice tells Grovenor Layton's tale, several narrate the murder of Martin Van Buren Griswold. And where the Chileans in the former are mute, nameless characters, the Chinese men in the latter have names—Fou Sin and Chou Yee, for example—and they speak on their own behalf. Make no mistake: *Murder of M. V. B. Griswold by Five Chinese Assassins* is a pamphlet produced by white newspapermen for white readers. Nonetheless, generated as it was in the Southern Mines, the actual particularities of social relations there provide more than just signposts for a familiar story. Indeed, these particularities threaten to spawn counternarratives quite at odds with the overarching tale the pamphlet tries to tell.

The pamphlet begins with a tribute to the murdered man, Martin Van Buren Griswold, who is the antithesis of Grovenor Layton. Although both were raised by loving parents in New York State, Martin never takes the "first false step" down the road of self-destruction. His origins are "highly respectable"; he is not only a namesake but a relative of the former president Martin Van Buren. A man "of very much more than ordinary vigor," Martin, unlike Grovenor, when faced with moral or material danger, responds with cool strength of character. He also exhibits appropriate racial self-confidence; according to the pamphlet writer, only "the utter contempt in which he held the whole [Chinese] race" can explain Martin's murder. His lack of regard for Chinese men, that is, "made him the more readily a victim to Asiatic cunning and treachery." As Martin's employer put it, in a fair fight Martin could have "whipped . . . fifty or an hundred such men as the Chinamen."[15]

When Martin leaves home at the age of twenty-one, he does not go to the city but rather embarks on a tour of the southern and western states, in order to prepare himself for "the vicissitudes of life." He settles for a time in Milwaukee, but then joins the overland migration for California, predicting—prior to the gold discovery—that "in less than two years the development of wealth on the Pacific slope of the Sierra Nevada . . . will loom up to an extent that will astonish the world." His party, however, detours to Oregon, where he first hears of the gold excitement. He sails for San Francisco. From there he heads for the Northern Mines, where he works "industriously and with good judgment" and takes out "a large sum of money." He returns to the Atlantic states, traveling through Mexico, where an altercation with "Greasers" allows Martin to demonstrate "a specimen of American prowess." Back in New York, he feels for the last time "the kindliest influence that entwines itself about the heart of a man—the influence of HOME." Thus fortified, Martin sets out on an arduous journey from Milwaukee to St. Paul to "the most remote stations of the Hudson Bay Company." Eventually, he returns to California, where he spends years crisscrossing the state before settling near Jackson in Amador County. Although Martin's "capacity, experience, [and] knowledge of the world" have fitted him to run his own business, he chooses instead to enter the employ of Horace Kilham as "general business manager and confidential clerk." It is while working for Kilham that Martin Van Buren Griswold is murdered.[16]

Unlike *Two Eras in the Life of the Felon Grovenor I. Layton*, which presents a seamless narrative, *Murder of M. V. B. Griswold by Five Chinese Assassins* ends this biographical sketch abruptly and moves on to a new section, "The Murder—The Trials, &c." It is as if the life of Grovenor Layton leads inevitably to its ignoble end, while M. V. B. Griswold's life in no way points to the manner of his death, so that the murder must be considered separately. This section is designed to convince the reader that "five Chinamen were present and participated, either directly or indirectly," in killing Griswold. From the start, however, the presence of five Chinese men in this pamphlet complicates the tale. In providing their names, the writer acknowledges that "it is difficult to spell Chinese names in English so as to retain the proper sound," foreshadowing the difficulties these men will bring to Anglo American storytelling. The writer settles on these transliterations from the Cantonese: Fou Sin and Chou Yee, for the two Amador County cooks who are friends; and Coon You, Coon See, and Ah Hung, for the three others who also seem to be acquainted. Fou Sin, Chou Yee, and Coon You, we learn, are convicted of murder and sentenced to be hanged. Ah Hung is never charged. Coon See is acquitted of murder, but convicted of the lesser charge of grand larceny. Coon See then commits suicide in his jail cell.[17]

According to this section of the pamphlet, the crime itself unfolds thus: Both M. V. B. Griswold and Fou Sin work for Horace Kilham, "an extensive ditch proprietor"—that is, a water company manager—and a banker of sorts who exchanges gold dust for specie. Griswold is Kilham's clerk and Fou Sin his cook. While Kilham is away in Sacramento, five Chinese men apparently commit the "ingeniously

MURDER
OF

M. V. B. GRISWOLD,

BY

FIVE CHINESE ASSASSINS;

FOU SIN---THE PRINCIPAL.

TOGETHER WITH

THE LIFE OF GRISWOLD,

AND THE STATEMENTS OF

FOU SIN, CHOU YEE AND COON YOU,

CONVICTED, AND

SENTENCED TO BE HUNG AT JACKSON, APRIL 16, 1858.

Illustrated with Correct Likenesses of the Murderers.

JACKSON:
T. A. SPRINGER & CO., PRINT.
1858.

Cover of the crime pamphlet *Murder of M. V. B. Griswold by Five Chinese Assassins,* with image of Fou Sin.

Reproduced by permission of the Huntington Library, San Marino, California.

conceived and dexterously executed" killing. Their primary aim is to rob Kilham's safe, which holds eight or nine thousand dollars. In order to steal the money, they must do away with Kilham's clerk. So Griswold is felled by a blow to the head, and the safe is emptied. Griswold's body is stashed underneath a bed in Fou Sin's room, and a board that almost reaches the floor is nailed to the bed rail so as to conceal the corpse. This section, however, is not written in narrative fashion but rather as a kind of catalogue of evidence that emerged from the inquest into Griswold's death and the trials of Fou Sin and his compatriots: the empty safe, Fou Sin's absence on Kilham's return, the body under the bed, a bloody shirt, sightings by white men of Chinese men in flight, gold and jewelry in Fou Sin and Chou Yee's possession. As the writer puts it, all of this "made up one of the strongest cases of circumstantial evidence of which there is any record."[18]

Just as the reader starts to piece this evidence together into a story, yet another section of the pamphlet begins, one with which the writer wrestles mightily so that it does not contradict what has come before. Here, statements appear that Fou Sin, Chou Yee, and Coon You made to newspapermen after conviction and before execution. A portrait of each man, drawn from an ambrotype, precedes his statement. The portrait and statement of Fou Sin go farthest in undermining the pamphlet's overarching narrative, though the consistency of all three men's accounts is also key. Fou Sin's portrait depicts a strong man with sturdy features who gazes directly at the camera, with no hint of guilt or remorse. He does not wear a customary queue; rather, his full head of hair hangs neatly to the nape of the neck. The writer of the pamphlet prefaces Fou Sin's statement by noting that Fou Sin was the "master spirit" of the crime, "vastly the superior of all the others." And indeed, Fou Sin's "capacity, experience, [and] knowledge of the world" exceed those of M. V. B. Griswold himself. He is fluent in English, and so he speaks to the newspapermen without an interpreter. He chronicles his life from his origins as the son of a· farmer and stonecutter in South China, to his many years working aboard British, French, American, and Russian ships, to his arrival in San Francisco in 1857 and his subsequent journey to Jackson, in the Southern Mines. According to Fou Sin, it was an old friend from his home district near Canton, a man named Chou Yee, who told him to look for work in Jackson and who lent him the thirty dollars it cost to travel there from San Francisco.[19]

Now begins Fou Sin's account of the crime at Horace Kilham's house. Once in Jackson, Fou Sin finds work cooking for the ditch proprietor Kilham. Chou Yee visits Fou Sin ·often, in part to see if Fou Sin can repay the thirty dollars advanced for the fare from San Francisco. During one such visit, three other Chinese—strangers to Fou Sin and Chou Yee—come to the house. They confirm with Fou Sin that his "master" is "very rich," and threaten to "rob the money out of the house." Fou Sin tells them not to do this while he is cooking there. But the next thing he knows, they are beating and choking Griswold, taking the key to the safe from the dying man's pocket, and emptying the safe of its contents. Now all five Chinese men—Fou Sin and Chou Yee as well as the strangers—must flee to avoid arrest. Fou Sin's statement continues with an account of their escape, the three strangers departing in one party and Fou Sin and Chou Yee in another. Both Fou Sin and Chou Yee disguise themselves by shaving their heads, and Fou Sin buys Chinese apparel to replace his Euro-American clothes. Their flight takes them from Jackson to Sacramento to the Northern Mines. In Marysville, however, an acquaintance of Fou Sin's betrays them, and they are arrested.[20]

Appended to this statement are answers Fou Sin gave to questions posed by examiners as well as a translation of a letter written to his father and brother. Fou Sin explains, for example, why one of his shirts was bloodied: it was hanging over the edge of the bed when Griswold's body was pushed underneath. He also explains why a deadly slungshot was found in his room: he made it in case he got into a fight at a Chinese brothel (a slungshot is a striking weapon that resembles a blackjack). In addition, he passes on what he has learned in jail about the two strangers, Coon See and Coon You, who were also arrested. According to Fou Sin, Coon See has said that he was "in jail for a long time in China for killing a man." Likewise, Coon You has said that he was "a robber and pirate" and a "great scoundrel" there. These denunciations notwithstanding, both Coon See and Coon You, as well as Chou Yee, add brief notes to the letter Fou Sin writes to his family explaining his fate. The pamphlet writer cannot help admiring the literary merit of this composite epistle. As translated by Charles Carvalho, Chinese interpreter for the city of San Francisco, Chou Yee writes, "My body hath gone before me, borne on clouds. My youth was coupled with twenty springs; I was unconscious of it, but thus it was." And Coon You, "The spirit will mount, borne by red incense, full of fragrance; the fulfillment, like a gem, is soon wrought." More and more, the "five Chinese assassins" threaten to break out of their characterization as cunning and treacherous devils and to appear instead as men with complicated affections and animosities, men alive to (what readers would consider) refined sensibilities.[21]

[From an Ambrotype by O. Hemenway, Jackson.]

CHOU YEE, THE Q RANCH COOK.

Image of Chou Yee from *Murder of M. V. B. Griswold by Five Chinese Assassins.*

Reproduced by permission of the Huntington Library, San Marino, California.

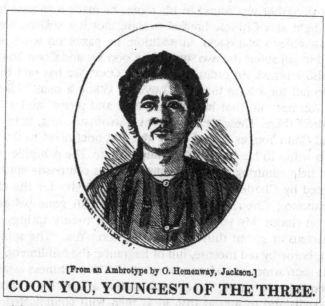

[From an Ambrotype by O. Hemenway, Jackson.]

COON YOU, YOUNGEST OF THE THREE.

Image of Coon You from *Murder of M. V. B. Griswold by Five Chinese Assassins.*

Reproduced by permission of the Huntington Library, San Marino, California.

To forestall this eventuality, the pamphlet employs several tactics. First, Fou Sin's portrait and statement are followed by those of Chou Yee and Coon You, which are less flattering. Chou Yee's portrait, for example, depicts a disheveled man: he looks away from the camera; his face is careworn; his hair hangs in uneven tangles. Coon You's likeness, meanwhile, must have looked feminized to eyes schooled in Anglo American conventions of gender. He is pictured with his hair drawn loosely into a queue, which is brought forward over one shoulder for emphasis. He gazes just above the camera's lens, lending an innocent air to his appearance. Both Chou Yee's and Coon You's statements are translated from the Chinese, underlining their foreignness, and the pamphlet writer does not preface either with admiring observations. Chou Yee says little about his background—only that he came to California from the Sandwich Islands and went to the Southern Mines, where he worked as a cook. Coon You's statement is similarly brief—though he mentions he is married—and is damningly contradicted in several particulars by an account he gave just after his conviction. In addition to setting these largely negative representations off against the more ambiguous representation of Fou Sin, the pamphlet writer also frequently interrupts the statements of all three men to point out apparent lies and inconsistencies. For example, where Fou Sin claims that Griswold was killed with a stick or club, and that his own slungshot was not used, the writer interjects, "The wounds on . . . Griswold's head . . . could scarcely have been made with a club. He must have been struck with the slungshot . . . or something of the kind." Finally, the pamphlet closes by reproducing the verdict of a coroner's jury in the jailhouse death of Coon See, who is found to have hanged himself by a rope made out of strips torn from his own shirt. Earlier, the writer has speculated that Coon See "appealed his case to the court of his own conscience, which convicted him . . . and receiving his sentence, [he] became his own executioner." This closing, then, tries to bring the reader back around to the positive guilt of the "five Chinese assassins."[22]

When the Southern Mines region began to write its own stories, the California Gold Rush became very complicated. Just as it was difficult to spell out Chinese names by means of the English alphabet, so too was it difficult to contain Chinese testimonials in an Anglo American narrative. Indeed, read in historical context, the statements of Fou Sin, Chou Yee, and Coon You point to a different unfolding of events surrounding M. V. B. Griswold's murder from what the pamphlet writer would have readers imagine. None of the convicted men suggest that Fou Sin and Chou Yee knew Coon You, Coon See, and Ah Hung. As for the four who were charged, Fou Sin and Chou Yee, on the one hand, and Coon You and Coon See, on the other, likely came from different native places in South China and felt little affinity for each other. California-bound Chinese came overwhelmingly from just eight districts in the Pearl River Delta area of south-central Guangdong Province: the "Three Districts," or Sam-yap; the "Four Districts," or Sze-yap; and the single district of Xiangshan. From what they told their interrogators, Fou Sin and Chou Yee probably came from Sam-yap, the area closest to the city of Canton. Coon You and Coon See probably came from Xiangshan.[23] Among Chinese immigrants, district origins drew important social boundaries. Hence it is not surprising that where Anglo American observers saw five Chinese men acting in concert, the Chinese men themselves saw something else altogether. For their part, Fou Sin and Chou Yee consistently blame the robbery and murder on the three strangers who came to Horace Kilham's headquarters that fateful morning—Coon You, Coon See, and Ah Hung. Coon See apparently gave no account of the crime before he was found hanged in his jail cell. Coon You, however, in one statement claims that Fou Sin and Chou Yee murdered Griswold—before he and Coon See arrived at Kilham's—and in another includes Coon See among the perpetrators. What this suggests is that two or three of these men might have joined forces to rob the safe where Kilham kept the proceeds of his ditchdigging and gold-dust-changing business. All five of them, however, are unlikely to have done so together.

As logical as all this seems when considered in historical context, such a reading of *Murder of M. V. B. Griswold by Five Chinese Assassins* was improbable in 1858. Those most apt to read in this manner—Chinese immigrants—for the most part were not literate in English. As audience, the publisher had in mind English-speaking Americans, as he put it, "the entire people, not only in California, but also in the Atlantic States." That the publisher intended to create among this people both local and national markets for the pamphlet is underlined by two strategies. First, he rushed the pamphlet to press after Fou Sin, Chou Yee, and Coon You were convicted, and put it on sale the day they were executed, when local attention to the crime and its punishment was at an all-time high. Second, when the pamphlet went on sale, postage was included in the purchase price; for fifty cents, anyone could both buy the pamphlet and send it to friends or relatives in the East.[24]

How might local and national audiences have read this pamphlet? White people in Amador County would have been shocked, outraged, and frightened by the crime. They might well have known

Griswold. They might have recognized Chou Yee, who had worked as a cook in area restaurants and residences for several months. And they certainly knew of Griswold's and Fou Sin's employer, Horace Kilham. Kilham had lived near Jackson since the early 1850s, and his house, which also served as an office, was a local gathering place. Kilham was well known as a prosperous "ditch proprietor," and he also ran an exchange business for miners laden with gold dust. In addition, he cultivated an oft-visited orchard and garden that included over 800 peach trees, 75 apple trees, and 200 grapevines— the only spot of its kind in the county. However shocking the crime, then, local readers must have felt compelled to grapple with its meaning. Indeed, on the day that Fou Sin, Chou Yee, and Coon You were hanged, officials estimated that four to five thousand people jammed the streets of Jackson.[25] Those unnerved by the crime would have applauded the pamphlet's efforts to impose order and logic on events, just as they seemed to appreciate the finality of retribution that the hangings represented.

Such responses, however, did not always extend beyond the immediate area. Much of the content of the pamphlet appeared first in the columns of Jackson's *Amador Weekly Ledger* (it was the *Ledger*'s publisher who printed the pamphlet). Other California newspapers reprinted or commented on some of the items the *Ledger* published. When the Jackson paper ran the portraits and statements of Fou Sin, Chou Yee, and Coon You, for example, the Sacramento *State Journal* noted, "The Amador *Ledger* comes to us this week with the portraits of the three Chinamen who were strangled for the murder of Martin Van Buren Griswold," but then declined to reprint the *Ledger* article. The *Ledger* editors were furious at the implication of this brief note, and shot back in their next issue, "If the *lawful* execution of three yellow-skinned Chinamen, who committed the most diabolical murder and robbery ever recorded in the annals of California crime, is to be termed '*strangling*' . . . then the *Journal* is welcome to use the expression." But the Sacramento writer should admit, the editors insisted, that his note "conveys the idea that the Chinamen were hung by a mob."[26] This was precisely the idea that the newspaper-and-pamphlet publisher wanted *not* to convey. After all, it was 1858, not 1848, and California criminals were punished within a state judicial system, not at the hands of local vigilantes. Were they not?

If the content of *Murder of M. V. B. Griswold by Five Chinese Assassins*, as it first appeared in the *Ledger*, could stir up this kind of rancor within a forty-mile radius of Jackson, one wonders how the pamphlet was received when local people sent copies to eastern friends and relatives. Indeed, all one can do is wonder, since no evidence of eastern reaction appears to have survived. If distribution of the pamphlet depended on individuals sending single copies through the mail, it seems unlikely that an extensive national audience ever developed. And the pamphlet does not seem to have been reprinted by an eastern publisher. In addition to these logistical problems, there would have been discursive problems as well in attracting a national readership. Put simply, the pamphlet told a complicated story that eastern readers were ill prepared to hear. Martin Van Buren Griswold himself would have been a familiar character—a cherished son of eastern parents who chases western opportunities, lighting out for the territories while holding in his heart "the influence of HOME." He is industrious and forward-looking (indeed, he predicts the Gold Rush) and does not hesitate to demonstrate "American prowess" to "Greasers." He becomes a clerk, a respectable entrée to an emerging middle class.

But M. V. B. Griswold is brutally murdered. And he is murdered not by customary western adversaries—say, Indians or Mexicans. He is murdered, it seems, by a world-traveled Chinese cook whose final act is to send a letter home to his family. What is more, this cook has a name—Fou Sin—and a story to tell, as do his countrymen, who are supposed to be co-conspirators. These co-conspirators, however, tell conflicting and confusing stories. And the one who is acquitted of murder charges, and who thus will not face execution, hangs *himself*—or at least that is what the coroner concludes. For eastern readers, then, the pamphlet would have ended with unsettling images: on the one hand, there is the only man *not* convicted of murder hanging by his neck in a jail cell; on the other, there are the three convicted men awaiting death. If readers had any doubt whatsoever about the guilt of the remaining three, then this last image could have been disturbing indeed. Most such readers would have been raised in a culture steeped in Christian iconography. And, short of the cross itself, there was no more powerful Christian image than that of three men facing public execution together—reminiscent as that was of the crucifixion of Jesus Christ alongside two common criminals. It was not an image that reflected well on public officials.

To Anglo American readers outside the region where the white clerk and Chinese cook lived, worked, and died, *Murder of M. V. B. Griswold by Five Chinese Assassins* would have told the wrong stories. *Two Eras in the Life of the Felon Grovenor I. Layton* had helped domesticate the Gold Rush for eastern readers by assuring them that true moral danger was located within the hearts of individual white men, where it could be mastered, not in the external trappings of western mines or eastern cities. At the same time, by portraying Grovenor Layton as both murderous villain and lynched victim—both subject and object—of his own story, and by eliding the murdered Chileans as nameless ciphers, the pamphlet participated in the taming of the Gold Rush as an essentially Anglo American event. *Murder of M. V. B. Griswold by Five Chinese Assassins*, by contrast, said that the danger white men faced in California was not within themselves, where self-restraint could keep it in check, but without, in the very social order the Gold Rush had fostered. No amount of hard work and home influence could defend against it. And that danger had a foreign face. It was not a familiar foreign face, either—not that of continental neighbors such as Mexicans or Indians. Worst of all, that foreign face was neither monolithic nor predictable—nor even consistently dangerous. It might be Fou Sin, son of a farmer and stonecutter, who was intelligent, worldly, and worried about his white employer only insofar as it concerned his own employment. It might be Coon You, a young husband whose innocent appearance contrasted with his incriminating statements. It might be Chou Yee, who looked diabolical enough, but who penned haunting phrases such as "My body hath gone before me, borne on clouds." When the Southern Mines region told its own tales, then, they were tales like these—global, complex, fragmented, multivocal. This was true even when the individuals telling the tales, such as the publisher of the *Amador Weekly Ledger*, came from social positions of dominance and privilege. No wonder national audiences turned a deaf ear to such stories so very long ago.

Tales told in the decade or so after the California Gold Rush sounded more like the story of Grovenor Layton and the nameless Chileans than like the story of M. V. B. Griswold, Fou Sin, Chou Yee, and the rest. But the fiction of the 1860s and early 1870s also introduced a new comic twist. This fiction elaborated on—even celebrated—the moral ambiguity of Gold Rush social relations in a manner unlike the crime pamphlets of the 1850s. Had Grovenor Layton's story been told by a Bret Harte or a Mark Twain, for instance, Grovenor would have been not only a fatally flawed but an infernally funny man, and the vigilantes who lynched him would have been pilloried as vainglorious prigs. No teller of such tales was more influential than Bret Harte, a native of New York State who emigrated to California when he was seventeen. Harte worked at a variety of jobs until he established himself as a writer and editor in the 1860s, with the help of no less a Gold Rush luminary than Jessie Benton Frémont.[27] As one historian puts it, it was Harte who "fixed the Gold Rush into formula for the nation."[28] Harte's oeuvre fills almost twenty volumes in all, but his reputation as storyteller of the Gold Rush rests on a handful of tales, the most famous of which include "Tennessee's Partner" and "The Luck of Roaring Camp." One can hardly overstate the impact these stories had in codifying collective memory of the Gold Rush for generations of Americans, for whom the event became one of colorful, unwashed, unshaven men who confront a moral vacuum in the mining camps, and who respond by struggling to build a new moral order appropriate to Gold Rush conditions. As late as 1969, when Joshua Logan and Alan Jay Lerner brought an unfortunate film version of Lerner and Frederick Loewe's Broadway musical *Paint Your Wagon* to the screen, moviegoers saw in Clint Eastwood's and Lee Marvin's characters men after Harte's own heart, albeit updated to 1960s sensibilities. Marvin's grizzled ne'er-do-well and Eastwood's innocent farm boy turned forty-niner could have stepped off the pages of any Harte story. To grasp the relationship between the Southern Mines and popular memory of the Gold Rush, then, one must attend to Harte's fiction.

First, consider "Tennessee's Partner," which was published in Harte's own periodical, the *Overland Monthly*, in 1869. This tale of two white miners, one named Tennessee and the other called simply Tennessee's Partner, opens in 1853, as Tennessee's Partner decides to leave the diggings for San Francisco in search of a wife.[29] He finds one closer to home, in Stockton, and brings her back to the cabin he shares with Tennessee in the mines. But Tennessee soon woos the woman away from his partner, and the lovers run off together. Then, however, the woman rids herself of Tennessee as well. So Tennessee returns to the old cabin, where his partner greets him "with affection." All is well between the two friends, but the rest of the men in the camp turn against Tennessee, not only because he has stolen a wife but because he is, in general, a gambler and a thief. After one especially flagrant crime, Tennessee is finally arrested and tried in a makeshift miners' court.

During the course of the trial, Tennessee's Partner appears, carrying a carpetbag filled with seventeen hundred dollars in gold, which he offers as payment for Tennessee's crime. He also offers a wry rebuke to a question posed about Tennessee's character:

> I come yar as Tennessee's pardner—knowing him nigh on four year, off and on, wet and dry, in luck and out o' luck. His ways ain't aller my ways, but . . . there ain't any liveliness as he's been

up to, as I don't know. And you sez to me, sez you—confiden-
tial-like, and between man and man—sez you, "Do you know
anything in his behalf?" and I sez to you, sez I—confidential-
like, as between man and man—"What should a man know of
his pardner?"

Neither the gold nor the rebuke influences the court, and Tennessee is
convicted and hanged. All his partner can do is gather up the body in
a donkey cart, where he has laid a rough-hewn casket filled with fra-
grant pine needles. The cart itself is decorated with willow slips and
buckeye blossoms, and in it Tennessee's Partner wheels the body away.
After burying his friend, however, Tennessee's Partner falls desperately
ill. Delirious on his deathbed, he feels himself walking up the hill near
their cabin and looking for Tennessee, who he fears may be staggering
home drunk. At the top of the hill, the two men spot each other, and
Tennessee's Partner sees that Tennessee is "all by himself, sober, and
his face a-shining." The story ends: "And so they met."

Harte's story did indeed capture something of the homosocial ties—
and tensions—of the California Gold Rush. The ties he breaks off suddenly in 1853, showing them to be overwhelmed by the tensions of
man against man in the mines. Such ties can be sustained only in
death, when Tennessee and his partner meet on the high hill of the
afterlife. In the Southern Mines, of course, such ties were rendered
anomalous primarily by the influx of white women from the eastern
United States. And tensions there, while they arose often enough
among white men, typically involved struggles for economic and cultural dominance defined in racial terms and dignified by the language
of citizenship. Indeed, although Harte meant to represent the moral
complexity of the mines, his stories represent a narrowing of the field
of moral conflict, in which relations of power among various human
communities, as opposed to those among individuals, rarely surface.

But something else was lost in Harte's vision. Acquaintances of
Harte claimed that he had modeled the relationship between
Tennessee and his partner on a story he had heard about two
Tuolumne County miners, Jason Chamberlain and John Chaffee.[30]
Jason and John, too, believed that they had served as prototypes for
the famous tale. In letters he wrote as he grew older, Jason often
called himself "Tennessee" and John "Old Pard."[31] If there is even a
shred of truth to the claimed connection between the actual and the
fictional partners (and there is no reason to believe there is not), then
the afterlife reunion of the devoted friends in "Tennessee's Partner" is
doubly ironic. For the decline of the Southern Mines brought no such

tragedy in the lives of Jason and John. The Massachusetts artisans, in fact, lived together near the town of Groveland for over fifty years. Neither ever married, and the voluminous archive they left behind holds no trace of intimate female companions. John dug gold for the rest of his life, with little success. Jason turned to gardening and, in time, to keeping a way station for travelers headed up to Yosemite Valley, which, by 1890, was a national park.

Jason had a guest book for the travelers who passed through on their way to the park, and some of the entries in that book suggest that his partnership with John was an intimate one indeed. One party quipped, "The artistic inclination of these gentlemen is quite apparent tho which one is the 'ladies man' we could not discover, each modestly declining the honor." Another man wrote simply, "These are men after my own Heart." A few days later, a visitor remarked on Groveland's natural beauty, but noted that the most curious bond created "by the convulsions of nature" was that between "the wedded batchelors." And yet another traveler, himself an old forty-niner, was even more explicit in his guest book entry:

> On Our Trip to the Yosemite Providence directed us to the Cheerful Cabin of Messrs Chamberlain and Chaffee Two Characteristic "49ers" whose attachment to each other has the true "Damon and Pythias" ring, that touches sentiments so welcome May their "Golden Wedding" to be celebrated in 1899 be a crowning event to their long history of Hospitality[32]

Jason and John did make it to their "Golden Wedding." In his diary for 1899, itself a gift from *Overland Monthly* editors, Jason wrote on the inside front cover, "This is the Jubilee Number or 50 Years Together."[33]

The partners would live with one another for four more years, until sickness forced John to travel down to the Bay Area for medical care in 1903. A guest book entry from this period indicates the toll John's illness took on Jason: "His meditative, absent look, and day dreams indicate that his mind, thought, anxiety are in Chaffee while he lingers in the East Bay Sanitorium at Oakland. A love could not miss his sweetheart more."[34] John never returned to Groveland. He died on July 31, 1903. Jason puttered around their homestead for a couple of months after John's death, picking apples, walking to town for his mail, and looking after his own failing health (he was eighty-one, and suffered from painful prostate troubles). The journal Jason kept for over half a century ends abruptly on October 16, 1903, with the terse entry "went for mail picked apples." Shortly thereafter,

John Chaffee and Jason Chamberlain, hearthside, in their seventies, after living half a century together in Tuolumne County.

Courtesy of the Bancroft Library.

Jason Chamberlain put the barrel of a shotgun in his mouth and pulled the trigger.[35]

This story of illness and grief is not easily accommodated by collective memory of the Gold Rush, though Bret Harte's tale prefigured the partners' deaths and offered a culturally intelligible narrative in which to fit their passing. But like most dominant cultural memories of California's rush for riches, this one narrows the field of vision considerably, cutting short as it does the intimate—and, no doubt in some cases, erotic—ties between men that the Gold Rush fostered. Indeed, no historical silence is so deafening as that which surrounds the intimacies among men who spent a night, or a lifetime. together in the foothills of the Sierra Nevada. Groveland was not Greenwich Village, to be sure. But neither was it a land of lonely hearts.

In the end, of course, the process of codifying collective memory of the California Gold Rush produced not one but many historical silences. Consider another of Bret Harte's famous stories, "The Luck of Roaring Camp," published in 1868.[36] Harte sets the scene in this manner:

> There was commotion in Roaring Camp. It could not have been a fight, for in 1850, that was not novel enough to have called together the entire settlement. The ditches and claims were not

only deserted, but "Tuttle's grocery" had contributed its gamblers, who, it will be remembered, calmly continued their game the day that French Pete and Kanaka Joe shot each other to death over the bar in the front room.

The commotion is created by a woman—a "very sinful woman" named Cherokee Sal—who is giving birth. She is not having an easy time of it, and the miners and gamblers occupy themselves by betting on the outcome: Will Sal live? Will the baby? If the baby lives, will it be a boy or a girl? What will be the color of the infant's skin? It does not take much imagination to guess at Sal's fate: such women rarely survive in nineteenth-century fiction. She dies in short order, but the baby, a boy, lives: "Mighty small specimen," exclaims one miner; "Has n't mor'n got the color," observes another.

The birth at Roaring Camp works a series of social miracles: first, the men file past the infant, who is wrapped in red flannel and lying in a candle box, bringing him the gifts of latter-day wise guys: a revolver, a slingshot, a golden spur, a diamond pin, and, then, a diamond ring (the giver remarking that he "saw that pin and went two diamonds better"). As time passes, the baby thrives on donkey's milk and attentive father figures, and the camp thrives too—so much so that the men christen the boy "The Luck" for the prosperity he brings. Wholesale regeneration follows. Men start to bathe and wash their clothes, and they begin to refrain from profanity. The Luck's cabin is whitewashed without and wallpapered within. Some even suggest inviting "one or two decent families" to live in Roaring Camp, so that The Luck can "profit from female companionship."

But this is where the new social order doubles back upon itself: to bring in married, white women ("decent" being an unsubtle code for white and married) is not to create something new but rather to install a familiar moral regime, in which white women assert moral influence and white men exercise self-control. Bret Harte knew this story. It was a story that middle-class Americans told about themselves through much of the nineteenth century. It was not a story that interested Harte. What interested him was a story for which there was no imaginable resolution—one in which white gold seekers create an alternative social order, every bit as moral as that presided over by white women in settled regions. When there is no imaginable resolution, however, death and destruction often ensue. Harte could not conceive of a world in which an unmarried Cherokee mother could live in harmony with non-native men—or else he thought his readers would not abide such a world. So Sal dies quickly, leaving behind her mixed-blood offspring. Destruction follows. It is winter, and the rivers that start in the Sierra Nevada are swelling their banks from snow in the mountains and rain in the foothills. A wall of water rushes into Roaring Camp, sweeping tents, trees, and tools in its wake, dumping them in the valley below. Among the debris is the whitewashed cabin, and with it goes "the pride, the hope, the joy, The Luck, of Roaring Camp." The dead infant is found in the arms of a man who tried and failed to save The Luck and who himself is dying too. "Tell the boys I've got The Luck with me now" are his last words, and, as Harte puts it, "The strong man, clinging to the frail babe . . . drifted away into the shadowy river that flows forever to the unknown sea."

This, then, is another piece of the Gold Rush of collective memory: an amoral community of men confronts a baby's birth and begins to build a world worthy of that child. It is an impossible social world, however, and it ends in sentimentalized destruction. But note too who lived in this world: not just characters named Sandy and Stumpy and Kentuck but ones named French Pete and Kanaka Joe and Cherokee Sal. Granted, these characters are all dead or dying; Pete and Joe have knocked each other off by the third sentence. Nonetheless, they represent a kind of shadow story that lurks around the edges of Harte's tale, and that almost takes center stage in the baby who brings not just luck but regeneration to Roaring Camp. Recall the miners' curiosity about the baby's "complexion," and the comment that the infant "has n't mor'n got the color"? This phrase derives from miners' habit of looking for "color"—that is, gold—in the dirt they washed out. Its use here tells us that, in the miners' eyes, the baby is light-skinned but not "white." The shadow story, then, is one about a multiracial, multiethnic social world, in which French men and Pacific Islanders live alongside Anglos from the eastern United States and Cherokee women from Indian Territory. Within a few pages, all that remains of this shadow world is a mixed-race child who becomes, momentarily, not the shame but The Luck of Roaring Camp.

And then The Luck dies, and so does Roaring Camp. Unlike "Tennessee's Partner," "The Luck of Roaring Camp" cannot be linked to any particular persons, places, or events in the Southern Mines. That does not mean, however, that the tale cannot be used to illuminate the troubled connection between history and memory, between the lived past of the Southern Mines, on the one hand, and popular representations of the California Gold Rush, on the other. Indeed, most of Harte's tales are not geographically specific; they represent a composite Gold Rush world. Roaring Camp, for example, is probably an imaginary mining community.[37] Yet Harte's stories, in their centering of Anglo American men as characters, draw more from the history of the Northern Mines than from that of the Southern Mines. Few readers have made or cared about this distinction, which may at first glance seem trivially historicist. Nonetheless, if one turns from sites of memory such as Harte's stories to the historical record of social relations in the Southern Mines, one can easily tell tales that suggest how dominant cultural memory has refracted history, casting a halo on the most basic inequities, the most blatant practices of power. In "The Luck of Roaring Camp," for example, a mixed-blood baby's death brings the possibility of an alternative social world—even a moral universe—to an end. In the Southern Mines, actual infants perished, some of them the offspring of intimate interethnic and interracial ties. But such deaths suggest different stories with different morals: stories of power as well as sentiment, stories of women as well as men, stories that start not only north but also south of the equator, stories of complex human beings rather than rough-hewn heroes with hearts of gold.

One last story, then—this one drawn from an inquest into the death of an unidentified infant, whose body was found in a mining shaft on Murphys Flat in Calaveras County in 1858. The entire record of this human drama—in which a woman and man had sex and conceived, the woman carried the fetus to term and gave birth, and then someone, perhaps the woman herself, smothered the baby and threw the body down a mining shaft—consists of just three pieces of paper. The first is in the handwriting of a coroner. "Information having come to me . . . that the Body of [a] dead Infant had been found," he writes, "I proceeded to the place where the Body lay." The next is written by a doctor. He states that the fetus was carried to term and then smothered after birth. He notes that the deceased is female, and says that she looks like "a white child and from white parents," although she "may be from a white father and [a] Chilano woman." Finally, a jury summoned by the coroner renders its verdict: the deceased is female; she was born living; and she was smothered "by some person or persons unknown."[38] No strong men clinging to frail babes here; this child was *not* The Luck of Murphys Flat.

Who was she? We cannot know for sure. But we can cast a wide net using the larger record of social relations in the Southern Mines to come up with a scenario that makes good historical sense. We know, for example, that the area jurors called Murphys Flat was a rich placer mining site as early as 1848. Miners used water from Angels Creek to wash gold-bearing dirt, looking for "color" in every pan, rocker, and sluice box. By 1858, when the body was found, the creek had proven insufficient, and a water company had built flumes and dug ditches to provide water to miners from the Stanislaus River.[39] By then, Murphys was one of the most famous spots in the Southern Mines. The unfortunate infant was born in the vicinity of this town. According to the doctor who examined her, she appeared to be the offspring of two white parents or of a white father and a Chilean mother. Like The Luck of Roaring Camp, the baby from Murphys Flat was light-skinned, but the doctor thought she might not be "white." His guess that it was the mother who may have been Chilean was no doubt based on social rather than somatic observations. First, Chileans had lived in and around Murphys since the Gold Rush began, and not all had left, even after the Chilean War and the imposition of the 1850 foreign miners' tax. Second, the early history of the Southern Mines, when Anglo men socialized freely with non-Anglo women, had established a pattern of interethnic encounters that continued past the boom years. So it was not difficult for the doctor to imagine that an Anglo man and a Chilean woman had kept company.

What sort of situation could lead a woman to carry a fetus to term, only to smother the baby after birth? We do not know, of course, that the mother killed the infant. But with death following so quickly after birth, the mother seems a likely suspect. There is no record by which we can assess individual motivation, but there is copious evidence of the parameters within which a person would have made choices in 1858. A pregnant woman, probably unmarried, living at this moment faced overwhelming constraints. First, she lived in an economic world that provided few opportunities for a woman to support even herself, to say nothing of a child. Second, she lived in a social and cultural world in which married, middle-class women from the eastern United States were increasingly setting the standards for acceptable behavior. These two constraints were intertwined. The arrival of married, middle-class women also brought an assault on some of the work—dealing cards, pouring drinks, selling sex—most readily available to unmarried women, further narrowing economic opportunities. Third—if the woman was, in fact, Chilean—she lived in a place where the number of Chileans was shrinking, not growing, and where there was now a decade of bad blood between her people and Anglo Americans. Finally, whatever this woman was facing, it seems likely that she was facing it on her own, that the man who fathered the baby had, as Anglo miners liked to put it, "vamosed." Under such circumstances, nurturing an infant and then raising a daughter might well have seemed an impossible task.

There is little else in the historical record to help us link these details together into a story. But there is one other piece of information we can glean from the Calaveras County inquest report: the baby from Murphys Flat was thrown in a mining shaft. Again, we have no direct evidence of the meaning a mother might have attached to such an act. But tossing a baby's body down a mining shaft seems a grim commentary on a historical moment that has come to be as celebrated as the California Gold Rush. We cannot know for sure the nature of this commentary any more than we can know for sure who committed this act. But it seems safe to suggest that the act did not constitute a compliment—to the father of the child, to men who were miners, to the Gold Rush itself. The depth of meaning embedded in a woman's gruesome decision to throw her infant daughter's dead body down a shaft toward the Mother Lode, *la veta madre*, is equal to anything we can plumb in a Bret Harte story.

But if I show that a document as thin as an inquest, when examined through the thick lens of historical context, can yield a past as richly textured as that portrayed in any great American short story, then I may seem to be straying from a commitment I made many pages ago—a commitment to write within the tension between history and memory rather than trying to resolve it. This was what I did when I told the tale of Joaquín Murrieta and Rosa Felíz de Murrieta, who are figures of memory just as surely as they are figures of history. Now I may seem to be saying that history tells better stories than memory because historians use documents and tell the truth while writers of fiction lie about our collective past. In fact, however, I offer my history as food for memory, and make only modest truth claims about the past I have constructed herein. In these final pages, I purposely have explored historical documents that are frustratingly fragmented, in order to turn back to my initial arguments—arguments that are not mine alone—about the similarity between the work of history and the work of memory. History and memory alike begin with fragments, with filaments, and then weave those filaments together into a fabric of the past intelligible to human eyes in the present. That fabric may not always be pretty, but if it is to be preserved, it must be useful. Because as human beings, we insist on wrapping ourselves in the mantle of the past; we warm our feet at old fires. If academic history and collective memory alike arise out of an impulse to know ourselves in the present by knowing our past, then there is little good to be gained by setting one way of knowing over or against the other.[40]

Nonetheless, I do believe that historians have a key contribution to make to our collective project, a distinctive dish to bring to the table. Historical perspectives on the workings of memory are crucial. Take, for example, Bret Harte's fiction, which for a century and a half has constituted square one for popular memory of the California Gold Rush in the United States. As such, it demands our attention, for it demonstrates who certain Americans have imagined themselves to be—particularly Americans who are white and male or who at least aspire to such social categories of dominance. It also yields clues about how the American nation itself has been conceived. In "The Luck of Roaring Camp," Sandy and Stumpy and Kentuck need no modifiers attached to their monikers; we assume they are white and American and male, quintessential Gold Rush participants. (Cherokee) Sal and (French) Pete and (Kanaka) Joe are, quite literally, other stories, other narratives, other nations. Harte's fiction, then, does not tell us much of anything about the people whom quintessential Gold Rush participants—quintessential Americans—have imagined themselves *not* to be.[41] After all, one can rummage around in stories such as "The Luck of Roaring Camp" only just so long searching for the shadow story of people who were not white and American and male. The tales of Sal and Joe and Pete remain embedded in solid rock, no matter how one tries to crush it and get at the gold. This is because it was not Harte's intention to make of Gold Rush gender and race relations much more than a quirky, colorful background to high-spirited portraits of Anglo American men.[42] Historians, however, can help turn backgrounds into foregrounds, portraits of individuals into pictures of crowds—now contending, now cooperating, now careening into artistic and political spaces heretofore unimagined.

But we must also ask for help, not only from one another but from all creators of collective memory—who are often better tellers of tales than are academic historians. We must turn in particular to those who are producing countermemories, stories and images and built environments doing battle with dominant narratives that reinscribe social inequities. My own understanding of California's Southern Mines, for example, has been informed not only by the work of countless other scholars but by sites of countermemory that I have visited or attended or otherwise encountered.[43] One of these was a gathering held in 1991 in what was once Nisenan country but is now Marshall Gold Discovery State Historic Park—the spot where white and native workers for John Sutter found gold in 1848. The gathering was called "Return to Gold Mountain: A Chinese American Pioneer Festival," and its purpose was both to rededicate two Chinese buildings in the park and to educate Californians about the earliest Chinese immigrants to the state. This was the first-ever commemoration of Chinese participation in the Gold Rush held in what is now called the gold country, and it took more ethnic Chinese up into the foothills than had been there for over a hundred years.[44] Another of these sites of countermemory is the *Del Rey Mural*, a panel painted by the Chicano muralist Antonio Bernal in 1968 on the wall of the United Farm Workers' Teatro Campesino Cultural Center. The six-by-fifteen-foot painting features eight leaders, historical and contemporary, held in esteem by participants in the Chicano movement of the 1960s. The two central figures in the mural are Cesar Chávez, leader of the United Farm Workers, and Joaquín Murrieta, scourge of the Southern Mines.[45] Yet another site of countermemory is Chaw'se, or Indian Grinding Rock State Historic Park, near Jackson in Amador County. This remarkable site, which is built around an outcrop of rock where native women once ground acorns, was constructed in part by Sierra foothill Indians in the late 1960s. It features both an indoor museum and an outdoor park with a reconstructed Miwok village from times past. The site includes a ceremonial roundhouse and gathering places for contemporary native people; each fall, for example, witnesses a "Big Time" celebration that marks the customary time of the acorn harvest.[46] These sites of countermemory offer up a Gold Rush that cannot just be grafted onto dominant collective memory, for they both people and plot the past anew. They offer a past in which all are repositioned; at the same time, they embody a hope for a more just and equitable future.

As we begin the second century and a half since the California Gold Rush began, we would do well to recognize that we live in an era of concentrated human diversity and congealed human inequity not wholly unlike that faced by gold seekers a hundred and fifty years ago, especially in the region that was known as the Southern Mines. There is so much that we have not yet learned from the Gold Rush. If we can remember it differently, perhaps we can use that memory to different ends.

Notes

Prologue: Joaquín Murrieta and the Bandits

1. Pierre Nora, "Between Memory and History: Les Lieux de Mémoire," *Representations*, no. 26 (Spring 1989): 7–25, esp. 19. This is the introduction to Nora's multivolume collaborative work on French collective memory, *Les Lieux de mémoire* (Paris: Éditions Gallimard, 1984–), which has been translated as *Realms of Memory: Rethinking the French Past*, trans. Arthur Goldhammer (New York: Columbia Univ. Press, 1996–). I am grateful to Dorothy Fujita Rony for conversations and suggested readings on history and memory.

2. Charles Howard Shinn, *Mining Camps: A Study in American Frontier Government*, ed. Rodman Wilson Paul (1884; reprint, Gloucester, Mass.: Peter Smith, 1970); Josiah Royce, *California, from the Conquest in 1846 to the Second Vigilance Committee in San Francisco: A Study of American Character* (1886; reprint, Santa Barbara: Peregrine, 1970); Rodman W. Paul, *California Gold: The Beginning of Mining in the Far West* (1947; reprint, Lincoln: Univ. of Nebraska Press, 1965); John Walton Caughey, *The California Gold Rush* (1948; reprint, Berkeley: Univ. of California Press, 1975) (originally titled *Gold Is the Cornerstone*); J. S. Holliday, *The World Rushed In: The California Gold Rush Experience* (New York: Simon and Schuster, 1981); Ralph Mann, *After the Gold Rush: Society in Grass Valley and Nevada City, California, 1849–1870* (Stanford: Stanford Univ. Press, 1982); David Goodman, *Gold Seeking: Victoria and California in the 1850s* (Stanford: Stanford Univ. Press, 1994); and Malcolm J. Rohrbough, *Days of Gold: The California Gold Rush and the American Nation* (Berkeley: Univ. of California Press, 1997).

3. Natalie Zemon Davis and Randolph Starn, "Introduction," Special Issue: Memory and Counter–Memory, *Representations*, no. 26 (Spring 1989): 1–6, esp. 5. Cf. David Thelen, "Memory and American History," Special Issue: Memory and American History, *Journal of American History* 75, no. 4 (March 1989): 1117–29. More recently, the *American*

Historical Review published a forum on history and collective memory, with articles by Susan A. Crane, Alon Confino, and Daniel James. James's essay, "Meatpackers, Peronists, and Collective Memory: A View from the South," advances the arguments most relevant to my concerns here. See *American Historical Review* 102, no. 5 (Dec. 1997): 1371–412, esp. 1404–12.

4. On the gold regions, see Paul, 91–115.

5. Writings on Joaquín Murrieta are legion. For a succinct summary, see Stan Steiner's entry in *Reader's Encyclopedia of the American West*, ed. Howard R. Lamar (New York: Harper and Row, 1977), 782–83; and the updated entry by Raul Ramos in *The New Encyclopedia of the American West*, ed. Howard Lamar (New Haven: Yale Univ. Press, 1998), 748. The latest film rendition of the life of Murrieta is *The Mask of Zorro* (1998), starring Antonio Banderas as the brother of Joaquín. In this film, Murrieta is relocated in a vague Mexican-era California prior to the Gold Rush.

6. Frank F. Latta, *Joaquín Murrieta and His Horse Gangs* (Santa Cruz, Calif.: Bear State Books, 1980). By far the most exhaustively researched account of Murrieta—Latta traveled extensively in the state of Sonora interviewing Murrieta associates and descendants, and he carefully studied written records as well—this book lacks the scholarly apparatus of footnotes and bibliography and is organized and written in a manner many academics will find exasperating. For its oral interviews alone, however, the book is worth the patience required to use it. Most of my references to this work are to information Latta gathered in interviews, though I have also made use of facsimile reproductions of documents therein.

7. See Pedro Castillo and Albert Camarillo, eds., *Furia y muerte: Los bandidos chicanos*, Monograph no. 4 (Los Angeles: Aztlán Publications, Chicano Studies Center, Univ. of California, Los Angeles, 1973), esp. 32–51. Castillo and Camarillo draw on the formulation of social banditry developed in E. J. Hobsbawm, *Primitive Rebels: Studies in Archaic Forms of Social Movements in the 19th and 20th Centuries* (New York: Praeger, 1959), and *Bandits* (London: Weidenfeld and Nicolson, 1969). The argument in *Furia y muerte* has been developed in Robert J. Rosenbaum, *Mexicano Resistance in the Southwest: "The Sacred Right of Self-Preservation"* (Austin: Univ. of Texas Press, 1981). For an excellent survey of the fate of Hobsbawm's thesis in Latin American history, and for useful suggestions for future research, see Gilbert M. Joseph, "On the Trail of Latin American Bandits: A Reexamination of Peasant Resistance," *Latin American Research Review* 25, no. 3 (1990): 3–53.

8. Latta, esp. 145–50, 167, 186, 213, 215–16.

9. Frank Latta, who gathered oral histories of Murrieta descendants from the 1920s through the 1970s, must also have had a hand in constructing this familial, male-oriented past.

10. Latta, 208, 212–13. On the order in which the earliest emigrant groups

reached the diggings, see Paul, 20–35; Caughey, 17–24; J. M. Guinn, "The Sonoran Migration," *Historical Society of Southern California Annual Publications* 8 (1909–11): 31–36; Doris M. Wright, "The Making of Cosmopolitan California: An Analysis of Immigration, 1848–1870," parts 1 and 2, *California Historical Society Quarterly* 19, no. 4 (Dec. 1940): 323–43, and 20, no. 1 (March 1941): 65–79; Richard H. Peterson, *Manifest Destiny in the Mines: A Cultural Interpretation of Anti-Mexican Nativism in California, 1848–1853* (1965; rev. ed., San Francisco: R and E Research Associates, 1975), 24–31.

11. Latta, esp. 177, 208, 212–14. On Mexican women emigrants, see, e.g., Paul, 26–27; Guinn, 32; Leonard Pitt, *The Decline of the Californios: A Social History of the Spanish-Speaking Californians, 1846–1890* (Berkeley: Univ. of California Press, 1966), 72; William Perkins, *Three Years in California: William Perkins' Journal of Life at Sonora, 1849–1852*, ed. Dale L. Morgan and James R. Scobie (Berkeley: Univ. of California Press, 1964), 103–4, 130–31, 251, 268, 292.

12. The Southern Mines were the first logical stopping point for emigrants traveling north from Mexico. Then, too, the Anglo majority in the Northern Mines early on became known as especially inhospitable to Spanish-speaking women and men, further encouraging Californios, Mexicans, Chileans, and Peruvians to concentrate in the southern region. See Paul, 106–15; Pitt, 48–68, 73–74; Dale M. Morgan and James R. Scobie, "Introduction," in Perkins, 1–57, esp. 32; Sister Colette M. Standart, "The Sonoran Migration to California, 1848–1856: A Study in Prejudice," *Southern California Quarterly* 58, no. 3 (Fall 1976): 333–57; Richard H. Peterson, "Anti-Mexican Nativism in California, 1848–1853: A Study of Cultural Conflict," *Southern California Quarterly* 62, no. 4 (Winter 1980): 309–27, esp. 310.

13. Walter Colton, *Three Years in California* (New York: A. S. Barnes, 1850), 276, 304.

14. Paul, 54–55.

15. At $16 an ounce, the gold would have been worth well over $3,000. Antonio Franco Coronel, "Cosas de California," trans. and ed. Richard Henry Morefield, in *The Mexican Adaptation in American California, 1846–1875* (1955; reprint, San Francisco: R and E Research Associates, 1971), 76–96, esp. 93–94. My thanks to Michael González for calling my attention to this translation of the original Coronel manuscript, which is at the Bancroft Library, Univ. of California, Berkeley.

16. Perkins, 106; R. A. Appling to John, March 31, 1853, transcript in Appling Family File, Mariposa Museum and History Center, Mariposa, Calif.

17. Perkins, 157–58, 268.

18. Latta, 30, 145–50, 167, 178, 227. On Indian-Mexican relations, see Edward H. Spicer, *Cycles of Conquest: The Impact of Spain, Mexico, and the United States on the Indians of the Southwest, 1533–1960* (Tucson: Univ. of Arizona Press, 1962), 46–85 (Mayos and Yaquis), 105–17 (Seris), and 229–61 (Western Apaches). On how U.S. expansion exac-

erbated conditions in northern Mexico, see David J. Weber, "American Westward Expansion and the Breakdown of Relations between Pobladores and 'Indios Bárbaros' on Mexico's Far Northern Frontier," *New Mexico Historical Review* 56, no. 3 (July 1981): 221–38, and *The Mexican Frontier, 1821–1846: The American Southwest under Mexico* (Albuquerque: Univ. of New Mexico Press, 1982), 83–105. On the relationship between these conditions and Sonoran emigration to California, see Standart.

19. See Albert L. Hurtado, *Indian Survival on the California Frontier* (New Haven: Yale Univ. Press, 1988).

20. See Spicer, 279–367.

21. These exclusionary and extortionate practices are detailed in chap. 4, "Mining Gold and Making War." See also Pitt, 48–68, and "The Beginnings of Nativism in California," *Pacific Historical Review* 30, no. 1 (Feb. 1961): 23–38; Morefield, *Mexican Adaptation* and "Mexicans in the California Mines, 1848–53," *California Historical Society Quarterly* 35, no. 1 (March 1956): 37–46; William Robert Kenny, "Mexican-American Conflict on the Mining Frontier, 1848–1852," *Journal of the West* 6, no. 4 (Oct. 1967): 582–92, and "Nativism in the Southern Mining Region of California," *Journal of the West* 12, no. 1 (Jan. 1973): 126–38; Standart; Peterson, *Manifest Destiny* and "Anti-Mexican Nativism."

22. Latta, 208, 212, 228, 291–92, 582–85.

23. Ibid., 286–92, 297–99; Perkins, 161–62; Deena J. González, "La Tules of Image and Reality: Euro-American Attitudes and Legend Formation on a Spanish-Mexican Frontier," in *Building with Our Hands: New Directions in Chicana Studies,* ed. Adela de la Torre and Beatríz M. Pesquera (Berkeley: Univ. of California Press, 1993), 75–90; and Janet Lecompte, "The Independent Women of Hispanic New Mexico, 1821–1846," *Western Historical Quarterly* 12, no. 1 (Jan. 1981): 17–35.

24. Latta, passim and esp. 399–467.

25. Hurtado, 32–54.

26. Latta, 85, 208, 212, 228. The first interviewee, Soledad Murrieta de Murrieta, was described to Latta as the family historian. The second, Elías Murrieta, remembered that his grandfather had accompanied Joaquín Murrieta to California and had never returned.

27. The standard reference on these ideas in late colonial New Mexico is Ramón A. Gutiérrez, *When Jesus Came, the Corn Mothers Went Away: Marriage, Sexuality, and Power in New Mexico, 1500–1846* (Stanford: Stanford Univ. Press, 1991). See also his "Honor Ideology, Marriage Negotiation, and Class-Gender Domination in New Mexico, 1690–1846," *Latin American Perspectives* 12, no. 1 (Winter 1985): 81–104, and "From Honor to Love: Transformations of the Meaning of Sexuality in Colonial New Mexico," in *Kinship Ideology and Practice in Latin America,* ed. Raymond T. Smith (Chapel Hill: Univ. of North Carolina Press, 1984), 237–63.

28. Standart, 335; Spicer, 113, 241; Stuart F. Voss, *On the Periphery of*

Nineteenth-Century Mexico: Sonora and Sinaloa, 1810–1877 (Tucson: Univ. of Arizona Press, 1982), 105–13.

29. A particularly trenchant critique of the cultural concept of honor itself appears in Lila Abu-Lughod, *Writing Women's Worlds: Bedouin Stories* (Berkeley: Univ. of California Press, 1993). Abu-Lughod effectively dismantles the "culture of honor" approach advanced in much historical and anthropological literature, by demonstrating the varieties of ways in which contemporary Bedouin women live in critical dialogue with cultural values of "honor" and "shame."

30. Latta, esp. 13–15, 85–86, 174–76, 208, 279–80, 292, 297–99. (The earlier page references are to interviews with Murrieta descendants and to Latta's assessment of their stories. The later ones are to an interview with the grandson of the Calaveras County second sheriff Ben Marshall, who echoes some of the contentions of the Murrieta family members.)

31. The inconsistency in the use of diacritical marks that begins here is intentional. A "Joaquin Muliati" appeared in the *San Joaquin Republican* (Stockton), May 7, 1853. "Joaquin Muriati" appeared in the text of the California state legislature's "Act to Authorize the Raising of a Company of Rangers," approved by Governor John Bigler on May 17, 1853, facsimile reproduction in Latta, 328.

32. Based on items published in the *San Joaquin Republican*, Jan.–May, 1853. Some historians have used San Francisco or other California newspapers to trace essentially the same story. See esp. Pitt's chapter on banditry entitled "The Head Pickled in Whiskey," in *Decline of the Californios*, 69–82. I have chosen the Stockton paper because of Stockton's unique relationship to the Southern Mines, where most of the events of 1853 took place. In particular, the *San Joaquin Republican* reprinted much of its material from the *Calaveras Chronicle* (Mokelumne Hill) and other newspapers in the Southern Mines that are no longer extant. For "the notorious outlaw, Joaquin," see Feb. 16, 1853; for "Joaquin Carillo," see, e.g., March 2, 1853.

33. See, e.g., *San Joaquin Republican*, Feb. 16, 1853.

34. Ibid., March 2, 1853.

35. Ibid.

36. Ibid., Jan. 26, 29, 1853.

37. Ronald Takaki lays the groundwork for such analysis in *Iron Cages: Race and Culture in Nineteenth-Century America* (New York: Alfred A. Knopf, 1979), though the theme is more implicit than explicit in his argument. See esp. 215–49. The later international implications are suggested in the chapter entitled "The Masculine Thrust toward Asia," 253–79.

38. *San Joaquin Republican*, Feb. 23, March 2, 1853.

39. Ibid., Feb. 23, 1853. On midnineteenth-century Anglo American notions of male gender, see, e.g., Charles E. Rosenberg, "Sexuality, Class and Role in Nineteenth-Century America," *American Quarterly* 35, no. 2 (May 1973): 131–53; G. J. Barker-Benfield, *The Horrors of the Half-Known*

Life: Male Attitudes toward Women and Sexuality in Nineteenth-Century America (New York: Harper Colophon, 1976), esp. 175–88; Elizabeth H. Pleck and Joseph H. Pleck, "Introduction," in *The American Man*, eds. Pleck and Pleck (Englewood Cliffs, N.J.: Prentice-Hall, 1980), 1–49, esp. 14–20, and essays in the section entitled "The Commercial Age," 145–215; J. A. Mangan and James Walvin, eds., *Manliness and Morality: Middle-Class Masculinity in Britain and America, 1800–1940* (Manchester: Manchester Univ. Press, 1987); E. Anthony Rotundo, *American Manhood: Transformations in Masculinity from the Revolution to the Modern Era* (New York: Basic Books, 1993). This story is complicated further by competing ideas about white manhood in the U.S. South, where notions of honor not unlike those described by Gutiérrez for colonial New Mexico were in ascendance. See discussion below.

40. *San Joaquin Republican,* March 2, 1853.

41. Along with the literature on Anglo manhood already cited, Takaki has influenced my argument here. It is perhaps telling that while Anglo accounts tend to describe Joaquín as dark-skinned, Murrieta family members insist that their forebear, like a good many of his kin, was *huero*—he had light skin and eyes and brown hair. Cf., e.g., *San Joaquin Republican,* Feb. 16, 1853; and Latta, 179, 183. Anglo men did indeed think about their "darker" selves during the Gold Rush. Describing one mining camp, e.g., the future Wisconsin governor Lucius Fairchild wrote in a letter home, "You never dreamed of such a rowdy hole as this is, all summer there was not an hour but what some one was drunk in the street & fights have become so common as not to excite any curiosity even to run & see them. . . . This is a true picture, Every body drinks freely, even myself have swallowed enough cocktails to float a skiff. . . . Gamblers, loafers, loose women, and all the scum of society are here. . . . This is the dark side of us." Lucius Fairchild, *California Letters of Lucius Fairchild*, ed. Joseph Schafer (Madison: State Historical Society of Wisconsin, 1931), 182.

42. *San Joaquin Republican,* Feb. 2, 1853.

43. Ibid., Jan. 29, 1853.

44. Ibid., March 2, 1853.

45. John Doble, farther north in Calaveras County at Volcano (Volcano is now in Amador County), noted on March 14, 1853, that (Miwok) Indians along Dry, Sutter, Amador, and Rancherie creeks—"an area in which there are no Mines & consequently no whites"—were harassing travelers. "They are supposed to be incited to rob and steal by the band of outlawed Mexicans & Chileans [!] known as Joaquins band." Reflecting a Feb. newspaper story, Doble wrote of Joaquín, "he is said to wear a shirt of mail so that all who have yet shot at him have not affected him." (The "shirt of mail" is a "coat of armor" in *San Joaquin Republican,* Feb. 16, 1853.) This is Doble's only mention of Joaquín or of Mexican banditry. See *John Doble's Journal and Letters from the Mines: Mokelumne Hill, Jackson, Volcano and San Francisco, 1851–1865,* ed.

Charles L. Camp (Denver: Old West Publishing, 1962), 148. Likewise, P. V. Fox, who was situated much farther south in Mariposa County—another supposed hotbed of banditry—noted mule thefts and murders just once in his diary. Reflecting popular sentiment, Fox wrote that the attacks "were supposed to be the work of Joaquin or his band who has created great excitement by his daring and unprovoked murders and robberies." See Journal entry, March 13, 1853, P. V. Fox Journals, Beinecke Library, Yale Univ., New Haven.

46. *The Journals of Alfred Doten, 1849–1903*, 3 vols., ed. Walter Van Tilburg Clark (Reno: Univ. of Nevada Press, 1973), 1:123–24. I have not seen the name Cladne used elsewhere in Anglo or Mexican accounts. Murrieta descendants recall an associate of Joaquín, El Famoso, named Claudio (Acevedo), who they claim helped Joaquín get revenge on the Anglo miners. See Latta, 95, 173. The *San Joaquin Republican*, Aug. 11, 1853, mentions a brother of Joaquín's named Claudio. Likewise, the first "historical" account of Murrieta, to be discussed at length below, identifies a "Claudio" as an important band member. See John Rollin Ridge [Yellow Bird], *The Life and Adventures of Joaquín Murieta, the Celebrated California Bandit* (1854; reprint, Norman: Univ. of Oklahoma Press, 1955), esp. 17–18. All of which is to say Doten's "Cladne" might have been a Murrieta associate or relative named Claudio. Or maybe not.

47. Doten, 1:140. Doten added that despite the "great excitement," he "could not learn the particulars very definitely."

48. Ibid., 1:141.

49. On this point, see chap. 4, "Mining Gold and Making War."

50. *San Joaquin Republican*, Feb. 23, March 30, May 4, 1853. And see the facsimile reproductions of Governor Bigler's Feb. 21 proclamation offering a $1,000 reward "for the apprehension and safe delivery of the said Joaquin Carillo into the custody of the sheriff of Calaveras county," and the Mariposa County petition to the governor to "call out a company of Rangers," dated April 20, both in Latta, 321, 324–26.

51. "An Act to Authorize the Raising of a Company of Rangers."

52. *San Joaquin Republican*, Feb. 23, 1853, and facsimile reproduction of the petition in Latta, 324–26.

53. *San Joaquin Republican*, June 8, 1853.

54. On Covarrubias, see Hubert H. Bancroft, "Pioneer Register and Index," in *The Works of Hubert Howe Bancroft*, vol. 19, *California* (San Francisco: A. L. Bancroft, 1885), 2:683–795, esp. 770; Donald E. Hargis, "Native Californians in the Constitutional Convention of 1849," *Historical Society of Southern California Quarterly* 36, no. 1 (March 1954): 3–13, esp. 12, n. 7; Pitt, 43.

55. All quotations from "Minority Report of J. M. Covarrubias," facsimile reproduction in Latta, 330–32.

56. Bancroft, 2:770; Pitt, 136, 143.

57. "Black hair" and "black eyes" were the only physical descriptions offered of the head of Joaquin Carillo in the governor's proclamation of Feb. 21, 1853. See facsimile reproduction in Latta, 321. On the declining fortunes of Californio men from families like the Carillos and Covarrubiases, see Pitt; and Albert Camarillo, *Chicanos in a Changing Society: From Mexican Pueblos to American Barrios in Santa Barbara and Southern California, 1848–1930* (Cambridge: Harvard Univ. Press, 1979).

58. "Act to Authorize the Raising of a Company of Rangers"; *San Joaquin Republican,* June 8, 1853 (the newspaper's spelling of two of the five names varies slightly—"Muliati" for "Muriati," "Corillo" for "Carillo").

59. Latta insists that Murrieta family memories can account for each of the five named Joaquins: "Joaquin Muriati" was Joaquín Murrieta, El Famoso; "Joaquin Ocomorenia" was actually Jesús Valenzuela, who adopted the alias Ochomorenio from a childhood incident involving *ocho merino* (eight sheep); "Joaquin Valenzuela" was Joaquín Valenzuela, brother of Jesús; "Joaquin Botellier" was Joaquín Botellas, an associate of Joaquín Murrieta; and "Joaquin Carillo" was Joaquín Manuel Carillo Murrieta, half brother of Joaquín, El Famoso, and full brother of Jesús Carillo Murrieta, who was hanged by the Anglo mob in the diggings. See 96, 127–28, 133–34. Important as all this may be, it does not explain why Anglos named only "Joaquins" as the objects of their search.

60. This would not be the last time Anglos tried to attenuate diversity through (mis)naming; soon thousands upon thousands of men from South China would all be called John Chinaman.

61. Report of Captain Harry Love to Governor John Bigler, Aug. 4, 1853, facsimile reproduction in Latta, 512–14; *San Joaquin Republican,* July 30, Aug. 2, 6, 11, 1853. Two of Love's rangers later offered their reminiscences of the battle at Cantúa to California newspapers. An article based on an interview with William Henderson appeared in the *Fresno Expositor,* Nov. 12, 1879, which is quoted at length in Latta, 511, 515–20, 584. Similarly, William Howard talked twice to reporters and gave somewhat different renditions of the events in the *Merced County Sun,* May 3, 1890, and the *San Francisco Bulletin,* Dec. 3, 1899, both quoted at length in Latta, 540–50, 554–56. Howard's daughter Jill L. Cossley-Batt pieced together her father's reminiscences in *The Last of the California Rangers* (New York: Funk & Wagnalls, 1928), esp. 157–93, which offers a third version of the story. The "last words" of Joaquin appear in *San Joaquin Republican,* Aug. 11, 1853; and *Fresno Expositor,* Nov. 12, 1879, quoted in Latta, 519. William Howard claimed in all three renditions of the battle that Joaquin was first shot and injured, that he then surrendered to one of Love's men, and that finally he was shot again and killed when other rangers rode up and believed he was resisting arrest. See Howard quoted in Latta, 542 and 559; and Cossley-Batt, 190.

62. Report of Captain Love; *San Joaquin Republican,* July 30, Aug. 2, 6, 11, 1853.
63. Report of Captain Love.
64. *Alta California* (San Francisco), Aug. 23, 1853, quoted in Joseph Henry Jackson, *Bad Company* (New York: Harcourt, Brace, 1949), 13. On the *Los Angeles Star* coverage, see Pitt, 80.
65. *San Joaquin Republican,* Aug. 2, 1853.
66. Report of Captain Love.
67. *San Joaquin Republican,* July 30 and Aug. 6, 1853.
68. Report of Captain Love.
69. *San Joaquin Republican,* Aug. 6, 1853.
70. Facsimile reproductions of the broadside appear in Latta, 601; and Ridge, xxxiv.
71. "Act to Authorize the Raising of a Company of Rangers"; Report of Captain Love.
72. "Minority Report of J. M. Covarrubias."
73. This analysis relies on a chastened reading of historical and anthropological scholarship on how ideas about honor have operated in various cultural contexts. For the most relevant analysis, see Gutiérrez, *When Jesus Came,* esp. 176–226. Background on "cultures of honor" can be found in Julian Pitt-Rivers, "Honor," in *International Encyclopedia of the Social Sciences,* 18 vols., ed. David L. Sills (New York: Macmillan, 1968); and J. G. Peristiany, ed., *Honour and Shame: The Values of Mediterranean Society* (Chicago: Univ. of Chicago Press, 1966). My reading of such works (as well as those cited on the U.S. South below) has been tempered primarily by Abu-Lughod.
74. For the various versions of when and why Byrnes recognized Joaquín, and what part he played in relation to the heads and hand, see *San Joaquin Republican,* July 30, Aug. 6 and 11, 1853; Report of Captain Love; William Henderson's account from *Fresno Expositor;* William Howard's three accounts from *Merced County Sun, San Francisco Bulletin,* and Cossley-Batt, 188–90; and Ridge, 155. Two Anglo old-timers told Latta in 1930 that Byrnes later admitted the rangers had not killed Murrieta at all, but some other man. Byrnes never came forward with this information, the men said, because the rangers' larger purpose had been accomplished: they got the heads and hand and broke up the gang. Latta, 585–86. Whatever one makes of these old-timers' tales, the stories are not inconsistent with the analysis developed below; the appearance of victory was all-important.
75. Leonard Withington Noyes Reminiscences, Essex Institute, Salem, Mass., transcription at Calaveras County Museum and Archives, San Andreas, Calif., 48. I am grateful to Willard Fuller of the Calaveras County Historical Society for calling my attention to this source.
76. See Elliot Gorn, "'Gouge and Bite, Pull Hair and Scratch': The Social Significance of Fighting in the Southern Backcountry," *American Historical Review* 90, no. 1 (Feb. 1985): 18–43. Gorn locates this rough-

and-tumble male world as far west as Mississippi and Arkansas, but it seems likely that southerners who moved on to Texas partook of a similar cultural milieux. The origins of Texas as part of Mexico also must have had an impact on the discourse of honor as it developed there. See also Bertram Wyatt-Brown, *Southern Honor: Ethics and Behavior in the Old South* (New York: Oxford Univ. Press, 1982); and Kenneth S. Greenberg, "The Nose, the Lie, and the Duel in the Antebellum South," *American Historical Review* 95, no. 1 (Feb. 1990): 57–74, and *Honor and Slavery: Lies, Duels, Noses, Masks, Dressing as a Woman, Gifts, Strangers, Humanitarianism, Death, Slave Rebellions, the Proslavery Argument, Baseball, Hunting, and Gambling in the Old South* (Princeton: Princeton Univ. Press, 1996).

77. The Calaveras County second sheriff Ben Marshall kept a journal in the early 1850s that has since been lost, but transcriptions of portions of that journal made by his son Frank Marshall, Sr., apparently survived. Frank Marshall, Jr., allowed Latta to use the transcribed (and in part rewritten) journal, and pieces of it are reproduced in Latta; see esp. 287–88. Leonard Noyes (who despised Ben Marshall) confirms the hanging of Sam Green, though he recalls that Green shot Alexander Long, not Bill Lang. See Noyes, 48.

78. If Latta is right that Martínez was of Chinese descent, then Martínez's father was probably a Chinese sailor aboard a European or American vessel that stopped at the Sonoran port city of Guaymas sometime around 1840. His mother would have been mestiza. See Latta, 120.

79. Ibid., 100.

80. Ibid., 560–68.

81. Ibid., 569–74.

82. See esp. Gutiérrez, *When Jesus Came*, esp. 176–206.

83. See Thurman Wilkins, *Cherokee Tragedy: The Ridge Family and the Decimation of a People*, 2d ed. (Norman: Univ. of Oklahoma Press, 1981); Gary E. Moulton, *John Ross: Cherokee Chief* (Athens: Univ. of Georgia Press, 1978); and James W. Parins, *John Rollin Ridge: His Life and Works* (Lincoln: Univ. of Nebraska Press, 1991). I began to develop these ideas in a talk entitled "Moral Stories: Telling Tales of the California Gold Rush," American Religious History Luncheon Series, Yale Univ., Jan. 29, 1990, and am grateful to participants in that colloquium for their comments. I particularly benefited from Philip J. Deloria's suggestions.

84. Parins, 61–75; Wilkins, 343–44; E. Raymond Evans, "Following the Rainbow: The Cherokees in the California Gold Fields," *Journal of Cherokee Studies* 2, no. 1 (Winter 1977): 170–75; and the documents in "The Cherokee Trail," in *Southern Trails to California in 1849*, ed. Ralph P. Bieber (Glendale, Calif.: Arthur H. Clark, 1937), 325–50.

85. John Rollin Ridge to Stand Watie, Sept. 23, 1853, quoted in Evans, 172. Original in Frank Phillips Collection of Southwestern History, Univ. of Oklahoma, Norman.

86. Ridge, 7–12.
87. Walter Nobel Burns, *The Robin Hood of El Dorado* (New York: Coward-McCann, [1932]). See Joseph Henry Jackson, "The Creation of Joaquin Murieta," *Pacific Spectator* 2, no. 2 (Spring 1948): 176–81, *Bad Company*, 3–40, and "Introduction," in Ridge. Jackson carefully traces the proliferation of Murrieta tales, though his argument differs from my own, in that he contends that the development of the "myth" of Murrieta is proof positive that no "actual" Murrieta ever existed. My own emphasis is on the interplay between history and memory, rather than on an opposition between mythic and actual pasts. See also Hector H. Lee, "The Reverberant Joaquín Murieta in California Legendry," *Pacific Historian* 25, no. 3 (Fall 1981): 39–47. On Hollywood's Murrieta, see Allen L. Woll, "Hollywood Bandits, 1910–1981," in *Bandidos: The Varieties of Latin American Banditry*, ed. Richard W. Slatta (New York: Greenwood Press, 1987), 171–79. There is something of a cottage industry in popular publications on Murrieta, which are sold especially in California gold country book and museum stores. See, e.g., William Secrest, *Joaquin: Bloody Bandit of the Mother Lode* (Fresno, Calif.: Sage-West Publishing, 1967); Remi Nadeau, *The Real Joaquin Murieta: California's Gold Rush Bandit: Truth v. Myth* (Santa Barbara: Crest Publishers, 1974).
88. Mrs. Lee Whipple-Haslam, *Early Days in California: Scenes and Events of the '50s as I Remember Them* (Jamestown, Calif.: Mother Lode Magnet, [1925]), 13, 18. Portions of this account were reprinted recently in Ruth B. Moynihan et al., eds., *So Much to Be Done: Women Settlers on the Mining and Ranching Frontier* (Lincoln: Univ. of Nebraska Press, 1990), 28–37.
89. Ridge, 158.
90. Ridge to Watie, and Ridge to Sarah Northrup Ridge, Oct. 5, 1855, quoted in Evans, 172–73. Originals in Frank Phillips Collection of Southwestern History, Univ. of Oklahoma, Norman.
91. See Michael Denning, *Mechanic Accents: Dime Novels and Working-Class Culture in America* (London: Verso, 1987), 3–4.
92. "Editor's Preface," in Ridge, 4
93. See Renato Rosaldo, "Imperialist Nostalgia," *Representations*, no. 26 (Spring 1989): 107–22, esp. 107–8.
94. Earle Ennis, "My Grandfather Debunks Murietta, Who Was a Sissy," *San Francisco Chronicle*, April 17, 1936. Ennis wrote a daily column for the *Chronicle*. For the *Chronicle*'s report on the opening of *The Robin Hood of El Dorado* in San Francisco, see "Wild Murietta to Live Again," *San Francisco Chronicle*, April 21, 1936. My thanks to Katherine Morrissey for tracking these articles down for me when I did not have access to them.
95. Cf. Robert E. McGlone, "Rescripting a Troubled Past: John Brown's Family and the Harpers Ferry Conspiracy," *Journal of American History* 75, no. 4 (March 1989): 1179–200. When Raymond F. Wood tried to

retrace some of Latta's steps in Sonora several decades later, Wood found that many whom Latta had interviewed had died or moved away. Those who were left had much vaguer recollections of their connection with Joaquín Murrieta. See Wood, "New Light on Joaquin Murrieta," *Pacific Historian* 14, no. 1 (Winter 1970): 54–65, esp. 63.

96. See Castillo and Camarillo; and cf. Rosenbaum. For an analysis of later critiques of this scholarly approach to banditry, see Joseph. For a thoughtful discussion of "social banditry" in the broader history of the U.S. West, see Richard White, *"It's Your Misfortune and None of My Own": A New History of the American West* (Norman: Univ. of Oklahoma Press, 1991), 334–37.

97. I have benefited in this analysis from Michael M. J. Fischer, "Ethnicity and the Post-modern Arts of Memory," in *Writing Culture: The Poetics and Politics of Ethnography,* ed. James Clifford and George E. Marcus (Berkeley: Univ. of California Press, 1986), 194–233.

98. Rodolfo Gonzales, *I Am Joaquín—Yo soy Joaquín: An Epic Poem* (1967; reprint, New York: Bantam Books, 1972), esp. 6, 44, 100. For discussion, see Bruce-Novoa, *Chicano Poetry: A Response to Chaos* (Austin: Univ. of Texas Press, 1982), 48–68; Julio A. Martínez and Francisco A. Lomelí, *Chicano Literature: A Reference Guide* (Westport, Conn.: Greenwood Press, 1985), 221–28; Marcienne Rocard, *The Children of the Sun: Mexican-Americans in the Literature of the United States,* trans. Edward G. Brown, Jr. (1980; Tucson: Univ. of Arizona Press, 1989), 260–61.

99. An important aspect of ethnic memory not discussed here is the *corrido,* the Mexican cultural practice of narrative balladry. Not surprisingly, Murrieta is the hero of a particularly anti-American *corrido.* See Alfred Arteaga, "The Chicano-Mexican Corrido," *Journal of Ethnic Studies* 13, no. 2 (Summer 1985): 75–105; and, for the *corrido* itself, John Donald Robb, *Hispanic Folk Music of New Mexico and the Southwest: A Self-Portrait of a People* (Norman: Univ. of Oklahoma Press, 1980), 165–66. The folklorist Hector Lee provides some preliminary notes on memory of Murrieta among California Mexican Americans in Lee, 45–46.

100. I may as well cite my own memory for this: while doing research between 1985 and 1990, I ran across numerous mentions of Murrieta, but seemed not to hold on to that information until I recalled a presentation on Castillo and Camarillo by Christine Marín in a graduate course during spring term 1980. The class on "frontier minorities" was taught by the historian Robert Trennert at Arizona State Univ., Tempe. Marín directs the Chicano Studies Collection at Arizona State's Hayden Library, and I have benefited from her support of my work for many years.

101. Paul, e.g., discusses all three California gold regions (Northern, Southern, and northwestern mines), but the story he tells of technological innovations developed to exploit first placers, then deep gravels, then quartz veins, and the corresponding evolution of social and political institutions, is a story that describes the Northern Mines best of all.

Two recent scholarly works on the Gold Rush, by Mann and Holliday, focus explicitly on the Northern Mines. I owe my interest in the Southern Mines to conversations with Howard Lamar, and in part to questions suggested by Jean-Nicolas Perlot, *Gold Seeker: Adventures of a Belgian Argonaut during the Gold Rush Years*, trans. Helen Harding Bretnor and ed. Howard R. Lamar (New Haven: Yale Univ. Press, 1985).

102. I have developed these arguments in greater detail in "'A Memory Sweet to Soldiers': The Significance of Gender in the History of the 'American West,'" *Western Historical Quarterly* 24, no. 4 (Nov. 1993): 495–517, reprinted in Clyde A. Milner II, ed., *A New Significance: Re-envisioning the History of the American West* (New York: Oxford Univ. Press, 1996), 255–78. I use terms like "women," "men," and "people of color" advisedly here, understanding their constructed nature and wanting to avoid the essentializing impulse that often accompanies their uncritical use. A problem more specific to their use in this setting arises from the fact that some nondominant peoples in California were *not* peoples of color in the sense in which that term generally is understood at the turn of the twenty-first century. In the Southern Mines, e.g., French-speaking immigrants were also targeted by the foreign miners' tax and sometimes allied themselves with Spanish-speaking miners in contesting Anglo dominance. My use of racial and ethnic labels is grounded in an understanding of how groups of people have been racialized and have racialized themselves in particular historical contexts. Other historians of western peoples and places have put this process of racialization at the center of their analysis. See, e.g., Lisbeth Haas, *Conquests and Historical Identities in California, 1769–1936* (Berkeley: Univ. of California Press, 1995); Neil Foley, *The White Scourge: Mexicans, Blacks and Poor Whites in Texas Cotton Culture* (Berkeley: Univ. of California Press, 1998). I also will have occasion to discuss a Calaveras County "hermaphrodite," who represents only the most obvious challenge to dominant oppositions between male and female in the Gold Rush. Exemplary collections of articles on gender relations in other U.S. historical contexts include Ava Baron, ed., *Work Engendered: Toward a New History of American Labor* (Ithaca: Cornell Univ. Press, 1991); Catherine Clinton and Nina Silber, eds., *Divided Houses: Gender and the Civil War* (New York: Oxford Univ. Press, 1992); and Margaret S. Creighton and Lisa Norling, eds., *Iron Men, Wooden Women: Gender and Seafaring in the Atlantic World, 1700–1920* (Baltimore: Johns Hopkins Univ. Press, 1996).

103. I place this in quotation marks partly in deference to its use in another (though not entirely unrelated) context: see Nancy K. Miller, "Changing the Subject," in *Coming to Terms: Feminism, Theory, and Politics*, ed. Elizabeth Weed (New York: Routledge, 1989), 3–16.

104. Important influences on my work here include Elsa Barkley Brown, "Polyrhythms and Improvization: Lessons for Women's History," *History Workshop Journal* 31–32 (1991): 85–90; Evelyn Brooks Higginbotham,

"African-American Women's History and the Metalanguage of Race,"
Signs 17, no. 2 (Winter 1992): 251–74; and Antonia I. Castañeda,
"Women of Color and the Rewriting of Western History: The Discourse,
Politics, and Decolonization of History," *Pacific Historical Review* 61, no. 4
(Nov. 1992): 501–33.

105. Latta, 619–25.

106. Ibid., 619–22, 633–37, quotation on 636. Latta provides a plausible argument that the "compañero" was Joaquín Manuel Carillo Murrieta
(half brother to Joaquín, El Famoso), known to Anglos as Joaquin
Carillo. I am agnostic. See 633, 640, 643–48.

107. I have been influenced in my reading of Rosa's constrained choices by
the unsentimental analysis of widowhood in Deena J. González, "The
Widowed Women of Santa Fe: Assessments on the Lives of an
Unmarried Population, 1850–1880," in *Unequal Sisters: A Multicultural
Reader in U.S. Women's History,* ed. Ellen Carol DuBois and Vicki L.
Ruiz (New York: Routledge, 1990), 34–50 (first published in *On Their
Own: Widows and Widowhood in the American Southwest, 1848–1939,*
ed. Arlene Scadron [Urbana: Univ. of Illinois Press, 1988]), and, in my
understanding of how women can live in critical dialogue with discourses of "honor," by Abu-Lughod. I have also benefited from
Sueann Caulfield's helpful and generous comments on these issues.

Chapter 1: On the Eve of Emigration

1. Although I use the term "emigrant" here, since I am talking about the
process of leaving homelands, for the most part I use the term
"immigrant" in this study and I use it with a particular meaning. An
"immigrant" is any non-native person in the Southern Mines, which
is to say that people who came to California from elsewhere in the
United States were "immigrants," as surely as, e.g., French and
Chilean Gold Rush participants were. All who came to the area in
response to the gold discovery were interlopers in Indian territory.

2. The quoted phrase, of course, is from J. S. Holliday, *The World Rushed In:
The California Gold Rush Experience* (New York: Simon and Schuster,
1981), which consists of the edited diaries and letters of William
Swain, letters to Swain from his family in New York State, and interpolations from other Anglo American forty-niners whose writings
help illuminate Swain's. It is one of the best Anglo personal accounts
of the Gold Rush, and easily the most ingeniously edited. But the
extravagance of the title bears little relationship to the wonderful particularities of the text, which documents primarily one white, eastern
family's twenty-two-month Gold Rush experience.

3. For a good contextualization of the Gold Rush in global economic history, see E. J. Hobsbawm, *The Age of Capital, 1848–1875* (1979; New
York: New American Library, 1984).

4. See Ralph J. Roske, "The World Impact of the California Gold Rush,

1849–1857," *Arizona and the West* 5, no. 3 (Autumn 1963): 187–232; Doris Marion Wright, "The Making of Cosmopolitan California: An Analysis of Immigration, 1848–1870," parts 1 and 2, *California Historical Society Quarterly* 19, no. 4 (Dec. 1940): 323–43, and 20, no. 1 (March 1941): 65–79. Like most who hazard into thinking about global connections, I have benefited from Eric R. Wolf, *Europe and the People without History* (Berkeley: Univ. of California Press, 1982); and the work of Immanuel Wallerstein, e.g., "The Rise and Future Demise of the World Capitalist System: Concepts for Comparative Analysis," in *The Capitalist World-Economy* (Cambridge: Cambridge Univ. Press, 1979), 1–36, though I am no doubt more influenced by the former than the latter. For an excellent critique of the world-systems approach in the Latin American and Caribbean context that stresses the importance of local developments, see Steve J. Stern, "Feudalism, Capitalism, and the World-System in the Perspective of Latin America and the Caribbean," *American Historical Review* 73, no. 4 (Oct. 1988): 829–72, and commentary, 873–97.

5. For immigrant population figures in 1852, see U.S. Bureau of the Census, *The Seventh Census of the United States: 1850* (Washington, D.C., 1853), in which is also printed "Population and Industry of California by the State Census for the Year 1852." For Miwok populations around the time of the Gold Rush, see Richard Levy, "Eastern Miwok," in *Handbook of North American Indians*, vol. 8, *California*, ed. Robert F. Heizer (Washington, D.C.: Smithsonian Institution, 1978), 398–413, esp. 402.

6. Clearly there were other important historical actors in the Southern Mines—Hawaiian, British, Yokuts, Peruvian, German, Australian, Cherokee, Irish, e.g.—many of whom I mention herein. But those identified with the groups I have highlighted were key participants in the stories I have chosen to tell in this book.

7. See, e.g., Leonard Pitt, *The Decline of the Californios: A Social History of the Spanish-Speaking Californians, 1846–1890* (Berkeley: Univ. of California Press, 1966); Jay Monaghan, *Chile, Peru and the California Gold Rush of 1849* (Berkeley: Univ. of California Press, 1973); Wright, part 1; Stuart F. Voss, *On the Periphery of Nineteenth-Century Mexico: Sonora and Sinaloa, 1810–1877* (Tucson: Univ. of Arizona Press, 1982), 33–74, 80–120; Fernando Henrique Cardoso and Enzo Faletto, *Dependency and Development in Latin America*, trans. Marjory Mattingly Urquidi (1971; Berkeley: Univ. of California Press, 1979), 29–41, 52–54; Tulio Halperín Donghi, "Economy and Society in Post-Independence Spanish America," Frank Safford, "Politics, Ideology and Society in Post-Independence Spanish America," Jan Bazant, "Mexico from Independence to 1867," and Simon Collier, "Chile from Independence to the War of the Pacific," in *Cambridge History of Latin America*, vol. 3, *From Independence to c. 1870*, ed. Leslie Bethell (Cambridge: Cambridge Univ. Press, 1985), 299–470, 583–613.

8. I owe much of the following discussion of conditions in Sonora before and after Mexican independence to Voss. See also Oakah L. Jones, Jr., *Los Paisanos: Spanish Settlers on the Northern Frontier of New Spain* (Norman: Univ. of Oklahoma Press, 1979), esp. 177–95; David J. Weber, *The Mexican Frontier, 1821–1846: The American Southwest under Mexico* (Albuquerque: Univ. of New Mexico Press, 1982); and Cynthia Radding, *Wandering Peoples: Colonialism, Ethnic Spaces, and Ecological Frontiers in Northwestern Mexico, 1700–1850* (Durham, N.C.: Duke Univ. Press, 1997).

9. Voss, 1–32. See also Evelyn Hu-DeHart, *Missionaries, Miners and Indians: Spanish Contact with the Yaqui Nation of Northwestern New Spain, 1533–1820* (Tucson: Univ. of Arizona Press, 1981); Jones, 177–91.

10. Voss, 33–47.

11. Ibid., 48–54, 64–72; Weber, 83–105; Evelyn Hu-DeHart, *Yaqui Resistance and Survival: The Struggle for Land and Autonomy, 1821–1910* (Madison: Univ. of Wisconsin Press, 1984), 18–55.

12. Voss, 80–111; Hu-DeHart, *Yaqui Resistance*, 56–67.

13. Voss, 111; Sister M. Colette Standart, "The Sonoran Migration to California, 1848–1856: A Study in Prejudice," *Southern California Quarterly* 58, no. 3 (Fall 1976): 333–57; Wright, part 1; Richard H. Peterson, "Anti-Mexican Nativism in California, 1848–1853: A Study in Cultural Conflict," *Southern California Quarterly* 62, no. 4 (Winter 1980): 309–27.

14. Hu-DeHart, *Yaqui Resistance*, p. 66.

15. Standart; Pitt, 48–68. On Coronel's cook, see prologue, "Joaquín Murrieta and the Bandits." Coronel's *peónes* had already migrated once from Sonora to Southern California.

16. Standart cites these figures from *El Sonorense* (Ures), April 26, 1850. See 343.

17. Ibid., 338, from *El Sonorense*, May 4, June 15, 1849.

18. Sylvia Marina Arrom, *The Women of Mexico City, 1790–1857* (Stanford: Stanford Univ. Press, 1985), 105–11; Elizabeth Kuznesof and Robert Oppenheimer, "The Family and Society in Nineteenth-Century Latin America: An Historiographical Introduction," *Journal of Family History* 10, no. 3 (Fall 1985): 215–34, esp. 226.

19. Arrom, 110–11, 154–205.

20. For Mexico City, see ibid., 129–34. For Latin America in general, see Kuznesof and Oppenheimer, 224, 226. I have not found direct confirmation of the prevalence of female–headed households in Yaqui pueblos. It is implied by Voss, and in Hu-DeHart, *Yaqui Resistance*.

21. The image of "cities of women" is suggested by Arrom and borrowed from Christine Stansell, *City of Women: Sex and Class in New York, 1789–1860* (New York: Alfred A. Knopf, 1986).

22. I owe this summary to Brian Loveman, *Chile: The Legacy of Hispanic Capitalism* (New York: Oxford Univ. Press, 1979), esp. 9–115. See also 2d ed. (1988). Page numbers cited herein are to 1st ed.

23. Ibid., 42–149.
24. Arnold J. Bauer, "Chilean Rural Labor in the Nineteenth Century," *American Historical Review* 76, no. 4 (Oct. 1971): 1059–83; and see Loveman, 97–98; Collier, 597–98.
25. Bauer, esp. 1069–74; Loveman, esp. 89, 145, 164; Collier, 597–98.
26. Monaghan, esp. 5–6; Abraham P. Nasatir, "Chilenos in California during the Gold Rush Period and the Establishment of the Chilean Consulate," *California Historical Quarterly* 53, no. 1 (Spring 1974): 52–70, esp. 61; George Edward Faugsted, Jr., *The Chilenos in the California Gold Rush* (1963; reprint, San Francisco: R and E Research Associates, 1973), esp. 16–17; Edwin A. Beilharz and Carlos U. López, "Introduction," in *We Were 49ers! Chilean Accounts of the California Gold Rush*, trans. and ed. Beilharz and López (Pasadena, Calif.: Ward Ritchie Press, 1976), xi–xx, esp. xiii–xv.
27. On Pérez Rosales, see Monaghan, 32–34, 55; Beilharz and López, eds., 1; and the writings of Pérez Rosales himself, esp. *Diario de un viaje a California, 1848–1849* (Buenos Aires: Editorial Francisco de Aguirre, 1971). And see *California Adventure*, trans. Edwin S. Morby and Arturo Torres–Rioseco (San Francisco: Book Club of California, 1947). I have relied primarily on a translated selection of his work, including a fragment of his manuscript diary from the Chilean Archivo Nacional, entitled "Diary of a Journey to California," in Beilharz and López, eds., 3–99, spot-checking *Diario de un viaje* for translations. For background on the Chilean independence and early national periods, see Loveman, 116–49.
28. Monaghan, 22, 32–34, 55; Beilharz and López, eds., 1; Loveman, 116–49.
29. Pérez Rosales, "Diary," 3, and *California Adventure*, 4, 9. The manuscript diary (in Beilharz and López) and the published version (trans. Morby and Torres-Rioseco) at first seem to contradict each other about whether Pérez Rosales took along two, three, or five laborers. Closer analysis suggests, though, that there were altogether five workers who accompanied the brothers—two tenant and three contract laborers.
30. Pérez Rosales, "Diary," 6, 46, 48, 50, 57, 58. Cf. Pérez Rosales, *California Adventure*.
31. Pérez Rosales, "Diary," 5, 27, 30. The Latin American historian Sueann Caulfield suggests that the *péon* whom Pérez Rosales called the "mulatto" may have been an Argentinean soldier or descendant.
32. Ibid., 6, 7, 11, 26, 56.
33. Ibid., 3–4, 6, 11, 12, 20.
34. I depend here on the research of the Tuolumne County historian Carlo M. De Ferrari. See "A Brief History of Stephen Spencer Hill: Fugitive from Labor," in *Gold Spring Diary: The Journal of John Jolly*, ed. De Ferrari (Sonora, Calif.: Tuolumne County Historical Society, 1966), 125–42.
35. See, e.g., Eugene D. Genovese, *The Political Economy of Slavery: Studies in*

the *Economy and Society of the Slave South*, 2d ed. (Middletown, Conn.: Wesleyan Univ. Press, 1989), esp. "The Origins of Slavery Expansionism"; Gavin Wright, *The Political Economy of the Cotton South: Households, Markets, and Wealth in the Nineteenth Century* (New York: W. W. Norton, 1978).

36. U.S. Bureau of the Census, Seventh Federal Population Census, 1850, National Archives, Washington, D.C., RG-29, M-432. See esp. the manuscript census schedules for Mariposa County, reel 35. Mariposa County had the highest proportion of African Americans of the three counties that constituted the Southern Mines in 1850 (Mariposa was nearly 5 percent black, while in Calaveras and Tuolumne less than 1 percent of the population was black). See U.S. Bureau of the Census, *Seventh Census of the United States: 1850* (Washington, D.C., 1853), for composite figures.

37. For context, see Thomas R. Hietala, *Manifest Design: Anxious Aggrandizement in Late Jacksonian America* (Ithaca: Cornell Univ. Press, 1985). On the slavery question specifically in California, see Eugene H. Berwanger, *The Frontier against Slavery: Western Anti-Negro Prejudice and the Slavery Extension Controversy* (Urbana: Univ. of Illinois Press, 1967), 60–77; and Rudolph M. Lapp, *Blacks in Gold Rush California* (New Haven: Yale Univ. Press, 1977), 126–57. See also Quintard Taylor, *In Search of the Racial Frontier: African Americans in the American West* (New York: W. W. Norton, 1998).

38. Berwanger, 64–77.

39. John Paul Dart, "A Mississippian in the Gold Fields: The Letters of John Paul Dart," ed. Howard Mitcham, *California Historical Society Quarterly* 35, no. 3 (Sept. 1956): 205–31, esp. 219, 221, 222, 223, 225.

40. Jefferson Martenet to Mother [Aug. 1853], Jefferson Martenet Collection, Huntington Library, San Marino, Calif. (hereafter cited as Huntington Library).

41. See, e.g., Bruce Laurie, *Artisans into Workers: Labor in Nineteenth-Century America* (New York: Hill and Wang, 1989), 58.

42. Jason P. Chamberlain to Mary E. Griswold, Oct. 12, 1899, Jason P. Chamberlain Letters, Huntington Library.

43. Diary entries, June 11 and 12, Aug. 2, 1903, Jason Chamberlain Diary no. 42, John Amos Chaffee and Jason Palmer Chamberlain Papers, Bancroft Library, Univ. of California, Berkeley.

44. For local accounts, see, e.g., Mrs. Robert Thom, comp., *Memories of the Days of Old, Days of Gold, Days of 49* ([Sonora, Calif.: The Banner Print, c. 1923]), 8; James G. White, "The Death of Tennessee's Pardner: The True Story of the Death of Jason P. Chamberlain," *Tuolumne County Historical Society Quarterly* 4, no. 3 (Jan.–March 1965): 122–24. On Bret Harte, see Kevin Starr, *Americans and the California Dream, 1850–1915* (New York: Oxford Univ. Press, 1973), esp. 49–50. On the connection between Chamberlain and Chaffee and Harte's story, see Fred Stocking, "The Passing of 'Tennessee' and his Partner," *Overland Monthly*, 2d ser.,

42 (1903): 539–43; Fletcher Stokes, "Fred Stocking and His Service to California Literature," *Overland Monthly*, 2d ser., 59 (1912): 105–14; and Jessie Heaton Parkinson, *Adventuring in California, Yesterday, Today, and Day before Yesterday, with Memoirs of Bret Harte's "Tennessee"* (San Francisco: Harr Wagner, 1921), 7–8, 42–43, 59–119. The later lives of Chamberlain and Chaffee and the significance of Bret Harte's story are addressed in the epilogue, "Telling Tales."

45. Laurie provides an excellent summary of nineteenth-century social and economic change that synthesizes earlier works; see esp. 15–112. For references to the scholarship he synthesizes, see his bibliographic essay, esp. 223–31. On the language of class as male, see Joan Scott, "On Language, Gender, and Working-Class History," in *Gender and the Politics of History* (New York: Columbia Univ. Press, 1988), 53–67; and cf. Stansell, esp. 130–54. See also Ava Baron, "Gender and Labor History: Learning from the Past, Looking to the Future," in *Work Engendered: Toward a New History of American Labor,* ed. Baron (Ithaca: Cornell Univ. Press, 1991), 1–46.

46. See Jonathan Prude, *The Coming of Industrial Order: Town and Factory Life in Rural Massachusetts, 1800–1860* (Cambridge: Cambridge Univ. Press, 1983). My thanks to David Montgomery for helping me clarify this key argument.

47. Nathan Chase to Jane Chase, March 5, 1852, Nathan Chase Letters, Beinecke Library, Yale Univ., New Haven.

48. These suggestions are based on the analysis developed in Mary P. Ryan, *Cradle of the Middle Class: The Family in Oneida County, New York, 1790–1865* (Cambridge: Cambridge Univ. Press, 1981), esp. 145–85; and Laurie, esp. 57. As for Chamberlain's and Chaffee's lifetime of labor, the fifty years of diaries kept by Chamberlain are primarily a record of their mining and agricultural work, as well as of occasional use of their skills as carpenter and wheelwright.

49. The summary of the lives of Mary and William Newell from 1849 to the mid-1850s is based on letters exchanged between family members found in the Joseph Pownall Papers, Huntington Library. All of the letters from this period are in boxes 1–4. For the mining association agreement, see Agreement for Mining Gold, Jan. 23, 1849, PW 276, box 1, Pownall Papers.

50. See, e.g., Mary Newell to William Newell, June 13, 1849, PW 762, Benjamin Harrison to William Newell, June 18, 1849, PW 342, box 1, Pownall Papers, as well as numerous references to the family bakery scattered throughout letters in boxes 1–4.

51. See, e.g., letters cited above; Benjamin Harrison to William Newell, Aug. 13, 1849, PW 343, Norman Newell to William Newell, March 17–28, 1850, PW 511, June 27, 1852, PW 512, box 1; William Newell to Mary Newell, Feb. 24, 1853, PW 522, box 2; William Newell to Mary Newell, Jan. 20, 1854, PW 514, box 3, Pownall Papers.

52. See Benjamin Harrison to William Newell, Aug. 13, 1849, PW 343, Oct.

31, 1849, PW 344, William Newell to Mary Newell, May 15, 1850, PW 518, box 1, Pownall Papers.

53. William Newell to Mary Newell, Feb. 4, 1851, PW 519, [Nov. 26, 1852], PW 521, box 1, Pownall Papers.

54. See, e.g., Nancy Cott, *The Bonds of Womanhood: "Woman's Sphere" in New England, 1780–1835* (New Haven: Yale Univ. Press, 1977); and Ryan, esp. 232 (for "launching pad").

55. See, e.g., Benjamin Harrison to Mary and William Newell, Jan. 4, 1855, PW 350, Feb. 4, 1855, PW 351, box 4; William Newell to Mary Newell, Dec. 12, 1853, PW 526, box 2, Pownall Papers. The analysis here depends heavily on arguments developed in Ryan.

56. See, e.g., Benjamin Harrison to Children, June 1, 1854, PW 346, July 10, 1854, PW 347, box 3; Mary Newell to Lucy Harrison, March 29, 1855, PW 765, Mary Newell to Benjamin Harrison, June 11, 1855, PW 790, Mary Newell to Lucy Harrison, Aug. 13, 1855, PW 766, Sept. 2, 1855, PW 767, Mary Newell to Benjamin and Lucy Harrison, Dec. 18, 1855, PW 795, box 4, Pownall Papers.

57. For more on Mary Harrison Newell and her family after William Newell's death, see chap. 6, "The Last Fandango."

58. See William Perkins, *Three Years in California: William Perkins' Journal of Life at Sonora, 1849–1852*, ed. Dale L. Morgan and James R. Scobie (Berkeley: Univ. of California Press, 1964), esp. 130–31, 218–19, 238, 243–44, 250, 251, 268, 303–4, 341, 343 (quotation on 243).

59. See *Laura Echeverria v. Juan Echeverria* (1857), District Court, Tuolumne County, Sonora, Calif.; *S. R. Mills and James Vantine v. Madame Emilie Henry* (1856), District Court, Mariposa County, Mariposa, Calif. For more examples of this sort, see chap. 6, "The Last Fandango."

60. I owe this summary of French regulationism to Jill Harsin, *Policing Prostitution in Nineteenth-Century Paris* (Princeton: Princeton Univ. Press, 1985), esp. xv–xxv. See also Alain Corbin, *Women for Hire: Prostitution and Sexuality in France after 1850*, trans. Alan Sheridan (Cambridge: Harvard Univ. Press, 1990).

61. See Harsin, 282–307. While I rely on Harsin here for the evidence she has gathered of same-sex eroticism in brothels, I am troubled by her analysis of these ties, which depicts them as sordid and unrelentingly coercive.

62. I am indebted to Reeve Huston for helping me find a concise way of conceptually linking the events of 1848. See also E. J. Hobsbawm, *The Age of Revolution, 1789–1848* (New York: Mentor/New American Library, 1962).

63. This summary is based on André Jardin and André-Jean Tudesq, *Restoration and Reaction, 1815–1848*, trans. Elborg Forster (Cambridge: Cambridge Univ. Press, 1983), esp. 191–204; Roger Price, ed., *Revolution and Reaction: 1848 and the Second French Republic* (London: Croom Helm, 1975), esp. the editor's introd., 1–72; John M. Merriman, *The Agony of the Republic: The Repression of the Left in*

Revolutionary France, 1848–1851 (New Haven: Yale Univ. Press, 1978), esp. xv–xxx, 1–24.

64. Merriman, passim.

65. Ibid., 4–5, 14, 162–63, 193–94.

66. Henry Blumenthal, "The California Societies in France, 1849–1855," *Pacific Historical Review* 25, no. 3 (Aug. 1956): 251–60; Gilbert Chinard, "When the French Came to California: An Introductory Essay," *California Historical Society Quarterly* 22, no. 4 (Dec. 1943): 289–314; Abraham P. Nasatir, "Introductory Sketch," in *French Activities in California: An Archival Calendar Guide* (Stanford: Stanford Univ. Press, 1945); Rufus Kay Wyllys, "The French of California and Sonora," *Pacific Historical Review* 1, no. 3 (Sept. 1932): 337–59; Howard R. Lamar, "Introduction," in Jean-Nicolas Perlot, *Gold Seeker: Adventures of a Belgian Argonaut during the Gold Rush Years*, trans. Helen Harding Bretnor and ed. Howard R. Lamar (New Haven: Yale Univ. Press, 1985), xv–xxxii, esp. xvii–xxi.

67. Karl Marx, *The Eighteenth Brumaire of Louis Bonaparte* (1852; New York: International Publishers, 1963), 84–85; A. P. Nasatir, "Alexandre Dumas fils and the Lottery of the Golden Ingots," *California Historical Society Quarterly* 33, no. 2 (June 1954): 125–42.

68. *Murder of M. V. B. Griswold by Five Chinese Assassins; Fou Sin—the Principal. Together with the Life of Griswold, and the Statements of Fou Sin, Chou Yee and Coon You, Convicted, and Sentenced to Be Hung at Jackson, April 16, 1858. Illustrated with Correct Likenesses of the Murderers* (Jackson, Calif.: T. A. Springer, 1858), 16.

69. Ibid., 16–17.

70. Ibid., 17.

71. Ibid., 16; Frederic Wakeman, Jr., *Strangers at the Gate: Social Disorder in South China, 1839–1861* (Berkeley: Univ. of California Press, 1966), 179–80; Yong Chen, "The Internal Origins of Chinese Emigration to California Reconsidered," *Western Historical Quarterly* 28, no. 4 (Winter 1997): 520–46, esp. 533–38.

72. See Sucheng Chan, *This Bittersweet Soil: The Chinese in California Agriculture, 1860–1910* (Berkeley: Univ. of California Press, 1986), 7–31; Yen Ching-Hwang, *Coolies and Mandarins: Chinese Protection of Overseas Chinese during the Late Ch'ing Period, 1851–1911* (Singapore: Singapore Univ. Press, 1985).

73. I owe this summary to Wakeman, *Strangers at the Gate*, and "The Canton Trade and the Opium War," in *The Cambridge History of China*, vol. 10, *Late Ch'ing, 1800–1911*, part 1, ed. John K. Fairbank (Cambridge: Cambridge Univ. Press, 1978), 163–212; and Jonathan D. Spence, *The Search for Modern China* (New York: W. W. Norton, 1990), 120, 128–32, 147–64, and *God's Chinese Son: The Taiping Heavenly Kingdom of Hong Xiuquan* (New York: W. W. Norton, 1996).

74. See Wakeman, *Strangers at the Gate*; John K. Fairbank, "The Creation of the Treaty System," and Philip A. Kuhn, "The Taiping Rebellion," in

Fairbank, ed., 213–63, 264–317; and Spence, *Search for Modern China*, 158–64, 168–78.

75. Earlier interpretations of Chinese emigration stressed the hardships created by overpopulation and western incursion (best symbolized by the Opium War) as major causes. See Chan; and June Mei, "The Socioeconomic Origins of Emigration: Guangdong to California, 1850 to 1882," in *Labor Immigration under Capitalism: Asian Workers in the United States before World War II*, ed. Lucie Cheng and Edna Bonacich (Berkeley: Univ. of California Press, 1984). More recently, Chen has argued convincingly that South China was "home to one of China's oldest and best developed market-oriented economies. Such an economy prepared merchants and experienced wage-earning laborers to voyage to the new market economy in gold-rush California" (quotation on 522).

76. Chan, 7–31; Mei; Chen.

77. *Murder of M. V. B. Griswold*, 15–31.

78. Ibid. On the development of water companies in the Southern Mines, see chap. 5, "Dreams That Died." For a full analysis of the crime pamphlet *Murder of M. V. B. Griswold* and for an account of what became of Foù Sin, Chou Yee, and Coon You, see epilogue, "Telling Tales."

79. U.S. Bureau of the Census, *Population of the United States in 1860; Compiled from . . . the Eighth Census* (Washington, D.C., 1864). See returns from Amador, Calaveras, Mariposa, and Tuolumne counties in Calif. On Chinese prostitutes, see Lucie Cheng Hirata, "Free, Indentured, Enslaved: Chinese Prostitutes in Nineteenth-Century America," *Signs* 5, no. 1 (Autumn 1979): 3–29; Sucheng Chan, "The Exclusion of Chinese Women, 1870–1943," in *Entry Denied: Exclusion and the Chinese Community in America, 1882–1943*, ed. Chan (Philadelphia: Temple Univ. Press, 1991), 94–146; and Judy Yung, *Unbound Feet: A Social History of Chinese Women in San Francisco* (Berkeley: Univ. of California Press, 1995), esp. 26–37. Conversations with Yukiko Hanawa about the practice of "selling daughters" in twentieth-century Japan have influenced my thinking about the emigration of nineteenth-century Chinese women.

80. Perlot, 84, 181–90, 223. Perlot was sure that Scipiano, or Cypriano, was leader of the Yosemites, a mixed band of Miwoks, Paiutes, and Yokuts. But by most accounts, the famous Tenaya was the Yosemite chief at this time. George Harwood Phillips, *Indians and Indian Agents: The Origins of the Reservation System in California, 1849–1852* (Norman: Univ. of Oklahoma Press, 1997), gives the clearest information on the identity of various foothill bands in this period. On the Yosemites and Awals, see esp. 37–38, 68–91, 141–44 passim.

81. Perlot, 84, 181, 224, quotation on 224.

82. The following summary of pre–Gold Rush Miwok history is based largely on Albert L. Hurtado, *Indian Survival on the California Frontier* (New Haven: Yale Univ. Press, 1988), esp. chaps. 1–5, except where

noted. See also Phillips, *Indians and Indian Agents* and *Indians and Intruders in Central California, 1769–1849* (Norman: Univ. of Oklahoma Press, 1993); and, for the larger regional context, Weber. The notion of Great Basin Indians as living on the "other side of the sky" comes from Scipiano's speech in Perlot, 224. The editor Howard Lamar explains that Miwoks "believed that the sky rested on the . . . Sierra Nevada; beyond that, another sky . . . extended to another chain of mountains and so on indefinitely." Although Scipiano mentioned only Monos as trading partners, a white woman who lived farther north in Tuolumne County remembered that Miwoks there traded with Paiutes as well. See Mrs. Lee Whipple-Haslam, *Early Days in California: Scenes and Events of the '50s as I Remember Them* (Jamestown, Calif.: Mother Lode Magnet, [1925]), 19.

83. On the Bay and Plains Miwoks, see Levy, esp. 398–400, 402. On the malaria outbreak, see Hurtado, 46; and Phillips, *Indians and Intruders*, 94.

84. See Perlot, 182.

85. From here on, I most often use the term "Miwok" to designate the Indians of that portion of the Sierra Nevada foothills in the drainage of the San Joaquin River. But it should be remembered that the "Miwok" bands to which I refer were often mixed groups of Sierra Miwoks, Plains Miwoks, mission Indians, and sometimes other peoples, such as Nisenans and Yokuts. A helpful model for describing such mixed communities, which formed as a consequence of conquest, is Richard White, *The Middle Ground: Indians, Empires, and Republics in the Great Lakes Region, 1650–1815* (New York: Cambridge Univ. Press, 1991), esp. 1–50.

86. Hurtado, 34–54; Weber, 60–68.

87. Weber, 198–99; Hurtado, 47–48.

88. Weber, 199, 204–5; Hurtado, 49, 55, 73–74.

89. Hurtado, 48, 55–71.

90. Ibid.

91. Ibid., 15–20, 69; Levy, 398, 402, 410–11.

92. Levy, 402–5; Hurtado, 15–20.

93. The significance of such non-Indian observations is discussed in chap. 2, "Domestic Life in the Diggings."

94. Hurtado, 15–20; Levy, 402–5. Perlot, 260–61, describes a Miwok deer hunt. On divisions of labor, cf., e.g., William Cronon, *Changes in the Land: Indians, Colonists, and the Ecology of New England* (New York: Hill and Wang, 1983), 39–40, 44–48, 52–53. For more evidence of male power among Miwoks as well as of male-female interdependence, see a speech apparently made by Cypriano, in which he carefully implores his womenfolk to "refrain from vice" and to be "obedient" to their husbands. *San Joaquin Republican*, July 7, 1853.

95. Perlot, 230–32.

96. Ibid.

Chapter 2: Domestic Life in the Diggings

1. Helen Nye to Mother, Jan. 6, 1853, Helen Nye Letters, Beinecke Library, Yale Univ., New Haven (hereafter cited as Beinecke Library); Journal entry, Nov. 12, 1849, William W. Miller Journal, Beinecke Library; Daniel B. Woods, *Sixteen Months at the Gold Diggings* (London: Sampson Low; New York: Harper and Brothers, [1851]), 86; Charles Davis to Daughter, Jan. 1, 1852, Charles Davis Letters, Beinecke Library.

2. Edmund Booth, *Edmund Booth, Forty-Niner: The Life Story of a Deaf Pioneer* (Stockton, Calif.: San Joaquin Pioneer and Historical Society, 1953), 22, 31, 33.

3. See Denise Riley, *"Am I That Name?": Feminism and the Category of "Women" in History* (Minneapolis: Univ. of Minnesota Press, 1988), esp. 6; and Evelyn Brooks Higginbotham, "African-American Women's History and the Metalanguage of Race," *Signs* 17, no. 2 (Winter 1992): 251–74, esp. 253–56.

4. My thinking here has been influenced by a growing literature on questions of male gender, including Mary P. Ryan, *Cradle of the Middle Class: The Family in Oneida County, New York, 1790–1865* (Cambridge: Cambridge Univ. Press, 1981); essays collected in J. A. Mangan and James Walvin, eds., *Manliness and Morality: Middle-Class Masculinity in Britain and America, 1800–1940* (Manchester: Manchester Univ. Press, 1987), and Mark C. Carnes and Clyde Griffen, eds., *Meanings for Manhood: Constructions of Masculinity in Victorian America* (Chicago: Univ. of Chicago Press, 1990); E. Anthony Rotundo, *American Manhood: Transformations in Masculinity from the Revolution to the Modern Era* (New York: Basic Books, 1993); George Chauncey, *Gay New York: Gender, Urban Culture, and the Making of the Gay Male World, 1890–1940* (New York: Basic Books, 1994); and Gail Bederman, *Manliness and Civilization: A Cultural History of Gender and Race in the United States, 1880–1917* (Chicago: Univ. of Chicago Press, 1995).

5. Much of the important scholarship on this and related points is summarized and critiqued in Thomas C. Holt, "Marking: Race, Race-Making, and the Writing of History," *American Historical Review* 100, no. 1 (Feb. 1995): 1–20. See esp. Barbara Jeanne Fields, "Ideology and Race in American History," in *Region, Race, and Reconstruction: Essays in Honor of C. Vann Woodward*, ed. J. Morgan Kousser and James M. McPherson (New York: Oxford Univ. Press, 1982).

6. Much of my thinking on this and related issues was originally influenced by Mrinalini Sinha, "Gender and Imperialism: Colonial Policy and the Ideology of Moral Imperialism in Late Nineteenth-Century Bengal," in *Changing Men: New Directions in Research on Men and Masculinity*, ed. Michael Kimmel (Newbury Park, Calif.: Sage Publications, 1987), 217–31. My emphasis on gender and race here, to the seeming exclusion of class, requires explanation. In the boom years of the Gold

Rush, relations of class were often obscured or even subsumed by the day-to-day salience of gender and race. This was in part because the means of getting gold during the initial boom was by placer (surface, individualized) mining rather than quartz (underground, industrialized) mining. Placer mining required almost no capital and did not necessarily entail a hierarchy among workers. Later, entrepreneurs in the Northern Mines developed hydraulic mining, a more capital-intensive means of exploiting surface deposits, whereby men shot powerful streams of water against hills assumed to be rich in "deep gravels." When hydraulic mining and quartz mining took hold, they were accompanied by an elaboration of class hierarchies. Class relations followed a different course in areas—like much of the Southern Mines—where insufficient water and underground deposits thwarted the development of hydraulic and quartz mining. For class making in the Southern Mines, see chap. 5, "Dreams That Died," and chap. 6, "The Last Fandango." The developments described in these chapters did not begin until about 1852. During the boom years in the Southern Mines, class contests and class solidarities often had as much to do with immigrants' memories of class in their homelands as with actual social relations structured through divisions of labor in the mines.

7. Analyses of productive versus reproductive labor particularly characterized Marxist-feminist thought of the 1970s and early 1980s. A culminating explication and critique appears in Joan Kelly, "The Doubled Vision of Feminist Theory," in *Women, History, and Theory* (Chicago: Univ. of Chicago Press, 1984), 51–64. See also the essays collected in Zillah Eisenstein, ed., *Capitalist Patriarchy and the Case for Socialist Feminism* (New York: Monthly Review Press, 1979); and Heidi Hartmann, "The Family as the Locus of Gender, Class, and Political Struggle: The Example of Housework," *Signs* 6 (Spring 1981): 366–94. For a trenchant analysis of the gendering of work in a different historical context, see Dana Frank, *Purchasing Power: Consumer Organizing, Gender, and the Seattle Labor Movement, 1919–1929* (New York: Cambridge Univ. Press, 1994). And for a crucial analysis of how reproductive work is not only gendered but also racialized, see Evelyn Nakano Glenn, "From Servitude to Service Work: Historical Continuities in the Racial Division of Paid Reproductive Labor," *Signs* 18, no. 1 (Autumn 1992): 1–43.

8. See Glenn; and Joan Scott, "Deconstructing Equality-versus-Difference: Or, the Uses of Poststructuralist Theory for Feminism," *Feminist Studies* 14, no. 1 (Spring 1988), 33–50. For other discussions of domestic themes in the Gold Rush, see David Goodman, *Gold Seeking: Victoria and California in the 1850s* (Stanford: Stanford Univ. Press, 1994), 149–87; Laurie F. Maffly-Kipp, *Religion and Society in Frontier California* (New Haven: Yale Univ. Press, 1994), esp. 148–80; Malcolm J. Rohrbough, *Days of Gold: The California Gold Rush and the American Nation* (Berkeley: Univ. of California Press, 1997), esp. 91–105.

9. See Richard Levy, "Eastern Miwok," in *Handbook of North American Indians*, vol. 8, *California*, ed. Robert F. Heizer (Washington, D.C.: Smithsonian Institution, 1978), 398–413, esp. 408–9. The Canadian observer is William Perkins, *Three Years in California: William Perkins' Journal of Life at Sonora, 1849–1852*, ed. Dale L. Morgan and James R. Scobie (Berkeley: Univ. of California Press, 1964), 122. The Belgian observer is Jean-Nicolas Perlot, *Gold Seeker: Adventures of a Belgian Argonaut during the Gold Rush Years*, trans. Helen Harding Bretnor and ed. Howard R. Lamar (New Haven: Yale Univ. Press, 1985), 188. See also *The Journals of Alfred Doten, 1849–1903*, 3 vols., ed. Walter Van Tilburg Clark (Reno: Univ. of Nevada Press, 1973), 1:212–13; Friedrich W. C. Gerstäcker, *Narrative of a Journey round the World* (New York: Harper and Brothers, 1853), 218.

10. Woods, 121. "Wigwam" was a term of Abenaki and Massachuset origin that described dwellings of eastern Indians, which often had an arched wooden framework overlaid with bark, rushes, or hides.

11. Ibid.; Journal entry, July 18, 1852, John Wallis Journal, Holt-Atherton Center for Western Studies, Univ. of the Pacific, Stockton, Calif.; Perkins, 103; Doten, 1:76.

12. J. D. Borthwick, *The Gold Hunters* (1857; Oyster Bay, N.Y.: Nelson Doubleday, 1917), 291. Cf. George W. B. Evans, *Mexican Gold Rush Trail: The Journal of a Forty-Niner*, ed. Glenn S. Dumke (San Marino, Calif.: Huntington Library, 1945), 244.

13. See, e.g., Journal entry, Jan. 10, 1851, George W. Allen Journals, Beinecke Library; Journal entry, March 28, 1853, Angus McIsaac Journal, Beinecke Library; Doten, 1:76–77 (Doten writes, "we vamosed aqui for the rich gulsh").

14. Borthwick, 252, and see 143, 302; Enos Christman, *One Man's Gold: The Letters and Journal of a Forty-Niner*, ed. Florence Morrow Christman (New York: Whittlesey House, McGraw-Hill, 1930), 132.

15. John Doble, *John Doble's Journal and Letters from the Mines: Mokelumne Hill, Jackson, Volcano and San Francisco, 1851–1865*, ed. Charles L. Camp (Denver: Old West Publishing, 1962), 40, 54.

16. Perlot, 100–1, 153.

17. Harvey Wood, *Personal Recollections of Harvey Wood* (Angels Camp, Calif.: Mountain Echo Job Printing Office, [c. 1878]), 16; Leonard Withington Noyes Reminiscences, Essex Institute, Salem, Mass., transcription at Calaveras County Museum and Archives, San Andreas, Calif., 37.

18. Journal entry, Dec. 18, 1852, McIsaac Journal.

19. Journal entry, Feb. 26, 1853, ibid.; Jesse R. Smith to Sister Helen, Dec. 23, 1852, Lura and Jesse R. Smith Correspondence, Huntington Library, San Marino, Calif. (hereafter cited as Huntington Library).

20. See Perkins, esp. 333. When Perkins left California in 1852, he did not return east, but sailed to Chile, where he eventually married a Chilean woman. In 1860, he moved with his family to Argentina, and there

spent the rest of his life as a businessman, journalist, and tireless pro-
moter of Argentinean economic development. See "Introduction,"
48–56.

21. Ibid., 101, 103. On Orientalism, see Edward W. Said, *Orientalism* (New
York: Pantheon, 1978).

22. These generalizations are based on wide reading in Gold Rush personal
accounts that describe household organization; an adequate citation of
the evidence would run several pages. But see, e.g., Moses F. Little
Journals, Beinecke Library, items 12 and 14, passim; John Amos Chaffee
and Jason Palmer Chamberlain Papers, Bancroft Library, Univ. of
California, Berkeley (hereafter cited as Bancroft Library), Chamberlain
Journals 1 and 2, passim; Doten, 1:91–250 passim; Perlot, 89–292 pas-
sim. Secondary accounts that address such issues include Rodman W.
Paul, *California Gold: The Beginning of Mining in the Far West* (1947;
reprint, Lincoln: Univ. of Nebraska Press, 1965), 72–73; John Walton
Caughey, *The California Gold Rush* (1948; reprint, Berkeley: Univ. of
California Press, 1975), 177–201; Ralph Mann, *After the Gold Rush:
Society in Grass Valley and Nevada City, California, 1849–1870* (Stanford:
Stanford Univ. Press, 1982), 17. Although I have not undertaken a full
statistical analysis of the 1850 census, even a spot-check through the
microfilm reels for Calaveras, Tuolumne, and Mariposa counties sup-
ports my contentions about household size: U.S. Bureau of the Census,
Seventh Federal Population Census, 1850, National Archives and
Records Service, RG-29, M-432, reels 33, 35, 36.

23. See, e.g., Journal entries, Oct. 20–Nov. 3, 1849, Miller Journal; Journal
entry, Jan. 16, 1853, McIsaac Journal; Journal entries, June 11–29,
1850, Allen Journals; Perlot, 215, 259–61; Doten, 1:76, 81; Doble, 94.

24. See, e.g., Doble, 38–39; Doten, 1:115–27 (Doten was keeping a store in
Calaveras County, and these pages record, in particular, the patronage
of Chinese, Mexicans, and Chileans); Helen Nye to Mother, Jan. 6,
1853, Nye Letters (Nye's husband was merchant at Don Pedro's Bar in
Tuolumne County); Account book entries, 1852–53, Little Journals,
item 13.

25. Leonard Pitt, *The Decline of the Californios: A Social History of the Spanish-
Speaking Californians, 1846–1890* (Berkeley: Univ. of California Press,
1966), 54, 104–5; Albert Camarillo, *Chicanos in a Changing Society:
From Mexican Pueblos to American Barrios in Santa Barbara and Southern
California, 1848–1930* (Cambridge: Harvard Univ. Press, 1979), 26. For
Anglo observations of the Californio cattle trade in the Gold Rush,
see, e.g., Journal entries, July 3 and Sept. 10, 1850, Timothy C. Osborn
Journal, Bancroft Library (a 1932 transcription of the handwritten
journal by Daniel Harris, entitled "The Heart of a 49er: The Diary of
Timothy Osborn," is also available).

26. See sources cited n. 24 above, and Charles Davis to Daughter, Jan. 5,
[1852], Davis Letters; Perlot, 153, 154, 159–60; Howard C. Gardiner, *In
Pursuit of the Golden Dream: Reminiscences of San Francisco and the*

Northern and Southern Mines, 1849–1857, ed. Dale L. Morgan (Stoughton, Mass.: Western Hemisphere, 1970), 95, 107, 164–65; Doble, 58.

27. Perlot, 56–57; cf. Evans, 200.

28. Gardiner, 95; cf. Perkins, 106.

29. Vicente Pérez Rosales, "Diary of a Journey to California," in *We Were 49ers! Chilean Accounts of the California Gold Rush,* trans. and ed. Edwin A. Beilharz and Carlos U. López (Pasadena, Calif.: Ward Ritchie Press, 1976), 3–99, esp. 70–77. For background on Pérez Rosales, see chap. 1, "On the Eve of Emigration."

30. Journal entries, Oct. 20, Nov. 15, and Dec. 19, 1852, Little Journals, item 12.

31. Perlot, 155–60. For similar troubles among Anglos, Mexicans, and French at San Antonio in Calaveras County, see A. Hersey Dexter, *Early Days in California* (Denver: Tribune-Republican Press, 1886), 20–26.

32. Journal entries, Dec. 21, 24, 25, 1852, Little Journals, item 12; Journal entries, Nov. 25, 27, 1851, Osborn Journal.

33. Journal entries, Oct. 13–Dec. 25, 1849, passim, Miller Journal. These friendly parties of black and white miners faced opposition from neighboring white southerners who resented the presence of free blacks in the area. See chap. 4, "Mining Gold and Making War." See also Perlot, 272. Leonard Withington Noyes hunted frequently and sold venison to a neighboring Mexican camp; see Noyes, 37. On the decline of game animals near Sonora over the early years of the Gold Rush, see Perkins, 261–62. For examples of men fishing, particularly during the fall salmon run, see Journal entries, Oct. 16–19, 1850, Allen Journals; Journal entry, Oct. 18, 1850, Osborn Journal; Journal entry, Oct. 19, 1852, P. V. Fox Journals, Beinecke Library.

34. Perlot, 272.

35. Journal entry, Nov. 26, 1849, Miller Journal; Woods, 123; A. W. Genung to Thomas, April 22, 1851, A. W. Genung Letters, Beinecke Library. On other gardens, see Doten, 1:85, 147–48, 151; Doble, 94.

36. Evans, 260–61. For other references to scarce vegetables and resulting health problems, see Perkins, 262; Borthwick, 57; Doble, 58; Journal entries, Aug. 12–24, 1851, Chamberlain Journal no. 1; Benjamin Butler Harris, *The Gila Trail: The Texas Argonauts and the California Gold Rush,* ed. Richard H. Dillon (Norman: Univ. of Oklahoma Press, 1960), 123 (on scurvy among Mexican miners); Lucius Fairchild, *California Letters of Lucius Fairchild,* ed. Joseph Schafer (Madison: State Historical Society of Wisconsin, 1931), 48, 63; Étienne Derbec, *A French Journalist in the California Gold Rush: The Letters of Étienne Derbec,* ed. Abraham P. Nasatir (Georgetown, Calif.: Talisman Press, 1964), 121–22, 140–41.

37. Perlot, 260; Doble, 245; Journal entries, Aug. 24, Sept. 6, 1852, Little Journals, item 12.

38. Journal entries, Oct. 24, Nov. 22, 24, 1852, ibid.; Journal entries, July 14, 1850, Jan. 12, Feb. 9, 1851, Allen Journals. And see Journal entry, Aug. 8, 1852, Fox Journals.

39. Journal entries, Dec. 22, 30, 1849, Jan. 1, 4, 5, 1850, Miller Journal.

40. Borthwick, 255–56, 302–3.

41. John Marshall Newton, *Memoirs of John Marshall Newton* (n.p.: John M. Stevenson, 1913), 48–50.

42. Gardiner, 166. Although Gardiner spent most of his time in the Southern Mines, this actually took place in the Northern Mines.

43. Journal entry Aug. 23, 1850, Osborn Journal; Josiah Foster Flagg to Mother, March 9, 1851, Josiah Foster Flagg Letters, Beinecke Library.

44. Journal entries, Aug. 23 and Oct. 14, 1850, Osborn Journal. For more on slavery in the gold fields, see chap. 1, "On the Eve of Emigration," and chap. 4, "Mining Gold and Making War"; and Rudolph M. Lapp, *Blacks in Gold Rush California* (New Haven: Yale Univ. Press, 1977), esp. 64–77.

45. Pérez Rosales, 46–56. On other instances in which sick or injured men took on added domestic tasks, see, e.g., Journal entries, Sept. 8–17, 1852, Little Journals, item 12. Timothy Osborn indicated men's fear of being seen as weak when he refused to stop working on an extraordinarily hot day, all so that no one could say "he was too delicate" to mine. Journal entry, Aug. 16, 1850, Osborn Journal.

46. Perlot, 258–71, esp. 259–60, 271. One other instance of white men forgoing weekly cooking rotations appears in the journal of Ben Bowen. Bowen—who worked a claim in present-day Amador County along with his father, brother Dave, and two other miners—reported a novel division of domestic labor: "Father and I do the cooking: he does the dishwashing part. Dave pays for his board at the rate of four dollars per week." Journal entry, Sept. 3, 1854, Ben Bowen Journal, Bancroft Library.

47. 1850 manuscript census, reel 35; Samuel Ward, *Sam Ward in the Gold Rush,* ed. Carvel Collins (Stanford: Stanford Univ. Press, 1949), 28, 149–52, 167; Charles Davis to Daughter, Jan. 5, [1852], and Jan. 6, 1854, Davis Letters. Julia Ward Howe would become a prominent participant in the U.S. woman movement and the author of "Battle Hymn of the Republic."

48. Charles Davis to Daughter, Jan. 5, [1852], and Jan. 6, 1854; Ward, 149, 152, 167; Fairchild, esp. 103–4; Christman, esp. 187.

49. Journal entry, April 18, 1852, Fox Journals; Ward, 168. Cf. Journal entry, July 3, 1850, Osborn Journal; Journal entry, March 30, 1851, Allen Journals. Mrs. Lee Whipple-Haslam (first name unknown), who came overland to California as a child, remembered, "The wonder and admiration of the Flat was our cow. Mother could have sold milk at any price." See *Early Days in California: Scenes and Events of the '50s as I Remember Them* (Jamestown, Calif.: Mother Lode Magnet, [1925]), 11. On women in dairy and poultry production, see, e.g., Joan M. Jensen, *Loosening the Bonds: Mid-Atlantic Farm Women, 1750–1850* (New Haven: Yale Univ. Press, 1986), and "Cloth, Butter, and Boarders: Women's Household Production for the Market," *Review of Radical*

Political Economics 12, no. 2 (Summer 1980): 14–24; John Mack Faragher, *Women and Men on the Overland Trail* (New Haven: Yale Univ. Press, 1979), esp. 51, and *Sugar Creek: Life on the Illinois Prairie* (New Haven: Yale Univ. Press, 1986), esp. 101–5.

50. On domestic failures, see, e.g., Journal entry, Dec. 22, 1849, Miller Journal; Doble, 54.

51. Christman, 126; William H. Newell to Mary Harrison Newell, Feb. 4, 1851, Joseph Pownall Papers, Huntington Library; Woods, 148; Journal entry, July 12, 1850, Osborn Journal.

52. Frank Marryat, *Mountains and Molehills; or, Recollections of a Burnt Journal*, ed. Robin Winks (1855; Philadelphia: J. B. Lippincott, 1962), 136; Dexter, 23–24; Borthwick, 342–44.

53. Borthwick, 342–43.

54. Hinton Rowan Helper, *The Land of Gold. Reality versus Fiction* (Baltimore: Henry Taylor, 1855), vi, 169.

55. Fairchild, 139. On gender as performative, see Judith Butler, *Gender Trouble: Feminism and the Subversion of Identity* (New York: Routledge, 1990), esp. 24–25, 33, 134–41.

56. Antonio Franco Coronel, "Cosas de California," trans. and ed. Richard Henry Morefield, in *The Mexican Adaptation in American California, 1846–1875* (1955; reprint, San Francisco: R and E Research Associates, 1971), 76–96, esp. 93–94; Derbec, 128. It is quite possible that Coronel exaggerated his cook's profits. But even if he doubled the amount she took in each day, her earnings would have been greater than those of the average miner in 1848. See "Appendix B: Wages in the California Gold Mines," in Paul, 349–50.

57. Perkins, 105–6.

58. Harris, 124; Silvia Marina Arrom, *The Women of Mexico City, 1790–1857* (Stanford: Stanford Univ. Press, 1985), 158–59, 192–93.

59. Pérez Rosales, 78–79.

60. Helen Nye to Sister Mary, Dec. 26, 1852, Feb. 8, March 14, 1853, May 20, 1855, Nye Letters. On Chinese cooks, see also Evans, 274.

61. Doble, 58; Derbec, 142: Whipple-Haslam, 3–4.

62. Noyes, 35; Christman, 132; Gardiner, 69; Journal entries, Aug. 10, 17, 31, 1849, Osborn Journal.

63. Doble, 245; Journal entries, Sept. 9, Nov. 22, 1852, Little Journals, item 12; Journal entries, Feb. 1, 8, 1851, Allen Journals; Journal entries, March 2–3, 1850, Miller Journal.

64. Journal entry, Jan. 1, 1850, Miller Journal; Woods, 98.

65. Perkins, 157–58.

66. Gardiner, 188–89.

67. Lapp, 49–93.

68. Gerstäcker, 225.

69. On the arrival of large numbers of Chinese starting in 1852, and on the reimposition of the foreign miners' tax, see chap. 5, "Dreams That Died."

70. See Ronald Takaki, *Strangers from a Different Shore: A History of Asian Americans* (Boston: Little, Brown, 1989), 92–94; and also Paul Ong, "An Ethnic Trade: The Chinese Laundries in Early California," *Journal of Ethnic Studies* 8, no. 4 (Winter 1981): 95–113.
71. Helper, 88–89, 96.
72. Ibid., esp. 36–44, 298–300. For contextualization of Helper's dim view of the Gold Rush, see Goodman, 24, 64, 136, 179, 205, 208. Helper's famous critique of southern slavery is *The Impending Crisis of the South: How to Meet It* (New York: Burdick Brothers, 1857).
73. Borthwick, 82, 361.
74. For a rich portrait of such patterns of sociability in the twentieth century, see Paul C. P. Siu, *The Chinese Laundryman: A Study in Social Isolation*, ed. John Kuo Wei Tchen (1953; New York: New York Univ. Press, 1987).
75. Journal entry, Sept. 6, 1849, Osborn Journal; William McCollum, *California as I Saw It. Pencillings by the Way of Its Gold and Gold Diggers. And Incidents of Travel by Land and Water*, ed. Dale L. Morgan (1850; reprint, Los Gatos, Calif.: Talisman Press, 1960), 160–61.
76. Harris, 113, 123, 132–34, 136. The term "male homosocial desire," of course, is Eve Kosofsky Sedgwick's: *Between Men: English Literature and Male Homosocial Desire* (New York: Columbia Univ. Press, 1985). The misquoted line from *Troilus and Cressida* is "One touch of nature makes the whole world kin." Given Harris's exuberance about male relationships in the Gold Rush, it is telling that when I first queried literary scholars about the source of the line, all suggested that it sounded very much like Walt Whitman, though none could identify the poem or essay. Yukiko Hanawa finally found the source for me and helped me think through the implications of Harris's misquotation, for which I am grateful. (Elsewhere Harris misquotes the line again as "one touch of whose nature made the whole world akin.")
77. Journal entries, Sept. 25, 29, 1850, Allen Journals.
78. Journal entries, Dec. 19–20, 1849, Miller Journal. On Irish immigrants and questions of race, see Noel Ignatiev, *How the Irish Became White* (New York: Routledge, 1995); David R. Roediger, *The Wages of Whiteness: Race and the Making of the American Working Class* (London: Verso, 1991), esp. 133–63.
79. See Susan M. Reverby, *Ordered to Care: The Dilemma of American Nursing, 1850–1945* (Cambridge: Cambridge Univ. Press, 1987), esp. 11–21; Barbara Melosh, *"The Physician's Hand": Work Culture and Conflict in American Nursing* (Philadelphia: Temple Univ. Press, 1982), esp. 3.
80. Evans, 250–51.
81. Dexter, 27–30.
82. See, e.g., Glenda Riley, *Women and Indians on the Frontier, 1825–1915* (Albuquerque: Univ. of New Mexico Press, 1984), esp. 76–81; William Cronon, *Changes in the Land: Indians, Colonists, and the Ecology of New England* (New York: Hill and Wang, 1983), 52–58, 92.

83. Likewise, Ephraim Delano told his wife that the Indians he saw lived primarily on acorns: "the women picks them and kerreys them in baskets." Sam Ward also "admired the ceaseless activity of the crones who went forth into the forest to gather acorns." Journal entries, Nov. 16, 17, 1852, Little Journals; Ephraim Delano to Wife, May 15, 1851, Ephraim Delano Letters, Beinecke Library; Ward, 136.

84. Doble, 42–50. Cf. Derbec, 154–56; Noyes, 74–75; Helper, 269–70; Gerstäcker, 210–11; Doten, 1:212.

85. Derbec, 155; Helper, 268; Christman, 180.

86. Gerstäcker, 217

87. See, e.g., Ryan; and essays collected in Carnes and Griffen, and Mangan and Walvin.

88. Perlot, 230–32. See full discussion in chap. 1, "On the Eve of Emigration."

89. Helen Nye to Sister Mary, Feb. 8, 1853, Nye Letters; Noyes, 75.

90. Journal entry, Oct. 20, 1849, Osborn Journal.

91. Gerstäcker, 217–18; Perlot, 181.

92. Ward, 51–52, 111, 125, 126–27, 136–37; George Phillips, *Indians and Indian Agents: The Origins of the Reservation System in California, 1849–1852* (Norman: Univ. of Oklahoma Press, 1997), 111–17. For further discussion of the Mariposa War and its aftermath, see chap. 4, "Mining Gold and Making War."

93. On the notion of vocational domesticity, see, e.g., Nancy F. Cott, *The Bonds of Womanhood: "Woman's Sphere" in New England, 1780–1835* (New Haven: Yale Univ. Press, 1977), esp. 74. Catharine Beecher popularized the idea in her *Treatise on Domestic Economy* (1841), which was in its ninth printing at the time of the Gold Rush; see Kathryn Kish Sklar, *Catharine Beecher: A Study in American Domesticity* (New York: W. W. Norton, 1976), 151–67.

94. Journal entry, Aug. 31, 1852, Little Journals, item 12; Benjamin Kendrick to Father, Sept. 25, 1849, Benjamin Franklin Kendrick Letters, Beinecke Library. Cf. Booth, 27. A. W. Genung to Mr. and Mrs. Thomas, Feb. 14, 1852, Genung Letters.

95. Christman, 204–5.

Chapter 3: Bulls, Bears, and Dancing Boys

1. Journal entry, Dec. 25, 1852, Angus McIsaac Journal, Beinecke Library, Yale Univ., New Haven (hereafter cited as Beinecke Library). For brief quotations, see Benjamin Kendrick to Father, Sept. 25, 1849, Benjamin Franklin Kendrick Letters, Beinecke Library; Joseph Pownall to Thomas Tharp, Aug. 5, 1850, Joseph Pownall Journal and Letterbook, Pownall Papers, Huntington Library, San Marino, Calif. (hereafter cited as Huntington Library); Journal entry, Sept. 7, 1850, Timothy C. Osborn Journal, Bancroft Library, Univ. of California, Berkeley (hereafter cited

as Bancroft Library); Journal entry, March 27, 1851, George Allen Journals, Beinecke Library; George W. B. Evans, *Mexican Gold Trail: The Journal of a Forty-Niner*, ed. Glenn S. Dumke (San Marino, Calif.: Huntington Library, 1945), 259; Jesse Smith to Sister Helen, Dec. 23, 1852, Lura and Jesse Smith Letters, Huntington Library. Examples of such lamentations about "society" are rife in Gold Rush personal accounts. Still, there is a less prevalent but not insignificant counter-tendency in the same kinds of sources for some Gold Rush participants to see themselves as involved in a different kind—for a few, even a *better* kind—of society. I will discuss such seemingly contradictory evidence below.

2. Here I rely on the argument developed by Denise Riley in her chapter entitled "'The Social,' 'Woman,' and Sociological Feminism," in *"Am I That Name?": Feminism and the Category of "Women" in History* (Minneapolis: Univ. of Minnesota Press, 1988), 44–66. In a less direct but no less crucial way, I draw on the earlier work of U.S. women's historians such as Kathryn Kish Sklar, *Catharine Beecher: A Study in American Domesticity* (New York: W. W. Norton, 1976); Nancy F. Cott, *The Bonds of Womanhood: "Woman's Sphere" in New England, 1780–1835* (New Haven: Yale Univ. Press, 1977); Mary P. Ryan, *Cradle of the Middle Class: The Family in Oneida County, New York, 1790–1865* (Cambridge: Cambridge Univ. Press, 1981).

3. U.S. Bureau of the Census, *Seventh Census of the United States: 1850* (Washington, D.C., 1853), hereafter cited as *1850 Census*.

4. J. D. Borthwick, *The Gold Hunters* (1857; Oyster Bay, N.Y.: Nelson Doubleday, 1917), 290.

5. Mrs. Lee Whipple-Haslam, *Early Days in California: Scenes and Events of the '50s as I Remember Them* (Jamestown, Calif: Mother Lode Magnet, [1925]), 2; Jesse Smith to Sister Helen, Dec. 23, 1852, Smith Letters.

6. See, e.g., Roy Rosenzweig, *Eight Hours for What We Will: Workers and Leisure in an Industrial City, 1870–1920* (Cambridge: Cambridge Univ. Press, 1983), 35–40, 240, n. 4; Bruce Laurie, *Artisans into Workers: Labor in Nineteenth-Century America* (New York: Hill and Wang, 1989), esp. 84–86, 168–70; Herbert G. Gutman, "Work, Culture, and Society in Industrializing America, 1815–1919," in *Work, Culture, and Society in Industrializing America: Essays in American Working-Class and Social History* (New York: Alfred A. Knopf, 1976), 3–78; and E. P. Thompson, "Time, Work-Discipline, and Industrial Capitalism," *Past and Present*, no. 38 (Dec. 1967), 56–97.

7. Here I am influenced by Joan Scott, "Gender: A Useful Category of Historical Analysis," *American Historical Review* 91, no. 5 (Dec. 1986): 1053–76, and "Deconstructing Equality-versus-Difference: Or, the Uses of Poststructuralist Theory for Feminism," *Feminist Studies* 14, no. 1 (Spring 1988): 33–50.

8. My thanks to Nancy Cott and Ann Fabian for initially helping me clar-

ify these arguments. Yukiko Hanawa and anonymous readers for *Radical History Review* helped me refine them even further, and for that I am very grateful.

9. See Albert L. Hurtado, *Indian Survival on the California Frontier* (New Haven: Yale Univ. Press, 1988); and chap. 4, "Mining Gold and Making War."

10. E. W. Gifford, "Central Miwok Ceremonies," *Anthropological Records* 14, no. 4 (1955): 261–318, esp. 295–99, and "Miwok Cults," *University of California Publications in American Archaeology and Ethnology* 18, no. 3 (1926): 391–408, esp. 397–98; and Richard Levy, "Eastern Miwok," in *Handbook of North American Indians*, vol. 8, *California*, ed. Robert F. Heizer (Washington, D.C.: Smithsonian Institution, 1978), 398–413, esp. 410–12.

11. Alfred Doten, *The Journals of Alfred Doten, 1849–1903*, 3 vols., ed. Walter Van Tilburg Clark (Reno: Univ. of Nevada Press, 1973), 1:238, 239–42.

12. Doten, 1:238, 239 (Doten's *Plymouth Rock* articles are reprinted along with his diary in these edited volumes); Gifford, "Central Miwok Ceremonies," 295–99.

13. Doten, 1:237, 240. Many thanks to Yukiko Hanawa for helping me rethink my interpretation of this event.

14. Such sources—argonauts' personal accounts and early twentieth-century ethnographies—are also usefully read as texts caught up in their own rules of representation, their own practices of separating self and other, subject and object. In the end, they tell us as much about mid-nineteenth- and early twentieth-century white constructions of reality as about Miwok spirituality and sociability in the same periods. See essays collected in James Clifford and George E. Marcus, eds., *Writing Culture: The Poetics and Politics of Ethnography* (Berkeley: Univ. of California Press, 1986).

15. On Doble's description of Miwok women's acorn processing, see chap. 2, "Domestic Life in the Diggings."

16. See John Doble, *John Doble's Journal and Letters from the Mines: Mokelumne Hill, Jackson, Volcano and San Francisco, 1851–1865*, ed. Charles L. Camp (Denver: Old West Publishing, 1962), 45, 48–52. Doble's description of this event does not match precisely practices for any of the dances the anthropologist E. W. Gifford identified among early twentieth-century Miwoks. This is no surprise; Miwok rituals were syncretic and constantly evolving over the nineteenth and early twentieth centuries, reflecting material changes in Miwok life and practices learned from other native Californians. Still, some ritual practices and regalia survived the half century that separated the Gold Rush years from the era of ethnographic fieldwork among Miwok people. In the 1920s, Gifford described the significance of birds and their feathers in Miwok ritual practices, the most important of which was the *kuksuyu* ceremony, in which the main dancer impersonated a revered bird or birdlike spirit. Other dances also featured

bird paraphernalia, and, according to Gifford, it was largely the presence of feathers that signified the sacredness of a dance, though Gifford himself acknowledged that the term "sacred" might not best describe what set these dances apart from others. Thus it seems safe to surmise that the preparations John Doble observed were for what might be termed a sacred dance. See Gifford, "Central Miwok Ceremonies," and "Miwok Cults." See also Levy, esp. 410–12.

17. Doble, 52.
18. The anthropologist was C. Hart Merriam; see his "The Mourning Ceremony of the Miwok, 1906," reprinted in *The California Indians: A Source Book*, ed. R. F. Heizer and M. A. Whipple, 2d ed. (Berkeley: Univ. of California Press, 1971), 520–32, esp. 528. See Doble, 41, 45–46, 52.
19. For more on religious themes during the Gold Rush, see Laurie F. Maffly-Kipp, *Religion and Society in Frontier California* (New Haven: Yale Univ. Press, 1994).
20. John B. McGloin, S.J., ed., "A California Gold Rush Padre: New Light on the 'Padre of Paradise Flat,'" *California Historical Society Quarterly* 40, no. 1 (March 1961): 49–67, esp. 58, 59.
21. William Hanchett, "The Question of Religion and the Taming of California, 1849–1854, Part I," *California Historical Society Quarterly* 32, no. 1 (March 1953): 49–56, esp. 51.
22. Pedro Isidoro Combet, "Memories of California," in *We Were 49ers! Chilean Accounts of the California Gold Rush*, trans. and ed. Edwin A. Beilharz and Carlos U. López (Pasadena, Calif.: Ward Ritchie Press, 1976), 151–85, esp. 164–65.
23. Borthwick, 298–99; cf. Benjamin Butler Harris, *The Gila Trail: The Texas Argonauts and the California Gold Rush*, ed. Richard H. Dillon (Norman: Univ. of Oklahoma Press, 1960), 144. Harris describes a drunken American comrade who threatened to tear down the Catholic church in San Andreas.
24. Thanks once again to Yukiko Hanawa for helping me reinterpret this event.
25. On overt and purposeful forms of resistance, see esp. chap. 4, "Mining Gold and Making War."
26. See Charles E. Rosenberg, "Sexuality, Class, and Role in Nineteenth-Century America," *American Quarterly* 35, no. 2 (May 1973): 131–53; E. Anthony Rotundo, "Learning about Manhood: Gender Ideals and the Middle-Class Family in Nineteenth-Century America," in *Manliness and Morality: Middle-Class Masculinity in Britain and America, 1800–1940*, ed. J. A. Mangan and James Walvin (Manchester: Manchester Univ. Press, 1987), 35–51, and *American Manhood: Transformations in Masculinity from the Revolution to the Modern Era* (New York: Basic Books, 1993); Howard Gadlin, "Private Lives and Public Order: A Critical View of the History of Intimate Relations in the U.S.," *Massachusetts Review* 17 (Summer 1976): 304–30; G. J. Barker-Benfield, *The Horrors of the Half-Known Life: Male Attitudes*

toward Women and Sexuality in Nineteenth-Century America (New York: Harper Colophon, 1976); Clyde Griffen, "Reconstructing Masculinity from the Evangelical Revival to the Waning of Progressivism: A Speculative Synthesis," in *Meanings for Manhood: Constructions of Masculinity in Victorian America*, ed. Mark C. Carnes and Clyde Griffen (Chicago: Univ. of Chicago Press, 1990), 183–204; Ryan; Gail Bederman, *Manliness and Civilization: A Cultural History of Gender and Race in the United States, 1880–1917* (Chicago: Univ. of Chicago Press, 1995).

27. On miners' declining daily yields, see Rodman W. Paul, *California Gold: The Beginning of Mining in the Far West* (1947; reprint, Lincoln: Univ. of Nebraska Press, 1965), 349–52. I owe my understanding of the ambiguous place of luck in nineteenth-century perceptions of economic advancement to Ann Vincent Fabian, *Card Sharps, Dream Books, and Bucket Shops: Gambling in Nineteenth-Century America* (Ithaca: Cornell Univ. Press, 1990).

28. See, e.g., sources cited n. 26 above; Cott; Sklar; Carl N. Degler, *At Odds: Women and the Family in America from the Revolution to the Present* (New York: Oxford Univ. Press, 1980); Robert L. Griswold, *Family and Divorce in California, 1850–1890: Victorian Illusions and Everyday Realities* (Albany: State Univ. of New York Press, 1982); Steven Mintz and Susan Kellogg, *Domestic Revolutions: A Social History of American Family Life* (New York: Basic Books, 1988). A good first look at the impact of white women's absence on white gold seekers appears in Andrew J. Rotter, "'Matilda for God's Sake Write': Women and Families on the Argonaut Mind," *California History* 58, no. 2 (Summer 1979): 128–41. See also Malcolm J. Rohrbough, *Days of Gold: The California Gold Rush and the American Nation* (Berkeley: Univ. of California Press, 1997), 91–105.

29. Journal entries, April 25, May 9, 16, 23, 30, June 20, 27, 1852, P. V. Fox Journals, Beinecke Library.

30. Journal entries, July 7, Nov. 17, 1850; Feb. 2, 9, 23, March 5, 1851, Osborn Journal.

31. Journal entry, Nov. 3, 1850, Allen Journals.

32. See, e.g., Journal entries, Nov. 3, 17, 1850; Jan. 19, Feb. 23, March 10, 16, [April 27], 1851, Lemuel Herbert Journal, Amador County Archives, Jackson, Calif.

33. Daniel B. Woods, *Sixteen Months at the Gold Diggings* (London: Sampson Low; New York: Harper and Brothers, [1851]), 104; Enos Christman, *One Man's Gold: The Letters and Journal of a Forty-Niner,* ed. Florence Morrow Christman (New York: Whittlesey House, McGraw-Hill, 1930), 181–82; Charles Peters, *The Autobiography of Charles Peters* (Sacramento: La Grave Co., [1915]), 16; Journal entry, May 19–25, 1851, Jason Chamberlain Journal no. 1, John Amos Chaffee and Jason Palmer Chamberlain Papers, Bancroft Library.

34. Étienne Derbec, *A French Journalist in the California Gold Rush: The Letters*

of Étienne Derbec, ed. Abraham P. Nasatir (Georgetown, Calif.: Talisman Press, 1964), 143–44; Borthwick, 308.

35. Quotations appear in Charles Davis to Wife, May 17, 1850, Charles Davis Letters, Beinecke Library; Woods, 97, 102; and Lucius Fairchild, *California Letters of Lucius Fairchild,* ed. Joseph Schafer (Madison: State Historical Society of Wisconsin, 1931), 186–87. Other references to prayer, hymn singing, and devotional reading include Derbec, 142; Journal entries, March 21, 1852, Feb. 27, March 9, 23, 1853, Fox Journals; Journal entries, July 18, Aug. 1, Oct. 10, 1852, Moses F. Little Journals, Beinecke Library; Christman, 144; Journal entry, Jan. 4, 1853, John Wallis Journal, Holt-Atherton Center for Western Studies, Univ. of the Pacific, Stockton, Calif.

36. Journal entry, Aug. 3, 1850, Allen Journals.

37. Journal entry, Dec. 3, 1851, Fox Journals.

38. Woods, 187–91.

39. For a good discussion of the practice of diary keeping in the nineteenth century, see Cott, 15–16.

40. Background on the men comes from Doten, 1:xviii–xx; Doble, xiii; the information provided by Emma B. Harris with the transcription of the Osborn Journal that is kept with the original; and from the three journals themselves.

41. Doten, 1:3–4, 84, 105, 107, 111, 112, 125, 141.

42. Reading these references is especially complicated because a relative of Doten's, after his death in 1903, saw fit to start erasing explicit descriptions of sexual activity in the fifty years of journals Doten left behind. The censor never completed the project, and hence the later diaries are filled with sexually explicit material. But the earlier volumes, which cover the Gold Rush years, are substantially altered. Still, the three references mentioned remain, if in abbreviated form, and they may stand for a greater number of sexual encounters in the mines. Ibid., 1:xii–xiii, 125–26, 150, 195.

43. Ibid., 1:125–26. On the Miwok practice of cutting hair when in mourning, see, e.g., Levy, 407; A. L. Kroeber, *Handbook of the Indians of California* (1925; reprint, St. Clair Shores, Mich.: Scholarly Press, 1976), 1:452; S. A. Barrett and E. W. Gifford, *Miwok Material Culture,* Bulletin of the Public Museum of the City of Milwaukee, vol. 2, no. 4 (Milwaukee, 1933), 222.

44. Most ethnographic works on Miwoks are concerned only with marriage practices and are silent about nonmarital sex. For an overview of the meanings of Indian-white cross-racial sex in the Gold Rush, see Hurtado, *Indian Survival,* 169–92, which, however, does not shed light specifically on Miwoks. Hurtado focuses on "alliances of convenience," prostitution, and forced sex. While influenced by Hurtado's careful work, I think the situation described here may allow for other interpretations as well. See also Hurtado, "When Strangers Met: Sex and Gender on Three Frontiers," in *Writing the Range: Race, Class, and*

Culture in the Women's West, ed. Elizabeth Jameson and Susan Armitage (Norman: Univ. of Oklahoma Press, 1997), 122–42; and Antonia I. Castañeda, "Sexual Violence in the Politics and Policies of Conquest: Amerindian Women and the Spanish Conquest of Alta California," in *Building with Our Hands: New Directions in Chicana Studies,* ed. Adela de la Torre and Beatríz M. Pesquera (Berkeley: Univ. of California Press, 1993), 15–33.

45. Doten, 1:75, 121, 122, 128, 130–34, 150, 152, 195, 243–51. (Doten refers to his hometown sweetheart as "M," for Martha, in journal entries here. His California sweetheart was also named Martha.) Marion Goldman has chronicled Doten's later life on the Comstock Lode in Nevada, and her research indicates that the old Doten was finally revived in the new mining area. See *Gold Diggers and Silver Miners: Prostitution and Social Life on the Comstock Lode* (Ann Arbor: Univ. of Michigan Press, 1981), 51–56.

46. Doble, 47, 114.

47. Ibid., 132, 178–81.

48. Ibid., 70, 83, 114, 149.

49. Journal entries, July 11, 18, Aug. 18, 24, Oct. 19, Nov. 16, 1850; Jan. 6, 1851, Osborn Journal. Osborn called his shorthand "phonography."

50. Ibid., e.g., Journal entries, Sept. 9, Oct. 18, 1850.

51. Ibid., Journal entries, Aug. 8, Sept. 17, Oct. 2, 1850. The Miwok man named Juan, e.g., explained to the Belgian miner Jean-Nicolas Perlot that his people tried to conceive children so that they would be born between March and June, and thus benefit in the early months of their lives from the natural abundance of spring, summer, and fall in the Sierra foothills. See Perlot, *Gold Seeker: Adventures of a Belgian Argonaut during the Gold Rush Years,* trans. Helen Harding Bretnor and ed. Howard R. Lamar (New Haven: Yale Univ. Press, 1985), 230.

52. Journal entries, Oct. 10, 1850, April 25, 1851, Osborn Journal.

53. Ibid., e.g., Journal entries, July 7, 11, Aug. 24, 25, 1850.

54. Ibid., Journal entry, Sept. 15, 1850. Similar, though more ambiguous, entries occur in the journal of Angus McIsaac, where constant references to the moon—once called the "horny moon"—and its silver light may signify ejaculation, or else simply fond memories of home. See Journal entries, Dec. 26, 1852, Jan. 22, 24, 25, Feb. 14, 15, 1853, McIsaac Journal.

55. Journal entries, Aug. 24, Dec. 10, 19, 1850, Osborn Journal.

56. *1850 Census.* By 1852, the population in the Southern Mines had more than doubled, to over 60,000, but male-female breakdowns are not available for all three counties in the aggregate statistics from the 1852 state census, which are published in the same volume as those from the 1850 federal census. In 1860, women still made up only about 19 percent of the population of the Southern Mines. U.S. Bureau of the Census, *Population of the United States in 1860; Compiled*

from . . . the Eighth Census (Washington, D.C., 1864). As for markets in heterosocial pleasures, one anonymous reader of an article-length version of this chapter has noted that such markets "flourished with full participation" by white men in the East as well—particularly, no doubt the reader means, in urban areas. S/he, of course, is correct. What was different about the Gold Rush was the physical absence of "respectable" middle-class white women, which meant that such "markets" could more easily stand in for "society" in the mining camps and supply centers of California. And what was unique about the Southern Mines, in particular, was a demography in which Anglo men barely constituted a majority. On markets in pleasure in the East, see Timothy J. Gilfoyle, *City of Eros: New York City, Prostitution, and the Commercialization of Sex, 1790–1920* (New York: W. W. Norton, 1992).

57. Christman, 179, 198. On the "Model Artists," see also William Perkins, *Three Years in California: William Perkins' Journal of Life at Sonora, 1849–1852*, ed. Dale L. Morgan and James R. Scobie (Berkeley: Univ. of California Press, 1964), 219–20.

58. Doten, 1:92, 227–28 (and cf. his description of the Fiddletown event to the *Plymouth Rock*, which ignores the dance hall stop, 1:232–33); Journal entry, Jan. 16, 1852, Wallis Journal; Doble, 104, 108. See also Journal entry, Dec. 30, 1850, Osborn Journal, on Stockton dance houses. My discussion of fandangos here focuses on male patrons. For a discussion of female workers in such establishments, see chap. 6, "The Last Fandango."

59. On the impact of the foreign miners' tax on Sonora, see chap. 4, "Mining Gold and Making War."

60. Perkins, 127–28.

61. Ibid., 161, 163, 201–2, 221–23, 305. Perkins is introduced in chap. 2, "Domestic Life in the Diggings."

62. Ibid., 103–4, 130–31, 218, 303–4. Elsewhere I have examined informal union among Mexican immigrant women, linking it to earlier cultural practices that proved particularly appropriate to mining areas. See "Sharing Bed and Board: Cohabitation and Cultural Difference in Central Arizona Mining Towns, 1863–1873," in *The Women's West*, ed. Susan Armitage and Elizabeth Jameson (Norman: Univ. of Oklahoma Press, 1987), 77–91. For a useful critique of this essay, see Antonia I. Castañeda, "Women of Color and the Rewriting of Western History: The Discourse, Politics, and Decolonization of History," *Pacific Historical Review* 61, no. 4 (Nov. 1992): 501–33, esp. 512, n. 21.

63. Perkins, 242–45, 268.

64. Ibid., 161–62, 218–19, 242–43, 260, 268. On women in Santa Fe, see Deena J. González, "La Tules of Image and Reality: Euro-American Attitudes and Legend Formation on a Spanish-Mexican Frontier," in de la Torre and Pesquera, eds., 75–90. French women's monopoly over the bars and gaming tables seems not to have lasted, and it may even

have been peculiar to the town of Sonora. Sources from the mid to late 1850s show that Spanish-speaking women in the Southern Mines frequently did such work. See chap. 6, "The Last Fandango."

65. English-speaking women—and they were few in number—Perkins dismissed altogether, calling the "loose" women from Australia and the United States "vulgar, degraded and brutish." Perkins, 243.

66. For the comparison to New York, see Gilfoyle.

67. Perkins, 251–52, 314. Perkins made this remark in response to the arrival of Elizabeth Le Breton Gunn, the wife of Lewis Gunn, a doctor and the publisher of the *Sonora Herald*, in 1851. For more on the Gunns, see chap. 6, "The Last Fandango." For the perspective of Elizabeth Gunn, see Lewis C. Gunn and Elizabeth Le Breton Gunn, *Records of a California Family: Journals and Letters of Lewis C. Gunn and Elizabeth Le Breton Gunn*, ed. Anna Lee Marston (San Diego: n.p., 1928). As this collection of family papers makes clear, the woman whom Perkins called a "descendant of the Puritans" descended from both English and French immigrants, hence her maiden name, Le Breton. Enos Christman, who worked for and lived with Lewis Gunn, was more enthusiastic about Elizabeth Gunn's arrival, noting that a "woman about a house produces a new order of things." See chap. 2, "Domestic Life in the Diggings," and Christman, 187.

68. My thanks to Yukiko Hanawa for helping me clarify my interpretation in this section.

69. Borthwick, 314–15; Perkins, 314. On Jewish merchants, see Robert E. Levinson, *The Jews in the California Gold Rush* (New York: KTAV Publishing, 1978), 23–60. Levinson notes that Perkins was also in competition with these merchants (p. 27).

70. Doble, 89–90; Perlot, 246. For more on Perlot, see chap. 1, "On the Eve of Emigration."

71. Friedrich Gerstäcker, *Narrative of a Journey round the World* (New York: Harper and Brothers, 1853), 236–37, 251.

72. Borthwick, 351; Harris, 112–13, 123; Journal entry, Aug. 4, 1850, Osborn Journal.

73. Ibid., Journal entries, Aug. 4, 25, 1850; John Marshall Newton, *Memoirs of John Marshall Newton* (n.p.: John M. Stevenson, 1913), 34, 36, 48.

74. Howard C. Gardiner, *In Pursuit of the Golden Dream: Reminiscences of San Francisco and the Northern and Southern Mines, 1849–1857*, ed. Dale L. Morgan (Stoughton, Mass.: Western Hemisphere, 1970), 216; Doten, 1:116.

75. There is one other possible clue, but it comes from a document generated almost three years after Doten's diary entry. Given the geographic mobility of Gold Rush participants, I hesitate to suggest that the individual to which the later source refers is the same person Doten called the "Chileno hermaphrodite." But s/he might be. In March of 1855, a storekeeper at Rich Gulch (the area Doten visited during his drunken spree in May 1852) named Eben Brooks was mur-

dered. During the inquest into Brooks's death, authorities interviewed a number of men who lived nearby, though a jury ultimately concluded that Brooks "came to his death by wounds inflicted by some person or persons unknown." One man interviewed, a Mexican miner named Marshall Gómez (from Matamoros, along the Rio Grande near Texas), testified that he had visited Brooks's store with two Anglos on the eve of the murder. Before he left, Gómez testified, "two Spaniards came into the store" and asked after "a Spaniard who had a large woman." Gómez told them that "there had been such a man below here." It is this "large woman" who I suggest may be Doten's "hermaphrodite." The conversation at Brooks's store was likely to have been conducted in Spanish, because although Gómez was in the store with two Anglos, the visitors directed their inquiry to him. Gómez himself was bilingual, and so he translated this conversation into English during the inquest. The Spanish term most likely to have been translated into English as "large woman" is *mujer grande*. If the "Spaniards" had meant to refer to a plump woman, they probably would have said *mujer gorda* or, more politely, *gordita*. So it seems unlikely that the "Spaniards" were simply looking for a rotund person. All of this suggests that it is possible that the "Spaniard who had a large woman" was a man who lived with an ambiguously gendered person who to some seemed a "hermaphrodite" and to others a "large woman," or *mujer grande*. What is strikingly similar about the evidence from 1852 and 1855 is that both Doten's "hermaphrodite" and Gómez's "large woman" were well known along the Mokelumne River and sought out by visitors—perhaps s/he was something of a spectacle in a social world filled with gender trouble. See Inquest, Eben N. Brooks (1855), Inquest Records, Calaveras County, Calaveras County Museum and Archives, San Andreas, Calif. I am grateful to Camille Guerin-Gonzales for helping me analyze this evidence.

76. See Judith Butler's reading of Michel Foucault, ed., *Herculine Barbin, Being the Recently Discovered Memoirs of a Nineteenth Century Hermaphrodite*, trans. Richard McDongall (New York: Colophone, 1980), in *Gender Trouble: Feminism and the Subversion of Identity* (New York: Routledge, 1990), 93–106. On women who passed as men in this period, see San Francisco Lesbian and Gay History Project, "'She Even Chewed Tobacco': A Pictorial Narrative of Passing Women in America," in *Hidden from History: Reclaiming the Gay and Lesbian Past*, ed. Martin Duberman, Martha Vicinus, and George Chauncey, Jr. (New York: Meridian/Penguin, 1989), 182–94; and the chapter entitled "Passing Women: 1782–1920," in *Gay American History: Lesbians and Gay Men in the U.S.A.*, ed. Jonathan Ned Katz (New York: Thomas E. Crowell, 1976), 209–79. On cross-dressing men, see, e.g., Gilfoyle, 135–38; and, for the late nineteenth century, George Chauncey, *Gay New York: Gender, Urban Culture, and the Making of the Gay Male World, 1890–1940* (New York: Basic Books, 1994), 33–45.

77. Journal entries, Dec. 19, 25, 1849, William Miller Journal, Beinecke Library. "The tallest kind of dancing" is Alfred Doten's phrase: Doten, 1:192.

78. Doten, 1:122, 167–68.

79. Derbec notes that even in San Francisco some dance halls were frequented only by men (p. 168).

80. Borthwick, 303–4; Harris, 140. Leonard Noyes also confirms the use of flour sacks for patches. See Leonard Withington Noyes Reminiscences, Essex Institute, Salem, Mass., transcription at Calaveras County Museum and Archives, San Andreas, Calif., 54. Hinton Rowan Helper discusses Haxall flour in *The Land of Gold: Reality versus Fiction* (Baltimore: Henry Taylor, 1855), 78–79.

81. Despite the recent profusion of scholarship on same-sex eroticism, the study of nineteenth-century sexual interactions between men is still in its early stages. In the late 1980s, the historians John D'Emilio and Estelle Freedman provided a useful overview of the boundaries and meanings of same-sex intimacy, spelling out the myriad evidentiary and interpretive problems in studying a phenomenon that did not become intelligible as a cultural category of "inversion" or "homosexuality" until decades later. More recently, Jonathan Ned Katz has begun to explore "the abundance of nineteenth-century American terms for men's affectional and sexual relations with men," which suggest "the possibility of an equally large, unmapped variety of relationships." See John D'Emilio and Estelle B. Freedman, *Intimate Matters: A History of Sexuality in America*, 2d ed. (1988; Chicago: Univ. of Chicago Press, 1997), 121–30; Jonathan Ned Katz, "Coming to Terms: Conceptualizing Men's Erotic and Affectional Relations with Men in the United States, 1820–1892," in *A Queer World: The Center for Lesbian and Gay Studies Reader*, ed. Martin Duberman (New York: New York Univ. Press, 1997), 216–35, esp. 231.

82. Katz, "Coming to Terms," 219. The term comes from the diaries of the sailor Philip Van Buskirk, quoted and analyzed in B. R. Burg, *An American Seafarer in the Age of Sail: The Erotic Diaries of Philip C. Van Buskirk, 1851–1870* (New Haven: Yale Univ. Press, 1994), esp. 75.

83. D'Emilio and Freedman, 123.

84. *Hanna Allkin v. Jeremiah Allkin* (1856), Calaveras County, District Court, Calaveras County Museum and Archives, San Andreas, Calif.

85. Doten, 1:68–69, 108, 109, 110, 173, 174. Similar references appear in diary entries on 75, 103, 127, 205, 213. For Whitman's language, see D'Emilio and Freedman, 123.

86. Cf. John Mack Faragher, *Sugar Creek: Life on the Illinois Prairie* (New Haven: Yale Univ. Press, 1986), 153–54; Martin Duberman, "'Writhing Bedfellows' in Antebellum South Carolina: Historical Interpretation and the Politics of Evidence," in Duberman et al., eds., 153–68; and E. Anthony Rotundo, "Romantic Friendship: Male Intimacy and Middle-Class Youth in the Northern United States, 1800–1900," *Journal of*

Social History 23, no. 1 (1989): 1–25, and *American Manhood,* esp. 84–85.

87. On such practices in northern Mexico, see Oakah L. Jones, Jr., *Los Paisanos: Spanish Settlers on the Northern Frontier of New Spain* (Norman: Univ. of Oklahoma Press, 1979), esp. 32, 61, 75, 106, 251. I am grateful to María Teresa Koreck for conversations on these matters.

88. See chap. 4, "Mining Gold and Making War."

89. Antonio Franco Coronel, "Cosas de California," trans. and ed. Richard Henry Morefield, in *The Mexican Adaptation in American California, 1846–1875* (1955; reprint, San Francisco: R and E Research Associates, 1971), 76–96, esp. 79–80, 88–89.

90. See Ann Vincent Fabian, "Rascals and Gentlemen: The Meaning of American Gambling, 1820–1890" (Ph.D. diss., Yale Univ., 1982), 53–59, and, more generally, Fabian, *Card Sharps.*

91. My thanks to William Cronon for helping me clarify this argument.

92. Noyes, 57. On the Murrieta family, see prologue, "Joaquín Murietta and the Bandits."

93. Noyes, 53–57.

94. Doten, 1:98–104.

95. Ibid., 1:88; Noyes, 51; Christman, 199–200; Journal entry, Nov. 7, 1852, Fox Journals.

96. Borthwick, 276–85, 336–37; Perkins, 273–77; Helper, 116–30, esp. 124; Frank Marryat, *Mountains and Molehills; or Recollections of a Burnt Journal,* ed. Robin Winks (1855; Philadelphia: J. B. Lippincott, 1962), 131; Noyes, 51; Christman, 199–200; Journal entry, Nov. 7, 1852; Fox Journals. A key difference between Clifford Geertz's Balinese cockfight, on the one hand, and California bull and bull-and-bear fights, on the other, was women's participation in the latter and the liminality that participation signaled in the realm of Gold Rush gender relations. See Geertz, "Deep Play: Notes on the Balinese Cockfight," in *The Interpretation of Cultures* (New York: Basic Books, 1973), 412–53, esp. 417–18, n. 4.

97. Borthwick, 276–83.

98. Ibid.; Marryat, 131.

99. For an overview, see Lisbeth Haas, "War in California, 1846–1848," in Special Issue: Contested Eden: California before the Gold Rush, *California History* 76, nos. 2 and 3 (Summer and Fall 1997): 331–55.

Chapter 4: Mining Gold and Making War

1. California Gold Rush scholarship includes Charles Howard Shinn, *Mining Camps: A Study in American Frontier Government,* ed. Rodman W. Paul (1884; reprint, Gloucester, Mass.: Peter Smith, 1970); Josiah Royce, *California, from the Conquest in 1846 to the Second Vigilance Committee in San Francisco: A Study in American Character* (1886; reprint, Santa Barbara, Calif.: Peregrine, 1970); Rodman W. Paul,

California Gold: The Beginning of Mining in the Far West (1947; reprint, Lincoln: Univ. of Nebraska Press, 1965); John Walton Caughey, *The California Gold Rush* (originally titled *Gold Is the Cornerstone*) (1948; reprint, Berkeley: Univ. of California Press, 1975); Ralph Mann, *After the Gold Rush: Society in Grass Valley and Nevada City, California, 1849–1870* (Stanford: Stanford Univ. Press, 1982); David Goodman, *Gold Seeking: Victoria and California in the 1850s* (Stanford: Stanford Univ. Press, 1994); and Malcolm J. Rohrbough, *Days of Gold: The California Gold Rush and the American Nation* (Berkeley: Univ. of California Press, 1997). Of the older works, only Royce's is concerned with what late twentieth-century historians would consider issues of social context and cultural meaning. All of the more recent works—those of Mann, Goodman, and Rohrbough—to varying degrees address such issues, and I have been guided by their approaches. My own approach centers issues of gender and race differently and sees the Gold Rush as a global as well as a national event.

2. The best account of these matters is found in Paul, 50–68, 91–123. On later economic development and class formation in the Southern Mines, see chap. 5, "Dreams That Died."

3. See Eric Foner, *Free Soil, Free Labor, Free Men: The Ideology of the Republican Party before the Civil War* (New York: Oxford Univ. Press, 1970), esp. 11–75, quotation on 17.

4. Cf. Tomás Almaguer, *Racial Fault Lines: The Historical Origins of White Supremacy in California* (Berkeley: Univ. of California Press, 1994).

5. Discussion based on Rudolph M. Lapp, *Blacks in Gold Rush California* (New Haven: Yale Univ. Press, 1977), esp. 126–57. See also Eugene H. Berwanger, *The Frontier against Slavery: Western Anti-Negro Prejudice and the Slavery Extension Controversy* (Urbana: Univ. of Illinois Press, 1967), 60–77.

6. Robert Givens to Father, Sept. 10, 1852, Robert Givens Letters, Bancroft Library, Univ. of California, Berkeley (hereafter cited as Bancroft Library), quoted in Lapp, 131, and see 293, n. 11.

7. Journal entry, Aug. 23, 1850, Timothy C. Osborn Journal, Bancroft Library.

8. Letter to Wife, May 20, 1853, Charles Davis Letters, Beinecke Library, Yale Univ., New Haven (hereafter cited as Beinecke Library). Cf. Letter to Wife, Jan. 6, 1853.

9. On southern trails, see Ralph Bieber, ed., *Southern Trails to California in 1849* (Glendale, Calif.: Arthur H. Clark, 1937), 17–62; Benjamin Butler Harris, *The Gila Trail: The Texas Argonauts and the California Gold Rush*, ed. Richard H. Dillon (Norman: Univ. of Oklahoma Press, 1960); and George W. B. Evans, *Mexican Gold Trail: The Journal of a Forty-Niner*, ed. Glenn S. Dumke (San Marino, Calif.: Huntington Library, 1945).

10. U.S. Bureau of the Census, *The Seventh Census of the United States: 1850* (Washington, D.C., 1853); and U.S. Bureau of the Census, Seventh Federal Population Census, 1850, National Archives, Washington, D.C., RG-29, M-432, reels 33–35, esp. reel 33 (Mariposa County).

11. Lapp, 126–57.
12. See Bill of Sale, dated Aug. 17, 1852, folder 1, and Tuolumne County Tax Receipts, 1857–1907, folder 13, in Thomas Gilman Collection, box 353, California State Library, Sacramento; and "Documents: California Freedom Papers," *Journal of Negro History* 3, no. 1 (Jan. 1918): 45–51, esp. 48–49. On the "Sunday claims," see Leonard Withington Noyes Reminiscences, Essex Institute, Salem, Mass., transcription at Calaveras County Museum and Archives, San Andreas, Calif., esp. 44.
13. The following account is derived from Carlo M. De Ferrari, "A Brief History of Stephen Spencer Hill: Fugitive from Labor," appended to John Jolly, *Gold Spring Diary: The Journal of John Jolly*, ed. De Ferrari (Sonora, Calif.: Tuolumne County Historical Society, 1966), 125–42. De · Ferrari's account is based on thorough research in local court records, newspaper articles, and family reminiscences. Stephen Spencer Hill and his master Wood Tucker are introduced in chap. 1, "On the Eve of Emigration."
14. Jolly, 66.
15. *San Joaquin Republican* (Stockton), Sept. 25, 1854, quoted in De Ferrari, "A Brief History," 138.
16. James Williams, *Life and Adventures of James Williams, a Fugitive Slave, with a Full Description of the Underground Railroad*, 3d ed. (San Francisco: Women's Union Print, 1874; reprint, San Francisco: R and E Research Associates, 1969), 34.
17. Journal entries, Oct. 13, 20, 22, 1849, William W. Miller Diary, Beinecke Library.
18. Charles Davis to Wife, Jan. 6, 1853, Davis Letters.
19. See Foner, 261–300, esp. 266.
20. Leonard Pitt, *The Decline of the Californios: A Social History of the Spanish-Speaking Californians, 1846–1890* (Berkeley: Univ. of California Press, 1966), esp. 57.
21. Theodore T. Johnson, *Sights in the Gold Region and Scenes by the Way* (New York: Baker and Scribner, 1849), 196.
22. *Alta California* (San Francisco), July 26, 1849.
23. Howard Lamar, "From Bondage to Contract: Ethnic Labor in the American West, 1600–1890," in *The Countryside in the Age of Capitalist Transformation*, ed. Steven Hahn and Jonathan Prude (Chapel Hill: Univ. of North Carolina Press, 1985), 293–324, esp. 31.
24. Cf. Almaguer, esp. 12–13, 32–37.
25. See Antonio Franco Coronel, "Cosas de California," trans. and ed. Richard Henry Morefield, in *The Mexican Adaptation in American California, 1846–1875* (1955; reprint, San Francisco: R and E Research Associates, 1971), 76–96, esp. 86.
26. Coronel claimed to have raised Augustin as a family member, though the young man's muteness may have been a marker of the childhood dislocation from his land and people (pp. 77–78). On *genízaros*, see

Ramón A. Gutiérrez, *When Jesus Came, the Corn Mothers Went Away: Marriage, Sexuality, and Power in New Mexico, 1500–1846* (Stanford: Stanford Univ. Press, 1991), esp. 149–56, 171–90. The work of Estevan Rael y Galvez (American Culture Program, Univ. of Michigan) also has helped me see Augustin's status.

27. Coronel, 86–87.
28. Ibid., 87.
29. See, e.g., Pitt, 54–55; William Robert Kenny, "Mexican-American Conflict on the Mining Frontier, 1848–1852," *Journal of the West* 6, no. 4 (Oct. 1967): 582–92, esp. 586.
30. Journal entry, June 22, 1850, Osborn Journal; cf. June 29, 1850.
31. Journal entries, June 27, Aug. 31, Dec. 20, 1850, ibid.
32. Daniel B. Woods, *Sixteen Months at the Gold Diggings* (London: Sampson Low; New York: Harper and Brothers, [1851]), 100.
33. I am deeply indebted to David Montgomery for helping me clarify this argument.
34. See *Alta California*, Dec. 31, 1849, Jan. 2, 7, 1850; Journal entries, Dec. 28, 1849, to Jan. 4, 1850, John Hovey Journal, Huntington Library, San Marino, Calif. (hereafter cited as Huntington Library), and Hovey's "Historical Account of the troubles between the Chilian and American Miners in the Calaveras Mining District, commencing Dec. 6, 1849, & ending Jan. 4, 1850," Huntington Library; Ramon Jil Navarro, "California in 1849," in *We Were 49ers! Chilean Accounts of the California Gold Rush,* trans. and ed. Edwin A. Beilharz and Carlos U. López (Pasadena: Ward Ritchie Press, 1976), 101–49; and James J. Ayres, *Gold and Sunshine: Reminiscences of Early California* (Boston: Richard G. Badger, Gorham Press, 1922), 46–63. On the Chilean War, see also Jay Monaghan, *Chile, Peru, and the California Gold Rush of 1849* (Berkeley: Univ. of California Press, 1973), esp. 243–48; and George Edward Faugsted, Jr., *The Chilenos in the California Gold Rush* (1963; reprint, San Francisco: R and E Research Associates, 1973), esp. 37–38. Neither Monaghan nor Faugsted used the Navarro account, which was not available in English translation until 1976.
35. *Alta California*, Dec. 31, 1849.
36. Ibid., Jan. 2, 1850.
37. Ibid., Jan. 7, 1850.
38. Journal entries, Dec. 28, 1849, to Jan. 4, 1850, Hovey Journal (quotation in Jan. 3 entry), and esp. Hovey, "Historical Account of the troubles between the Chilian & American Miners."
39. Navarro, 103–4.
40. Ibid., 111–15.
41. Ibid., 116–21.
42. Ibid., 122–26.
43. Ibid., 127–30.
44. Ibid., 130–33.
45. Ibid., 134–42.

46. Ibid., 143–49.

47. Ibid., 137–38, 145.

48. Ayres, 44–46.

49. Ibid., 46–48.

50. Ibid., 48–50.

51. Ibid., 50–53.

52. Ibid., 53–54.

53. Ibid., 54–57.

54. Ibid., 57–58.

55. On the importance of such frontier tales in the 1890s, see, e.g., Richard White, "Frederick Jackson Turner and Buffalo Bill," in *The Frontier in American Culture*, ed. James R. Grossman (Chicago: Newberry Library; Berkeley: Univ. of California Press, 1994), 6–55; and Susan Lee Johnson, "'A Memory Sweet to Soldiers': The Significance of Gender in the History of the 'American West,'" *Western Historical Quarterly* 24, no. 4 (Nov. 1993): 495–517, esp. 497–98 (reprinted in *A New Significance: Re-envisioning the History of the American West*, ed. Clyde Milner II [New York: Oxford Univ. Press, 1996]). On the meanings of "civilization" at the turn of the twentieth century, see Gail Bederman, *Manliness and Civilization: A Cultural History of Gender and Race in the United States, 1880–1917* (Chicago: Univ. of Chicago Press, 1995).

56. Ayres, 59–60.

57. Ibid., 60–63.

58. See Nina Silber, *The Romance of Reunion: Northerners and the South, 1865–1900* (Chapel Hill: Univ. of North Carolina Press, 1993).

59. Jay Monaghan provides an anticommunist reading of Neruda's success with the Murrieta opera, 217–18. I am grateful to Susan Larsen (Department of Literature, Univ. of California, San Diego) for telling me about the Moscow performance of a musical play based on Neruda's opera in the winter of 1988 under the title "Zvezda i smert' Khoakina Mur'ety, chilijskogo razboijnika, podlo ubitogo v Kalifornii 23 iulja 1853 goda" [The star and death of Joaquín Murieta, a Chilean bandit foully murdered in California on 23 July 1853]. Larsen writes, "This production premiered in 1983 in the Lenin Komsomol Theater under the direction of Mark Zakharov. The 'star' of the title refers to Joaquin's love interest, Teresa, who, as I recall, is gang-raped by a bunch of Rangers . . . dressed in checkered cowboy shirts. . . . The play is sort of a schlocky rock musical and, according to the program, uses slides of engravings of the Mexican artist Posada and documentary photos from the Soviet Committee of Solidarity with Chilean Democrats. The theater is one of the main Moscow theaters and in the 80's was considered one of the more liberal and progressive stages in the country." Personal communication, Oct. 19, 1992.

60. I first saw a slightly different translation of lines from this *"Cancion Masculina"* in Monaghan, 217. This particular song does not appear in the standard English translation, which is based on a later version of

the opera. The translator Ben Belitt says this later version was "the text finally preferred by the poet himself." See Pablo Neruda, *The Splendor and Death of Joaquin Murieta,* trans. Belitt (New York: Farrar, Straus and Giroux, 1972), 181–82. My thanks to Camille Guerin-Gonzales for helping me find the original version in Neruda, *Fulgor y muerte de Joaquín Murieta* (Santiago: Empresa Editoria Zig-Zag, 1966), 78, and for helping me think about the translation.

61. Samuel McNeil, *McNeil's Travels in 1849 to, through, and from the Gold Regions, in California* (Columbus, Ohio: Scott and Bascom, 1850), 3. On the middle-class project, see, e.g., Mary P. Ryan, *Cradle of the Middle Class: The Family in Oneida County, New York, 1790–1865* (Cambridge: Cambridge Univ. Press, 1981); and, in the English context, Leonore Davidoff and Catherine Hall, *Family Fortunes: Men and Women of the English Middle Class, 1780–1850* (Chicago: Univ. of Chicago Press, 1987).

62. "Proceedings of a Meeting of the People of Lower Mocalime Bar, Oct. 14, 1849," Amador County Archives, Jackson, Calif.

63. Woods, 115. Alfred Doten records the same expulsion in *The Journals of Alfred Doten, 1849–1903,* 3 vols., ed. Walter Van Tilburg Clark (Reno: Univ. of Nevada Press, 1973), 1:65–66.

64. William Shaw, *Golden Dreams and Waking Realities; Being the Adventures of a Gold-Seeker in California and the Pacific Islands* (London: Smith Elder, 1851), esp. 56, 64, 86–87.

65. Ibid., 87–88.

66. Secondary accounts of the imposition of the foreign miners' tax include Pitt, *Decline of the Californios,* 60–68, and "The Beginnings of Nativism in California," *Pacific Historical Review* 30, no. 1 (Feb. 1961): 23–38; Richard H. Peterson, *Manifest Destiny in the Mines: A Cultural Interpretation of Anti-Mexican Nativism in California, 1848–1853* (San Francisco: R and E Research Associates, 1975), 48–59, "The Foreign Miners' Tax of 1850 and Mexicans in California: Exploitation or Expulsion?" *Pacific Historian* 20, no. 3 (Fall 1976): 265–72, and "Anti-Mexican Nativism in California, 1848–1853: A Study in Cultural Conflict," *Southern California Quarterly* 62, no. 4 (Winter 1980): 309–27; William Robert Kenny, "Mexican-American Conflict on the Mining Frontier, 1848–1852," *Journal of the West* 6, no. 4 (Oct. 1967): 582–92, and "Nativism in the Southern Mining Region of California," *Journal of the West* 12, no. 1 (Jan. 1973): 126–38.

67. Antoine Alphonse Délèpine to Father, Aug. 20, 1850, Délèpine Papers, California State Library, Sacramento (hereafter cited as California State Library), from a typescript translation by C. R. Délèpine.

68. See Friedrich W. C. Gerstäcker, "The French Revolution," trans. George Cosgrave, *California Historical Society Quarterly* 17, no. 1 (March 1938): 3–17. Cosgrave's translation is from Gerstäcker's *Scènes de la vie californienne* (Geneva, 1859), which is itself a translation of his *Californische*

Skizzen (Leipzig, 1856). See also Gerstäcker, *Narrative of a Journey round the World* (New York: Harper and Brothers, 1853), esp. 209.

69. Jamestown, as well as Columbia, was called American Camp, but these events seem to have taken place in or near the settlement that would become Columbia. See "Introduction" in William Perkins, *Three Years in California: William Perkins' Journal of Life at Sonora, 1849–1852*, ed. Dale L. Morgan and James R. Scobie (Berkeley: Univ. of California Press, 1964), 19, n. 10, 39–40; Erwin G. Gudde, *California Gold Camps*, ed. Elisabeth K. Gudde (Berkeley: Univ. of California Press, 1975), 78–80.

70. *Stockton Times*, May 25, June 1, 1850; Gerstäcker, "The French Revolution," esp. 4–5.

71. On William Perkins as "Leo," see "Appendix" in Perkins, 395–405.

72. *Stockton Times*, May 25, June 1, 1850; Perkins, 153–56; Gerstäcker, "The French Revolution," 4–5.

73. *Stockton Times*, May 25, 1850.

74. Ibid., May 25, June 1, 1850; Harris, 132; and Perkins, 153–56, 251; cf. the account apparently published in the *Sonora Herald* in 1852 (copies of the *Sonora Herald* are no longer extant) and reprinted in J. Heckendorn and W. A. Wilson, *Miners and Business Men's Directory for the Year Commencing January 1st, 1856. Embracing a General Directory of the Citizens of Tuolumne . . . Together with the Mining Laws of Each District, a Description of the Different Camps, and Other Interesting Statistical Matter* (Columbia, Calif.: Clipper Office, 1856), 38–40.

75. *Stockton Times*, May 25, 1850; Harris, 133.

76. *Stockton Times*, May 25, June 1, 1850; Harris, 133; Perkins, 155; Heckendorn and Wilson, 39.

77. Gerstäcker, "The French Revolution," 4–10.

78. Ibid., 14–15.

79. Ibid., 12.

80. *Stockton Times*, May 25, June 1, 1850; Heckendorn and Wilson, 39.

81. *Stockton Times*, June 1, 1850.

82. See chap. 5, "Dreams That Died."

83. *Stockton Times*, Aug. 10, 1850, March 15, 1851.

84. Heckendorn and Wilson, 40; *Stockton Times*, July 20, 1850.

85. *Stockton Times*, July 20, 1850.

86. Woods, 140–42.

87. *Stockton Times*, June–July 1850, passim.

88. Ibid., July 27, 1850; Heckendorn and Wilson, 42–43. Other accounts of the attempted expulsion of "foreigners" from Tuolumne County, and from Sonora in particular, include Enos Christman, *One Man's Gold: The Letters and Journals of a Forty-Niner*, ed. Florence Morrow Christman (New York: Whittlesey House, McGraw-Hill, 1930), 171–78; and Edmund Booth, *Edmund Booth, Forty-Niner: The Life Story of a Deaf Pioneer* (Stockton, Calif.: San Joaquin Pioneer and Historical

Society, 1953), 27. A few days after reporting on the meeting at Sonora, the *Stockton Times* noted with pleasure that "the inhabitants of George Town" had taken an "opposite position to the adjacent town of Sonora," having passed resolutions stating "That all men shall have permission to live in this Camp without being molested." *Stockton Times*, Aug. 3, 1850.

89. Harris, 132; Heckendorn and Wilson, 43 (emphasis in original).

90. John Baker to Julia Ann Baker, Sept. 20, Nov. 8, 1853, John W. H. Baker Correspondence, Holt-Atherton Center for Western Studies, Univ. of the Pacific, Stockton, Calif.; Eduard Vischer, "A Trip to the Mining Regions in the Spring of 1859," part 2, trans. Ruth Frey Axe, *California Historical Society Quarterly* 11, no. 4 (Dec. 1932): 321–38, esp. 322–23; Journal entry, May 23, 1857, Harriet Jane (Kirtland) Lee, "Journal of a Trip Through the Southern Mines" [1857], California State Library (typescript from original); [Henry S. Brooks], "Hornitos, Quartzburgh and the Washington Vein, Mariposa County," *California Mountaineer* 1 (1861): 335, quoted in Paul, 112. As early as 1851, the Belgian Jean-Nicolas Perlot found Hornitos a very diverse place. Business was conducted in both English and Spanish, and in the street "all possible tongues" were spoken. Perlot saw native people there as well. See Perlot, *Gold Seeker: Adventures of a Belgian Argonaut during the Gold Rush Years*, ed. Howard R. Lamar and trans. Helen Harding Bretnor (New Haven: Yale Univ. Press, 1985), 95.

91. *Stockton Times*, esp. June–July 1850, passim.

92. Account of Expenditures for 1851, Tuolumne County Sheriff George Work, PW 1029, Joseph Pownall Collection, Huntington Library.

93. For reports on Sonora's vigilance committee in the summer of 1851, see *San Joaquin Republican* (the *Stockton Times* became the *San Joaquin Republican* in May 1851) and *Alta California,* June–July 1851, passim, and esp. *San Joaquin Republican,* July 16, 1851; Heckendorn and Wilson, 44; Perkins, 224–42; and Christman, 189–98, quotation on 197.

94. See prologue, "Joaquín Murrieta and the Bandits."

95. Coronel, 77.

96. Ibid., 77–78.

97. Ibid., 78–82.

98. See James J. Rawls, "Gold Diggers: Indian Miners in the California Gold Rush," *California Historical Quarterly* 55, no. 1 (Spring 1976): 28–45, esp. 32, and *Indians of California: The Changing Image* (Norman: Univ. of Oklahoma Press, 1984), 115–33, esp. 121–22. Albert L. Hurtado contends that Weber's employees were Miwok, not Yokuts. Given that white observers tended to identify Indians by band location or name of a presumed chief, it is often difficult to tell from contemporary sources which Indians were present in a given situation. The restructuring of native communities that accompanied missionization, secularization, and widespread disease complicates identification further.

See Hurtado, *Indian Survival on the California Frontier* (New Haven: Yale Univ. Press, 1988), 112.

99. Noyes, 45. On the locations of the Murphy brothers' camps, see Gudde, 132–33.

100. Étienne Derbec, *A French Journalist in the California Gold Rush: The Letters of Étienne Derbec,* ed. Abraham P. Nasatir (Georgetown, Calif.: Talisman Press, 1964), 148.

101. See Rawls, "Gold Diggers," 37, and *Indians of California,* 124–25; Hurtado, 112–14; and Annie R. Mitchell, "Major James D. Savage and the Tulareños," *California Historical Society Quarterly* 28, no. 4 (Dec. 1949): 323–41.

102. Woods, 83; Lafayette Houghton Bunnell, *Discovery of the Yosemite and the Indian War of 1851 Which Led to That Event* (1880; Yosemite National Park, Calif.: Yosemite Association, 1990), 243; *Stockton Times,* Jan. 1, 1851.

103. For background, see chap. 1, "On the Eve of Emigration."

104. Journal entries, Aug. 10, Sept. 17, Oct. 4, 1850, Osborn Journal; Gerstäcker, *Narrative,* 218.

105. Samuel Ward, *Sam Ward in the Gold Rush,* ed. Carvel Collins (Stanford: Stanford Univ. Press, 1949). Ward is introduced in chap. 2, "Domestic Life in the Diggings." As noted, Julia Ward Howe was a participant in the nineteenth-century woman movement and author of the "Battle Hymn of the Republic." Brother Sam was married for a time to Emily Astor, the granddaughter of the fur trade capitalist John Jacob Astor, but she had since died in childbirth. At the time of the Gold Rush, Sam Ward was unhappily remarried and had lost his family's banking fortune. See "Introduction" in Ward, 3–16.

106. Ward, esp. 23–25. For more on Ward among the Indians, see George Harwood Phillips, *Indians and Indian Agents: The Origins of the Reservation System in California, 1849–1852* (Norman: Univ. of Oklahoma Press, 1997), 111–17, 127–31; and my discussion below.

107. Ephraim Delano to Wife, April 2, 1851, Ephraim Delano Letters, Beinecke Library; Perlot, 218.

108. Perlot, 218–19.

109. J. D. Borthwick, *The Gold Hunters* (1857; Oyster Bay, N.Y.: Nelson Doubleday, 1917), 275. On the pre–Gold Rush history of Sierra Miwoks, see chap. 1, "On the Eve of Emigration."

110. Woods, 86; Evans, 219–22; and see Bunnell, esp. 243.

111. Doten, 1:67.

112. Journal entry, March 8, 1850, Miller Journal.

113. *Stockton Times,* Jan. 8, 29, 1851.

114. Derbec, 23; Gilbert Chinard, "When the French Came to California: An Introductory Essay," *California Historical Society Quarterly* 22, no. 4 (Dec. 1943): 289–314, esp. 312; Abraham P. Nasatir, trans. and ed., "Alexandre Dumas fils and the Lottery of the Golden Ingots," *California Historical Society Quarterly* 33, no. 2 (June 1954): 125–42,

esp. 128; Lucius Fairchild, *California Letters of Lucius Fairchild*, ed. Joseph Schafer (Madison: State Historical Society of Wisconsin, 1931), 99–100. For the skirmish in which Indians participated, see Hovey, "Account of the troubles between the American Miners and the Frenchmen." For the newspaper quotations, see *Stockton Times*, Jan. 1, 1851.

115. *Stockton Times*, Jan. 8, 29, 1851.
116. Noyes, 39.
117. Ibid., 39–40.
118. Hurtado, 114; Mitchell, 325–27; Phillips, 37–56; Harris, 147–48; *Stockton Times*, Jan. 1, 4, 22, 1851; Robert Eccleston, *The Mariposa Indian War, 1850–1851: Diaries of Robert Eccleston: The California Gold Rush, Yosemite, and the High Sierra*, ed. C. Gregory Crampton (Salt Lake City: Univ. of Utah Press, 1957), iii–iv, 15–26, 131–41; and Bunnell, esp. 1–16.
119. The other personal narrative of these events is Lafayette Houghton Bunnell's reminiscence (cited above), first published in 1880.
120. Eccleston, 25–111 passim; *Stockton Times*, Jan. 29, 1851; cf. Bunnell, passim.
121. Eccleston, e.g., 15, 49, 67–68, 69–70, 86; cf. Bunnell, 74–76. On the Yosemites, see Phillips, 37–38.
122. Eccleston, 48, 64; and Bunnell, 49.
123. Harris, 148; Eccleston, 79, n. 15; Hurtado, 136; Francis Paul Prucha, *The Great Father: The United States Government and the American Indians* (1984; abridged ed., Lincoln: Univ. of Nebraska Press, 1986), 130–31.
124. Eccleston, 28–29; Hurtado, 136; Prucha, 130–31.
125. Hurtado, 114–15, 136–37; Prucha, 130–31; Perlot, 124–25; Mitchell, 327–34; Phillips, 132–54.
126. Hurtado, 115–16; Mitchell, 334–49; Phillips, 144–50. On Murrieta, see Prologue, "Joaquín Murrieta and the Bandits."
127. Hurtado, 153–57.
128. Ward, 19–49, quotations on 31, 46–47; Phillips, 111–17. On the Ward family, see "Introduction" in Ward, 3–16.
129. Ward, 44–45, 53, 55–64, quotations on 53, 55, 62–63.
130. Ibid., 125, 126–27, 136–40, 161–63. It is the historian Albert Hurtado who has made the most convincing arguments about Indian survival in California; see *Indian Survival on the California Frontier*.
131. Perlot, esp. 161, 165–66.
132. Ibid., 169–70.
133. Ibid., 181–235, quotation on 224. For more on this interaction, see chap. 1, "On the Eve of Emigration."
134. Indeed, writing his reminiscences many years later in his native Belgium, Perlot waxed romantic about the Miwok people he had once known, wondering what had became of them: "It could be that today . . . they dress, live, speak, and think like us: they would then have succeeded in becoming civilized, or rather would have exchanged

their civilization for ours. If that is the case, alas! what have they gained?" See Perlot, 235.

Chapter 5: Dreams That Died

1. *San Joaquin Republican* (Stockton), Sept. 25, 1852. The identity of this correspondent is unknown, but internal evidence suggests that it was an Anglo American man.

2. *The Golden Era* (San Francisco), Sept. 17, 1854. For background on Lorena Hays, see the editor's summaries in *To the Land of Gold and Wickedness: The 1848–59 Diary of Lorena L. Hays,* ed. Jeanne Hamilton Watson (St. Louis: Patrice Press, 1988), 1–14, 198–229.

3. *The Golden Era,* Sept. 17, 1854; Hays, 261.

4. Chap. 4, "Mining Gold and Making War," details these conflicts, each of which has been named rather extravagantly as a "war" or "revolution" by participants or later chroniclers. I use these exaggerated terms as a shorthand to identify what were actually more limited and localized conflicts. Only the event known as the Mariposa War came close in scale to living up to its sobriquet.

5. U.S. Bureau of the Census, *Population of the United States in 1860; Compiled from . . . the Eighth Census* (Washington, D.C., 1864) (hereafter cited as *1860 Census*).

6. The impact of the arrival of aspiring middle-class white women in the Southern Mines is detailed in chap. 6, "The Last Fandango."

7. For average daily yields, see Rodman W. Paul, *California Gold: The Beginning of Mining in the Far West* (1947; reprint, Lincoln: Univ. of Nebraska Press, 1965), 116–23, 349–52. Interestingly, Paul notes that his estimates "do not apply to the Chinese" (p. 349). For quotations, see A. W. Genung to Friend Thomas, April 22, 1851, A. W. Genung Correspondence, Beinecke Library, Yale Univ., New Haven (hereafter cited as Beinecke Library); *San Joaquin Republican,* Feb. 2, 1853. Genung did not say whether his estimates for the yields of the first and second diggings were for an individual or a team of miners.

8. A good account of the hope California represented for emigrating Chinese appears in Ronald T. Takaki, *Strangers from a Different Shore: A History of Asian Americans* (Boston: Little, Brown, 1989), 31–42. For the quotations, see *San Joaquin Republican,* Dec. 10, 1858 (reprinted from the *Jackson Sentinel*), June 26, 1854 (reprinted from the *Mariposa Chronicle*), and Dec. 21, 1856 (reprinted from Mokelumne Hill's *Calaveras Chronicle*). As for use of the name John, Chinese men returned the favor. One 1850s pictorial lettersheet (illustrated stationery used for letters sent home) depicts a group of Chinese miners passing a white man on a trail, and the text reads, "Strings of Chinamen pass, and greet you in broken English with 'how you do, John?'—we are all *Johns* to them, and they to us" (see illustration p. 304). California Lettersheet Facsimiles, Huntington Library, San Marino, Calif. (hereafter cited as

Huntington Library). This mutual name-calling, of course, was not reciprocal in meaning, since Chinese were greeting Anglos with a name common among Anglos, while Anglos were addressing Chinese with a foreign sobriquet.

9. Journal entries, Dec. 11, 26, 27, 1850, Dec. 16, 1853, Timothy C. Osborn Journal, Bancroft Library, Univ. of California, Berkeley (hereafter cited as Bancroft Library); *San Joaquin Republican,* Oct. 10, 1857 (reprinted from *Mariposa Democrat).* See also Paul, 130; Ping Chiu, *Chinese Labor in California, 1850–1880: An Economic Study* (Madison: State Historical Society of Wisconsin, 1967), 17; and Stephen Williams, *The Chinese in the California Mines, 1848–1860* (1930; San Francisco: R and E Research Associates, 1971), 38–40.

10. According to Makoto Kowta of California State Univ., Chico, Chinese miners, drawing on knowledge of traditional Chinese water-lifting devices, may have contributed significantly to the development of new technology used to remove water from riverbeds. Personal communication, March 12, 1999. An 1858 newspaper article described another use for such pumps: "In the bed of Jackson creek . . . a company of Chinamen . . . have sunk a large hole, and run two tom heads of water into it, for the purpose of washing the pay-dirt at the bottom without raising it out. All the water thus thrown into the hole, besides the considerable quantity which otherwise collects, is thrown out by a pump driven by tread-mill power. Three Chinamen are employed to tread the mill." *San Joaquin Republican,* July 9, 1858 (reprinted from *Jackson Sentinel).*

11. See chap. 4, "Mining Gold and Making War."

12. J. D. Borthwick, *The Gold Hunters* (1857; Oyster Bay, N.Y.: Nelson Doubleday, 1917), 144, 254–55.

13. See, e.g., Mrs. Lee Whipple-Haslam, *Early Days in California: Scenes and Events of the '50s as I Remember Them* (Jamestown, Calif.: Mother Lode Magnet, [1925]), 30.

14. See Chiu, 23–25. In addition to those discussed below, see, e.g., expulsions at Clinton and Agua Frio documented in the *San Joaquin Republican,* Sept. 13, 1854 (from the *Jackson Sentinel),* and April 29, 1856, respectively.

15. Some scholarly works cite an even earlier—1849—expulsion of Chinese from Chinese Camp in Tuolumne County. See, e.g., Chiu, 12. From what I have been able to determine, most rely for this information on an undocumented account published in Theodore H. Hittell, *History of California,* vol. 4 (San Francisco: N. J. Stone, 1898), 102. I have found no contemporary documentation of this event (from newspapers, letters, diaries, or reminiscences), and so have chosen not to consider it here. Hittell's account is of a party of sixty Chinese miners employed by British men (and supervised, interestingly, by Sonorans). There *is* contemporary documentation of British men early on bringing a

smaller party of Chinese under contract to Tuolumne County, but this account has the Chinese miners leaving their British employers of their own volition. See *Stockton Times*, March 23, 1850. Ping Chiu has also found good evidence of instances where British employed Chinese on a contract basis (see pp. 12, 147, n. 10). Nonetheless, I can find no contemporary documentation of such contract laborers' being expelled from the mines in 1849 or 1850.

16. For the Columbia location of the 1850 conflicts, see chap. 5, "Mining Gold and Making War." For Bigler's message, see California Legislature, Journal of the Senate, *Journal of the Third Session of the Legislature of the State of California* (San Francisco, 1852), 373–78.

17. *Daily Alta California*, May 15, 1852. For another mention of this meeting, see *San Joaquin Republican*, May 19, 1852. Similar disturbances took place in the Northern Mines in May 1852. See Ralph Mann, *After the Gold Rush: Society in Grass Valley and Nevada City, California, 1849–1870* (Stanford: Stanford Univ. Press, 1982), 54–56.

18. *Daily Alta California* (San Francisco), May 15, 1852. On the "discovery" of gold at Columbia, see, e.g., J. Heckendorn and W. A. Wilson, *Miners and Business Men's Directory for the Year Commencing January 1st, 1856. Embracing a General Directory of the Citizens of Tuolumne . . . Together with the Mining Laws of Each District, a Description of the Different Camps, and Other Interesting Statistical Matter* (Columbia, Calif.: Clipper Office, 1856), 6; Hero Eugene Rensch, "Columbia, a Gold Camp of Old Tuolumne: Her Rise and Decline, Together with Some Mention of Her Social Life and Cultural Strivings" (Berkeley, 1936, for State of California, Department of Natural Resources, Division of Parks, under auspices of Works Progress Administration), 5–7; and Edna Bryan Buckbee, *The Saga of Old Tuolumne* (New York: Press of the Pioneers, 1935), 90–91.

19. This argument, so far as it concerns the racialization of class in nineteenth-century California, is hardly new. Alexander Saxton advanced it in *The Indispensable Enemy: Labor and the Anti-Chinese Movement in California* (Berkeley: Univ. of California Press, 1971). By now consideration of how class has been constructed in racial terms is de rigueur, though many historians unfamiliar with U.S. western racial politics have conceived of race largely in black/white terms. See, e.g., David R. Roediger, *The Wages of Whiteness: Race and the Making of the American Working Class* (London: Verso, 1991). Alexander Saxton has greatly expanded and usefully updated his arguments in *The Rise and Fall of the White Republic: Class Politics and Mass Culture in Nineteenth-Century America* (London: Verso, 1990). What *is* new about my argument is that it pushes the process Saxton describes (in *Indispensable Enemy*) for the later nineteenth century backward in time, locating white men's antipathy to Chinese workers in a period before either white or Chinese men were employed routinely as wage laborers. More predictably, what

is also new is that my argument sees class formation in gendered as well as racialized terms. Here I follow the lead of feminist scholars such as those represented in Ava Baron, ed., *Work Engendered: Toward a New History of American Labor* (Ithaca: Cornell Univ. Press, 1991).

20. For the measures considered in the state legislature, see California Legislature, Journals of the Senate and Assembly (1852), passim, especially material related to "An Act to enforce contracts and obligations to perform work and labor," "An Act to prevent coolie labor in the mines, and to prevent involuntary servitude," "A Bill to protect the State of California against the introduction of foreigners of bad character," "An Act to prevent foreigners becoming chargeable to the State of California," and "An Act to protect mining interests, and to prevent excessive emigration from Asia to the State of California." Also relevant are "Report of the Committee on Mines and Mining Interests" (appendix, pp. 829–35); "Report of the Committee on the Governor's Special Message, in Relation to Asiatic Emigration" (appendix, pp. 731–37); and "Minority Report of the Select Committee on . . . 'An Act to enforce contracts and obligations to perform work and labor'" (appendix, pp. 669–75). The foreign miners' tax was proposed in the senate as "An Act to provide for the protection of foreigners, and to define their liabilities and privileges." It became law on May 4, 1852.

21. *San Joaquin Republican,* April 21, 1852.

22. There was a sharp decrease in Chinese immigration the year after the foreign miners' tax was imposed (1853), but immigration rates shot back up the following year and remained steady throughout the rest of the 1850s. See Chiu, 142.

23. *San Joaquin Republican,* Feb. 11, June 24, July 6, 1855.

24. George H. Bernhard Reminiscences, Bernhard-Patterson Family File, Mariposa Museum and History Center, Mariposa, Calif. (there are two versions of Bernhard's brief reminiscences in this file; these quotations are from the 1944 version).

25. *San Joaquin Republican,* Aug. 7, 1856.

26. *Alta California* (weekly edition), May 15, 1852.

27. E. Sawtell to James W. Mandeville, Jan. 30, 1853, James Wylie Mandeville Papers, Huntington Library. Mandeville was not only Sawtell's assemblyman but his creditor as well. See letters from Sawtell dated April 5, 1853, and Sept. 18, 1854, and the deed to a mining claim dated April 13, 1853, all in the same collection.

28. Takaki, 82. For a detailed account of the actual revenue received from the foreign miners' tax, see the tables in Chiu, 23, 28, 29.

29. *Daily Alta California,* May 15, 1852; Sucheng Chan, *This Bittersweet Soil: The Chinese in California Agriculture, 1860–1910* (Berkeley: Univ. of California Press, 1986), 25–26; Takaki, 35–36.

30. *San Joaquin Republican,* April 28, 1852.

31. I follow Chiu's lead here and introduce new evidence that further docu-

ments his contentions about the connections between anti-Chinese and anticapitalist agitation. See Chiu, esp. 12–16. Chiu probably overstated white miners' anxiety over the coming of "company mining" in the Southern Mines. Water companies, more than mining companies, were the entrepreneurial venture of choice in the Southern Mines.

32. *Alta California* (steamer edition), May 15, 1852; Rensch, 67–68; *San Joaquin Republican*, Aug. 7, Oct. 6, 1852.

33. Certificate of Incorporation of the Tuolumne County Water Company (TCWC), Sept. 4, 1852, PW 1030, Joseph Pownall Papers, Huntington Library.

34. Two early summaries of water companies in Tuolumne County appeared in the *San Joaquin Republican*, Aug. 7, Oct. 6, 1852, and an updated report appeared Oct. 9, 1855. The Tuolumne County Water Company was the largest venture of its kind in the Southern Mines. Another sizable company was organized in Calaveras County in June of 1852, which came to be known as the Mokelumne Hill Canal and Mining Company. See Paul, 161–62; *San Joaquin Republican*, June 30, 1852, Feb. 24, 1856.

35. *San Joaquin Republican*, March 14, 16 (from the *Columbia Clipper*), 1855; Rensch, 68–77; [Herbert O. Lang], *A History of Tuolumne County. Compiled from the Most Authentic Records.* (San Francisco: B. F. Alley, 1882), 166–67.

36. Within weeks of the meeting, e.g., newspaper subscribers in Sonora, Stockton, and even San Francisco all were reading that "the Tuolumne County Water Company . . . refuse water on anything like reasonable terms." As a result, readers learned, "the miners are almost all provoked and indignant." *Alta California*, Feb. 11, 1853; cf. *San Joaquin Republican*, Feb. 16, 1853 (from the *Sonora Herald*).

37. These anti-Chinese activities are described and analyzed in chap. 6, "The Last Fandango."

38. The following narrative and analysis concentrates on events in Tuolumne County, in part because of the rich documentation available and in part because the TCWC was the most extensive of the water companies established in the Southern Mines. For evidence of a miners' strike against the Mokelumne Hill Canal and Mining Company, see, e.g., *San Joaquin Republican*, Feb. 23, 24, March 5, 9, 1856.

39. TCWC List of Land Transactions, 1852–92; and TCWC List of Reservoir Locations, 1855–56, PW 1170, Pownall Papers, Huntington Library.

40. TCWC Account Book, 1852–53, PW 972; and, e.g., TCWC Payroll for Week Ending Jan. 22, 1853, PW 1081, Pownall Papers, Huntington Library.

41. See, e.g., TCWC Salary Resolutions for Jan. 1, 1858, Feb. 1, 1858, PW 1214 and PW 1215, Pownall Papers, Huntington Library.

42. *San Joaquin Republican*, March 16, 1855.

43. Ibid.

44. John Jolly, *Gold Spring Diary: The Journal of John Jolly, and Including a Brief*

History of Stephen Spencer Hill, Fugitive from Labor, ed. Carlo M. De Ferrari (Sonora, Calif.: Tuolumne County Historical Society, 1966), esp. 81, 87, 102–3, 104. John Jolly, who was British, was one of the allies of Stephen Spencer Hill, the black man who purchased his freedom from his white master Wood Tucker in 1853. When an agent of Tucker's tried to re–enslave Hill and seize his property the following year, Jolly and others rallied on Hill's behalf. Jolly's commitment to "free labor" in the diggings seems to have run deeper than that of most white men. See chap. 4, "Mining Gold and Making War."

45. Petition of Columbia "Traders, Mechanicks and business men" to the TCWC, March 18, 1855, PW 229, Pownall Papers, Huntington Library. An interesting outcome of this alliance between miners, merchants, and the CSRWC was the publication in 1856 of Heckendorn and Wilson, *Miners and Business Men's Directory,* which avoided, so far as possible, mention of the TCWC, while giving wide exposure to the CSRWC. See esp. 6–7, 25, 33.

46. Joseph Pownall to [R. A. Robinson], March 19, 1855, PW 555, and Joseph Pownall, Journal and Letterbook, 1849–54, PW 553, Pownall Papers, Huntington Library. Another TCWC manager who may have been ambivalent about company policies is William Newell, who early on worked as company secretary. Newell left the TCWC in spring 1853, not long after the Columbia miners first protested high water rates. There is no direct evidence that he did so because of the protests. But when the CSRWC formed, Newell's father-in-law (who had been to Columbia and knew the local business and political climate) wrote to his daughter and son-in-law, "I kept expecting to see in the Columbia Papers that William had joined the New Water Company, but I dont see his Name as yet." This suggests that William may have been sympathetic to the miners' demands—and also well qualified for a job with a rival company. See, e.g., William Newell to Mary Newell, April 24, 1853, PW 523, and Benjamin Harrison to Mary and William Newell, Feb. 4, 1855, PW 351, Pownall Papers, Huntington Library. For more on the Newells, see chap. 1, "On the Eve of Emigration," and chap. 6 "The Last Fandango."

47. Joseph Pownall to [R. A. Robinson], March 19, 1855, PW 555, Pownall Papers, Huntington Library. On Coffroth, see, e.g., Buckbee, 83–88.

48. Since Democrats constituted the majority party in the diggings, this crisis was by definition a crisis among Democrats. For scholars interested in this topic, and in its connection to the local politics of water companies, there would be no better place to begin research than in the Mandeville Papers and the Pownall Papers, both at the Huntington Library.

49. Joseph Pownall to [R. A. Robinson], March 19, 1855, PW 555, Pownall Papers, Huntington Library.

50. Minutes of the TCWC Stockholders' Meetings, 1852–1900, PW 975,

Pownall Papers, Huntington Library. The following document Mandeville's role as TCWC stockholder and trustee; all are located in the Mandeville Papers, Huntington Library: Receipt from TCWC to Mandeville, July 17, 1852; Andrew Jay Hatch to Mandeville, March 4, 1853; Hamilton Ellerson to Mandeville, March 7, 1853; Samuel R. Goddard to Mandeville, March 20, 1853; Cyrus Lennan to Mandeville, Sept. 12, 1853; R. A. Robinson to Mandeville, Jan. 10, 1854 (here TCWC Secretary Robinson sends Mandeville a dividend check and assures him that the miners' complaints against the company are "nothing but a flash in the pan"); George S. Evans to Mandeville, March 20, 1855; John McGlenchy to Mandeville, March 25, 1855.

51. *Union Democrat* (Sonora, Calif.), April 21, 1855, cited in Buckbee, 87–88. James Mandeville, too, faced such a challenge, though the dispute seems to have been unrelated to water company politics. In 1854, a Sonora businessman challenged Mandeville to a duel for calling him an "abolitionist" and a "defaulter." Mandeville refused, denouncing the practice of dueling in terms similar to those of TCWC President Dobie. He also retracted his insults, admitting, "I have no personal knowledge of your sentiments in relation to the first accusation, nor of your condition in relation to the second." D. A. Enyart to Mandeville, March 8, 1854; Mandeville to D. A. Enyart, March 15, 1854; and Mandeville to Benjamin S. Lippincott, April 3, 1854, Mandeville Papers, Huntington Library.

52. *San Joaquin Republican*, Aug. 8, 1855.

53. T. B. Dryer to Joseph Pownall, Oct. 20, 1855, PW 284, Pownall Papers, Huntington Library. For newspaper coverage of both Coffroth's "somerset" and Know-Nothing challenges and victories, see *San Joaquin Republican*, July 14, Aug. 15, Sept. 16, 1855, Feb. 21, 1856.

54. Certificate of Incorporation of the Tuolumne County Water Company, Sept. 4, 1852, PW 1030, Pownall Papers, Huntington Library.

55. I have not located business papers for the Columbia and Stanislaus River Water Company. These figures appeared in the *San Joaquin Republican*, Oct. 9, 1855.

56. See, e.g., Heckendorn and Wilson, 7; Rensch, 77.

57. *San Joaquin Republican*, Nov. 27, 1856.

58. The following description is derived from Rensch, 88–90; and Buckbee, 273–75.

59. This "Miners' Union" is significant because historians routinely cite a later date—1863, to be precise—for the beginnings of organized labor in western mining. It was in 1863 that hardrock miners formed a union on Nevada's Comstock Lode. See, e.g., Richard E. Lingenfelter, *The Hardrock Miners: A History of the Mining Labor Movement in the American West, 1863–1893* (Berkeley: Univ. of California Press, 1974). I note this mention of a "Miners' Union" with the hope that future

researchers will be able to find more than passing reference to it, and thus analyze its relationship to the labor movement that later developed in western hardrock mining.

60. See Paul, 345–52.

61. This summary relies on Rensch, 90–92; and Buckbee, 280–81. The quotation is from the *Sacramento Union*, May 10, 1859, quoted in Rensch, 91. Documentation for the TCWC purchase appears in TCWC List of Land Transactions, 1852–92; and TCWC List of Reservoir Locations, 1855–56, PW 1170, Pownall Papers, Huntington Library. The purchase price was $149,307.18.

62. The best explanation of the geographic distribution of gold deposits in California is in Paul, 91–115. Mann provides the best account of the placers-to-gravels-and-quartz trajectory in the Northern Mines in general and Nevada County in particular, and of the social consequences of that trajectory.

63. *Stockton Times*, Oct. 5, 12, 18, 1850. For later arguments, see *Stockton Times*, Jan. 29, April 9, 1851, and *San Joaquin Republican*, April 3, 1852.

64. *San Joaquin Republican*, Jan. 24, 1854, April 17, 1855. Another article claimed such superiority for Calaveras, Tuolumne, and Mariposa counties collectively. See Sept. 25, 1855.

65. *San Joaquin Republican*, Oct. 15, 1857.

66. For a copy of the document by which the Alvarados conveyed Las Mariposas to Frémont, see John Charles Frémont, *The Expeditions of John Charles Frémont*, vol. 2, *The Bear Flag Revolt and the Court-Martial*, ed. Mary Lee Spence and Donald Jackson (Urbana: Univ. of Illinois Press, 1973), 2:297–300. The purchase price was $3,000. As Leonard Pitt has shown, Larkin forced Alvarado into conveying this property to Frémont in order to satisfy prewar debts. See Pitt, *The Decline of the Californios: A Social History of the Spanish-Speaking Californians, 1846–1890* (Berkeley: Univ. of California Press, 1966), 36.

67. J. C. Frémont, 2:299.

68. Ibid., 2:34–38, 299, quotation on 35.

69. For speculations about Jessie Benton Frémont that are beyond the scope of this chapter, see my essay "The United States of Jessie Benton Frémont: Corresponding with the Nation," *Reviews in American History* 23, no. 2 (June 1995): 219–25, which is a review of the fine collection *The Letters of Jessie Benton Frémont*, ed. Pamela Herr and Mary Lee Spence (Urbana: Univ. of Illinois Press, 1993). The overview of Benton Frémont's life and the introductions to each section of letters in this collection are indispensable (for the period covered here, see esp. xvii–xxx, 3–10, 63–70, 187–91). See also Herr, *Jessie Benton Fremont* (New York: Franklin Watts, 1987).

70. *San Joaquin Republican*, Aug. 6, 1856.

71. Here I rely on the analysis of the historian Mary Lee Spence. See J. C. Frémont, *The Expeditions of John Charles Frémont*, vol. 3, *Travels from 1848 to 1854*, ed. Mary Lee Spence (Urbana: Univ. of Illinois Press,

1984), 3:xxxvi–xxxvii. The bill that actually passed, the Land Act of 1851, was introduced by Frémont's fellow senator from California, William Gwin. It permitted appeals on Land Commission decisions, a provision that was seen as favorable to Anglo Americans.

72. *Stockton Times*, Nov. 23, 1850. The editorial suggested that where Frémont wanted to "immortalize himself by eradicating the Aztec from North America," Anglos should instead embrace Mexicans in California as unrivaled "hewer[s] of wood and . . . drawer[s] of water."

73. Ibid., Dec. 7, 1850.

74. Ibid., Jan. 1, 1851.

75. *Alta California*, Dec. 24, 1850, reprinted in J. C. Frémont, 3:213–20.

76. This summary, too, relies on Spence's work. See J. C. Frémont, 3: lxx–lxxiii.

77. Ibid., 3:xxxix–xliv. See also Albert Hurtado, *Indian Survival on the California Frontier* (New Haven: Yale Univ. Press, 1988), 140–41.

78. Spence notes these remarks of Lafayette Houghton Bunnell, J. C. Frémont, 3:xliii. See Bunnell, *Discovery of the Yosemite and the Indian War of 1851 Which Led to That Event* (1880; Yosemite National Park, Calif.: Yosemite Association, 1990), esp. 232, 242–44. On the Mariposa War and on Savage, see chap. 4, "Mining Gold and Making War."

79. J. C. Frémont, 3:xliv–xlv, 51–53; Bayard Taylor, *Eldorado or Adventures in the Path of Empire* (1850; Lincoln: Univ. of Nebraska Press, 1988), 84–85.

80. For an excellent account of Mariposa business affairs, see Spence's summary in J. C. Frémont, 3:xliv–lii. Benton is quoted on xlix. By 1853, Hoffman no longer worked on Frémont's behalf. Spence suggests that Frémont never paid Hoffman for his services. See also Spence, "David Hoffman: Frémont's Mariposa Agent in London," *Southern California Quarterly* 60 (Winter 1978): 379–403.

81. J. C. Frémont, 3:xliv. Spence has succeeded in this task beyond all reasonable expectations.

82. Ibid., 3:lix, lxiii, lxix, and see survey maps reprinted on lxiv–lxv, lxviii.

83. Ibid., 3:lix–lxiii, lxix.

84. *San Joaquin Republican*, April 7, 1855.

85. Ibid., Jan. 10, June 30, 1852.

86. Ibid., Nov. 13, 1852.

87. Ibid., Aug. 6, 1856. For another conflation of Frémont's financial and political aspirations, see ibid., July 20, 1856: "Col. Fremont's political principles are as much a matter of uncertainty as the extent and value of the gold mines on his Mariposa claim."

88. Ibid., Aug. 24, 1856. Cf. Sept. 16, 1856 (reprinted from the *Calaveras Chronicle*): "A well known colored resident of Mokelumne Hill, named Peter Sykes, has been missing for the past few weeks, and much anxiety was felt by lovers of gumbo on account of his mysterious absence. It is now ascertained that Peter is stumping the state for Fremont. . . .

It required some persuasion to start Pete on his mission as he announced himself more in favor of draw poker than Fre–monte."

89. See J. B. Frémont, 67.

90. Hays, 270; *San Joaquin Republican*, July 20, 1856.

91. See, e.g., *San Joaquin Republican*, Aug. 31, 1856, June 24, 1857, July 30, 1858.

92. Ibid., Jan. 25, 1857.

93. Ibid., June 24, 25, Oct. 8, 1857, March 6, 17, June 25, 1858.

94. Ibid., Oct. 16, 1857 (from *Mariposa Gazette*); see also Bunnell, 284.

95. *San Joaquin Republican*, Feb. 6, 1858 (from *Mariposa Gazette*).

96. See J. B. Frémont, 193, 194–95.

97. Ibid., 195, 199; *San Joaquin Republican*, April 24, 1858.

98. J. B. Frémont, 187, 195.

99. Ibid., 194–95. The editors of Jessie's correspondence indicate that the Frémonts brought two maids back from France in the mid-1850s, and Mémé may have been one of these. She is mentioned frequently in Jessie's correspondence as the children's nurse. See ibid., 62, n. 7, 126, 135, 143, 162, 183. I can find nothing in Jessie's published correspondence to indicate who Rose was or when she entered the Frémonts' employ.

100. On Albert Lea, see ibid., 54, 55, n. 3, 194, 195, 203, 206. In the fall of 1860, Lea was convicted of murdering his estranged wife in San Francisco, and the Frémonts campaigned to get his death sentence commuted to life imprisonment. Jessie herself wrote a long letter on his behalf to the *Alta California* (printed Feb. 27, 1861, reprinted in J. B. Frémont, 235–37). The Frémonts' campaign failed, and Lea was hanged. See Herr, 317–18. On Isaac, see J. B. Frémont, 199, 201, n. 2 (here, the editors quote Jessie from her own *Souvenirs of My Time* [Boston: D. Lothrop, 1887], 196–98), 206, 215, 216, 229–30.

101. J. B. Fremont, *Letters*, 195. Cf. Mann, 111–12, 247, tables 26 and 27. Mann's figures show the small number of servants at work in middle-class homes in the Northern Mines. I have not done a comparable statistical analysis for the Southern Mines, but extensive reading in letters, diaries, and reminiscences of aspiring middle-class people there suggests a similar underreliance on servants when compared with middle-class homes in the East. In *Far-West Sketches* (Boston: D. Lothrop 1890), Jessie Benton Frémont indicates that she also employed Indian women to do domestic work (112–13). Cf. Albert L. Hurtado, "'Hardly a Farmhouse—a Kitchen without Them': Indian and White Households on the California Borderland Frontier in 1860," *Western Historical Quarterly* 13 (1982): 245–70.

102. J. B. Frémont, *Letters*, 43.

103. Ibid., 198–99; J. B. Frémont, *Far-West Sketches*, 103–5.

104. J. B. Frémont, *Letters*, 205–8, quotations on 205.

105. Indeed, the miners' and settlers' association and the Hornitos League

may have been one in the same, or else the former may have developed into the latter. See ibid., 188, 207–8, n. 1; Herr, 295–300; Andrew Rolle, *John Charles Frémont: Character as Destiny* (Norman: Univ. of Oklahoma Press, 1991), 181–82.

106. See chap. 4, "Mining Gold and Making War."

107. Jessie Benton Frémont thought that the miners who opposed her husband were from Hornitos. See *Far-West Sketches*, 59.

108. For Jessie Benton Frémont, the term "border ruffian" no doubt had a very specific referent. It would have evoked the pro-southern Missourians who had struggled to secure Kansas as a slave state starting in 1854. The Missourians were led by David Atchison, U.S. senator and bitter rival of Jessie's father, Thomas Hart Benton. I am indebted to the historian Ralph Mann for pointing this out. As Mann notes, calling opponents of her father and husband "border ruffians" reduced them to the status of southern "white trash," thereby negating their legitimacy. For contemporary analyses of the category "white trash," see Matt Wray and Annalee Newitz, eds., *White Trash: Race and Class in America* (New York: Routledge, 1997).

109. *San Joaquin Republican,* July 14, 1858.

110. Ibid.; J. B. Frémont, *Letters,* 207–8, n. 1.

111. J. B. Frémont, *Letters,* 206.

112. Ibid., 205–7.

113. Herr, 298–99. According to Herr, Jessie "described this confrontation only in her unpublished memoirs. While she may have dramatized the story, Lily [Jessie's daughter], eighteen at the time, corroborates it in her *Recollections,* adding that she accompanied her mother to the tavern" (p. 466, n. 13). See Elizabeth Benton Frémont, *Recollections of Elizabeth Benton Frémont,* comp. I. T. Martin (New York: F. H. Hitchcock, 1912). Jessie Benton Frémont's unpublished memoirs are located at the Bancroft Library, but throughout this section, I am relying on the careful readings of these memoirs by her biographer Herr and the historian Mary Lee Spence. Benton Frémont does not mention the visit to the saloon in *Far-West Sketches* (see pp. 53–83).

114. Quoted in J. B. Frémont, *Letters,* 190, 246; and Herr, 319, 338.

115. J. B. Frémont, *Letters,* 208–9.

116. *San Joaquin Republican,* July 18, 1858.

117. See, e.g., ibid., July 30, Aug. 13, Oct. 29, 1858. "The Fremont Outrage" described how Frémont men violently evicted a young fellow from a house he was "fitting . . . up to be used as a store." See ibid., Dec. 1, 7, 1858.

118. J. B. Frémont, *Letters,* 207.

119. As early as the 1860s, hardrock miners on Nevada's Comstock Lode kept in union halls "complete sets of prospecting gear for loan" to union men. See Lingenfelter, 53. And as late as the 1920s in Butte, Montana, "underground miners still roamed the nearby mountains in the sum-

mer, prospecting and staking claims in search of gold." See Mary Murphy, *Mining Cultures: Men, Women, and Leisure in Butte, 1914–41* (Urbana: Univ. of Illinois Press, 1997), 19.

Chapter 6: The Last Fandango

1. John Robertson to Wade Johnston, Nov. 5, 1901, Effie Johnston Collection in Brame Papers, Holt-Atherton Center for Western Studies, Univ. of the Pacific, Stockton, Calif. (hereafter cited as Holt-Atherton Center). Effie Enfield Johnston, daughter of Wade Johnston, wrote down many of the stories her father told about his early years in Calaveras County, some of which have been reproduced in a series called "Wade Johnston Talks to His Daughter," in *Las Calaveras: Quarterly Bulletin of the Calaveras County Historical Society* 17, no. 3 (April 1969); 18, no. 1 (Oct. 1969); 18, no. 3 (April 1970); 19, no. 1 (Oct. 1970); 19, no. 4 (July 1971); 20, no. 2 (Jan. 1972); 21, no. 1 (Oct. 1972).

2. Robertson's use of the term "civilized" had a particular meaning at the turn of the century, when, as Gail Bederman has shown, middle-class white people were reformulating ideas about manhood to incorporate a new emphasis on virility and racial superiority that came together in a discourse of "civilization." See Bederman, *Manliness and Civilization: A Cultural History of Gender and Race in the United States, 1880–1917* (Chicago: Univ. of Chicago Press, 1995). To date, historians (including myself) have not sufficiently analyzed the extent to which the conquest of the North American West contributed to this discourse. I began to suggest this in "'A Memory Sweet to Soldiers': The Significance of Gender in the History of the 'American West,'" *Western Historical Quarterly* 24, no. 4 (Nov. 1993): 495–517, reprinted in *A New Significance: Re-Envisioning the American West,* ed. Clyde Milner II (New York: Oxford Univ. Press, 1996), 255–78.

3. For a stunning counterexample about a different time and place—a model of regional history in which conflict is seen as central—see Katherine G. Morrissey, *Mental Territories: Mapping the Inland Empire* (Ithaca: Cornell Univ. Press, 1997).

4. *San Joaquin Republican* (Stockton), Sept. 25, 1852; *The Golden Era* (San Francisco), Sept. 17, 1854. See discussion of these two divergent accounts of change in chap. 5, "Dreams That Died."

5. I am grateful to Dorothy Fujita Rony (Asian American Studies, Univ. of California, Irvine) for sharing her early work on this topic. The quotation comes from her unpublished paper "The 1854 Chinese War of Weaverville, California," Yale Univ., 1990, which focuses on a battle of this sort that took place in the Shasta-Trinity diggings of northwestern California.

6. See Anthony Shay, "Fandangos and Bailes: Dancing and Dance Events in Early California," *Southern California Quarterly* 64, no. 2 (Summer 1982):

99–113. A "fandango" was distinguished from the dance event among elite Spanish Mexicans called a "baile." For men as patrons of early Gold Rush fandangos, see chap. 3, "Bulls, Bears, and Dancing Boys."

7. *San Joaquin Republican,* July 30, 1851 (from the *Sonora Herald*).

8. Ibid.

9. See, e.g., *San Joaquin Republican,* Aug. 9, Oct. 25, 1853, March 11, April 11, Nov. 22, Dec. 13, 1854, May 3, July 31, Nov. 20, 1855, Aug. 24, 1856.

10. Ibid., July 28, 1852 (from the *Sonora Herald*). Copies of most issues of the *Sonora Herald* are no longer extant—hence my reliance on articles reprinted in Stockton papers.

11. On these events, see chap. 4, "Mining Gold and Making War."

12. See U.S. Bureau of the Census, *Seventh Census of the United States: 1850* (Washington, D.C., 1853), and *Population of the United States in 1860; Compiled from . . . the Eighth Census* (Washington, D.C., 1864) (hereafter cited as *1860 Census*).

13. On class making, see, e.g., Mary P. Ryan, *Cradle of the Middle Class: The Family in Oneida County, New York, 1790–1865* (Cambridge: Cambridge Univ. Press, 1981); and cf. Leonore Davidoff and Catherine Hall, *Family Fortunes: Men and Women of the English Middle Class, 1780–1850* (Chicago: Univ. of Chicago Press, 1987).

14. For background on Mary Harrison Newell, see chap. 1, "On the Eve of Emigration."

15. For the TCWC's role in class formation in the Southern Mines, see chap. 5, "Dreams That Died."

16. William Newell to Mary Newell, April 24, 1853, PW 523; July 28, 1853, PW 524; and "Articles of Copartnership between B. M. Brainard and W. H. Newell," April 25, 1853, PW 76, Joseph Pownall Papers, Huntington Library, San Marino, Calif. (hereafter cited as Huntington Library).

17. See, e.g., Journal entries, Oct. 20, 24, Dec. 17, 1853, Jan. 20, July 2, Aug. 26, Sept. 28, Dec. 10, 1854, Clementine H. Brainard Journal, Bancroft Library, Univ. of California, Berkeley (hereafter cited as Bancroft Library).

18. For details on Pownall's role in the miners' strike against the TCWC, see chap. 5, "Dreams That Died."

19. Mary Newell to Benjamin and Lucy Harrison, Dec. 18, 1855, PW 793; Mary Newell to Lucy Harrison, April 17, 1856, PW 769; Benjamin Harrison to Lucy Harrison, April 18, 1856, PW 356; "Receipt from Hotel International, San Francisco," March 17, 1857 (a receipt for Mary and Joseph Pownall's honeymoon suite, for which Joseph paid $32 for a stay of four days), PW 146, Pownall Papers, Huntington Library. For Pownall's status in the TCWC, see Minutes of Board Meetings, May 1856–Nov. 1859, Tuolumne County Water Company Correspondence and Papers, 1853–1905, vol. 2, Bancroft Library. For Pownall's concerns about his marital status, see Pownall Journal and

Letterbook, PW 553, passim, Pownall Papers; for the quotation, see the letter therein labeled Joseph Pownall to "dear Friend" [1854].

20. For an overview of antebellum reform, see Ronald G. Walters, *American Reformers, 1815–1860* (New York: Hill and Wang, 1978). For an excellent account of the urban worlds of leisure that so incensed reformers in the East, see Timothy J. Gilfoyle, *City of Eros: New York City, Prostitution, and the Commercialization of Sex, 1790–1920* (New York: W. W. Norton, 1992). A helpful overview of reform efforts that impinged on sexual practices appears in John D'Emilio and Estelle B. Freedman, *Intimate Matters: A History of Sexuality in America*, 2d ed. (Chicago: Univ. of Chicago Press, 1997), esp. 139–45.

21. See Lewis Perry, *Childhood, Marriage, and Reform: Henry Clarke Wright, 1791–1870* (Chicago: Univ. of Chicago Press, 1980), esp. 172–82; and Anna Lee Marston, ed., *Records of a California Family: Journals and Letters of Lewis C. Gunn and Elizabeth Le Breton Gunn* (San Diego: n.p., 1928), esp. 3–15.

22. Marston, ed., 156–58, 170.

23. See, e.g., Brainard's support for temperance and Sabbatarianism expressed in Journal entries, Dec. 17, 18, 1853, July 4, Oct. 4, 1854.

24. For these references to Lorena Hays, see chap. 5, "Dreams That Died."

25. Lorena L. Hays, *To the Land of Gold and Wickedness: The 1848–59 Diary of Lorena L. Hays*, ed. Jeanne Hamilton Watson (St. Louis: Patrice Press, 1988), 1–14, 198–229.

26. Ibid., esp. 231–33, 235, 237–49, 252–57, 263–65, quotations on 238, 252, 255; *The Golden Era* (San Francisco), Sept. 17, 1854.

27. Hays, esp. 249, 251, 253, 259–61, quotation on 261. On the murders and the subsequent siege of Spanish-speaking communities in Amador County, see Larry Cenotto, *Logan's Alley: Amador County Yesterdays in Picture and Prose*, 2 vols. (Jackson, Calif.: Cenotto Publications, 1988), 1:159–73.

28. For his part, James accused Chloe of sleeping with a man named John Burridge and of leaving home only "for the purpose of having adulterous intercourse" with Burridge. See *James B. Cooper v. Chloe C. Cooper* (1857–58), District Court, Amador County, Jackson, Calif. (hereafter cited as Amador County District Court Records).

29. *Mary Jane Anderson v. James W. Anderson* (1857), Amador County District Court Records.

30. *Mary Ann Hayes v. Nicholas Hayes* (1860), District Court, Tuolumne County, Sonora, Calif. (hereafter cited as Tuolumne County District Court Records).

31. According to the *1860 Census*, U.S. citizens constituted 45.55 percent of the population of the four counties that made up the Southern Mines in 1860: Amador, Calaveras, Tuolumne, and Mariposa. White U.S. citizens constituted 44.75 percent of the enumerated population (blacks, including those designated as "mulattos," made up 1.8 percent of the U.S. population and .9 percent of the total population).

32. Cf. Ralph Mann, *After the Gold Rush: Society in Grass Valley and Nevada City, California, 1849–1870* (Stanford: Stanford Univ. Press, 1982), 56–59, who describes similar campaigns, in the two major towns of the Northern Mines. Some references to such activities in the Southern Mines are quite brief. Writing to his wife from Mokelumne Hill in 1853, for example, the dentist John Baker noted, "There has been an endeavor in the part of some citizens to improve the state of society in this place recently. Two of the worst house in town were indicted at our court last week as nuiscences and one was fined $250, the other case was continued to the next term." John Baker to Julia Ann Baker, Oct. 21, 1853, John W. H. Baker Correspondence, Holt-Atherton Center.

33. Journal entry, Brainard Journal, Dec. 17, 1853.

34. Hays, 258–59; cf. Journal entry, Brainard Journal, Dec. 18, 1853: "I do hope that merchants will decide soon to close their stores on the Sabbath and then we may hope for a reformation in Columbia."

35. *San Joaquin Republican*, Feb. 6, 1855, June 25, 1856 (the latter is reprinted from the *Weekly Columbian*); *Volcano Weekly Ledger*, Jan. 26, 1856.

36. See *Volcano Weekly Ledger*, June 28, Dec. 13, 1856, Feb. 28, July 18, 1857; *San Joaquin Republican*, Oct. 16, 1857.

37. Journal entries, March 21–24, 1854, Brainard Journal; *[Phoebe] Quimby v. Z. M. Quimby* (1852), Tuolumne County District Court Records. That this incident evoked increasing class tensions in Columbia is suggested by the fact that Thomas Cazneau, six months after this party, became a founding officer of the Columbia and Stanislaus River Water Company, the company that challenged the Tuolumne County Water Company by building the famed "Miners' Ditch." See chap. 5, "Dreams That Died." He also managed the first theater in Columbia, which no doubt became a site of moral ambiguity—if not outright moral peril—to the emerging white middle class. See Hero Eugene Rensch, "Columbia, a Gold Camp of Old Tuolumne: Her Rise and Decline, Together with Some Mention of Her Social Life and Cultural Strivings" (Berkeley, 1936, for State of California, Department of Natural Resources, Division of Parks, under auspices of Works Progress Administration), 73; Edna Bryan Buckbee, *The Saga of Old Tuolumne* (New York: Press of the Pioneers, 1935), 96, 267.

38. See Robert L. Griswold, *Family and Divorce in California, 1850–1890: Victorian Illusions and Everyday Realities* (Albany: State Univ. of New York Press, 1982), esp. 76.

39. *Mary Ann Chick v. Alfred Chick* (1859), District Court, Calaveras County, San Andreas, Calif. (hereafter cited as Calaveras County District Court Records); *Emily Davis v. O. S. Davis* (1860), Tuolumne County District Court Records.

40. *Sarah E. Philbrick v. William H. Philbrick* (1860), Amador County District Court Records.

41. *Joseph L. Hall v. Celia E. Hall* (1860), Tuolumne County District Court Records.

42. For background, see chap. 3, "Bulls, Bears, and Dancing Boys," and chap. 4, "Mining Gold and Making War."

43. *The People v. French Mary* (1857), Court of Sessions, Tuolumne County, Sonora, Calif. (hereafter cited as Tuolumne County Court of Sessions Records). Cf. *The People v. John Doe and Richard Roe* (1856), Tuolumne County Court of Sessions Records.

44. The saloons of Clement and Follet are mentioned in *Alfred Washburn v. Francis Williams* (1855) and *Alfred Washburn v. Sam Lord* (1856), District Court, Mariposa County, Mariposa, Calif. (hereafter cited as Mariposa County District Court Records). Clement's saloon is also mentioned in the *San Joaquin Republican*, Sept. 13, 1856 (reprinted from the *Mariposa Democrat*).

45. *S. R. Mills and James Vantine v. Madame Emilie Henry* (1856), Mariposa County District Court Records.

46. The 1852 state census lists a forty-year-old Chilean woman named Elibe Ortiz in Calaveras County, and this may be the Isabel Ortis (who also went by the names Elisa and Elizabeth) of the 1858 court records cited below. But, as we shall see, Ortis linked her property ownership in Amador County to the contested land grant of Californio Andrés Pico, suggesting familiarity with the disposition of Mexican land claims in California. Such familiarity might have been more likely for an ethnic Mexican than for a Chilean. Chilean names in the 1850 and 1860 federal census as well as the 1852 state census are indexed in Carlos U. López, *Chilenos in California: A Study of the 1850, 1852 and 1860 Census* (San Francisco: R and E Research Associates, 1973), see esp. 60.

47. *Inquest, Francisco [Arayo]* (1858), Inquest Records, Calaveras County, Calaveras County Museum and Archives, San Andreas, Calif.

48. *Natividad Shermenhoof v. John Shermenhoof* (1856) and *Natividad Shermenhoof v. John Shermenhoof, W. W. Cope, and James F. Hubbard* (1858), Amador County District Court Records. Another copy of the divorce record can be found in Amador County Legal Records, box 1370, folder 6, California State Library, Sacramento (hereafter cited as Amador County Legal Records). Natividad accused John of violence and of trying to compel her to "open a house of prostitution." For his part, John accused Natividad of squandering his earnings in "riotous and dissipated living." He claimed she left him only to place herself "in a better condition to carry on an uninterrupted illicit intercourse with one Frederick Schober." Schober was a German butcher in Jackson, where a street still bears his name. See Cenotto, 2:223.

49. *A. C. Brown v. Isabel Ortis and John McKay* (1858), Amador County District Court Records; *John McKay v. His Creditors* (1858), County Court, Amador County, Jackson, Calif. Documents for both cases can also be found in Amador County Legal Records, boxes 1368 and 1369.

50. On Andrés Pico, see Leonard Pitt, *The Decline of the Californios: A Social History of Spanish-Speaking Californians, 1846–1890* (Berkeley: Univ. of California Press, 1966), esp. 34–35, 139–40, 145.

51. The literature on California land claims is vast. See, e.g., Pitt; and Albert Camarillo, *Chicanos in a Changing Society: From Mexican Pueblos to American Barrios in Santa Barbara and Southern California, 1848–1930* (Cambridge: Harvard Univ. Press, 1979). For another perspective, see Paul W. Gates, *Land Law in California: Essays on Land Policies* (Ames: Iowa State Univ. Press, 1991). On the meanings that Californios attached to dispossession, see Rosaura Sánchez, *Telling Identities: The Californio testimonios* (Minneapolis: Univ. of Minnesota Press, 1995).

52. See, e.g., *Volcano Weekly Ledger,* June 7, 1856, in which an editor warns that if Pico continues to press his claim, he will face "the hard fisted yeomanry of the mountains," whose insurgence will resemble the "Anti-Rent . . . troubles in New York." Lorena Hays Bowmer's husband, John—a merchant, not a yeoman—may have participated in the settlers' league that organized in opposition to the Arroyo Seco grant. See Hays, 265, 417, n. 86. On the Mariposa Estate, see chap. 4, "Mining Gold and Making War."

53. I use "juridical" in both ordinary and academic senses of the word. In the first and most obvious sense, Ortis entered into the legal controversies over land tenure then underway in California. But the term "juridical" also has been used by Michel Foucault and scholars influenced by his work to refer to the ways in which systems of power (among them, legal systems) not only regulate or even prohibit certain kinds of people but actually produce and reproduce those kinds of people through the very practices that are assumed to constitute regulation and prohibition. In this sense, then, Ortis was not simply a Mexican or Chilean woman who managed fandangos and who thereby ran afoul of Anglo American law. She was a person engaged in an economic activity who became, in part through the imposition of the law, a representative of a cultural category. On juridical power, see, e.g., Michel Foucault, *Discipline and Punish: The Birth of the Prison,* trans. Alan Sheridan (1975; New York: Vintage Books, 1979); Judith Butler, *Gender Trouble: Feminism and the Subversion of Identity* (New York: Routledge, 1990).

54. *A. C. Brown v. Isabel Ortis and John McKay* (1858), *John McKay v. His Creditors* (1858), and see Amador County Legal Records, box 1368, folders 12 and 13, and box 1369, folder 8. The quoted material is from documents in this latter folder.

55. Cf. Deena J. González, "La Tules of Image and Reality: Euro-American Attitudes and Legend Formation on a Spanish-Mexican Frontier," in *Building with Our Hands: New Directions in Chicana Studies,* ed. Adela de la Torre and Beatríz M. Pesquera (Berkeley: Univ. of California Press, 1993), 75–90.

56. This information about Armsted and Philippa Brown is drawn from the work of the Amador County historian Larry Cenotto (2:182–85). As for Philippa, she was actively engaged in efforts to supplant polyglot sites of heterosocial leisure with "respectable" gatherings. In early 1858, for example, she was among a group of women who planned a "Calico Party," the proceeds of which were to go toward the building of a schoolhouse in Jackson. After the ball, the managers met at Philippa's home and decided how the funds would be appropriated. The women appointed Armsted Brown to "receive the funds and pay out the same" for the schoolhouse. See *Amador Weekly Ledger,* Jan. 2, 16, 1858.

57. *Laura Echeverria v. Juan Echeverria* (1857), Tuolumne County District Court Records.

58. Ibid.

59. Ibid.

60. Ibid.

61. For historiographical context, see Camille Guerin-Gonzales, "Conversing across Boundaries of Race, Ethnicity, Class, Gender, and Region: Latina and Latino Labor History," *Labor History* 35, no. 4 (Fall 1994): 547–63.

62. Throughout, my argument has been guided by the work of Elsa Barkley Brown and Evelyn Nakano Glenn, particularly as it relates to the relational nature of differences among women. See, e.g., Brown, "Polyrhythms and Improvization: Lessons for Women's History," *History Workshop Journal* 31–32 (1991): 85–90; and Glenn, "From Servitude to Service Work: Historical Continuities in the Racial Division of Paid Reproductive Labor," *Signs* 18, no. 1 (Autumn 1992): 1–43.

63. *San Joaquin Republican,* Oct. 8, 1858.

64. *1860 Census.*

65. See Lucie Cheng Hirata, "Free, Indentured, Enslaved: Chinese Prostitutes in Nineteenth-Century America," *Signs* 5, no. 1 (Autumn 1979): 3–29, esp. 13–18; Sucheng Chan, "The Exclusion of Chinese Women, 1870–1943," in *Entry Denied: Exclusion and the Chinese Community in America, 1882–1943,* ed. Chan (Philadelphia: Temple Univ. Press, 1991), 94–146; and Judy Yung, *Unbound Feet: A Social History of Chinese Women in San Francisco* (Berkeley: Univ. of California Press, 1995), esp. 26–37. My account of Chinese prostitution in the Southern Mines relies on the analysis in these groundbreaking works. See also Takaki, 118–19.

66. According to Lucie Cheng Hirata, it was in 1854 that the secret societies gained control of Chinese prostitution, inaugurating a period of organized trade that peaked around 1870 but lasted into the early twentieth century. The Hip Yee Tong monopolized the trade in the years under consideration here. See Hirata, 8–13. On the relative importance of tongs and other social organizations among Chinese immigrants, see Eve Armentrout-Ma, "Urban Chinese at the Sinitic Frontier: Social Organization in United States' Chinatowns, 1849–1898," *Modern Asian Studies* 17, no. 1 (1983): 107–35.

67. *San Joaquin Republican,* Sept. 18, 22, Oct. 2, 1854.

68. Ibid., Aug. 27, 28, Sept. 16, 1857, June 4, 5, 6, 7, 12, Aug. 10, 1858. The details of the Columbia fire appear in the Aug. 27 and 28, 1857, articles. For more on western perceptions of Chinese opium use, in particular, see Jonathan D. Spence, *The Chan's Great Continent: China in Western Minds* (New York: W. W. Norton, 1998.)

69. *San Joaquin Republican,* Oct. 9, 1854.

70. Receipt Issued by the Jackson Town Marshal's Office, Sept. 15, 1854; and *The People v. A. C. Brown, E. H. Williams, Hiram Allen, T. Hinckley, and Ellis Evans* (1854), Amador County Court of Sessions, Amador County Archives, Jackson, Calif. My thanks to Larry Cenotto for pointing out these materials to me. See also Cenotto, 1:39, 53, 60.

71. *The People v. Chinaman John* (1856), and *The People v. John Doe a Chinaman* (1856), Tuolumne County Court of Sessions Records; *Mary Babbit v. Horace Babbit* (1858), Amador County District Court Records; *Amador Weekly Ledger,* June 26, 1858.

72. See, e.g., Yung, 33–34.

73. Hirata, esp. 13, 19.

74. *Amador Weekly Ledger,* July 3, 1858. Cf. *San Joaquin Republican,* June 15, 1858.

75. Yung, 31.

76. *Amador Weekly Ledger,* May 2, 1857. An account of a marriage ceremony for a Chinese woman and man—called by the editor "a John and a Johness, with unwritable names"—appears in the same newspaper on May 8, 1858. Significantly, this couple chose to marry according to Anglo American law in Amador County, with a local judge presiding.

77. Ibid., July 18, 1857.

78. For an excellent preliminary survey of the sources, both primary and secondary, on the Weaverville War, see Rony. This unpublished essay also provides interpretive themes that have influenced my analysis. I am grateful to Dorothy Fujita Rony for sharing her work with me.

79. The *San Joaquin Republican* followed all of these conflicts, often drawing on reports from local correspondents and on articles published in smaller papers in the Southern Mines such as the *Calaveras Chronicle* (Mokelumne Hill), the *Mariposa Gazette,* the *San Andreas Independent,* and the *Union Democrat* (Sonora). For accounts in the *San Joaquin Republican,* see May 29, 31, June 9, 1854; Jan. 26, Feb. 3, 8, Sept. 25, 26, Oct. 26, 28, Nov. 13, 1856.

80. See, e.g., Rony; Armentrout-Ma; Sucheng Chan, *This Bittersweet Soil: The Chinese in California Agriculture, 1860–1910* (Berkeley: Univ. of California Press, 1986); Gunther Barth, *Bitter Strength: A History of the Chinese in the United States, 1850–1870* (Cambridge: Harvard Univ. Press, 1964); June Mei, "Socioeconomic Origins of Emigration: Guangdong to California, 1850 to 1882," in *Labor Immigration under Capitalism: Asian Workers in the United States before World War II,* ed. Lucie Cheng and Edna Bonacich (Berkeley: Univ. of California Press,

1984); Yong Chen, "The Internal Origins of Chinese Emigration to California Reconsidered," *Western Historical Quarterly* 28, no. 4 (Winter 1997): 520–46.

81. In addition to sources cited above, see Frederic Wakeman, Jr., *Strangers at the Gate: Social Disorder in South China, 1839–1861* (Berkeley: Univ. of California Press, 1966). That conflicts were rooted in local disputes as well as homeland strife is suggested by an account of an 1856 battle at Knight's Ferry, on the border between Stanislaus and Tuolumne counties. Although a correspondent wrote to the *San Joaquin Republican* (Sept. 26, 1856) that the fight was "Hongkong vs. Canton," his letter indicated that "the trouble grew out of a mining dispute."

82. Isaac Cox, *Annals of Trinity County* (1858; Eugene: Univ. of Oregon Press, 1940), cited in Rony; see esp. n. 6.

83. See Wakeman.

84. *San Joaquin Republican*, May 29, 31, June 9, 1854.

85. On the apparently aborted Bear Valley fight, see ibid., Jan. 26, Feb. 3, 8, 1856.

86. *San Joaquin Republican*, Oct. 26, 28, Nov. 13, 1856. One reader of this chapter suggested that perhaps fights such as these among *any* group of Gold Rush participants would have been seen as entertainment—that spectatorship of these battles may not have been as racialized as I argue it was. I have not, however, found reference to such ritualized spectatorship of conflicts among any other group, and the language of these white spectators is overtly and virulently racialized.

87. Ibid., Feb. 3, Sept. 26, 1856.

88. See chap. 3, "Bulls, Bears, and Dancing Boys."

89. *San Joaquin Republican*, Sept. 20, 1853 (from the *Calaveras Chronicle*). The dentist John Baker wrote to his wife about a similar demonstration in Mokelumne Hill a month later: "about 20 or 30 Indians with sticks and bones, dressed in all manner of fantastic shapes went through the town stopping in front of the largest houses and singing, drumming with sticks & c, dancing meanwhile in the rudest Indian manner." John Baker to Julia Ann Baker, Oct. 21, 1853, Baker Correspondence, Holt-Atherton Center.

90. Marston, 249.

91. George H. Bernhard Reminiscences, Bernhard-Patterson Family File, Mariposa Museum and History Center, Mariposa, Calif. (there are two version of Bernhard's brief reminiscences in this file; these quotations are from the 1944 version).

92. Leonard Withington Noyes Reminiscences, Calaveras County Museum and Archives, San Andreas, Calif. (typescript transcription of original from Essex Institute, Salem, Mass.), 75.

93. See chap. 4, "Mining Gold and Making War."

94. See Noyes, 73. Noyes thought these Miwoks had built a sweat lodge, but his description of the structure and its use makes it sound much more

like an assembly house. See S. A. Barrett and E. W. Gifford, *Miwok Material Culture* (1933; Yosemite National Park: Yosemite Natural History Association, n.d.), 200–206.

95. That such tactics proved advantageous not only in the short run but in the long run is evident in the continuous occupancy of Miwok villages in this area well into the early twentieth century. Six Mile Rancheria, for example, which was four miles from the immigrant town of Murphys, was occupied by Sierra Miwoks from the 1830s until the 1930s. Murphys Rancheria, which was even closer to the immigrant town, seems not to have been an established village during the Gold Rush, but Miwok people lived there from the 1870s to the 1910s. People at both villages continued to combine customary subsistence practices with market-based strategies: men worked in the mines; women worked as domestics in private homes; and Miwok families raised vegetable gardens. In addition, residents of Murphys Rancheria continued to welcome non-Indians to ceremonial gatherings called *kote* (in English, these are generally referred to as "big time" festivities). See James Gary Maniery, *Six Mile and Murphys Rancherias: A Study of Two Central Sierra Miwok Sites*, San Diego Museum Papers, no. 22 (San Diego: San Diego Museum of Man, 1987).

96. Bernhard (1944 version); Noyes, 75.

97. See Craig D. Bates, "Miwok Dancers of 1856: Stereographic Images from Sonora, California," *Journal of California and Great Basin Anthropology* 6, no. 1 (1984): 6–18, esp. 15, 17. This article reproduces excellent stereographic images of Miwoks who danced in the streets of Sonora (note that one of these illustrations is also reproduced in this chapter).

98. Bernhard (1944 version). On the meanings of blackface minstrelsy, see Alexander Saxton, *The Rise and Fall of the White Republic: Class Politics and Mass Culture in Nineteenth-Century America* (London: Verso, 1990), 165–82; and Eric Lott, *Love and Theft: Blackface Minstrelsy and the American Working Class* (New York: Oxford Univ. Press, 1993).

99. That is to say that few Miwoks in the 1850s were able to read newspapers and talk back to printed immigrant representations of native peoples.

100. *Amador Weekly Ledger*, Jan. 26, 1858.

101. *San Joaquin Republican*, Feb. 9, 1853 (from the *Sonora Herald*).

102. J. Heckendorn and W. A. Wilson, *Miners and Business Men's Directory, for the Year Commencing Jan. 1st, 1856. Embracing a General History of the Citizens of Tuolumne . . . Together with the Mining Laws of Each District, a Description of the Different Camps, and Other Interesting Statistical Matter* (Columbia, Calif.: Clipper Office, 1856).

103. On the rivalry between the TCWC and the CSRWC and its implications for class formation in the Southern Mines, see chap. 5, "Dreams That Died."

104. Heckendorn and Wilson, 8.

105. Ibid.

Epilogue: Telling Tales

1. Carol Von Pressentin Wright, "Exploring the Mother Lode," *New York Times*, Sunday, May 16, 1993, Travel section.

2. This argument, of course, relies on Benedict Anderson, *Imagined Communities: Reflections on the Origin and Spread of Nationalism* (London: Verso, 1983); and also on thoughts provoked by essays collected in *Cultures of United States Imperialism*, ed. Amy Kaplan and Donald E. Pease (Durham, N.C.: Duke Univ. Press, 1993).

3. See, e.g., David S. Reynolds, *Beneath the American Renaissance: The Subversive Imagination in the Age of Emerson and Melville* (New York: Alfred A. Knopf, 1988), 171–77. See also Michael Denning, *Mechanic Accents: Dime Novels and Working-Class Culture in America* (London: Verso, 1987).

4. *Two Eras in the Life of the Felon Grovenor I. Layton. Who Was Lynched by the Vigilance Committee, at Sonora, Tuolumne County, California, June 17th, 1852. For Robbery, Murder, and Arson, He Having Robbed Three Chilians, Two Men and One Woman, of Ten Thousand Dollars in Gold Dust, at Mormon Gulch, Murdered and Burned Them, Together with Their Cabin, May 28th, 1852* (New Orleans, Charleston, Baltimore, and Philadelphia: A. R. Orton, 1852); *Murder of M. V. B. Griswold by Five Chinese Assassins; Fou Sin—the Principal. Together with the Life of Griswold, and the Statements of Fou Sin, Chou Yee and Coon You, Convicted and Sentenced to Be Hung at Jackson, April 16, 1858. Illustrated with Correct Likenesses of the Murderers* (Jackson, Calif.: T. A. Springer, 1858). T. A. Springer also published the *Amador Weekly Ledger*.

5. *Two Eras in the Life of the Felon Grovenor I. Layton*, 1–32.

6. Ibid., 32–36.

7. Ibid., 36–38.

8. Ibid., 38–39.

9. I won't cite all of the places where I haven't found Grovenor Layton in the historical record, but they are numerous. My thanks to Mary Coomes for double-checking the *San Joaquin Republican* for me, and to Martin Ridge and Peter Blodgett for helping me think of even more places not to find Grovenor. For newspaper reports of Sonora vigilance committee activity in the summer of 1851, see the *San Joaquin Republican* and the *Alta California* (San Francisco), June and July 1851, passim, and esp. *San Joaquin Republican*, July 16, 1851. See also William Perkins, *Three Years in California: William Perkins' Journal of Life at Sonora, 1849–1852*, ed. Dale L. Morgan and James R. Scobie (Berkeley: Univ. of California Press, 1964), 224–42; and Enos Christman, *One Man's Gold: The Letters and Journal of a Forty-Niner*, ed. Florence Morrow Christman (New York: Whittlesey House, McGraw-Hill, 1930), 189–98. I would like to argue as well that on the very day Grovenor was supposed to have been hanged (June 17, 1852), sources show that the town of Sonora was still smoldering from a destructive

fire that had broken out just after midnight—making it not a good day for a lynching. But, in fact, sources differ as to whether the fire broke out just after midnight on June 17 or June 18. See, e.g., *Alta California,* June 20, 1852; Journal entry, June 18, 1852, John Wallis Journal, Holt-Atherton Center for Western Studies, Univ. of the Pacific, Stockton, Calif.; Perkins, 219; J. Heckendorn and W. A. Wilson, *Miners and Business Men's Directory, for the Year Commencing January 1st, 1856. Embracing a General Directory of the Citizens of Tuolumne . . . Together with the Mining Laws of Each District, a Description of the Different Camps, and Other Interesting Statistical Matter* (Columbia, Calif.: Clipper Office, 1856), 37; and [Herbert O. Lang], *A History of Tuolumne County. Compiled from the Most Authentic Records.* (San Francisco: B. F. Alley, 1882), 86. So it goes.

10. Analytically, the distinction may be a small one, but historically, it means the difference between lives and deaths imagined, on the one hand, and lives and deaths experienced, on the other. As for the subject of gain in the nineteenth century, I rely on Ann Vincent Fabian, *Card Sharps, Dream Books, and Bucket Shops: Gambling in Nineteenth-Century America* (Ithaca: Cornell Univ. Press, 1990).

11. For multiple references to the crimes of Hill and the murder of Snow, see the sources cited in n. 9 above. For the quotation, see Perkins, 237. For more on the historical context for this vigilance activity, see chap. 4, "Mining Gold and Making War."

12. The only more unlikely last straw would have been the cheating and killing of Mexican or Indian gold seekers. Given the recent U.S.-Mexican War and centuries of Indian-white conflict, even eastern readers probably would have balked at a story that ended with a white man lynched for such crimes. Unlike Mexicans and Indians, Chileans were largely unknown to eastern audiences, and so were more likely to fill the curious narrative niche they fill in this pamphlet.

13. For this argument, see William Cronon, *Nature's Metropolis: Chicago and the Great West* (New York: W. W. Norton, 1991).

14. See Fabian; and Mary P. Ryan, *Cradle of the Middle Class: The Family in Oneida County, New York, 1790–1865* (Cambridge: Cambridge Univ. Press, 1981). For a wonderful example of the worries gold seeking provoked, see E. L. Cleaveland, *Hasting to Be Rich. A Sermon Occasioned by the Present Excitement Respecting the Gold of California, Preached in the Cities of New Haven and Bridgeport, Jan. and Feb. 1849* (New Haven, Conn.: J. H. Benham, 1849). My thanks to Ann Fabian for introducing me to this sermon.

15. *Murder of M. V. B. Griswold by Five Chinese Assassins,* 5–6.

16. Ibid., 6–11.

17. Ibid., 12.

18. Ibid., 13–14.

19. Ibid., 15–31, esp. 15–17. For more on Fou Sin's life story, see chap. 1, "On the Eve of Emigration."

20. Ibid., 18–22.
21. Ibid., 22–27.
22. Ibid., 12, 14–31.
23. The pamphlet does not record information about the district origins of Fou Sin, Chou Yee, Coon You, and Coon See as carefully as one would wish. The writer thought that Fou Sin said he was born in "Canton county," and elsewhere notes that both Fou Sin and Chou Yee "were originally from the Canton district" (ibid., 14, 16). Similarly, the writer thought that Coon You said that he "belonged to the Cheung people," which I have taken to mean that he was from Xiangshan (Heungshan or Chungshan). Elsewhere the writer notes that both "Coon You and Coon See belonged to the Yin Foo party or company of Chinamen" (ibid., 14, 30). I have been unable to find reference in Chinese American historiography to any district organization, secret society, or surname association that approximates the designation "Yin Foo." The closest is the district organization (huiguan or hui-kuan) formed by immigrants from Xiangshan in 1852, variously transliterated as Yeung-wo, Yanghe, and Yang-ho. Nonetheless, the pamphlet consistently suggests that Fou Sin and Chou Yee shared a native place, as did Coon You and Coon See. For the district origins of Chinese emigrants and on social organization in Chinese America, I rely on Eve Armentrout-Ma, "Urban Chinese at the Sinitic Frontier: Social Organizations in United States' Chinatowns, 1849–1898," *Modern Asian Studies* 17, no. 1 (1983): 107–35, esp. 109–19; June Mei, "Socioeconomic Origins of Emigration: Guangdong to California, 1850 to 1882," in *Labor Immigration under Capitalism: Asian Workers in the United States before World War II*, ed. Lucie Cheng and Edna Bonacich (Berkeley: Univ. of California Press, 1984), 219–45, esp. 224–27; Sucheng Chan, *This Bittersweet Soil: The Chinese in California Agriculture, 1860–1910* (Berkeley: Univ. of California Press, 1986), 16–26, and *Asian Americans: An Interpretive History* (Boston: Twayne, 1991), 63–67; Ronald I. Takaki, *Strangers from a Different Shore: A History of Asian Americans* (Boston: Little, Brown, 1989), 118–19; and Gunther Barth, *Bitter Strength: A History of the Chinese in the United States, 1850–1870* (Cambridge: Harvard Univ. Press, 1964), esp. 87–90.
24. For the quotation, see the "Advertisement" printed on the pamphlet's first page of text: *Murder of M. V. B. Griswold by Five Chinese Assassins*, 3 (unnumbered). For the date the pamphlet went on sale and the postage-paid purchase price, see *Amador Weekly Ledger* (Jackson), April 10, 17, 1858.
25. For Kilham's orchard and garden and for the crowd at the hangings, see *Amador Weekly Ledger*, May 2, Aug. 22, Sept. 12, 1857, April 17, 1858.
26. Ibid., April 24, 1858 (the *State Journal* note is quoted here).
27. See Pamela Herr and Mary Lee Spence, eds., *The Letters of Jessie Benton Frémont* (Urbana: Univ. of Illinois Press, 1993), esp. 185, 234, 235, n. 3, 334–35.

28. Kevin Starr, *Americans and the California Dream, 1850–1915* (New York: Oxford Univ. Press, 1986), 49–50.

29. Harte's story is often reprinted. For the original, see *Overland Monthly,* 1st ser., 3 (1869). A useful collection of Harte's Gold Rush stories is *Bret Harte's Gold Rush,* ed. Reuben H. Margolin (Berkeley, Calif.: Heyday Books, 1997).

30. Chamberlain and Chaffee are introduced in chap. 1, "On the Eve of Emigration." Their lives are documented in the John Amos Chaffee and Jason Palmer Chamberlain Papers, Bancroft Library, Univ. of California, Berkeley; and Jason P. Chamberlain Correspondence, Huntington Library, San Marino, Calif. On the connection between "Tennessee's Partner" and Chamberlain and Chaffee, see Fred Stocking, "The Passing of 'Tennessee' and his Partner," *Overland Monthly,* 2d ser., 42 (1903): 539–43; Fletcher Stokes, "Fred Stocking and His Service to California Literature," *Overland Monthly,* 2d ser., 59 (1912): 105–14; and James G. White, "The Death of Tennessee's Pardner: The True Story of the Death of Jason P. Chamberlain," *Tuolumne County Historical Society Quarterly* 4, no. 3 (Jan.–March 1965): 122–24. My thanks to the Tuolumne County historian Carlo M. De Ferrari for conversations about Chaffee and Chamberlain. Mr. De Ferrari grew up near the men's homestead, and no doubt knows more about them than any other living person.

31. See, e.g., Jason Chamberlain to [Bicknell], Nov. 23, 1897, Chaffee and Chamberlain Papers. In this particular letter, Chamberlain also explains the origins of his and Chaffee's association with the story: "Bret Harte was connected with the Overland Monthly and we had a friend and old Partner that was secretary of the company Bret Harte told our friend he was going to write a story and call it Tennessee's Partner Our Friend said he knew a character that would just fill the bill for Tennessee's Partner and when Chaffee went to the City a year ago he was introduced as Tennessee's Partner and was a big surprise to the Partner as he had never heard any thing about the matter before."

32. See Guest Book (1895–1903), Chaffee and Chamberlain Papers. The guest book entries quoted are dated June 9, 11, and 20, 1895. Similar entries continue through 1903, when both men died. In his discussion of the making of a gay male world in New York City's Greenwich Village in this period, George Chauncey notes that "in some contexts calling men 'artistic' became code for calling them homosexual." Although this was quite a different historical context—rural and western—most of the travelers who stopped at Chamberlain and Chaffee's on their way to Yosemite and who wrote in the guest book were from urban areas where such semiotic codes were being developed. Of course, almost no one would have used the term "homosexual" to describe the relationship between Chamberlain and Chaffee at the turn of the century. But I think it not unlikely that future research, by tracing the visitors who wrote in Chamberlain and Chaffee's guest book, will be able

to link the partners to regional variants of the emerging gay worlds Chauncey documents. See *Gay New York: Gender, Urban Culture, and the Making of the Gay Male World, 1890–1940* (New York: Basic Books, 1994), passim and esp. 229. Even more relevant, Jonathan Ned Katz is engaging in a crucial study of intimate relationships between men in the nineteenth century, in which he is uncovering both the varieties of male same-sex bonds and the range of language used to describe those bonds. For example, college-educated men frequently used references to "Damon and Pythias"—and other famous male couples, historical and mythological, of ancient Greece and Rome—to signify intimate male relationships, as travelers did when they visited Chamberlain and Chaffee. Similarly, visitors referred to the two men as "David and Jonathan," a biblical reference commonly used to denote male intimacies in the nineteenth century. In addition to the guest book entries cited above, see, e.g., those dated June 23 and July 9, 1903. See Katz, "Coming to Terms: Conceptualizing Men's Erotic and Affectional Relations with Men in the United States, 1820–1892," in *A Queer World: The Center for Lesbian and Gay Studies Reader,* ed. Martin Duberman (New York: New York Univ. Press, 1997), 216–35, esp. 221.

33. Jason Chamberlain Diary no. 38 (1899), Chaffee and Chamberlain Papers.

34. Entry dated June 27, 1903, Guest Book, Chaffee and Chamberlain Papers.

35. Diary entries, Aug. 2, Oct. 16, 1903, Jason Chamberlain Diary no. 42, Chaffee and Chamberlain Papers; and White.

36. This story is also often reprinted. For the original, see *Overland Monthly,* 1st ser., 1 (1868). For another reading of this story, see Blake Allmendinger, *Ten Most Wanted: The New Western Literature* (New York: Routledge, 1998), 65–78.

37. See Erwin G. Gudde, *California Gold Camps,* ed. Elisabeth K. Gudde (Berkeley: Univ. of California Press, 1975), 293.

38. *Inquest [Unknown Infant]* (1858), Inquest Records, Calaveras County, Calaveras County Museum and Archives, San Andreas, Calif.

39. Gudde, 232–33. For a good account of social relations in the Murphys area, see Leonard Withington Noyes Reminiscences, Essex Institute, Salem, Mass., transcription at Calaveras County Museum and Archives, San Andreas, Calif.

40. For related arguments, see Richard White, *Remembering Ahanagran: Storytelling in a Family's Past* (New York: Hill and Wang, 1998).

41. Here my argument is influenced by Camille Guerin-Gonzales, *Mexican Workers and American Dreams: Immigration, Repatriation, and California Farm Labor, 1900–1939* (New Brunswick, N.J.: Rutgers Univ. Press, 1994), esp. 2–8, and by years of conversation with the author that are stretching into a lifetime.

42. Some of Harte's stories that focus on Chinese characters, even as they helped codify stereotypes, also advanced critiques of white anti-

Chinese activity (critiques that frequently were not recognized and certainly were not shared by many readers). See Takaki, 104–8; Jonathan D. Spence, *The Chan's Great Continent: China in Western Minds* (New York: W. W. Norton, 1998), 126–29, 134–39.

43. The work in progress of David Glassberg, Department of History, Univ. of Massachusetts, Amherst, will help immeasurably in understanding sites of memory in the "gold country"; e.g., "Remapping the Gold Country" (paper presented at the Western History Association Annual Conference, Sacramento, Calif., Oct. 16, 1998).

44. I attended this commemorative celebration in Oct. 1991. Organizers produced a pamphlet entitled *Return to Gold Mountain: The Life of the Early Chinese in California* (Sacramento: Chinese American Council of Sacramento, 1991). The festival was conceived by Peter C. Y. Leung, Asian American Studies, Univ. of California, Davis, who also served as co-chair of the planning committee. Wesley Yee chaired the planning committee.

45. I have not visited the Del Rey Mural, but it is reproduced, described, and analyzed in *Signs from the Heart: California Chicano Murals*, ed. Eva Sperling Cockcroft and Holly Barnet-Sánchez (Venice, Calif.: Social and Public Art Resource Center, 1990; Albuquerque: Univ. of New Mexico Press, 1993), 22, 26–27.

46. I have visited this park, which is located off Highway 88 near Jackson, many times. The State of California produces a useful brochure about the park entitled "Chaw'se, Indian Grinding Rock State Historic Park," California Department of Parks and Recreation, Sacramento, 1994. The periodical *News from Native California* (published by Heyday Books in Berkeley, Calif.) prints quarterly events calendars in which such gatherings as the Big Time festivities are listed.

$\mathcal{S}$elected Bibliography

I. Archival and Manuscript Sources

Amador County Archives, Jackson, Calif.
>Herbert, Lemuel. Journal.
>*The People v. A. C. Brown, E. H. Williams, Hiram Allen, T. Hinckley, and Ellis Evans* (1854), Amador County Court of Sessions.
>Proceedings of a Meeting of the People of Lower Mocalime Bar.

Amador County Courthouse, Jackson, Calif.
>County Court Records.
>District Court Records.

Bancroft Library, Univ. of California, Berkeley
>Bowen, Ben. Journal.
>Brainard, Clementine H. Journal.
>Chaffee, John Amos, and Jason Palmer Chamberlain. Papers and Correspondence.
>Franklin, Lucy A. (Harrison). Papers and Correspondence.
>Osborn, Timothy C. Journal.
>Pownall Family Papers.
>Tuolumne County Water Company. Papers and Correspondence.

Beinecke Library, Yale Univ., New Haven, Conn.
>Allen, George W. Journals.
>Bourne, Julia A. C. Correspondence.
>Chase, Nathan. Correspondence.
>Davis, Charles. Correspondence.
>Delano, Ephraim. Correspondence.
>Flagg, Josiah Foster. Correspondence.
>Fox, P. V. Journals.
>Genung, A. W. Correspondence.
>Kendrick, Benjamin Franklin. Correspondence.

Little, Moses F. Journals.
McIssac, Angus. Journal.
Miller, William W. Journal.
Nye, Helen. Correspondence.
Post, J. H. Correspondence.
Spicer, Julius A. Correspondence.
Watson, Nelson. Correspondence.

Calaveras County Museum and Archives, San Andreas, Calif.
Calaveras County Court Records, District Court Cases.
Calaveras County Court Records, Inquests.
Noyes, Leonard Withington. Reminiscences. Transcription of original from Essex Institute, Salem, Mass.

California State Library, Sacramento, Calif.
Amador County Legal Records.
California Legal Records.
Délèpine, Antoine Alphonse. Papers and Correspondence.
Gilman, Thomas. Papers.
Laws of Chinese Camp Relating to the Mines and Mining Claims.
Lee, Harriet Jane (Kirtland). Journal.
Pennell, William Doyle. Correspondence.
Tuolumne County Records.
Tuolumne County Water Company Papers.

Holt-Atherton Center for Western Studies, Univ. of the Pacific, Stockton, Calif.
Baker, John W. H. Correspondence.
Brame Papers. Effie Johnston Collection.
Wallis, John. Journal.

Huntington Library, San Marino, Calif.
California Lettersheet Facsimiles.
Chamberlain, Jason P. Correspondence.
Hovey, John. Journal.
———. "Historical Account of the troubles between the Chilian and American Miners in the Calaveras Mining District"
———. "Account of the troubles between the American Miners and the Frenchmen of the Garde Mobile at Mokelumne Hill, Calif."
Mandeville, James Wylie. Papers and Correspondence.
Martenet, Jefferson. Papers and Correspondence.
Pownall, Joseph. Papers and Correspondence.
Smith, Lura and Jesse R. Correspondence.

Mariposa Museum and History Center, Mariposa, Calif.
Appling Family File.
Bernhard-Patterson Family File.

Clark Family File.
Counts Family File.

Mariposa County Courthouse, Mariposa, Calif.
District Court Records.
Court of Sessions Records.

Tuolumne County Courthouse, Sonora, Calif.
District Court Records.
Court of Sessions Records.

II. Government Documents

California Legislature. Journals of the Senate and Assembly. *Journal of the Third Session of the Legislature of the State of California.* San Francisco, 1852.
U.S. Bureau of the Census. *The Seventh Census of the United States: 1850.* Washington, D.C., 1853.
————. Seventh Federal Population Census, 1850. National Archives. Washington, D.C. RG-29, M-432, reels 33–35.
————. *Population of the United States in 1860; Compiled from . . . the Eighth Census.* Washington, D.C., 1864.

III. Newspapers

Alta California (San Francisco), scattered issues, 1849–58.
Amador Weekly Ledger (Jackson) (continues *Weekly Ledger*), 1857–58.
The Golden Era (San Francisco), scattered issues, 1852–57.
Stockton Times, 1850–51.
San Joaquin Republican (continues *Stockton Times*), 1851–58.
San Francisco Chronicle, scattered issues, 1936.
Volcano Weekly Ledger, 1855–57.
Weekly Ledger (Jackson) (continues *Volcano Weekly Ledger*), 1857.

IV. Published Primary Sources

Ayers, James J. *Gold and Sunshine: Reminiscences of Early California.* Boston: Richard G. Badger, Gorham Press, 1922.
Booth, Edmund. *Edmund Booth, Forty-Niner: The Life Story of a Deaf Pioneer.* Stockton, Calif.: San Joaquin Pioneer and Historical Society, 1953.
Borthwick, J. D. *The Gold Hunters.* 1857. Oyster Bay, N.Y.: Nelson Doubleday, 1917.
Bunnell, Lafayette Houghton. *Discovery of the Yosemite and the Indian War of 1851 Which Led to That Event.* 1880. Yosemite National Park, Calif.: Yosemite Association, 1990.

Burns, Walter Noble. *The Robin Hood of El Dorado*. New York: Coward-McCann, [1932].

Carson, James H. *Early Recollections of the Mines and a Description of the Great Tulare Valley*. Stockton, Calif.: [San Joaquin Republican], 1852.

Christman, Enos. *One Man's Gold: The Letters and Journal of a Forty-Niner*. Edited by Florence Morrow Christman. New York: Whittlesey House, McGraw-Hill, 1930.

Cleaveland, E. L. *Hasting to Be Rich. A Sermon Occasioned by the Present Excitement Respecting the Gold of California, Preached in the Cities of New Haven and Bridgeport, Jan. and Feb. 1849*. New Haven, Conn.: J. H. Benham, 1849.

Colton, Walter. *Three Years in California*. New York: A. S. Barnes, 1850.

Combet, Pedro Isidoro. "Memories of California." In *We Were 49ers! Chilean Accounts of the California Gold Rush*. Translated and edited by Edwin A. Beilharz and Carlos U. López. Pasadena, Calif.: Ward Ritchie Press, 1976.

Coronel, Antonio Franco. "Cosas de California." Translated and edited by Richard Henry Morefield. In *The Mexican Adaptation in American California, 1846–1875*. 1955. Reprint, San Francisco: R and E Research Associates, 1971.

Cossley-Batt, Jill L. *The Last of the California Rangers*. New York: Funk and Wagnalls, 1928.

Dart, John Paul. "A Mississippian in the Gold Fields: The Letters of John Paul Dart." Edited by Howard Mitcham. *California Historical Society Quarterly* 35, no. 3 (Sept. 1956): 205–31.

Délèpine, Alphonse Antoine. *To My Children: A Simple Narrative of My Travels*. Sonora, Calif.: Banner Printing Co. for Harold Mojonnier, 1963.

Derbec, Étienne. *A French Journalist in the California Gold Rush: The Letters of Étienne Derbec*. Edited by Abraham P. Nasatir. Georgetown, Calif.: Talisman Press, 1964.

Dexter, A. Hersey *Early Days in California*. Denver: Tribune-Republican Press, 1886.

Doble, John. *John Doble's Journal and Letters from the Mines: Mokelumne Hill, Jackson, Volcano and San Francisco, 1851–1865*. Edited by Charles L. Camp. Denver: Old West Publishing, 1962.

"Documents: California Freedom Papers." *Journal of Negro History* 3, no. 1 (Jan. 1918): 45–51.

Doten, Alfred. *The Journals of Alfred Doten, 1849–1903*. 3 vols. Edited by Walter Van Tilburg Clark. Reno: Univ. of Nevada Press, 1973.

Eccleston, Robert. *The Mariposa Indian War, 1850–1851: Diaries of Robert Eccleston: The California Gold Rush, Yosemite, and the High Sierra*. Edited by C. Gregory Crampton. Salt Lake City: Univ. of Utah Press, 1957.

Evans, George W. B. *Mexican Gold Trail: The Journal of a Forty-Niner*. Edited by Glenn S. Dumke. San Marino, Calif.: Huntington Library, 1945.

Fairchild, Lucius. *California Letters of Lucius Fairchild*. Edited by Joseph Schafer. Madison: State Historical Society of Wisconsin, 1931.

Frémont, Elizabeth Benton. *Recollections of Elizabeth Benton Frémont.* Compiled by I. T. Martin. New York: F. H. Hitchcock, 1912.

Frémont, Jessie Benton. *Far-West Sketches.* Boston: D. Lothrop, 1890.

————. *The Letters of Jesse Benton Frémont.* Edited by Pamela Herr and Mary Lee Spence. Urbana: Univ. of Illinois Press, 1993.

Frémont, John Charles. *The Expeditions of John Charles Frémont.* Vol. 2, *The Bear Flag Revolt and the Court-Martial.* Edited by Mary Lee Spence and Donald Jackson. Urbana: Univ. of Illinois Press, 1973.

————. *The Expeditions of John Charles Frémont.* Vol. 3, *Travels from 1848 to 1854.* Edited by Mary Lee Spence. Urbana: Univ. of Illinois Press, 1984.

Gardiner, Howard C. *In Pursuit of the Golden Dream: Reminiscences of San Francisco and the Northern and Southern Mines, 1849–1857.* Edited by Dale L. Morgan. Stoughton, Mass.: Western Hemisphere, 1970.

Gerstäcker, Friedrich W. C. "The French Revolution." Translated by George Cosgrave. *California Historical Society Quarterly* 17, no. 1 (March 1938): 3–17.

————. *Narrative of a Journey round the World.* New York: Harper and Brothers, 1853.

Gonzales, Rodolfo. *I Am Joaquín—Yo soy Joaquín: An Epic Poem.* 1967. Reprint, New York: Bantam Books, 1972.

Gunn, Lewis C., and Elizabeth Le Breton Gunn. *Records of a California Family: Journals and Letters of Lewis C. Gunn and Elizabeth Le Breton Gunn.* Edited by Anna Lee Marston. San Diego: n.p., 1928.

Harlan, Jacob Wright. *California '46 to '88.* 1883. Oakland: n.p., 1896.

Harris, Benjamin Butler. *The Gila Trail: The Texas Argonauts and the California Gold Rush.* Edited by Richard H. Dillon. Norman: Univ. of Oklahoma Press, 1960.

Harte, Bret. *Bret Harte's Gold Rush.* Edited by Reuben H. Margolin. Berkeley, Calif.: Heyday Books, 1997.

————. "The Luck of Roaring Camp." *Overland Monthly,* 1st ser., 1 (1868).

————. "Tennessee's Partner." *Overland Monthly,* 1st ser., 3 (1869).

Hays, Lorena. *To the Land of Gold and Wickedness: The 1848–59 Diary of Lorena L. Hays.* Edited by Jeanne Hamilton Watson. St. Louis: Patrice Press, 1988.

Heckendorn, J., and W. A. Wilson. *Miners and Business Men's Directory for the Year Commencing January 1st, 1856. Embracing a General Directory of the Citizens of Tuolumne…Together with the Mining Laws of Each District, a Description of the Different Camps, and Other Interesting Statistical Matter.* Columbia, Calif.: Clipper Office, 1856.

Helper, Hinton Rowan. *The Impending Crisis of the South: How to Meet It.* New York: Burdick Brothers, 1857.

————. *The Land of Gold: Reality versus Fiction.* Baltimore: Henry Taylor, 1855.

Johnson, Theodore T. *Sights in the Gold Region and Scenes by the Way.* New York: Baker and Scribner, 1849.

Johnston, Effie Enfield. "Wade Johnston Talks to His Daughter." In *Las*

    Calaveras: Quarterly Bulletin of the Calaveras County Historical Society 17–21 (1969–72).

Jolly, John. *Gold Spring Diary: The Journal of John Jolly, and Including a Brief History of Stephen Spencer Hill, Fugitive from Labor*. Edited by Carlo M. De Ferrari. Sonora, Calif.: Tuolumne County Historical Society, 1966.

[Lang, Herbert O.] *A History of Tuolumne County. Compiled from the Most Authentic Records*. San Francisco: B. F. Alley, 1882.

The Life of Joaquin Murieta the Brigand Chief of California; Being a Complete History of His Life, from the Age of Sixteen to the Time of His Capture and Death at the Hands of Capt. Harry Love, in the Year 1853. San Francisco: Office of the "California Police Gazette," 1859.

Loring, James Lovell. *Gold Rush Adventures of James Lovell Loring*. Introduction by Arthur L. Loring. Edited by Alexis A. Praus and Ruth Howard. Kalamazoo, Mich.: Kalamazoo Public Museum, 1963.

McCollum, William. *California as I Saw It. Pencillings by the Way of Its Gold and Gold Diggers. And Incidents of Travel by Land and Water*. 1850. Reprint, edited by Dale L. Morgan. Los Gatos, Calif.: Talisman Press, 1960.

McNeil, Samuel. *McNeil's Travels in 1849, to, through, and from the Gold Regions in California*. Columbus, Ohio: Scott and Bascom, 1850.

Marryat, Frank. *Mountains and Molehills; or, Recollections of a Burnt Journal*. 1855. Reprint, edited by Robin Winks. Philadelphia: J. B. Lippincott, 1962.

Marx, Karl. *The Eighteenth Brumaire of Louis Bonaparte*. 1852. New York: International Publishers, 1963.

Moerenhout, Jacques Antoine. *The Inside Story of the Gold Rush*. Edited and translated by Abraham P. Nasatir. San Francisco: California Historical Society, 1935.

Murder of M. V. B. Griswold by Five Chinese Assassins; Fou Sin—the Principal. Together with the Life of Griswold, and the Statements of Fou Sin, Chou Yee and Coon You, Convicted, and Sentenced to Be Hung at Jackson, April 16, 1858: Illustrated with Correct Likenesses of the Murderers. Jackson, Calif.: T. A. Springer, 1858.

Nadeau, Remi. *The Real Joaquin Murieta: California's Gold Rush Bandit: Truth v. Myth*. Santa Barbara: Crest Publishers, 1974.

Navarro, Ramon Jil. "California in 1849." In *We Were 49ers! Chilean Accounts of the California Gold Rush*. Translated and edited by Edwin A. Beilharz and Carlos U. López. Pasadena: Ward Ritchie Press, 1976.

Neruda, Pablo. *Fulgor y muerte de Joaquín Murieta*. Santiago: Empresa Editoria Zig-Zag, 1966.

———. *The Splendor and Death of Joaquin Murieta*. Translated by Ben Belitt. New York: Farrar, Straus and Giroux, 1972.

Newton, John Marshall. *Memoirs of John Marshall Newton*. N.p.: John M. Stevenson, 1913.

Parkinson, Jessie Heaton. *Adventuring in California, Yesterday, Today, and Day before Yesterday, with Memoirs of Bret Harte's "Tennessee."* San Francisco: Harr Wagner, 1921.

Pérez Rosales, Vicente. *California Adventure*. Translated by Edwin S. Morby and Arturo Torres-Rioseco. San Francisco: Book Club of Calif., 1947.

———. *Diario de un viaje a California, 1848–1849*. Buenos Aires: Editorial Francisco de Aguirre, 1971.

———. "Diary of a Journey to California." In *We Were 49ers! Chilean Accounts of the California Gold Rush*. Translated and edited by Edwin A. Beilharz and Carlos U. López. Pasadena, Calif.: Ward Ritchie Press, 1976.

Perkins, William. *Three Years in California: William Perkins' Journal of Life at Sonora, 1849–1852*. Edited by Dale L. Morgan and James R. Scobie. Berkeley: Univ. of California Press, 1964.

Perlot, Jean-Nicolas. *Gold Seeker: Adventures of a Belgian Argonaut during the Gold Rush Years*. Translated by Helen Harding Bretnor. Edited by Howard R. Lamar. New Haven: Yale Univ. Press, 1985.

Peters, Charles. *The Autobiography of Charles Peters*. Sacramento: La Grave Co., [1915].

Pierce, Hiram Dwight. *A Forty-Niner Speaks*. Oakland, Calif.: Keystone-Inglett Printing Co. for Sarah Wiswall Meyer, 1930.

Ridge, John Rollin [Yellow Bird]. *The Life and Adventures of Joaquín Murieta, the Celebrated California Bandit*. 1854. Reprint, Norman: Univ. of Oklahoma Press, 1955.

Secrest, William. *Joaquin: Bloody Bandit of the Mother Lode*. Fresno, Calif.: Sage–West Publishing, 1967.

Shaw, William. *Golden Dreams and Waking Realities; Being the Adventures of a Gold–Seeker in California and the Pacific Islands*. London: Smith Elder, 1851.

Steele, Reverend John. *In Camp and Cabin: Mining Life and Adventure, in California during 1850 and Later*. Lodi, Wisc.: J. Steele, 1901.

Stocking, Fred. "The Passing of 'Tennessee' and his Partner." *Overland Monthly*, 2d ser., 42 (1903).

Stokes, Fletcher. "Fred Stocking and His Service to California Literature." *Overland Monthly*, 2d ser., 59 (1912).

Taylor, Bayard. *Eldorado or Adventures in the Path of Empire*. 1850. Lincoln: Univ. of Nebraska Press, 1988.

Thom, Mrs. Robert, comp. *Memories of the Days of Old, Days of Gold, Days of 49*. [Sonora, Calif.: The Banner Print, c. 1923].

Two Eras in the Life of the Felon Grovenor I. Layton. Who Was Lynched by the Vigilance Committee, at Sonora, Tuolumne County, California, June 17th, 1852. For Robbery, Murder, and Arson, He Having Robbed Three Chilians, Two Men and One Woman, of Ten Thousand Dollars in Gold Dust, at Mormon Gulch, Murdered and Burned Them, Together with Their Cabin, May 28th, 1852. New Orleans, Charleston, Baltimore, and Philadelphia: A. R. Orton, 1852.

Vischer, Eduard. "A Trip to the Mining Regions in the Spring of 1859." Parts 1 and 2. Translated by Ruth Frey Axe. *California Historical Society Quarterly* 11, no. 3 (Sept. 1932): 224–46; and 11, no. 4 (Dec. 1932): 321–38.

Ward, Samuel. *Sam Ward in the Gold Rush*. Edited by Carvel Collins. Stanford: Stanford Univ. Press, 1949.

Whipple-Haslam, Mrs. Lee. *Early Days in California: Scenes and Events of the '50s as I Remember Them*. Jamestown, Calif.: Mother Lode Magnet, [1925].

Williams, James. *Life and Adventures of James Williams, a Fugitive Slave, with a Full Description of the Underground Railroad*. 3d ed. San Francisco: Women's Union Print, 1874. Reprint, San Francisco: R and E Research Associates, 1969.

Wood, Harvey. *Personal Recollections of Harvey Wood*. Angels Camp, Calif.: Mountain Echo Job Printing Office, [c. 1878].

Woods, Daniel B. *Sixteen Months at the Gold Diggings*. London: Sampson Low; New York: Harper and Brothers, [1851].

V. Secondary Sources

Abu-Lughod, Lila. *Writing Women's Worlds: Bedouin Stories*. Berkeley: Univ. of California Press, 1993.

Allmendinger, Blake. *The Cowboy: Representations of Labor in an American Work Culture*. New York: Oxford Univ. Press, 1992.

———. *Ten Most Wanted: The New Western Literature*. New York: Routledge, 1998.

Almaguer, Tomás. *Racial Fault Lines: The Historical Origins of White Supremacy in California*. Berkeley: Univ. of California Press, 1994.

Anderson, Benedict. *Imagined Communities: Reflections on the Origin and Spread of Nationalism*. London: Verso, 1983.

Armentrout-Ma, Eve. "Urban Chinese at the Sinitic Frontier: Social Organization in United States' Chinatowns, 1849–1898." *Modern Asian Studies* 17, no. 1 (1983): 107–35.

Armitage, Susan, and Elizabeth Jameson, eds. *The Women's West*. Norman: Univ. of Oklahoma Press, 1987.

Arrom, Sylvia Marina. *The Women of Mexico City, 1790–1857*. Stanford: Stanford Univ. Press, 1985.

Arteaga, Alfred. "The Chicano-Mexican Corrido." *Journal of Ethnic Studies* 13, no. 2 (Summer 1985): 75–105.

Bancroft, Hubert H. "Pioneer Register and Index." In *The Works of Hubert Howe Bancroft*, vol. 19, *California*. San Francisco: A. L. Bancroft, 1885.

Barker-Benfield, G. J. *The Horrors of the Half-Known Life: Male Attitudes toward Women and Sexuality in Nineteenth-Century America*. New York: Harper Colophon, 1976.

Baron, Ava, ed. *Work Engendered: Toward a New History of American Labor*. Ithaca: Cornell Univ. Press, 1991.

Barrett, S. A., and E. W. Gifford. *Miwok Material Culture*. Bulletin of the Public Museum of the City of Milwaukee, vol. 2, no. 4. Milwaukee, 1933. Reprint, Yosemite National Park, Calif.: Yosemite Natural History Association, n.d.

Barth, Gunther. *Bitter Strength: A History of the Chinese in the United States, 1850–1870*. Cambridge: Harvard Univ. Press, 1964.

Bates, Craig D. "Miwok Dancers of 1856: Stereographic Images from Sonora, California." *Journal of California and Great Basin Anthropology* 6, no. 1 (1984): 6–18.

Bauer, Arnold J. "Chilean Rural Labor in the Nineteenth Century." *American Historical Review* 76, no. 4 (Oct. 1971): 1059–83.

Bederman, Gail. *Manliness and Civilization: A Cultural History of Gender and Race in the United States, 1880–1917*. Chicago: Univ. of Chicago Press, 1995.

Beilharz, Edwin A., and Carlos U. López, eds. "Introduction." In *We Were 49ers! Chilean Accounts of the California Gold Rush*. Pasadena, Calif.: Ward Ritchie Press, 1976.

Berwanger, Eugene H. *The Frontier against Slavery: Western Anti-Negro Prejudice and the Slavery Extension Controversy*. Urbana: Univ. of Illinois Press, 1967.

Bethell, Leslie, ed. *Cambridge History of Latin America*. Vol. 3, *From Independence to c. 1870*. Cambridge: Cambridge Univ. Press, 1985.

Bieber, Ralph, ed. *Southern Trails to California in 1849*. Glendale, Calif.: Arthur H. Clark, 1937.

Blumenthal, Henry. "The California Societies in France, 1849–1855." *Pacific Historical Review* 25, no. 3 (Aug. 1956): 251–60.

Brown, Elsa Barkley. "Negotiating and Transforming the Public Sphere: African American Political Life in the Transition from Slavery to Freedom." *Public Culture* 7, no. 1 (Fall 1994): 107–46.

———. "Polyrhythms and Improvization: Lessons for Women's History." *History Workshop Journal* 31–32 (1991): 85–90.

Brown, Elsa Barkley, and Gregg D. Kimball, "Mapping the Terrain of Black Richmond." *Journal of Urban History* 21, no. 3 (March 1995): 296–346.

Brown, Ronald C. *Hard-Rock Miners: The Intermountain West, 1860–1920*. College Station: Texas A&M Univ. Press, 1979.

Bruce-Novoa. *Chicano Poetry: A Response to Chaos*. Austin: Univ. of Texas Press, 1982.

Buckbee, Edna Bryan. *The Saga of Old Tuolumne*. New York: Press of the Pioneers, 1935.

Burg, B. R. *An American Seafarer in the Age of Sail: The Erotic Diaries of Philip C. Van Buskirk, 1851–1870*. New Haven: Yale Univ. Press, 1994.

Butler, Judith. *Gender Trouble: Feminism and the Subversion of Identity*. New York: Routledge, 1990.

Camarillo, Albert. *Chicanos in a Changing Society: From Mexican Pueblos to American Barrios in Santa Barbara and Southern California, 1848–1930*. Cambridge: Harvard Univ. Press, 1979.

Cardoso, Fernando Henrique, and Enzo Faletto. *Dependency and Development in Latin America*. Translated by Marjory Mattingly Urquidi. 1971. Berkeley: Univ. of California Press, 1979.

Carnes, Mark C., and Clyde Griffen, eds. *Meanings for Manhood: Constructions of Masculinity in Victorian America.* Chicago: Univ. of Chicago Press, 1990.

Castañeda, Antonia I. "Sexual Violence in the Politics and Policies of Conquest: Amerindian Women and the Spanish Conquest of Alta California." In *Building with Our Hands: New Directions in Chicana Studies,* edited by Adela de la Torre and Beatríz M. Pesquera. Berkeley: Univ. of California Press, 1993.

———. "Women of Color and the Rewriting of Western History: The Discourse, Politics, and Decolonization of History." *Pacific Historical Review* 61, no. 4 (Nov. 1992): 501–33.

Castillo, Pedro, and Albert Camarillo, eds. *Furia y muerte: Los bandidos chicanos.* Monograph no. 4. Los Angeles: Aztlán Publications, Chicano Studies Center, Univ. of California, Los Angeles, 1973.

Caughey, John Walton. *The California Gold Rush.* 1948. Reprint, Berkeley: Univ. of California Press, 1975.

Cenotto, Larry. *Logan's Alley: Amador County Yesterdays in Picture and Prose.* 2 vols. Jackson, Calif.: Cenotto Publications, 1988.

Chan, Sucheng. *Asian Americans: An Interpretive History.* Boston: Twayne, 1991.

———. "Chinese Livelihood in Rural California: The Impact of Economic Change, 1860–1880." *Pacific Historical Review* 53, no. 3 (Aug. 1984): 273–307.

———. "The Exclusion of Chinese Women, 1870–1943." In *Entry Denied: Exclusion and the Chinese Community in America, 1882–1943,* edited by Sucheng Chan. Philadelphia: Temple Univ. Press, 1991.

———. *This Bittersweet Soil: The Chinese in California Agriculture, 1860–1910.* Berkeley: Univ. of California Press, 1986.

Chauncey, George. *Gay New York: Gender, Urban Culture, and the Making of the Gay Male World, 1890–1940.* New York: Basic Books, 1994.

"Chaw'se, Indian Grinding Rock State Historical Park." Sacramento: California Department of Parks and Recreation, 1994.

Chen, Yong. "The Internal Origins of Chinese Emigration to California Reconsidered." *Western Historical Quarterly* 28, no. 4 (Winter 1997): 520–46.

Chinard, Gilbert. "When the French Came to California: An Introductory Essay." *California Historical Society Quarterly* 22, no. 4 (Dec. 1943): 289–314.

Chiu, Ping. *Chinese Labor in California, 1850–1880: An Economic Study.* Madison: State Historical Society of Wisconsin, 1967.

Clifford, James, and George E. Marcus, eds. *Writing Culture: The Poetics and Politics of Ethnography.* Berkeley: Univ. of California Press, 1986.

Clinton, Catherine, and Nina Silber, eds. *Divided Houses: Gender and the Civil War.* New York: Oxford Univ. Press, 1992.

Cockcroft, Eva Sperling, and Holly Barnet-Sánchez, eds. *Signs from the Heart: California Chicano Murals.* Venice, Calif.: Social and Public Art

Resource Center, 1990; Albuquerque: Univ. of New Mexico Press, 1993.

Coomes, Mary L. "From Pooyi to the New Almaden Mercury Mine: Cinnabar, Economics, and Culture to 1920." Ph.D. diss., Univ. of Michigan, 1999.

Corbin, Alain. *Women for Hire: Prostitution and Sexuality in France after 1850.* Translated by Alan Sheridan. Cambridge: Harvard Univ. Press, 1990.

Cott, Nancy F. *The Bonds of Womanhood: "Woman's Sphere" in New England, 1780–1835.* 1977. 2d ed. New Haven: Yale Univ. Press, 1997.

Creighton, Margaret S., and Lisa Norling, eds. *Iron Men, Wooden Women: Gender and Seafaring in the Atlantic World, 1700–1920.* Baltimore: Johns Hopkins Univ. Press, 1996.

Cronon, William. *Changes in the Land: Indians, Colonists, and the Ecology of New England.* New York: Hill and Wang, 1983.

———. *Nature's Metropolis: Chicago and the Great West.* New York: W. W. Norton, 1991.

Davidoff, Leonore, and Catherine Hall. *Family Fortunes: Men and Women of the English Middle Class, 1780–1850.* Chicago: Univ. of Chicago Press, 1987.

Davis, Natalie Zemon, and Randolph Starn. "Introduction." Special Issue: Memory and Counter-Memory. *Representations,* no. 26 (Spring 1989): 1–6.

Davis, W. N., Jr. "Research Uses of County Court Records, 1850–1879, and Incidental Intimate Glimpses of California Life and Society." Parts 1 and 2. *California Historical Quarterly* 52, no. 3 (Fall 1973): 241–66; and 52, no. 4 (Winter 1973): 338–65.

De Ferrari, Carlo M. "A Brief History of Stephen Spencer Hill: Fugitive from Labor." Appended to John Jolly, *Gold Spring Diary: The Journal of John Jolly,* edited by Carlo M. De Ferrari. Sonora, Calif.: Tuolumne County Historical Society, 1966.

Degler, Carl L. *At Odds: Women and the Family in America from the Revolution to the Present.* New York: Oxford Univ. Press, 1980.

D'Emilio, John, and Estelle B. Freedman. *Intimate Matters: A History of Sexuality in America.* 2d ed. Chicago: Univ. of Chicago Press, 1997.

Denning, Michael. *Mechanic Accents: Dime Novels and Working-Class Culture in America.* London: Verso, 1987.

Deutsch, Sarah. *No Separate Refuge: Culture, Class, and Gender on an Anglo-Hispanic Frontier in the American Southwest, 1880–1940.* New York: Oxford Univ. Press, 1987.

Driesbach, Janice T., Harvey L. Jones, and Katherine Church Holland. *Art of the Gold Rush.* Oakland: Oakland Museum of California, Crocker Art Museum, and Univ. of California Press, 1998.

Duberman, Martin. "'Writhing Bedfellows' in Antebellum South Carolina: Historical Interpretation and the Politics of Evidence." In *Hidden from History: Reclaiming the Gay and Lesbian Past,* edited by Martin Duberman et al. New York: Meridian/Penguin, 1989.

Duberman, Martin, Martha Vicinus, and George Chauncey Jr., eds. *Hidden from History: Reclaiming the Gay and Lesbian Past*. New York: Meridian/Penguin, 1989.

Dubofsky, Melvyn. *We Shall Be All: A History of the Industrial Workers of the World*. Chicago: Quadrangle Books, 1969.

Eisenstein, Zillah, ed. *Capitalist Patriarchy and the Case for Socialist Feminism*. New York: Monthly Review Press, 1979.

Emmons, David M. *The Butte Irish: Class and Ethnicity in an American Mining Town, 1875–1925*. Urbana: Univ. of Illinois Press, 1989.

Evans, E. Raymond. "Following the Rainbow: The Cherokees in the California Gold Fields." *Journal of Cherokee Studies* 2, no. 1 (Winter 1977): 170–75.

Fabian, Ann Vincent. *Card Sharps, Dream Books, and Bucket Shops: Gambling in Nineteenth-Century America*. Ithaca: Cornell Univ. Press, 1990.

———. "Rascals and Gentlemen: The Meaning of American Gambling, 1820–1890." Ph.D. diss., Yale Univ., 1982.

Fairbank, John K., ed. *Cambridge History of China*. Vol. 10, *Late Ch'ing, 1800–1911*. Part 1. Cambridge: Cambridge Univ. Press, 1978.

Faragher, John Mack. *Sugar Creek: Life on the Illinois Prairie*. New Haven: Yale Univ. Press, 1986.

———. *Women and Men on the Overland Trail*. New Haven: Yale Univ. Press, 1979.

Faugsted, George Edward, Jr. *The Chilenos in the California Gold Rush*. 1963. Reprint, San Francisco: R and E Research Associates, 1973.

Fields, Barbara Jeanne. "Ideology and Race in American History." In *Region, Race, and Reconstruction: Essays in Honor of C. Vann Woodward*, edited by J. Morgan Kousser and James M. McPherson. New York: Oxford Univ. Press, 1982.

Fischer, Michael M. J. "Ethnicity and the Post-modern Arts of Memory." In *Writing Culture: The Poetics and Politics of Ethnography*, edited by James Clifford and George E. Marcus. Berkeley: Univ. of California Press, 1986.

Foley, Neil. *The White Scourge: Mexicans, Blacks and Poor Whites in Texas Cotton Culture*. Berkeley: Univ. of California Press, 1998.

Foner, Eric. *Free Soil, Free Labor, Free Men: The Ideology of the Republican Party before the Civil War*. New York: Oxford Univ. Press, 1970.

Foucault, Michael. *Discipline and Punish: The Birth of the Prison*. Translated by Alan Sheridan. 1975. New York: Vintage Books, 1979.

———. *The History of Sexuality*. Vol. 1, *An Introduction*. Translated by Robert Hurley. 1976. New York: Vintage Books, 1990.

Frank, Dana. *Purchasing Power: Consumer Organizing, Gender, and the Seattle Labor Movement, 1919–1929*. New York: Cambridge Univ. Press, 1994.

Gadlin, Howard. "Private Lives and Public Order: A Critical View of the History of Intimate Relations in the U.S." *Massachusetts Review* 17 (Summer 1976): 304–330.

Gates, Paul W. *Land Law in California: Essays on Land Policies*. Ames: Iowa State Univ. Press, 1991.

Geertz, Clifford. *The Interpretation of Cultures*. New York: Basic Books, 1973.

Genovese, Eugene D. *The Political Economy of Slavery: Studies in the Economy and Society of the Slave South*. 2d ed. Middletown, Conn.: Wesleyan Univ. Press, 1989.

Gifford, E. W. "Central Miwok Ceremonies." *Anthropological Records* 14, no. 4 (1955): 261–318.

———. "Miwok Cults." *University of California Publications in American Archaeology and Ethnology* 18, no. 3 (1926): 391–408.

Gilfoyle, Timothy J. *City of Eros: New York City, Prostitution, and the Commercialization of Sex, 1790–1920*. New York: W. W. Norton, 1992.

Glassberg, David. "Remapping the Gold Country." Paper Presented at the Western History Association Annual Conference, Sacramento, Calif., Oct. 16, 1998.

Glenn, Evelyn Nakano. "From Servitude to Service Work: Historical Continuities in the Racial Division of Paid Reproductive Labor." *Signs* 18, no. 1 (Autumn 1992): 1–43.

Goldman, Marion. *Gold Diggers and Silver Miners: Prostitution and Social Life on the Comstock Lode*. Ann Arbor: Univ. of Michigan Press, 1981.

González, Deena J. "La Tules of Image and Reality: Euro-American Attitudes and Legend Formation on a Spanish-Mexican Frontier." In *Building with Our Hands: New Directions in Chicana Studies*, edited by Adela de la Torre and Beatríz M. Pesquera. Berkeley: Univ. of California Press, 1993.

———. "The Widowed Women of Santa Fe: Assessments on the Lives of an Unmarried Population, 1850–1880." In *On Their Own: Widows and Widowhood in the American Southwest, 1848–1939*, edited by Arlene Scadron. Urbana: Univ. of Illinois Press, 1988. Reprinted in *Unequal Sisters: A Multicultural Reader in U.S. Women's History*, edited by Ellen Carol DuBois and Vicki L. Ruiz. New York: Routledge, 1990.

Goodman, David. *Gold Seeking: Victoria and California in the 1850s*. Stanford: Stanford Univ. Press, 1994.

Gorn, Elliot. "'Gouge and Bite, Pull Hair and Scratch': The Social Significance of Fighting in the Southern Backcountry." *American Historical Review* 90, no. 1 (Feb. 1985): 18–43.

Greenberg, Kenneth S. *Honor and Slavery: Lies, Duels, Noses, Masks, Dressing as a Woman, Gifts, Strangers, Humanitarianism, Death, Slave Rebellions, the Proslavery Argument, Baseball, Hunting, and Gambling in the Old South*. Princeton: Princeton Univ. Press, 1996.

———. "The Nose, the Lie, and the Duel in the Antebellum South." *American Historical Review* 95, no. 1 (Feb. 1990): 57–74.

Griffen, Clyde. "Reconstructing Masculinity from the Evangelical Revival to the Waning of Progressivism: A Speculative Synthesis." In *Meanings for Manhood: Constructions of Masculinity in Victorian America*. Edited by Mark C. Carnes and Clyde Griffen. Chicago: Univ. of Chicago Press, 1990.

Griswold, Robert L. *Family and Divorce in California, 1850–1890: Victorian*

Illusions and Everyday Realities. Albany: State Univ. of New York Press, 1982.

Gudde, Erwin G. *California Gold Camps*. Edited by Elisabeth K. Gudde. Berkeley: Univ. of California Press, 1975.

Guerin-Gonzales, Camille. "Conversing across Boundaries of Race, Ethnicity, Class, Gender, and Region: Latina and Latino Labor History." *Labor History* 35, no. 4 (Fall 1994): 547–63.

———. *Mexican Workers and American Dreams: Immigration, Repatriation, and California Farm Labor, 1900–1939*. New Brunswick, N.J.: Rutgers Univ. Press, 1994.

Guinn, J. M. "The Sonoran Migration." *Historical Society of Southern California Annual Publications* 8 (1909–11): 31–36.

Gutiérrez, David G. *Walls and Mirrors: Mexican Ameicans, Mexican Immigrants, and the Politics of Ethnicity*. Berkeley: Univ. of California Press, 1995.

Gutiérrez, Ramón A. "From Honor to Love: Transformations of the Meaning of Sexuality in Colonial New Mexico." In *Kinship Ideology and Practice in Latin America*, edited by Raymond T. Smith. Chapel Hill: Univ. of North Carolina Press, 1984.

———. "Honor Ideology, Marriage Negotiation, and Class–Gender Domination in New Mexico, 1690–1846." *Latin American Perspectives* 12, no. 1 (Winter 1985): 81–104.

———. *When Jesus Came, the Corn Mothers Went Away: Marriage, Sexuality, and Power in New Mexico, 1500–1846*. Stanford: Stanford Univ. Press, 1991.

Gutman, Herbert G. "Work, Culture, and Society in Industrializing America, 1815–1919." In *Work, Culture and Society in Industrializing America: Essays in American Working-Class and Social History*. New York: Alfred A. Knopf, 1976.

Haas, Lisbeth. *Conquests and Historical Identities in California, 1769–1936*. Berkeley: Univ. of California Press, 1995.

———. "War in California, 1846–1848." In Special Issue: Contested Eden: California Before the Gold Rush. *California History* 76, nos. 2 and 3 (Summer and Fall 1997): 331–55.

Hanchett, William. "The Question of Religion and the Taming of California, 1849–1854, Part I." *California Historical Society Quarterly* 32, no. 1 (March 1953): 49–56.

Hargis, Donald E. "Native Californians in the Constitutional Convention of 1849." *Historical Society of Southern California Quarterly* 36, no. 1 (March 1954): 3–13.

Harsin, Jill. *Policing Prostitution in Nineteenth-Century Paris*. Princeton: Princeton Univ. Press, 1985.

Hartmann, Heidi. "The Family as the Locus of Gender, Class, and Political Struggle: The Example of Housework." *Signs* 6 (Spring 1981): 366–94.

Herr, Pamela. *Jessie Benton Fremont*. New York: Franklin Watts, 1987.

Hietala, Thomas R. *Manifest Design: Anxious Aggrandizement in Late Jacksonian America*. Ithaca: Cornell Univ. Press, 1985.

Higginbotham, Evelyn Brooks. "African-American Women's History and the

Metalanguage of Race." *Signs* 17, no. 2 (Winter 1992): 251–74.

Hirata, Lucie Cheng. "Free, Indentured, Enslaved: Chinese Prostitutes in Nineteenth-Century America." *Signs* 5, no. 1 (Autumn 1979): 3–29.

Hittell, Theodore H. *History of California*. Vol. 4. San Francisco: N. J. Stone, 1898.

Hobsbawm, E. J. *The Age of Capital, 1848–1875*. 1979. New York: New American Library, 1984.

———. *The Age of Revolution, 1789–1848*. New York: Mentor/New American Library, 1962.

———. *Bandits*. London: Weidenfeld and Nicolson, 1969.

———. *Primitive Rebels: Studies in Archaic Forms of Social Movements in the 19th and 20th Centuries*. New York: Praeger, 1959.

Holliday, J. S. *The World Rushed In: The California Gold Rush Experience*. New York: Simon and Schuster, 1981.

Holt, Thomas C. "Marking: Race, Race-Making, and the Writing of History." *American Historical Review* 100, no. 1 (Feb. 1995): 1–20.

Hu-DeHart, Evelyn. *Missionaries, Miners and Indians: Spanish Contact with the Yaqui Nation of Northwestern New Spain, 1533–1820*. Tucson: Univ. of Arizona Press, 1981.

———. *Yaqui Resistance and Survival: The Struggle for Land and Autonomy, 1821–1910*. Madison: Univ. of Wisconsin Press, 1984.

Huginnie, Andrea Yvette. "'Strikitos': Race, Class, and Work in the Arizona Copper Industry, 1870–1920." Ph.D. diss., Yale Univ., 1991.

Hunter, Tera W. *To 'Joy My Freedom: Southern Black Women's Lives and Labors after the Civil War*. Cambridge: Harvard Univ. Press, 1997.

Hurtado, Albert L. "'Hardly a Farmhouse—a Kitchen without Them': Indian and White Households on the California Borderland Frontier in 1860." *Western Historical Quarterly* 13 (1982): 245–70.

———. *Indian Survival on the California Frontier*. New Haven: Yale Univ. Press, 1988.

———. "When Strangers Met: Sex and Gender on Three Frontiers." In *Writing the Range: Race, Class, and Culture in the Women's West*, edited by Elizabeth Jameson and Susan Armitage. Norman: Univ. of Oklahoma Press, 1997.

Ignatiev, Noel. *How the Irish Became White*. New York: Routledge, 1995.

Jackson, Joseph Henry. *Bad Company*. New York: Harcourt, Brace, 1949.

———. "The Creation of Joaquin Murieta." *Pacific Spectator* 2, no. 2 (Spring 1948): 176–81.

James, Daniel. "Meatpackers, Peronists, and Collective Memory: A View from the South." *American Historical Review* 102, no. 5 (Dec. 1997): 1371–1412.

Jameson, Elizabeth. *All That Glitters: Class, Conflict, and Community in Cripple Creek*. Urbana: Univ. of Illinois Press, 1998.

Jameson, Elizabeth, and Susan Armitage, eds. *Writing the Range: Race, Class, and Culture in the Women's West*. Norman: Univ. of Oklahoma Press, 1997.

Jardin, André, and André-Jean Tusdeq. *Restoration and Reaction, 1815–1848*. Translated by Elborg Foster. Cambridge: Cambridge Univ. Press, 1983.

Jensen, Joan M. "Cloth, Butter, and Boarders: Women's Household Production for the Market." *Review of Radical Political Economics* 12, no. 2 (Summer 1980): 14–24.

———. *Loosening the Bonds: Mid-Atlantic Farm Women, 1750–1850.* New Haven: Yale Univ. Press, 1986.

Johnson, David A. *Founding the Far West: California, Oregon, and Nevada, 1840–1890.* Berkeley: Univ. of California Press, 1992.

Johnson, Drew Heath, and Marcia Eymann, eds. *Silver and Gold: Cased Images of the California Gold Rush.* Iowa City: Univ. of Iowa Press for Oakland Museum of California, 1998.

Johnson, Susan Lee. "'A Memory Sweet to Soldiers': The Significance of Gender in the History of the 'American West.'" *Western Historical Quarterly* 24, no. 4 (Nov. 1993): 495–517. Reprinted in *A New Significance: Re-Envisioning the History of the American West*, edited by Clyde A. Milner II. New York: Oxford Univ. Press, 1996.

———. "Sharing Bed and Board: Cohabitation and Cultural Difference in Central Arizona Mining Towns, 1863–1873." *Frontiers* 7, no. 3 (1984). Reprinted in *The Women's West*, edited by Susan Armitage and Elizabeth Jameson. Norman: Univ. of Oklahoma Press, 1987.

———. "The United States of Jessie Benton Frémont: Corresponding with the Nation." *Reviews in American History* 23, no. 2 (June 1995): 219–25.

Jones, Oakah L, Jr. *Los Paisanos: Spanish Settlers on the Northern Frontier of New Spain.* Norman: Univ. of Oklahoma Press, 1979.

Joseph, Gilbert M. "On the Trail of Latin American Bandits: A Reexamination of Peasant Resistance." *Latin American Research Review* 25, no. 3 (1990): 3–53.

Kaplan, Amy, and Donald E. Pease, eds. *Cultures of United States Imperialism.* Durham, N.C.: Duke Univ. Press, 1993.

Katz, Jonathan Ned. "Coming to Terms: Conceptualizing Men's Erotic and Affectional Relations with Men in the United States, 1820–1892." In *A Queer World: The Center for Lesbian and Gay Studies Reader*, edited by Martin Duberman. New York: New York Univ. Press, 1997.

———. *Gay American History: Lesbians and Gay Men in the U.S.A.* New York: Thomas E. Crowell, 1976.

Kelley, Joan. "The Doubled Vision of Feminist Theory." In *Women, History, and Theory*. Chicago: Univ. of Chicago Press, 1984. (First published in *Feminist Studies* 5, no. 1 [Spring 1979].)

Kenny, William Robert. "Mexican-American Conflict on the Mining Frontier, 1848–1852." *Journal of the West* 6, no. 4 (Oct. 1967): 582–92.

———. "Nativism in the Southern Mining Region of California." *Journal of the West* 12, no. 1 (Jan. 1973): 126–38.

Kroeber, A. L. *Handbook of the Indians of California.* 1925. Reprint, St. Clair Shores, Mich.: Scholarly Press, 1976.

Kuznesof, Elizabeth, and Robert Oppenheimer. "The Family and Society in Nineteenth-Century Latin America: An Historiographical Introduction." *Journal of Family History* 10, no. 3 (Fall 1985): 215–34.

Lamar, Howard. "From Bondage to Contract: Ethnic Labor in the American West, 1600–1890." In *The Countryside in the Age of Capitalist Transformation*, edited by Steven Hahn and Jonathan Prude. Chapel Hill: Univ. of North Carolina Press, 1985.

———, ed. *The New Encyclopedia of the American West*. New Haven: Yale Univ. Press, 1998.

———, ed. *Reader's Encyclopedia of the American West*. New York: Harper & Row, 1977.

Lapp, Rudolph M. *Blacks in Gold Rush California*. New Haven: Yale Univ. Press, 1977.

Latta, Frank F. *Joaquín Murietta and His Horse Gangs*. Santa Cruz, Calif.: Bear State Books, 1980.

Laurie, Bruce. *Artisans into Workers: Labor in Nineteenth-Century America*. New York: Hill and Wang, 1989.

Lecompte, Janet. "The Independent Women of Hispanic New Mexico, 1821–1846." *Western Historical Quarterly* 12, no. 1 (Jan. 1981): 17–35.

Lee, Hector H. "The Reverberant Joaquín Murieta in California Legendry." *Pacific Historian* 25, no. 3 (Fall 1981): 39–47.

Levinson, Robert E. *The Jews in the California Gold Rush*. New York: KTAV Publishing, 1978.

Levy, Richard. "Eastern Miwok." In *Handbook of North American Indians*. Vol. 8, *California*, edited by Robert F. Heizer. Washington, D.C.: Smithsonian Institution, 1978.

Limerick, Patricia Nelson. *The Legacy of Conquest: The Unbroken Past of the American West*. New York: W. W. Norton, 1987.

Lingenfelter, Richard E. *The Hardrock Miners: A History of the Mining Labor Movement in the American West, 1863–1893*. Berkeley: Univ. of California Press, 1974.

López, Carlos U. *Chilenos in California: A Study of the 1850, 1852 and 1860 Census*. San Francisco: R and E Research Associates, 1973.

Lott, Eric. *Love and Theft: Blackface Minstrelsy and the American Working Class*. New York: Oxford Univ. Press, 1993.

Loveman, Brian. *Chile: The Legacy of Hispanic Capitalism*. New York: Oxford Univ. Press, 1979.

McGloin, John B., S. J., ed. "A California Gold Rush Padre: New Light on the 'Padre of Paradise Flat.'" *California Historical Society Quarterly* 40, no. 1 (March 1961): 49–67.

McGlone, Robert E. "Rescripting a Troubled Past: John Brown's Family and the Harpers Ferry Conspiracy." *Journal of American History* 75, no. 4 (March 1989): 1179–200.

Maffly-Kipp, Laurie F. *Religion and Society in Frontier California*. New Haven: Yale Univ. Press, 1994.

Mangan, J. A., and James Walvin, eds. *Manliness and Morality: Middle-Class Masculinity in Britain and America, 1800–1940*. Manchester: Manchester Univ. Press, 1987.

Maniery, James Gary. *Six Mile and Murphys Rancherias: A Study of Two Central*

Sierra Miwok Sites. San Diego Museum Papers, no. 22. San Diego: San Diego Museum of Man, 1987.

Mann, Ralph. *After the Gold Rush: Society in Grass Valley and Nevada City, California, 1849–1870.* Stanford: Stanford Univ. Press, 1982.

Martínez, Julio A., and Francisco A. Lomelí. *Chicano Literature: A Reference Guide.* Westport, Conn.: Greenwood Press, 1985.

Mei, June. "Socioeconomic Origins of Emigration: Guangdong to California, 1850 to 1882." In *Labor Immigration under Capitalism: Asian Workers in the United States before World War II,* edited by Lucie Cheng and Edna Bonacich. Berkeley: Univ. of California Press, 1984.

Melosh, Barbara. *"The Physician's Hand": Work Culture and Conflict in American Nursing.* Philadelphia: Temple Univ. Press, 1982.

Merriam, C. Hart. "The Mourning Ceremony of the Miwok, 1906." Reprinted in *The California Indians: A Source Book.* Edited by R. F. Heizer and M. A. Whipple. 2d ed. Berkeley: Univ. of California Press, 1971.

Merriman, John M. *The Agony of the Republic: The Repression of the Left in Revolutionary France, 1848–1851.* New Haven: Yale Univ. Press, 1978.

Miller, Nancy K. "Changing the Subject." In *Coming to Terms: Feminism, Theory, and Politics,* edited by Elizabeth Weed. New York: Routledge, 1989.

Mintz, Steven, and Susan Kellog. *Domestic Revolutions: A Social History of American Family Life.* New York: Basic Books, 1988.

Minnick, Sylvia Sun. *Samfow: The San Joaquin Chinese Legacy.* Fresno, Calif.: Panorama West Publishing, 1988.

Mitchell, Annie R. "Major James D. Savage and Tulareños." *California Historical Society Quarterly* 28, no. 4 (Dec. 1949): 323–41.

Monaghan, Jay. *Chile, Peru and the California Gold Rush of 1849.* Berkeley: Univ. of California Press, 1973.

Morefield, Richard Henry. *The Mexican Adaptation in American California, 1846–1875.* 1955. Reprint, San Francisco: R and E Research Associates, 1971.

———."Mexicans in the California Mines, 1848–53." *California Historical Society Quarterly* 35, no. 1 (March 1956): 37–46.

Morrissey, Katherine G. *Mental Territories: Mapping the Inland Empire.* Ithaca: Cornell Univ. Press, 1997.

Mouat, Jeremy. *Roaring Days: Rossland's Mines and the History of British Columbia.* Vancouver: Univ. of British Columbia Press, 1995.

Moulton, Gary E. *John Ross: Cherokee Chief.* Athens: Univ. of Georgia Press, 1978.

Moynihan, Ruth B., Susan Armitage, and Christiane Fischer Dichamp, eds. *So Much to Be Done: Women Settlers on the Mining and Ranching Frontier.* Lincoln: Univ. of Nebraska Press, 1990.

Murphy, Mary. *Mining Cultures: Men, Women, and Leisure in Butte, 1914–41.* Urbana: Univ. of Illinois Press, 1997.

Nasatir, Abraham P. "Alexandre Dumas fils and the Lottery of the Golden Ingots." *California Historical Society Quarterly* 33, no. 2 (June 1954): 125–42.

———. "Chilenos in California during the Gold Rush Period and the Establishment of the Chilean Consulate." *California Historical Quarterly* 53, no. 1 (Spring 1974): 52–70.

———. *French Activities in California: An Archival Calendar Guide.* Stanford: Stanford Univ. Press, 1945.

News from Native California, 1990–.

Nora, Pierre. "Between Memory and History: Les Lieux de Mémoire." *Representations,* no. 26 (Spring 1989): 7–25.

———. *Realms of Memory: Rethinking the French Past.* Translated by Arthur Goldhammer. New York: Columbia Univ. Press, 1996–.

Ong, Paul. "An Ethnic Trade: The Chinese Laundries in Early California." *Journal of Ethnic Studies* 8, no. 4 (Winter 1981): 95–113.

Parins, James W. *John Rollin Ridge: His Life and Works.* Lincoln: Univ. of Nebraska Press, 1991.

Pascoe, Peggy. *Relations of Rescue: The Search for Female Moral Authority in the American West, 1874–1939.* New York: Oxford Univ. Press, 1990.

Paul, Rodman W. *California Gold: The Beginning of Mining in the Far West.* 1947. Reprint, Lincoln: Univ. of Nebraska Press, 1965.

Peristiany, J. G., ed. *Honour and Shame: The Values of Mediterranean Society.* Chicago: Univ. of Chicago Press, 1966.

Perry, Lewis. *Childhood, Marriage, and Reform: Henry Clarke Wright, 1791–1870.* Chicago: Univ. of Chicago Press, 1980.

Peterson, Richard H. "Anti-Mexican Nativism in California, 1848–1853: A Study of Cultural Conflict." *Southern California Quarterly* 62, no. 4 (Winter 1980): 309–27.

———. "The Foreign Miners' Tax of 1850 and Mexicans in California: Exploitation or Expulsion?" *Pacific Historian* 20, no. 3 (Fall 1976): 265–72.

———. *Manifest Destiny in the Mines: A Cultural Interpretation of Anti-Mexican Nativism in California, 1848–1853.* 1965. Rev. ed. San Francisco: R and E Research Associates, 1975.

Phillips, George Harwood. *Indians and Indian Agents: The Origins of the Reservation System in California, 1849–1852.* Norman: Univ. of Oklahoma Press, 1997.

———. *Indians and Intruders in Central California, 1769–1849.* Norman: Univ. of Oklahoma Press, 1993.

Pitt, Leonard. "The Beginnings of Nativism in California." *Pacific Historical Review* 30, no. 1 (Feb. 1961): 23–38.

———. *The Decline of the Californios: A Social History of the Spanish–Speaking Californians, 1846–1890.* Berkeley: Univ. of California Press, 1966.

Pitt-Rivers, Julian. "Honor." In *International Encyclopedia of the Social Sciences,* edited by David L. Sills. 18 vols. New York: Macmillan, 1968.

Pleck, Elizabeth H., and Joseph H. Pleck, eds. *The American Man.* Englewood Cliffs, N.J.: Prentice-Hall, 1980.

Price, Roger, ed. *Revolution and Reaction: 1848 and the Second French Republic.* London: Croom Helm, 1975.

Prucha, Francis Paul. *The Great Father: The United States Government and the American Indians.* 1984. Abridged ed. Lincoln: Univ. of Nebraska Press, 1986.

Prude, Jonathan. *The Coming of Industrial Order: Town and Factory Life in Rural Massachusetts, 1800–1860.* Cambridge: Cambridge Univ. Press, 1983.

Radding, Cynthia. *Wandering Peoples: Colonialism, Ethnic Spaces, and Ecological Frontiers in Northwestern Mexico, 1700–1850.* Durham, N.C.: Duke Univ. Press, 1997.

Rawls, James J. "Gold Diggers: Indian Miners in the California Gold Rush." *California Historical Quarterly* 55, no. 1 (Spring 1976): 28–45.

———. *Indians of California: The Changing Image.* Norman: Univ. of Oklahoma Press, 1984.

Rensch, Hero Eugene. "Columbia, a Gold Camp of Old Tuolumne: Her Rise and Decline, Together with Some Mention of Her Social Life and Cultural Strivings." Berkeley, 1936, for State of California, Department of Natural Resources, Division of Parks, under auspices of Works Progress Administration.

Return to Gold Mountain: The Life of the Early Chinese in California. Sacramento: Chinese American Council of Sacramento, 1991.

Reverby, Susan M. *Ordered to Care: The Dilemma of American Nursing, 1850–1945.* Cambridge: Cambridge Univ. Press, 1987.

Reynolds, David S. *Beneath the American Renaissance: The Subversive Imagination in the Age of Emerson and Melville.* New York: Alfred A. Knopf, 1988.

Riley, Denise. *"Am I That Name?": Feminism and the Category of "Women" in History.* Minneapolis: Univ. of Minnesota Press, 1988.

Riley, Glenda. *Women and Indians on the Frontier, 1825–1915.* Albuquerque: Univ. of New Mexico Press, 1984.

Robb, John Donald. *Hispanic Folk Music of New Mexico and the Southwest: A Self-Portrait of a People.* Norman: Univ. of Oklahoma Press, 1980.

Rocard, Marcienne. *The Children of the Sun: Mexican-Americans in the Literature of the United States.* Translated by Edward G. Brown, Jr. 1980. Tucson: Univ. of Arizona Press, 1989.

Roediger, David R. *The Wages of Whiteness: Race and the Making of the American Working Class.* London: Verso, 1991.

Rohrbough, Malcolm J. *Days of Gold: The California Gold Rush and the American Nation.* Berkeley: Univ. of California Press, 1997.

Rolle, Andrew. *John Charles Frémont: Character as Destiny.* Norman: Univ. of Oklahoma Press, 1991.

Rony, Dorothy Fujita. "The 1854 Chinese War of Weaverville, California." Unpublished paper, Yale Univ., 1990.

Rosaldo, Renato. "Imperialist Nostalgia." *Representations,* no. 26 (Spring 1989): 107–22.

Rosenbaum, Robert J. *Mexicano Resistance in the Southwest: "The Sacred Right of Self-Preservation."* Austin: Univ. of Texas Press, 1981.

Rosenberg, Charles E. "Sexuality, Class, and Role in Nineteenth-Century America." *American Quarterly* 35, no. 2 (May 1973): 131–53.

Rosenzweig, Roy. *Eight Hours for What We Will: Workers and Leisure in an Industrial City, 1870–1920.* Cambridge: Cambridge Univ. Press, 1983.

Roske, Ralph J. "The World Impact of the California Gold Rush, 1849–1857." *Arizona and the West* 5, no. 3 (Autumn 1963): 187–232.

Rotter, Andrew J. "'Matilda for God's Sake Write': Women and Families on the Argonaut Mind." *California History* 58, no. 2 (Summer 1979): 128–41.

Rotundo, E. Anthony. *American Manhood: Transformations in Masculinity from the Revolution to the Modern Era.* New York: Basic Books, 1993.

———. "Learning about Manhood: Gender Ideals and the Middle-Class Family in Nineteenth-Century America." In *Manliness and Morality: Middle-Class Masculinity in Britain and America, 1800–1940,* edited by J. A. Mangan and James Walvin. Manchester: Manchester Univ. Press, 1987.

———. "Romantic Friendship: Male Intimacy and Middle-Class Youth in the Northern United States, 1800–1900." *Journal of Social History* 23, no. 1 (1989): 1–25.

Royce, Josiah. *California, from the Conquest in 1846 to the Second Vigilance Committee in San Francisco: A Study of American Character.* 1886. Reprint, Santa Barbara: Peregrine, 1970.

Ryan, Mary P. *Cradle of the Middle Class: The Family in Oneida County, New York, 1790–1865.* Cambridge: Cambridge Univ. Press, 1981.

Said, Edward W. *Orientalism.* New York: Pantheon, 1978.

San Francisco Lesbian and Gay History Project. "'She Even Chewed Tobacco': A Pictorial Narrative of Passing Women in America." In *Hidden from History: Reclaiming the Gay and Lesbian Past,* edited by Martin Duberman et al. New York: Meridian/Penguin, 1989.

Sánchez, Rosaura. *Telling Identities: The Californio testimonios.* Minneapolis: Univ. of Minnesota Press, 1995.

Saxton, Alexander. *The Indispensable Enemy: Labor and the Anti-Chinese Movement in California.* Berkeley: Univ. of California Press, 1971.

———. *The Rise and Fall of the White Republic: Class Politics and Mass Culture in Nineteenth-Century America.* London: Verso, 1990.

Schlissel, Lillian, Vicki L. Ruiz, and Janice Monk, eds. *Western Women: Their Land, Their Lives.* Albuquerque: Univ. of New Mexico Press, 1988.

Scott, Joan. "Deconstructing Equality-versus-Difference: Or, the Uses of Poststructuralist Theory for Feminism." *Feminist Studies* 14, no. 1 (Spring 1988): 33–50.

———. "Gender: A Useful Category of Historical Analysis." *American Historical Review* 91, no. 5 (Dec. 1986): 1053–75.

———. *Gender and the Politics of History.* New York: Columbia Univ. Press, 1988.

Sedgwick, Eve Kosofsky. *Between Men: English Literature and Male Homosocial Desire.* New York: Columbia Univ. Press, 1985.

Shay, Anthony. "Fandangos and Bailes: Dancing and Dance Events in Early California." *Southern California Quarterly* 64, no. 2 (Summer 1982): 99–113.

Shepard, William Finley. "Parisian Paupers in the California Gold Rush." *Conference of California Historical Societies Proceedings* (1955): 31–45.

Shinn, Charles Howard. *Mining Camps: A Study in American Frontier Government.* Edited by Rodman Wilson Paul. 1884. Reprint, Gloucester, Mass.: Peter Smith, 1970.

Silber, Nina. *The Romance of Reunion: Northerners and the South, 1865–1900.* Chapel Hill: Univ. of North Carolina Press, 1993.

Sinha, Mrinalini. "Gender and Imperialism: Colonial Policy and the Ideology of Moral Imperialism in Late Nineteenth-Century Bengal." In *Changing Men: New Directions in Research on Men and Masculinity,* edited by Michael Kimmel. Newbury Park, Calif.: Sage Publications, 1987.

Siu, Paul C. P. *The Chinese Laundryman: A Study in Social Isolation.* Edited by John Kuo Wei Tchen. 1953. New York: New York Univ. Press, 1987.

Sklar, Kathryn Kish. *Catharine Beecher: A Study in American Domesticity.* New York: W. W. Norton, 1976.

Snitow, Ann, Christine Stansell, and Sharon Thompson, eds. *Powers of Desire: The Politics of Sexuality.* New York: Monthly Review Press, 1983.

Spence, Jonathan D. *The Chan's Great Continent: China in Western Minds.* New York: W. W. Norton, 1998.

———. *God's Chinese Son: The Taiping Heavenly Kingdom of Hong Xiuquan.* New York: W. W. Norton, 1996.

———. *The Search for Modern China.* New York: W. W. Norton, 1990.

Spence, Mary Lee. "David Hoffman: Fremont's Mariposa Agent in London." *Southern California Quarterly* 60 (Winter 1978): 379–403.

Spicer, Edward H. *Cycles of Conquest: The Impact of Spain, Mexico, and the United States on the Indians of the Southwest, 1533–1960.* Tucson: Univ. of Arizona Press, 1962.

Standart, Sister Colette M. "The Sonoran Migration to California, 1848–1856: A Study in Prejudice." *Southern California Quarterly* 58, no. 3 (Fall 1976): 333–57.

Stansell, Christine. *City of Women: Sex and Class in New York, 1789–1860.* New York: Alfred A. Knopf, 1986.

Starr, Kevin. *Americans and the California Dream, 1850–1915.* New York: Oxford Univ. Press, 1973.

Stern, Steve J. "Feudalism, Capitalism, and the World-System in the Perspective of Latin America and the Caribbean." *American Historical Review* 73, no. 4 (Oct. 1988): 829–72, and commentary, 873–97.

Takaki, Ronald T. *Iron Cages: Race and Culture in Nineteenth-Century America.* New York: Alfred A. Knopf, 1979.

———. *Strangers from a Different Shore: A History of Asian Americans.* Boston: Little, Brown, 1989.

Taylor, Quintard. *In Search of the Racial Frontier: African Americans in the American West.* New York: W. W. Norton, 1998.

Thelen, David. "Memory and American History." Special Issue: Memory and American History. *Journal of American History* 75, no. 4 (March 1989): 1117–29.

Thompson, E. P. "Time, Work-Discipline, and Industrial Capitalism." *Past and Present*, no. 38 (Dec. 1967): 56–97.

Vance, Carole S., ed. *Pleasure and Danger: Exploring Female Sexuality.* 1984. New York: Pandora/HarperCollins, 1992.

Voss, Stuart F. *On the Periphery of Nineteenth-Century Mexico: Sonora and Sinaloa, 1810–1877.* Tucson: Univ. of Arizona Press, 1982.

Wakeman, Frederic, Jr. *Strangers at the Gate: Social Disorder in South China, 1839–1861.* Berkeley: Univ. of California Press, 1966.

Wallerstein, Immanuel. "The Rise and Future Demise of the World Capitalist System: Concepts for Comparative Analysis." In *The Capitalist World Economy.* Cambridge: Cambridge Univ. Press, 1979.

Walters, Ronald G. *American Reformers, 1815–1860.* New York: Hill and Wang, 1978.

Watts, Jennifer. "From the Photo Archives: 'That's no woman . . . .'" *The Huntington Library, Art Collections, and Botanical Gardens Calendar.* July–Aug. 1998.

Weber, David J. "American Westward Expansion and the Breakdown of Relations between Pobladores and 'Indios Bárbaros' on Mexico's Far Northern Frontier." *New Mexico Historical Review* 56, no. 3 (July 1981): 221–38.

———. *The Mexican Frontier, 1821–1846: The American Southwest under Mexico.* Albuquerque: Univ. of New Mexico Press, 1982.

White, James G. "The Death of Tennessee's Pardner: The True Story of the Death of Jason P. Chamberlain." *Tuolumne County Historical Society Quarterly* 4, no. 3 (Jan.–March 1965): 122–24.

White, Richard. "Frederick Jackson Turner and Buffalo Bill." In *The Frontier in American Culture*, edited by James R. Grossman. Chicago: Newberry Library; Berkeley: Univ. of California Press, 1994.

———. *"It's Your Misfortune and None of My Own": A New History of the American West.* Norman: Univ. of Oklahoma Press, 1991.

———. *The Middle Ground: Indians, Empires, and Republics in the Great Lakes Region, 1650–1815.* New York: Cambridge Univ. Press, 1991.

———. *Remembering Ahanagran: Storytelling in a Family's Past.* New York: Hill and Wang, 1998.

Wilkins, Thurman. *Cherokee Tragedy: The Ridge Family and the Decimation of a People.* 2d ed. Norman: Univ. of Oklahoma Press, 1981.

Williams, Stephen. *The Chinese in the California Mines, 1848–1860.* 1930. San Francisco: R and E Research Associates, 1971.

Wolf, Eric R. *Europe and the People without History.* Berkeley: Univ. of California Press, 1982.

Woll, Allen L. "Hollywood Bandits, 1910–1981." In *Bandidos: The Varieties of Latin American Banditry*, edited by Richard W. Slatta. New York: Greenwood Press, 1987.

Wood, Raymond F. "New Light on Joaquin Murrieta." *Pacific Historian* 14, no.
    1 (Winter 1970): 54–65.

Wray, Matt, and Annalee Newitz, eds. *White Trash: Race and Class in America*.
    New York: Routledge, 1997.

Wright, Doris M. "The Making of Cosmopolitan California: An Analysis of
    Immigration, 1848–1870." Parts 1 and 2. *California Historical Society
    Quarterly* 19, no. 4 (Dec. 1940): 323–43, and 20, no. 1 (March 1941):
    65–79.

Wright, Gavin. *The Political Economy of the Cotton South: Households, Markets,
    and Wealth in the Nineteenth Century*. New York: W. W. Norton, 1978.

Wyatt-Brown, Bertram. *Southern Honor: Ethics and Behavior in the Old South*.
    New York: Oxford Univ. Press, 1982.

Wyllys, Rufus Kay. "The French of California and Sonora." *Pacific Historical
    Review* 1, no. 3 (Sept. 1932): 337–59.

Wyman, Mark. *Hard Rock Epic: Western Miners and Industrial Revolution,
    1860–1910*. Berkeley: Univ. of California Press, 1979.

Yen Ching–Hwang. *Coolies and Mandarins: Chinese Protection of Overseas
    Chinese during the Late Ch'ing Period, 1851–1911*. Singapore: Singapore
    Univ. Press, 1985.

Yung, Judy. *Unbound Feet: A Social History of Chinese Women in San Francisco*.
    Berkeley: Univ. of California Press, 1995.

Index

Note: Page numbers in *italics* refer to illustrations.